OXFORD HISTORICAL MONOGRAPHS

LUCCA 1369–1400

Politics and Society in an Early Renaissance City-State

BY

CHRISTINE MEEK

OXFORD UNIVERSITY PRESS
1978

Oxford University Press, Walton Street, Oxford OX2 6DP
OXFORD LONDON GLASGOW NEW YORK
TORONTO MELBOURNE WELLINGTON CAPE TOWN
IBADAN NAIROBI DAR ES SALAAM LUSAKA
KUALA LUMPUR SINGAPORE JAKARTA HONG KONG TOKYO
DELHI BOMBAY CALCUTTA MADRAS KARACHI

British Library Cataloguing in Publication Data
Meek, Christine
Lucca, 1369–1400.—(Oxford historical monographs).
1. Lucca—History 2. Lucca—Politics and government
I. Title II. Series
945'.53 DG975.L82 78-40086

ISBN 0-19-821866-4

Set by Malvern Typesetting Services Ltd
and printed in Great Britain by
Billing & Sons Limited, Guildford, London and Worcester

ACKNOWLEDGEMENTS

I have incurred many debts in the course of writing this book. I would like especially to thank D. M. Bueno de Mesquita, who first suggested Lucca to me as a subject for research, and who offered much valuable advice and assistance both when I was working on the D.Phil. thesis on which the book is based and when I came to re-write it for publication. Dr. G. A. Holmes, as sub-editor for the series, patiently read through several drafts and made many helpful suggestions as to substance and style, though I am, of course, responsible for any errors that remain. I have also benefited from discussions with two other students of Lucchese history, Dr. T. W. Blomquist and Dr. Duane Osheim.

The preparation of this book involved many visits to the Archivio di Stato in Lucca, which the friendliness and helpfulness of the staff there made pleasant as well as profitable. I would like to thank particularly the present Director, Professor Vito Tirelli, his predecessor, Dr. Domenico Corsi, Dr. Antonio Romiti, Dr. Giorgio Tori, Carlo Gabrielli Rosi, Ivo Giannecchini, Angelo Pasquini, Anselmo Pierantoni, Giovanni Fiorani, Adolfo Frediani, Duilio Matteoni, Bruno Gelli and Rinaldo Pozzi.

CONTENTS

PART IV: THE CONSOLIDATION OF THE GUINIGI REGIME

ABBREVIATIONS

A.S.L.	Archivio di Stato, Lucca
A.S.F.	Archivio di Stato, Firenze
A.S.P.	Archivio di Stato, Pisa
A.S.S.	Archivio di Stato, Siena
Anz. Av. Lib.	Series *Anziani Avanti la Libertà* (A.S.L.)
Anz. Temp. Lib.	Series *Anziani al Tempo della Libertà* (A.S.L.)
Delib.	*Deliberazioni*, Series *Anziani al Tempo della Libertà* (A.S.L.)
Min.	*Minute di Riformagioni*, Series *Anziani al Tempo della Libertà* (A.S.L.)
Reg.	*Regesto del R. Archivio di Stato di Lucca*, Vol. II, ed. L. Fumi, Lucca, 1903
Rif.	*Riformagioni Pubbliche*, Series *Consiglio Generale* (A.S.L.)
R.I.S.	Rerum Italicarum Scriptores
Sign. Cart. Miss.	*Signori: Carteggio Missive* (A.S.F.)
Tommasi	G. Tommasi, 'Sommario della storia di Lucca, MIV al MDCC', *Archivio Storico Italiano*, Ser. i, Vol. X (1847)

Note

In the case of the Riformagioni and some other series the modern pagination has been quoted for the sake of clarity, as one volume often contains several sets of foliation.

INTRODUCTION: THE GOVERNMENT OF LUCCA

For the Lucchese 1369 was no ordinary year; it was in that year that Lucca regained the independence she had lost over fifty years before, and was able to take her place once more as an independent Tuscan city-state. She had had a long history as a self-governing community. After playing an active role as a Guelf city earlier, she reached the height of her power at the end of the thirteenth and beginning of the fourteenth century, when she was second only to Florence in Tuscany. In a league of 1282 Florence was to provide 166 knights and Lucca 114—slightly more than Siena with 104—out of a total *taglia* of 500 knights. But her decline began soon afterwards. In 1300 the faction struggles of Blacks, led by the degli Obizi family, against Whites, led by the Antelminelli and Ciapparoni families, caused an outbreak of internal violence, which resulted in the exile of the entire White party. Further internal troubles soon after led to a victory for the popular cause, consolidated in the Statute of 1308, which provided for a broadly based popular government and placed many of the leading families under legal disabilities as 'potentes et casastici', but Lucca was further weakened by the departure of many of the wealthiest and most powerful families into voluntary exile. And worse was to follow, for on 14 June 1314 Uguccione della Faggiuola, captain of Pisa, attacked Lucca with the aid of the Lucchese Ghibelline and White exiles, notably Castruccio Castracani degli Antelminelli. Lucca was bitterly divided by internal factions and was unable to put up effective resistance. The city was taken by force, and burned and sacked for three days. Apart from the loss of life and destruction of property in the actual sack, many Guelfs fled from the city, and about 300 families, including the Obizi, were banished.

In 1316 Uguccione was supplanted in Lucca by Castruccio Castracani, who by 1320 had succeeded in getting himself made *signore* for life. He strengthened his position still further by obtaining an imperial vicariate over Lucca and Pistoia and their bishoprics and that of Luni in 1324, and in 1325 having his eldest son, Arrigo, elected captain-general and rector of the city. He also built an imposing castle, known as the Augusta, within the walls of Lucca. His rule lasted from 1316 until his death in 1328 and in this period he raised Lucca to a position of importance in Italy that she was never to approach again. He pursued a policy of expansion in all directions, putting himself at the head of the Ghibelline party in Tuscany and seeking the alliance of other Italian Ghibellines. He succeeded in extending his authority over Pistoia, and when this was opposed by Florence and her allies he defeated them at the battle of Altopascio in 1325. The Italian expedition of Lewis of Bavaria, with whom he was already on good terms, offered him further opportunities to extend his power. Pisa resisted the Emperor because of his alliance with Castruccio, but he took the city after a brief siege and Castruccio's authority was soon established there too, despite imperial guarantees of Pisan autonomy. In November 1327 the Emperor granted Castruccio the title of duke of Lucca, Pistoia, Luni, and Volterra in hereditary right, though he never obtained actual possession of Volterra. In May 1328 an imperial vicariate over Pisa followed. Castruccio was present at the imperial coronation in Rome in January 1328 and was further honoured with the titles of Count of the Sacred Lateran Palace and Senator of Rome. He recovered Pistoia, which had risen in rebellion, and was threatening Florence itself when he suddenly died on 3 September 1328. The external expansion and military glory of Castruccio's rule may have made it acceptable to the Lucchese, but the rule of a Ghibelline *signore*, even one of Lucchese birth, was probably unpopular in a city that was traditionally both Guelf and a free republic. After Castruccio's death it quickly became clear how insecurely based his power had been, and Lucca was to pay heavily for the brief period of military glory. The worst period of Lucchese history began on his death.

Although the Emperor had granted Castruccio the title of duke of Lucca in hereditary right, he refused to accept the succession of his young sons, and instead sold the vicariate of Lucca to Francesco Castracani, their uncle and enemy. But effective control passed to a band of German mercenaries, who seized the city on 15 April 1329. Their only thought was to sell it to the highest bidder, and after entering into negotiations with both Pisa and Florence they finally sold it to Gherardo Spinola of Genoa for 60,000 florins. His rule was weak and short-lived. He proved powerless to defend the city against the attempts of Florence to take it by force, and the Lucchese themselves sought the protection of John of Bohemia, who was then in Italy. He and his son, the future Emperor Charles IV, ruled the city through a vicar from March 1331 to October 1333, but the collapse of their power elsewhere in Italy obliged them to dispose of Lucca. Again Lucca was sold with the Lucchese themselves having no say in their fate. Francesco Castracani received an imperial vicariate over Coreglia, and Lucca itself was sold to the brothers Marsilio, Pietro, and Rolando Rossi of Parma. They also held Parma as imperial vicars and when they lost it to Mastino della Scala of Verona they sold Lucca to him as well. The rule of the Scaligeri lasted a little longer, from November 1335 to August 1341, but they found it difficult to hold the city from distant Verona, especially after they lost Parma in May 1341. Again Lucca was put up for sale, and both Florence and Pisa hoped to buy it. In August 1341 Mastino della Scala agreed to sell Lucca to Florence for 250,000 florins, though this price was later much reduced. But the Pisans, on having their offer refused, laid siege to the city, and Pisa and Florence struggled for the possession of it. Despite the Pisan besiegers some Florentine forces managed to enter the city and take formal possession on 25 September 1341, but the Pisans were far from defeated and after an eleven-month siege the Florentines were finally obliged to surrender, and by 6 July 1342 Lucca had fallen to the Pisans.

Since the death of Castruccio, Lucca had passed from one outside ruler to another with no account being taken of her wishes, and had finally fallen into the hands of her ancient rival and enemy, Pisa. The terms which the Pisans granted in 1342 were generous. There was to be an offensive and defensive alliance between the two cities for fifteen years, and certain fortresses disputed between them were to go to Pisa. Pisa was to have the custody of Lucca, the Augusta and certain other fortresses at Lucchese expense, but only for the duration of the war with Florence, and she was not to interfere in the administration of Lucca. It is unlikely that these or any other terms could have rendered Pisan rule really acceptable to Lucca, but they were not to be kept, and the period of Pisan rule which lasted for over twenty-five years was regarded by the Lucchese as Babylonian servitude. Though the oppressive character of Pisan rule has sometimes been exaggerated it is nevertheless true that a large proportion of the revenues of Lucca went to Pisa for the costs of the custody of the city, that the Pisans quickly extended their control over much of the Lucchese *contado*, and that they came to interfere more and more in Lucchese internal affairs, nominating the Podestà, the chancellor, and the Anziani, and allowing Lucchese officials only a limited degree of autonomy. In agreements with Florence made in 1342 and 1343, Pisa agreed to cede to Florence certain Lucchese territories in the Garfagnana, Valdinievole, and elsewhere, and to pay Florence an indemnity of 100,000 florins at the rate of 7,000 florins a year, of which she made Lucca pay a third.

The Lucchese quickly began to attempt to procure their freedom. Some were led to support the efforts of the Antelminelli to recover the lordship of Castruccio, preferring the rule of the Antelminelli to that of Pisa. But a better hope was to induce the Emperor to free Lucca. The Pisans had no imperial confirmation of their rule over Lucca, and when Charles IV visited Italy in 1354/5 Lucchese hopes were high. He does seem seriously to have contemplated freeing Lucca from Pisan rule, but despite an attempted rising against the Pisans in Lucca, and despite every petition and offer that the Lucchese could make to the Emperor, Charles IV not only failed to grant the Lucchese their freedom, but even granted the Pisans an imperial vicariate over the city on 9 March 1355. This meant that although the original fifteen-year alliance between the two cities expired in 1357, the Lucchese could no longer have any hope of recovering their independence. In fact Pisan rule became harsher with the renewal of war with Florence in 1362. Lucca was called upon to fight on the Pisan side and to contribute to the expenses of the war, and as the Pisans had good reason to doubt Lucchese loyalty more restrictive measures were imposed. Meetings of more than four persons were forbidden without a licence and eventually all

Lucchese between the ages of fourteen and seventy, except for Ghibellines, were ordered out of the city and into the suburbs. Either because they were provoked by these measures or because they in any case preferred Florentine rule to that of Pisa, a group of Lucchese did conspire to admit the Florentines. The plot was discovered and eleven Lucchese were executed for their part in it. Pisa again had to make peace on unfavourable terms, and again Lucca was called upon to pay a share of the indemnity.

In the aftermath of the unsuccessful war against Florence Pisa had elected a doge, Giovanni dell'Agnello. This election may have applied to Lucca as well, and the Lucchese were later obliged to elect him captain-general, governor, and defender of the city for life, and authorize him to appoint his sons to these offices. Lucca's position seems to have deteriorated under Giovanni dell'Agnello; arbitrary acts and financial exactions increased, and Pisan rule was probably harsher during the 1360s than it had been earlier. The Lucchese were therefore even more anxious to obtain their freedom, and the second visit to Italy of the Emperor Charles IV in 1368 raised their hopes of doing so. Again the Lucchese pressed him to free the city, offering large sums as an inducement to grant them their liberty. Dell'Agnello hoped to obtain confirmation of his position, and he also made offers, but his rule came to an end when a balcony on which he was standing collapsed and he broke a thigh, so that he was incapacitated at a critical moment. But this did not free Lucca from the rule of Pisa, and her position long remained in doubt. The Emperor himself arrived in Lucca in September 1368 and took over the government directly, but it was some months before he made clear what his intentions for the city were after he had gone. Despite the efforts of the Lucchese to induce the Emperor to free them from Pisan rule, it was not until 6 April 1369 that he finally did so, and even then the decision was partly the result of his own deteriorating relations with Pisa. The anniversary of the day the Emperor declared Lucca free, and revoked any grants and privileges giving Pisa authority over her, was to be celebrated long after as the feast of liberty, but this did not in itself settle the question of Lucca's future. The end of Pisan rule did not mean that Lucca at once became self-governing.

Lucca was now a city directly subject to the Emperor. While he remained there the government was in his hands, and there was a possibility that he might grant an imperial vicariate over the city to some outside power. This danger was avoided, but Lucca did not become self-governing even when the Emperor departed, for at the beginning of July 1369 he appointed Guy of Boulogne, Cardinal-bishop of Porto, as imperial vicar there. The Cardinal was to have the custody of the city for three years, and the administration was conducted in his name and that of the Anziani. He seems to have nominated the Anziani and the Podestà and to have confirmed elections to other offices. His power was especially great in foreign policy, but he could also issue decrees on general matters of policy and administration and the most important officials of Lucca had to take an oath of loyalty to him. The Lucchese had full control of the revenues, but had to pay the Cardinal 40,000 florins a year as the cost of the custody and administration of the city. The limitations imposed upon their freedom by the presence of an imperial vicar were probably resented by the Lucchese, but they proved to be only temporary. On 12 March 1370 the Cardinal, presumably with the consent of Charles IV, granted the Lucchese a diploma in which he invested present and future Anziani with the title of imperial vicars, and confirmed them in other legislative, administrative, and judicial powers.[1] Charles IV himself had already granted them the right to strike coinage, set up a university, create notaries, legitimize bastards and legalize adoptions.[2] At the end of March 1370 the Cardinal left the city and the Lucchese were then free to rule themselves without further interference from their nominal overlord.

The reorganization of the administration had begun even before the Cardinal left. One of the first changes was the redivision of the city, something that had been contemplated

[1] Imperial vicariate over Tuscany, *Capitoli*, 3, ff. 94–95v, 2 July 1369, Cardinal's diploma to the Lucchese, *Capitoli*, 3, ff. 96–8, and *Capitoli*, 31, pp. 343–50, 12 Mar. 1370. For the Cardinal and his administration, O. Banti, 'Una anno di storia lucchese (1369–1370)', in *La 'libertas lucensis' del 1369*, Accademia Lucchese di Scienze, Lettere e Arti, Studi e Testi IV (Lucca, 1970), esp. pp. 44–52.

[2] *Capitoli*, 3, ff. 72v–73v, 75–75v, 76–76v. J. C. Lünig, *Codex Italiae Diplomaticus*, Vol. II, part II, section VIII, no. x, col. 2225–6.

since 1362.[3] In 1370 Lucca still retained its ancient division into five areas, called *porte*. These five *porte* were the basis for the election of officials and councillors and for the distribution of taxes and for other obligations. This theoretically produced an equal distribution and had perhaps once done so in fact, but Lucca had suffered many vicissitudes since they were instituted. Not only had the population declined, but changes had taken place in its distribution within the city, so that already in 1362 the men of Porta S. Donato, Porta S. Frediano, and Porta S. Gervasio had complained of inequalities in assessments which meant that some of them were paying three times as much as men of equal wealth in the other *porte*.[4] Nothing permanent had been done at that time, but in February 1370 a *balìa* was authorized to reorganize the administrative divisions of the city, so as to make them more equal.[5] This *balìa* instituted a new division of the city into three *terzieri*, named S. Martino, S. Paolino, and S. Salvatore, after the cathedral and two of the principal churches.[6] These three *terzieri* became the basis of the political organization of the city and of appointments to many offices and the distribution of some taxes and forced loans. The re-division of the city meant that the colleges and councils also had to be reorganized. This was quickly done, so that the first college of Anziani arranged in *terzieri* took office on 1 March 1370 and the first councils on 15 March.[7]

But these changes were only a beginning. It was agreed in November 1370 that Lucca needed a new Statute, as the laws laid down under the rule of the Pisans and other tyrants had

[3] *Anz. Av. Lib.* 42, p. 57, 21 Apr. 1362. The plan was for a redivision into five *porte* with the same names as before.

[4] *Anz. Av. Lib.* 42, p. 57, 21 Apr. 1362. In June 1363 an *imposita* of 10,000 florins was divided among the five *porte* as follows, Porta Borghi, 1,120 florins, Porta S. Frediano 2,550, Porta S. Donato 2,530, Porta S. Pietro 570, Porta S. Gervasio 3,230 florins, which suggests that the inequalities of size and resources were very great, *Anz. Av. Lib.* 42, p. 267, 23 June 1363.

[5] *Rif.* 2, p. 214, 2 Feb., p. 219, 5 Feb. 1370.

[6] *Rif.* 1, p. 220, 6 Feb. 1370. S. Paolino was formed by uniting the old *porte* of S. Donato and S. Pietro; S. Salvatore from S. Frediano and Porta Borghi; S. Martino from Porta S. Gervasio and part of the *borghi* not included in S. Salvatore.

[7] *Rif.* 1, pp. 229–30, 16 Feb., p. 231, 19 Feb. 1370. The college of Anziani was to consist of three Anziani per *terziere* and a Gonfaloniere drawn from each *terziere* in turn. The General Council was reduced to 180 members and the Council of Fifty to thirty-six members.

not been dictated by principles of justice, and in any case the latest Statute was now some thirty years old.[8] *Statutarii* were elected, but various delays prevented the completion of the new Statute before July 1372.[9] The new Statute was arranged in four books; the first dealt with the government of the city, the second with criminal jurisdiction, and the last two with civil jurisdiction and procedure and with the *contado*.

The Statute confirmed decisions about the form of government that had already been taken. Lucca was to be ruled by a college consisting of nine Anziani and a Gonfaloniere di Giustizia, a General Council of 180 members and a smaller council of thirty-six members. The *tasca* of Anziani was to be renewed every two years, that is the colleges of Anziani were elected for two years at a time. The Anziani were chosen by a straightforward system of election, not as in Florence by a system of drawing lots on the basis of lists of citizens declared eligible. The Anziani were elected by the Anziani and council of Thirty-Six in office at the time and six *invitati* from each *terziere* in the presence of a religious. Those elected were then arranged into colleges, each to hold office for two months. This important task was done by nine sorters, three of them Anziani and the others members of the Thirty-Six. The sorters were also to choose from among those elected Anziani the men most fitted to be Gonfalonieri di Giustizia. The names of each college were then written on separate pieces of paper and locked in a chest, to be drawn out in the council of Thirty-Six eight days before the term of office of the previous college expired. No one could refuse the office of Anziano, but a number of *spiccinati* were elected to fill any vacancies that should occur through death, illness, absence from Lucca, or some other cause.[10]

[8] *Rif.* 2, pp. 137–9, 13 Nov. 1370. The Statute compiled in 1342, when Lucca was under Pisan rule, was still in force. Since the earliest surviving statute of 1308 there had been new statutes or modifications in 1316, 1331, and 1336. See *Statuto del Comune di Lucca 1308* in *Memorie e Documenti per Servire all'Istoria del Principato Lucchese*, Vol. III, part III, introduction pp. ix–xvi.

[9] *Rif.* 2, pp. 137–9, 13 Nov., p. 151, 23 Nov. 1370, p. 318, 28 June 1371, *Min.* 2, f. 4v, 21 Apr., f. 20, 2–4 May, f. 46v, 18 June 1371. *Rif.* 3, pp. 137–8, 7 Dec., p. 149, 10 Dec., p. 154, 14 Dec. 1371. The Statute was proclaimed *Rif.* 3, p. 366, 31 July 1372. It is no. 6 in the series *Statuti del Comune di Lucca.*

[10] *Statuto*, 1372, I, iiii, vi, vii.

The General Council consisted of 180 members, sixty from each *terziere*, and was elected for a year at a time, beginning 15 March each year, by the Anziani and a *balìa* of twelve members of the Thirty-Six, four per *terziere*.[11] The council of Thirty-Six held office for six months at a time, beginning mid-March and mid-September, and was elected by the Anziani and four citizens per *terziere* from the old council, who also elected the new General Council in March. The Thirty-Six consisted of four *gonfalonieri* and eight ordinary councillors for each *terziere*.[12] The *gonfalonieri* also had duties in the defence of the city in case of riot or other disturbance. Each *gonfaloniere* had four *pennonieri* under him, and they had the duty of appearing armed with the banners entrusted to them and of calling the other citizens inscribed under their banner to appear in arms on the command of the Gonfaloniere di Giustizia in time of danger.[13]

Anziani, and members of the General Council and Thirty-Six had to be at least twenty-five years of age, of legitimate birth, and Lucchese citizens, originating from the Lucchese state and holding citizenship for at least twenty years. But certain noble families were excluded from the offices of Anziano, *gonfaloniere* and *pennoniere*,[14] and there were also restrictions designed to prevent any one family gaining excessive power and to ensure that as large a number of citizens as possible would have the opportunity of holding office as Anziano and councillor. Two brothers or father and son could not sit in the same council, and no one could be a member of the General Council in two consecutive years.[15] In the Thirty-Six there was a 'vacation' of a year before a *gonfaloniere* could be re-elected and six months in the case of an ordinary councillor.[16] For the Anziani the 'vacation' was a year, and three years for the Gonfaloniere di Giustizia. In addition only one member of a family could be Anziano in the same college, only one member of a family could be Gonfaloniere in two

[11] *Statuto* I, xxii.
[12] *Statuto* I, xviii.
[13] *Statuto* I, xviiii, xx, xxi.
[14] *Statuto* I, viii, xx, *Rif*. 1, pp. 454–8, 31 July 1370. Addition to the Statute f. 149, 18 Aug. 1372.
[15] *Statuto* I, xxii.
[16] *Statuto* I, xviii.

years, and there was to be a four-month 'vacation' between brother and brother or father and son.[17]

The General Council was the highest authority in the state, and certain things could only be decided there. All contracts made by Lucca had to be read out and voted there, and only the General Council could commit Lucca to any obligations or alienate any of her property or jurisdiction. A dispensation from the General Council was necessary to quash certain sentences or to do anything that was prohibited by statute.[18] But most things connected with the ordinary administration could be done in the council of Thirty-Six. The Anziani and the Thirty-Six acting together could make laws and decrees, elect many officials and authorize money for all extraordinary expenses.[19] The Anziani acting alone could make mandates for ordinary expenses, receive and answer letters, and deal with day-to-day administration and policy, except in things expressly reserved to the General Council or Thirty-Six. They could also elect men to sit in the councils as *invitati* with the same speaking and voting rights as ordinary councillors. Two-thirds of the councillors had to be present to form a quorum, but two-thirds of those present, both councillors and *invitati*, formed a majority.[20]

In the college of Anziani too matters had to be formally put to the vote, and seven votes were necessary to pass a measure. The Gonfaloniere di Giustizia had certain special functions. He took precedence over the other Anziani and made the first reply to embassies to the college, though he could not give a final reply until the Anziani had debated the matter. He also made the proposals in council meetings and in times of crisis could have the 'vexillum' brought out and ring the bells to summon the *gonfalonieri* and *pennonieri* to arms. But these things could only be done with the agreement of the Anziani.[21] The nine Anziani also took it in turns to act as preceptor of the college, keeping the seal and opening and reading the letters addressed to the Anziani.[22]

[17] *Statuto* I, viii, ix.
[18] *Statuto* I, xv, III, lvi, lvii.
[19] *Statuto* I, xv, xxii.
[20] *Statuto* I, xi, xiii–xv, xxii.
[21] *Statuto* I, xiii.
[22] *Statuto* I, xiiii.

Apart from the Anziani and councils there were certain other important offices that were a permanent part of the administration of the city. There were the *conducterii*, responsible along with the Anziani for the hiring and supervision of mercenaries and castellans.[23] The *conducterii* were Lucchese citizens elected to the office by the college of Anziani and the retiring *conducterii*. The Statute of 1372 provided that there should be six of them, holding office for four months, but that three *conducterii* should be elected every two months, so that there would always be three old ones and three new ones.[24] There were later modifications in these regulations. In 1381 the *conducterii* were reduced to three, holding office for three months, and a *tasca* of *conducterii* was to be made for a year at a time.[25] There may have been further changes later, and the *conducterii* were one of the bones of contention between the factions in 1392. After the events of May 1392 further changes were made. There was to be a *tasca* of eighteen *conducterii* elected each year, to hold office three at a time for periods of two months each. These regulations were still in force in 1400.[26]

Another important office was that of the *secretarii*. Their duty was the supervision of spies and scouts and other things that needed to be kept secret, hence their name. The office developed gradually. The need to provide secretly for various negotiations and the sending of letters and envoys was discussed in September 1369, and a *balìa* of fifteen was elected, with the power to commit particular matters to a smaller *balìa*.[27] In September 1371 a *balìa* of one citizen per *terziere* was authorized for three months to supervise the sending of spies.[28] In December 1371 the Anziani were authorized to elect three Lucchese citizens every three months for this and each set of *secretarii* could spend up to fifty florins without being

[23] *Statuto* I, xxvii–xxviii, xxx–xxxii, xxxviii. There were certain limitations on whom they could appoint and for how long.

[24] *Statuto* I, xxvii.

[25] *Rif.* 7, p. 365, 17 Dec. 1380.

[26] *Rif.* 12, pp. 118–20, 26 May 1392.

[27] *Rif.* 1, pp. 87–8, 11 Sept., p. 91, 17 Sept. 1369. Money was provided for this 1 Oct. 1369, pp. 109–10.

[28] *Rif.* 3, p. 53, 19 Sept. 1371. The Anziani had been authorized to elect one or more (presumably per *terziere*) for three months with authority to spend up to 150 florins, *Rif.* 2, p. 183, 3 Jan. 1371.

required to render any account of it.[29] One of the three *secretarii* sat with their successors for the first month in order to inform them of secret matters.[30] The decree of 22 December was only to last for a year, but such an office was clearly useful and it was to become a permanent part of the machinery of government. Information about the *secretarii* is necessarily scanty, but the names of those elected are often recorded and there are very frequent authorizations of sums of money beyond the fifty florins which each set of *secretarii* could spend without the need for any special mandate. The *secretarii* apparently continued to hold office for three months at a time until 1392, when some changes were made. There were still to be three *secretarii*, but they were to hold office for six months, not three, and the *secretarii* for a whole year were to be elected by the college of Anziani for November and December each year.[31]

There were other offices that were part of the regular machinery of government, such as the *pacificatores*, whose duty it was to settle disputes and quarrels among Lucchese citizens and subjects and arrange reconciliations,[32] and the governors of the *dovana salis*, who were responsible for the administration of the salt-tax and for safeguarding the interests of the creditors of the public debt, which was connected with it.[33] There were also many *ad hoc* commissions or *balìe*, which were not part of the regular machinery of government, but which were responsible for taking many of the most important decisions. It was common for the General Council or the Thirty-Six to appoint one of these *balìe* to settle some specific question rather than settling it outright in the council itself. The use of *balìe* must have done much to solve the problem of executive efficiency in a government where periods of office were short and men of little experience might be elected to councils. Able and experienced citizens could be chosen for *balìe*. This use of *balìe* must have given a degree of continuity to the government, for the same names appear

[29] *Rif.* 3, p. 167, 22 Dec. 1371.
[30] *Rif.* 3, p. 293, 1 May, p. 351, 1 July 1372.
[31] *Rif.* 12, p. 117, 26 May 1392.
[32] *Rif.* 3, pp. 206–7, 10 Jan. 1372.
[33] See below, Chapter 3, pp. 56–7.

again and again among the membership of *balìe*. This clearly had its dangers for a republican regime, as it was a means by which an oligarchical group of wealthy, powerful, and experienced citizens could gain an undue influence over the government.

The office of chancellor also probably gave a degree of continuity to the government. Until 1370 there was only one chancellor, but it was then found that there was too much work for a single chancellor, even with notaries to assist him, and the office was divided into two. There was to be a chancellor of the commune, responsible for the records of councils, for contracts and the documents relating to mercenaries and castellans. There was also to be a chancellor of the Anziani, responsible for their letters, provisions, and mandates. Each chancellor was to have one notary, and there were regulations about their salaries, the fees to be paid by citizens for chancery documents, and the proportion of these fees that was to go to Lucca, the chancellors and their notaries.[34] This decree laid down that the chancellors, who must be Lucchese citizens, should hold the office for one year only, and that there should be a year's 'vacation' before they could be re-elected. But in practice these 'vacations' were ignored. The chancellors were regularly re-elected; they usually held the office for several consecutive years, and ser Guido Manfredi of Pietrasanta was re-elected every year from 1 January 1382 and was still in office in 1400.

The office of Podestà still continued in Lucca and was regarded as the most important office in the state. The Podestà held office for six months and was paid a large salary for himself and his retinue, which had to include three knights, one of whom was to act as captain of the *contado*, and two lawyers to act as judges. The Podestà himself had to be a knight from a city at least sixty miles from Lucca, and no one who was an exile from his own city or who had been Podestà of Lucca within the last three years was eligible.[35] The election of the Podestà was regarded as a very important matter and was to be done in the General Council. The Podestà continued to

[34] *Rif.* 1, pp. 438–40, 17 July 1370.

[35] *Statuto*, 1372, I, xxiiii. Oath taken by the Podestà I, xxv.

be chosen very carefully. Occasionally a doctor of laws was elected, if a suitable knight could not be found, and occasionally a Podestà's term of office might be extended, though never for more than six months and usually only for three. In general the regulations about his election were carefully observed. But despite the care with which the Podestà was still chosen, the office was far less important than it had been in the thirteenth century.[36] The Podestà no longer had any political power, but he was still an important judicial and police official, responsible for the arrest and trial of suspects from the city and *distretto*, with higher jurisdiction over the *contado* also.[37]

Another important official was the *major sindicus*, who also exercised the functions of judge of appeals and major official of the gabelle. He had to be a doctor of laws from a city at least fifty miles from Lucca. He was elected for six months, and his most important duty was to 'sindicate' other Lucchese officials, that is to hold an inquiry into their actions while in office, hearing and investigating complaints against them.[38]

The Lucchese state still retained its old divisions into city, *suburbio*, *distretto* and *contado* proper.[39] The *suburbio* consisted of the parishes nearest to the city, such as Sorbano, Pontetetto, S. Alessio, and Monte S. Quirico. The *distretto* was the area beyond these but within six miles of the city, the six miles over which Lucca had had her earliest grants of jurisdiction. It included Pieve di Compito, Marlia, Lammari, S. Gennaro, and Massaciuccoli.[40] The *suburbio* and the *distretto* were situated in the plain near Lucca, and as they were not far distant from the city required no special administration beyond their own elected consuls and the Lucchese officials, many of whom also had authority in the city.

The rest of the Lucchese state, much of which was mountainous, was organized into nine vicariates, Camaiore, Pietrasanta, Massa Lunense, Valdriana, Valdilima, Coreglia,

[36] S. Bongi (ed.) *Inventario del R. Archivio di Stato in Lucca*, Vol. II, p. 303.

[37] G. Tommasi, 'Sommario della Storia di Lucca dal MIV al MDCC', *Archivio Storico Italiano*, Ser. i, Vol. X (1847), pp. 149-51. *Statuto*, 1372, Lib. II, III, IV.

[38] *Statuto*, 1372, I, xxvi. Tommasi, p. 147.

[39] Also the *borghi* or suburbs, but Borgo S. Frediano had been included in the *terzieri* of S. Salvatore and S. Martino in the re-division of the city.

[40] *Statuto*, 1308, I, xlii. Tommasi, p. 141.

Castiglione, Gallicano, and Camporgiano. These were administered by vicars, who were responsible for the maintenance of law and order, the collection of dues and the general execution of decrees relating to the *contado*. The vicars presided at the courts of the vicariates, which had jurisdiction in certain civil and criminal cases, though for some they had to be assisted by a doctor of laws elected by the college of judges to be judge of that particular vicariate, and other cases were reserved to the court of the Podestà. The vicars had to be Lucchese citizens, preferably knights, elected for six months at a time, and they could not be re-elected to the same vicariate immediately.[41] Certain border communes were administered separately under a *podestà*. Casola and Pugliano formed the *podesteria* of Ultra Iugum.

There were also certain places in the *contado* to which special regulations applied. There were enclaves in Lucchese territory over which the bishop of Lucca and the canons of S. Martino had jurisdiction. The canons had rights over the villages of Massarosa, Fibbialla, Gualdo, and Ricetri,[42] the bishop over Moriano, Aquilea, Sesto, and Decimo, though his jurisdiction had once been more extensive.[43] These enclaves were a potential nuisance to Lucca; criminals and debtors might take refuge there and defy her authority. But it was not in the interests of the bishop and chapter to permit this; wrongdoers from their lands might take refuge in Lucchese territory. The Church also found that it sometimes lacked the power to enforce order even within its own jurisdiction,[44] and was therefore glad to be able to call on Lucchese assistance. It was usually possible to come to terms with the bishop and canons. Agreements were made for terms of years that allowed Lucchese officials to arrest criminals within ecclesiastical territory, sharing the fines, and imposed upon the bishop's

[41] *Statuto*, 1372, III, ci, cii.

[42] *Rif*. 4, pp. 376-7, 22 Apr. 1374. Tommasi, p. 141.

[43] Tommasi, p. 141. The bishop only claimed jurisdiction over these four *Rif*. 5, p. 6, 11 Jan. 1375. He had earlier claimed other places, including Collodi and Villa Basilica, *Rif*. 1, pp. 27-8, 5 Aug. 1369, but *balìa* elected to defend Lucchese rights, p. 30, 6 Aug. 1369.

[44] For example petitioners said in 1379 that it was difficult to obtain justice because the bishop was not holding a court 'e se pure la tenesse non pare che abbia potentia desser ubidito', *Rif*. 7, p. 75, 23 Apr. 1379.

subjects the same gabelles that those of Lucca paid. These agreements were regularly renewed.[45]

Some of the most important places in the *contado* were big enough to have special institutions. The town of Pietrasanta had a population of perhaps 2,500,[46] and had six Anziani.[47] The town of Camaiore was divided into four quarters, each with a captain, and Coreglia also had four officials.[48] In 1370 there is a mention of six officials called 'consules maris' at Motrone. They were to have full authority over the organization of the port of Motrone.[49] This may only have been a temporary measure, for nothing more is heard of them. Even in these larger places the defence of fortresses was organized from Lucca, and most of the other places in the *contado* were little more than villages and had no independent organization of their own.

[45] Agreements with the bishop. *Rif.* 3, p. 296, 3 May 1372, *Rif.* 4, pp. 184–5, 25 June 1373, *Min.* 2, f. 280v, 24 May 1379, Rif. 7, pp. 582–3, 23 Oct. 1381, *Rif.* 8, p. 39, 22 Jan. 1382 with the canons of S. Martino, *Rif.* 4, pp. 376–7, 22 Apr., p. 380, 23 Apr. 1374, *Rif.* 9, p. 233, 27 Nov. 1384, p. 325, 23 Mar. 1385. Copies of an agreement with the bishop, *Capitoli*, 32, pp. 4–6, 9–13, 24 May 1379, with the canons *Capitoli*, 33, pp. 509–11.

[46] *Rif.* 8, p. 497, 29 Apr. 1383. It had 2,172 *bocche* for the salt tax.

[47] *Min.* 3, (not foliated), 23 June 1383, to hold office for July, August, and September. There is a loose folio in *Min.* 4 containing the names of six Anziani for Pietrasanta for October, November, and December 1389.

[48] *Min.* 3, 23 June 1383.

[49] *Rif.* 2, p. 175, 22 Dec. 1370.

PART I

The Economic Basis of the Lucchese State

1

LUCCA IN 1369: THE CONTRACTED CITY

In April 1369 Lucca was again free, but after decades of rule by various outside powers there were many aspects of her position that needed clarifying. It was necessary to define the boundaries of the newly independent state and some declaration of Lucca's position and rights with regard to the Emperor needed to be made. The government and administration of both city and state needed to be reordered; the existing statute of the commune dated from 1342, and one of the first actions of the Lucchese after regaining their independence was to set about compiling a new one.

One of the first matters that needed to be settled was the extent of the newly independent Lucchese state. Lucca had attained her widest boundaries about 1306, a few years before she first fell under the rule of a foreign lord. Since then she had lost much territory to her neighbours; Pisa, Florence, Pistoia and some of the nobles of the Lunigiana had all made gains at her expense. There were also complications. Territory disputed between Lucca and Pisa had been formally returned to Pisa while Lucca was under Pisan rule. Pisa had also ceded Lucchese territory to Florence during this period. Lucca did not recognize all these losses of territory. The Lucchese felt that in recovering the independence they had enjoyed in the early fourteenth century, they should also control the same territory that they had ruled then; many villages and castles which she no longer held are named as part of the Lucchese state in the Statute of 1372.[1] It was obviously necessary to clear up some of these confusions, especially with regard to Pisa, and to make clear exactly what territory the Emperor was freeing from Pisan rule. He therefore made a declaration of Lucchese territory 6 June 1369.[2] The villages and castles of the

[1] *Statuto del Comune di Lucca*, 1372. Series *Statuti del Comune di Lucca*, 6, Lib. III, cap. xciii.

[2] Copies in *Capitoli*, 3, ff. 71–2, and *Capitoli*, 31, pp. 305–8. Also Lünig, *Codex Italiae Diplomaticus*, Vol. II, part ii, section viii, no. viii, cols. 2223–34.

suburbio and Six Miles were mentioned by name and Lucca's rights over the vicariates of Massa Lunense, Camaiore, Pietrasanta, Camporgiano, Castiglione, Barga, Coreglia, Valdilima, and Valdriana with all their dependencies were guaranteed, though the dependencies were not mentioned by name. Rights over other important places, Motrone, Viareggio, Rotaio, Montecarlo, Bientina, Collodi, Monteclaro, Veneri, and S. Pietro in Campo were also specifically guaranteed, and the right to use Motrone as a port, to sail the sea and unload goods at Motrone was especially mentioned.

In a separate document issued the same day the Emperor reserved Lucchese rights over certain lands held by Florence, although he had earlier granted the Florentines an imperial vicariate over them. They were mainly lands in the Valdinievole and Valdarno between Lucca and Florence and included Pescia, Uzzano, Buggiano, Stignano, Montecatini, Monsummano, Montevettolini, Pietrabuona, Fucecchio, S. Croce, Castelfranco, S. Maria a Monte, Montecalvoli, Montefalcone, Orentano, Galleno, Staffoli, and Montopoli.[3] But although this guarantee was certainly made at the request of the Lucchese, and they were doubtless gratified to have their rights in this area reserved, the imperial guarantee remained a dead letter. Florence had long held actual possession of these territories and continued to do so.[4]

In fact Lucca began her new period of liberty with much narrower boundaries than she had had at the turn of the century. In 1306 her territory had stretched to the river Magra in the north, and she had held places like Pontremoli, Carrara, and Sarzana. In the south her territory had reached the Arno, including places like Fucecchio, Castelfranco, and S. Croce, and also villages on the far side of the Arno like Montopoli, Colleoli, Treggiaia, and Montecastello.[5] The coastline had been her boundary on the west and in the east her territory had reached the Apennines, and she had held such places as Serravalle and Lizzano in Pistoiese territory,

[3] *Capitoli*, 3, f. 74^{v}, 6 June 1369.

[4] The contemporary Lucchese chronicler, Giovanni Sercambi, names some of these places and others as held by Florence in 1398, *Le Chroniche Lucchesi*, ed. S. Bongi, (Rome, 1892), Vol. II, p. 124.

[5] *Statuto del Comune di Lucca 1308*, printed in *Memorie e Documenti per Servire all'Istoria del Principato Lucchese*, Vol. III, part iii, Lib. I, cap. xlii.

through her rule over Pistoia jointly with Florence.[6] By 1369 her losses were considerable. Florence had gained most at Lucchese expense — as well as the places named by Charles IV she also held an enclave in Lucchese territory in the Garfagnana, consisting of Sommocolonia and the important centre of Barga.[7] In the south Pisa held some castles which had once been held by Lucca and which the Lucchese still claimed, though in many cases these were places that had long been disputed between the two cities. The Lucchese chronicler, Sercambi, names twenty-nine villages and castles, including Bientina and Montecalvo, which he asserts were Lucchese castles held by Pisa.[8] Lucca had also suffered more recent losses to Milan in the north. Sercambi relates how in 1369, while fighting was still going on against Pisa, the men of Sarzana expressed a wish that they and the rest of Lunigiana might return to Lucchese obedience and offered the keys of the town to Lucca. But the forces in Lucchese service hesitated and thus gave Alderigo degli Antelminelli the opportunity to leave the camp secretly and take possession of Sarzana and the rest of Lunigiana in the name of Bernabò Visconti of Milan.[9] In this way Lucca suffered a further loss of territory at the very moment of recovering her independence. Because of this and the other losses she had suffered since 1306, she ruled a more limited territory after 1369 than she had done at the beginning of the fourteenth century. Her northern boundary now reached no further than Massa. In the south her territory no longer reached the Arno and places like Montecarlo, Veneri, Collodi, S. Gennaro, and Villa Basilica were now border villages on the frontier with Florence.

Lucca certainly ruled a smaller state than she had done in the early fourteenth century, but were the city itself and the territory that remained to her seriously impoverished? The misfortunes suffered in the earlier fourteenth century, the foreign rulers, the losses of territory, the financial exactions were bitterly felt by the Lucchese, but did they have a serious and permanent effect on her prosperity? Basic to any dis-

[6] G. Tommasi, 'Sommario della storia di Lucca dal MIV al MDCC', *Archivio Storico Italiano*, Ser. i, Vol. X (1847), pp. 141-2.

[7] Also Altopascio, Sercambi, II, p. 124.

[8] Sercambi, II, pp. 120-1.

[9] Sercambi, I, p. 168.

cussion of Lucca's prosperity or decline in the later fourteenth century is the question of population. Unfortunately it is difficult to find figures that can be used as the basis for an estimate. There are two sets of figures, both connected with the levying of *estimi*, that at first sight seem to provide some kind of indication of the population of the city after 1369. They are figures taken from the books of the *Massa* or public debt for the years 1368–73 and figures for the *Estimo* of 1397. But on closer examination both turn out to have serious disadvantages. The *Estimo* of 1397[10] lists roughly 1,483 persons. They are not, however, heads of households or adult males. They include a number of widows and other women who had property in their own right, and also two or more brothers, where they were joint heirs; in fact anyone who had sufficient property to be assessed. There would obviously be difficulty in deciding what multiplier to use. But there is also the further difficulty that the lists are not sufficiently comprehensive. Clergy, monks, and nuns were exempt, and so were aliens. But more serious is the omission of those who were too poor to be assessed. The decree establishing the *Estimo* had provided for the exemption of those declared to be 'povere e miserabili persone'[11] and this was observed, as there are few assessments under thirty florins. It was apparently not only the very poor who were exempt, for, as a man's assessment was to be only half the total valuation of his goods, it would take property worth sixty florins to produce an assessment of thirty florins.[12] There must have been many in Lucca who did not have goods worth sixty florins. Using a multiplier of 3·5, the 1,483 *estimati* would produce a population of only 5,191. Even using a multiplier of 5, which it would be hard to justify, would only produce a population of 7,415. To this should be added something for clergy, aliens, and the poor, but how many is a matter of guesswork. The figures for the *Estimo* of 1397 are

[10] There is a copy of this, though not contemporary, in the Biblioteca Governativa in Lucca, MS. 925, ff. 249–58.

[11] *Rif.* 13, p. 39, 18 June 1397 'intendendo sempre che di ciascuno de dicti stimi debbiano essere tracte libere et exempte le povere e miserabili persone. Et quelli sintendano in questo caso poveri et miserabili che seranno per poveri et miserabili dichiarati da dicti dieci citadini per terzieri'.

[12] It is not known what type of property was liable to assessment or whether allowances were made for debts or dependents.

clearly not sufficiently comprehensive to form a reliable basis for the calculation of the population.

The other set of figures, those of the creditors of the *Massa* for 1368–73, is at first sight more promising. Unfortunately it is not known on what principles the forced loans included in the *Massa* were assessed, and particularly whether or not the poor were exempt. The books themselves show many very small holdings of a florin, half a florin, or even less, and some very humble people, such as 'Masseo Junctini, portator' or 'Domina Vanna, recollectrix puerorum', were included. But if assessment was comprehensive enough to include some creditors drawn from the humbler ranks of society, it is far less certain that it did so uniformly. Though four or five widely distributed loans are included in the *Massa*, many of the smaller creditors had holdings in only one or two. If there were humbler citizens who were included in only one such loan, there may have been others who were not assessed in any at all. There is also the possibility that some smaller creditors had sold their holdings before the books were compiled and thus disappeared from the records. Poorer citizens did tend to sell their credits; only 495 persons are listed for the *terziere* of S. Martino for 1373–5 as against 637 for 1368–72.[13]

There are other problems in the use of these figures. The book for the *terziere* of S. Salvatore for 1368–73 is missing, and the figures for the other *terzieri* vary considerably, 800 persons for S. Paolino and 637 for S. Martino.[14] If the number for S. Salvatore lay somewhere between, there may have been about 720. This would be a total for all three *terzieri* of 2,157. There is still the problem of finding a multiplier. A multiplier of 5 would produce a population of about 10,785, but like the figures for the *Estimo* of 1397 the creditors of the *Massa* were not heads of households, and a multiplier of 3·5 is certainly to be preferred for figures based on financial levies, as for figures based on oaths.[15] This would produce a population of only about 7,550, which confirms one's doubts about the comprehensiveness of these figures. One would probably be justified in adding something for the poor who were not included in

[13] *Imprestiti*, nos. 11 and 13.
[14] *Imprestiti*, nos. 10 and 11.
[15] E. Cristiani, *Noblità e popolo nel comune di Pisa* (Naples, 1962), p. 166.

these forced loans, as well as for aliens and clergy, including monks and nuns, but this carries one into the realms of conjecture. However, a population of something in the region of 10,000 would not be out of line with evidence for the population of Lucca earlier and with figures for neighbouring cities in the late fourteenth century. Beloch estimated the population of Lucca at about 15,000 in 1331 on the basis of the oath taken to John of Bohemia and his son. Some 4,746 persons took this oath, including adult sons as well as fathers, groups of brothers and some widows, not just heads of households.[16] The population of Pisa has been estimated at about

[16] K. J. Beloch, *Bevölkerungsgeschichte Italiens*, Vol. II (Berlin, 1939), pp. 165–6. There is a wide discrepancy between this figure of 15,000 or a little more for 1331 and the figure of 40,000 for 1334 given by D. Herlihy, *Pisa in the early Renaissance* (New Haven, 1958), p. 43. Herlihy quotes figures given by C. Sardi, *Le contrattazioni agrarie del medio evo studiate nei documenti lucchesi* (Lucca, 1914), p. 138, who in turn derived them from S. Bongi, *Inventario del R. Archivio di Stato in Lucca,* Vol. II, pp. 22–3. This estimate is based on figures for wine imported into the city and involves the assumption that each adult drank five to six barrels a year. It is probably not a very reliable basis for an assessment of population, as the amount of wine imported in any year would depend on other factors in addition to the size of population. Also the figure quoted applies only to 1334; one cannot speak, as Herlihy does, of the same amount being consumed 'every year'. The oath of allegiance to John of Bohemia seems to have been taken by all adult Lucchese and to have been carefully administered, those temporarily absent swearing on their return or taking the oath by proxy during their absence, *Capitoli*, 52, pp. 3–301. It is probably a more reliable basis for the estimate of population than figures based on a tax on the import of wine. Evidence of population density based on the area enclosed by the city walls also supports the lower figure. The area enclosed was about 75 hectares and a total population of 15,000 would mean a density of 200 to the hectare, though in fact some of those who took the oath lived in the suburbs. A density of 200 to the hectare would be fairly high; in the early fourteenth century Florence seems to have had about 150 to the hectare, though Pisa had about 205 in the late thirteenth century. A population of 40,000 for Lucca would mean over 530 to the hectare. This is extremely improbable, especially as Lucca lay in a flat plain, so there were no mountains, as in Siena, to cause the population to be abnormally closely concentrated. See discussion by J. C. Russell, *Medieval Regions and their Cities* (Newton Abbot, 1972), p. 45. However there is little to support his suggested figure of 23,800 for Lucca, as it is based on an assumption that the 'men' who took the oath to John of Bohemia were the same proportion of the total population of Lucca as the 11,710 heads of families listed in Siena for 1328 were of the total population of that city. It has already been seen that those taking the oath of 1331 were not heads of families. Russell also assumes that something can be added for the population of the suburbs of Lucca, but the oath-takers included at least some living outside the city walls. Accepting a population of 15,000 involves of course an even higher wine consumption than the five or six barrels per person calculated by Herlihy, but for impressive wine consumption in other cities, W. M. Bowsky, *The Finance of the Commune of Siena, 1287–1355* (Oxford, 1970), pp. 146–51, and E. Fiumi, 'Sui rapporti economici tra città e contado nell'età communale', *Archivio Storico Italiano*, Vol. CXIV (1956), pp. 29–30.

15,000 at the end of the fourteenth century and 10,000 in 1427–9.[17] Pisa was certainly still a larger city than Lucca in the late fourteenth century, as she had been in the twelfth and thirteenth.[18] Lucca would not have been able to plead her smallness and poverty as successfully as she did in order to keep down her obligations in leagues if she had been equal in size to Pisa. The smallness and decline of Lucca is a constant theme in late fourteenth-century records, even in internal discussions where there is no question of evading any outside obligation. Lucca's smallness was self-evident; 'come a voi signori e manifesto la cita e picola e con poghi citadini'.[19] Though there are no figures on which any reliance can be placed it is by no means improbable that Lucca had a population of only about 10,000 in the last decades of the fourteenth century.

A rather more accurate estimate is possible of the population of the *contado*. In 1383 a census of the inhabitants over the age of five was made for the salt tax, and these figures survive. The 'bocche' numbered 24,297.[20] With those under the age of five added the total would perhaps be about 30,000. The census only included the vicariates, not the *suburbio* or the *distretto* of Six Miles. But their population can perhaps be estimated. In 1381 an assessment had been made for the *cerne*, the militia of the *contado*. In this the Six Miles and *suburbio* had to produce 600 men to the 2,000 men provided by the vicariates.[21] If the population was in the same ratio, as seems probable, there would be about 7,290 'bocche' over the

[17] B. Casini, *Aspetti della vita economica e sociale di Pisa dal catasto del 1428–9* (Pisa, 1965), pp. 9–11. C. Violante, 'Imposte dirette e debito pubblico a Pisa nel medio evo', in *L'Impôt dans le cadre de la ville et de l'état*, Colloque Internationale, *Pro Civitate*, Collection Histoire (Brussels, 1966), pp. 78–9.

[18] Herlihy, *Pisa in the Early Renaissance*, pp. 42–3. Lucca's second circle of walls were begun about 1200, half a century after those of Pisa, and the area enclosed was only 75 hectares as opposed to the 114 hectares for Pisa north of the Arno or 185 including Kinsica. In 1355 Pisan revenues were 141,000 florins, including 36,000 she received annually from Lucca, and this and their relative obligations in leagues would suggest that Pisa was appreciably larger than Lucca in the fourteenth century.

[19] *Rif.* 8, p. 222, 12 Aug. 1382. Efforts after 1369 to revive the silk industry and introduce the manufacture of good quality woollen cloth were designed at least partly 'ut civitas civibus et eorum famulis repleatur', *Rif.* 7, pp. 544–5, 20 Aug., pp. 628–30, 2 Dec. 1381.

[20] *Rif.* 8, pp. 497–9, 29 Apr. 1383.

[21] *Rif.* 7, pp. 481–2, 26 Apr., pp. 489–90, 20 May 1381.

age of five, perhaps about 9,000 inhabitants altogether, including young children. This would be about 39,000 for the *contado* and *distretto* together, though something would have to be added for certain castles that were administered separately, to obtain a figure for the population of the Lucchese state as a whole.[22] As in the case of the city there are many indications of decline in the population of the *contado*. Again it is a constant theme in petitions and other records.[23] Many petitioners speak of a decline only in general terms, but others quote figures to support their claims. Examples of such figures are the case of Vegghiatore, which in 1342 had forty men and in 1370 had only twelve,[24] S. Lorenzo, pieve di Massa Macinara, which had once had eleven men, but in 1370 had only four,[25] or Schiappa which had seven men in 1378, though it had once had twice as many.[26] There were even more impressive declines. Ruota had once had 150 men, but in 1381 it had only sixteen.[27] Castiglione had once had 800 men, but had declined to eighty by 1384.[28] These can hardly have been typical, but a less severe decline was clearly general.

Causes for this decline in population in both the city and

[22] This is a relatively high ratio of rural to urban population for a city that was a centre of trade and industry, P. J. Jones, 'Medieval agrarian society in its prime: Italy', in *Cambridge Economic History*, Vol. I (Second edition, Cambridge, 1966), pp. 245-7. It is appreciably higher even than relatively unindustrialized Pistoia, see the figures given by D. Herlihy, *Medieval and Renaissance Pistoia* (New Haven, Conn., 1967), pp. 76-7 and Table 3, Population Urban and Rural, 1219-1569, p. 76, also pp. 112-14. For Siena, W. M. Bowsky, 'The impact of the Black Death on Sienese government and society', *Speculum*, Vol. XXXIX (1964), pp. 5-11. But it seems that in the sixteenth century the Lucchese state was comparatively densely populated, with 130,000 inhabitants to 1410 sq. km, a density for the entire state of 92 inhabitants per sq. km. Florence, with 300,000 inhabitants to 5,799 sq. km, had a density of only 52 inhabitants per sq. km, though the city of Florence had almost 60,000 inhabitants to Lucca's 24,000, Beloch, *Bevölkerungsgeschichte Italiens*, Vol. II, pp. 474-6. For evidence of heavy population in the Lucchese contado in the sixteenth century, M. Berengo, *Nobili e mercanti nella Lucca del Cinquecento* (Turin, 1965), pp. 305-6. Also G. Cherubini, 'Qualche considerazione sulle campagne dell'Italia centro-settentrionale tra l'XI e il XV secolo', *Rivista Storica Italiana*, Vol. LXXIX (1967), p. 137. This unusually high density of rural population may also apply to the fourteenth century.

[23] See below, Chapter 4, pp. 78–97.

[24] *Rif.* 1, p. 300, 9 Apr. 1370.

[25] *Rif.* 1, p. 265., 5 Mar. 1370.

[26] *Rif.* 6, pp. 568-9, 14 May 1378.

[27] *Rif.* 7, pp. 569-70, 19 Sept. 1381.

[28] *Rif.* 9, p. 66, 4 Mar. 1384.

contado are not far to seek. As far as the city was concerned the political troubles of Lucca in the fourteenth century had led to repeated waves of emigration on a scale that can hardly have failed to have caused serious losses. Apart from emigration, losses may also have resulted from the wars of the fourteenth century. Though there had been wars in earlier centuries, those of the fourteenth century were probably more serious and more damaging, especially the sack of Lucca in 1314 and the siege of the city in 1342, but there were a number of other years when there was campaigning in the Lucchese state and her territory suffered severely. Outbreaks of plague must also have had an effect. Apart from the Black Death in 1348 there had been at least one other outbreak before 1369 and there were to be others later. Some places in the *contado* specifically attribute the decline in their population to deaths from plague.

A smaller *contado* and a decline in the population of what remained and of the city itself must have led to a decrease in Lucca's resources. In addition her main industry, the manufacture of silk cloth, had also declined, partly as a result of the emigration of Lucchese silk-workers and increasing competition from other centres of production. It is difficult to be sure of the extent to which the various foreign rulers contributed to the decline of Lucchese prosperity. There must have been much destruction of property in the sack of 1314. The wars of Castruccio Castracani and the building of the Augusta were costly and the costs had to be borne by the Lucchese. Much is heard of financial exactions under the Pisans. At times Pisa took direct control of the Lucchese revenues; at others she left the Lucchese to administer their own finances, demanding a fixed sum each year, and also making the Lucchese contribute to extraordinary payments, such as war indemnities. These exactions by a foreign ruler were regarded as unjust and oppressive, and were bitterly resented, but it is doubtful if they were really unreasonable or beyond Lucca's capacity to pay, let alone severe enough to damage her prosperity permanently. Figures such as 35,000 or 40,000 florins a year do not seem to be unduly high, as this was to cover the costs of the defence and custody of the city and state. Though Lucca's revenues were somewhat reduced in this period and she does seem to have had some difficulty in raising the sums she had to pay to Pisa and the additional sum of about 8,000 florins she needed each year for the expenses for which she was directly responsible, little if any of the money Lucca paid ever reached Pisa; it was spent in Lucca itself on payments to Pisan forces there and other local expenses.[29] The possession of Lucca seems to have brought Pisa no direct financial benefit and at times to have been a burden. After the revolt of 1355 Pisa was apparently obliged to contribute to the cost of the defence and administration of Lucca out of her own pocket.[30] During the war with Florence that began in 1362 Lucca had to contribute a share of the cost and this involved the payment of large sums as *prestanze*,[31] but in 1369 she still had the resources to make the exceptional financial efforts necessary to buy her freedom from Charles IV.

If it is difficult to estimate the effect of Pisan rule on Lucchese prosperity, there seems little doubt that the recovery of her independence involved heavy obligations and was a serious strain on her resources. The payments she had to make in 1368–70 were heavy, and she began her independence deeply in debt. She had obtained her freedom by outbidding the Pisans for imperial favour. There must also have been many presents to influential courtiers and heavy incidental expenses in entertaining the Emperor and Empress and the Patriarch of Aquilea and their following for several months. The Lucchese were expected to make a contribution to imperial campaigns against Pisa and to the building of the

[29] Lucca was directly responsible for the payment of 2,333⅓ florins to Florence as her third share of the war indemnity of 7,000 florins a year. She also had to spend an agreed sum varying between 800 and 1,000 florins a year on the repair of fortresses, and pay certain salaries and other expenses that had been estimated at 5,000 florins a year in 1345, *Capitoli*, 19, ff. 46^{v}–47. In many years the sums recorded as passing through the hands of the Lucchese treasurer were insufficient to cover these expenses and the annual payment to Pisa, and the difference must have been made up from loans, *Ragionieri della Camera e del Comune*, nos. 3–9.

[30] A.S.P. *Comune A* 60, f. 32^{v}, 7 June 1355. Complaints of Pisan citizens and *contadini* of the burden of guard duty in Lucca, A.S.P. *Comune A*, 56, ff. 67–67^{v}, 12 Oct. 1349.

[31] Lucca never had to pay more than a quarter of the total of any *prestanza* raised in Pisa and Lucca jointly, but the sums she had to contribute were large, 12,500 florins in April 1363, a further 12,500 florins in June and 15,000 florins, which she was able to get reduced to 12,000 florins, in August of the same year, *Anz. Av. Lib.* 42, p. 233, 5 Apr., p. 264, 19 June, p. 286, 29 Aug., p. 289, 30 Aug. 1363. This was at a time when

Castello Cezareo in Lucca itself.[32] The Emperor also demanded a direct payment of 100,000 florins for the liberation of Lucca, and Sercambi makes it sound as though this were only one of the payments made to him.[33] Lucca could not afford to refuse this sum and had no choice but to promise it, though it was quite beyond her resources to pay it by Christmas 1369, the term originally set. A figure of 100,000 florins was probably about a year and a half's revenue at this time, and Lucca was able to satisfy the Emperor's demands only by having 50,000 of the 100,000 florins transferred to the Papacy and borrowing the rest from Florence, Niccolò d'Este of Ferrara and Francesco Carrara of Padua.[34] In addition Lucca had to agree to pay 40,000 florins a year to the imperial vicar whom Charles IV left in Lucca, to cover the costs of the custody of the city and the salaries of officials. When the imperial vicar left in 1370 gifts and a further payment of 20,000 florins were made to him.[35] Sercambi puts the total amount that Lucca had to pay in these years at 300,000 florins.[36] Though it is not easy to see how he arrived at this figure and it is probably an overestimate, there can be no doubt that the costs of obtaining her liberty were great and that Lucca's resources were seriously strained. She had the greatest difficulty in paying off the debts she had contracted in 1368–70, and it was not until 1387 that Lucchese debts to outside powers were finally settled.[37] Lucca also had to borrow from her own citizens, and the public debt, originating in loans contracted in 1368–70 to pay the costs of the recovery of her independence, was still in existence in 1400.

In general it can be said that Lucca had declined greatly by 1369 in comparison with her position in the first years of the fourteenth century, when she had been at the height of her power. In 1369 her territory was much reduced, and although there is a lack of clear evidence, it is probable that the

---

the ordinary revenues of Lucca were in Pisan hands.

[32] Sercambi, I, pp. 144–72.

[33] Sercambi, I, p. 174.

[34] Copy of the obligation to pay Charles IV 100,000 florins, *Capitoli*, 4, ff. 32–3, 4 June 1369. *Anz. Av. Lib.* 46, p. 9, 12 June 1369.

[35] *Capitoli*, 31, pp. 337–8.

[36] Sercambi, I, p. 174.

[37] See below, Chapter 3, p. 57.

population both of the city and the *contado* had suffered a serious contraction. Lucchese prosperity had also almost certainly declined, although it would be difficult to attribute it to any one cause, such as over-taxation by the Pisans. Lucca no longer had a near monopoly in the silk industry in Northern Italy. Her own silk industry had declined and other cities had become serious rivals. Finally she started her new independence heavily burdened with debts, mostly contracted in 1369–70. In 1369 her continuance as an independent state must have seemed problematical. As a small, weak state, surrounded by powerful neighbours, she had to fight for survival in the first few years after 1369.

2

INDUSTRIAL AND COMMERCIAL WEALTH

SITUATED at an important junction on the *via francigena*, one of the main roads from the north to Rome, controlling a stretch of coastline and enjoying since at least 1081 the right to navigate off Motrone, Lucca was favourably placed geographically and important commercial clauses in treaties made in the twelfth century and later show her taking advantage of this to develop her trade. She also engaged in industrial activity. She had, of course, many kinds of craftsmen, such as tailors and shoemakers, catering only for a limited home market, but she also had industries that were of more than local importance. There was iron-mining, apparently on some scale, in the hills around Pietrasanta, and in Lucca itself wool and linen cloth, leather-work, and gold and silversmiths' work of high quality were produced for export as well as local consumption. But far and away the most important industry in Lucca was the silk industry, described in a petition in 1375 as 'una dota precipua et un dono singulare da dio precedente'.[1] It was essentially an export industry and depended on widespread trading contacts. The raw materials came from abroad. The raw silk came from the Greek Empire, Asia Minor, Syria, Persia, Georgia and the shores of the Caspian Sea, and even from distant Cathay. Silk was also produced in Spain, Sicily and parts of Italy. There are occasional mentions of Lucchese silk in the fourteenth and fifteenth centuries, but Lucca certainly never produced enough silk herself to supply the needs of her industry, and was

[1] *Rif.* 5, p. 149, 21 Dec. 1375. For pre-fourteenth-century Lucchese trade and industry, Tommasi, Lib. I, chapters 2–5 and Appendix of documents pp. 48–118; T. W. Blomquist, 'Trade and Commerce in thirteenth-century Lucca', unpublished doctoral dissertation, Department of History, University of Minnesota (Minneapolis, 1966) and 'The Castracani family of thirteenth-century Lucca', *Speculum*, Vol. XLVI, (1971), pp. 459–76. Also C. E. Meek, 'The trade and industry of Lucca in the fourteenth century', in T. W. Moody (ed.), *Historical Studies VI* (London, 1968), pp. 39–58, where some of the things dealt with in this chapter are treated in greater detail.

therefore dependent upon imported raw materials. The dye-stuffs, grain or kermes, indigo, woad, saffron, and some of the gold thread used was also imported.[2] The silk industry was a luxury industry, producing rich and costly cloths like *baldacchino*, *imperiale*, damask, brocade, velvet, and cloth of gold and silver that were used for ecclesiastical vestments and hangings, as well as for clothing for noble and princely houses. There were also lighter-weight silks, like sendal, sarsenet, and taffeta, which were primarily used for clothing. Virtually all this silk cloth was exported. In the fourteenth century sumptuary laws forbade the Lucchese themselves to wear rich cloths of silk and gold.[3]

The Lucchese silk industry reached the height of its prosperity and fame in the thirteenth century, with Lucchese silks listed in inventories not only in Italy but also in Northern Europe and numerous contracts for the sale and purchase of silk and the manufacture of silk cloth preserved in the notarial records.[4] In the fourteenth century a decline began, largely as

[2] There is a considerable literature on the Lucchese silk industry, notably F. Edler, 'The Silk Trade of Lucca during the thirteenth and fourteenth centuries', unpublished doctoral dissertation, Department of History, University of Chicago (Chicago, 1930); C. Massei, *Dell'Arte della Seta in Lucca* (Lucca, 1843); L. Ciucci, *L'Arte della Seta in Lucca* (Como, 1930); E. Lazzareschi, *L'Arte della Seta in Lucca*, Seconda Settimana Lucchese, May 1930; T. Bini, *I Lucchesi a Venezia* (Lucca, 1853); S. Bongi, *Della Mercatura Lucchese nei secoli XIII e XIV*, in *Atti della R. Accademia Lucchese*, Vol. XXIII (1884), pp. 443–521, and reprinted with additions Lucca, 1884. More generally, F. Podreider, *Storia dei Tessuti d'Arte in Italia* (Bergamo, 1928); F. Michel, *Recherches sur le commerce, la fabrication et l'usage des étoffes de soie, d'or et d'argent et autres tissus precieux en occident, principalement en France, pendant le moyen âge*, 2 vols. (Paris, 1852–4); W. Heyd, *Histoire dû commerce du Levant au moyen âge*, tr. Furcy Raynaud, 2 vols. (Leipzig, 1923); *La Pratica della Mercatura di Francesco Balducci Pegolotti* (ed. Allan Evans) Medieval Academy of America, 1936. There is much valuable information in *L'Arte della Seta in Firenze*, an anonymous treatise of the late fourteenth or early fifteenth century, published by G. Gargiolli (Florence, 1868); also *Lo Statuto della Corte dei Mercanti in Lucca del MCCCLXXVI* (ed. A. Mancini, U. Dorini, and E. Lazzareschi (Florence, 1927).

[3] For these and other types of silk cloth *Statuto della Corte dei Mercanti*, Lib. IV, 16–21, 23–31, 33–6, and pp. 190–5; Michel, *Recherches*, Vol. 1, pp. 172–3, 211, 243–5, 253–6, 354–8; Pegolotti, pp. 415, 429, 434. Sumptuary laws, *Anz. Av. Lib*. 42, p. 6, 8 Jan. 1362, *Rif*. 7, pp. 285–9, 28 June 1380.

[4] Bini, *I Lucchesi a Venezia*, pp. 16–19, 42–4, 75–6; Bongi, *Della Mercatura Lucchese*, pp. 36, 38–40; Ciucci, *Dell'Arte della Seta*, p. 22; Lazzareschi, *L'Arte della Seta*, pp. 6–8; Podreider, *Storia dei Tessuti d'Arte*, pp. 32–3; Edler, *The Silk Trade of Lucca*, pp. 24–6, 99; 'Inventaire du Trésor du Saint-Siège sous Boniface VIII', *Bibliothèque de l'École des Chartes*, Vol. XLVII (1886), pp. 649–50. The importance of the silk industry to Lucca is shown by the fact that 18 of the 36 consuls and 21 of the

a result of political disturbances. Repeated revolutions and changes of regime caused waves of emigration of Lucchese silk workers to Florence, Bologna, Venice, Genoa, and elsewhere. Even in the thirteenth century Lucca had not been the only north Italian city producing silks; Florence, Venice, and Genoa also had silk industries, but the Lucchese industry had been the most highly developed and her products the most sought after. When her silk-workers began to emigrate in the fourteenth century, taking with them the skill and trade secrets on which the superiority of Lucchese silks depended, they were sure of a warm welcome in other Italian cities and were given every encouragement to engage in silk production there. According to a sixteenth-century writer, 300 families and their dependants left Lucca for other Italian cities and for France, Germany, or England, so that 'sericorum pannorum ars, qua soli Lucenses in Italia et divitiis affluebant et gloria florebant ubique exerceri coepta'.[5] Over thirty Lucchese families were living in Venice between 1310 and 1340, and according to Venetian chroniclers there were 300 Lucchese silk-workers living there.[6]

Emigration on this scale could hardly fail to harm the Lucchese industry and benefit that of other cities. The Lucchese in Bologna claimed in 1343 that 'si fanno quazi tante sendada in Bologna quante si facciano a Luccha', and their industry was so powerful that their silks were able to rival those of Lucca in the markets of France and the Low Countries.[7] The Lucchese government made efforts to check emigration and the spread of the secrets of Lucchese silk manufacture to other cities. It is unlikely that the decree of Castruccio Castracani forbidding Lucchese who were in exile to engage in silk manufacture had any effect, but during the period of

36 councillors who governed the Court of Merchants were to be silk merchants. The others were drawn in equal numbers from three groups, the manufacturers and importers of woollen cloth; the bankers, jewellers, and goldsmiths; the apothecaries, mercers, and all other trades governed by the Court.

[5] N. Tegrimi, *Vita Castruccii Antelminelli, Lucensis Duci 1301-1328*, R.I.S., Tom. XI (1727), col. 1320-1.

[6] Bini, *I Lucchesi a Venezia*, pp. 174-8; G. Livi, 'I Mercanti di Seta Lucchesi in Bologna nei secoli XIII e XIV', *Archivio Storico Italiano*, Ser. iv, Vol. VII (1881), pp. 29-55, esp. pp. 35-7; Edler, *The Silk Trade of Lucca*, pp. 18-21, 181-3.

[7] Livi, 'I Mercanti di Seta Lucchesi', p. 41; Edler, *The Silk Trade of Lucca*, pp. 178-80.

Pisan rule efforts were made to attract exiles back by offers of immunities and tax exemptions. The Lucchese in Bologna used these offers as a bargaining lever to exact better terms from the Bolognese government for remaining there, but some exiles did return from other places. Lucchese records show that twenty-three families took up the immunity between 30 July and 24 December 1343, a further twenty in 1346 and sixteen in 1347. The missing volumes for 1344 and 1345 may well have recorded the return of other families, and others had probably returned before with some change of regime and offer of political amnesty. But many families remained abroad permanently, and many of those that did return were merchants and bankers rather than silk-workers.[8]

It has sometimes been assumed that Lucca's trade and industry recovered rapidly and automatically when she regained her independence in 1369,[9] but there is little evidence that this happened. The assumption rests partly on the belief that large numbers of citizens returned from exile in the years 1368–70. This belief is supported by statements of Giovanni Sercambi, but there are no lists, as there are for 1343 and 1346–7, and it is difficult to find more than a few examples of men who did return in this period, and even these few were not necessarily silk-workers.[10] It seems probable that

[8] Edler, *The Silk Trade of Lucca*, p. 176; Livi, 'I Mercanti di Seta Lucchesi', pp. 37–41. Men returning, *Anz. Av. Lib.* 21, (30 July–23 Dec. 1343), *Anz. Av. Lib.* 24, (1346), and 26 (1347). Livi, pp. 46–7 gives slightly different numbers of families and dates their return 12 Jan.–7 June 1343, but the names show he is basing his statements on the same sources. There had been offers of amnesty in 1331 and later, and *Curia de'Ribelli e de'Banditi*, 3 records those returning and claiming their property at various dates after this.

[9] For example Ciucci, *Dell'Arte della Seta*, p. 27, 'Nel giro brevissimo di pochi mesi la città passò dalla desolazione al più florido stato . . . quasi che il movimento del traffico non si fosse mai interotto.'

[10] 'Tornònno molti ciptadini ricchi et possenti & amadori di Luccha, da Genova, Vinegia, Parigi, Vignone e d'altri paesi', Sercambi, I, p. 171, also pp. 173, 190. There are some references to men returning, *Rif.* 1, p. 334, 4 May, p. 401, 22 June 1370, *Rif.* 4, p. 326, 5 Feb. 1374, *Delib.* 132, f. 6, 29 May 1371, but they were not very numerous, nor were they important citizens or necessarily connected with trade or industry. Dino di Vanni Malapresa, a merchant whose family had been absent since 1314, expressed a desire to return. *Delib.* 132, f. 13, 20 June 1371, and some other merchants, such as Giuffredo Cenami, Bartolomeo Faitinelli, Orlandino Volpelli, and Enrico Sandei, who are known to have been living abroad at times before 1369, returned from Venice. But they left relatives or factors in Venice and carried on their business in both cities, sometimes returning there after 1369, so they cannot be regarded as returned exiles.

many were too firmly settled abroad by 1369 to think of uprooting themselves. Certainly there were many families of Lucchese origin established in Venice and other cities, whose names no longer appear in Lucchese documents. There were, however, a number of foreign silk-workers living in Lucca in the last thirty years of the fourteenth century. They seem to have come in the 1370s and 1380s, though a few had come before 1369. The *Riformagioni* and notarial records give the names of more than twenty Venetians, eight Florentines and another fifteen or more from other Italian cities and in one case from Flanders. But despite the possible return of some Lucchese and immigration from other cities, the Lucchese industry does not seem to have made rapid progress after 1369. At a meeting of the weavers' gild in 1376 there were 104 present and another thirteen signed the decrees later. This is appreciably fewer than the 164 who had attended a similar meeting in 1358, which suggests that the industry had declined still further rather than recovering since the end of Pisan rule.[11] Nor do the figures for the numbers engaged in the trade in silks after 1369 suggest that there was any rapid or immediate expansion. The declarations of the numbers and names of their employees, which all firms of silk merchants had to make to the Court of Merchants each year, survive for the years 1371, 1372, and 1381. The size and composition of a firm was very fluid, and there are considerable variations from year to year. In 1371 there were ninety firms employing a total of 316 persons. In 1372 there were seventy-five firms employing a total of 285 persons and in 1381 eighty-two firms employing 311 persons.[12]

[11] *Protocolli* of ser Bartolomeo Buonmese, *Archivio de'Notari*, no. 123, 25 Apr. 1376. For 1358 *Protocolli* of ser Niccolò Lupori, referred to in Bini, *I Lucchesi a Venezia*, pp. 63-4, and Edler, *The Silk Trade of Lucca*, p. 68. The 164 silk weavers are said to be 'duo partes et ultra satis de tribus partibus hominum universitatis', that is presumably a quorum. Bini, followed by Edler, concluded, however, that the total number of weavers in Lucca was at least 240, but it is likely that far more than the minimum number necessary to form a quorum would be present.

[12] *Corte de'Mercanti*, 82, ff. 3-12^v, 40-41^v (1371), 83, ff. 2-9 (1372); 84, ff. 4-12^v (1381). The figures for 1381 should perhaps be a little higher, as folios 12^v-39 are missing and the next section does not begin until f.18, according to the table of contents. But there were probably some blank folios, so that the missing names, if any, would not be very numerous. These were men employed in the trade in silks, not including weavers or others engaged in manufacturing. There were 10 firms of *tintores*

The Lucchese themselves in petitions and decrees made to aid the silk industry stressed its continuing decline after 1369 and the increasing competition it was having to face from other cities equally or better suited to the manufacture of silk. They sometimes took as gloomy a view of the future of the industry as they did of its past and its present, as when in 1381 it was stated that the industry 'declinavit et declinat et magis dubitetur declinatura in futurum'.[13] But efforts were made to assist it by abolishing import duties on first some and then all types of silk coming into the city, and appointing officials to ensure supplies.[14] Efforts were made to ensure that all silks manufactured in Lucca should be of the highest quality.[15] A new statute of the Court of Merchants, begun in 1376 though not completed until 1381, included detailed regulations to ensure good workmanship in the dyeing and weaving of silk, and forbade the use of inferior types of silk, gold, and silver. Only authorized persons could buy or sell materials used in silk manufacture, and dyers and other workmen were not permitted to do work on their own account or to accept commissions from any who were not silk merchants. To make control easier all weavers in Lucca had to be registered, and all work begun had to be declared to the Court. Finished cloth was examined for quality and that which met the Court's minimum standards was sealed with an official seal. No cloth was to be offered for sale without this seal, and the penalty for forging it was death. The seal was intended as a guarantee of the quality of Lucchese goods, and efforts were made to publicize these new regulations as widely as possible.[16]

---

et cocitores sete in 1371, and 11 in 1372, *Corte de'Mercanti*, 82, ff. 30–1; 83, ff. 38–38v. There were 12 firms of *tintores* and 2 firms of *cocitores* in 1381, *Corte de'Mercanti*, 84, ff. 43–43v, 46. There were also 14 firms of *tintores et cocitores* in 1407, *Corte de Mercanti* 85, ff. 34–35v, but some may not have been concerned with silk dyeing.

[13] *Rif.* 7, p. 628, 2 Dec. 1381.

[14] *Rif.* 4, p. 140, 25 May 1373, p. 398, 26 May 1374, *Rif.* 7, pp. 544–5, 20 Aug. 1381.

[15] A petition of the consuls of the Court of Merchants, incorporated into the statute, claimed that 'multa et multa sete laboreria fiat in dicta civitate lucana, que sunt vilia imperfecta non bona male atque calunpniose laborata, et talia propter que etiam alia lucana·laboreria per totum orbem ab omnibus vitantur et vilipenduntur', *Statuto*, pp. 1–2.

[16] *Statuto* Lib. I, 9, Lib. IV, 13, 37–8, 40–4, 52, 64, 68 and additions pp. 183–4, 30 July 1381, p. 198, 25 June 1382. *Corte de'Mercanti*, 16, ff. 4–5, 23 Feb. 1389.

Efforts were also made to afford protection to the Lucchese silk industry by forbidding the import and sale in Lucca of cloth of silk or gold manufactured outside the Lucchese state. The export of raw and partly worked silk was also prohibited, and instruments and tools used in the manufacture of silk cloth were not to be taken out of the city, 'ad fine che lo mestieri della seta piu non si spanda in delle strane parti'.[17] In April 1381 a further decree was passed forbidding any throwsters or weavers to leave the city or *distretto* to engage in silk manufacture elsewhere, and ordering all those who had already left to return within four months. But this kind of prohibition was virtually impossible to enforce, and it is unlikely to have had much effect. It seems to have proved impossible even to prevent the export of looms and other instruments used in the manufacture of silk; for the prohibition was repeated in 1389, when it was said that they were being exported daily.[18]

There are virtually no provisions relating to the silk industry in the records of council meetings for the last decade of the fourteenth century, when in any case the records become less full, but some indication of the state of the industry can be obtained from figures taken from the customs accounts. There are figures for about half the years 1369–1410, when the series stops, and there are also figures for 1339 and 1351.[19] On the basis of these figures the nineteenth-century Lucchese archivist, Salvatore Bongi, stated that Lucca exported 125,000 *libbre* of worked silk of various kinds in 1339 and that this had dropped to 50,000 *libbre* by 1351. He added that samples of the figures for the years after 1369 showed no signs of a rapid recovery.[20] But these figures must be regarded with caution. They are not annual averages, but are taken from two isolated

[17] *Statuto* Lib. IV, 41, also 40, 42–4. Decree of 15 Nov. 1370 referred to when confirmed, *Rif.* 3, p. 123, 19 Nov. 1371. There were similar measures to protect the wool industry in Pistoia, Herlihy, *Medieval and Renaissance Pistoia*, pp. 157–8.

[18] *Statuto*, pp. 176–7, 22 Apr. 1381, *Rif.* 11, p. 154, 9 Nov. 1389, *Corte de'Mercanti*, 16, ff. 20v–21, 12 Oct. 1389.

[19] Series *Gabella Maggiore*, nos. 10–50, 1329–1433, but the records for the years after 1410 are fragmentary. The references for the years quoted are nos. 10–11 (1339), no. 13 (1351), nos. 17–18 (1378), no. 22 (1386), nos. 26–7 (1389), nos. 27–8 (1390), no. 34 (1396), no. 38 (1401), no. 45 (1410).

[20] S. Bongi, *Inv.* II, p. 246.

years, one of which was very shortly after the Black Death. Also, on examining the records they are found to be based on figures for four months of each year only, January, February, March, and August 1339, and January, February, May, and June 1351. The totals vary greatly from month to month; almost three times as much silk was exported in February 1339 as in March of the same year. A comparison with figures for the period after 1369 shows that exports varied greatly and unpredictably from month to month for years in which figures for the whole year survive. It is clearly dangerous to assume that figures for the whole year can be worked out simply by multiplying those for the existing four months by three. But although the totals for 1339 and 1351 cannot be regarded as reliable, there can be no doubt that there had been a decline in silk exports by 1369. There are figures for a number of complete years in the later fourteenth century, and in only one case does the total for a whole year exceed that for the four months of 1339. That was in 1378, when slightly under 35,000 *libbre* of silk were exported. It seems probable that there had been a further decline since 1351, and there are no signs of recovery towards the end of the fourteenth century or in the early years of the fifteenth. There seems indeed to have been a further decline; fewer than 30,000 *libbre* of silk were exported in 1386, fewer than 25,000 in 1389, about 22,000 in 1390, about 14,000 in 1396 and 1401, and under 10,000 in 1410. These figures support certain statements in Sercambi about the decline of the silk industry. He speaks about 1392 of the 'pogo fare della seta'.[21] Under the year 1419 he speaks at length about the troubles of the silk industry, asserting that the disorders in France in this period had caused the Lucchese a loss of 150,000 florins, and that as a result of this little or no silk working was being done in Lucca and the Lucchese were being driven to emigrate again.[22] Declarations of silk firms to the Court of Merchants show that in 1407 there were only sixty-four firms employing 131 persons.[23] Similar figures for 1488 show that there were eighty-eight firms employing about

[21] In his 'Nota ai Guinigi', written about 1392. Printed in Vol. III of *Chroniche Lucchesi*, p. 405.

[22] Sercambi, III, pp. 251–2.

[23] *Corte de'Mercanti*, 85, ff. 3–12^{v}.

210 persons, but not all of these were silk merchants, and many of those that traded in silks, also engaged in general trade as well.[24] This suggests that there may have been little improvement in the situation even quite late in the fifteenth century, though there is some evidence in chroniclers and in a Lucchese memoir that the industry had recovered by the early sixteenth century, and silk-working was still done in Lucca in the eighteenth century.[25]

But in the last twenty years of the fourteenth century the decline of the Lucchese silk industry was sufficiently serious for an attempt to be made to revive the wool industry in Lucca to supplement the declining profits of the silk industry. It was also hoped to prevent any further decline in the population of the city by providing an alternative means of livelihood for some of those already living there, and to encourage immigration from other cities. There had earlier been a wool industry of some importance in Lucca, but in the fourteenth century it seems to have greatly declined. Though it is unlikely that woollen cloth production had ceased completely, the number of references to it before 1381 is not great, and it is probable that it was not in a very flourishing state.[26] In that year, however, a general invitation was issued to all *forenses* to come and settle in Lucca and engage in the wool industry there, offering as an inducement a five-year period of freedom from actions for debts contracted outside the Lucchese state, provided they were not owed to Lucchese citizens. In addition the city undertook to build at public expense the fulling works, dye-works, and tenters necessary for the industry, authorizing the expenditure of up to 2,000 florins.[27] The highest hopes

[24] *Corte de'Mercanti*, 86, ff. 1-7^v, 9^v-11^v, 12^v, 14. Five more men were approved as merchants, 26 June 1488, ff. 15-15^v.

[25] Bongi, *Inv.* II, pp. 246-7. Ciucci, *Dell'Arte della Seta*, p. 31, figures given by sixteenth-century writers for pre-1534, 3,000 looms, 20,000 workers employed and 360,000 *libbre* of silk exported, but it is difficult to believe such a recovery possible by the early sixteenth century.

[26] For the wool industry in the thirteenth century T. W. Blomquist, 'The Drapers of Lucca and the marketing of cloth in the mid-thirteenth century', in *Economy, Society and Government in Medieval Italy*, essays in memory of Robert L. Reynolds, ed. D. Herlihy, R. S. Lopez, and V. Slessarev (Kent, Ohio, 1969), pp. 68-9. Also C. E. Meek, 'The Trade and Industry of Lucca', pp. 47-8.

[27] *Rif.* 7, pp. 628-9, 2 Dec., p. 657, 30 Dec. 1381, *Rif.* 8, pp. 60-1, 26 Feb., p. 87, 11 Apr., p. 209, 29 July 1382, p. 437, 27 Jan. 1383. *Min.* 3 (not foliated), 24 Feb. 1382.

were entertained for the development of the industry. It was even suggested that there would be a shortage of houses for the newcomers if as many came as was hoped, and that it would therefore be wise to set about building new ones on the many empty plots within the city walls.[28] Some difficulties were encountered. The cost of developing the wool industry was found to be considerable, and a number of agreements were made to let the various buildings and subcontract the building of others to individuals and groups, so as to spare Lucca any further expense and even bring in an income.[29] But the city was so determined to develop the industry that it authorized further large sums of money to be spent when it was petitioned that the industry was being held back for lack of adequate tenters and fulling and dye-works.[30] In 1391 after the fulling works had been out of action for some months owing to the failure of the water supply, which Lucca was responsible for maintaining, they were once more taken over by the commune.[31]

Despite these difficulties the effort to develop the wool industry met with some success. In February 1387 the immunity granted to those coming to Lucca to engage in the wool industry was renewed for another ten years in view of the good effects it had had so far. It was stated that the number engaged in it was increasing daily, so it would bring great benefit to the city.[32] Fortunately we are not obliged to rely on the dubious statements of interested parties to estimate the success of the wool industry. The Lucchese Archives contain a list of those immigrants who came and registered their names in the chancery with the date, their place of origin, and often the branch of the industry in which they specialized.[33] This

[28] *Rif.* 8. p. 250, 8 Sept. 1382.

[29] *Rif.* 8, pp. 271-3, 26 Sept. 1382, pp. 466-7, 2 Mar. 1383.

[30] 'Defectu purgi tiratorii et tintorie dicta ars non multum coalescat', *Rif.* 11, p. 236, 23 Feb. 1390.

[31] *Rif.* 11, pp. 428–9, 20 Feb. 1391.

[32] 'Ars lane que a pauco tempore citra in civitate lucana incepit vires assumere multum utilitatis et commodi attulerit civitati et civibus lucanis et quottidie multiplicentur gentes artem illam exercentes', *Rif.* 10, p. 225, 24 Feb. 1387. To assist the industry the import of certain types of cheap cloth was prohibited, *Rif.* 10, p. 285, 7 June 1387, but there was later a shortage of this kind of cloth and its import was allowed once more, *Rif.* 12, p. 272, 27 Feb. 1393.

[33] Series *Sentenze e Bandi,* 538, ff. 26–41. It is headed 'Hic describuntur omnes tam

shows that 147 workers of the *arte della lana* came to Lucca between 1382 and 1400 and another fifty-seven before 1417, when the list stops. Over fifty came in the first three years, mainly from Florence. The invitation to wool workers was general, but it was probably directed particularly to Florentines. In the years after the defeat of the *Ciompi* rising many Florentine artisans were ready to seek new homes. One of the first to come was the early leader of the rising, Michele di Lando,[34] and many other Florentines followed, a total of eighty-five before 1400. After the first few years the flow of immigrants slackened, but a handful still came each year. Apart from Florence they came from other Tuscan cities, Pistoia, Prato, Siena, and especially Pisa, with a few from other Italian cities, and one from as far away as Famagusta in Cyprus. Immigration on this scale, together with government subsidies for mills and other buildings, should have been sufficient to give the industry a good start in Lucca, and fifteenth-century records show that wool cloth making was active there, even if it never seriously competed with Florence or Prato.[35]

It is more difficult to speak with any certainty of the development of Lucchese trade in this period. The Lucchese had long been accustomed to trading far afield and in the late fourteenth century they had organized communities in Paris, Bruges, London, Avignon, Montpellier, Genoa, and Venice.[36] There were also individuals or groups of Lucchese in such places as Çatalonia, Cologne, and Prague, and one firm even sent an agent as far as Damascus.[37] The book of the acts

magistri quam discipuli qui veniunt ad civitatem lucanem pro dicta arte facienda secundum ordinem propterea celebratum.'

[34] *Sentenze e Bandi*, 538, f. 26. He was granted Lucchese citizenship the same day, *Rif.* 8, p. 83, 28 Mar. 1382.

[35] Bongi, *Inv.* II, p. 258, *Della Mercatura Lucchese*, pp. 17–18. The books of the sensals, which survive from 1408 onwards, show buying and selling of wool, much of the trade in the hands of Florentines. Many of the firms listed for 1407 under the 'titulus pannariorum et lanariorum', *Corte de'Mercanti*, 85, ff. 14–19v, were from Florence, Pisa and elsewhere.

[36] They were granted a degree of autonomy and the right to make their own statutes, *Rif.* 1, p. 99, 24 Sept. 1369. References to such statutes of the community in Venice, *Rif.* 2, p. 82, 29 Sept. 1370, and Genoa, *Rif.* 6, p. 264, 27 May 1377. Also L. Mirot, 'Études lucquoises: la colonie lucquoise à Paris XIIIe–XIVe siècles', *Bibliothèque de l'Écoles des Chartes*, Vol. LXXXVIII (1927), pp. 50–86.

[37] *Protocolli* of ser Niccolò Turinghelli, *Archivio de'Notari*, no. 242 (not foliated),

of the Lucchese community in Bruges for the years 1377–1404 has survived and this, together with the volumes of the records of the Court of Merchants in Lucca, gives some idea of the scale on which they operated. Forty-six Lucchese attended a meeting in Bruges 6 September 1377,[38] though between thirty and forty was more usual in the succeeding years. The period covered by the *Libro*, the end of the fourteenth and early years of the fifteenth century, seems to have been the period of greatest prosperity of the Lucchese community there. In the later fifteenth century the numbers had dropped to about twelve. The largest single company in Lucca itself was the Guinigi company, which had twenty-two members in 1371, with branches in Pisa, Naples, and Bruges. In 1372 it had twenty members and branches in Genoa, Venice, Naples and Bruges, and in 1381 sixteen members with branches in Rome, Pisa, Bruges, and London.[39] This, the largest Lucchese company, could not compare with the great Florentine firms of the first half of the fourteenth century, nor even with the Medici company later, which employed sixty people in 1469, but these Florentine firms seem to have been exceptionally large for the period.[40] A number of Lucchese firms employed ten or more, including the Panichi, Balbani, and Boccella companies.[41] The Rapondi company, which had its centre outside Lucca and therefore did not have to declare its membership to the Court of Merchants, seems to have numbered six or eight, but its operations were extensive, with branches active in Bruges, Paris, Avignon, Venice, and

18 Oct. 1376 (Catalonia); *Libro della communità de'mercanti lucchesi in Bruges*, ed. E. Lazzareschi (Milan, 1947), p. 43, 6 Feb. 1379, p. 85, 24 Aug. 1381, p. 197, Aug. 1393, also *Reg*. no. 1225, 1 Dec. 1384 (Cologne). *Rif.* 7, p. 653, 26 Dec. 1381 (Prague). *Protocolli* of ser Filippo Lupardi, *Archivio de'Notari*, no. 160 (not foliated), 16 Mar. 1384 (Damascus).

[38] *Libro della communità*, p. 5, 6 Sept. 1377.

[39] *Corte de'Mercanti*, 82 ff. 11v (1371), no. 83, f. 7 (1372), no. 84, f. 11 (1381).

[40] R. de Roover, 'The organisation of trade', in *Cambridge Economic History*, Vol. III (Cambridge, 1963), pp. 85–6.

[41] Panichi, *Corte de'Mercanti*, 82, f. 10v, no. 83, f. 9. no. 84, f. 12v (in partnership with Bartolomeo Michaelis). Balbani, no. 82, f. 4v (numbered only nine), no. 83, f. 6, no. 84, f. 10. Boccella, no. 82, f. 6, no. 83, f. 4v, no. 84, f. 9v. The partnership of Giuffredo Cenami and Francesco and Pietro Martini had nineteen members in 1381, *Corte de'Mercanti*, 84, f. 11v.

perhaps London.[42] There are no figures for other prosperous, and perhaps numerous, companies which had their centres in Avignon or Venice, like those of Enrico Sandei or Bartolomeo di Michele Moccindente, and consequently did not have to declare their members in Lucca.

These companies traded in Lucchese products, especially luxury silk goods, but they had many other interests. They were by no means dependent on Lucchese industry for their trade, and the decline of the silk industry did not necessarily mean the decline of the Lucchese merchant companies. Indeed the customs accounts show that Lucchese merchants were dealing in silk goods manufactured in Bologna and elsewhere. There are numerous entries for payments of toll for passage only on silks going through Lucchese territory on their way to the sea at Motrone or Pisa, or north by the land route. They came mostly from Bologna, though there are also entries for silks coming from Florence and Venice. The quantities involved are large, usually much larger than the quantities being exported from Lucca, and this transit trade was mostly in the hands of Lucchese merchants, though non-Lucchese are occasionally mentioned. Most leading Lucchese merchants seem to have engaged in this trade with rival cities, and it must have done much to minimize the ill-effects of the decline of the Lucchese silk industry on the city's trade, though it can hardly have helped check the decline of the silk industry in Lucca itself.

Apart from engaging in the silk trade with other cities, many Lucchese were engaged in trading enterprises that had no connection with their own city. Matteo Cattani, for example, is found importing 144 pieces of wool cloth of 'Vervi' and 'Coltray' worth 3,600 florins from northern Europe to Venice.[43] Pierotto Scatizza was treasurer to the king of France and the Sbarra family acted as royal moneyers.[44] Dino Rapondi and his brothers engaged in moneylending on a large

[42] L. Mirọt, 'Études lucquoises: la société des Raponde: Dine Raponde', *Bibliothèque de l'École des Chartes*, Vol. LXXXIX (1928), pp. 299–389. *Libro della communità*, declarations of merchants and their factors under various years.

[43] *Protocolli* of ser Domenico Lupardi, *Archivio de'Notari*, no. 281, ff. 82^{v}–83, 1 June 1388.

[44] L. Mirot, 'La colonie lucquoise', pp. 63–4, 72–6. L. Mirot, 'Études lucquoises: les Isbarre monnayeurs royaux, Augustin Isbarre', *Bibliothèque de l'École des Chartes*, Vol. LXXXVIII (1927), pp. 275–314. Pierotto Scatizza, *Rif.* 1, p. 308, 15 Apr. 1370.

scale, and acted as suppliers of arms and surveyors of military defences, as well as supplying luxury goods to the princes and nobles of France and the Low Countries.[45] Other companies, such as the Trenta and the Forteguerra, operated on a large scale in northern Europe. In 1370 Philip the Bold, duke of Burgundy, was in Forteguerra Forteguerra's debt to the extent of 17,185 francs.[46] In addition to their commercial activities the Guinigi company also acted as financiers and bankers. For about fifteen years from 1376 they acted as papal bankers, transferring funds, advancing the Pope credit, and handling sums that ran into hundreds of thousands of florins.[47]

Though little is known of the stages of development of any of these Lucchese companies, it was probably still possible to make a fortune in the late fourteenth century. Certainly there is evidence that despite the decline of the silk industry and despite the financial difficulties in which the commune of Lucca frequently found itself, there was a considerable degree of personal wealth in the city. Lucca still seems to have had a reputation for wealth as her citizens found to their cost, when in 1384 their envoy wrote of an armed company that threatened to invade Lucchese territory that he could not get it into their heads that Lucca was not full of gold and precious cloths, and that it was useless for him to tell them how poor she was.[48] It was found necessary in 1362 and again in 1380 to legislate against extravagance in dress and excessive expenditure on dowries and wedding festivities.[49] One of the reaons given for this legislation was that the expenditure which had become customary was beyond the means of many citizens, but it apparently continued afterwards, for there are

[45] Mirot, 'La société des Raponde', p. 299. For the role of Dino Rapondi in the service of Philip the Bold, R. Vaughan, *Philip the Bold* (London, 1962), pp. 73, 171, 220–1.

[46] L. Mirot, 'Études lucquoises: Forteguerra Forteguerra et sa succession', *Bibliothèque de l'École des Chartes*, Vol. LXXXIX (1928), pp. 299–389. *Libro della*

[47] For the commercial and banking activity of the Guinigi see below, Chapter 11, pp. 200–2.

[48] *Reg.*, no. 1188, 3 Jan. 1384. Lucca still had something of this reputation in the early sixteenth century, M. Berengo, *Nobili e Mercanti nella Lucca del Cinquecento* (Turin, 1965), p. 53, note 2.

[49] *Anz. Av. Lib.* 42, p. 6, 8 Jan. 1362. See also Tommasi, 'Sommario della Storia di Lucca', Appendix of documents, pp. 93–118. *Rif.* 7, pp. 285–9, 28 June 1380, *Rif.* 8, p. 325, 27 Nov. 1382.

a number of records of condemnations for breaches of these sumptuary laws.

There are other signs of private wealth in the city. Many of the leading merchant families were building palaces and endowing chapels, and individuals were able to lend large sums to the commune. Simone Boccella and Dino Guinigi lent 12,000 florins, and Bartolomeo di Michele Moccindente 5,000 in 1369, and there are a number of other loans of comparable size.[50] According to a seventeenth-century writer, who claimed to be basing his assertions on the public records, the fortune of Francesco and Dino Guinigi alone amounted to 200,000 florins—almost three times the annual revenue of the commune—without counting the wealth of the other numerous members of the family.[51] The Rapondi fortune has been assessed at 100,000 florins; Dino Rapondi was able to leave a particular bequest of 20,000 *scudi* to his brother Jacobo in his will, in addition to a general share of his property, and he had paid a ransom of 10,000 florins for another brother, Piero, in 1398.[52] Wills preserved in the notarial records give hints as to the wealth of individuals, though as they usually take the form of a list of charities and bequests with the residue left to a particular heir or heirs without stating its total, they do not give a full or clear picture of a man's wealth. The will of Bonagiunta di Simone Bonagiunta, for example, contains only smallish bequests, and does not give the impression that he was a rich man, yet an inventory included with it shows that he had property worth about 70,000 florins.[53] The will of Enrico Sandei made shortly before his death in 1387 shows him to have been an extremely wealthy man. He was able to contemplate legacies of 15,000 florins to each of four or five sons, and he also left

[50] *Anz. Av. Lib.* 45, p. 49, 27 June 1369, *Rif.* 2, p. 259, 22 Apr. 1371, *Rif.* 8, p. 169, 16 June 1382. For the commissioning of chapels and works of art, E. Lazzareschi, 'Angelo Buccinelli e gli altri pittori lucchesi del Trecento', *Bollettino Storico Lucchese*, Vol. X (1938), pp. 137–64.

[51] B. Beverini, *Annali Lucchesi* (Lucca, 1830), Lib. III, p. 9, 'Solos Franciscum ac Dinum ad CC florenorum aureorum millia in censu habuisse publicis tabulis constat.' Other figures he gives are accurate.

[52] L. Mirot, 'La société des Raponde', pp. 301, 306, Dino Rapondi's will, pp. 378–81.

[53] *Protocolli* of ser Domenico Lupardi, *Archivio de'Notari*, no. 283, will, ff. 145v–147, 11 Oct. 1390, inventory ff. 174–183v.

legacies totalling perhaps 5,000 florins and the exceptionally large dowry of 2,500 florins to his infant daughter, Giovanna. He made his sons joint heirs of the residue whose total is unstated, but was probably considerable.[54]

The figures of the *Estimo* of 1397 show that there were many other wealthy men in Lucca. The figures do not represent the total of a man's property, but rather an assessment to serve as a basis for taxation. These assessments were made by five groups of commissioners. The highest and the lowest estimates were cancelled and the average of the other three worked out. Half of this was to be the figure of each man's assessment. The sources make it clear that both movable and immovable property was liable to assessment, but there is no indication of exactly how it was assessed and what deductions, if any, were allowed. Nevertheless the figures demonstrate the existence of wealthy men in Lucca in the late fourteenth century. The highest assessment was that of Bonaccorso Bocci with 16,666 florins. Next came Lazzaro di Francesco Guinigi with 14,332 florins and Baldassare Guinigi with 14,000. The total for the Guinigi family was 58,160 florins, and though no other family or individual approached this figure, there are a number of assessments of 12,000 or 13,000 florins, which, as they represented property worth at least twice these figures, must have denoted wealthy men.[55]

These wealthy men were all merchants and bankers. Most of them would own at least some land in the *contado*, which would provide them with some of the supplies they needed for their own households, but it does not seem to have been an important element in their wealth. This came from trade, industry, and banking. It is often difficult to distinguish between merchants and manufacturers; many of the leading merchants also engaged in silk manufacture as entrepreneurs. Lucchese merchants continued to trade in Lucchese silks, and these continue to appear in inventories in France and Flanders, but the silk industry was in a serious state of decline in the late fourteenth century, and Lucchese merchants also engaged in many other branches of trade and in finance,

[54] *Protocolli* of ser Domenico Lupardi, *Archivio de'Notari*, no. 280, ff. 44^v–47^v, 31 Jan. 1387.

[55] Lucca, Biblioteca Governativa, MS. 925, ff. 249–58.

banking and money lending. There are no figures for these activities, which in any case lay to a large extent outside Lucca. But it seems probable that the silk industry became less important to the Lucchese merchants, and that the profits of general trade and banking became a more important element in their wealth. This must have meant that they were less seriously affected by the decline of the silk industry than they might otherwise have been, and it may well have done something to mitigate the effects of this decline in Lucca generally.

3

THE FINANCES

THE Lucchese archives are especially rich in sources for the financial history of the commune. Records of many *proventus* are preserved in minute detail, often covering a period of more than a century.[1] But this does not apply to all sources of revenue and there are many gaps, so that it would be difficult to calculate the total revenues of the state with any accuracy were it not for two other types of record, the series *introito-esito* of the central treasury,[2] and the series *ragionieri della camera e del comune*.[3] The two series supplement each other, though the *ragionieri* accounts contain much less detail, but unfortunately for the period 1369–1400 neither is continuous after April 1381,[4] and the year 1380 is the last for which revenues for a whole year can be calculated.

In the year 1372 the total revenue passing through the hands of the *camarlingo generale* was 81,216 florins,[5] but in the years that followed it was considerably below this figure. It was 66,531 florins for the twelve months February 1374 to January 1374,[6] 65,571 for the year 1377,[7] 67,777 for 1378,[8] and 70,862 for 1380.[9] The considerably higher figure for 1372 is explained by certain temporary tax increases imposed in 1371 and by the inclusion in the ordinary revenues of the yield of a forced loan of 15,000 florins from the *contado* and *distretto*, which produced 5,100 florins in the first six months of 1372 and 8,474 florins in the second.[10] The revenues passing through the hands of the *camarlingo generale* probably averaged 60,000–65,000 florins a year in the years 1373–5 and 65,000–70,000 in the years 1375–80. The trend seems to have been upwards after 1377, but the increase is not great and as there are figures for only three years after 1377 it would be dangerous to generalize.[11]

[1] S. Bongi (ed.), *Inventario del R. Archivio di Stato in Lucca*, Vol. II (Lucca, 1876), pp. 3–192.

[2] Series *Camarlingo Generale*, nos. 79–83, *Introito-esito*.

[3] Series *Ragionieri della camera e del comune*, nos. 11–14. Bongi, *Inv.* II, pp.

186-9. The *ragionieri* were accountants employed by the commune to audit the accounts of the *camarlingo generale* and other treasurers for the separate dues and levies that made up the communal revenues and of any other citizens through whose hands public money had passed. Their function, however, was to determine the responsibility of individuals and grant them quittance, not to work out the totals of communal revenues, so that if some branch of the revenues had been taken out of the hands of the treasurer usually responsible for it and was being administered separately there would be no reason for the *ragionieri* to comment on this.

[4] Bongi, *Inv.* II, p. 7 notes lacune for 1379–82 and 1390–1404. In fact for the period 1383–90 only the *introito-esito* for Nov. and Dec. 1383 and the *introito* for Oct. Nov. Dec. 1389 survive. Series *Camarlingo Generale* no. 83.

[5] *Ragionieri*, 11, *introito* for the first semester ff. 81v-82v, *esito* ff. 83-83v, for the second semester *introito* ff. 2-5v, *esito* ff. 6-56. (There are a number of different foliations). Accounts are partly in florins and partly in £.*s*.*d*. of Lucchese *piccioli*, which varied in value at this time from £5. 1*s*. to £5. 5*s*. per florin. The totals have been given in florins worked out at the rate current each year.

[6] *Ragionieri*, 12 (various foliations). Feb.-Mar., *introito*, ff. 49-51v, *esito*, ff. 52-78, Apr.-May *introito*, ff. 84-87, *esito* ff. 88v-100v (incomplete), June-July *introito*, ff. 13-14v, *esito*, ff. 15-29v, Aug.-Sept. *introito*, ff. 39-40, *esito*, ff. 40v-56v, Oct.-Nov. *introito*, 63-64v, *esito*, ff. 66-81v, Dec. 1374-Jan. 1375 *introito*, ff. 7-12, *esito*, f. 12v (*esito* in summary form with total only).

[7] *Ragionieri*, 13 (various foliations). For the first semester *introito* ff. 1-5v, *esito*, ff. 6-95, for the second semester *introito*, ff. 26-32, *esito*, ff. 33-143.

[8] *Ragionieri*, 13. For the period 8 Jan.-16 Mar. 1378 *introito* ff. 155-158v, *esito* ff. 159-201, for the period 28 Mar.-5 July 1378 *introito*, ff. 12-14v, *esito*, ff. 15-70. *Camarlingo Generale*, no. 82 *introito* for the second semester, ff. 2-5v, *esito*, ff. 6-49v, though this is not complete. (*Camarlingo Generale*, no. 82 has several lots of foliation.)

[9] *Ragionieri*, 14. Accounts for Jan.-Feb., Mar.-Apr. and Oct. 1380 are on unfoliated pages. May-June *introito*, ff. 3-5, *esito*, ff. 5v-41, July, Aug. Sept., *introito*, ff. 63–65, *esito*, ff. 65v–83 and continues on unfoliated pages, Nov.–Dec. *introito*, ff. 7-9v, *esito*, ff. 10-38. *Ragionieri*, 12 also records figures for the period of eleven months Feb.-Dec. 1375, when the total was 55,317 florins. Feb.-Mar. *introito*, ff.21-24v, *esito*, f. 25 (in summary form with total only), Apr.-May *introito*, ff. 26-29v, *esito*, f. 30 (total only), June *introito*, ff. 22-24, *esito*, ff. 24v-25v, second semester of 1375 *introito*, ff. 3-8v, *esito*, f. 9 (total only). There are also figures for the thirteen months Jan. 1373-Jan. 1374, when the total was 76,250 florins. *Ragionieri*, 11, Jan., Feb., Mar., *introito*, ff. 75-77v, *esito*, ff. 78-106, Apr.-May *introito*, ff. 116v-118v, *esito*, ff. 119-148, June-July *introito*, ff. 13-14v, *esito*, ff. 15-28, Aug.-Sept. *introito*, ff. 34-35v, *esito*, ff. 36-38, Oct.-Nov. *introito*, ff. 60-61v, *esito*, ff. 62-77v. *Ragionieri*, 12, Dec. 1373-Jan. 1374 *introito*, ff. 2-4v, *esito*, ff. 5-27v. As receipts did not apparently vary greatly from season to season, this probably represents totals of about 62,077 florins for 1373 and 60,345 for 1375.

[10] These totals formed a separate *titulus* in the *introito* of the *camarlingo generale* for the first and second semesters of 1372, *Ragionieri*, 11, ff. 57-57v, ff. 2-5v. There are also separate accounts for the treasurer for this forced loan, which show that he received 5,100 florins, said to be for the *prima paga*, 1 Jan.-31 May and 5,131 florins for the *seconda paga* 29 May-20 Aug. 1372, f. 79. This account is clearly not complete, but a further 1,454 florins for the rest of the third *paga* was received 7 Jan.-23 Feb. 1373, f. 107.

[11] For upward trends in the receipts of gabelles in other Tuscan cities in the later fourteenth century D. Herlihy, 'Direct and indirect taxation in Tuscan urban finance ca. 1200–1400' in *Finances et Comptabilité Urbaines du XIIIe au XVIe siècle*, Collection *Pro Civitate* (Brussels, 1964), p. 399.

But the revenues passing through the hands of the *camarlingo generale* did not represent the whole of the revenues of Lucca. In some cases salaries and other expenses were deducted from the yield of a particular *proventus* and only the surplus paid into the central treasury, and one of the most productive taxes,[12] the *dovana salis* or salt gabelle, was administered separately. There are few clear indications of its precise yield. In the first three months of 1370 it produced £25,443. 2s. 3d. *picc.*, the equivalent of 4,988 florins £4. 6*s*. 8*d*. at the then current rate of £5. 2*s*. *picc*. per florin.[13] The salt gabelle was paid in two instalments each year, so it perhaps produced about 10,000 florins.[14] There were, however, quite heavy expenses to be decucted; at least 847 florins was paid for the purchase of salt in the first six months of 1370. But the salt gabelle apparently produced enough to cover the costs of the interest payments on the public debt. This was reckoned by Sercambi to cost 300 florins a month or 3,600 florins a year in 1423,[15] but in the late fourteenth century it certainly cost more. The debt totalled at least 92,363 florins in the last decade of the century, when the interest rate was 5 per cent. Before 1378 the rate of interest had been 10 per cent, though the total debt may have been slightly less. After the reduction of the interest rate to 5 per cent there was assumed to be a surplus in the revenues of the *dovana salis* after these charges had been met, and this surplus was to be paid into a special deposit. Under a new assessment for the salt gabelle made in 1383 the yield from forced sales to

[12] 'principaliori membro introytus civitatis lucane', *Delib*. 132, f. 38, 8 Feb. 1374.

[13] *Camarlingo Generale*, no. 80, ff. 82v–83. This includes one instalment of the salt tax which was paid twice a year. The same citizen was treasurer of the *dovana salis* in October, November and December 1369, when receipts were £3,406. 12*s*. 3*d*. *picc*., ff. 81–2. The *dovana salis* produced 8,232 florins, £6,029. 7*s*. 8*d*. *picc*. gross in the first six months of 1372, but there had been an increase of a third in the price of salt, *Ragionieri*, 11, ff. 81v–82v.

[14] In 1355 the *dovana salis* had yielded £40,151. 14*s*. 5*d*. *picc*., equivalent to roughly 9,230 florins. Of this £36,486. 14*s*. 8*d*. *picc*. or 8,383 florins was surplus after expenses and was paid to the *camarlingo generale*. The rate per florin in 1355 was £4. 7*s*. *picc*. *Ragionieri*, 8. For a similar salt monopoly in other cities, W. M. Bowsky, *The Finance of the Commune of Siena 1287–1355* (Oxford, 1970), pp. 56–60, C. M. de la Roncière, 'Indirect taxes or "gabelles" at Florence in the fourteenth century: the evolution of tariffs and problems of collection', in N. Rubinstein (ed.) *Florentine Studies* (London, 1968), pp. 158–61, Herlihy, 'Direct and indirect taxation', pp. 392–3.

[15] Sercambi, III, p. 355.

Lucchese subjects should have been 8,941 florins a year, though it is doubtful if this new assessment was ever fully enforced.[16] In addition there were the profits of sales to the inhabitants of Lucca, the suburbs and the Six Miles, who were not obliged to receive a fixed amount of salt each year, but who had to buy what they needed from the commune. The cost of purchasing the salt and administering the tax would have to be deducted, but the total yield may well have equalled or even exceeded that for 1370 in the later years of the fourteenth century.[17]

Apart from the salt monopoly, the revenues of Lucca came mainly from the gabelles, in Lucca usually called *proventus*. These were largely, though not exclusively, indirect taxes,[18] of which the most important was the *proventus sigilli gabelle maioris* or customs duty on the more valuable kinds of goods entering or leaving the city.[19] In 1377 it produced 11,302 florins, over one-sixth of the total of 65,571 florins for that year. Duties were paid separately on the entry of wine, bread, and flour, animals for slaughter, and certain other types of goods.[20] There were further taxes on the sale of bread, wine,

[16] *Rif.* 8, pp. 497-9, 29 Apr. 1383, but immediate concessions had to be made which would have reduced the yield to 6,531 florins for the next three years, and further concessions had to be made later, *Rif.* 8, p. 618, 10 Oct. 1383, *Rif.* 11, p. 349, 25 Nov. 1390, *Rif.* 12, pp. 49-50, 20 Feb. 1392.

[17] It may well have yielded more than in 1370. In 1387 Piero di Ciuchino Panichi, who was acting as treasurer of the *dovana salis* when he went bankrupt, had received 3,571 florins and £19,692 *picc.*, equal to about 7,395 florins in all. He was treasurer for six months, but may not have received all the money due for that period before he fled, *Protocolli* of ser Domenico Lupardi, *Archivio de'Notari*, no. 280, ff. 173v–174v, 19 Dec. 1387.

[18] Bowsky, *Finance of the Commune of Siena*, pp. 114-18 correctly points out that, though historians customarily refer to gabelles as indirect taxes, they in fact included some direct taxes and other levies. Roncière, 'Indirect taxes or "gabelles"', pp. 140-92 and Herlihy, 'Direct and indirect taxation', esp. pp. 398-9 for the importance of gabelles elsewhere. There was by this date no *dazio* or direct property tax in Lucca, as there was at Siena slightly earlier, Bowsky, pp. 98-113, 282-3. For direct taxation in Tuscan communes at an earlier date, Herlihy, pp. 393-8, E. Fiumi, 'Fioritura e decadenza dell'economia fiorentina III' *Archivio Storico Italiano*, Vol. CXVII (1959), pp. 440-9, also 'L'imposta diretta nei comuni medioevali della Toscana' in *Studi in onore di Armando Sapori* (Milan, 1957), Vol. I, pp. 327-53.

[19] *Statuto della Gabella Maggiore*, series *Gabella Maggiore*, 1, gives details of most of the sources of revenue, including the rates of duty charged on the various types of goods. It was compiled in 1372, but includes a number of revisions 1372-1443.

[20] *Proventus cassarum vini, proventus farine, proventus macelli, proventus cassarum generalium*, etc.

and oil retail within the city,[21] and similar taxes were paid in the suburbs and in the *distretto*.[22] There was a tax of 2*s*. in the £1 on all money received as rents and a tax at rates varying from 8*d*. to 2*s*. in the £1 on alienations of immovables by sale or exchange or as legacies or dowries.[23] Citizens living in the *contado*, known as *cives silvestres*, whose food had not paid gabelles for entry into the city, paid a special tax to compensate the Lucchese *camera* for the loss.[24] There was a tax of 16*d*. in the £1 on the salaries of many officials,[25] and payments for licences for pawnbrokers.[26] There were also many small taxes on such things as mills, market gardens, the checking of weights and measures, boats, innkeepers, prisoners, gambling, and prostitutes, and many other things, which produced only small sums.[27] There were also gabelles on the entry and exit of goods in each vicariate and on retail sales there, though the inhabitants were sometimes allowed to compound for these.[28]

The revenues of Lucca may be compared with those of her neighbours. The ordinary revenues of Florence seem to have produced about 300,000 florins a year in the late fourteenth century, though she was able to raise very much larger sums by the use of *prestanze*.[29] The relative receipts from ordinary revenues of Florence and Lucca in the late fourteenth century seem to have been much as they were in the 1330s. In 1334 about £240,000, roughly the equivalent of 70,000 florins at the then current rate of £3. 9*s*. 1*d*. per florin, passed through

[21] These together with the *gabella maggiore* produced 33,890 florins, or half the total revenue passing through the hands of the *camarlingo generale* in 1377.

[22] *Proventus burgorum et subburgorum, proventus vini, panis et olei sex miliarum.*

[23] *Proventus pensionum et livellorum, proventus dotium, testamentorum, venditionum et alienationum.*

[24] *Proventus civium silvestrium.*

[25] *Proventus datie salariorum officialium.*

[26] *Proventus feneratorum et hospitatorum.*

[27] For these and others, Bongi, *Inv.* II, pp. 22-8. There were also various legal dues and fines for offences, but these produced only trivial sums that were a very small proportion of the total, c.p. earlier Herlihy, 'Direct and indirect taxation', pp. 389-90. Other Tuscan cities had very similar gabelles, Bowsky, *The Finance of the Commune of Siena*, Chapter VI, pp. 114-65, Roncière, 'Indirect taxes or "gabelles"', pp. 140-92.

[28] Composition for the gabelles with the vicariates of Castiglione and Camporgiano, *Rif.* 3, p. 221, 6 Feb. 1372, with certain other communes, *Rif.* 3, p. 240, 21 Feb., p. 386, 8 Aug. 1372, *Rif.* 5, p. 318, 5 May 1376.

[29] For sums raised by *prestanze* in 1375-8, G. A. Brucker, *Florentine Politics and Society 1343-1378* (Princeton, 1962), p. 315. In the 1390s sums as high as 1,300,000 florins could be raised in a single year, M. B. Becker, *Florence in Transition*, Vol. II,

the hands of the Lucchese treasurer,[30] and Florence had about 300,000 florins a year in 1336–8.[31] A comparison with Pisa is perhaps more profitable. Pisa had had revenues of 141,000 florins in 1355, but this had included an annual payment of 36,000 florins from Lucca. Without this Pisan revenues would amount to 105,000 florins.[32] The Pisan archives contain no records for the revenues at a later date, but if the total was similar to that for 1355, the difference between the resources of Pisa and those of Lucca is less than might have been expected. Lucca was able to plead poverty with some success in such matters as negotiations for leagues with her neighbours. She was able to escape any fixed *taglia* at all before 1379, when Pisa was heavily burdened, for example with a *taglia* of 200 lances and 400 foot soldiers in 1371.[33] Even after 1379 Lucca was called upon to provide a much smaller contingent than Pisa.

In normal times Lucca could hope that the ordinary revenues would be adequate to cover expenditure. But the expenses of recovering her liberty had been very great, and the revenues of 60,000–65,000 florins a year would have been quite

---

Studies in the Rise of the Territorial State (Johns Hopkins, 1968), pp. 162, 168–9. Also M. B. Becker, 'Economic change and the emerging territorial state', *Studies in the Renaissance*, Vol. XIII (1966), p. 36 and 'Problemi della finanza pubblica fiorentina della seconda metà del Trecento e dei primi del Quattrocento', *Archivio Storico Italiano*, Vol. CXXXIII (1965), p. 434, 452–3, but see also L. Martines in *Speculum*, Vol. XLIII (1968), pp. 689–92. For sums raised by *prestanze* averaging 271,307 florins a year over nine years in the 1390s, A. Molho, *Florentine Public Finances in the Early Renaissance, 1400–1433* (Cambridge, Mass., 1971), p. 63.

[30] Series *Camarlingo Generale*, nos. 7 and 8. This includes about £35,000 *picc.* from the *dovana salis*. Bongi, *Inv.* II, p. 28 gives the figure of £353,359. 17*s.* 10*d. picc.*, equivalent to 110,000 florins, for the year 1337. In the 1350s during the period of Pisan rule Lucchese revenues do not seem to have exceeded 50,000 florins except in 1354, S. Bongi, *Bandi Lucchesi del Secolo Decimoquarto* (Bologna, 1863), p. 391, series *Ragionieri*, 3–9. I hope to analyse Lucchese revenues in greater detail for the whole fourteenth century at a later date.

[31] Bongi, *Inv.* II, p. 28. E. Fiumi, 'Fioritura e decadenza III', pp. 450–2, Herlihy, 'Direct and indirect taxation', p. 387, Becker, *Florence in Transition*, Vol. II, p. 169. Statistics for Florence in 1336–8, Villani, *Cronica*, Lib. IX, caps. 91–3.

[32] Figures for Pisa in 1355 are based on statements made by the Pisans to Charles IV 10 May 1355, A.S.P. *Comune A 60*, ff. 2–2ᵛ. P. Silva, 'Il governo di Pietro Gambacorta in Pisa', *Annali della R. Scuola Normale Superiore di Pisa*, Vol. XXIII (1912), p. 107. C. Violante, 'Imposte dirette e debito pubblico a Pisa nel medioevo', in *L'Impôt dans le cadre de la ville et de l'état*, Collection Pro Civitate (Brussels, 1966), p. 70.

[33] *Capitoli*, 24, cap. vi, p. 372. Another copy *Capitoli*, 31.

inadequate to pay the large sums that Lucca had to find in a short period of time, even in ordinary circumstances. But in the last years of Pisan rule Lucca had not had control of her own revenues and only recovered this in March 1369.[34] The problem of finding large sums of money in a short space of time could only be solved by heavy borrowing both from Lucchese citizens and from foreign states. Florence lent 29,000 florins,[35] Niccolò d'Este, lord of Ferrara lent 12,000,[36] and Francesco Carrara, lord of Padua 10,000.[37] In addition the Pope accepted the transfer of 50,000 of the 100,000 florins Lucca owed to the Emperor. All these loans were for a comparatively short period of time, apparently a year or little more in each case, so that Lucca began her independence under a heavy burden of debt, all of which had to be repaid in the near future.

In the first years after the recovery of her independence, and especially in the years 1369–71, the Lucchese *Riformagioni* are full of discussions of financial problems, which are rarely found in later years. There was constant shortage of ready money for such ordinary expenses as the payment of salaries of officials, castellans, and mercenary soldiers and other costs of defence. The money usually had to be found by borrowing from some wealthy citizen. The rate of interest that had to be paid in order to find men willing to lend rose from 10 per cent in June 1369 to 12 per cent by the end of the year,[38] and as much as 18 per cent was apparently paid.[39] Even so it was not always possible to find voluntary lenders, and money had to be raised by forced loans, although this was distasteful and regarded only as a last resort. But forced loans had to be used more and more frequently,[40] both limited ones where a

[34] *Anz. Av. Lib.* 45, p. 1, 24 Mar. 1369.

[35] *Reg.* no. 48. *Rif.* 2, p. 270, 23 Apr., p. 271, 25 Apr. 1371.

[36] *Rif.* 3, p. 87, 26 Oct. 1371. [37] *Rif.* 1, p. 298, 8 Apr. 1370.

[38] *Anz. Av. Lib.* 45, pp. 33–4, 12 June 1369, *Rif.* 1, p. 165, 30 Dec. 1369.

[39] Series *Camarlingo Generale*, no. 80, *introito-esito*, 23 June 1370. I have found no parallels in Lucca to the interest rates of 20 per cent, 30 per cent or more on voluntary loans as at Siena in the earlier fourteenth century, Bowsky, *Finance of the Commune of Siena*, pp. 190–7. Interest rates on forced loans were lower, though 10 per cent was usual, pp. 178–81. For rates of 30–40 per cent on voluntary loans in Florence in the 1430s, Molho, *Florentine Public Finances*, pp. 174–5.

[40] *Rif.* 1, pp. 133–4, 8 Nov., p. 149, 29 Nov. 1369, p. 381, 31 May 1370. *Rif.* 2, p. 96, 7 Oct., p. 109, 25 Oct. 1370.

number of wealthy citizens were chosen to pay a fixed sum, and in October 1370 a general *estimo* on all Lucchese citizens.[41] The general financial position of the city was such that citizens were seldom willing to lend without security[42] and it was usual to assign a particular *proventus* for the repayment of each loan. This of course led to further difficulties in the months ahead, as the money that should have been coming in for current expenses was tied up in the repayment of past loans. So further borrowing was necessary, and by the end of 1370 assignments of *proventus* to take effect only after one, or even more, previous loans had been repaid from it are not uncommon. For the security of creditors it had been decreed that such assignments should on no account be cancelled or annulled. The city prided itself on fair treatment of its creditors, but the revenues had been so far anticipated that it was difficult to keep promises and avoid arbitrary measures. Creditors were forced to relend sums they had received as repayment of earlier loans,[43] and on 10 May 1370 the suspension of assignments already made was authorized by the large majority of 150–10.[44] Efforts were also made to improve the administration of the revenues and effect economies where possible.[45]

But the measure which was to have the most important and permanent effect was the establishment of the *Massa*

[41] *Rif.* 2, pp. 102–5, 20 Oct. 1370. There seems to have been opposition to this; it was passed by 124–38, an unusually high figure of votes against, and it was stipulated that it should be used as a basis for forced loans only until mid-January 1371. It was referred to as 'seca seu taxa' and was to be assessed by five groups of nine Lucchese citizens, each group making its assessment separately. The largest and the smallest of these were to be cancelled and the average of the other three was to be each man's *seca*. The total of the *seca* was to be 3,000 florins a month with assessments ranging upwards from a minimum of 6*d*. a day. Anything paid was to be regarded as a loan and the Anziani were to assign revenues for its repayment.

[42] An example is the case of Bartolomeo di Michele Moccindente, who lent 5,000 florins in July 1369 'et perche lo stato di questa terra non era ancora ben rifermo, launde lo dicto Bartolomeo non vedea da potere liberamente servire per esser certo di riaverli, volse che alcuni citadini e mercadanti li fusseno obligati . . .', *Rif.* 8, p. 169, 16 June 1382.

[43] *Rif.* 1, p. 338, 5 May 1370.

[44] *Rif.* 1, pp. 348–9, 10 May 1370. Similar provision *Rif.* 2, pp. 123–4, 7 Nov. 1370, passed by 129–13.

[45] *Rif.* 1, p. 430, 13 July, p. 431, 14 July, p. 447, 20 July 1370. *Rif.* 2, pp. 118–19, 4 Nov., p. 158, 5 Dec. 1370.

Creditorum.[46] The commune needed to regain control of the *proventus* which were pledged for the repayment of loans. This was done by uniting all the many separate loans secured on different *proventus* into one, and securing it on a single *proventus*, the *dovana salis*. Interest was to be paid at the rate of 10 per cent, and the revenues of the *dovana salis* were to be regarded as pledged for this. This assignment was on no account to be revoked.[47] Officials were to be appointed for the administration of the *Massa*, and should any further loans be necessary, they were to be assigned on the *dovana salis* on the same terms. The establishment of this consolidated public debt, known in future as the *Dovana Salis et Massa Creditorum*, both simplified the administration of the city's finances and gave greater security to creditors. They were in future sure of interest at the fairly high rate of 10 per cent[48] though they could no longer hope for the immediate repayment of their capital. But the debt was not envisaged as per-

[46] It does not seem that Lucca had had a consolidated public debt earlier, but the practice was familiar in Tuscan cities, and Lucchese citizens seem to have had shares in the Pisan public debt. Documents in the series *Archivio Guinigi* show that members of the Guinigi family were receiving interest on holdings in the Pisan public debt as well as that of Lucca after 1384, series *Archivio Guinigi*, no. 151, *Memorie di Michele Guinigi*, ff. 2^v, 10^v (1387), 16^v (1389), 20^v (1391), 24 (1392), 25 (1394), 30 (1396). It is probable that these holdings in the Pisan public debt derived from forced loans paid by the Lucchese in 1362–4 while under Pisan rule. At least a part of these sums seems to have been included in the Pisan public debt, Violante, 'Imposte dirette e debito pubblico', p. 71. The Lucchese public debt and the circumstances leading to its establishment are treated more fully in 'Il debito pubblico nella storia finanziaria di Lucca nel secolo XIV°', *Actum Luce*, Vol. III (1974) pp. 7–46.

[47] *Rif.* 2, pp. 194–5, 24 Jan. 1371. There is evidence of an earlier attempt to consolidate the city's debts and assign them on the *dovana salis*. There are references to a book in which all loans were to be written; 10 per cent interest was to be paid, and all the revenues of the *dovana salis* were to be reserved for this, *Anz. Av. Lib.* 45, pp. 33–4, 12 June 1369. A book of loans does seem to have been kept (*Rif.* 1, pp. 115–16, 12 Oct. 1369, p. 298, 8 Apr., p. 321, 26 Apr. 1370), but many separate loans were issued, other revenues were pledged for them, the revenues of the *dovana salis* were used for other purposes and higher rates of interest than 10 per cent were paid.

[48] Bongi, *Inv.* II, p. 193. The rate of 10 per cent, though high, probably meant a reduction in the rate of interest for some creditors. 12 per cent and more had been paid earlier, and at least some loans at these higher rates of interest must still have been outstanding. In Lucca the salt gabelle alone apparently produced sufficient revenue to cover interest payments on the public debt; in Pisa other *proventus* had to be assigned in addition, Violante, 'Imposte dirette e debito pubblico', p. 72 and in Florence a large proportion of several of the most important gabelles was devoted to *Monte* charges, Roncière, 'Indirect taxes or "gabelles" ', p. 145. For the use of the salt gabelle to guarantee and repay voluntary loans elsewhere, Bowsky, *Finance of the Commune of Siena*, pp. 59–60 and note 50.

manent in 1371; it was hoped that it could be gradually paid off in the not too distant future. Any money left over after the expenses of the purchase and distribution of salt and the payment of interest to the creditors was to be used for the repayment of the principal to each creditor *pro rata*. The decree of 24 January 1371 was confirmed on 28 and 31 January[49] in further decrees that made the position of the creditors even more secure by providing that no alterations could be made in the regulations of the *Massa* without their consent, and that six citizens, who must be creditors of the *Massa*, should be elected as governors every six months to oversee its administration. A decree of 16 March 1371[50] brought certain categories of loan, not previously included, within the *Massa*, and further strengthened the authority of the six governors.

The establishment of the *Massa Creditorum* relieved some of Lucca's more pressing financial problems, but in the next two years this was more than counterbalanced by the need to find large sums for the repayment of debts contracted in 1369. The largest sum Lucca owed outside the city, the 50,000 florins owed to the Papacy, had originally been due for repayment in December 1369, but Urban V and Gregory XI agreed first of all to delays and then to accept payment in small sums each year, and it was 1387 before the debt was finally cleared.[51] Lucca's other creditors were far less accommodating. The debt of 29,000 florins to Florence was still intact in April 1371, despite Florentine recriminations.[52] Though Florence also agreed to accept payment in instalments, the last of these was to be paid no later than January 1373. Lucca almost managed to pay within this term; the Gonfaloniere stated on 7 January 1373 that only 4,000 florins was still outstanding and that this would be paid, though with difficulty, in February.[53] The debt owed to Niccolò d'Este also

[49] *Rif.* 2, p. 198, 28 Jan.; pp. 200–1, 31 Jan. 1371.

[50] Series *Offizio Sopra il Sale*, no. 1, ff. 17–18.

[51] *Reg.*, nos. 9 (11 Dec. 1369); 29 (17 Aug. 1370); 41 (9 May 1371); 548 (16 Jan. 1376). Though Urban VI, finding himself in need of money after the outbreak of the Schism, asked for payment of the remainder in 1379, the last of the debt was only paid off in 1387, *Reg.*, nos. 705 (29 Jan. 1379); 1334 (7 Sept. 1387).

[52] Florence made demands 'cum instantia' . . . 'etiam pro retardatis et frustratoriis responsionibus repetat indignanter', *Rif.* p. 171, 16 Dec. 1370, pp. 267–9, 23 Apr. 1371, *Min.* 2, ff. 24v–25, 18 May 1371.

[53] *Rif.* 3, p. 479, 7 Jan. 1373. *Reg.*, nos. 48–9 (13 Aug. 1371); 95 (4 Apr. 1372).

led to recriminations. Lucca asked for a delay on the grounds of 'impotentia', offering payment in instalments beginning 1 January 1372, but d'Este, who needed the money for war, wanted the whole sum at once and was indignant at Lucca's failure to pay.[54] In view of his demands and the threats which accompanied them, Lucca did all that she could to pay him at least part of the sum as soon as possible, but it was still February 1372 before anything could be paid.[55] D'Este at once demanded the rest. Lucca made great efforts and was apparently able to pay the debt off by the end of July or the beginning of August 1372.[56] The other loan from an outside power, the 10,000 florins from Francesco Carrara of Padua, was rather more complicated, as it had not been lent to Lucca direct but to fifteen Lucchese citizens living in Venice, who then lent it to Lucca. Therefore, when Francesco Carrara demanded repayment, Lucca did not scruple to deny that she owed him anything and refer him to the Lucchese community in Venice, at the same time ordering her citizens there to repay the debt.[57] These citizens complained with some justification that they had been unfairly treated; the *proventus* assigned to them for the 10,000 florins they had borrowed from Carrara and lent to Lucca had been revoked when they had received only about 1,000 florins from them, though they still remained bound to Carrara for 10,000.[58]

In addition to the need to repay these debts Lucca had to meet other extraordinary expenses in these years; 6,000 florins had to be paid to the company of Lutz of Landau[59] and 12,000

[54] *Rif.* 3, p. 19, 11 Aug.; p. 87, 26 Oct. 1371. *Reg.*, no. 54 (10 Sept. 1371). In a letter dated 10 November 1371 he wrote 'de qua responsione sic inhonesta mirati sumus non modicum et ex ipsa quamplurimum conturbati, et merito, nullo modo credentes talem a vobis recipere responsivam debentibus considerare necessitatem nobis imminentem', *Rif.* 3, p. 117, 16 Nov. 1371.

[55] *Reg.*, nos. 77 (5 Jan. 1372); 83 (30 Jan. 1372); 91 (5 Mar. 1372).

[56] *Rif.* 3, p. 268, 10 Apr.; p. 300, 10 May; p. 301, 13 May 1372. *Reg.*, nos. 118 (19 July 1372); 120 (23 July 1372). *Rif.* 3, p. 479, 7 Jan. 1373.

[57] *Rif.* 1, p. 298, 8 Apr. 1370. *Reg.*, nos. 129, 133, 135 (5, 11, and 13 Sept. 1372); 188 (7 Mar. 1373).

[58] *Rif.* 2, pp. 249–50, 14 Apr. 1371. It is not clear how, when or by whom this debt was repaid, but 2,666 florins were still outstanding many years later; for in 1384 a Lucchese citizen visiting Padua reported that Carrara was angry with Lucca, accusing her of ingratitude. Provision was then made to repay him the money still owed, and give him gifts of Lucchese silks worth 500 florins to placate him, *Rif.* 9, p. 76, 16 Mar.; p. 97, 26 Apr. 1384.

[59] *Rif.* 2, p. 213, 22 Feb. 1371.

to purchase certain castles in the Garfagnana from Alderigo degli Antelminelli.[60] There are signs of serious financial strain in 1371; ambassadors refused to go and men would not accept offices because the salaries were too low.[61] Loans had to be raised and *proventus* pledged as before the establishment of the *Massa*.[62]

But to find sums like the 29,000 florins for Florence special measures had to be taken.[63] All the tolls and gabelles with one or two minor exceptions were increased by 50 per cent until the debts were paid off. This was done by the rather devious method of altering the value of Lucchese *piccioli* from the current rate of £5. 5*s*. to the florin to £3. 10*s*. This new rate was to apply to all private transactions as well as to the payment of dues to the commune, but prices were to be reduced so that what cost 3*d*. at the old rate was to cost 2*d*. at the new rate. In addition an increase of 50 per cent was decreed in a recent *imposita*, the price of salt was increased by a third and a special tax was imposed on all wine produced. But these measures were not apparently sufficient to raise the necessary sums; for a couple of weeks later the 'gabella cultrarum terrarum' was imposed. This was a tax on land at the rate of 15*s*. (at £3. 10*s*. to the florin) per *cultra* on arable land and 10*s*. per *cultra* on vineyard, two thirds to be paid by the landlord and one third by the tenant.[64]

These heavy taxes show the effort Lucca had to make to pay off her debts, and they must have been a serious burden on her citizens and subjects. There were in fact protests and opposition and some of the measures had to be modified or rescinded. In the face of many complaints of unfairness in the assessment of the *imposita* a measure of relief had to be granted.[65] After many petitions had been received from

[60] *Rif.* 2, p. 259, 22 Apr. 1371. Also 1,100 florins to buy back Tereglio and 800 florins for Bargilio, *Rif.* 2, p. 326, 27 June 1371, *Rif.* 3, p. 57, 23 Sept. 1371.

[61] *Rif.* 2, p. 191, 22 Jan., p. 211, 7 Feb., pp. 233–4, 16 Mar., pp. 237–8, 26 Mar., p. 298, 7 June, pp. 332–3, 30 June 1371.

[62] *Rif.* 2, p. 254, 19 Apr., p. 259, 22 Apr. 1371.

[63] *Rif.* 2, pp. 268–9, 23 Apr., pp. 271–2, 25 Apr. 1371. *Min.* 2, f. 10^{v}, 23 Apr. 1371.

[64] *Rif.* 2, pp. 280–1, 7 May 1371. Like the *imposita* this was a loan, not a form of direct taxation and was to be written on the *Massa*.

[65] *Min.* 2, f. 15^{v}, and *Rif.* 2, p. 273, 28 Apr. 1371. *Min.* 2, ff. 13^{v}–15, 27 Apr. there

contadini asking for the abolition of the wine tax and the 'gabella cultrarum terrarum' it was agreed that they should pay instead an *imposita* of 15,000 florins in fifteen monthly instalments of 1,000 florins each, and following further petitions those who had already paid the 'gabella cultrarum terrarum' were reimbursed.[66] The change in the value of the florin was found to cause confusion and it was restored to its old rate, though the increases in the gabelles were retained until the debts were paid off.[67] In addition to these efforts to raise money by special taxes, Lucca still had to resort to short-term loans, pledging the *proventus* for their repayment.[68] But by the beginning of January 1372 the worst was over. With the money to Niccolò d'Este entirely paid, and only 4,000 florins still owing to Florence, Lucca was able to abolish the special tax increases, and by making some economies provide that in future expenditure should not exceed the revenues.[69]

In the years that followed, Lucca never again had to face such a serious financial crisis, though her situation was never easy. She often used the argument of her poverty to avoid burdens such as a definite *taglia* in leagues. To some extent these were excuses to evade responsibilities; Lucca often seems to have been getting away fairly lightly and her citizens were far less burdened with *imposite* and other special levies than were the citizens of Florence and some other neighbouring states. Had the safety of the state been involved, she would have raised the money somehow. But her pleas of poverty also had some justification. Poverty was quite frequently mentioned in quite ordinary discussions of internal matters in the council, where there was no question of evading any outside payment.[70] Lucchese revenues barely covered ordinary

was a discussion in which many citizens expressed opinions, but no conclusion was reached. There are voting figures down the margin, showing votes like 36–34, 39–32, 42–28, 45–25, 45–26. Other petitions *Rif.* 2, pp. 285–6, 21 May, p. 323, 22 June 1371.

[66] *Rif.* 3, p. 89, 29 Oct., pp. 95–100, 30 Oct. 1371 (distribution of the 1,000 florins among the various communities of the Lucchese *contado*). *Rif.* 3, p. 215, 23 Jan. 1372.

[67] *Rif.* 2, p. 341, 4 July 1371, *Rif.* 3, p. 106, 3 Nov. 1371.

[68] *Rif.* 2, p. 309, 14 June, p. 326, 27 June 1371, *Rif.* 3, pp. 113–14, 13 Nov. 1371, pp. 199–200, 1 Jan., p. 253, 10 Mar., p. 268, 10 Apr., pp. 325–6, 15 June 1372.

[69] *Rif.* 3, pp. 479–80, 7 Jan., a *balìa* authorized p. 482, 8 Jan., p. 483, 12 Jan., pp. 492–6, 20 Jan. 1373.

[70] For example the work on the bridge of S. Quirico was not proceeding 'propter

expenditure, and emergency expenses were common.[71] Efforts to reduce expenditure were frequent,[72] and it was quite often necessary to borrow the interest of the *Massa*[73] or increase the price of salt.[74]

In these years two major reforms of Lucca's financial system were introduced, the establishment of the *deposita* and the reorganization of the *Massa*. The *deposita* in no way increased the revenue or reduced expenditure, but it was to prove of the greatest usefulness in preventing the need to borrow quite small sums for immediate needs. Lucca had often found herself temporarily without ready money to meet very minor and ordinary expenses, which were well within her means. The best way to deal with this problem was to keep a sum of money in reserve to be drawn upon in such cases. The first recorded attempt to set up a reserve of this kind was in 1377.[75] It provided for a fund of 15,000 florins, to be taken from the *dovana salis*. Whenever money was withdrawn from it the sum was to be made up again as soon as possible, so that there would always be 15,000 florins in reserve. This is the only reference to such a fund at this date, and as the year 1377 was a particularly difficult one, the decree may have remained a dead letter. It is not mentioned in the decree of 8 January 1381, which established a similar fund, this time of 20,000 florins.[76] The 20,000 florins were to be placed in the hands of the Lucchese banker, Giovanni Cagnuoli. There are no references in the *Riformagioni* to him spending it, but this was

carentiam pecunie et tenuitatem introitum', *Rif.* 4, p. 213, 18 July 1373, also Ponte S. Pietro, *Rif.* 5, p. 71, 24 May 1375. A *balìa* to decide how many mercenaries Lucca needed for her defence decreed that as the city lacked the money for these the price of salt was to be increased, *Rif.* 4, p. 328, 13 and 14 Feb. 1374.

[71] Payment to Conrad Wettingher *Rif.* 4, p. 260, 22 Nov., pp. 265–6, 4 Dec. 1373, p. 299, 15 Jan. 1374. Need to hire more forces, *Rif.* 4, pp. 328–9, 13 Feb. 1374, payment of 7,000 florins to Hawkwood, *Rif.* 5, p. 90, 9 July, pp. 93–4, 14 July 1375 and other smaller payments to armed companies, *Rif.* 6, p. 621, 4 Aug. 1378, *Min.* 2, ff. 192–3, 11 Aug. 1378, 2,300 florins to a company of Italians, *Rif.* 7, p. 93, 24 May 1379.

[72] *Rif.* 6, p. 203, 5 Mar., p. 282, 24 June, pp. 312–13, 29 July, p. 425, 14 Dec. 1377. *Rif.* 7, pp. 128–9 and *Min.* 2, ff. 366–7, 8 Aug. 1379, *Rif.* 7, p. 168, 4 Nov. 1379.

[73] *Rif.* 4, p. 423, 2 July, pp. 501–2, 20 Nov. 1374. *Rif.* 5, pp. 90–1, 9 July, pp. 93–4, 14 July, pp. 94–5, 15 July 1375. *Rif.* 6, pp. 13–14, 22 July 1376.

[74] *Rif.* 4, pp. 501–2, 20 Nov. 1374.

[75] Series *Offizio Sopra il Sale*, no. 1, ff. 25–26^{v}, 21 July 1377.

[76] *Rif.* 7, p. 402, 8 Jan. 1381.

a confidential matter that might well not have been recorded, and when he died shortly before 14 August 1383 he had rather more than 20,000 florins in his possession, which suggests that the *deposita* may have been functioning between January 1381 and August 1383.[77]

After the death of Giovanni Cagnuoli the administration of the *deposita* was reorganized.[78] Each treasurer of the *dovana salis* was to place any surplus there might be at the end of his period of office in the *deposita*, which was to be kept in the Gonfaloniere's room in the Palazzo della Signoria. The fund was to be administered by the Gonfaloniere, three keepers of the keys, and three citizens elected for this.[79] Books were to be kept, but the amount in the *deposita* at any one time was not to be revealed, and even the Gonfaloniere would know only the sums withdrawn and deposited during his term of office. The *deposita* began to function smoothly from 1384, and withdrawals and deposits are quite frequently recorded in the *Riformagioni* and occasionally in the *Minute* and *Deliberazioni*. It was used for the kind of extraordinary payments which had previously caused such difficulties; payments to *condottieri* and armed companies,[80] the purchase of corn, the payment of hired soldiers, the costs of fortification and the final instalment of the 50,000 florins owed to the Papacy.[81]

In these years payments into the *deposita* appear more frequently than withdrawals from it, and the sums withdrawn were probably more than covered by the deposits, though in

[77] *Rif.* 8, p. 583, 16 Aug. 1383, where it was stated that he had spent the money on the mandate of the Anziani. The sums given are 10,993 florins and £52,610. 19*s*. 1*d*. *picc.* The sum of 20,529 florins and £8. 11*s*. 4*d*. *picc.* was repaid on behalf of his heirs, who were minors, *Rif.* 9, p. 33, 9 Jan., p. 146, 14 July 1384.

[78] *Rif.* 9, p. 37, 20 Jan. 1384, where it is stated 'quod hactenus ordinatum fuit pro conservatione libertatis et felicis status civitatis lucane quod de denariis dovane et masse salis lucani comunis fieret depositum quod ad evitandos infestos casus semper teneretur paratum'.

[79] These were Giovanni Mingogi, Martino Arnolfini and Michele Guinigi, who held the office indefinitely.

[80] 3,000 florins were paid to Coucy, *Rif.* 9, p. 179, 4 Sept. 1384, 2,120 to the company of Taddeo Pepoli and Boldrino da Panicale, *Rif.* 9, pp. 329-30, 11 Apr. 1385, 4,300 to John Beltoft, *Rif.* 9, p. 395, 2 Sept. 1385, and 6,500 to Eberhard Suyler, Bertrand de la Salle and others, *Rif.* 10, p. 363, 23 Dec. 1387.

[81] *Rif.* 10, p. 329, 13 Sept. 1387, *Rif.* 11, p. 110, 17 Aug. 1389, p. 446, 13 Mar., p. 505, 26 Aug., p. 513, 3 Sept., p. 542, 26 Nov. 1391, *Rif.* 12, p. 318, 25 Aug. 1393 (to send aid to Marchese d'Este).

view of the provisions for secrecy 20 January 1381 some transactions may not have been recorded. There is a gap in the *Riformagioni* for 1395–7 and when the series begins again there are more records of withdrawals than of deposits; a total of 18,059 florins is recorded as having been withdrawn and only 5,500 paid in between 29 March 1397 and 19 July 1400.[82] These were years of war against Pisa and also of internal tension. In such times the *deposita* must have proved especially useful as a reserve from which ready money could be obtained quickly and easily. It many times proved its value in the years 1384–1400 as a means of meeting unexpected expenses without the need to borrow at interest, pledging the *proventus* for repayment as had happened in 1369–72. On the whole it was administered wisely, and the temptation to use such a convenient source of ready cash recklessly was resisted. Even in the years of war and crisis at the end of the century, when money was taken from it more freely, and the surplus of the *dovana salis*, instead of being placed in the *deposita*, was used for more immediate needs, deposits were still made whenever possible.

The other major reform in Lucca's financial system concerned the *Massa Creditorum*. Lucca's burden of debt was heavy. Silva regarded Pisa's public debt of 65,000 florins as enormous, as the revenues were probably only about 100,000 florins a year.[83] Lucca's debt was perhaps about 60,000–70,000 in 1368–73, when her ordinary revenues were about 60,000–65,000 florins a year and the public debt seems to have increased considerably by 1375, reaching a total of perhaps 90,000 florins.[84] Though the extent of her indebtedness could not be compared with that of Florence, whose public debt has been estimated at 1,250,000 florins in 1367, with carrying charges of 135,414 florins a year when the ordinary revenues were only about 300,000 florins,[85] she nevertheless probably found it a heavy burden. If the debt was about 90,000 florins the interest charges alone would have been about 9,000 florins

[82] Withdrawals, *Rif.* 13, p. 28, 29 Mar., p. 35, 4 May, p. 37, 19 May, p. 50, 18 July 1397, p. 118, 18 Mar. 1398, p. 348, 19 July 1400. Deposits, *Rif.* 13, p. 298, 30 Dec. 1399, *Min.* 4 (not foliated), 26 Feb. 1399.

[83] Silva, *Governo*, p. 117, Violante, 'Imposte dirette e debito pubblico', pp. 74–5.

[84] See Note on the *Massa*, pp. 75–6.

[85] Becker, *Florence in Transition*, Vol. II, pp. 177–8.

a year, apart from the costs of administration. The measures of 1376–8 were clearly designed to reduce this burden.

When the *Massa* had been established in January 1371 there had been no restrictions on holdings changing hands by purchase or other means, and the annual interest had been fixed at 10 per cent. Changes in the years 1376–8 prohibited alienation of holdings, except to the commune of Lucca, and reduced the interest to 5 per cent. The first hint of these changes comes in July 1376, when the governors of the *Massa* decreed that they and their successors 'liceat et possint a creditoribus dicte masse vendere volentibus emere medietatem crediti cuiusque creditoris dando de tribus denariis unum ipsi creditori vendere volenti'.[86] The purpose of the decree is made clear by the heading 'modis minuendi debitum masse creditorum'. Though the price to be paid was only a third of the face value of the holdings, it probably represented something like the market price at this time, since no repayments of the principal had been made since the establishment of the *Massa* and payments of interest seem to have been very irregular.[87] There was no compulsion to sell and no impediment to creditors selling their holdings to others. It would, of course, be of great advantage to the commune to use what money was available to buy up credits at $33\frac{1}{3}$ per cent rather than begin the repayment of the debt at face value.[88] The next year the purchase of credits at a third of their face value from men wishing to sell was again authorized. Only half the total holding of original creditors would be purchased, but men who had bought up other men's holdings could sell the whole of these to the commune. It was specifically stated that no one was compelled to sell, but this time alienation of credits

[86] *Rif.* 6, p. 21, 25 July 1376.

[87] Becker, 'Problemi della finanza pubblica fiorentina', p. 455 records that Florentine state bonds changed hands at 35–6 per cent, and in 1378 they were fetching as little as 13 per cent of their face value, Becker, *Florence in Transition*, Vol. II, p. 192. For fluctuations in the market price of credits in the Venetian public debt, G. Luzzatto, *Il debito pubblico della repubblica di Venezia dagli ultimi decenni del XIII° secolo alla fine del XV°* (Milan, 1963), pp. 99, 162–3, 190, 198, 206, 210–13, 234–5. The rate ranged from 99 per cent to 17–18 per cent of face value, and in some cases Venice took action with the aim of raising their value.

[88] For the purchase of credits in the market by the state in Venice, Luzzatto, *Il debito pubblico*, pp. 113–15, 191–2, 195–6. F. C. Lane, 'The funded debt of the Venetian republic, 1262–1482', in his *Venice and History* (Baltimore, 1966), p. 87.

except to the commune was prohibited.[89]

But more radical changes were shortly made. In a special meeting of the General Council in September 1378 new ordinances for the *Massa* were proposed. The rate of interest from 1 January 1372 to 1 January 1379 was to be reduced to 5 per cent, and reckoned at simple not compound interest. Anyone who had bought up other men's holdings on the *Massa* was to be obliged to sell these to the commune at a third of their face value. From 1 January 1379 any original creditor who wished to do so could sell up to half his holding to the commune at a third of its face value, and sale or alienation to anyone else was prohibited.[90] These were clearly important and far reaching changes. The interest rate was cut by half with retrospective effect. Alienation was now prohibited except to the commune, which would not buy more than half the holding of any original creditor and would pay only a third of its face value, and men who had bought other creditors out would be compelled to sell the whole of the credits they had purchased to Lucca at this rate. The interest at 10 per cent had been high. Interest rates on the public debt in many other cities were lower. Only Siena paid as much as 10 per cent.[91] The rate was 5 per cent in Florence from 1345, though 10 per cent was paid later and higher rates were sometimes paid by inscribing

[89] Series *Offizio Sopra il Sale*, no. 1, f. 26, 21 July 1377.

[90] *Rif.* 6, pp. 658-60, 17 Sept. 1378 'prima che dal primo die che la massa sordinoe cioe da Kal. gennaio del MCCCLXXII fine a Kal. gennaio proximo del MCCCLXXVIIII si debbia rendere cinque per centonaio senza mettere fructi in capitale. Et a quelli che dapoi vavessero aquistato ragione da quel di che acquistato vavessero fine a Kal. gennaio superscripto et per lo dicto Kal. quello che per arrieto avuto se navesse si debbia sbattere et l'resto ponere sopral capitale et chi meno che fine al superscripto tempo vitenesse lidicti per tanto meno debbia esser proveduto.

Secondo che infra qui et Kal. gennaio superscripto chiunque ae comperato alcuno denaro o ragione di denari nella superscripta massa sia tenuto et debbia farne vendita al comune di Lucha per lo terso denaro a pena del doppio. El comune o li dovanieri per lo comune comperare al dicto termine.

Item che dal superscripto Kal. inansi sianno tenuti li dovanieri a pena di floreni C per uno di rendere a ciascuno della dicta massa conto a ragione di cinque per cento lanno facendo lo pagamento ogni sei mesi pro rata. El camarlingho alloro richiesta di cosi pagare alla dicta pena.

Item che dal superscripto Kal. gennaio innansi chiunque ara denari nella superscripta massa possa vendere al comune di Lucha et non adaltra persona ne in alcuno modo alienare fine in della meta dicio che avra in della dicta massa per lo terso denaro di quella somma che vendere vorrae.'

[91] B. Barbadoro, *Le finanze della repubblica fiorentina* (Florence, 1929), p. 676.

lenders for two or three times the sum they had in fact lent,[92] and 8 per cent was paid on the new *Mons Libertatis* in 1390.[93] Genoa paid 8 per cent,[94] Pisa 5 per cent and Venice 4 or 5 per cent.[95] Arbitrary reductions of interest were made in other cities also; the interest was reduced by two-thirds in Florence[96] and from 10 per cent to 5 per cent in Pisa in 1370.[97]

In some respects the administration of the public debt in Lucca was similar to that in other cities. In Genoa the administration was entirely in the hands of the creditors, and in Lucca, as in Pisa, the creditors shared in the administration of the debt.[98] But in some respects Lucchese creditors were worse off than those of other cities. After 1378 credits were not negotiable as they were elsewhere. In Florence and Venice state bonds were in demand as a form of investment and were also an object of speculation.[99] In some cities the sale of credits was discouraged by what were in effect taxes on such sales; in Venice lower rates of interest were paid on credits that had

[92] Barbadoro, *Le finanze*, pp. 632–3, 667–70, 672, 676. Becker, *Florence in Transition*, Vol. II, pp. 161, 173–5, 177–8, and 'Problemi della finanza pubblica fiorentina', pp. 442–3. Matteo Villani, Lib. VIII, cap. 71, Marchionne di Coppo Stefani, rubr. 520, 799, 883.

[93] H. Sieveking, 'Studio sulle finanze genovesi nel medioevo', *Atti della Società Ligure di Storia Patria*, Vol. XXXV (1905), p. 193. Becker, 'Problemi della finanza pubblica fiorentina', p. 452 for other higher rates, 7 per cent, 8 per cent in the late fourteenth and early fifteenth century.

[94] Sieveking, 'Studio sulle finanze genovesi nel medioevo', p. 190.

[95] Barbadoro, *Le finanze*, p. 676, Silva, *Governo*, pp. 111–12, Violante, 'Imposte dirette e debito pubblico', pp. 72, 78, G. Luzzatto, *Studi di Storia Economica Veneziana* (Padua, 1954), pp. 213–15 and *Il debito pubblico*, pp. 158, 179–81, Lane, 'The funded debt of the Venetian republic', p. 87.

[96] Barbadoro, *Le finanze*, p. 676. Reduced to 5 per cent in 1380, Becker, *Florence in Transition*, Vol. II, pp. 197–8. N. Rodolico, *I Ciompi, una pagina di storia del proletariàto operaio* (Florence, 1945), pp. 188–9.

[97] Barbadoro, *Le finanze*, p. 676, Silva, *Governo*, pp. 111–12, Violante, 'Imposte dirette e debito pubblico', pp. 71–2. Also defaulting on interest payments, Becker, *Florence in Transition*, Vol. II, pp. 168–9. Suspensions of interest payments in Venice, Luzzatto, *Il debito pubblico*, pp. 139, 153, and reduction of the interest rate from 5 per cent to 4 per cent, p. 158, also pp. 179–82, 239–41, 247–8.

[98] Sieveking, 'Studio sulle finanze genovesi del medioevo', pp. 195–7, Silva, *Governo*, pp. 119–20.

[99] For Florence, Barbadoro, *Le finanze*, pp. 632, 666, Sieveking, 'Studio sulle finanze genovesi del medioevo', pp. 202–3, Becker, *Florence in Transition*, Vol. II, pp. 159, 175, 197, Brucker, *Florentine Politics and Society*, pp. 19–20, Marchionne di Coppo Stefani, rubr. 727. For Venice, Luzzatto, *Il debito pubblico*, pp. 158, 162–3, 181–3, 188, 195–6, 202–3, Lane, 'The funded debt of the Venetian republic', pp. 87–8.

changed hands and in Pisa they were counted at only half their face value after the financial reform of 1370, and from 1378 at only a third of face value, with the government also having first refusal in sales of credits.[100] Like other cities Lucca permitted the assignment of credits for debts and fines, and also for dowries at their face value,[101] but she treated her creditors unusually harshly in prohibiting alienation except to the state. The early books of the *Massa* show that wealthy capitalists had been buying up small credits of a few florins from poor men and especially from communes in the *contado* on some scale. The citizens of the *terziere* of S. Salvatore alone had purchased credits totalling 9,273 florins 8*s*. and 6*d*. *a oro*, and there were probably purchases on a similar scale for S. Martino and S. Paolino.[102] The possibility of redeeming credits of this order of magnitude on such favourable terms was clearly of great advantage to the commune.

It would have been surprising had there not been opposition to these measures. The *Riformagioni* account gives the impression that they went through smoothly. On 17 September 1378 the preliminary dispensation to enable the proposals to be discussed[103] was passed by 129–32 and the proposals themselves by 122–40, only a few more negative votes than usual. But there is evidence that the proposed changes had been thoroughly discussed for some months and much opposition to them overcome. In March 1378 there had been a

[100] Sieveking, 'Studio sulle finanze genovesi del medioevo', pp. 202–3, Barbadoro, *Le finanze*, pp. 666, 678–9, Silva, *Governo*, p. 113, 122–3, Violante, 'Imposte dirette e debito pubblico', pp. 72, 76, Luzzatto, *Il debito pubblico*, pp. 181–2, N. Rodolico, *La democrazia fiorentina nel suo tramonto* (Bologna, 1905), p. 280.

[101] For example *Rif.* 12, p. 178, 26 Aug. 1392 and others recorded in the books of the *Massa*. But if cash were required for a dowry, the rule that the holding must be sold to the state at a third of face value and that only half the total holding would be bought still applied. In Pisa after the reform of 1370 debtors of the commune and those condemned to fines had three times the sum involved cancelled from their holding in the public debt, Violante, 'Imposte dirette e debito pubblico', p. 72. In Venice the transfer of credits for fines was allowed at face value, but their use for dowries may have been at a reduced rate, Luzzatto, *Il debito pubblico*, pp. 62–3, 191.

[102] Series *Imprestiti*, 14, for the *terziere* of S. Salvatore 1379–95. The other books of this set have not survived, but no. 10 for S. Paolino 1368–73 shows purchases totalling 6,163 florins.

[103] Penalties had been laid down for those proposing changes in the *Massa*, *Rif.* 2, p. 198, 28 Jan. 1371, and it was therefore necessary to grant a dispensation from this before they could be discussed.

discussion of methods of easing Lucca's financial position, in which it had been proposed that, while interest that had been paid in cash for 1371–8 should remain at 10 per cent, that not actually paid should be reckoned at 5 per cent, and that for three years from 1 January 1378 it should be 4 per cent.[104] On this occasion it was agreed in principle that the regulations governing the *Massa* should be changed and a *balìa* was appointed to work out the details. There are several entries in the *Minute di Riformagioni* for the summer months of 1378 that probably refer to these proposed changes in the ordinances of the *Massa*. An entry which is undated but comes between entries dated 15 and 21 June, proposed a discussion of the ordinances of the *Massa* in view of Lucca's need for money. The necessary preliminary dispensation was defeated 105–46, and though it was put to the vote at least twice more, it was defeated each time.[105] There was another meeting on 22 June 1378 when the dispensation was proposed at least five times and voted at least three times without success.[106] The *Minute* version of the discussion on 17 September 1378 shows that

[104] *Rif.* 6, pp. 539–40, and *Min.* 2, f. 162v, 24 Mar. 1378. 'Quod ratio masse dovane salis videri debeat a die qua prius formata fuit in anno N.D. MCCCLXXII usque ad Kalendas Januarii proxime preteriti anni N.D. MCCCLXXVIII et meritum seu benefitium solutum in pecunia numerata intelligatur omnibus dicte masse creditoribus datum ad ratum decem per centenario pro quolibet anno dictorum quinque annorum. Residuum vero non solutum in pecunia numerata tamen pro toto dicto intermedio tempore vel parte ipsius ponatur ad ratum et computum cuiuslibet creditoris ad ratum quinque pro quolibet centenario in quolibet anno. Et a dictis Kalendis Januarii citra comune lucanum reddere debeat et assignare super et de proventu salis cuilibet creditori ad ratum quatuor pro centenario pro quolibet anno. De quibus quatuor pro centenario duo pro centenario expendi et investiri debeant in emtione creditorum masse salis vendere volentium ad ratum trigintatrium et tertii pro quolibet centenario incipiendo ab illis creditoribus qui emerent credita aliorum in dicta massa salis pro dictis emtionibus tamen. Reliqui vero duo pro centonario restituantur pro rata cuilibet creditori dicte masse salis. Totum vero residuum proventus dicte masse salis excepta quantitate necessaria ad futuram emtionem salis et exceptis duobus milibus florenorum solvi debendis quolibet mense Januarii Camere Apostolice possit comune lucanum et domini Antiani sine aliqua requisitione consiliariorum vel camerarii dicte masse salis expendere et expendi facere in suis occurrentibus necessitatibus sicut et quomodo possunt aliam pecuniam lucani comunis perventam et perveniendam ad manus generalis camerarii lucani comunis. Et hic ordo a Kalendis mensis Januarii superscripti MCCCLXXVIII durare debeat per tres annos proxime secuturos.'

[105] *Min.* 2, f. 186, 15–21 June 1378.

[106] *Min.* 2, ff. 187v–188, 22 June 1378. The only figures recorded are 119–49. There were 36 *invitati*.

both the dispensation and the proposals themselves were defeated the first time, and only passed after some modification.[107] The opposition to a measure that halved the interest with retrospective effect and seriously restricted alienation of holdings was clearly much greater than would appear from the *Riformagioni* and there was probably much discussion and persuasion behind the scenes before it was finally passed.

Even after these reforms Lucca's chronic financial difficulties continued. Problems were caused by the not infrequent need to buy off armed companies[108] and extra defence costs during the outbreaks of plague in 1383 and 1390. Efforts at economy were made,[109] but it was often necessary to borrow to pay for defence or ensure food supplies. On several occasions the interest of the *Massa* was borrowed,[110] or money was taken from the *dovana salis* or *abundantia*,[111] or it was necessary for private citizens to come to the aid of the state.[112] Efforts were made to collect the revenues more efficiently, particularly by a more rigorous application of the salt monopoly. Any immunities or privileges granted to *contadini* were to be revoked at once if they had no fixed date, and others were not to be renewed when they expired.[113] Shortly afterwards a new assessment of 'bocche' for the salt tax was ordered.[114] In a series of measures in June 1388 it was

[107] *Min.* 2, ff. 217–18, 17 Sept. 1378. The votes were 118–42 on the dispensation and 98–63 on the proposals.

[108] Payments to the English *condottieri* John Hawkwood and Richard Ramsey, *Rif.* 8, p. 593, 30 Aug., p. 667, 7 Dec. 1383. *Rif.* 9, pp. 32–3, 7 Jan., p. 248, 19 Dec. 1384, p. 321, 21 Mar. 1385.

[109] *Rif.* 8, p. 56, 19 Feb. 1382, p. 494, 28 Apr., p. 605, 6 Sept., p. 624, 25 Oct., p. 664, 4 Dec. 1383, *Rif.* 12, p. 234, 27 Dec. 1392, p. 413, 17 Feb. 1394.

[110] *Rif.* 8, p. 586, 25 Aug., pp. 623–4, 25 Oct. 1383, *Rif.* 10, p. 491, 26 June and again p. 581, 8 Dec. 1388.

[111] *Rif.* 8, p. 521, 25 May, p. 540, 23 June, pp. 543–4, 27 June, p. 568, 25 July, p. 573, 31 July 1383. *Min.* 4, (not foliated), 28 Mar., 11 Dec. 1389. *Rif.* 11, p. 110, 17 Aug. 1389. *Min.* 4, (not foliated), 12 Mar., 27 Aug., 7 Dec. 1390, 3 Nov. 1391. *Rif.* 12, p. 55, 21 Feb., p. 76, 23 Mar., p. 170, 2 Aug. 1392. *Min.* 4, (not foliated), 30 Aug., 21 Dec. 1392, 8, 10 and 30 Jan., 22 Feb., 29 Apr., 19 June, 7 Nov. 1397, 26 Apr., 30 May, 19 June, 17 July 1398.

[112] Michele Guinigi and Lando Moriconi paid 9,000 florins to purchase corn, *Rif.* 11, pp. 106–7, 21 July 1389. 150–200 of the richest citizens were elected to buy 25–150 sacks each, *Min.* 4 (not foliated), 26 July, 12 Aug. 1389.

[113] *Rif.* 7, p. 480, 26 Apr. 1381.

[114] *Rif.* 7, pp. 487–8, 17 May, p. 492, 22 May 1381.

proposed to distribute salt in the city and the suburbs on the same basis as it was done in the *contado*. Lucca had the monopoly of the sale of salt in the city and suburbs, but there was no obligation on the inhabitants to buy any fixed amount, and it was alleged that the amount sold there was far less than might have been expected considering the size of the population. In addition a tax was imposed on wine, again assessed according to the population. The import duty on silk from the 'mare magiore' was reimposed and a change in the value of the florin was decreed. The florin which then stood at £5 *picc*. Lucchese was to be worth £3. 15*s*. which, it was said, would bring Lucca into line with other cities like Florence, Prato, Pistoia, and Pisa, and would benefit both the city and individuals.[115] It was in effect an increase in the gabelles. But the result of all these measures was apparently disappointing and an official was appointed to prevent frauds.[116] There were further efforts in 1394 to increase the revenues by higher gabelles and forced distribution of salt in the city and suburbs.[117]

But expenditure increased in the following years, owing primarily to the war with Pisa and the consequent need to maintain more forces. Despite efforts to avoid the necessity of forced loans, a general *estimo* had to be decreed in 1397.[118] The Gonfaloniere in proposing this, stressed the seriousness of the dangers to Lucchese independence and the vital need of money for war, both trying to appeal to patriotic feelings and stressing that the burden would be by no means unbearable, if shared equally according to each man's capacity. Different

[115] *Rif.* 10, pp. 485–6, 19 June 1388.

[116] *Rif.* 10, p. 553, 21 Oct. 1388, a *balìa* was appointed to review the whole question, provided they did nothing that might reduce the revenues, 'cum introitus gabelle proventus et obventiones lucani comunis non respondeant eo modo quo verisimiliter deberent consideratis augmentationibus noviter factis'.

[117] 'perche avuto consideratione a le bocche di Luca et de borghi e soborghi et a la quantita del sale che se spacciato et spaccia a minuto al calamaio si vede quasi per meta esser ingannata', *Rif.* 12, pp. 423–4, 9 Mar., pp. 444–6, 29 Apr. 1394. A census was apparently made for the purpose, but no figures survive either for 1388 or 1394. But it seems that forced distribution of salt in the city was put into effect, for in decreeing a reduction in the price of salt 25 Nov. 1390 it was stated that citizens as well as *contadini* were about to default on the second *paga* of the salt tax because the price was too high, *Rif.* 11, p. 348.

[118] *Rif.* 13, pp. 38–40, 18 June 1397. *Rif.* 12, p. 413, 17 Feb. 1394 it had been specified that there was not to be an *estimo* or *prestantia*.

methods of assessment were laid down according to whether or not citizens were willing to declare their property. Only half the estimated value of each man's property was to be used as the basis for payment and 'poveri et miserabili persone' were to be exempt . This was not a form of direct taxation, for like the 'taxa' of 1370, it was to be regarded as a loan. Anything paid for this *estimo* was to be written into the *Massa* and 5 per cent interest would be paid, though, unlike other holdings in the *Massa* these new credits were to be freely alienable and any citizen might lend on behalf of another, if both were agreed. The number of assessments was 1,483, and a general *estimo* of this kind, based on each man's capacity to pay seems an obvious way to raise the necessary money. But for the Lucchese it was a last resort, to be accepted only when all else failed and when the very existence of the state was felt to be at stake.[119] It was to be used 'solo quando lo nostro comune fusse ad extremo bisogno' and was only to be valid for three years. Anything borrowed on the basis of this *estimo* was to be repaid at the earliest possible date, as soon as peace was restored and Lucca was able to reduce her expenditure. There is no official record of how much was raised on the basis of this *estimo* or indeed that anything was, but it is mentioned by Sercambi, who asserts that 'molti ciptadini se partiranno per le gravesse'.[120]

But these last years of the century were wholly exceptional because of the war with Pisa. In time of war Lucca quickly found herself in serious difficulties, as she had done earlier in 1369–71, and the events of 1396–1400 and the financial crisis that resulted demonstrate the wisdom of her policy earlier in refusing to be drawn into wars among her neighbours. Apart from the crisis caused by the war with Pisa, Lucca's financial position was probably much the same at the end of the century as it had been in the early years after 1371. Some improve-

[119] For reluctance to accept direct taxation based on an assessment of wealth, Becker, *Florence in Transition*, Vol. II, pp. 154–5, 170–2, 176–7, 180, 192–6, also 'Economic change', pp. 11-12, 25-8, and 'Problemi della finanza pubblica fiorentina', pp. 437-9. For Pisa, Violante, 'Imposte dirette e debito pubblico', pp. 73-4, and Silva, *Governo*, pp. 114-17.

[120] Sercambi, II, p. 82. For the names of the *estimati* and their assessments, Lucca, Biblioteca Governativa, MS. 925, ff. 249-58. There is no record in the books of the *Massa* of anything paid on this *estimo*, but separate books would probably be kept, especially as the terms were not the same as for earlier *Massa* holdings.

ments had been effected, notably the establishment of the *Massa Creditorum* and the *deposita*, but it had never been possible to pay off the public debt, as had been intended; the debt was still virtually intact in 1411. The revenues were barely adequate in time of peace and any reduction in receipts due to plague or invasion or any increase in expenditure due to the need to buy off an armed company, hire more soldiers or buy corn in time of shortage rendered emergency measures necessary. There were frequently repeated efforts to keep down expenditure and maintain and increase the revenues. But these crises seem to have been comparatively minor ones. By exercising a little care the revenues could be made to cover expenditure. Lucca's position was certainly no worse than that of her neighbours, and probably better than that of at least some of them. There was no parallel in Lucca to the Florentine system of deficit financing.[121] If it was never possible to pay off the public debt as had been hoped, it does not seem to have increased after about 1375, at any rate until 1396/7, at a time when the Florentine *Monte* grew enormously from about 500,000 florins in 1345 to 3,000,000 florins by 1400 and the Venetian public debt reached about 5,000,000 ducats in 1386.[122] The *Massa* never came to play anything like the predominant role in Lucchese public life that the *Monte* played in Florence or Venice.[123]

Though Lucca sometimes had recourse to voluntary short term loans from small groups of citizens, she did not have to impose *prestanze* of the kind common in Venice, Florence or

[121] Becker, *Florence in Transition*, Vol. II, pp. 160-1, 179-80, 188-91, 198-9, and 'Economic change', p. 36 and 'Problemi della finanza pubblica fiorentina', pp. 442, 449-50. But Lucca probably lacked the underlying economic strength to make such a policy possible. There was no increase in the Sienese public debt as in Florence, Bowsky, *Finance of the Commune of Siena*, pp. 294-6.

[122] Becker, *Florence in Transition*, Vol. II, pp. 151-2, 169, 181. A. Molho, 'The Florentine oligarchy and the *balìe* of the late Trecento', *Speculum*, Vol. XLIII (1968), p. 39, relying on Becker's notes. For Venice Doge Mocenigo claimed in 1423 that the Venetian public debt was 6,000,000 ducats, having been reduced from 10,000,000 since he became doge, Luzzatto, *Il debito pubblico* pp. 212-13. The debt had apparently been about 5,000,000 ducats in 1386, but it had been possible to reduce it 1389-1402, pp. 196-8.

[123] Becker, *Florence in Transition*, Vol. II, pp. 152-3, 155, 158-62, 200. For the fifteenth-century L. F. Marks, 'The financial oligarchy in Florence under Lorenzo', in E. F. Jacob (ed.), *Italian Renaissance Studies* (London, 1960), esp. pp. 127-8. Luzzatto, *Il debito pubblico*, pp. 6-7.

Pisa.[124] These *prestanze* have sometimes been seen as a source of profit to the lenders. They may perhaps have been preferred by the well-to-do, if the alternative was direct non-interest bearing and non-returnable taxation.[125] But the view that *prestanze* were a source of profit depends on high interest rates of 10 per cent, 15 per cent or even 20 per cent.[126] Interest rates were lower in Lucca and it is unlikely that she could have afforded to pay such rates, especially as one would have to assume a financial situation serious enough to cause her to have recourse to forced loans in the first place. F. C. Lane argued that Venetians were willing to invest in the public debt even at 5 per cent interest, but this was for credits bought at less than face value so that the real rate of return would be much higher.[127] The view that the Florentine *Monte*, in which many *prestanze* were eventually incorporated, gave a good return at 5 per cent, also depends on credits being freely transferable.[128] In Lucca holdings in the public debt were not transferable after 1378, except for the special category arising from the *estimo* of 1397, and returns would thus be more modest.

It has been argued that *prestanze* were demaging to a mercantile and industrial society, as they diverted capital from

[124] Becker, *Florence in Transition*, Vol. II, pp. 160–2, 177, 188–92, 198–9. As much as 1,300,000 florins was raised by forced loans in the single year 1393, and there were other high figures for the 1390s, Becker, 'Problemi della finanza pubblica fiorentina', pp. 434, 452–3, Molho, *Florentine Public Finances* pp. 63–4 and 'The Florentine oligarchy', pp. 38–46. For the 1370s, Brucker, *Florentine Politics and Society*, pp. 196, 315. For Pisa, Violante, 'Imposte indirette e debito pubblico', pp. 75–6 and Silva, *Governo*, p. 127. For the enormous importance of forced loans in Venice, Luzzatto, *Il debito pubblico*, esp. pp. 6–7.

[125] Brucker, *Florentine Politics and Society*, pp. 92–3. Becker, *Florence in Transition*, Vol. I, *The Decline of the Commune* (Baltimore, Md., 1967), p. 25, *Florence in Transition*, Vol. II, pp. 155, 170–2.

[126] Molho, 'The Florentine oligarchy', p. 39. Becker, *Florence in Transition*, Vol. II, p. 155. Also E. Cristiani, *Nobiltà e popolo nel comune di Pisa* (Naples, 1962), pp. 306–7.

[127] Lane, 'The funded debt of the Venetian Republic', pp.87–8. Luzzatto argues that even 4 per cent was a good return if credits had been bought for less than their face value, *Il debito pubblico*, p. 158.

[128] Becker, *Florence in Transition*, Vol. II speaks of a brisk traffic in *Monte* shares, p. 158. Brucker, *Florentine Politics and Society*, p. 92. But fiscal expedients often gave actual returns of 10 per cent or 15 per cent, Becker, *Florence in Transition*, pp. 161–2, 174–5, and interested parties are found arguing that 5 per cent was insufficient to attract the capital needed, p. 169. Also Molho, 'The Florentine oligarchy', p. 39.

[129] E. Fiumi, 'Sui rapporti economici tra città e contado nell'età communale',

other more profitable enterprises,[129] and they certainly seem to have been a serious burden in some Italian states.[130] It is probable that, as G. A. Brucker said no one really wished to pay *prestanze*,[131] though they did offer some return in the form of inerest and the hope of eventual repayment and were preferable to direct taxation. The Lucchese clearly regarded them as something undesirable, to be avoided if at all possible, and only to be resorted to if all else failed.[132] Except for the crisis years immediately after 1369 and during the war with Pisa at the end of the century Lucca was able to avoid *prestanze*. Though her efforts to raise extra money by such means as increasing the gabelles perhaps hit the poorer citizens especially hard, these measures were relatively limited. In 1390 the Gonfaloniere compared Lucca's record in matters of finance and taxation favourably with that of her neighbours saying

> neuno nostro vicino lo credesse perche non pure a citadini di Luca e stata gloriosa utilita ilben vivere ma etiando et da lungi et da presso di meglio vivere che alcuna altra cita di questo paese a preso fama et non senza cagione per che dove laltre terre con viva ragione via piu di noi potenti non senza graveze e molestie di compagne non senza graveze dimposte e dismesurate carestie e mortali guerre sono state dove idio a noi a conceduto gratia dirippararsi da le insidii de vicini da le graveze de le compagne senza cavare di borsa sforsatamente denaio a persona.[133]

He clearly felt that Lucchese had something to congratulate themselves on in having been able to avoid forced loans and it is by no means impossible that Lucchese subjects bore a lighter burden of taxation and that Lucca had to call for fewer financial sacrifices from her citizens than did other neigh-

---

Archivio Storico Italiano, Vol. CXIV (1956), p. 38, 'Fioritura e decadenza III', p. 458.

[130] In Florence some citizens preferred to pay a smaller assessment and give up their claim to interest or repayment, Molho, 'The Florentine oligarchy', pp. 39-40, Becker, *Florence in Transition*, Vol. II, pp. 199-200. This was also the case in Venice, where some citizens were also obliged to sell their old holdings at far less than their face value in order to pay new forced loans at the full rate, Luzzatto, *Il debito pubblico*, pp. 135, 158-64, 166-76.

[131] In a private communication quoted in Bowsky, *Finance of the Commune of Siena*, pp. 286, note 29. The whole question of the profitability of *prestanze* is discussed pp. 285-7.

[132] For reluctance in Florence, Brucker in Bowsky, *Finance of the Commune of Siena*, p. 286, note 29. Becker, *Florence in Transition*, Vol. II, pp. 191-2.

[133] *Rif.* 11, p. 371, 16 Dec. 1390.

bouring cities that pursued a more active and ambitious external policy.[134]

NOTE ON THE MASSA

It is not easy to make even an estimate of the total of the Lucchese public debt at any particular date. Only one of the sets of four books, that is one for each of the three *terzieri* of Lucca and one for the communes of the Lucchese *contado* and citizens living outside Lucca, survives complete, nos. 17–20 in the series *Imprestiti* covering the years 1396–1411. The totals were then 23,473 florins for S. Paolino, 25,523 for S. Martino, 25,777 for S. Salvatore and 17,588 for the communes and absent citizens, a total of 92,361 florins.

This is considerably higher than the figures available for the first years after the establishment of the *Massa*. *Imprestiti* 10, for the *terziere* of S. Paolino 1368–73 shows original credits of 13,056 florins, plus 6,163 florins of credits purchased from others by the citizens of S. Paolino. *Imprestiti* 11 for S. Martino 1368–73 shows 17,159 florins original credits and about 543 florins of purchased credits, though the latter are probably not complete. *Imprestiti* 12 for S. Salvatore 1368–73 is a fragment, showing purchased credits only, to a total of 3,451 florins. It can only be guessed what the credits held by the communes and absent citizens amounted to at this time. It may have been proportionally more than in 1396–1411, as the communes at least were among those most likely to sell their holdings.

Imprestiti 13 for S. Martino 1373–5 shows a total of 25,642 florins credits, not counting 6,020 florins unpaid accumulated interest. This is appreciably more than the 17,159 florins of 1368–73 and is even a little higher than the figure of 25,523 florins for 1396–1411. The increase on the figure for 1368–73 cannot be accounted for by accumulated interest, for that was recorded separately. It is unlikely that purchases account for it. There is no indication of these in the book, and in any case if the increase were the result of purchases of credits, the total would have fallen again by 1396, as the purchasers would have

[134] For the connection between *prestanze* and war and an active external policy, Becker, *Florence in Transition*, Vol. II, pp. 156, 160–5, 177–9, 188–92, Molho, *Florentine Public Finances*, pp. 3–4, 9–11, Luzzatto, *Il debito pubblico*, pp. 134–9, 196–8, 237–8. Also Bowsky, *Finance of the Commune of Siena*, p. 282, and note 14.

been obliged to resell what they had bought as a result of the changes in the *Massa* in 1378. The increase is more likely to have resulted from further borrowings by Lucca after 1373. Perhaps when the interest paid on holdings in the *Massa* was re-borrowed, this was added to the original credits.

It seems probable that the total debt was over 90,000 florins in 1396–1411 (allowing for possible errors and duplicated entries, one of which may not have been cancelled). The debt was probably appreciably less in 1368–73, perhaps 60,000–70,000 florins, depending on the amount held by the communes of the Lucchese *contado*. The increase perhaps took place chiefly 1373–5. Lucca was comparably heavily indebted, as her annual revenues in 1373–80, excluding the yield of the salt gabelle, were only 60,000–70,000.

4

THE RESOURCES OF THE *CONTADO*

In the last thirty years of the fourteenth century, in addition to being much reduced in extent, the Lucchese *contado* was in serious economic crisis. Her troubled history in the earlier fourteenth century had not been without repercussions on the *contado*, and there is much evidence of serious economic difficulties in the thirty or forty years before the recovery of Lucchese independence. As soon as the series *Anziani Avanti la Libertà* begins in 1330 there are records of many petitions from individual communes and groups of communes for respites in the payment of dues or debts or for tax relief because of poverty, depopulation, and economic difficulties resulting from wars and other causes. As early as 1333 the commune of Capella S. Stefano di Tassignano, pieve S. Paolo, petitioned that it was reduced from the 120 and more men that it used to have to only about twenty-five and that most of their houses had been burnt and they were reduced to poverty and wretchedness.[1]

There were certain years of especial difficulty. There were general decrees for the benefit of many men of the communes of the suburbs and Six Miles whose property had been burnt and destroyed in enemy attacks in September and November 1336.[2] The damage done in the area immediately surrounding Lucca in the siege of 1341–2 brought a spate of petitions for respite in the payment of debts owed to Lucca and to individuals.[3] But quite apart from these especially difficult

[1] *Anz. Av. Lib.* 4, p. 39, 24 May 1333. Fifty men had taken the oath of allegiance to John of Bohemia 31 May 1332, *Capitoli*, 52, p. 467.

[2] *Anz. Av. Lib.* 12, p. 101, 29 Nov. 1336. There were several renewals of these grants later, the last of them until 1 July 1341, *Anz. Av. Lib.* 12, pp. 108, 118, 121, 7 July 1337, *Anz. Av. Lib.* 13, pp. 103, 107, 111, 114, 14 July 1338, *Anz. Av. Lib.* 14, pp. 113–16, 24 July 1339, *Anz. Av. Lib.* 16, pp. 57–8, 11 Jan. 1341. There had been grants of reductions of *estimo* to some of these communes earlier because of enemy attacks, *Anz. Av. Lib.* 5, p. 56, 12 Feb. 1334, referring to an earlier grant of 31 Oct. 1332.

[3] *Anz. Av. Lib.* 18, p. 92, 5 Nov., p. 98, 12 Nov., pp. 106, 107, 109, 18 Nov., p.

years there was a steady stream of petitions complaining of sufferings in war or natural disasters, depopulation, impoverishment, indebtedness and taxes and dues that were beyond the capacity of the men of the communes of the Lucchese *contado* to pay, and asking for reductions, immunities, and respites in the payment of debts. A number of villages had been abandoned completely and their former inhabitants asked for tax concessions and immunities to help them to return and rebuild them.[4] Others were much reduced. S. Martino in Vignale, pieve S. Stefano, had only five men remaining, the others being 'profugi et vagabundi'.[5] Burciano, in the vicariate of Gallicano, which had obtained a reduction of its assessment from seventeen hearths to twelve in 1343, petitioned in 1358 that it only had six men instead of the eighty or so that it had once had.[6] Only four men remained in Valpromaro, in the vicariate of Camaiore, sixteen others having left,[7] Schiava, in the same vicariate, was reduced from seventeen to five,[8] and there were a number of other communes that were reduced to only two or three men.[9]

The Lucchese authorities did what they could with temporary grants of immunity and tax relief, permanent

---

111, 23 Nov., p. 117, 29 Nov., p. 118, 30 Nov., pp. 149, 151, 17 Dec. 1342. A general reference to many petitions, *Anz. Av. Lib.* 18, p. 124, 30 Nov. 1342. Military operations around Pietrasanta, Monteggiori and elsewhere in the Lucchese state resulted in similar petitions later, *Anz. Av. Lib.* 21, p. 138, 4 Nov., p. 150, 28 Nov., p. 152, 29 Nov., p. 176, 12 Dec. 1343, *Anz. Av. Lib.* 24, p. 61, 11 Apr., p. 91, 13 June 1346, *Anz. Av. Lib.* 26, p. 7, 11 Jan. 1347.

[4] Bolognana, vicariate of Barga, *Anz. Av. Lib.* 13, p. 35, 6 Mar. 1338. Cerasomma, *Anz. Av. Lib.* 16, pp. 93–4, 17 Mar. 1341. Vegghiatore, *Anz. Av. Lib.* 18, p. 96, 6 Nov. 1342. Ponte S. Pietro, *Anz. Av. Lib.* 24, p. 110, 11 July 1346. S. Martino in Colle, *Anz. Av. Lib.* 26, p. 95, 16 Apr. 1347.

[5] *Anz. Av. Lib.* 7, p. 14, 14 May 1334.

[6] *Anz. Av. Lib.* 21, p. 33, 28 July 1343. *Anz. Av. Lib.* 39, p. 41, 23 Jan. 1358.

[7] *Anz. Av. Lib.* 24, p. 70, 16 May 1346. The books of the *estimo* of the Lucchese contado go some way towards confirming this; *Estimo* no. 83 (for the year 1346) and no. 76 (for 1347–8) list the names of eight *estimati* in Valpromaro, while no. 69 (for 1374) lists only five. However *estimati* were not necessarily the same as residents. *Estimo* no. 75 (for 1394–6) lists four men *estimati* in Valpromaro, two of whom lived elsewhere, but it also lists nine men not of Valpromaro. *Estimo* no. 135 (for 1410) lists only one *estimatus* of Valpromaro and he lived in Loppeglia, but it also lists fifteen *forenses*.

[8] *Anz. Av. Lib.* 41, p. 165, 6 Aug. 1361.

[9] For example Palaria, pieve di Compito, *Anz. Av. Lib.* 7, p. 3, 12 Apr. 1334, Palmatoria, pieve S. Pancrazio, *Anz. Av. Lib.* 24, p. 71, 16 May 1346, Chiatri, *Anz. Av. Lib.* 41, p. 18, 29 Jan. 1361.

reductions in the assessments of communes or individuals, or respites in payment of dues or debts 'ut melius valeant respirare',[10] but these seem to have had little permanent effect. The general situation seems to have deteriorated rather than improved and in January 1360 a *balìa* was appointed 'ad providendum circa gravedines et onera comitatinorum et comunium lucani comitatus fortie et districtus'.[11] Another outbreak of plague and Lucca's involvement in war with Florence as an ally of Pisa led to further difficulties and in November 1362 it was urged that it was very necessary to make a new *estimo*

> per che dal tempo che lo stimo fu fatto in qua per li casi et novita occorse sono molto mutate et variate le condictioni de comuni et del [sic] homini et molti comuni ancora venuti a niente et facti perdenti li quali se fusseno uniti et agiunti con altri comuni li homini di quelli che sono fuggiti per le gravezze che non ponno sostenere ritornerenno et ancora molti et molti comuni sono per mancare et venire meno per le gravezze che vegnono loro secondo lo vecchio stimo le quali non ponno sostenere per lo mancamento del homini et delle persone dellor comuni li quali dal tempo del dicto stimo in qua sono facti perdenti.[12]

This gloomy picture of the situation does not seem to be exaggerated. Certainly there are many references to *contadini* leaving their communes because they were called upon to pay dues that were beyond their capacity. Four men of Bargecchia, in the vicariate of Camaiore, petitioned in June 1363 that everyone had left in the last eighteen months or so because they could not pay the dues imposed upon them. The commune was deserted, but the petitioners wished to return and claimed that doubtless some of the others would do the same if given concessions.[13] The men of Schiava petitioned that there had been twenty-four men before the recent mortality, and that though only four now remained they were being made to pay according to the *estimo* made more than twenty-two years previously, so that unless they were shown

[10] *Anz. Av. Lib.* 12, p. 64, 19 Oct. 1336.

[11] The decree establishing this *balìa* has not survived, but it is referred to as having been set up 31 Jan. 1360, *Anz. Av. Lib.* 41, p. 18, 29 Jan. 1361. Also *Anz. Av. Lib.* 42, p. 157, 28 Nov. 1362, where it is said to have been set up to consider many petitions from communes that were so impoverished and depopulated as to be unable to pay their customary dues.

[12] *Anz. Av. Lib.* 42, pp. 157–8, 28 Nov. 1362.

[13] *Anz. Av. Lib.* 42, p. 252, 3 June 1363.

mercy they too would have to leave.[14] Concessions were made, and in December 1365 the doge, Giovanni dell'Agnello, authorized the Lucchese Anziani to arrange for the remaking of the *estimo* of the entire Lucchese *contado*.[15] The defectiveness of the sources for the last few years of Pisan rule makes it impossible to discover whether the situation improved, as it may have done to a certain extent with the end of the war with Florence, or whether petitions for relief continued to come in. But even if there was some temporary improvement, there is ample evidence of serious and deeply rooted economic difficulties in the period before 1369. They dated back at least to 1330 and probably much earlier, and as the problems of depopulation, impoverishment, and indebtedness resulting from warfare and destruction were by 1369 exacerbated by plagues, the government of the newly independent Lucchese state inherited a difficult situation in which it was virtually impossible to find measures that would have much permanent effect.

And when Lucca recovered her liberty the *contado* expected to feel an immediate benefit, and there was a flood of petitions for relief and immunity. Whole vicariates petitioned[16] as well as many individual communes. Treppignana, in the vicariate of Gallicano, was granted immunity from all obligations except the customary gabelles and salt tax for three years, because of its obviously poor and miserable condition.[17] Trassalico, in the same vicariate, and the commune of Gallicano itself were granted similar immunities for ten years in answer to a petition and to encourage fidelity.[18] Castelnuovo, in the vicariate of Castiglione, was granted a twelve year immunity,[19] and many other communes also petitioned successfully for tax relief. A few got a reduction in the number of hearths at which they were assessed; Coreglia

[14] *Anz. Av. Lib.* 42, p. 275, 4 Aug. 1363.

[15] *Anz. Av. Lib.* 44, p. 21, 15 Dec. 1365. The work was certainly begun; some fragments of this *estimo* dated 1368, survive in *Estimo* no. 39.

[16] For example Pietrasanta and Massa Lunense, *Delib.* 131, ff. 9-9^{v}, 11-13, 10 Apr. 1370.

[17] 'Considerantes evidentem paupertatem et miserabilem conditionem', *Rif.* 1, p. 31, 7 Aug. 1369.

[18] *Rif.* 1, p. 53, 22 Aug., p. 65, 29 Aug. 1369.

[19] *Rif.* 4, pp. 415-16, 23 June 1374, referring to an earlier immunity granted 16 Nov. 1370.

was reduced from thirty-eight to thirty hearths, and Pèrpoli from ten hearths to eight.[20] Others obtained relief in the form of a reduction of the amount of salt they were obliged to buy each year.[21] Of course, communes petitioning for tax relief might be expected to exaggerate their impoverishment, but their petitions were almost always granted, often after an inquiry into the truth of their complaints, so they were probably substantially true. The petitioners themselves often gave details and figures to support their requests for relief. Cascio, in the vicariate of Gallicano, spoke of the death of adults and children, and the shortage of food and other necessities.[22] The men of S. Lorenzo, pieve di Massa Macinara, petitioned that there were only four men remaining in the commune, one of whom was blind; there used to be eleven.[23] The men of S. Alessio, near Lucca itself, petitioned that only three men remained, five others having left with their families.[24] Vegghiatore in the vicariate of Camaiore had declined from forty men to twelve,[25] Montegiano in the same vicariate had only five men,[26] S. Filippo dei Sobborghi had only three, two of them very old, and petitioned that eight or nine others had left to go and live in Lucca.[27]

Some places attributed their misfortunes directly to the wars and other disturbances of this period. The men of the suburbs and country parishes around Lucca itself petitioned for relief because of the devastations they had suffered at the hands of the mercenary soldiers of Bernabò Visconti, armed companies and other such attacks.[28] The men of Cerasomma petitioned

[20] Coreglia, *Rif.* 1, p. 67, 31 Aug. 1369, *Rif.* 8, p. 121, 29 Apr. 1382. Pèrpoli, *Rif.* 1, p. 120, 15 Oct. 1369.

[21] *Rif.* 1, p. 73, 31 Aug. 1369.

[22] 'Morte hominum et puerorum', *Rif.* 1, p. 73, 31 Aug. 1369. Seventeen men of Cascio had taken the oath to John of Bohemia 11 Jan. 1332, *Capitoli*, 52, p. 623.

[23] *Rif.* 1, p. 265, 5 Mar. 1370.

[24] *Rif.* 1, p. 290, 31 Mar. 1370. Thirty-one men of S. Alessio had taken the oath to John of Bohemia 24 May 1332, *Capitoli*, 52, p. 427.

[25] *Rif.* 1, p. 300, 9 Apr. 1370.

[26] *Rif.* 5, p. 14, 15 Jan. 1375.

[27] *Rif.* 5, pp. 190–1, 14 Jan. 1376. 'Et tucti li altri homini li quali soleano habitare in della dicta contrata di Sancto Filipo sono partiti e venuti a stare e habitare in della citta di Lucca e in de borghi e anosi facto dare perscripto a consoli in delle bandiere delle contrate in delle quali dimorano per fare le factioni reali e personali della citta di Lucca sicome cittadini di Lucca, li quali homini sono octo o vero nove.'

[28] *Rif.* 1, p. 199, 10 Jan. 1370. For similar problems in the Pisan *contado*, Silva, *Governo*, p. 136.

that they had been robbed and their houses burnt by the Pisans, so that they could no longer live there.[29] S. Donnino petitioned that it had been much impoverished by the wars,[30] and S. Alessio that it had lost many men who were dead or who had left the commune because of the troubles and attacks of Pisans and Lombards.[31] The men of Massa Lunense petitioned that they were on the borders and therefore suffered first. In addition to requesting a reduction of their gabelle, they asked either that arrangements be made to defend them adequately or that they be given leave to make a truce with the men of Carrara and Sarzana.[32] The men of S. Vitale also petitioned that they were near enemy territory and had suffered severely, and asked either that peace be made or that mercenaries be stationed in their territory to defend them.[33] Taxation added to their difficulties. Customary payments which were bearable in ordinary times would weigh much more heavily if wars, devastation, and deaths had reduced their capacity to pay. Communes where some of the inhabitants had died or left found themselves in particular difficulties. Unless they could get a reduction in their assessment, the men who remained would find themselves paying the dues of those who no longer lived there as well as their own. This might prove the last straw and cause the remaining inhabitants to leave also. The men of S. Alessio asked for such a reduction, urging that they too would be obliged to leave, as they could not pay the dues of the absent men as well as their own.[34]

In fact petitions, though couched in humble terms, often had a sting in the tail in the form of a threat to leave if relief

[29] *Rif.* 1, p. 263, 5 Mar. 1370.

[30] *Rif.* 1, pp. 368–9, 22 May 1370.

[31] *Rif.* 1, p. 403, 22 June 1370.

[32] They claimed they acted as 'quasi clipeus et primum signaculum ad sagittam' and asked 'quod circa defensionem ipsorum per comune lucanum debeat provideri vel quod ipsis licentia concedatur faciendi cum hominibus et comunitatibus Sarezane Carrarie et aliis finitimis subiectis atque suppositis Bernabovi et aliis inimicis comunis lucani truguam [*sic*] seu compositionem perpetuam vel ad tempus cum illis pactis conventionibus et modificationibus cum quibus dicto comuni placuerit faciendi et firmandi', *Rif.* 2, p. 15, 3 Aug. 1370.

[33] *Rif.* 1, p. 444, 18 July 1370.

[34] *Rif.* 1, p. 403, 22 June 1370. E. Fiumi, 'Sui rapporti economici tra città e contado nell'età comunale', *Archivio Storico Italiano*, Vol. CXIV (1956), p. 36 for the practice of making those who remained pay the dues of absent ones.

was not granted. These were no idle threats. Other neighbouring states were also suffering from depopulation and extended a warm welcome to immigrants. Emigration was, in fact, a serious problem and efforts were made to check it. Poor men, who suffered a crop failure, a plague, or an enemy attack, would be unable to pay their rents and dues, and might well flee the state as a way of escaping from their debts and difficulties. The Lucchese authorities were aware of this problem, and the matter was raised in the council in July 1369, where it was stated that so many *contadini* had already left because of debts of this kind that the *contado* 'quasi sit incultus'. A *balìa* appointed to consider remedies decreed that those who had already left were to be free of actions for debts owed to individuals for three years if they returned, and those who still remained were to have a similar respite for one year.[35] But this probably had little effect, for less than a year later it was stated that 'propter duras exactiones que fiunt a comitativis multi discesserint ac plurimi sint, ut dicitur, recessuri'. In an effort to remedy this a general respite from arrest and imprisonment for unpaid rents and other debts was granted to the men of the Distretto of Six Miles.[36] Yet depopulation still continued. A petition of October 1374 is prefaced by the statement that 'multe terre propter carentiam agricultorum inculte sint et remaneant',[37] and another in January 1375 began 'per plures consules et comunia lucani comitatus sit expositum et humiliter supplicatum quod propter mortalitates et sinistra tempora retroacta ipsa comunia suis sint depopulata et vacuata hominibus et ad minimum numerum hominum sint reducta'.[38] A little over a year later a number of Lucchese citizens petitioned that 'per li disconcii carichi delle bocche e del sale la maggiore parte delli habitanti in de soborghi di Luccha sono dipartiti da uno anno

[35] *Rif.* 1, p. 14, 20 July 1369. For attempts to check emigration and attract immigrants in other Italian states, Silva, *Governo*, pp. 140–2, 148. E. Fiumi, *Storia economica e sociale di San Gimignano* (Florence, 1961), p. 173. W. M. Bowsky, 'The impact of the Black Death upon Sienese government and society', *Speculum*, Vol. XXXIX (1964), pp. 26, 31–2. E. Carpentier, *Une ville devant la peste, Orvieto et la Peste Noire de 1348* (Paris, 1962), pp. 207–8, 215.

[36] *Rif.* 2, p. 236, 17 Mar. 1371.

[37] *Rif.* 4, p. 481, 25 Oct. 1374.

[38] *Rif.* 5, p. 7, 11 Jan. 1375.

in qua e li soborghi sono per essere in tutto abondonati'.[39] As well as these general assertions that the Lucchese *contado* was being depopulated because of the emigration of its inhabitants, there is evidence of its effects on particular places; nine men of Aramo, for example, complained that other more substantial families had left.[40]

These men had not necessarily left the Lucchese state entirely. Men often moved from one commune to another. Some of the men from Granciglia had gone to Castelnuovo.[41] Three of the families that had left Aramo had gone no further than Lucca.[42] It was particularly easy for men from the suburbs and country parishes around Lucca to move into the city, and it exercised a considerable force of attraction over them. A petition complained too that it was the richest families that moved into the city, and that this left the poor to pay their taxes.[43] But in at least some cases men fled from the Lucchese state entirely. It might take very little to make them do so. Petitioners from the *contado* claimed that men who were condemned to small fines for gabelle or other similar offences, and who were unable to pay them, left the Lucchese state, so that Lucca was losing many men for small cause.[44] The men of Bergiole, in the *podesteria* of Ultra Iugum, petitioned against oppression by the officials of the *dovana salis*, adding that some families there had already left and gone to live in the territory of Bernabò Visconti and the Malaspina, which was only a quarter of a mile away, and more would leave if the burdens increased.[45]

One method of assisting communes that were in temporary difficulties has already been mentioned, that of freeing them from certain payments for a term of years. This had the advantage of costing Lucca nothing, for the amount to be paid by the whole vicariate remained unchanged. But grants of this

[39] *Rif.* 5, p. 205, 12 Feb. 1376.

[40] *Rif.* 8, p. 525, 30 May 1383. Twenty-two men of Aramo had taken the oath to John of Bohemia 22 Dec. 1331, *Capitoli*, 52, p. 646.

[41] *Rif.* 8, p. 313, 6 Nov. 1382.

[42] *Rif.* 8, p. 525, 30 May 1383.

[43] 'Li ricchi sono venuti e vegnono ad habitare in citta e li poveri con le loro familliole non potendo sostenere sono dipartiti et tucto die si diparteno', *Rif.* 5, p. 205, 12 Feb. 1376.

[44] *Rif.* 6, p. 489, 23 Jan. 1378.

[45] *Rif.* 8, p. 526, 30 May 1383.

kind could themselves impoverish other communes, for communes that had not obtained immunities had to pay the share of those that had, as well as their own. This naturally produced complaints from *contadini* that they were being forced to pay other people's taxes. The unfairness as well as the heaviness of these payments was resented. Certain communes in the vicariate of Gallicano, for example, petitioned that, though they totalled only sixty-seven hearths and the other communes of the vicariate totalled 112, they had been made to pay two thirds of a sum of 360 florins imposed on the vicariate, because the others had immunities and therefore paid nothing. They complained that Lucchese officials were now trying to make them pay the remaining third.[46] This is by no means an isolated complaint, and it was clearly a matter about which *contadini* felt strongly.

A more equitable remedy was the union of two or more small communes into one. The initiative for this often came from the communes themselves. Montegiano and Pieve a Elici, in the vicariate of Camaiore, for example, petitioned that they might be united 'ad omnia onera supportanda ut ea facilius propter talem unionem valeant tollerare'.[47] Volmiano and Vitiana, in the vicariate of Coreglia, produced a treaty of union they had drawn up, asking that it should be confirmed.[48] Lucca lost nothing by such unions, as the obligations and dues of the communes thus united remained unchanged, but the communes themselves gained, for they now needed to make only one appearance in the courts and keep only one set of officials and 'nuntii'—messengers each commune was obliged to maintain in order to keep in touch with Lucca. The Lucchese government had already approved the idea of the union of small communes of the *contado* in principle, and the Anziani were authorized to do all they could to promote them.[49] But no commune was to be compelled to

[46] *Rif.* 4, p. 53, 25 Feb. 1373. Other complaints, *Rif.* 3, p. 168, 22 Dec., p. 171, 23 Dec. 1371, *Rif.* 4, p. 172, 13 June 1373. Complaints of men evading obligations on the grounds of alleged Lucchese citizenship, *Rif.* 1, p. 501, 9 Apr. 1370, *Rif.* 3, p. 253, 10 Mar. 1372.

[47] *Rif.* 5, p. 14, 15 Jan. 1375.

[48] *Rif.* 7, pp. 315–16, 29 Aug. 1380.

[49] *Rif.* 5, p. 7, 11 Jan. 1375. For similar measures in Siena in the years immediately after the Black Death, Bowsky, 'The impact of the Black Death', p. 25, and in Pisa, Silva, *Governo*, pp. 144–5.

union,[50] and no commune was to be made liable for the debts of another.[51] The government also insisted that an inquiry should be made by the vicar before a union was confirmed to ensure that the other communes of the vicariate would not suffer loss as a result.[52]

In at least one case a union proved a disappointment to smaller communes. The communes of Granaiola and Lugnano in the vicariate of Coreglia petitioned that they had been induced to unite with Terezane and Bugliano on the grounds that it would reduce expenses and also replace past bad feeling by peace. But they found that in fact they paid more and that the bad feeling had increased rather than diminished.[53] Granaiola was freed, but the others remained united, until following further complaints the union was dissolved.[54] But in other cases unions were more successful, and they were popular with *contadini*. Eight unions were confirmed the same day on 28 June 1378.[55] The reason usually given for asking to be united was that one or both of the communes was very small. Pugliano and Metra in the *podesteria* of Ultra Iugum were very close together and had eight and two and a half hearths respectively.[56] Puticciano had two men when it was united with Anchiano, and Serra three when it was united with Corsagna, in the vicariate of Coreglia.[57] Meati was almost uninhabited when it was united with Fagnano, pieve di Flesso.[58]

Union could alleviate the difficulties of some small communes, but it did nothing about the basic problem, which was depopulation. This was a problem common to Tuscan cities and some recent studies have tended to stress that the demographic crisis was at the basis of the economic difficulties

[50] *Rif.* 10, p. 26, 13 Feb. 1386.

[51] *Rif.* 9, pp. 325–6, 23 Mar. 1385.

[52] *Rif.* 9, pp. 98–9, 26 Apr. 1384.

[53] *Rif.* 9, pp. 334–5, 19 Apr. 1385. The numbers taking the oath to John of Bohemia in October 1331 had been 11 from Granaiola, 13 from Lugnano, 19 from Terezane and 22 from Bugliano, *Capitoli*, 52, pp. 679–81.

[54] *Rif.* 10, p. 358, 26 Nov. 1387.

[55] *Rif.* 6, pp. 590–1, 28 June 1378.

[56] *Rif.* 9, pp. 124–5, 16 June 1384.

[57] *Rif.* 10, p. 314, 28 Aug. 1387. Ten men of Puticciano had taken the oath to John of Bohemia 11 Oct. 1331, *Capitoli*, 52, p. 682. Anchiano is not listed. Thirteen men of Serra and 41 of Corsagna had taken the oath on the same day, *Capitoli*, 52, pp. 681–2.

[58] *Rif.* 12, p. 85, 21 Apr. 1392.

of the period.[59] Herlihy calculated that the rural population of Pistoia fell from about 31,000 in 1244 to less than 9,000 in 1401, a fall of over seventy per cent with the disappearance of many rural settlements and a shortage of agricultural labour leading to land falling out of cultivation.[60] Figures for Prato show a decline from 7,690 *bocche* in 1339 to 4,707 in 1427, a fall of 38·7 per cent in the countryside with an even sharper decline in the city itself.[61] The *contado* of S. Gimignano saw a decline from 852 hearths in 1332 to 468 by 1350 and 250 by 1427–9, a decline of 77 per cent in the number of hearths, though an increase in the average number of persons per hearth meant that the decline in population was less sharp.[62] Lucca has no sources from which such precise calculations can be made. She may have been in a less serious position than some of her neighbours. It has already been noted that her *contado* seems to have been relatively densely populated in the mid-sixteenth century, and this may also have been so in the fourteenth century. Certainly she seems to have had a higher ratio of rural to urban population than some of her neighbours.[63] But if her territory was still more densely populated than that of some neighbouring cities, it is nevertheless clear that there had been a decline from early fourteenth-century levels. Complaints that men had died or left, and that com-

[59] See especially Fiumi, *Storia economica e sociale di San Gimignano*, pp. 224–5. Also E. Cristiani, 'Città e campagna nell'età comunale in alcune pubblicazioni dell'ultimo decennio', *Rivista Storica Italiana*, Vol. LXXV (1963), p. 844. For the importance of the demographic upsurge to earlier Florentine development, E. Fiumi, 'Fioritura e decadenza dell'economia fiorentina III', *Archivio Storico Italiano*, Vol. CXVII (1959), pp. 486–7.

[60] D. Herlihy, *Medieval and Renaissance Pistoia, the Social History of an Italian Town*, 1200–1430 (New Haven, Conn., and London, 1967), pp. 68–72.

[61] E. Fiumi, *Demografia, movimento urbanistico e classi sociali in Prato dall'età comunale ai tempi moderni* (Florence, 1968), p. 135. The number of hearths in the *contado* declined more sharply than the number of *bocche*, from 1786 to 943, a fall of 47.2 per cent.

[62] Fiumi, *Storia economica e sociale di San Gimignano*, pp. 154, 171–2. For Florence E. Fiumi, 'Fioritura e decadenza dell'economia fiorentina II', *Archivio Storico Italiano* Vol. CXVI (1958), pp. 476–82, but lack of figures for the period between the early thirteenth century and 1350 prevents a clear picture from emerging. For Orvieto, Carpentier, *Une ville devant la peste*, pp. 216–20. Also P. J. Jones, 'Medieval agrarian society in its prime: Italy', in *Cambridge Economic History*, Vol. I 2nd edn., Cambridge, 1966), pp. 362–5.

[63] See Chapter 1, pp. 25–6 and note 22. Herlihy, *Medieval and Renaissance Pistoia*, pp. 76–7, and Table 3.

munes that were once large and flourishing were now small and impoverished are so frequent that there can be no doubt of the seriousness of the situation. Though some of the places that were in difficulties were small mountain villages that had perhaps always been struggling, the problem was by no means confined to them, and large villages in the rich agricultural land around Lucca itself are also found petitioning for relief.[64] Lucca attempted to prevent peasants from leaving the state, but even if successful, these efforts would only prevent the situation from getting worse. To effect any real improvement more was needed, and Lucca also tried to encourage immigration by offering immunities to men from outside the state who came to live in Lucca. In 1370 certain men of Sanminiato, forced to leave their homes when Florence captured the town, petitioned to be allowed to come to Lucca with their families, and asked for an immunity.[65] Their request was favourably received and it was decreed that Sanminiatesi and other *forestieri* who had come to live and work in the Lucchese state since 1 January 1370 or who should come in future, were to be exempt from military service, all loans and *imposite* and other taxes except the salt gabelle. They were to register with the Chancery within fifteen days of their arrival, and the immunity was to last for five years.[66]

In 1374 an immunity was offered specifically to peasants. All *forestieri* coming to Lucca as farmers in the next two years were to be free from all taxes and obligations on person or property, except customs duties and the salt tax for five years.[67] Two years later the immunity was not only renewed for a further three years, but was also extended to Lucchese subjects who had left the state ten or more years ago and who now wished to return. They were also offered a five year respite from actions for debt.[68] These grants of immunity probably had some effect; there are records of some men

[64] *Rif.* 1, p. 263, 5 Mar., p. 290, 31 Mar. 1370, *Rif.* 2, p. 236, 17 Mar. 1371, *Rif.* 7, p. 108, 22 June 1379.

[65] *Rif.* 1, p. 243, 25 Feb. 1370.

[66] *Rif.* 1, p. 251, 26 Feb. 1370. It seems possible, however, that the Sanminiatesi were not allowed to remain for long. There were protests from Florence, and Lucca seems to have agreed to their expulsion, see Chapter 6, p. 139 note 45.

[67] *Rif.* 4, p. 481, 25 Oct. 1374.

[68] *Rif.* 6, pp. 85–6, 24 Oct. 1376.

registering with the Chancery. But Lucca was not the only Tuscan city trying to attract immigrants. Other states were also suffering from depopulation and were competing for immigrants, and some states offered greater inducements than Lucca did. Pisa, for example, offered a ten year immunity, as against Lucca's five.[69] It would clearly be to the peasants' advantage to move from one state to another, but it seems likely that the immigrants attracted by offers of immunities would be counterbalanced by those leaving in order to obtain similar concessions elsewhere.

As well as attempts to attract *forestieri* and induce Lucchese emigrants to return to the *contado* in general, there were also efforts to repopulate particular places. The reasons for this were often military. Veneri, for example, was near the border with Florence and also near important roads. It had been deserted for ten years, but efforts were made to induce its old inhabitants, who were living in nearby Collodi and S. Gennaro, to return by offering them and any *forestieri* who were prepared to settle there an immunity for eight years. As well as tax exemptions, they were to be free from actions for debts contracted in the last twenty-five years, and were to have food and other supplies free of gabelle.[70] The men of Cerasomma petitioned successfully that they and any *forestieri* who were prepared to settle there should be granted a ten-year immunity to aid the recovery of the commune after it had been burnt by the Pisans.[71] Efforts were made to induce men to settle in Motrone, offering immunities since 'nisi fiat illis qui ibidem habitare voluerint immunitas et exemptio nullus ibidem lares proprios destinaret'.[72] Similar attempts were made to repopulate the commune of Pugliano, inducing up to thirty men from the surrounding area to settle there,[73] and to rebuild the village of Sasso at the foot of the hill, after the fortress had been destroyed.[74]

[69] Silva, *Governo*, p. 141, Herlihy, *Medieval and Renaissance Pistoia*, pp. 157-8, Jones, 'Medieval agrarian society in its prime: Italy', p. 363, for general efforts by Italian states to attract immigrants.

[70] *Rif.* 3, pp. 421-2, 15 Nov. 1372. A *balìa* was appointed to consider their petition, *Rif.* 3, p. 425, 17 Nov., its decision pp. 431-2, 25 Nov. 1372.

[71] *Rif.* 1, p. 263, 5 Mar. 1370.

[72] *Rif.* 2, p. 175, 22 Dec. 1370.

[73] *Rif.* 4, p. 212, 15 July 1373.

[74] *Rif.* 8, pp. 674-6, 18 Dec. 1383.

Had the recovery of liberty in 1369 been followed by a couple of decades of peace, free of plagues and other disasters, this might have done much to aid the recovery of the *contado*. But there were further outbreaks of plague in 1373, 1383, 1392, and 1400, and several attacks by armed companies and other hostile forces. So the same kind of petition as had been presented in 1369 and 1370 continued to come in. A man of S. Andrea de Tempagnano in the Six Miles petitioned that he was unable to pay certain dues owing to the devastation his lands had suffered at the hands of Giovanni degli Obizi.[75] Ruota petitioned in 1376 that it had been attacked by the English Company, robbed and partially burnt. Three men had been killed and the rest taken prisoner.[76] Apparently the inhabitants had not fully recovered from this attack seven years later, for they mentioned it when petitioning to be exempt from paying a share in the salary of a new official, a petition that was granted.[77] The vicariate of Massa suffered particularly. The English Company had attacked and devasted it, and its inhabitants had to be pardoned for failing to fulfil their obligations.[78] They suffered again at the hands of the Sire de Coucy in 1384. He had camped there and his men had robbed and burnt in the surrounding region, totally destroying some property, so that the *estimo* of the area had to be reduced.[79]

There are examples of the same commune petitioning again and again. Corfino, in the vicariate of Castiglione, is one of these. It had been captured by Alderigo degli Antelminelli in the war in the Garfagnana and many of its inhabitants were killed and the houses robbed and burnt. The men remaining petitioned that they had returned and would rebuild the houses, but they were very poor and had contracted heavy debts. They were granted immunities in 1372, and these were extended when they petitioned again the next year.[80] Their

[75] *Rif.* 4, p. 536, 28 Dec. 1374. Other houses there had been burnt, men had been unable to work the land, and as the harvest was poor that year in any case, there was a shortage of cereals.

[76] *Rif.* 5, p. 191, 14 Jan. 1376.

[77] *Rif.* 7, pp. 569–70, 19 Sept. 1381.

[78] *Rif.* 6, p. 128, 20 Dec. 1376.

[79] *Rif.* 9, p. 190, 28 Sept., p. 235, 30 Nov. 1384.

[80] *Delib.* 132, f. 21, 30 July 1371, *Rif.* 3, p. 309, 20 May 1372, referring to an earlier immunity due to expire 1 July. *Rif.* 3, pp. 311–12, 21 May 1372 a *balìa* extended this immunity until 22 Feb. 1373.

assessment was reduced from thirty-seven hearths to twenty for a term of years, but when the time came for the assessment to be raised again they petitioned once more, and by 1383 they were still assessed at only twenty-four hearths.[81]

Corfino, with thirty-seven hearths, was quite a big village, but even larger places could be seriously impoverished by repeated wars and plagues. The commune of Castiglione itself is an example of this. The men of Castiglione petitioned that because of the wars and plagues, which had been there not once but several times in a few years, they were reduced to the last extremity; yet they still had to pay the same dues and services as they had in the past, when they had been powerful and flourishing and rightly regarded as the head of the province.[82] In another petition a few months later they gave more precise details of their decline. They had once numbered 800 good men, but they were now reduced to eighty. Over forty of their best men had died in the plague of 1383, and only about thirty of the eighty men remaining were fit to bear arms, the rest of the inhabitants being old and poor. And the outlook for the future was no brighter, for there were very few children, only sixteen under the age of fourteen. If they were not exaggerating, their *estimo* of ninety hearths out of the 390 for the whole vicariate was clearly unrealistic. They asked for a reduction of their *estimo* and salt tax, and also for assistance from neighbouring communes in guarding Castiglione, stressing its strategic importance. They also asked that a five-year immunity be offered to *forestieri* who were prepared to settle there, though they added gloomily 'benche non sperino che persona civegni'.[83]

In fact many petitions provide evidence that the depopulation of the *contado* continued in the last twenty years of the fourteenth century. The parish of S. Dalmazio had only three men,[84] and Ruota had only sixteen, including the very

[81] *Rif.* 4, p. 111, 28 Apr. 1373, *Rif.* 6, pp. 237–8, 13 Apr. 1377, *Rif.* 7, pp. 478–9, 22 Apr. 1381, *Min.* 3 (not foliated), 6 Dec. 1383.

[82] 'Totius provincie caput', *Rif.* 8, pp. 637–8, 31 Oct. 1383.

[83] *Rif.* 9, pp. 66–7, 4 Mar. 1384. Their claim that they once had 800 men seems to apply to the period just before 1348. It may well be an exaggeration, but 235 men took the oath to John of Bohemia in December 1331 and the list may not be complete, *Capitoli* 52, pp. 657–62.

[84] *Rif.* 7, pp. 439–40, 9 Jan. 1380.

old and the very young, instead of the 150 it had once had.[85] Montefegatesi had only twenty men, and was in a mountainous and barren region.[86] General references to communes that are empty or almost empty are frequent; many communes are 'gentibus et hominibus vacua'[87] and certain communes in the Distretto of Six Miles are 'multum diminuta et vacua hominibus'.[88] Many communes are declined and there are many others where no one lives,

> seu sevientis mortalitatis contagio qua mortales propter peccata corripiuntur seu locorum damnato situ multa comunia comitatus quasi ad desolationem et exterminium ultimum devenerunt nam aliquod uno aliud duobus et aliud tribus vel paucis pluribus ut plurimum habitatur ex quo homines ibi habitantes apti non sunt nec sufficientes ad onera incumbentia sicut exactis temporibus bonorum omnium abundantes infuturum quodlibet subeunda.[89]

Some places were totally deserted. When the vicar went to the commune of Granciglia to investigate its failure to pay the salt tax, he found the place deserted.[90] Castelnuovo petitioned that Cerrètoli in the vicariate of Castiglione had been deserted for twelve years, and asked that it be united with Castelnuovo. An inquiry was made and it was found that Cerrètoli was indeed deserted.[91]

The usual remedies were tried. Places that petitioned for relief on the grounds of poverty were often freed from part of their dues, and communes continued to be united with others to save expenses. Efforts to attract *forestieri* into the Lucchese state continued. The order authorizing the five year immunity to be granted to peasants coming to live and work in the Lucchese state was renewed for a further four years in 1380, and it was provided that they should have the same wood and pasture rights in the places they settled as did Lucchese subjects.[92] In 1385 the order was renewed again, but this time

[85] *Rif.* 7, p. 569, 19 Sept. 1381.

[86] *Rif.* 8, p. 50, 3 Feb. 1382.

[87] *Rif.* 9, p. 352, 23 Mar. 1385.

[88] *Rif.* 10, p. 267, 10 May 1387.

[89] *Rif.* 11, p. 177, 17 Dec. 1389. The situation was similar in neighbouring states. Depopulation continued in the Pisan *contado* in the later fourteenth century, Silva, *Governo*, pp. 149–53, 162.

[90] *Rif.* 8, p. 313, 6 Nov. 1382.

[91] *Rif.* 8, pp. 207–8, 21 July 1382, the union was agreed, p. 273, 29 Sept. 1382.

[92] *Rif.* 7, p. 443, 10 Jan. 1380. For the importance of such rights in the sixteenth century, M. Berengo, *Nobili e mercanti nella Lucca del Cinquecento* (Turin, 1965), pp. 314–16, 321, 329–41.

the immunity was to be for ten years, not five, thus giving greater inducement to *forestieri* to settle in Lucchese territory and bringing Lucca into line with Pisa and certain other neighbouring cities.[93] Two years later the privilege of freedom from actions for debt granted to *forestieri* coming for the *arte della lana* was extended to peasants in the hope that it would induce many more to come.[94] Every effort was made too to prevent Lucchese subjects from emigrating. It was believed that one of the reasons that caused men to leave the state was inability to pay fines they had incurred. As councillors pointed out, if men emigrated because they could not pay their fines, Lucca got neither the money nor the men. In 1374 eighteen men of Massa Lunense, who had been fined for exporting corn from the Lucchese state, were granted a reduction in the amount they had to pay, because among other reasons 'summe expediat procurare et habere laboratores terre in comitatu lucano'.[95] Four years later a scale was established for the reduction of fines, so that men need only pay 25 per cent or even 10 per cent to be free of any further obligations.[96] Later the same year this principle was extended still further, so that not only those condemned for gabelle offences, but also those condemned for more serious crimes could obtain pardon by paying only a part of their fine. This was done partly because *banniti* were a potential danger to the state, but also partly 'cum Lucana civitas et eius comitatus indigeat repleri hominibus et incolis'.[97] Later even those condemned 'in persona', that is for the most serious crimes, were pardoned, except for rebels and traitors.[98] These measures were again

[93] 'Ut lucanus comitatus colonis vacuus repleatur et inculta agrorum equorum extirpatis vepribus et acutis carduis bacho atque cerere revirescant', *Rif.* 9, p. 291, 5 Feb. 1385. Those *forestieri* who had already settled in Lucca were to have their five year immunity extended to ten in order to induce them to stay in the Lucchese contado.

[94] *Rif.* 10, p. 248, 29 Mar. 1387.

[95] *Rif.* 4, pp. 282–3, 25 Oct. 1374.

[96] *Rif.* 6, pp. 489–90, 23 Jan. 1378.

[97] *Rif.* 6, pp. 579–80, 1 June 1378. For crimes against individuals they also needed to have peace with the victim or his heirs.

[98] *Rif.* 8, pp. 543–4, 27 June, pp. 549–50, 30 June, pp. 682–4, 26 Dec. 1383. Further scales of payment were established later, *Rif.* 9, p. 409, 6 Oct. 1385, *Rif.* 10, p. 32, 16 Feb. 1386, *Rif.* 11, p. 85, 14 May 1389.

partly to remove a source of danger to the state, but also partly to supply the *contado* with peasants, especially after the population had been further depleted in the plague of 1383. Apparently quite large numbers of *banniti* were prepared to take advantage of these scales of reduced payments for pardon.[99]

In this case there was no conflict between the financial interest of Lucca and the desires of the *contadini*. As a member of the council said 'utile esset lucrari pecunias et homines'.[100] But Lucca's financial needs sometimes caused conflict with the *contadini*. This happened when Lucca began a new assessment of *bocche* for the salt tax. Everyone in the *contado* over the age of five had to receive a certain amount of salt each year, the quantity, and especially the price, fluctuating according to Lucca's financial need. In 1381, as there had not been a new declaration of *bocche* for many years and the situation had become very confused owing to changes in the population and grants of exemption of reductions in the number of *bocche*, a new count was ordered.[101] The Lucchese government was aware that there would be a temptation for *contadini* to conceal some of their *bocche* and extremely heavy penalties were laid down to deter them. But despite these penalties and the offer of a share in the fines to informers, there were widespread concealments and underestimates of the number of *bocche*. There are many references to 'buccis omissis'.[102] But even when the remission of fines incurred for a first false declaration was granted,[103] some *contadini* still refused to declare the true facts. In a number of cases several false declarations were made and *contadini* tried every subterfuge they could think of to avoid making accurate returns.[104] The new assessment was finally declared 29 April

[99] *Rif.* 6, pp. 651–2, 9 Sept. 1378. *Banniti* as a danger to the state, *Rif.* 7, p. 38, 19 Feb. 1379.

[100] *Min.* 2, p. 295, 19 Feb. 1379.

[101] *Rif.* 7, pp. 487–8, 17 May, p. 492, 22 May 1381. A new assessment had been ordered in 1376, but never apparently carried out, *Rif.* 5, p. 201, 8 Mar. 1376.

[102] *Rif.* 8, p. 138, 6 May, p. 225, 22 Aug., p. 283, 4 Oct. 1382, pp. 482–3, 29 March 1383.

[103] *Rif.* 8, pp. 225–6, 22 Aug., p. 232, 24 Aug., pp. 239, 243, 28 Aug. 1382.

[104] *Rif.* 8, pp. 312–13, 6 Nov. 1382.

1383, though inquiries and fines for false declarations were still being discussed two years later.[105]

The new assessment was said to be so much heavier than the old one that a reduction of between a fifth and a quarter was made for the first three years, so that *contadini* could get accustomed to the heavier payments [106] The new assessment would have been of great benefit to Lucca, but it seems probable that it was never fully enforced. In October 1383 after another outbreak of plague, it was decreed that because of Lucca's financial difficulties the next payment of the salt tax should be on the new assessment but to prevent complaints only two thirds of what was due should be exacted, though this was still heavier than the old assessment.[107] In 1390 the whole question of the salt tax had to be reconsidered. Large numbers of communes were in arrears, some of them dating back as far as 1370. The council was told 'che certo si comprende che per lo carico del sale che si da a forestieri che vegnano adabitare nel nostro terreno molti forestieri lassano di venirci che civerrebbeno e de venuti molti ne sono andati che sarrebbeno rimasi.' To remedy this the amount of salt that *forestieri* could be forced to buy was strictly limited, and the officials of the communes where they settled were forbidden to try and make them pay more. But it was not only *forestieri* who found the new salt tax a crushing burden. On the same occasion the council was told 'che veramente alquanti comuni piccoli e di pochi homini sono si venuti meno per esservi morti in quelli buona parte deloro doppo lamposta del sale facta che per neuno modo possano pagare le loro paghe del sale. Et se non visi provede in tutto sabandonano.' The council authorized alleviations of the salt tax for such communes, which were said not to be very numerous.[108] Apart from this the price of salt had already been reduced, and in 1392 it was necessary to reduce it again.[109]

[105] *Rif.* 8, pp. 497–9, 29 Apr. 1383, *Rif.* 9, p. 325, 23 Mar. 1385.
[106] *Rif.* 8, pp. 497–9, 29 Apr. 1383.
[107] *Rif.* 8, p. 618, 10 Oct. 1383.
[108] *Rif.* 11, pp. 374–6, 16 Dec. 1390.
[109] *Rif.* 11, p. 349, 25 Nov. 1390, and a reduction for three years, *Rif.* 12, p. 50, 20 Feb. 1392.

It is doubtful if the last decade of the fourteenth century saw any improvement in the situation in the Lucchese *contado*. It is true that there are relatively few petitions for tax relief, but this is almost certainly the result of changes in the character of the sources. There is a gap in the *Riformagioni* in the period 1394–7, and for reasons connected with the internal politics of the city the records for the period 1392–1400 are very meagre. It would be surprising if there had been any improvement in the situation. Twice in this decade there were outbreaks of plague, and apart from attacks by armed companies Lucca became involved in a war with Pisa, in which the *contado* must have suffered heavily. Such evidence as there is for 1390–1400 supports this. Many communes and individuals failed to pay their dues at the proper term because of the damage done by an armed company and the plague of 1392. One of the reductions in the price of salt was said to be because 'tam cives quam subditi nimium expensis et dannis attriti ob adventum gentium armorum et etiam mortalitatis sevitiam'.[110] Six communes of the vicariate of Camporgiano asked to be united because they were all much reduced by the plague and other misfortunes.[111] In 1395 it was necessary to reduce the *estimo* of Meati because almost all the inhabitants had left.[112]

These were all before the war with Pisa and the second plague in 1400. This outbreak of plague was exceptionally severe,[113] and the war with its raids and counter-raids, robbing, burning, and cattle-theft must have hit the *contado* hard.[114] It is unlikely, therefore, that after thirty years of periodic attacks and four outbreaks of plague the Lucchese

[110] *Rif.* 12, p. 50, 20 Feb. 1392.

[111] *Rif.* 12, p. 323, 21 Dec. 1392.

[112] *Delib.* 133, ff. 39v–40, 31 Mar. 1395. After a petition by a man who had come from S. Angelo in Campo four years previously and was not *estimatus* in Meati, the exactor was authorized to make an inquiry. He reported 'comune ipsum Meate quasi inhabitatum est et nichilominus extimum non parvum habet et in vero de extimatis nullum ibi habitare reperio . . . pro maiori parte hominum in dicto comuni extimatorum extra lucanum territorium exisse et esse videtur'. Meati had been united with Fagnano in 1392. It was agreed that the petitioner should pay only personal burdens in Meati, as he was still *estimatus* jointly with his father in S. Angelo in Campo.

[113] Sercambi, II, pp. 396–7; III, pp. 4–5.

[114] Sercambi, II contains an extremely detailed account of these campaigns.

contado was in a much better condition in 1400 than it had been in 1369.

The problem of ensuring adequate corn supplies was something that affected both city and *contado*. Like other Italian cities of the period Lucca had difficulty in ensuring food supplies for her urban population. Notarial records show that many citizens owned land in the Six Miles, which they leased to tenants for corn rents. Probably the majority of citizens obtained at least part of their supplies in this way. There were also corn merchants who brought supplies to the city by way of trade. There are no figures for the amount of corn Lucca needed annually nor the proportion of her needs that could be supplied from her own *contado*. She was probably rather more self-sufficient than Florence, which, it was calculated, grew enough corn to supply her own needs for only about five months of the year. Lucchese territory included the rich agricultural plain near the city itself and in the vicariates of Camaiore and Pietrasanta, but much of the rest of the state was mountainous, and it is unlikely that Lucca was entirely self-sufficient even in a good year. There were corn shortages or difficulties of some kind every year from 1369 to 1376, and again from 1380 to 1385, and in 1388, 1389, and 1392. After this the records are less full, but there is no reason to suppose that the situation had improved.

In times of shortage the government intervened directly, particularly if the corn shortage coincided with a period of war or fear of invasion by armed companies, for it realized the danger of a starving or discontented populace at such a time.[115] Corn was imported from Pisa, Genoa, the Papal

[115] *Rif.* 9, p. 246, 11 Dec. 1384, *Rif.* 10, p. 581, 8 Dec. 1388. Imports are frequently said to be 'ne . . . populus aut libertas periculum patiatur', or some similar phrase. Other cities had the same preoccupations, Fiumi, 'Sui rapporti economici', pp. 38–62, and 'Fioritura e decadenza dell'economia fiorentina III', pp. 466–78, Silva, *Governo*, pp. 162–4, Herlihy, *Medieval and Renaissance Pistoia*, pp. 124–5, 156–8, Bowsky, *Finance of the Commune of Siena*, pp. 33–42. Lucca had similar problems in the sixteenth century, Berengo, *Nobili e mercanti*, pp. 292–3, stressing the contrast between the rich agricultural land of the Six Miles and part of the vicariate of Camaiore and the barren mountainous character of much of the rest of the Lucchese *contado*. The distribution of the *tassa frumenti* of August 1377 illustrates this. The vicariate of Camaiore had to produce 7,000 *staia*, Pietrasanta 4,500 from the communes of the vicariate and 4,500 from Pietrasanta itself and the vicariate of Massa 5,000. The vicariate of Coreglia had to produce 4,000, Valdilima 3,000, Gallicano and Camporgiano 1,000 each, Castiglione 600, and Valdriana none at all. These

States, Sicily, and even farther afield.[116] Lucca had a permanent granary where corn from previous years was stored to ensure a supply in case of emergency,[117] and she insisted that Pietrasanta set up a similar granary.[118] There was also a permanent *balìa* 'super abundantia' in the city, whose members were replaced at regular intervals, and which was responsible for overseeing and ensuring supplies. Efforts were made to have as much corn as possible sown in the *contado*.[119] Export was always discouraged and was strictly forbidden on pain of heavy fine in times of shortage.[120] Import of corn into the city was encouraged by the frequent reduction or abolition of the gabelles for short periods in time of need. Attempts were made to ensure that *contadini* sent what supplies they should to Lucca, both for the corn rents they owed to private individuals and the supplies which they were obliged by custom to provide for the maintenance of certain officials, and a 'tassa' to supply the city. This was distributed proportionately among the various communes of the *contado*.[121] Lucchese subjects were also obliged to declare what supplies of corn they had, and records were to be kept at the gates of Lucca of the amount of corn imported. But these regulations proved very difficult to enforce. Officials called by such titles as 'cercatores', 'sollicitatores', or 'scrutatores bladii' were appointed to go round the *contado* searching out concealed

figures contrast strongly with those for the communes of the 'sobborghi' and Six Miles, where figures of 2,000 or 3,000 and even as many as 4,500 and 5,300 *staia* are allotted to single communes, *Rif.* 6, pp. 341-9, 23 August. 1377.

[116] *Anz. Av. Lib.* 45, pp. 18-19, 9 May 1369, *Rif.* 1, p. 7, 19 July 1369, *Delib.* 131, f. 27v, 8 June 1370, *Rif.* 2, p. 145, 22 Nov. 1370, *Rif.* 3, pp. 59-60, 27 Sept. 1371, *Rif.* 8, p. 673, 16 Dec. 1383, *Rif.* 11, pp. 108-10, 24 July 1389, *Min.* 4, (not foliated), 21 Jan. 1392. On at least one occasion the Lucchese government arranged to buy corn in Bruges, *Reg.* no. 815, 21 Feb. 1381.

[117] *Rif.* 7, pp. 327-8, 2 Sept., p. 337, 16 Sept. 1380, *Rif.* 10, pp. 309-10, 14 Aug. 1387.

[118] Pietrasanta was to buy 40,000 *staia* to begin this, and a further 10,000 *staia* a year, as well as sowing 3,500 *staia* in her own territory, *Rif.* 7, p. 124, 1 Aug., p. 140, 31 Aug., p. 169, 6 Nov. 1379, p. 307, 20 Aug. 1380, pp. 539-40, 13 Aug. 1381. Pietrasanta several times petitioned against this obligation.

[119] *Rif.* 10, pp. 20-2, 12 Jan. 1386.

[120] *Delib.* 131, ff. 28v-29, 12 June 1370, *Delib.* 132, f. 8, 10 June 1371, *Rif.* 5, p. 75, 30 May 1375, *Rif.* 9, pp. 447-8, 13 Dec. 1385, *Rif.* 10, pp. 20-2, 12 Jan. 1386.

[121] *Rif.* 6, p. 336, 18 Aug., pp. 341-9, 23 Aug. 1377, *Rif.* 7, pp. 267-9, 11 June 1380.

supplies.[122] Many *contadini* were found to be concealing or illegally exporting corn, but the penalties laid down for this were found to be too severe and could not be enforced without causing peasants to flee, thus depopulating the countryside still further.[123]

A degree of disorder and violence in the countryside seems to have been normal. There are many references to disorders in individual places in the Lucchese *contado* and at times disorder seems to have become more general. In June 1369 it was complained that there were many robberies and acts of violence with *contadini* ceasing to be obedient to Lucca.[124] A few years later in 1377 provision was made 'pro minuendis guerris que sunt in lucana diocesi',[125] and again in 1387 it was urged that something must be done about the many serious crimes and homicides committed in Lucchese territory.[126] Despite efforts to suppress violence, there were further discussions of disorder in the *contado* in 1389 and 1390,[127] and in 1394 the Gonfaloniere urged that men and money were needed 'cum in tantum hominum nequitia creverit, tantumque sceleratorum temeritas adoleverit quod vix civitates et castra ab eorum discursionibus ab externis et domesticis tractatibus intra murorum ambitus tute sint'.[128]

One of the causes of this endemic disorder was the existence of numbers of *banniti* in the Lucchese state. In 1372 it was complained that there were many *banniti* and robbers on the roads, attacking men and holding them to ransom,[129] and shortly afterwards it was said that the road along the sea coast to Pisa was unsafe because of robbers and *banniti*.[130] *Banniti*

[122] *Rif.* 4, p. 211, 15 July 1373, *Rif.* 5, p. 88, 4 July 1375, *Rif.* 7, p. 119, 21 July 1379, p. 463, 27 Feb. 1380. *Reg.*, no. 47, 12 Aug. 1371.

[123] *Rif.* 3, pp. 60–1, 27 Sept. 1371, *Rif.* 4, pp. 434–5, 14 July, pp. 482–3, 25 Oct. 1374, *Rif.* 7, p. 561, 11 Sept. 1381. Corn found concealed, *Rif.* 4, pp. 490–1, 2 Nov. 1374.

[124] *Anz. Av. Lib.* 45, p. 31, 4 June 1369.

[125] *Rif.* 6, pp. 361–3, 10 Sept. 1377.

[126] *Rif.* 10, pp. 281–4, 7 June 1387.

[127] *Rif.* 11, pp. 111–12, 18 Aug. 1389, p. 280, 12 June 1390. This was partly because of the need to protect Lucca from invasions during the war in Tuscany and Lombardy.

[128] *Rif.* 12, p. 413, 17 Feb. 1394.

[129] *Rif.* 3, p. 364, 31 July 1372.

[130] *Delib.* 133, f. 2, 9 Jan, 1376.

seem to have been responsible for the disorders of 1387, and they are often mentioned in the later years of the century as a potential threat to Lucca, plotting with the city's enemies and perhaps succeeding in capturing some Lucchese castle.[131] Not all *banniti* had committed serious crimes. Many had committed comparatively minor offences and been condemned only to fines. But if they were unable to pay these and have their banns cancelled, they were obliged to live as outlaws in order to avoid being captured and imprisoned by the authorities. It was realized that if such men were pardoned or a part of their fines remitted, they might settle down to a peaceful life.[132] Massa petitioned that eight men who had fled for some offence might be allowed to return for the sake of the peace of the vicariate, which would otherwise be threatened by the existence of 'tot extrinsecos'.[133] The measures taken for the pardon of *banniti* generally would also have a good effect in discouraging disorder in the *contado*.

But *banniti* were only one cause of disorder and violence. Perhaps a more serious cause was the factiousness and riotousness of the Lucchese *contadini* themselves. Many communes of the *contado* seem to have had two warring factions and this easily led to murders and other acts of violence. The two factions in Treppignana caused an outbreak of violence there in 1371,[134] and there were similar troubles in Menabbio, Sesto Moriano, Gallicano, Pieve di Compito, and many other places.[135] The men of Villa Basilica held a 'publicum parlamentum et consilium', in which they decreed the expulsion of certain men from the commune. As an example to others they were heavily punished for this, as it was deemed an insult to Lucca.[136]

In some cases violence was caused by just one or two trouble-makers. A certain Niccolò Vanelli caused trouble that led to

[131] *Rif.* 10, pp. 546–7, 11 Sept. 1388, *Rif.* 11, pp. 111–12, 18 Aug, 1389, *Rif.* 12, p. 135, 7 June 1392, *Rif.* 13, p. 15, 26 Jan. 1397.

[132] *Rif.* 10, pp. 546–7, 11 Sept. 1388.

[133] *Rif.* 5, p. 338, 15 May 1376.

[134] *Min.* 2, f. 51, 25 June 1371.

[135] *Min.* 2, ff.21^v–22^v, 5 May 1371, ff. 108–108^v, 14 May 1377, *Rif.* 5, p. 77, 8 June 1375, p. 314, 30 Apr. 1376, *Delib.* 132, ff. 88–88^v, 6 Aug. 1375, *Delib.* 133, ff. 116^v–117^v, 26 Aug. 1377, *Rif.* 7, p. 554, 2 Sept. 1381, *Rif.* 8, p. 93, 17 Apr., pp. 145–6, 27 May, p. 271, 26 Sept. 1382, *Rif.* 12, p. 128, 29 May 1392.

[136] *Rif.* 8, pp. 147–8, 27 May 1382.

violence in Coreglia.[137] In the vicariate of Massa there was a certain Iuntarone da Colle who 'e molto odiato'.[138] At Verni in the vicariate of Gallicano a few arrogant young men were said to be causing trouble.[139] In 1387 it was stated generally that serious crimes and homicides were being committed in the *contado*, 'e questo proceda per gran parte da persone che si fanno nel dicto contado, distrecto e forsa capo et segno favoregiando aiutando et consigliando quelli che anno voglia di malfare'.[140]

In some cases violence broke out between two neighbouring communes over boundary disputes, disagreements about pasture rights, or about *estimi* or customary obligations. There were dissensions between Serra, Corsagna and Anchiano because Corsagna claimed rights over territory belonging to Serra.[141] A serious dispute, involving riots, wounding, and homicide, between the neighbouring communes of Silico and Bargecchia in the vicariate of Castiglione probably had a similar origin.[142]

There were disputes, disorders, and violence also in the towns of Pietrasanta and Camaiore. There were disputes in Pietrasanta between the town and the communes of the vicariate about payment of dues,[143] and also disputes within the town itself. There were complaints about the excessive salaries of an unnecessarily large number of officials and about attempts to evade guard duty. There were also complaints that about ten men were monopolizing offices in the town, and that there were attempts to evade taxes and other obligations by making fictitious sales and alienations of property.[144] There was ill-feeling in the town and occasional

[137] *Rif.* 5, pp. 55–6, 6 Apr. 1375.

[138] *Reg.*, no. 78, 10 Jan. 1372.

[139] *Rif.* 10, p. 355, 21 Nov. 1387.

[140] *Rif.* 10, p. 281, 7 June 1387.

[141] *Rif.* 5, p. 111, 16 Oct. 1375.

[142] *Min.* 3 (not foliated), 12 July 1382, *Rif.* 8, p. 204, 16 July 1382.

[143] *Delib.* 131, ff. 17v–18, 3 May 1370, *Delib.* 132, f. 7v, 7 June 1371, *Rif.* 5, pp. 125–6, 12 Nov. 1375. There was to be a new *estimo*, *Rif.* 6, pp. 173–4, 14 Jan., pp. 174–5, 24 Jan. 1377 sentence of arbiters in a dispute over this *estimo*.

[144] *Rif.* 5, p. 52, 29 Mar. 1375, *Rif.* 7, pp. 40–1, 23 Feb. 1379, *Rif.* 8, p. 456, 29 Dec. 1385, *Rif.* 10, pp. 27–8, 14 Feb. 1386. For similar problems in Pisa Silva, *Governo* pp. 144, 156–7, and Siena, Bowsky, *Finance of the Commune of Siena*, p. 251.

disturbances,[145] but Pietrasanta was much less of a trouble spot than Camaiore.

In Camaiore too there were disputes between the town and the vicariate about customary obligations. Efforts were made to settle these by making a new *estimo*,[146] but further disputes arose later over the building of the wall of Camaiore and the obligations of the communes of the vicariate to help guard the town.[147] These disputes were serious, leading to violence and murder.[148] The internal disturbances were equally serious—it was said in 1371 that 'rixas, homicidia et vulnera et inquietationes pessimas' did not cease day or night in Camaiore.[149] In October 1374 certain of the leading trouble-makers were removed from the town and made to live in Lucca, and arrangements were made for certain exiles of Camaiore to return and make peace.[150] But trouble continued. There had been more violence and murders, and in August 1378 the two parties were induced to make a truce, agreeing not to attack each other before January, [151]

In January 1379 Chello di Poggio, who had recently been vicar there, made suggestions for the improvement of the administration of Camaiore in the hope of bringing the disputes there to an end. He suggested that there should be a *tasca* for the captains of Camaiore, and that it should be made by the Lucchese Anziani. Previously the captains had been elected in Camaiore itself, and the elections had been influenced by

[145] 'Novitatibus' there, *Min.* 2, f. 26, 20 May 1371. A man was dismissed from office because he had enemies there and had caused a riot, *Rif.* 7, p. 106, 16 June 1379.

[146] *Delib.* 132, ff. 57-57^{v}, 27 Nov. 1371, ff. 74-74^{v}, 12 Jan., ff. 83-84^{v}, 12 June 1372, *Rif.* 3, p. 402, 16 Sept. 1372, a *bargello* was appointed in the vicariate of Camaiore.

[147] *Rif.* 4, p. 407, 16 June 1374, *Delib.* 132, ff. 42-42^{v}, 6 Apr. 1374, *Delib.* 133, ff. 115-16, 22 July 1377, *Rif.* 8, p. 444, 7 Feb. 1383.

[148] *Delib.* 132, ff. 116^{v}-117, 17 Sept., ff. 131-2, 26 Sept. 1375, also loose folio at the end, dated 26 Sept. 1375. It was decreed that ten men of Camaiore and one of Corsanico were to be compelled to live in Lucca, and if anyone else in their absence made themselves 'caput partis', they too were to be compelled to live in Lucca. *Rif.* 5, p. 120, 29 Oct. 1375 the Anziani and *balìa* for these disputes stated that they were acting, 'volentes sopire discordias dissentiones et hodia hominum burgi et vicarie Camaioris unde tanta homicidia latrocinia et maleficia cotidie fuerunt commissa'.

[149] *Rif.* 2, p. 293, 3 June 1371. *Delib.* 132, f. 9^{v}, 14 June 1371, a man was condemned for killing another during a truce.

[150] *Rif.* 5, p. 120, 29 Oct., pp. 159-60, 29 Dec. 1375.

[151] *Rif.* 6, p. 632, 16 Aug. 1378.

party feeling there. He also suggested that the chancellor of Camaiore, in the past a *forestiere* chosen by the men of Camaiore, should in future be a Lucchese citizen chosen by the Lucchese Anziani, and that he should also hold the post of captain of the guard in Camaiore.[152] These suggestions were accepted, and the situation seems to have improved, for less is heard of disorder in Camaiore, though there were still occasional outbreaks.[153]

The Lucchese government was always very active in trying to prevent disorder in the *contado*. Various measures were possible, though it was difficult to find a permanent cure. One possibility was simple repression. At times of particularly serious disorders more *famuli* were added to the retinue of the *bargello*,[154] or additional *bargelli* were elected. In June 1387 it was decreed that there should be four *bargelli* instead of the usual one for the next six months.[155] In 1389 there were to be two *bargelli* and a *visconte* for the lands of the bishop in an effort to suppress disorder.[156] In 1392 a Captain of the *Contado* was elected, and this office later became permanent.[157] It was found to be effective in suppressing disorder, but the expense was a serious disadvantage. As well as appointing extra officials to suppress disorder in the *contado* generally, special officials could be sent to particular trouble spots. Extra mercenaries were stationed in Montecarlo in 1374,[158] and a *podestà* was appointed for Pieve di Compito in 1381 after violence had broken out there, for experience had shown that there were no murders in a place where there was a

[152] *Rif.* 7, pp. 8–9, 11 Jan. 1379. A *balìa* appointed to consider these proposals decreed that the six *sestieri* of Camaiore be united into three with the parts outside the walls making a fourth *quartiere*, and that Chello di Poggio's other suggestions be adopted, *Rif.* 7. pp. 11–12, 16 Jan. 1379.

[153] *Delib.* 133, ff. 20–20v, 16 Jan. 1381. In this case certain men of Camaiore seized the *rocca* and it took a military expedition to dislodge them.

[154] *Rif.* 10, p. 143, 2 Dec. 1386, though this was because of the arrival of the Pope rather than because of disorders in the Lucchese state. *Rif.* 11, p. 503, 13 Aug. 1391, *Rif.* 12, p. 413, 17 Feb., p. 425, 10 Mar. 1394.

[155] *Rif.* 10, pp. 282–4, 7 June 1387.

[156] *Rif.* 11, pp. 111–12, 18 Aug. 1389 and again *Rif.* 11, p. 503, 13 Aug. 1391.

[157] *Rif.* 12, p. 135, 7 June 1392, *Rif.* 13, p. 102, 9 Jan., p. 137, 22 July 1398, p. 223, 3 Feb., p. 255, 10 July 1399, p. 303, 12 Feb., p. 317, 24 Mar., p. 350, 4 Aug. 1400.

[158] *Rif.* 4, p. 396, 26 May 1374, also a reorganization of the administration to quieten the place.

podestà.[159] Similar measures were taken at Verni, Trassalico, Sasso, and other places.[160]

When disorder was caused by local factiousness efforts were made to induce the factions to come to peace. One of the functions of the *pacificatores* was to arrange formal pacifications,[161] but these were not always easy to enforce. It was stated in 1377 that such peace terms were often broken, and the Anziani decreed heavy penalties for this.[162] But this in itself caused further difficulties. When fighting broke out again in Pieve di Compito after a pacification, many men fled for fear of the fines and other penalties they knew they had incurred, so that several communes were almost deserted.[163] Another method of dealing with local factions was to remove the leading trouble-makers. This had been done in the case of Camaiore in 1375.[164] When there was violence in Moriano the leading men of the two parties were kept in prison in Lucca for several months and made to find sureties before they were released.[165] The men of Montecarlo were made to give hostages for their good behaviour.[166] Two men from Bargecchia and Silico were sent to another village,[167] and the removal of trouble-makers in the *contado* in general was authorized in 1387.[168] Other remedies were tried. Where the dispute was about some customary obligation, a commission

[159] *Rif.* 7, p. 554, 2 Sept. 1381. 'Et altra volta se veduto per experientia che a gittato buona ragione che mentre chel podesta vestato neuna uccisione vestata facta', *Rif.* 8, pp. 145-6, 27 May 1382.

[160] *Delib.* 132, ff. 88-88^{v}, 6 Aug. 1375, *Rif.* 10, p. 355, 21 Nov. 1387, *Rif.* 13, p. 15, 26 Jan. 1397.

[161] Pacifications were made at Menabbio, *Min.* 2, ff. 21^{v}-22^{v}, 5 May 1371, Treppignana, *Min.* 2, f. 51, 25 June 1371, Moriano, *Rif.* 7, pp. 412-13, 29 Jan. 1381, Colle and Castelvecchio, *Rif.* 8, p. 93, 17 Apr., pp. 145-6, 27 May 1382, Pieve di Compito, *Rif.* 8, pp. 160-2, 11 June, p. 271, 26 Sept. 1382.

[162] *Rif.* 6, pp. 361-2, 10 Sept. 1377.

[163] *Rif.* 8, p. 271, 26 Sept. 1382. Those not guilty of homicide were pardoned, but there was renewed fighting there later, *Rif.* 8, p. 422, 8 Jan. 1383.

[164] *Rif.* 5, p. 120, 29 Oct. 1375.

[165] *Rif.* 7, p. 410, 24 Jan., pp. 412-13, 29 Jan., p. 429, 7 Mar. 1381.

[166] *Rif.* 8, p. 115, 23 Apr. 1382 it was petitioned that a number of boys, sons of the men involved in these troubles, had been in Lucca as hostages for eight years. Their exchange for others was permitted.

[167] *Rif.* 8, p. 204, 16 July 1382.

[168] They were to be granted Lucchese citizenship and made to live in Lucca, *Rif.* 10, p. 281, 7 June 1387, and again p. 421, 4 Feb. 1388.

could be appointed to settle the matter.[169] It was recognized too that in some cases poverty and misery caused crime and sometimes amnesties were issued for past violence in the hope of future peace.[170]

But it was not really possible to prevent violence and disorder in the *contado*. The root causes, local factions, disputes over boundaries or pasture rights, rivalries between neighbouring villages, and the activities of *banniti* continued.[171] It does not seem that there was any improvement in the situation in this period. Indeed violence caused by *banniti* seems to have increased in the last decade of the century. Rather less is heard of local factions and disputes, though this may be due to the nature of the sources, and disorder in the *contado* does not seem to be connected with the internal factions of Lucca itself. But the situation in the last years of the century during the war between Milan and Florence, and more serious, the war between Lucca and Pisa from 1395 onwards led to an increase in the activities of *banniti*, though Lucca continued to fight this by appointing a regular Captain of the *Contado* and doing all she could to repress violence.

It is perhaps appropriate at this point to consider the general nature of Lucca's administration of her *contado* and to discuss whether the sources suggest that it involved the exploitation and oppression of her subjects.[172] It has been seen

[169] *Min.* 3 (not foliated), 12 July 1382, *Rif.* 12, p. 128, 29 May 1392, *Rif.* 13, pp. 50-2, 25 July 1397.

[170] Eight men of the vicariate of Massa Lunense were allowed to pay a modest fine 'ad hoc ne dicta vicaria qua hactenus dei gratia in pace et tranquillitate permansit modo per tot extrinsecos valeat perturbari et considerata pauperitate eorum qui propter paupertatem et ut habeant unde viverent et pro oneribus supportandis maxime armorum talia attentasse dicuntur', *Rif.* 5, p. 338, 15 May 1376. *Rif.* 10, pp. 281-4, 7 June 1387, even while taking stringent measures to suppress crime, it was recognized that 'molta misericordia' sometimes led men to commit such offences. Also *Rif.* 8, p. 204, 16 July, p. 271, 26 Sept. 1382.

[171] These problems were by no means confined to Lucca or to the fourteenth century. There was chronic violence in the Pistoiese *contado*, Herlihy, *Medieval and Renaissance Pistoia*, pp. 198-9, 207-10. There were also factions and other disorders in the Lucchese *contado* in the sixteenth century, Berengo, *Nobili e mercanti*, pp. 341-56.

[172] The view especially of R. Caggese, 'La Repubblica di Siena e il suo contado nel secolo decimoterzo', *Bullettino Senese di Storia Patria*, Vol. XIII (1906), and *Classi e Comuni Rurali nel Medioevo Italiano*, 2 vols. (Florence, 1907-9), challenged by E. Fiumi, 'Sui rapporti economici tra città e contado nell'età comunale', *Archivio Storico Italiano*, Vol. CXIV (1956), pp. 18-68. Also discussions by E. Cristiani, 'Città e

that many places in the *contado* were in difficulties and that gabelles and other fiscal demands were among the things to which they attributed their decline. Lucca certainly imposed some obligations that were both heavy and unpopular; the *tassa frumenti* is a case in point, and so is the obligation to maintain a granary imposed upon Pietrasanta, though this seems to have been somewhat mitigated by later provisions and Lucca even lent Pietrasanta 2,500 *staia* of corn.[173] Lucca also demanded military service from her subjects and assistance in the building, repair, and manning of fortresses. These obligations could be heavy in themselves and were often much resented, though they were for the defence of the peasants' own localities, but again the burden might be reduced. Lucca abandoned a scheme that provided her with an effective body of defenders in 1383 partly because the *contado* petitioned against the heavy burden, and she might be prepared to grant quite generous subsidies for the building of walls and fortresses and even for garrisoning them.[174]

It would be extremely valuable to be able to assess the relative weight of *contado* and city taxation, but in fact for Lucca it is by no means easy even to calculate the sums received from city and *contado* respectively.[175] It is true that by the late fourteenth century the city no longer had the direct tax, called *lira* or *estimo*, while for the *contado* the *estimo* was retained. It was indeed still extremely important; there are many references to it and communities in the *contado* quite

campagna nell'età comunale in alcune pubblicazioni dell'ultimo decennio', *Rivista Storica Italiana*, Vol. LXXV (1963), pp. 829–45 and Bowsky, *Finance of the Commune of Siena*, pp. 225–55, 291–2.

[173] *Tassa frumenti, Rif.* 6, pp. 341–9, 23 Aug. 1377. Pietrasanta, *Rif.* 7, p. 124, 1 Aug., p. 169, 6 Nov. 1379, p. 307, 20 Aug. 1380, p. 540, 13 Aug. 1381. Though there are many decrees concerning food supplies, Lucchese sources would bear out Fiumi's contention that the rigour with which they were applied varied greatly according to the general supply situation, 'Sui rapporti economici', pp. 42–62 and 'Fioritura e decadenza dell'economia fiorentina III', pp. 471–8.

[174] *Rif.* 8, p. 591, 29 Aug. 1383. For Lucchese defence policy in general pp. 119–27.

[175] It is doubtful if for Lucca one could speak with the precision Herlihy does in asserting that the Pistoiese *contado* was paying direct taxes six times as high as the city in the 1280s and 57 per cent of the total in 1427, *Medieval and Renaissance Pistoia*, pp. 144, 184–8, or Becker in calculating that the Florentine *contado* was contributing 40–50 per cent of total ordinary revenue, *Florence in Transition*, Vol. I, p. 4, 'Economic change', p. 37, 'Problemi della finanza pubblica fiorentina', pp. 460–2. Fiumi calculates that the city and *contado* paid dues in proportions of 75 per cent to 25 per cent in 1336–8, 'Sui rapporti economici', pp. 29–30.

frequently petitioned for its reassessment. But it does not seem to have been the basis for any direct taxation payable to Lucca. The direct levy called the *taglia delle cinquantasettemila lire e pedoni*, which had been primarily for the maintenance of armed forces, had lapsed under Pisan rule and was not revived.[176] The *estimo* was the basis for the division of customary local payments for such things as the salaries of officials, the building and repair of roads, walls, and defences, the garrisoning of fortresses, and perhaps the costs of the *cerne* and the candle local communities had to carry in the S. Croce procession in Lucca, though in at least some cases these obligations were divided between communes partly by hearths and between individuals in the communes partly by 'testa' as well as 'lira'.

The receipts of the Lucchese treasurer did include the 'gabella' of each of the vicariates and some other communities. These consisted of gabelles on such things as bread, wine, and meat sold locally, and on contracts and tolls on goods passing through certain places, or of fixed sums that represented a composition for such gabelles. These levies did not differ in kind, and were considerably fewer in number and lower in yield than those imposed in Lucca itself.[177] Where the local community paid a composition this was usually at its own request.[178]

[176] Bongi, *Inv.*, II, p. 28. Discussed by Fiumi, 'Sui rapporti economici', p. 31. The *dovana salis* was based on a special count of *bocche*, not on the *estimo*.

[177] In 1377 the various gabelles or compositions of the vicariates produced about 7,800 florins. The tax on wine, bread and oil in the Six Miles produced about 1,180 florins. With the yield of fines imposed by vicars and certain payments for the salaries of officials, guard of fortresses etc. the total from the *contado* was about 9,340 florins. Meanwhile the *cassa generalia*, *cassa vini*, *proventus vini venalis*, *proventus medie uncie panis*, *proventus farine* and *proventus macelli*, that is taxes on city food supplies, produced nearly 23,000 florins and the *gabella maggiore* about 11,000. Perhaps a proportion of such taxes as the *cassa vini* should be regarded as *contado* taxation, but it was probably a tax on consumers rather than producers, and in any case some of the producers must have been citizens with land in the *contado*. Other levies included some things like retentions on the salaries of officials, including non-Lucchese officials and mercenaries, that can hardly be regarded as city taxation, but most other dues were probably primarily levies on the city, though the *distretto* or Six Miles, which was legally and administratively separate from the *contado* proper, may have paid a share of some other minor dues, like taxes on weights and measures, brick and tile works, boats, etc. *Ragionieri*, 13, ff. 1-5^{v}, 26-32 (different foliations).

[178] These compositions were on a local and temporary basis. There was no general composition like the Sienese 'contado gabelle' of the late thirteenth and early

One levy that applied only to the *contado* and not to the city, at least until 1388, was the compulsory purchase of a fixed quantity of salt each year. The quantities and the price were certainly fixed with the financial needs of Lucca in mind and this monopoly was a lucrative source of revenue, but the burden was often less in practice than in theory. The fact that the new assessment of 1383, based on an actual count of the current number of *bocche*, was much heavier than the old means that *contadini* had been paying on a relative under-assessment for at least a number of years past, and it has been seen that the Lucchese government, despite the financial need that had caused it to undertake a new assessment in the first place, allowed immediate concessions that with modifications were renewed later. Nor does the salt monopoly seem to have been applied very rigorously, or even always very efficiently; in 1390 there were found to be arrears that dated back as far as 1370 in some cases, and some of them were represented by concessions to communities which had not been cancelled in the books.[179] It is doubly regrettable that the yield of the *dovana salis* is unclear, for though by no means all of it came from compulsory sales to *contadini*, a good proportion undoubtedly did, and it would have given some indication of the relative weight of the tax burden they bore. But even if it yielded a total of 10,000 florins, this, though heavy, would not seem unduly oppressive in the face of 60,000–70,000 florins from other sources, the great majority of it from the city and suburbs.

The same problems apply to extraordinary impositions. In the first years after the recovery of her independence Lucca was obliged to impose forced loans and the *contado* as well as the city was required to contribute. But again it is difficult to work out the relative burden on city and *contado*. The 'gabella

---

fourteenth century, Bowsky, *Finance of the Commune of Siena*, pp. 226–8.

[179] But a man of Palmatoria, pieve S. Pancrazio, petitioning that he could not pay the salt gabelle for the absent *bocche* as well as his own assessment, said bluntly 'quello comune e venuto meno per le troppe graveze del dicto sale', *Rif.* 8, p. 359, 27 Dec. 1382. Arrears *Rif.* 11, p. 375, 16 Dec. 1390. Becker, *Florence in Transition*, Vol. II, pp. 182–4, 186–7, 195, argues that Florence was tightening up her *contado* administration, so that it was no longer possible for communes to be 10 or 15 years in arrears and there were attempts to exact back dues, but Molho, *Florentine Public Finances*, p. 35, quotes places that were 20 years in arrears in the early fifteenth century.

cultrarum terrarum', for example, was to be paid one third by the tenant and two thirds by the landlord, and landlords must in at least some, and perhaps many, cases have been citizens. The 15,000-florin *imposita* that replaced the 'gabella cultrarum terrarum' is one of the few precise figures for a levy on the *contado*, but though it was a large sum, it must be remembered that payment was in instalments spread over fifteen months, and that it was a forced loan, eventually included in the *Massa*, not a form of direct taxation. Also gabelles had been increased by 50 per cent and citizens were being required to make other substantial contributions at the same time. It has already been seen that it is difficult to ascertain the proportion of *Massa* credits held by *contado* communes, because they seem to have been especially likely to sell their holdings. The proportions of 17,588 florins for the communes and other non-residents of the city to 23,473, 25,523 and 25,777 florins for the three city *terzieri* certainly understates the burden on the *contado*, especially as the 17,588 florins includes something like 9,000 florins of credits held by Lucchese citizens living in Venice and elsewhere.[180] But in later years Lucca was able to avoid *prestanze* and the *contado* as well as the city would benefit from this.

A genuine concern for the welfare of the *contado* as a whole can be detected. It is not uncommon for enquiries to be made to ensure that no other community will be damaged if concessions are made to a neighbour, and if anyone *estimatus* in the *contado* was granted citizenship, his commune was relieved of the amount of his *estimo*. There were constant efforts, often spurred on by petitions from the *contado*, to prevent some *contadini* from escaping their obligations by falsely claiming Lucchese citizenship or making fraudulent donations of their property to Lucchese citizens or to the Church.[181] Communes

[180] *Rif.* 2, pp. 268–9, 23 Apr., pp. 271–2, 25 Apr., pp. 280–1, 7 May 1371. *Min.* 2, f. 10^v, 23 Apr. 1371. *Rif.* 3, p. 89, 29 Oct., pp. 95–100, 30 Oct. 1371. For holdings in the *Massa*, series *Imprestiti* nos. 17–20 (1396–1411), and see Chapter 3, pp. 75–6.

[181] *Rif.* 11, p. 301, 9 Apr. 1370, *Rif.* 3, p. 253, 10 Mar. 1372. *Rif.* 9, p. 456, 29 Dec. 1385, *Rif.* 10, p. 27, 14 Feb. 1386. For reduction of the *estimo* where *contadini* had become citizens and similar attempts to defraud the treasury in Siena, Bowsky, *Finance of the Commune of Siena*, pp. 79–82, 237, 251. For general complaints of unfairness in *estimi*, *Rif.* 1, p. 127, 26 Oct. 1369, p. 345, 6 May 1370. In 1382 a great effort was made to share the burden of labour services more fairly. Communes were

presenting petitions often asked for 'misericordia', and the council in granting them often claims to be taking pity on them, something that may well be more than an empty formula. Of particular interest are two petitions that show a sense of the common interests of city and *contado* and even a willingness on the part of citizens to sacrifice some of their claims against *contadini* in order to assist the recovery of the *contado*. In February 1376 a petition concerning the depopulation of the 'sobborghi' was presented not by the inhabitants of the 'sobborghi' themselves but by a group of citizens, who pointed out that this depopulation

e et esser puo in grave danno preiudicio et vergogna del nostro comune e delle singulari persone per molte cagioni et ragioni et massimamente considerato che ungni biada che si ricollie in de soborghi e sempre presta alla citta e ungni cazo di fortuna. Et considerato che li habitandi in de soborghi sono le prime guardie delle mura della citta. Et considerato che per gravasse si debbiano partire et che per la loro partita li orti et giardini debbiano boschi divenire come gia funno per simili gravesse. Et considerato che si da privilegio a forestieri che venisseno quine o in del contado ad habitare maggioremente si denno li nostri originarii mantenere.

The 'sobborghi' were the rural parishes beyond the 'borghi' or suburbs, but not yet in the Six Miles. The petition shows that they were at least partly agricultural and the citizens sponsoring the petition may have had land there.[182] The same sense of the common interests of citizens and inhabitants of the *contado* is made even clearer by the second petition, referring to a wider area. The petitioner was again a citizen, Bernardo Bernardini, a goldsmith, who informed the council:

che per la absentia di molti contadini li quali per debiti daffitti et daltre cagioni contracti et facti per lo sinistro tempo passato della tirannia de pisani molte terre del contado de Luca et poderi rimangnano sodi et non lavorati li quali cotali contadini ritornando et stando si lavorerenno et molto terreno del quale al presente nulla utilita sicava, si ramene di che fare

---

arranged into six 'collonelli'. The official of the 'restauro' was to impose as few labour services as possible and to keep careful records of those that were imposed. At the end of the year those communes that had done less than average were to pay money and those that had done more were to receive payment, *Rif.* 8, pp. 274–9, 30 Sept. 1382.

[182] *Rif.* 5, p. 205, 12 Feb. 1376. The names of the petitioners were Fredo Martini, Bendinello Castiglione, Jacobo Ronghi, Biagio Guiducci, Fasino Boccansocchi, Niccolò di Poggio and there were said to be many others whose names are not given. Fiumi, 'Sui rapporti economici' pp. 21–5, 62–4, 67–8 for common interests of city and *contado*.

grande utilita della re publica come e grande danno et scurita non esser lavorate pregasi alla signoria vostra per parte di Bernardo Bernardini orafo cittadino di Lucha che avendo rispecto alla publica utilita videgnate provedere et stantiare col consillio bisognevile siche vallia che ciaschuno contadino lo quale non e sbandito per maleficio lo quale e absente dalla citta e contado di Luca possa venire stare et ritornare liberamente et siguramente in avere et in persona dal di del dicto stantiamento a cinque anni in del quale tempo non possa essere preso ne ditenuto ne molestato in avere o in persona per cagione dalcuno afficto ritenuto et non pagato dallano di MCCCLXX indirieto o per cagione dalcuno altro debito facto dal dicto anno indirieto rimanendo nientedimeno ferme et salde contra di loro le ragioni delloro creditori alli quali neuno tempo sintenda correre in del dicto spatio et tempo di cinque anni.

This was agreed, and a moratorium of five years before they could pursue claims for unpaid rents and other debts must have meant a sacrifice for some citizens, though it was realized that it was in the interests of both citizens and *contadini* in the long run that *contadini* should be able to return and till the land they held of citizens once more.[183]

The lack of fiscal records for the last two decades of the fourteenth century makes it impossible to discuss whether Lucca increased her financial pressure on the *contado* as Florence did.[184] There was perhaps less temptation for her to do so, as her financial position, though not easy, was not as strained as that of Florence. There is no parallel in Lucca to Florentine proposals to impose taxes or extract money from the *contado* as an alternative to heavier impositions in the city,[185] and legislative records suggest that she was still willing to listen to petitions and grant relief to the countryside. When she imposed extra burdens it seems to have been fairly even-handedly between city and *contado*. If in 1388 she imposed a tax on wine in the *contado*, she took action at the same time to increase the gabelles in the city, and one of the most far-reaching measures of the late fourteenth century was the decision to impose forced purchases of salt in the city as well as

[183] *Rif.* 4, p. 167, 10 June 1373. There are other grants of moratoria on rents and even the cancellation of arrears that must have involved a financial sacrifice for many citizens, *Rif.* 2, p. 236, 17 Mar. 1371, *Rif.* 3, p. 87, 26 Oct. 1371, *Rif.* 11, p. 37, 22 Feb. 1389.

[184] Becker, *Florence in Transition*, Vol. II, pp. 181-90, 'Economic change', pp. 32–7, 'Problemi della finanza pubblica fiorentina', pp. 444–8, 460–5. Molho, *Florentine Public Finances*, pp. 25–45.

[185] Becker, *Florence in Transition*, Vol. II, pp. 181, 189, 193.

the *contado*.[186] There is no evidence that the *Estimo* of 1397 applied to the *contado*.

In general the situation of the *contado* cannot be regarded as happy. The difficulties were largely due to depopulation and other causes beyond the control of the government. The population had fallen, but officials' salaries still had to be paid and the same area defended and administered. Burdens clearly were often heavy. But this did not apply only to the *contado*; a reduced city population was also liable to military service and had to pay heavy gabelles on food and other essentials.[187] If petitions for tax relief are evidence that some places in the *contado* were in difficulties, there are many communities that are not recorded as petitioning, and some of those that did were in only temporary difficulties due to some special cause.[188] If in 1379 the Six Miles petitioned for a new *estimo* on the familiar grounds that some men had left the area or fallen into poverty since the last one, it was also claimed that others had become rich and were therefore not paying their proper share.[189] The *contado* as a whole was being called upon to pay dues and undertake obligations that were heavy and perhaps unpopular, but they did not necessarily represent an undue share of the burdens. The government was prepared to grant concessions to places in serious difficulties. There was an awareness of the common interests of city and *contado* and there is no reason to believe that the city was engaging in deliberate oppression or excessive exploitation of the territory over which it ruled.

[186] *Rif.* 10, pp. 485-6, 19 June 1388. The increased gabelles and the imposition of salt in the city were the first two measures and the wine tax the third, if they were not enough. It was pointed out that other cities imposed heavy dues on wine, including 30 *bolognini* the *carro* in the Florentine *contado*. It was also pointed out that the cause of these tax increases was the need to make payments to armed companies so that the *contado* would not be devastated.

[187] *Rif.* 11, p. 348, 25 Nov., p. 370, 16 Dec. 1390 provides evidence of distress in the city as well as the *contado* due to wars, plagues and the difficulties suffered by the 'mestieri' with profits reduced while expenses remained the same, so that 'sia di somma necessita di provedere si a la cita come al contado et distrecto in quello che possibile sia acio che li homini piu alleviati et contenti in ogni caso si trovino al bene comune con la persona et avere disposti et aparechiati'. The price of salt was reduced *Rif.* 11, p. 348, 25 Nov. 1390 and this was renewed *Rif.* 12, p. 49, 20 Feb. 1392.

[188] Fiumi, 'Sui rapporti economici', p. 35-6, petitions for relief were not signs of continuous wretchedness.

[189] 'Multi homines et persone quorumlibet comunium ditati sunt qui tempore extimi vigentis pauperes existebant et sic qui modo possunt secundum eorum potentiam onera non subeunt', *Rif.* 7, p. 108, 23 June 1379.

PART II
External Relations

5
INTRODUCTION

In 1369 Lucca was again free and able to take her place as an independent city-state. But she had many problems. Her independence especially in the first few years after 1369 was precarious; she had lost it before and might do so again, as more powerful states than Lucca were to do before the end of the fifteenth century. The fact that Lucca was successful in preserving her independence until 1799 should not be allowed to obscure the difficulties. By no means all the Lucchese themselves were optimistic about the city's future in 1369; Bartolomeo di Michele Moccindente, lending 5,000 florins in July 1369, insisted on elaborate securities 'perche lo stato di questa terra non era ancora ben rifermo . . . per esser certo di riaverli'.[1]

In many ways Lucca's main problems were internal. Her most pressing concern was reconstruction. She needed to reorganize her government, provide for the defence of her state and restore her industry and commerce. She had been obliged to buy her liberty from Charles IV and this left her deeply in debt. Her smallness and her poverty meant that she was not inclined to an adventurous foreign policy, which would in any case hardly have been possible. The Lucchese were at pains to stress the smallness of their state, its poverty, and their own lack of ambition, so that they were 'una quantità trascurabile'.[2] Lucchese foreign policy was, in fact, virtually entirely negative. They wished only to remain on good terms with everyone so that they could restore their city in peace. They would undoubtedly have been glad, had it been possible, to have had no foreign policy at all, but because of Lucca's position in Tuscany, the attitude of her neighbours, and her own needs, this was not possible.

[1] *Rif.* 8, p. 169, 16 June 1382.

[2] *Reg.*, no. 972, 4 Sept. 1382. Similar statements nos. 517, 785, 805, 810, 873, 933, 946, 953.

Though Lucca's military and economic resources were modest compared with those of Milan, Florence, or even Pisa, she was not entirely negligible. Her state, though small, was in an important strategic position. She controlled a stretch of coastline, which included the port of Motrone. Florence had occasionally turned to Motrone in the past when her quarrels with Pisa had led her to abandon Porto Pisano, and though she might perhaps prefer the Sienese alternative of Talamone, she was to use Motrone again in the last decade of the fourteenth century. Even more important than her coastline and the possibility of using Motrone as a port was Lucca's strategic position controlling the roads and passes from the north. Lucca lay on the *via francigena*, which connected Siena and Rome with Northern Italy. The road from the south crossed the Arno at Fucecchio and passed through Lucca, continuing via the pass of Pontremoli across the Apennines to Parma, Milan, and the north. Lucca was therefore in a position to close the passes to invaders and to grant or refuse passage to forces travelling between Rome or Naples and the north.

If her strategic position meant that her alliance was sought, in her own interests Lucca could not afford to be isolated. She was a small state with powerful neighbours. Pisa and Florence had fought for possession of Lucca in 1341/2, and although Pisa, now under the pacific rule of Pietro Gambacorta and in any case much declined, offered no very serious threat to Lucchese liberty, the Lucchese were still suspicious of Florence and there were from time to time rumours of her hostile intentions towards Lucca. The Visconti state, too, bordered on that of Lucca at Sarzana, which had been Lucchese until lost to the Visconti in 1369. There had been a determined effort to capture Lucca herself in 1369/70 and the Lucchese had much cause to distrust the Visconti in the first years after 1369. Lucca was very conscious of her vulnerable position as a small, weak state surrounded by very much more powerful and potentially hostile neighbours. The Gonfaloniere in 1392 said 'mirabantur cuncti qualiter tam parva civitas intra tot potentissimos populos et tam claras potentias posita in tanta libertate et tam tranquillo et pacifico statu se gubernaret et regeret'.[3] This sense of being encircled by potential enemies

[3] *Rif.* 12, pp. 98–9, 15 May 1392. Also *Reg.*, no. 2000, 7 Feb. 1374.

comes out very clearly in Sercambi's chronicle. Under the year 1398 he devotes a whole section to listing Lucca's neighbours and the possessions they had nearest to the Lucchese borders. He reviews the past conduct of each of these states towards Lucca, seeing many of them as enemies and advising that precautions be taken even against those that are at present friendly. He advised that all Lucchese castles on the borders be carefully guarded against dangers.[4] The same fear that even states that were apparently friends and allies might be secret enemies is apparent in negotiations for leagues; Lucca was unwilling to agree that she could not make peace without the consent of any ally who was assisting her, for fear that such an ally might nourish 'odium occultum' and be aiding her 'fallaciter'.[5]

With this sense of being in an embattled position surrounded by more powerful neighbours, any of whom might be potential enemies, the Lucchese naturally took an active interest in the plans and movements of other Italian states, maintaining observers and sending out spies to report on rumours of any activities that might constitute a threat to their security. A particular problem in the late fourteenth century was invasion by companies of adventurers and unemployed mercenaries. Even a large state like Florence might be obliged to ransom her territory, but the danger was very much greater for a small state like Lucca. The threat from armed companies was one of the things that induced Lucca to join leagues. Her own forces would be inadequate to defend her against a determined attack, and however much she might mistrust her neighbours, she needed to have allies on whom she could call for aid. For Lucca the ideal situation would have been one in which she could remain on good terms with Florence, Milan, Pisa, and the Papacy all at once, but because of the rivalries and ambitions of these states this was rarely possible for long.

Lucca's aims in foreign policy were limited and purely defensive. She had, of course, territorial claims against a number of her neighbours, which a more powerful state might have pursued. Lucca had not forgotten these claims. A large

[4] Sercambi, II, pp. 121–44.

[5] Document headed 'limitationes pactorum fiendorum', relating to the league of 23 July 1380 in *Capitoli*, 32, p. 38.

number of villages and fortresses she had long since lost were listed as part of the Lucchese state in the Statute of 1372.[6] Sercambi too lists much Lucchese territory held by Florence, Pisa, and others, and complains bitterly that Florence made no attempt to return this territory when Lucca was in close alliance with her in 1395, so that she clearly intended to keep it.[7] There are even occasional hints of Lucchese attempts to claim lost territory. In the peace negotiations of 1374/5 they raised the question of their claim to Sarzana and Lunigiana. It was rumoured that these lands were to come into the possession of the Papacy, and Lucca could hardly let her claim to territory, some of which she had lost only in 1369, go by default.[8] In 1389 she not only objected to a clause in a proposed league that would have involved recognition of Florence as holding *de iure* 'una grande e magiore parte del nostro contado', but was even in negotiation with a *condottiere* for aid in its recovery.[9] But the Lucchese were realists. While not prepared to recognize the loss of territory that had been taken from them by force, its reconquest, or even attempts to recover it by other means, was no part of their general policy. They must have realized that only if there were a general upheaval in Italy would they have any chance of recovering their lost territory, and that if they attempted to do so on their own they were more likely to suffer further losses.

The aims of Lucchese foreign policy were thus almost entirely negative. The Lucchese wanted simply to survive at all as an independent state, and also as far as possible to escape humiliations and embarrassments. It was Lucca's policy to remain on good terms with as many of her neighbours as possible. She wanted to avoid committing herself too heavily to any one neighbouring state or entering into an exclusive alliance with any single power, maintaining good relations with others as a counterbalance. Lucca was not of the first rank, or even of the second, among Italian states, but she had not yet sunk into such complete insignificance that she was content to

[6] *Statuto del Comune di Lucca*, 1372, Lib. III, cap. xciiii, series *Statuti*, no. 6.

[7] Sercambi, II, pp. 122–5.

[8] *Reg.*, no. 475 and below p. 143.

[9] *Reg.*, nos. 1397, 1423–4 and below pp. 171–2. They also countered Pisa's territorial claims with claims of their own in 1397, *Reg.*, no. 1771.

rely for defence and protection on a client relation with one of her more powerful neighbours, a relation which might well have proved to be the first step towards her complete absorption into a neighbouring state. Lucca still had her share of civic pride, and her citizens were angry when her territory was violated, her opinion ignored, or her dignity disregarded. Their feelings of frustration at their powerlessness to prevent this are often apparent in Lucchese documents. But the Lucchese themselves were obliged to pursue a policy of which they were a little ashamed. They were obliged to stress their own insignificance, to return a soft answer, to avoid committing themselves to a course of action until they were sure what their neighbours' attitude was, and to avoid doing anything that might give offence to anyone. The Lucchese pursued this line of policy consciously and deliberately. They summed it up very clearly in a graphic phrase as 'nostra flexibilitas et tractabilitas cum vicinis', and felt the need to apologize for it.[10] But this kind of negative, cautious, and inglorious foreign policy was the only possible one for a state in Lucca's position, if she was to achieve her main aim which was simply to survive at all as an independent state.

The problem of defence was obviously a serious one for a state that saw many of its neighbours as potential enemies and had land borders on three sides and no natural frontiers. Lucca had to provide as best she could against possible attacks by armed companies in peace-time and by invading armies in time of war, and also against acts of violence by her own *banniti*. To maintain adequate forces permanently was very costly, and in the last thirty years of the fourteenth century Lucca can be seen experimenting with various forms of defence forces in the hope of finding a system which combined economy with a reasonable degree of efficiency.

Her own citizens had military obligations and might be sent on military expeditions in considerable numbers. In September 1370 so many citizens were absent because of the war in the Garfagnana that the quorum for the General Council was reduced from 120 to 80.[11] Citizens who were

[10] *Anz. Temp. Lib.* 530, ff. 8–8^v, 24 Nov. 1374. No. 460 in *Reg.*

[11] *Rif.* 2, pp. 76 and 79, 20 Sept. 1370. References to Lucchese citizens going with armies, *Rif.* 1, p. 471, 18 Dec. 1370, *Rif.* 2, p. 160, 11 Dec., p. 167, 13 Dec. 1370.

called upon to serve in the army were liable to a fine if they failed to do so, and even if they were ill or absent from the city they had to provide a substitute.[12] In addition to service in armies Lucchese citizens might be sent to garrison some particular place in the *contado* which was exposed to attack in troubled times.[13] *Contadini* too were liable for military service. Lucca sometimes took men of the *contado* into her service as mercenaries on a regular basis, both as infantry and as cavalry, despite prohibitions of this in the statutes,[14] but ordinary peasants also had to do military service. For this they were organized into *cerne*, which were periodically reviewed. In 1381 the *cerne* of the vicariates numbered 2,000 men, arranged into two groups so that 1,000 men could be called upon at any one time. The *cerne* of the Six Miles produced another 600 men in two groups of 300 men each, while the lands of the bishop of Lucca provided fifty, and those of the cathedral chapter twenty-four. There were detailed regulations about the arms they should carry and their wages. The aim was that there should always be a body of men on which Lucca could rely. The *cerne* were to meet regularly 'ad barsaglandum', and if anyone died or became unfit for service another should take his place. The *cerne* cost Lucca little or

---

Lucchese citizens were organized under *gonfaloni* and *pennoni* (*Statuto* 1372, Lib. 1, caps. xix–xxi), but it is not clear whether those recorded as serving in armies were organized on this basis. However, it was possible in 1392 for a party in Lucca to urge that mercenaries be dismissed and Lucca guarded by the *gonfaloni* and *pennoni* (Sercambi, I, p. 276). Though this suggestion was connected with the internal faction struggles, it shows that the organization by *gonfaloni* and *pennoni* still retained some vigour.

[12] *Delib.* 132, ff. 120v–121, 19 June 1373, ff. 50–50v, 26 Aug. 1374.

[13] *Rif.* 8, p. 292, 20 Oct. 1382, *Rif.* 9, p. 313, 1 Mar. 1385. Payments were made 6 Apr. 1370 to 18 citizens sent to Motrone and 37 to Pietrasanta, series *Camarlingo Generale*, no. 80, *Introito-esito*, f. 59v. Payments also to 188 men going to the war in the Garfagnana 1373, including many leading citizens, *Ragionieri*, no. 11, ff. 122v–124. The system continued later; 5 Feb. 1392 many citizens and *contadini* are said to have done service in guarding fortress in a time of crisis, and not yet been paid, *Rif.* 12, p. 46. For paid service by Florentine citizens in a rather earlier period, D. Waley, 'The army of the Florentine republic from the twelfth to the fourteenth century', in N. Rubinstein (ed.), *Florentine Studies* (London, 1968), esp. pp. 72, 76–8, 95.

[14] *Rif.* 4, p. 80, 15 Mar., pp. 226–7, 29 Aug. 1373, p. 294, 1 Jan. 1374, *Rif.* 5, p. 33, 25 Feb., p. 43, 21 Mar. 1375, *Rif.* 6, p. 6, 6 July 1376, p. 429, 18 Dec. 1377, *Rif.* 7, p. 158, 30 Sept. 1379, p. 246, 24 Jan., p. 251, 4 Feb., p. 241, 12 Mar., p. 253, 26 Apr., p. 348, 10 Nov. 1380, *Rif.* 8, p. 37, 22 Jan. 1382, pp. 591–2, 29 Aug., p. 593, 30 Aug. 1383.

nothing, as they were paid by their own localities, though they were under the authority of the central government and their captains were Lucchese citizens.[15] This was by no means a mere paper army. The *cerne* were called out quite frequently. They might be ordered to serve in an army,[16] but more frequently they were called upon to serve as guards and defenders of Lucca, Pietrasanta, or some other centre.[17] In 1380 over 600 men were summoned and sent to guard Lucca, Montecatinello, Aquilea, Brancalo, Matraia, and other fortresses.[18]

Sometimes defenders for Lucca were summoned without reference to the *cerne*. In 1383 an experiment was made of choosing from each vicariate thirty-six men skilled in arms and 'libertatis lucane ferventissimi zelatores', who should be divided into three groups, each to serve for a month at a time at a wage of eight florins a month.[19] This perhaps produced a more effective force than the *cerne*, but the experiment was short-lived, as it was found to be too expensive for Lucca, and her subjects petitioned that such service was an intolerable burden.[20] The *cerne* too were found to be costly, though their pay was lower, and the obligation to serve in them gave rise to

[15] They were reorganized in 1376 and 1381. *Rif.* 4, pp. 122–3, 11 May 1373, *Rif.* 5, p. 195, 24 Jan. 1376, *Rif.* 6, pp. 39–41, 13 Aug. 1376, *Rif.* 7, p. 79, 28 Apr. 1379. Their captains were to be Lucchese citizens, *Rif.* 6, p. 52, 25 Aug. 1376. The lists for the 1376 reorganization survive in series *Milizie della Campagna*, no. 1, *Cerna del Contado 1376*. For 1381, *Rif.* 7, p. 348, 10 Nov. 1380, pp. 481–2, 26 Apr. 1381, *Rif.* 8, p. 474, 10 Mar. 1383. Provisions for filling gaps left in the *cerne* through deaths, *Rif.* 8, p. 587, 26 Aug. 1383. The *cerne* are said to have been recently renewed, *Min.* 4 (not foliated), 8 Dec. 1392, but there are no further details of this. For military service by Florentine *contadini* in an earlier period, Waley, 'The army of the Florentine republic', p. 105. For Siena, W. M. Bowsky, 'City and contado: military relationships and communal bonds in fourteenth-century Siena', in A. Molho and J. A. Tedeschi (eds.), *Renaissance Studies in Honor of Hans Baron* (Dekalb, Ill., 1971), esp. pp. 79–80, 90–3. The use of peasant militia continued in Florence until the 1350s and 1360s, but was increasingly ineffective militarily and ceased soon after, C. C. Bayley, *War and Society in Renaissance Florence* (Toronto, 1961), pp. 17–20, 25–6, 30–1, 34–6, 54–8. Also M. Mallett, *Mercenaries and their Masters, Warfare in Renaissance Italy* (London, 1974), pp. 43–6.

[16] *Rif.* 4, p. 172, 13 June 1373, *Delib.* 132, ff. 50–50^{v}, 26 Aug. 1374.

[17] *Rif.* 4, p. 294, 1 Jan. 1374, *Delib.* 132, f. 30^{v}, 30 Dec. 1373, *Rif.* 7, p. 241, 12 Mar. 1380, *Min.* 3 (not foliated), 22 Oct. 1384, 8 Mar. 1385.

[18] *Rif.* 7, pp. 514–15, 22 June 1381.

[19] *Rif.* 8, p. 542, 25 June 1383. This was during the emergency caused by the plague of 1383.

[20] *Rif.* 8, p. 591, 29 Aug. 1383.

frequent complaints from Lucchese subjects.[21] Efforts were made to reduce the expenses of defence by building walls and ditches around Lucca so that fewer defenders would be needed, and by reducing the wages of the *cerne*.[22] But Lucca continued to look to the *contado* for extra defenders in time of need, summoning them either from the *cerne* or from some particular district of the *contado*.[23]

The defence of fortresses in the *contado* was a special case giving rise to separate problems. The fortresses were necessary for the guard of frontiers, roads, and important points in the *contado*, and in times of danger *contadini* could seek refuge in them. New fortification works were sometimes undertaken. Camaiore petitioned for walls and a *rocca* to be built, and this was done at great expense over the next few years.[24] The walls of the *burgi* of Lucca were also rebuilt.[25] But elsewhere fortresses were sometimes destroyed because the expense of guarding them was too great,[26] or alterations were made to them so that fewer guards would be necessary.[27] Keeping

[21] *Rif.* 1, p. 301, 9 Apr. 1370, *Rif.* 9, p. 297, 19 Feb. 1385.

[22] *Rif.* 9, p. 297, 19 Feb., p. 360, 7 June 1385.

[23] *Rif.* 9, p. 191, 1 Oct. 1384, p. 351, 18 May 1385, *Min.* 3, (not foliated), 24 Aug., 2 Dec. 1386, 29 Apr. 1387, *Min.* 4 (not foliated), 18 Nov. 1391, *Rif.* 12, p. 46, 5 Feb., p. 178, 26 Aug. 1392, *Rif.* 13, p. 340, 24 June 1400.

[24] *Rif.* 4, pp. 349–50, 11 Mar. 1374, *Delib.* 132, ff. 42–42^{v}, 6 Apr., f. 43, 23 Apr. 1374, *Rif.* 4, p. 408, 18 June, pp. 519–20, 7 Dec. 1374, *Rif.* 5, p. 115, 17 Oct. 1375. At one point the authorities seem almost to have despaired of ever seeing the work completed. A loose folio in *Delib.* 132, dated 26 Sept. 1375 provides 'quod Camaiore et burghum Camaioris nullo modo muretur totaliter quia esset impossibile et numquam posset compleri propter lapides qui ibi non sunt et propter intollerabile onus quod esset tote vicarie et quia postea ibi non essent homines ad custodiam ipsius', but this whole passage is marked 'vacat'. Lucca lent Camaiore 500 florins for the wall, later converting it from a loan into an outright gift, *Rif.* 7, p. 94, 23 May 1379, p. 233, 5 Mar. 1380, p. 521, 8 July 1381. The walls were finished by 21 Nov. 1381, *Rif.* 7, pp. 616–17. Fortifications elsewhere, *Rif.* 5, p. 69, 9 May 1375 (Capannori), p. 196, 25 Jan. 1376 (S. Gennaro), *Rif.* 6, p. 8, 9 July 1376, (Pedona), *Rif.* 7, p. 382, 31 Dec. 1380 (Ruota), pp. 639–40, 7 Dec. 1381 (Sasso).

[25] *Rif.* 5, pp. 194–5, 24 Jan., pp. 229–30, 21 Feb. 1376, *Rif.* 6, pp. 334, 336, 17 Aug. 1377, *Rif.* 8, p. 443, 7 Feb. 1383, *Rif.* 9, p. 113, 24 May 1384, p. 297, 19 Feb. 1385, *Rif.* 10, p. 37, 26 Feb. 1386, pp. 420–1, 4 Feb., p. 529, 30 Aug. 1388, *Rif.* 11, p. 59, 5 Mar. 1389, *Min.* 4 (not foliated), 6 May, 9 Sept., 18 Nov. 1390, 7 Apr., 21 July 1391.

[26] *Rif.* 1, p. 474, 23 July 1370 (Gallicano), p. 477, 24 Aug. 1370 (Treppignana), *Rif.* 4, p. 447, 9 Aug. 1374 (Pugliano), *Rif.* 8, p. 587, 26 Aug., p. 618, 12 Oct., p. 624, 25 Oct., p. 674, 18 Dec. 1383 (Sasso). Destruction of useless fortresses in general proposed *Min.* 2, f. 30, 22 May 1371.

[27] *Rif.* 4, pp. 225–6, 29 Aug. 1373 (Dallo), p. 425, 6 July 1374 (Verrucchio).

fortresses in good repair, particularly in times of comparative peace, presented a problem. There were officials whose duty it was to oversee this, but it was frequently found that fortresses were being allowed to fall into disrepair or that they lacked arms and other essential supplies.[28] Lucca felt that the *contado* should contribute to the cost of repairing fortresses, and in August 1377 decreed that all communes that had fortresses and all vicariates should pay something towards this.[29] But in some cases the obligations of particular communes were governed by local custom, and disputes arose over whether Lucca or the local communes should bear the cost.[30]

Apart from the cost of repairs, the guard of fortresses was a heavy burden. Important fortresses were usually kept by Lucchese citizens or by hired castellans, who had to give sureties and were paid a salary. A salary of perhaps as much as 12 florins a month to the castellan with payments also to each of the guards was a great expense, and in the interests of economy Lucca occasionally agreed to entrust the guard of even quite important fortresses to local men,[31] as was often done with those of less importance. In that case she might pay a subsidy to the local community; she paid 1 florin a month to the men of Schiappa,[32] and 2 florins a month for six months to Castelnuovo and later 24–30 florins a year.[33] But entrusting the guard of fortresses to local men was not always satisfactory from a security point of view. At S. Gennaro, which was on the border, guard was being neglected,[34] and at Castelnuovo, another key fortress, the inhabitants were merchants, coming

[28] *Rif.* 1, pp. 17–18, 27 July, p. 87, 11 Sept. 1369, p. 195, 4 Jan. 1370, *Delib.* 132, ff. 52–52v, 27 Oct. 1371, *Rif.* 5, p. 86, 24 June 1375, p. 299, 9 Apr. 1376, *Rif.* 6, p. 20, 25 July , pp. 92–3, 18 Nov. 1376, *Rif.* 7, p. 407, 23 Jan. 1381.

[29] *Rif.* 6, p. 334, 17 Aug. 1377. Also *Delib.* 132, ff. 58v–59, 30 Nov. 1371, concerning the fortresses of the vicariate of Castiglione.

[30] *Rif.* 7, p. 32, 16 Feb. 1379, *Rif.* 9, p. 331, 17 Apr. 1385, *Delib.* 132, ff. 58v–59, 30 Nov. 1371 concerning the obligations of the exempt and the non-exempt communes of the vicariate of Castiglione.

[31] *Rif.* 1, p. 317, 22 Apr., p. 353, 11 May 1370. *Delib.* 132, ff. 128v–130, 25 Sept. 1375 there were reductions in the number of sergeants in various castles as part of a general attempt to reduce expenditure and S. Quirico and Schiappa were handed over to local men.

[32] *Rif.* 5, p. 110, 11 Oct. 1375.

[33] *Rif.* 5, p. 109, 6 Oct. 1375, *Rif.* 12, p. 425, 10 Mar. 1394.

[34] *Rif.* 10, p. 17, 5 Jan. 1386.

in day and night, so that the castle was said to be ill-guarded, and might easily be surprised by enemies.[35] Often guard duty had to be taken out of the hands of local men once more and entrusted to a *podestà* or captain, who was a Lucchese citizen.[36] But local inhabitants were frequently called on to pay all or part of the cost of castle guard. The men of Montefegatesi had to pay 10 florins in six months,[37] and the vicariate of Coreglia had to pay 216 florins, later reduced to 180, for the guard of Coreglia, Tereglio, and Ghivizzano.[38]

Probably nothing caused greater resentment in the *contado* than the duties of castle guard or the obligation to pay subsidies for fortresses. Petitions for relief were frequent,[39] and were often expressed in strong terms. The men of Montefegatesi felt themselves to be 'enormiter aggravatos' by the subsidy of 20 florins a year they had to pay for the fortress.[40] The men of Castiglione complained that it was impossible for them to guard Verrucchio and they were not going to do so, though they only disobeyed because they were 'impotenti'.[41] The burden was indeed sometimes heavy, as in the case of Schiappa, which had only seven men, and yet had to pay 1 florin a month as subsidy and keep a man in the fortress each night.[42] In the face of the flood of petitions Lucca often had to grant relief and bear the expense herself.

But a very much greater expense was the maintenance of hired soldiers. Despite her limited resources Lucca kept a permanent force of mercenaries even in peace time and these were a vital element in her defence system. The number of

[35] *Rif.* 9, p. 285, 12 Jan. 1385.

[36] *Rif.* 5, p. 117, 4 Jan. 1376, *Rif.* 6, p. 72, 26 Sept., p. 96, 21 Nov. 1376, pp. 226–7, 16 Mar. 1377.

[37] *Rif.* 5, p. 110, 8 Oct. 1375.

[38] *Rif.* 5, p. 110, 6 Oct. 1375, *Rif.* 6, p. 82, 15 Oct. 1376, p. 319, 3 Aug. 1377, *Rif.* 7, p. 150, 26 Sept. 1379.

[39] Examples, *Rif.* 4, p. 172, 13 June, p. 220, 9 Aug. 1373, *Rif.* 6, p. 321, 3 Aug. 1377, *Rif.* 7, pp. 39–40, 30 Aug.; pp. 150–1, 26 Sept. 1379, pp. 548–9, 21 Aug. 1381, *Rif.* 9, p. 457, 29 Dec. 1385.

[40] *Rif.* 7, p. 439, 9 Jan. 1380. They offered to keep the castle themselves if subsidized by Lucca. Also *Rif.* 11, pp. 255–6, 28 Mar. 1390, *Rif.* 13, p. 16, 7 Feb. 1397.

[41] They petitioned 'quod eis erat impossibile custodire terram nostram Verrucchii Garfagnane nec ipsius terre custodie intendere posse sed potius propter impotentiam inobedientes existere', *Delib.* 132, ff. 95^{v}–96, 13 Aug. 1375.

[42] *Rif.* 6, pp. 568–9, 14 May 1378.

hired forces she kept at any one time varied considerably. In January 1377, when trying to economize, she reduced the number she kept to 60 'pagas' of cavalry, 150 *pavesarii* and 50 crossbowmen,[43] but a year later it was stated that the minimum number necessary was 80 'barbutas' and 20 Hungarians with 200 pavesarii and 200 crossbowmen.[44] In emergencies Lucca hired more than the usual number,[45] and in the last few years of the century, when involved in war with Pisa, she had 50 lances of cavalry and 35 'bannerias' of infantry in 1397 and 44 'bannerias' in 1400.[46] At 18 florins per month for each lance 50 lances would cost 900 florins a month or 10,800 florins a year. Two hundred crossbowmen at 4 florins a month each cost 9,200 florins a year and 200 *pavesarii* at three florins a month 7,200 florins a year.

The cost of hired soldiers was certainly the largest single item in Lucchese expenditure. In 1377, when the total recorded expenditure by the *camarlingo generale* was 65,571 florins, Lucca spent 21,311 florins, nearly a third of the total, on mercenaries alone, quite apart from other sums for castellans, arms, and other defence costs.[47] In the period January–June 1376, out of 34,107 florins spent, 10,026 was spent on mercenaries.[48] The cost of the mercenaries Lucca had in 1400 must have been at least 23,000 florins, though there are no figures for the total revenues in this year. But the *Mandatorie* show that expenditure on defence in 1397 was much greater than this. 39,947 florins £2. 16*s*. *picc*. was spent on mercenaries and a further 11,107 florins £1. 7*s*. on

[43] *Rif.* 3, pp. 492–3, 20 Jan. 1373. For the increasing use of mercenaries in Italian cities generally, Bayley, *War and Society in Renaissance Florence*, pp. 5–58, Mallett, *Mercenaries and their Masters*, pp. 13–57.

[44] *Rif.* 4, p. 329, 15 Feb. 1374. *Rif.* 6, p. 313, 29 July 1377, 20 'bannerias' of infantry, 12 of them crossbowmen and 8 *pavesarii*.

[45] *Rif.* 5, p. 135, 7 Dec. 1375 she hired another 50 crossbowmen for four months.

[46] *Rif.* 13, p. 35, 4 May 1397, p. 323, 26 Apr. 1400.

[47] According to *Ragionieri della camera e del comune*, no. 13, the total expenditure on defence was 29,342 florins £1. 8*s*. 11*d*. *picc*. (Various foliations; *esito* for first semester ff. 6–95, second semester ff. 33–143.) But *Camarlingo Generale*, no. 103, *Mandatorie* shows the total expenditure authorized by the Anziani for defence was 35,862 florins £3. 18*s*. 9*d*. *picc*.

[48] Series *Ragionieri della camera e del comune*, no. 12, ff. 9–76. In 1370 when recorded expenditure was about 60,000 florins, mercenaries, castellans etc. cost 18,588. But this was a time of confusion in the Lucchese finances and probably neither figure is complete. *Camarlingo Generale*, no. 80.

castellans and other defence costs, a total of 51,054 florins £4. 3*s. picc.*[49] Unless the revenues were very much higher than they had been in the 1370s, a far higher proportion than a third, as earlier, must have been spent on defence. But the last few years of the century were probably quite exceptional. The figures that Sercambi gives for the year 1423, a time of peace, show that expenditure on defence could be very much lower. He gives the total expenditure as 4,623 florins a month or 55,476 a year, of which 1,012 florins a month, or 12,144 a year, was spent on hired soldiers.[50]

Though expenditure of rather under a third of the annual revenue, except for the last years of the century, compared favourably with the military expenditure of other cities, such as Florence, Lucca tried to reduce these expenses. One way of obtaining semi-professional soldiers at small cost was to pardon *banniti* in return for military service to the commune. *Banniti* would be pardoned fines, though not more serious penalties, if they served Lucca for six or eight months either without pay or at a very small salary.[51] *Contadini* also might be hired as mercenaries at low rates of pay,[52] but Lucca continued to need hired professional soldiers as well, and their pay remained her largest single item of expenditure. There was also the possibility of calling upon her allies for military aid in time of need,[53] and Lucca did on occasions do so,[54] but she

[49] *Camarlingo Generale*, no. 110, *Mandatorie*, castellans, ff. 195–252, cavalry, ff. 260–304, infantry, ff. 308–351^{v}, 355–359^{v}, 364–387. Expenditure on defence had been heavy in the first half of the fourteenth century; in the period Nov. 1335 to Apr. 1336, when a total of £113, 532. 17*s. picc.* was spent, £71,566. 2*s.* 4*d. picc.* was spent on mercenaries, Bongi, *Inv.* II, pp. 21–9.

[50] Sercambi, III, pp. 350–9. For very high figures of Florentine military expenditure in the late fourteenth and early fifteenth centuries, Becker, *Florence in Transition*, Vol. II, pp. 160–1, 165, 190, Molho, *Florentine Public Finances*, pp. 3–4, 9–11, 15. But expenditure varied enormously according to whether it was a time of peace of war. For some Pisan figures, Silva, *Governo*, p. 108.

[51] *Rif.* 7, pp. 246–7, 20 Apr. 1380, *Rif.* 8, pp. 590–1, 28 Aug., pp. 682–3, 26 Dec. 1383.

[52] For example two lances from the *contado* were hired at twelve florins a lance, *Rif.* 6, p. 6, 6 July 1376.

[53] It is doubtful whether Lucca's own defences against a determined attack were ever very effective. In 1373 when threatened by the company of Conrad Wettingher, Lucca wrote that she could defend herself for a short period, but if the company stayed long in her territory her liberty would be in danger, *Reg.*, no. 386, 15 Dec. 1373.

[54] For example March to May 1370, *Rif.* 2, p. 148, 22 Nov. 1370. Aid from

did not rely on this for her ordinary defence to any serious extent. She found that allied forces could do as much damage in her territory as those of the enemy, and in later years she was cautious about calling them in,[55] though glad to have the possibility of doing so as a last resort in time of real danger.

These problems of defence deeply influenced the general lines of Lucchese foreign policy, though as a small state with limited resources she rarely had much scope for the exercise of initiative in her relations with other powers. Her vulnerable position meant that she needed to be on good terms with as many of her neighbours as possible to prevent threats to her liberty, and to ensure that if her state were endangered she had allies upon whom she could call. The limited nature of her resources, however, made her reluctant to enter leagues that involved potentially heavy financial commitments. She can therefore be seen in the 1370s and 1380s pursuing the deliberately negative, cautious, inglorious foreign policy which she herself described as 'nostra flexabilitas et tractabilitas cum vicinis' to such good effect that she was able to avoid isolation, enter leagues with her neighbours on very favourable terms and emerge unscathed even from embarassing and potentially dangerous situations where circumstances compelled her to choose between two neighbours or allies.

Florence, Pistoia, the Papacy and the Count of Savoy, *Rif.* 4, p. 108, 23 Apr., p. 149, 30 May 1373, pp. 487–8, 31 Oct. 1374.

[55] Complaints 'quod tam a gentibus amicorum quam inimicorum territorium leditur' in the negotiations for the league of 1380, *Capitoli*, 32, p. 40, *Min.* 2, ff. 389–90v. Also instructions to ambassadors going to Pavia May 1389, *Reg.*, no. 1397.

6

1369–1375

LUCCA took her place as an independent state at a difficult time. The years 1370–5 were a confused period of shifting alliances with Florence resisting Visconti attempts to intervene in Tuscany, and with papal policy towards Milan a further factor leading to local disturbances and wars. In the first few years after 1369 Lucca's relations with Bernabò Visconti, lord of Milan, were her main problem in foreign affairs. In May 1369 he had obtained possession of Sarzana with the assistance of Alderigo degli Antelminelli, whom he then made his *visconte* there.[1] Lucca thus lost a piece of territory which she regarded as rightly hers, and found herself with a powerful neighbour whose *visconte* was a member of the family of Castruccio Castracani and an enemy of the city. But Bernabò's ambitions went far beyond the acquisition of a few towns and villages on the borders of Lucchese territory. He hoped to control the entire state and perhaps Pisa and Sanminiato as well by obtaining an imperial vicariate over them from Charles IV.[2] Despite strenuous efforts to induce him to make this grant, the Emperor eventually made other arrangements for the city, appointing his kinsman, Guy of Boulogne, Cardinal Bishop of Porto, imperial vicar for three years,[3] but

[1] Sercambi, I, p. 168. *Cronica di Pisa di Ranieri Sardo*, ed. O. Banti, (Rome, 1963), pp. 188–9. Tommasi, pp. 235–6. In June 1369 Charles IV made Bernabò imperial vicar in Sarzana.

[2] It was rumoured that the Emperor would be willing to grant this, *La Cronica Domestica di messer Donato Velluti*, ed. I. del Lungo and G. Volpe (Florence, 1914), pp. 269, 276–7. Bernabò claimed in a letter to Urban V dated 16 May 1370 that he had in fact obtained it. G. Pirchan, *Italien und Kaiser Karl IV* (Prague, 1930), Vol. II, p. 225, Doc. No. 138. Fondazione Treccani degli Alfieri, *Storia di Milano*, Vol. V (Milan, 1955), pp. 457–8.

[3] First revoking any previous vicariate, with express mention of Bernabò Visconti, A. Theiner, *Codex Diplomaticus Dominii Temporalis Sancti Sedis*, Vol. II (Rome, 1861), nos. 452, 453, 13 June 1369. The Emperor also undertook that no one whom the Pope regarded as an enemy of the Church should be appointed in future, and Bernabò made offers of money and men in the hope of obtaining papal consent to his appointment as imperial vicar, Donato Velluti, pp. 280–1, Fondazione Treccani degli

later the same year Bernabò saw another opportunity of acquiring Lucca, when in August the cardinal asked for aid against the Florentines, who were besieging Sanminiato. Part of the force of 1,500 men at arms that he sent in response to this request went to Lucca where they attempted a *coup de main* against the city.[4] This initial attempt was unsuccessful, but the Visconti forces, which included Alderigo and Orlando degli Antelminelli, remained in and around Lucca awaiting their opportunity to try again, and they were joined by many enemies of the existing regime. According to Sercambi many Lucchese appealed to the Pope over the head of the cardinal, and the Pope instructed him not to rely on Milanese aid.[5]

But the danger remained acute, and on the night of 20 August the Visconti forces made another attempt to gain control of the city, which came very near to being successful. Some of the Lucchese rose to defend their city, but many were confused and apathetic, seeing the Visconti attempt as a chance to be rid of the irksome authority of the imperial vicar. After a night of confused fighting the *coup* failed more because of the lack of co-operation between Gianotto Visconti and Alderigo degli Antelminelli, who made a bid for the *signorìa* of Lucca on his own account, than because of any defence measures taken by the Lucchese.[6] The next day Alderigo made a further attempt to win the city for himself, but met with no support from the Visconti forces and was arrested and imprisoned. The Lombards were thrown into confusion and retired to the suburbs, pillaging and burning as they went.[7] With the failure of the Visconti attempt against Lucca the acute danger was over, though Bernabò himself was at Sarzana with 2,000 men at arms in December and the Visconti forces retiring from Sanminiato passed through

---

Alfieri, *Storia di Milano*, Vol. V, pp. 458–60. The Lucchese did everything they could to prevent any outsider being appointed imperial vicar of Lucca, *Reg.*, no. 1989, letter of the Cardinal Bishop of Porto to the Pope, 15 Sept. 1369.

[4] Sercambi, I, pp. 175–6. Sozomeno Pistoriensis, R.I.S. Tom. XVI, col. 1089.

[5] Sercambi, I, pp. 176–7. Donato Velluti, p. 283.

[6] Sercambi saw the situation as extremely dangerous, 'avendo le genti lombarde preso la piazza & i ciptadini sbarratosi, di vero, se Alderigo avesse voluto esser a una colle genti lumbarde di Milano a pititione di messer Bernabò, Lucca era a gravi pericolo, e a certo sere' venuto facto che sere' stata di messer Bernabò', I, pp. 176–181.

[7] Sercambi, I, pp. 181–3. Donato Velluti, pp. 284–5.

Lucchese territory on their way back to Sarzana.[8]

In view of the hostile intentions Bernabò had shown towards her it is not surprising that Lucca was among the members of the anti-Visconti leagues of 31 October 1369[9] and 25 March 1370. Silva pointed out that there were two versions of this second league with very similar preambles, but the first version dated 25 March stated that it was directed against aggressors 'praesertim domini Bernabovis de Vicecomittibus, non obstante quocumque vicariatu quem se habere pretendat', while the second, dated 3 April, does not mention Bernabò by name, though it does contain the reference to an alleged imperial vicariate.[10] Pisa accepted only the second form, but the Lucchese apparently found no difficulty in accepting the first, despite the fact that it was more openly directed against Bernabò. Perhaps they were aware that greater caution would have been pointless, for in 1370 Bernabò made further attempts to gain direct control of Lucca and other parts of Tuscany. In May 1370 he arranged a *condotta* for four months with Giovanni dell'Agnello, the ex-doge of Pisa and Lucca, which contained provisions for the re-conquest of Lucca as well as Pisa.[11] Further evidence of Bernabò's hostile intentions towards Lucca in these months is provided by a letter of the Pisans to Gregory XI, in which they related that an ambassador had come from Milan offering to assist them if they wanted to recover Lucca 'et in casu quod ad

[8] Sardo, pp. 196–9. Silva, *Governo*, pp. 57–8. 4 Jan. 1370 eight florins and eighteen soldi were paid for two messengers sent to Pontremoli 'ad scienda nova de domino Bernabove', *Rif.* 1, p. 196.

[9] The Lucchese did not have full control of their affairs at this date, as they were still under the authority of the cardinal.

[10] Silva, *Governo*, pp. 60–2. *Capitoli* 24 contains copies of both versions, pp. 187–99, 207–18. Lucca was a junior partner in this league, as, while Florence and the Papacy undertook not to make peace without each other's consent, they were bound only to see that Lucca was included and her interests safeguarded, but not to obtain her consent. She was also exempt from the obligation to provide any fixed number of forces for the league and from certain expenses.

[11] If Giovanni dell'Agnello captured Pisa he was to pay half the costs of the army and help in every way 'donec dominus obtinuerit civitatem Luce seu concordiam fecerit cum Luchanis'. This *condotta* is quoted in F. Landogna, 'La politica dei Visconti in Toscana', *Bollettino della Società Pavese di Storia Patria*, Vol. XXVIII (1928), pp. 80–3, Silva, *Governo* pp. 62–4. The original is in the Archivio di Stato di Pisa, series *Diplomi Roncioni*, dated 11 May 1370 (Pisan style 1371). See also Landogna, 'Le relazioni tra Bernabò Visconti e Pisa nella seconda metà del secolo XIV', *Archivio Storico Lombardo*, Vol. L (1923), pp. 136–43.

recuperationem non vellemus intendere antedictam, ipse ad illam intenderat pretendens se illius civitatis constitutum vicarium a Caesarea maiestate'.[12] In the event Giovanni dell'Agnello and his followers concentrated their efforts against Pisa and did not prove a serious danger to Lucca, though they did a certain amount of damage in her territory.[13] A more serious threat came from the Antelminelli, who invaded the Lucchese state with Milanese support in May. Parts of the Garfagnana, including the important centres of Castiglione, Castelnuovo, and the fortress of Sasso, surrendered to them, and at one point much of the vicariate of Camporgiano was in rebellion. In this crisis Lucca appealed to Florence for aid, and the Florentines assisted her both in the Garfagnana and in the defence of the passes on the road down the Versiliese coast from Lunigiana.[14] She sent aid again in 1371; when Gallicano rebelled and surrendered to Alderigo it was quickly recovered with the aid of 'alquanti Barghigiani li quali ci concedeo il comune di Firenza'.[15] Terms were finally made with Alderigo in 1371, under which he was paid 12,000 florins for the restitution of the castles he held in the Garfagnana and the Antelminelli had their property restored, though they were not allowed to return to Lucca.[16]

[12] The letter is undated, but comes between letters dated 20 and 26 July 1371 (Pisan style), A. S. P. *Comune A. 79*, f. 164ᵛ, quoted in Silva, *Governo*, Appendix, Doc. I pp. 295–6.

[13] They forced the defences Lucca had set up at Motrone and Pietrasanta, 'uccidendo assai Lucchesi, e presono prigioni assai', Sardo p. 200. Soz. Pist. col. 1089. *Delib.* 131, f. 6, 21 Apr. 1370.

[14] *Rif.* 1, pp. 348–9, 10 May 1370. Sercambi, I, p. 103, Sardo, p. 192. Lucca's policy was a combination of armed resistance and negotiation, *Delib.* 131, ff. 19ᵛ–20, 8 May, ff. 22–22ᵛ, 22 May, f. 23ᵛ, 24 May, f. 24, 26 May, ff. 26ᵛ–27, 3 June 1370. *Reg.*, no. 19, 24 May 1370. Florentine aid, Sercambi, I, pp. 203–4, *Rif.* 2, p. 148, 22 Nov. 1370, A. S. F. *Consulte*, 11, ff. 18–19, 1 May, ff. 23–23ᵛ, 6 May, f. 50ᵛ, 24 June, f. 65, 23 July 1370. Niccolò d'Este also sent aid, *Reg.*, no. 19. A truce was negotiated with Bernabò Visconti 11 Nov. 1370, Soz. Pist. col. 1091, *Rif.* 2, pp. 110–11, 29 Oct., p. 115, 31 Oct. 1370, and with Alderigo Antelminelli 4 Dec., *Rif.* 2, p. 153, 23 Nov., p. 159, 5 Dec. 1370.

[15] Sercambi, I, p. 205.

[16] *Rif.* 2, pp. 217–19, 2 Mar. pp. 231–3, 16 Mar., p. 256, 21 Apr., pp. 259–60, 22 Apr. 1371. *Min.* 2, f. 17, 28 Apr. 1371. *Reg.* nos. 30, 33, 35, 42, 52. There is a copy of the agreement in *Capitoli*, 24, pp. 245–58. The treaty does not seem to have produced lasting peace immediately. In May the Anziani complained that the Antelminelli 'come seme della pianta che sempre a pericolata la nostra terra s'atentano cose contro la pace', *Delib.* 132, f. 5, 23 May 1371. Also *Reg.* no. 43, 23 May 1371. In June there was further fighting over the castle of Tereglio, which the Antelminelli had occupied,

The league against the Visconti and other aggressors was renewed in October 1371. The *Minute di Riformagioni* contain one of the rare fuller accounts of the council meeting where the renewal was discussed, and it is therefore possible to get a more detailed and intimate picture of the view the Lucchese took of certain important questions of foreign policy at this time.[17] Firstly she was opposed, as were Siena and Pisa, to the attempts of Florence to exclude the Papacy from the league. She did not share Florentine hostility to papal expansion and had a strong sense of gratitude to the Papacy for assistance and support in the recovery of her independence.[18] Lucca's other main concern in the negotiations was to avoid committing herself to the maintenance of a fixed number of men in the service of the league. The instructions to the Lucchese ambassadors show concern above all that Lucca's obligations in the new league should not be any greater than they had been in the old.[19] The reasons for this reluctance were, of course, financial. The short-term loans Lucca had contracted with Florence, Niccolò d'Este and others were now falling due, and she was quite unable to pay them without sharp increases in taxation and further loans.[20] She was, therefore, extremely reluctant to undertake further obligations, though she did not wish to be left out of a league which included the other Tuscan cities and which would afford her protection against any further attacks by the Visconti or by armed companies such as that of Lutz of Landau, to which she had recently been obliged to pay money

---

Delib. 132, ff. 9ᵛ-10, 14 and 17 June 1371, *Rif.* 2, p. 314, 15 June, p. 326, 27 June 1371. An ambassador had been appointed to approve peace with Alderigo as early as 19 May, but the ratification was still under discussion in June, *Rif.* 2, p. 282, and *Min.* 2, f. 25, 19 May, f. 36ᵛ, 8 June, f. 65ᵛ, 14 July 1371. The Anziani ratified the agreements concerning Tereglio, *Rif.* 2, p. 345, 14 July 1371.

[17] *Min.* 2, ff. 78-78ᵛ, 16 July 1371.

[18] Soz. Pist. col. 1091, the meeting of the Tuscan communes was 'ut Ecclesia non extenderet vires suas in Tuscia'. L. Mirot, *La Politique pontificale et le retour du Saint-Siège à Rome en 1376* (Paris, 1899), p. 28. Silva, *Governo*, pp. 169-70. The Papacy made some efforts to influence the Lucchese, *Delib.* 132, f. 14ᵛ, 22 June 1371, *Rif.* 3, p. 11, 5 Aug. 1371.

[19] *Min.* 2, ff. 78-78ᵛ, 16 July 1371. *Reg.*, no. 51, instructions to the ambassadors going to Florence in August.

[20] She was in fact considering asking the Pope to lend her the money to pay Florence, as she had not been able to raise it any other way, counsel of Jacobo Rapondi, *Min.* 2, f. 178ᵛ, 16 July 1371.

she could ill afford.[21] Lucca's insistence on these limitations was one of the reasons for the protracted discussions in Florence, but she was finally successful. Though a *taglia* was laid down for the other states and Pisa had to maintain 200 lances and 400 infantry, and even little Arezzo had to keep 56 lances and 112 infantry, Lucca need only provide 'illam quantitatem gentis armigere equestris et pedestris quam poterit bona fide', and she was also exempted from the provision that any extra expenses should be borne by the member within whose territory they had been incured.[22]

Lucca had joined the anti-Visconti league, but she took no very active part in the war. The main theatre of war was Lombardy rather than Tuscany and there was never any question of Lucca contributing forces for use there. In fact these years during which Lucca was a member of a league fighting a war against Bernabò Visconti were to see a marked improvement in her relations with Milan, so that by 1374, and perhaps even earlier, they had become cordial. At the same time there was a deterioration in her relations with Florence and to a less extent the Papacy. The improvement in her relations with Bernabò seems to have begun very shortly after the conclusion of the league. There is a letter from Ambrogio Visconti as early as November 1371, reproving certain nobles for having made attacks on the Lucchese and threatening to inform his father.[23] In 1372 the Lucchese seem to have been attempting to avoid giving offence to Milan, even at the cost of giving their allies grounds for complaint. They appear to have undertaken not to grant passage or supplies to the forces of the

[21] *Rif.* 2, p. 213, 22 Feb. 1371. Agreements in *Capitoli*, 31, p. 395, 31 Mar. and p. 401, 4 Apr. 1371. Lucca had to borrow this money from a private citizen, *Rif.* 3, p. 70, 6 Oct. 1371.

[22] 'Quod comune Lucanum ad dictas expensas teneatur solum et dumtaxat iuxta eorum potentiam secundum bonam intentionem et fidem', copies of the league, *Capitoli*, 24, pp. 265–81, and 31, pp. 449–72. Lucca ratified it 30 Oct. 1371, *Rif.* 3, pp. 91–2. The negotiations were very long drawn out, as the league was not finally concluded until 24 October, though the ambassadors had first met in July. Some of the concessions to Lucca were the result of hard bargaining, and there were limitations on the allies' obligations towards her, Silva, *Governo*, p. 170.

[23] Letter to Lucchese that his father's intention was 'quod amici ipsius et adherentes habeant pacem cum habentibus pacem cum ipso', *Anz. Temp. Lib.* 529, f. 12^v, 14 Nov. 1371. This is no. 70 in *Reg.* Letter from the Lucchese Anziani to Ambrogio Visconti on the same subject, *Anz. Temp. Lib.* 529, f. 15, 12 Dec. 1371.

Church, despite their membership of the league,[24] and as early as June 1373 they regarded acts of violence against their subjects by men at arms in Visconti pay as a cause for complaint and demand for redress, rather than as natural and inevitable signs of Visconti hostility. They were apparently in a position to ask for redress, with every expectation of getting it, and to recall their past acts of friendship to the Visconti. Their relations with Bernabò were such that they could threaten to appeal to him personally, if his officials failed to give them satisfaction.[25] When in December 1373 the company of Conrad Wettingher, which was said to be on its way to Lombardy to take service with Galeazzo Visconti, invaded Lucchese territory, they complained to him, but they added 'nec putamus hec de intentione vestre celsitudinis aut placito processisse, cum numquam cogitaverimus nec cogitamus aliquid in detrimentum vestre dominationis vel dedecus attemptare', ending with a request for suitable compensation 'celeriter sicut honori potentie vestre congruit'.[26] While Wettingher and his company were still on Lucchese territory, Bernabò sent an embassy to Lucca. The exact purpose of this embassy is unknown, but it was probably connected with the improvement of Visconti relations with Lucca.[27] Certainly by

[24] On several occasions they denied knowledge of forces passing through their territory or claimed they had been too weak to prevent it, *Reg.* nos. 67, 89, 144, 151, 152, 155. They excused themselves, however, when asked to grant the Visconti supplies, no. 159.

[25] *Delib.* 132, f. 120^{v}, 19 June 1373, instructions to ser Taddeo Malpigli, ambassador to messer Ranalduccio, Bernabò's captain in Lunigiana. He was to say that the Lucchese were sure that neither Bernabò nor his captain had known anything of this, and remind him that Lucca had recalled her subjects who were in the service of the Church in Lunigiana and done other favours, threatening to appeal to Bernabò himself if his captain failed to give them satisfaction.

[26] *Anz. Temp. Lib.* 529, f. 131, 30 Dec. 1373. This is no. 394 in *Reg.* Printed in full in L. Zerbi, *I Visconti di Milano e la signoria di Lucca* (Como, 1894), pp. 26–7 and in Landogna, 'La politica dei Visconti in Toscana', Appendix, Doc. II, pp. 118–19.

[27] The Lucchese Anziani wrote 8 Jan. 1374 'que vive vocis oraculo dominus Ranalduccius orator vester ex parte vestre magnitudinis nos explicuit intelleximus, sibique intentionis nostre responsum dedimus super materia quam narravit', *Anz. Temp. Lib.* 529, f. 132^{v}, *Reg.*, no. 398. Landogna, 'La politica dei Visconti in Toscana', p. 91. Zerbi regarded this embassy as an important turning point in Lucca's relations with Milan, suspicion and veiled hostility being replaced by friendship, with the Lucchese appealing to Bernabò for protection. This change did take place, but it can be traced back beyond January 1374. Lucca was already on friendly terms with the Visconti in 1373 and was trying to avoid giving them offence in 1372. The

1374 Lucca's relations with Bernabò seem to have been cordial and she had perhaps made some formal peace with him.[28]

Bernabò was quickly able to make the Lucchese feel the practical value of his friendship. When they invoked his aid against the nobles of Gomola, Fogliano, and Rolandino da Teano, who were molesting Lucchese subjects within the Lucchese state, his reply was all they could wish. He made it clear that such attacks were 'totaliter contra mentem et intentionem nostram, quia non intendimus quod per gentes subditos nec adherentes nostros comuni lucano nec aliquibus hominibus et subditis suis fiat aliqua iniuria vel offensa.' He wished the Lucchese to be treated 'tamquam amici nostri humane et favorabiliter', and they should be compensated and those responsible for the attacks punished 'quemadmodum ipsa fecissent contra subditos nostros'.[29] Bernabò made no secret of this understanding with the Lucchese, addressing them as 'amici karissimi' and ordering that they should be treated as his friends, at least 'dummodo non faciant contra statum et honorem nostrum'.[30] Thus long before a general truce was made between the league and Bernabò on 4 June 1375, the Lucchese were on excellent terms with him. They enjoyed his protection and continued to address him in the next few years as 'spes certissima nostri presidii'[31] and 'protector . . . confidentissime noster . . . magnificentiam

improvement in relations can perhaps be traced back even further, but there were also expressions of hostility; Bernabò Visconti was referred to as 'tiranno perfido' and believed to have raised the castle of Minucciano in rebellion, *Rif.* 2, p. 56, 27 Aug. 1370. As late as 25 Feb. 1373, reporting to the Pope the arrival of Ambrogio Visconti at Pontremoli with a small force, the Lucchese referred to it as 'pro adiutorio viperei Bernabonis', *Anz. Temp. Lib.* 529, f. 65, 25 Feb. 1373. *Reg.*, no. 183.

[28] *Anz. Temp. Lib.* 529, ff. 142v–143, 23 Apr. 1374, Reg. no. 429, the Lucchese wrote to Guido Savino of Fogliano to complain of attacks on her territory, and threatened to appeal to Bernabò 'cum quo pacis federa obtinemus'. Similar letter 13 May 1374 to the Podestà and Captain of Reggio, *Anz. Temp. Lib.* 529, ff. 143v–144, *Reg.*, no. 433

[29] *Anz. Temp. Lib.* 530, ff. 2v–3, *Reg.*, no. 445, letters to the Lucchese Anziani and to the Savini. Printed in full in Zerbi, *I Visconti di Milano*, pp. 28–9 and Landogna, 'La politica dei Visconti in Toscana', Appendix, Docs. III and IV, pp. 119–20. Similar letter to the officials of Reggio, *Anz. Temp. Lib.* 530, f. 2v, 24 July 1374.

[30] *Anz. Temp. Lib.* 530, f. 2v, 24 July 1374. Landogna, 'La politica dei Visconti in Toscana', Appendix, Doc. IV., pp. 119–20.

[31] *Anz. Temp. Lib.* 530, f. 76, 18 Dec. 1376. *Reg.*, no. 599. Printed in full in Landogna, 'La politica dei Visconti in Toscana', Appendix, Doc. VII, p. 122.

vestram in qua spes omnia nostra viget et quam singularissiman affectionem vocemur' and to express their gratitude 'quoniam firmiter ex beneficiis que a Magnificentia Vestra nobis concessa sunt et in defensionem invenimus hanc civitatem ut alteram vestrarum fuisse preservatam a vestra celsitudine ac protectione utilissima conservatam.'[32]

The improvement in Lucca's relations with the Visconti was bound to have repercussions on her relations with the Papacy. Though the Lucchese acted as members of the league in some respects and, whatever they might say to Visconti officials, allowed their shores to be used by ships taking men and supplies to church lands in Lunigiana, and granted passage through their territory,[33] they seem to have fallen briefly into disfavour with the Papacy. There were complaints over a Lucchese decree forbidding their subjects to take service outside the Lucchese state. Lucca claimed that this decree was not directed against the Church in particular, but was general and was designed to check disorder among her subjects, who had been reduced to peace only with great difficulty, and to prevent them favouring Bernabò 'quia non modici districtuales nostri ad stipendia Bernabonis accedere preparabant'.[34] The Lucchese sent their chancellor, ser Pietro de'Beati of Bologna as ambassador to Gregory XI to allay any

[32] *Anz. Temp. Lib.* 530, f. 98, 29 July 1378. *Reg.*, no. 670. Printed in full in Landogna, 'La politica dei Visconti in Toscana', Appendix, Doc. VIII, pp. 122–3. There was, of course, an element of diplomatic courtesy in these expressions. Lucca had not entirely forgotten her earlier well-founded distrust, and could cite as cause for suspicion of Pisa her close association with the Lombards, *Anz. Temp. Lib.* 530, f. 8^{v}, 24 Nov. 1374, 'nam noti sunt Pisani et notissima est amicitia quam servant cum Lombardis nec possent amicitiam illam deserere'. *Reg.*, no. 460.

[33] *Reg.*, nos. 149, 153, 168. They also published the Emperor's letters of deprivation against Bernabò, *Reg.*, no. 147, 20 Oct. 1372. But they refused supplies and certain other demands they considered excessive, *Reg.*, nos. 149, 172. Also nos. 176, 182–3.

[34] *Anz. Temp. Lib.* 530, f. 65^{v}, 26 Feb. 1373. *Reg.*, no. 184. They told a very different story to Bernabò's officials. When asking for a grievance to be remedied they wrote 'che per benevolmente vicinare molti de nostri subditi li quali erano al soldo della chieza in Lunigiana per nostri decreti avemo costrecti partirsi dal dicto soldo et etiamdo a instantia del dicto messer Ranalduccio per ben vicinare avemo facto acumiatare dal nosso terreno di Massa Lunigiana tucti li homini del Vecciale'. This suggests that the general prohibition against taking service outside the Lucchese state harmed the Church more than it did the Visconti, apart from the fact that the Church, as an ally of Lucca, may well have expected more favourable treatment. *Delib.* 132, f. 120^{v}, 19 June 1373. Also *Reg.*, nos. 60, 67, 140. The prohibition on taking military service outside the state was repeated, 11 Nov. 1373, *Delib.* 132, f. 26^{v}.

suspicions the Pope might have of Lucca.[35] This he was able to do, and in December the Pope wrote to Jacobo de Itro, Archbishop of Otranto, the apostolic nuncio, that he was entirely satisfied with their explanations.[36]

The deterioration in Lucca's relations with Florence was more serious and more long-lasting. In the first year or two after her liberation Lucca's relations with Florence had been good. She had enjoyed Florentine support and had cause to be grateful to Florence for the loan of 29,000 florins, though perhaps Sercambi was not alone in suspecting that Florence had made this loan in the hope of reducing Lucca to client status.[37] But by 1372 relations had cooled considerably, mainly because of a dispute over a road built by the Florentines at Stallatoio on land they claimed belonged to the commune of Uzzano and was thus part of the Florentine state. But Lucca claimed that it was within her territory, and complained bitterly that the Florentines had taken the law into their own hands, building the road before the territorial dispute had been settled and committing unnecessary acts of violence on Lucchese territory in the course of its construction.[38] Lucchese opinion was further inflamed by

[35] Ser Pietro was also distributing gifts to men of influence at the Curia, *Reg.*, nos. 198, 202, 207, 293. Reports of papal suspicions of Lucca, *Reg.*, nos. 190, 294.

[36] *Reg.*, nos. 328–9, 383. Not all the complaints were on the papal side. Lucca protested strongly that Azzolino and Niccolò Malaspina, who raised the castle of Pugliano in rebellion in March 1373 had been aided and encouraged by Church officials in Lunigiana, *Reg.*, no. 215, 1 April, 1373. Also *Rif.* 4, p. 119, 4 May 1373. Men in the service of the bishop of Luni were also involved, *Reg.*, no. 259, 24 May 1373.

[37] Sercambi, II, p. 123. O. Banti, 'Un anno di storia Lucchese (1369–70): dalla dominazione pisana alla restaurazione della liberta', in *La "libertas lucensis" del 1369, Carlo IV e la fine della dominazione pisana*, Accademia Lucchese di Scienze, Lettere e Arti, Studi e Testi IV (Lucca, 1970), pp. 49–50. G. A. Brucker, *Florentine Politics and Society 1343–1378* (Princeton, 1962), pp. 268–9 takes a more favourable view of Florentine motives for assisting Lucca in this period. To describe Lucca as depending on Florentine subsidies for survival, however, is an overstatement. This 25,000 florins (29,000 in Lucchese documents) is the only loan Florence made to Lucca and was for the exceptional expenses of the purchase of her independence. Though Lucca seems to have considered borrowing from Florence the 20,000 florins she had to pay the Cardinal on his departure in 1370, she never actually did so, *Capitoli*, 31, pp. 337–8.

[38] 'Gentes vestre et multi armata manu quod expediens sive necessarium eis non erat, ad ipsam stratam accesserunt, ipsamque, sicut placuit, effecerunt', *Anz. Temp. Lib.* 529, f. 57, 19 Nov. 1372. *Reg.*, nos. 132, 163. The Lucchese pointed out that their neighbours would take 'allegressa et piacere' at the quarrel between them and 'al Comune di Firense ne seguitera infamia, et vergogna alluno Comune et allaltro', *Anz.*

Florence's refusal to commit the matter to a neutral third party and by the end of 1373 relations had deteriorated to a point at which Sercambi could record that Florence had 'facta raunata di molte genti da cavallo per prendere Luccha' and that it was only when her plans became known and defence measures taken that Florence saw that 'in Luccha era tal guardia et ch'abilmente aver non si potea, dimostrando il comune di Firenza tal brigata non esser raunata socto quell'acto, mandò la dicta gente a Pistoia et quella prese'.[39]

The invasion of Wettingher gave rise to further suspicions of this kind. It represented an even greater threat than such attacks by armed companies usually did, because he had an understanding with Giovanni degli Obizi and other Lucchese exiles, who accompanied him.[40] He had been in Florentine service until his *condotta* expired, and Lucca suspected that the Florentines had encouraged or at least condoned this attack on them, complaining that 'in su loro terreni, unde si sperava et spera aiuto et favore, si facciano raunamenti nocivi alla nostra libertade et al nostro stato'.[41] Colour was lent to these suspicions by the fact that a number of Lucchese exiles were living in Florence and Lucchese requests for their ex-

---

Temp. Lib. 529, ff. 58-58^{v}, 23 Nov. 1372, *Reg.*, no. 164, where dated 26 Nov. 1372. Florentine sources show that Lucca had some cause for complaint, and that Florence had no intention of giving her satisfaction. Speakers in the Florentine council advised 'quod si Lucani ambaxiatores possunt contentari verbis de via Stallatorii fiat, si non autem eis petentibus commictatur vertens questio in aliquem confidentem de iure terminanda et procuretur haberi arbiter confidens qui ius comunis defendat et interim perfectioni strate seu dicte vie opera soliciter detur', A. S. F. *Consulte* 12, f. 69, 5 Nov. 1371, also f. 69^{v}, 6 Nov. 1371. The Florentines felt as strongly as did the Lucchese about the matter, G. A. Brucker, *Florentine Politics and Society,* p. 75.

[39] *Reg.*, no. 167, 8 Dec. 1372. Sercambi, I, pp. 207-8, where he dates it 1372. He also records a plot in August 'di far tractato in Lucca a pititione de' Fiorentini insieme con messer Iohanni delli Opizi'.

[40] The Florentine priors warned Lucca of his approach as early as 21 Nov. 1373, *Reg.*, no. 359. The company was said to be on its way to Lombardy to take service with Galeazzo Visconti, but a Lucchese envoy in Pisa warned the Anziani that 'la verita e ch'elli e conducto a petissione di vostri lucchezi per IIII mesi a XII fiorini lo mese per lancia', and that when they approached the city three fortresses in the *contado* would rise in rebellion, *Anz. Temp. Lib.* 529, f. 121^{v}, 23 Nov. 1373. *Reg.*, no. 364. Lucchese defence measures, *Reg.*, nos. 365, 367, 372, 374, 384-6, 396, 404. *Rif.* 4, p. 260, 22 Nov. 1373, p. 487, 31 Oct. 1374. Sercambi, I, pp. 208-9.

[41] *Anz. Temp. Lib.* 529, f. 120^{v}, 23 Nov. 1373, in a letter to the Lucchese ambassadors in Florence. *Reg.*, no. 361. They wrote to the Florentines in similar terms and heard that the Florentines 'abbino preso disdegno' at their letters. *Anz. Temp. Lib.* 529, f. 122^{v}, *Reg.*, nos. 362, 370, also no. 365.

pulsion had had no effect.[42] The Lucchese Anziani wrote to their ambassadors in Florence 6 December 1373 'sapemo da diverse parti messer Iohanni delli Opizi, Iuntarone, Lorenso e Guasparino e piu altri sono e sono stati gia a buon di, in Firense in Sancta Maria Novella aluogo de frati predicatori e quine anno facte talliare bandiere e favizi continuamente tractati e ordinamenti contra la nostra libertade'.[43] One of the ambassadors, Dino Malapresa, had a 'carissimus amicus, dignissimus fide' in Florence, who told Dino for sure that Giovanni degli Obizi was in Florence hidden in the house of a friend, 'et quod ipse est venturus cum aliquibus intentionibus consulendo tamquam amicus quod attendatur ad bonam custodiam et specialiter ad frontieras et etiam civitatem'.[44] Lucca always kept a careful watch for anything that could threaten her liberty, and might have been over-anxious and exaggerated the danger, but she was understandably angry at the failure of Florence to expel exiles such as Giovanni degli Obizi, whom she had good reason to fear. Florence's attitude contrasted strongly with Lucca's own willingness to oblige Florence in 1370 by expelling exiles from Sanminiato, who did not represent anything like such a serious threat to Florence.[45] The Lucchese were not alone in suspecting Florentine good faith. A letter from Gregory XI shows that there were rumours that Florence was aiding Wettingher's company, and the Sienese chronicler, Donato di Neri, refers to it as 'le genti de'Fiorentini'.[46]

Lucca could not afford to offend Florence by showing her distrust too openly, but relations remained cool throughout

[42] *Reg.*, nos. 355, 370, 372.

[43] *Anz. Temp. Lib.* 529, f. 126. *Reg.*, no. 380.

[44] *Rif.* 4, pp. 265–6, letter of 2 Dec. discussed in the General Council, 4 Dec. 1373.

[45] When Sanminiato finally fell to Florence a number of its inhabitants had petitioned to be allowed to live in Lucca. The Lucchese had agreed and granted them certain immunities, *Rif.* 1, p. 243, 25 Feb. p. 270, 11 Mar. 1370. But when shortly afterwards there were protests from Florence, Lucca agreed to expel them on the grounds that 'Florentinorum fraternitas adeo tenaciter mentibus Lucanorum inhereat quod ea que suspiciosa sint ipsis sunt non minus quam si comuni lucano forent suspitioni vigilantibus oculis advertenda', *Rif.* 2, p. 51, 22 Aug. 1370. Sercambi states that the Sanminiatesi 'vennero a Luccha, et quine sono stati e stanno facciendo loro arti', I, p. 184, but this seems to be incorrect, for in May 1383 Lucca claimed in a letter to Florence that she had expelled about 300 men of Sanminiato at Florence's request, *Anz. Temp. Lib.* 530, f. 198, 9 May 1383. *Reg.*, no. 1079.

[46] *Reg.*, no. 404, 13 Jan. 1374. *Cronaca Senese di Donato di Neri*. R.I.S. new series, Tom. XV, part vi, fasc. 7, p. 653.

the summer of 1374.[47] In the autumn, however, a reconciliation was brought about by the efforts of certain private citizens, messer Guelfo de'Pugliesi of Prato and others, who had taken refuge in Lucca when the plague was raging in the rest of Tuscany. At the instance of messer Guelfo the Lucchese sent an embassy to Florence in October 1374 'ut omnis de mentibus et conceptis Florentinorum offuscatio et indignationis nebula detergatur'.[48] The ambassadors were to express general good-will rather than to make any concrete proposals, assuring the Florentines of Lucchese affection and asking for their support,

> prima ricordando lantiche amistadi state tra questi comuni et in casa et fuor di chasa, et le grandissime spese et operactioni chel comune di Fiorensa a senpre facte accio che Lucha non sia subiugata et rimanga in sua libertate le quali sono manifeste a tucto lo mondo. Appresso che, come si possano ricordare li antichi, senpre che Lucha e stata libera, sia recta et governata col consiglio et aiuto di Firense, come di loro padre. Et posto che Luchesi per le varietadi passate non si ricordasseno di queste cose antiche, quello che ora nuovamente lo Comune di Firense aopero a riparare con messer lo imperadore chella nostra libertade non ci fusse levata et con parole et con servirci di denari, non de essere uscito di mente a Luchesi.[49]

This not entirely accurate account of history and the humble tone elicited a favourable reply from Florence. In a meeting of the General Council 19 October 1374 the Lucchese ambassadors related the 'responsione gratissima' of the Florentine priors and one of them, Francesco Guinigi, spoke of the brotherly love and zeal for the popular regime of Lucca shown by the Florentines, who 'lucanos tractare intendunt et cupiunt in omnibus velut fratres et pro conservando bonum statum popularem et libertatem civitatis lucane in omnibus casibus opportunis sicuti per eorum defensa et propria libertate totam ipsorum potentiam et personas exponere'.[50] At the beginning of November an embassy came to Lucca from Florence to express goodwill and support and to assure the Lucchese that the Florentines intended to take action against anyone making attempts against Lucchese liberty, as if it were

[47] *Reg.*, nos. 379–80, 401, 405–7, 413, 422. Silva, *Governo*, pp. 174–5.

[48] *Rif.* 4, p. 476, 19 Oct. 1374.

[49] *Anz. Temp. Lib.* 530, ff. 5–6, instructions to the ambassadors going to Florence October 1374. *Reg.*, no. 456.

[50] *Rif.* 4, pp. 476–7, 19 Oct. 1374.

against their own state, and that any Lucchese in Florentine territory was to be treated as if he were a Florentine.[51] In this way a formal reconciliation was effected with many expressions of brotherly love and goodwill on both sides, and arrangements were made to reward messer Guelfo and others who had helped to bring it about.[52]

Unfortunately for Lucca the political situation was such that she could not improve her relations with one state without arousing suspicions elsewhere. In November 1374 the Lucchese wrote to their chancellor and ambassador in Florence, ser Pietro de'Beati, that the Florentines should inform the Pope of the true facts, in case he heard rumours that 'in alcuna delle terre vicine a Luccha et per alcuni malivoli e stato mormorato con parole dizoneste dello amore e fratellansa nuovamente mostrato e rinovellato intra lo comune di Firense et quelli di Luccha'.[53] The Lucchese thought it necessary to send ser Pietro to the Pope to discuss the embassies passing between Lucca and Florence 'ad excusadum conceptos rancores et rememorandum antiqua servitia et amicitiam singularem inter Lucanos et Florentinos'. He was to set out the Lucchese position in a way that, if it represents Lucca's real views, casts doubts on the sincerity of her reconciliation with Florence. He was to point out that Lucca was surrounded by more powerful states and had many rivals, and that if she engaged in disputes and took up arms to defend her rights she found it an unequal struggle, and was more likely to suffer further injury than to avenge herself. Therefore her citizens had to dissimulate and to bear insults in order to survive and maintain themselves within their narrow confines. They had been reconciled with Florence to prevent the Florentines from doing them harm, not to forget the past, but to keep more careful watch. The Pope was to be assured that no league had been concluded with Florence, but only 'una apparens amicitia que utilis est nobis', and the causes of 'nostra flexibilitas et tractabilitas cum vicinis' were to be demonstrated to him.[54]

[51] *Rif.* 4, p. 492, 4 Nov. 1374. [52] *Rif.* 4, p. 477, 19 Oct. 1374, p. 495, 7 Nov. 1374.

[53] *Anz. Temp. Lib.* 530, f. 7, 7 Nov. 1374. *Reg.*, no. 458.

[54] *Anz. Temp. Lib.* 530, ff. 8–8^{v}, 24 Nov. 1374. *Reg.*, no. 460. Similar embassies were sent to the Cardinal in Bologna and the Marchese of Ferrara to explain this renewed friendship with Florence, *Reg.*, no. 461, 28 Nov. 1374.

7

1375-1378

THE need to explain this renewal of friendship with Florence was partly a result of the changed political situation in Italy. Florence and the Papacy, which were usually found in alliance, had begun to drift apart, and Florence was looking to Milan as an ally. This situation was to result in the War of the Eight Saints (1375-8), in which Florence and the smaller Tuscan communes were ranged with Milan against the Papacy. This caused great embarrassment to the Lucchese, whose sole desire was to remain at peace and on good terms with everyone. They had recently renewed friendly relations with Florence and were on excellent terms with Milan. Despite memories of Pisan rule and occasional causes of friction, their relations with Pisa were also generally good.[1] But Lucca wanted above all to remain on good terms with the Papacy, to which she was bound by ties of gratitude and interest. Apart from many other benefits she had derived from the Papacy, notably the money lent at the time of the recovery of her independence, the aid of the forces of the Church, which the Pope had instructed his officials to provide on any request from Lucca, was most valuable in being usually prompt,

[1] Boundary disputes and other questions had recently been settled, but there were still causes of friction, and Silva exaggerates the harmony between the two cities. The memory of Pisan rule was still recent and even casual references to this period in Lucchese documents take for granted its tyranny and injustice, e.g. *Rif.* 1, p. 41, 20 Aug. 1369, *Rif.* 2, pp. 137-9, 13 Nov. 1370, *Rif.* 9, p. 44, 10 Feb. 1384. The Lucchese still occasionally betrayed distrust; they were anxious that Sarzana should never be entrusted to the Pisans, whose friendship with the Lombards was well known, *Anz. Temp. Lib.* 530, f. 8^{v}, 24 Nov. 1374, *Reg.*, no. 460. There were suspicions that the Pisans intended to occupy the tower of Monte S. Giuliano and Lucchese forces were sent out by night for its defence, *Delib.* 132, f. 77^{v}, 26 June 1375. They were anxious that the rectorship of the hospital of S. Pellegrino in Alpi should not go to a Pisan, a thing about which Lucca 'possit merito subspicari cum innantum sit Pisanis habere Lucanos hodio et ipsis velle prodesse et damnari cumque loci situs nisi per fidos custodiatur et gubernetur multa possint affere et civitati et civibus detrimenta', *Rif.* 8, p. 221, 12 Aug. 1382. General suspicion of the Pisans *Reg.*, 2000, 7 Feb. 1374. But in the negotiations preceding the War of the Eight Saints Pisa and Lucca were in a similar position and took the same attitude, Silva, *Governo*, pp. 68-9, 177.

generous, and disinterested, and without the danger to Lucchese liberty that aid from other Italian powers might bring. An alliance with Florence and Milan against the Papacy, which Lucca was urged to join, disrupted her policy of friendship with all her neighbours and reliance on the support of the Papacy. Neutrality was impossible; the forces of the belligerent states would require transit through her territory and supplies from her *contado*.

But Lucca and the other minor Tuscan states were expected to take a more active part, and were urged by both Florence and Milan to join the league. Like Pisa, Lucca was extremely reluctant to do so. Neither state wished to join a league which would involve them in war, especially war with the Papacy against which they had no real grievance. They had nothing to gain from the league and all their traditions were against it.[2] If Lucca did join the league, it would be because she was dragged along reluctantly in the wake of Florence and she would be unlikely to prove a very whole-hearted ally. But despite her unwillingness to be involved in a league against the Pope, she realized that to remain faithful to the Church would mean isolating herself from her neighbours and exposing herself to dangers against which the Pope might be unable to send effective help in time. It would obviously have been an advantage had the Pope been in Italy, and in the negotiations preceding the War of the Eight Saints, Lucca frequently urged him to return from Avignon to Rome.[3]

Meanwhile negotiations for a peace or truce with Bernabò went ahead between December 1374 and June 1375. In these negotiations the Lucchese, who were represented by their chancellor, ser Pietro de'Beati, were chiefly concerned with the fate of Sarzana and Lunigiana, the return of the Pope to Rome and their own security if the Church should dismiss its

[2] Silva, *Governo*, pp. 177–83, though as Lucca was already on good terms with Milan, she cannot have objected to the league on the grounds that it meant alliance with Milan.

[3] As he planned to do; for example in a letter of 8 Oct. 1374 he announced the date of his arrival as the September of the following year. *Reg.*, no. 455. Florentine fears of the Pope's arrival, A.S.F. *Consulte*, 14, ff. 100v–101v, 7 Nov. and f. 102, 8 Nov. 1376. The Lucchese also hoped for the arrival of the Emperor, *Reg.*, no. 493, 17 Apr. 1375, and spoke of the Pope and the King of the Romans 'qui de proximo sunt venturi ut publice divulgatur'. *Delib.* 132, f. 74, 19 May 1375.

forces. But in February they were already writing to their envoy of the danger that could result to Tuscany from Florentine distrust of the Papacy and of the advantages to be gained from ending this suspicion.[4] The question of a new league of Tuscan communes was apparently already in the air; for the Lucchese ambassador going to Florence was instructed that if he were approached about such a league, he should reply: 'pensano li comuni di Toschana essere in legha con Santa Chiesa per pacti che ancora sono in vigore, unde ora muovendosi a nuova legha, il papa primamente non richiestone, dubitano chessia materia al sancto padre non che da meravigliarsene, ma di prendere grande suspecto et turbamento,' adding 'lo mondo pare chessia tucto in commotione'.[5] The Lucchese assured the Pope that they bowed to his counsel about this new league, which was being promoted by the Florentines and not, as he had been informed, by Lucca and Pisa.[6] At this time the Lucchese are again found making small presents to men of influence at the Curia, and they discussed the question of finding protectors there in a letter to their chancellor.[7]

A truce for a year was signed with Bernabò and Galeazzo Visconti on 4 June 1375. Forces dismissed by the Church then attacked Tuscany, and, although Lucca had forseen the danger and taken precautions, she was not able to save her territory from attack and had to buy the company off.[8] The attack had serious consequences, as the Florentines believed

[4] *Rif.* 5, pp. 10-11, 13 Jan., pp. 13-14, 14 Jan. 1375. *Reg.*, nos. 472, 16 Jan., 475, 10 Feb. 1375.

[5] *Anz. Temp. Lib.* 530, ff. 23-24, 17 Apr. 1375, *Reg.*, no. 493. The Pisans made the same point, Silva, *Governo*, p. 179. Mention of the 'responsionibus Pisanorum et Lucanorum' about the league, ASF. *Consulte*, 13, f. 49, 21 Apr. 1375.

[6] *Reg.*, no. 503, 13 May 1375.

[7] *Reg.*, nos. 503, 13 May 1375; 507, 3 June 1375; 528, 19 Aug. 1375.

[8] The Pope had warned them of the danger and sent aid, *Reg.*, nos. 511, 21 June 1375; 514, 30 June 1375. Lucchese precautions, *Reg.*, nos. 501–2, 511, *Rif.* 5, p. 75, 30 May, p. 77, 8 June, pp. 78-9, 12 June, pp. 79-82, 13 June, p. 86, 24 June, p. 88, 4 July 1375. *Delib.* 132, f. 77^{v}, 20 June, ff. 79^{v}-80, 25 June, f. 79, 27 June 1375. Though the sum Lucca had to pay was only 7,000 florins, she had great difficulty raising it, and it was not until February 1376 that the final instalment was paid, though the agreement has specified payment by 5 Aug. 1375, *Rif.* 5, pp. 90-1, 9 July 1375, pp. 222-3, 16 Feb. 1376. Lucca, like Siena and Florence, tried to raise money from the clergy, *Delib.* 132, f. 84, 18 July 1375. Also private loans and borrowing interest on the *Massa*, *Delib.* 132, f. 87, 28 July, ff. 112^{v}-113, 10 Sept. 1375. Damage done by the Society, *Rif.* 5, p. 191, 14 Jan. 1376, *Rif.* 6, p. 128, 20 Dec. 1376.

that the Cardinal of Bologna had connived at it, and this proved the last straw in Papal-Florentine relations. Florence made a league with Bernabò Visconti on 24 July 1375 to last five years and directed against the Church, though it was not to come into effect until the year's truce the Visconti had with the Church expired on 4 June 1376.[9] In the preceding weeks both Florence and Milan had sent ambassadors to Lucca to urge the need for joint action against the danger of outside attacks.[10] Lucca had made favourable replies, while at the same time keeping the Church informed of the course of events and urging that the Pope should not delay his return to Italy.[11] But on 25 July 1375 the Florentines formally announced their league with Bernabò concluded the previous day, and offered favourable conditions for Lucca to adhere. The issue thus became clear.

Lucca wrote to the Cardinal of Bologna informing him of this and saying that, while they had in no way changed their attitude to the Church, they recognized the necessity of uniting with their neighbours so as to avoid imminent dangers, if they could.[12] Lucca hoped in fact to be able to join the league without offending the Pope. They hoped that he could be made to see the difficulties of their position and be persuaded that they joined the league only because they dared not remain isolated from their neighbours, and that it made no difference to their attachment to the Papacy. But ser Pietro de'Beati had already advised them against joining, as it would be impossible for them to do so without offending the Pope, and Gregory XI himself began to counter Florentine propaganda in favour of

[9] A. Gherardi, 'La Guerra degli Otto Santi', *Archivio Storico Italiano*, Ser. iii, Vols. V-VIII (1867-8), Vol. V, pp. 35-131. There was provision for any place rebelling against the Church to be received into the league.

[10] *Reg.*, nos. 2004, 14 July 1375; 516, 19 July 1375; 517, 23 July 1375.

[11] They had stressed their own weak position, which made it impossible for them to take an independent line. They wrote 'quod licet nostra civitas passus habeat fortissimos et istrictos, tamen comunitatem nostram inter alias Tuscie comunitates minimam putabamus, quod alie Tuscie civitates facient et nos etiam faciemus, ad quas ipse cum simili ambasciata se accessurum esse dicebat', *Anz. Temp. Lib.* 530, f. 49v, 23 July 1375, *Reg.*, no. 517. They sent ser Pietro de'Beati a copy of a letter from Florence, so that he might inform the Pope, *Reg.*, no. 518, 28 July 1375.

[12] *Reg.*, no. 2005, 28 July 1375. The same day they wrote to Florence of their joy at the news of the league, adding that if Galeazzo Visconti also joined, 'erit securitas et gaudium duplicatum', *Anz. Temp. Lib.* 530, f. 50, 28 July 1375, *Reg.*, no. 519. Also no. 520, 31 July 1375.

the league, exhorting them not to be deceived by the Florentines 'qui vestram quietam turbare et devotionem depravare forsitan niterentur et vicinorum suorum libertatem in servitutem redigunt quando possunt'.[13] For the Lucchese the ideal solution would have been for the Pope also to have joined the league, thus making it general; they wrote to ser Pietro 'opportet Ecclesiam in factis suis aliter quam verbis providere et non credat per oratorem placare mentes tam ferocissime concitatas. Certe, si posset honorifice dictam novam ligam intrare, esset, nostro parvo iudicio, ad tempus remedium salutare'.[14] But even if this ideal solution proved impossible of achievement, the Lucchese argued that they at least should join the league, urging that the destruction of Lucca could be of no possible benefit to the Pope, and even going so far as to argue that if they were members of the league they could act as spies and give the Pope and the Cardinal of Bologna much useful information, which they would not otherwise have.[15]

Lucca and the other Tuscan communes that had not yet joined the league continued to be courted by both sides. Gregory XI continued his attempts at reconciliation with Florence, and even hoped to arrange a definite peace with the Visconti.[16] Meanwhile he urged the Lucchese to remain faithful to the Church, writing numerous letters and sending Lucca copies of his letters to Florence.[17] The Florentines on the other hand did all they could to induce the Lucchese to enter the

[13] *Reg.*, no. 525, 10 Aug. 1375. Ser Pietro de'Beati's warning, *Reg.*, no. 2006, 1 Aug. 1375.

[14] *Reg.*, no. 526, 11-14 Aug. 1375. The Pope was trying to make the league general, no. 544, Dec. 1375, and this solution also appealed to the Pisans, who were still urging it in February 1376, Silva, *Governo*, pp. 183-5.

[15] *Reg.*, no. 526, 11-14 Aug. 1375 in a letter to ser Pietro de'Beati.

[16] *Reg.*, no. 527, 13 Aug. 1375. He urged the Lucchese to send their envoys for the peace by 30 Nov., *Reg.*, no. 531, 23 Sept. 1375. *Rif.* 5, p. 128, 15 Nov. 1375, a sindic to the Pope for peace was elected.

[17] He expressed regret at the damage Lucca had suffered from Hawkwood's company, and ordered his officials to grant any future Lucchese request for aid, *Reg.*, nos. 521-2, 3 Aug. 1375. Also nos. 2006, 1 Aug. 1375; 533, 538, 540, 541, 6 Oct.-25 Nov. 1375. A measure of the intense diplomatic activity is that several times the gate of Lucca was opened at night, which required a special decree, *Delib.* 132, f. 97, 14 Aug. for Ruggero Cane, Bernabò's ambassador, f. 97v, 19 Aug. 1375 it was decreed that it could be opened twice, and there was a further decree the same night to open it again.

league. They urged Bernabò to send forces to Tuscany to show that the league was a military reality, and to deny that he was allied to the Papacy, as Gregory XI claimed in his letters to the Tuscan communes. 'E sapete quanto questa novella vale a torre dall'animo a'Pisani, a'Lucchesi e a'Senesi che a nostra lega non vengano. E pero, ci pare oggi piu che mai necessario che la gente della lega venga, e venire a qualche atto manifesto per lo quale apparisca di fuori la volunta di messer Bernabò e nostra'.[18] At the end of November 1375 Florence was able to announce that Siena had joined the league, urging the Lucchese to follow their example 'reiectis que vobis in contrarium movent rationibus. O quanta firmitas, quantaque securitas statui vestre libertatis accedit si huic coniungi decreveritis societati'.[19] Lucca granted passage to Bernabò's forces at the request of Florence, and congratulated the Florentines on the adherence of Siena, but showed no sign of following suit.[20] In December she was still advising the Pope to make peace with the Visconti and to hasten his return to Italy, and she took up again her previous suggestion that the league should become general, 'come per la Sua Santita si cerchava, et domandata fu per la regina di Napoli'. She added that her attitude was leading her into difficulties with her neighbours, 'sentiamo manifestamente dalli vicini essere favoregiati li nostri isbanditi et ribelli, onde per guardia delle nostre fortesse ci conviene molte et diverse spese sostenere'.[21]

Gregory XI continued to praise Lucchese fidelity, but in a letter of 30 January 1376 he wrote that he had heard from

[18] Gherardi, 'La Guerra degli Otto Santi', *Archivio Storico Italiano*, Ser. iii, Vol. VI, part ii, Docs. 76–7, p. 244, 21 Oct. 1375. Silva, *Governo*, pp. 180–1. Cronica di Pisa, R.I.S., Vol. XV, col. 1070, relates that the Visconti sent 1,500 horsemen who passed through the Lucchese state, 23 Nov. 1375. For these *Delib.* 133, f. 25^{v}, 2 Sept. 1376. The Florentines also tried to clear up a number of small matters, such as the opening of Lucchese letters and an attack on the Lucchese castle of Sasso, which Lucca alleged was made by Florentine subjects from Barga, Gherardi, 'La Guerra degli Otto Santi', Doc. 72, 13 Oct. 1375, Doc. 81, 25 Oct. 1375.

[19] A.S.F. *Cart. Sign. Miss.* 16, f. 49^{v}, 28 Nov. 1375. Also quoted in Silva, *Governo*, pp. 181–2, n. 5.

[20] Gherardi, 'La Guerra degli Otto Santi', Doc. 45, 12 Sept. 1375, Doc. 95, 15 Nov. 1375. *Reg.*, no. 542, 4 Dec. 1375.

[21] *Anz. Temp. Lib.* 530, ff. 53^{v}–54^{v}, December 1375. *Reg.*, no. 544. Also no. 2002, 2 June 1375 concerning a plot by Giovanni degli Obizi against Pietrasanta, Camaiore and Massa.

their ambassadors that they were wavering.[22] He urged that it was both dishonourable and against their interests to join the league, but the Lucchese had by then elected their sindics and 1 February 1376 the Florentines were able to inform Siena of the arrival of the delegates of Pisa and Lucca.[23] Pisa and Lucca finally entered the league together, co-operating in the negotiations. Their long delay and obvious reluctance obtained favourable terms for them and they were able to enter the league in a somewhat watered-down form. Unlike the other members they were not obliged to maintain any fixed number of troops, but were to provide such aid as they could spare case by case. The league was also to be confined to the territories of the contracting parties 'ita quod extra dicta territoria defensa vel offensa nullatenus extendantur', as the Pisans and presumably also the Lucchese wished, and not extended against any aggressor and in any territory, as the Florentines had desired. Pisa and Lucca were not bound to aid their allies within lands belonging to the Church which had been occupied by other members of the league.[24] In this way, though they were in alliance with two states actively hostile to the Church and which had incited rebellions within the states of the Church itself, the scope of the league was narrowed, and they were less likely to find themselves called upon to act against the Church and were able to dissociate themselves from the occupation of Church lands.

Lucca had joined the league, but she was to prove a lukewarm and unsatisfactory ally. Her entry into the league did not prevent her from replying favourably to a letter from

[22] *Reg.*, nos. 546-9, 5-18 Jan. 1376, but no. 522, 30 Jan. 1376 he wrote 'iam vos vacillare . . . et virtutem vestre constantie in instabilitatis vicium, ex illorum, qui vos opprimunt, nonnullas vestras terras detinent tirannice occupatas et vos sibi totaliter subicere satagunt, deceptabili seductione mutari'.

[23] *Rif.* 5, pp. 185-6, 14 Jan. 1376. The sindics were the same as those elected 12 Aug. 1375. Silva, *Governo*, p. 183, Landogna, 'La politica dei Visconti in Toscana' pp. 98–100 and Doc. V, p. 121. The agreement was not finally signed until 12 Mar. 1376, and there were still difficulties to be overcome; as late as 2 Mar. 1376 the Lucchese Anziani wrote to their ambassadors in Florence about 'quel capitolo cosi nuovo, che ora all'ultimo vi fu giunto et dato', *Anz. Temp. Lib.* 530, f. 57, *Reg.*, no. 554.

[24] Copy of the league *Capitoli*, 25, pp. 3-14. The other members were not obliged to aid Pisa and Lucca with any fixed number of troops. Silva, *Governo*, pp. 186-7. The league was approved by Bernabò Visconti, 30 May 1376, Gherardi, 'La Guerra degli Otto Santi', Doc. 234.

the Emperor Charles IV in favour of the Church, and Gregory XI remained unaware for some months that Lucca had joined the league, and continued to urge her to remain faithful.[25] In July 1376 Pisa and Lucca made another attempt to bring about peace,[26] but by then sentences of excommunication had already been passed against Florence and the Visconti and hostilities began. Lucca and the other cities that had joined the league only reluctantly were faced with two problems in this situation; whether or not to observe papal censures and expel the Florentines from their territory, and whether or not to send military aid to Florence, as the terms of the league required. Lucca's attitude to these problems seems to have been inspired by a desire to avoid giving offence to the Pope at all costs, even though this must give rise to complaints from the Florentines. Lucca alone of the allies expelled the Florentines from her territory,[27] and although she did not refuse military aid to Florence, she met demands with delays and excuses.[28] In June the Lucchese wrote that they were ready, as required by the league, and for the common good, to oppose the Bretons, whom they heard were approaching, but their inactivity was already causing dissatisfaction in Florence, for the Florentines wrote 'tempus de somno surgere, tempus est sincere delectionis affectum per operam demonstrare'.[29] The Lucchese replied that they lacked the men to send aid to Florence with the Bretons invading their territory by two routes but the Florentines were not satisfied with these excuses, writing again that it was not the time for sleep, and urging

[25] Emperor's letter, *Reg.*, no. 556, 26 Mar. 1376. Lucchese reply, no. 562, 11 May 1376. Letters from the Pope, *Reg.*, nos. 558, 561, 576, 17 Apr.–1 July 1376. He was apparently still unaware of Lucca's defection in August, when he ordered the bishop of Lucca to raise the interdict under which he had placed the city as a result of a quarrel over the *commenda* of the abbey of S. Ponziano. The Pope pointed out that the Church had particular need of the devotion of her faithful subjects at this time. *Reg.*, nos. 589–90, 13 Aug. 1376. Also nos. 574, 582–3, 585–9, 591. *Rif.* 6, pp. 28–9, 2 Aug. 1376. Landogna, 'La politica dei Visconti in Toscana', p. 101.

[26] A. Segre, 'Dispacci di Cristoforo da Piacenza', *Archivio Storico Italiano*, Ser. v, Vol. XLIII, (1909), pp. 87–93, 17 July 1376.

[27] Gherardi, 'La Guerra degli Otto Santi', Doc. 286, 31 July 1376. *Reg.*, no. 582, 3 Aug. 1376.

[28] *Reg.*, no. 559, 23 Apr. 1376.

[29] *Anz. Temp. Lib.* 530, f. 61^{v}, 23 June 1376, *Reg.*, no. 569. Also nos. 567, 1–13 June 1376; 570, 18 June 1376. Gherardi, 'La Guerra degli Otto Santi', Docs. 261, 23 June, 265, 24 June 1376.

them to send aid as the terms of the league bound them to do, 'nunc sciemus quali erga nos et libertatem Italie mente sitis'.[30] But the Lucchese only repeated that they did not have enough men for their own guard, and do not seem to have sent aid to Florence that year. There was probably some truth in their assertion that they could not spare any forces. They naturally needed more for their own defence at this time, and there was also some difficulty in finding mercenaries, especially cavalry.[31] But they were also reluctant to risk offending the Pope by taking part in hostilities against him, even though they had joined the league.

This failure to send military aid was not the only cause for Florentine dissatisfaction with Lucca. She complained of the expulsion of her citizens from Lucca in accordance with papal decrees, and suspected Lucca of aiding her enemies.[32] The Lucchese had apparently similar suspicions of Florence, for in December the Florentines complained that many citizens were daily brought before the magistrates in Lucca accused of trying to raise places in the Lucchese state in rebellion at the instigation of Florence.[33] The Florentines also feared that Pisa or Lucca might receive the Pope on his return to Italy, and discussed sending embassies to dissuade them.[34] But if the papal war placed a strain on Lucca's relations with Florence, she seems to have remained on excellent terms with Bernabò Visconti. She received letters from Bernabò and Regina della Scala, expressing goodwill, and in December she replied to further letters, informing her of the inclination of Gregory XI

[30] *Anz. Temp. Lib.* 530, f. 61v, 24 June 1376, *Reg.*, no. 571. Also no. 575, 30 June 1376. The Pisans similarly refused Florence aid on the grounds that Pisa herself was more directly threatened, Silva, *Governo* p. 189.

[31] More crossbowmen were hired and the garrisons of fortresses increased, *Rif.* 5, p. 138, 7 Dec. 1375. The hire of more infantry was authorized to make up for the lack of cavalry, *Rif.*, 5, pp. 309-10, 26 Apr. 1376.

[32] Gherardi, 'La Guerra degli Otto Santi', Doc. 286, 31 July 1376. Lucca promised that in future Florentine citizens would be treated like Lucchese, *Reg.*, no. 581, 3 Aug. 1376. Lucca had earlier been obliged to deny that she was implicated in a plot against Florentine fortresses, or that Bretons hostile to Florence were in her territory, *Reg.*, no. 578, 14 July, in reply to a Florentine letter of 12 July, no. 579, 16 July 1376.

[33] Gherardi, 'La Guerra degli Otto Santi', Doc. 326, 10 Dec. 1376. It was perhaps in this connection that Lucca wrote the same day that she was sending a citizen who was fully informed on what the Florentines had written to them, *Reg.*, no. 598, 10 Dec. 1376.

[34] A.S.F. *Consulte*, 14, ff. 100v-101v, 7 Nov. 1376, f. 102, 8 Nov. 1376.

towards peace, and offering to recommend the city to Count Lutz of Landau, so that she should come to no harm from his forces.[35]

The Pope had returned to Italy at the end of 1376, reaching Livorno by 7 November, and negotiations for peace began soon afterwards. The Lucchese hastened to write to him, asking to be included in the negotiations.[36] Though these came to nothing and the war continued, the Florentines seem to have made no further requests for aid, and Lucca was able to reduce her forces.[37] When the negotiations were resumed a year later, there was a suggestion that they should take place in Lucca, but the Lucchese refused to receive the Pope and Bernabò Visconti, making the excuse that they could not do so without the consent of the Emperor.[38] The conference took place in Sarzana instead, and Lucca made preparations to honour the papal delegates passing through her state on their way to the conference, and to defend herself in view of the 'magnam armigerorum comitivam' they would bring with them.[39] When the negotiations were resumed in Rome after the death of Gregory XI and the election of Urban VI, Lucca kept a careful watch on events until peace was signed at the end of July 1378.[40]

The conclusion of peace meant the end of Lucca's difficulties in remaining on good terms with the Pope without offending her powerful neighbour Florence. During the war she had avoided serious danger by her policy of 'flexibilitas et tractabilitas cum vicinis'. Her understanding with the Visconti and enjoyment of Bernabò's protection continued

[35] *Reg.*, nos. 563, 12 May 1376; 565, 24 May 1376; 599, 18 Dec. 1376. Landogna 'La politica dei Visconti in Toscana', Doc. VII, p. 122. Also *Reg.*, nos. 604–5, Jan. 1377. Small matters of raids on Lucchese territory by *banniti* and an attack on the Visconti by a dismissed Lucchese mercenary were quickly dealt with, *Reg.*, nos. 664, 30 May 1378 and 669, 21 July 1378.

[36] *Reg.*, no. 609, 18 Feb. 1377. Silva, *Governo*, p. 193.

[37] *Rif.* 6, p. 313, 29 July 1377.

[38] Instructions to the Gonzaga ambassador, 7 Nov. 1377, Osio, *Documenti Diplomatici*, p. 193. Zerbi, *I Visconti di Milano*, p. 36, Landogna, 'La politica dei Visconti in Toscana', p. 101. Fondazione Treccani degli Alfieri, *Storia di Milano*, Vol. V (Milan, 1955), p. 491.

[39] *Reg.*, nos. 2016–21. *Rif.* 6, pp. 519–20, 17 Feb. 1378. *Min.* 2, ff. 136v–137, 17 Feb. 1378. *Delib.* 133, f. 98, 5 Mar. 1378.

[40] *Reg.*, nos. 665–6, 11 June 1378. Peace announced, no. 672, 29 July 1378, *Min.* 2, f. 207, 29 July 1378.

after the war, and she did not forfeit the favour of the Papacy. For, although she had joined the league, she had done so with evident reluctance, only after much delay, and in a form that did not bind her to aid any ally in occupying Church lands. Even after she had committed herself to the extent of joining the league, she had continued to play a double game, making friendly professions and promises to Florence, but observing the interdict and sending the Florentines no aid, in order to avoid unnecessarily offending the Papacy.

8

1378-1385

BUT the end of the war did not mean the beginning of a period of quiet. The next few years were disturbed by expeditions of foreign princes and invasions of armed companies, which were partly the indirect result of the Schism, which began 20 September 1378 with the election of Clement VII. The Schism had little direct effect on Lucca. She had greeted the election of Urban VI with joy and remained faithful to him, despite visits from French and Clementine ambassadors.[1] But the Schism affected Lucca and the other Tuscan cities indirectly in that it led to increased activity by armed companies and to the expeditions of Charles of Durazzo, Louis of Anjou, and Enguerrand de Coucy to Naples, where rival candidates to the succession were supported by rival popes.[2]

These dangers led to proposals for joint action by the Tuscan cities. When invited to take part in a conference to discuss this in April 1379, Lucca agreed in principle, but took the opportunity to voice certain complaints against Florence. The Lucchese rebel, Giovanni degli Obizi, had been received in Pistoia, and when Lucca had requested that Florence have him expelled she had been told that this was beyond the scope of Florentine authority in Pistoia.[3] She had not been satisfied with this reply, and now urged Perugia, who was promoting

[1] The election of an Italian pope 'quasi celicum portentium a cunctis et in omnium oculis mirabile videatur', *Rif.* 6, p. 552, 29 Apr. 1378. Embassies on behalf of Clement VII, *Reg.*, nos. 696, 25 Dec. 1378; 709, 5 Mar. 1379. These were received courteously enough to displease Urban VI and Paolo bishop of Lucca, *Reg.*, nos. 699, 8 Jan. 1379; 710, 9 Mar. 1379.

[2] Rumours of invasions of armed companies, *Reg.*, nos. 706, 715, 724-5, 735-7, 741, 2039-58. *Min.* 2, f. 304, 23 Mar. 1379. Lucca was invaded by Otto of Brunswick, *Reg.*, no. 720, 27 Apr. 1379, and had to make payments to the Companies of St. George and the Star 'quia de duobus malis minus malum eligendum est', *Rif.* 7, p. 60, 18 Mar. p. 93, 24 May, pp. 223-4, 30 Dec. 1379. As the Lucchese wrote in a letter, it was necessary to be on the watch constantly 'tot et tam variis insurgentibus periculis sotietatum nunc Anglicorum, nunc Theotonicorum, nunc Italorum que omnia expensas exigunt et damna atque pericula comminantur', *Rif.* 7, p. 69, 4 Apr. 1379.

[3] *Reg.*, nos. 713, 28 Mar.; 715, 29 Mar. 1379.

the proposed league, to use her influence with Florence, adding that if her anxiety on this account could only be allayed she would be better able to unite for the common good.[4] Though she sent her orators to Florence for the negotiations, Lucca was not among the signatories of the league concluded in October.[5] Her main reason for not joining was probably financial. Her ambassadors were instructed to explain that 'la cagione che ae sempre spaventato il Comune di Lucca di venire a legha principalmente e il non sentirsi poderoso alle spese che quella richiede'.[6] They returned too to the complaint that the Florentines were permitting Lucchese rebels to be received in their territory, pointing out that the need to provide against this danger increased Lucca's expenses, and also made them less anxious to join the league 'perche non saper vedere, se da nemici capitali che avemo su l'uscio ci convien guardare, a che sia utile far legha contra quelli dalla lungha'. But they did not make the expulsion of Lucchese rebels from Florentine territory a condition of their entry into the league, and the passage about the exiles was omitted in a later version of the ambassadors' instructions. It was presumably, therefore, not failure to gain satisfaction on this point that kept Lucca from joining the league.

All the other points in the instructions to the Lucchese ambassadors were concerned with Lucca's obligations in the projected league. The ambassadors were to take with them a copy of the last league and to refer to certain special terms made for Lucca then, pointing out that concessions were even more necessary now that their position had deteriorated because of the damage they had suffered. They did not wish to be bound to a definite *taglia* or a fixed share of expenses at all, but to provide according to their means for each case as it arose, the other members having the same limited obligations towards them. They also wanted provisions that any member

[4] *Reg.*, no. 721, 27 Apr. 1379. They had already sought and obtained the good offices of the Cardinal of Padua in this matter, *Reg.*, no. 718, 8–23, Apr. 1379.

[5] The members included Florence, Bologna, and Perugia, but not Lucca, Pisa, or Siena, *Reg.*, nos. 730, 21 June 1379; 746, 18 Oct. 1379.

[6] *Min.* 2, ff. 277–277^{v}, 29 June 1379. Instructions to the ambassadors going to Florence. This is *Reg.*, no. 731. A later version added further clauses; that the league should be for a term of years, not indefinite; that it should not extend outside the lands of the members, and that any building of defences or movements of forces within the state of one of the members should only be done with that member's consent.

of the league attacked by another member would be assisted by the rest, and that any possessions recovered by the league would be returned free of charge to the member who had lost it. Their concern to avoid expenses is clear from these conditions. In October, after the league was concluded, they were offered the opportunity to adhere with a *taglia* of 100 lances.[7] But in the course of the negotiations they had mentioned 25 lances as the most they could contribute, if they had to accept a fixed *taglia*, for they had no more and could pay no more. This was probably true. Lucca was trying to keep her expenses down at this time, and certainly could not have afforded to keep 100 lances, which would have cost her well over 20,000 florins a year. These financial conditions were Lucca's main concern in the negotiations, for her ambassadors were instructed 'fate quanto potete di venire in dicta legha al soprascritto modo, e se cosi e, deglaltri capitoli che facessero non ci curiamo molto, si veramente che niuno contra chi la presente legha potesse venire non si mentovi a nome'.[8]

The negotiations for the league of 1379 had begun under the pressure of the threat from the Company of the Star, and Lucca became less enthusiastic about the league as the danger receded, and more reluctant to commit herself to the expenses of a league with neighbours, some of whom she believed to be aiding her exiles. It was not until the next year, when Charles of Durazzo was about to pass through Italy to the conquest of Naples that negotiations began again. The league was finally concluded 23 July 1380, this time with Lucca among the signatories.[9] There are several documents relating to these negotiations, instructions to ambassadors, 'limitationes' and preliminary drafts,[10] which show particularly clearly Lucca's

[7] *Anz. Temp. Lib.* 530, ff. 115v, 18 Oct. 1379, *Reg.*, no. 746.

[8] *Min.* 2, ff. 277–277v, 29 June 1379, *Reg.*, no. 731.

[9] Lucca was among those threatened by the Company of St. George, part of which was in his service. According to Marchionne di Coppo Stefani rubr. 851, she had to pay 5,000 florins in Apr. 1380, and only escaped more through Florentine support. *Rif.* 7, p. 240, 12 Mar., pp. 244–5, 24 Mar., p. 246, 20 Apr., p. 253, 26 Apr. 1380. Silva, *Governo*, p. 208.

[10] There is a fair copy of the league, a rough copy with many corrections and marginal notes, and a document headed 'limitationes pactorum fiendorum' in *Capitoli*, 32, pp. 21–80. There is another version of the latter in *Min.* 2, ff. 390–390v, and also a double folio of notes relating to the terms of the league, loose, in *Capitoli*, 32.

main aims in foreign policy at this period.

Lucca had to accept a fixed *taglia* in this league, but the figure of 25 lances was lower than the 40 suggested at one stage in the negotiations and many fewer than the 100 lances suggested in 1379, and must be considered extremely moderate compared with the 200 each of Pisa or Siena, or the 220 of Perugia. Lucca was at pains to stress that even a *taglia* of 25 lances taxed her resources to the utmost, 'mostrando di farlo con grande fatica di Comune', and she obtained express exemption from any other expenses.[11]

Several clauses show the great caution Lucca exercised to avoid suffering harm or making enemies. The forces of the league were not to be allowed to enter Lucchese territory except at Lucca's express request, because allied forces could do as much damage as those of the enemy.[12] Lucca had wished the scope of the league to be general, 'non faciendo mentionem de domino vel tiranno'.[13] She argued that more general phrases would include lords and tyrants, but her real reason was probably a desire to do nothing that might give offence to Bernabò Visconti, who was not included in the negotiations. The other cities wished the phrase about a lord or tyrant to remain, and Lucca therefore accepted this, but she obtained exemption from a clause which provided for the forces of the league to go outside the territory of the allies. Her motive for this was 'quod nobis non expedit tum ratione impotentie tum ratione inimicitie non captande'.[14] She set great store by this clause and her ambassadors were instructed to resist any attempts to cancel it, with further emphasis on the point about not making enemies,

et ideo faciatis omnimodo quod illa clausula remaneat et non sit cassata . . . nam scitis quod ingredi territoria aliena est causa quirendi magnas inimicitias eorumdem. Et posito quod dici potest quod cum gentibus armorum lige posset talibus inimicitiis resisti tamen talis resistentia

[11] For the proposal of a *taglia* of 40 lances, *Capitoli*, 32, p. 37. Even little Arezzo had to provide 50 lances, if she joined. The only other place with a *taglia* as low as 25 lances was Città di Castello. Several of the documents relating to the league stress Lucca's inability to provide more or to undertake other expenses.

[12] 'Scitis enim quod tam a gentibus amicorum quam inimicorum territorium leditur', *Min.* 2, ff. 390–390^{v}, rough copy of the league, *Capitoli*, 32, cl. xviiii, p. 51 and p. 40.

[13] *Min.* 2, ff. 390–390^{v}, *Capitoli*, 32, p. 21. *Reg.* no. 768, 27 June 1380.

[14] *Min.* 2, ff. 390–390^{v}, *Capitoli*, 32, p. 21.

non esset sine damno intollerabili Lucani comunis. Et etiam si finita liga postea non reciperetur Lucanum comune ad ligam posset totaliter opprimi quod Lucanum comune evitare intendit.[15]

The matter of the Lucchese *banniti* was still a live issue. Lucca insisted on and obtained exemption from a clause that would have allowed *banniti* who had been granted citizenship of another city two or more years previously to remain there. Lucca objected to this 'quia secundum ea nostri ribelles et imbanniti qui quisierunt civilitatem in terris colligatorum seu qui ibidem nati essent possent impune teneri. Nos autem omnes expellere teneremus, quod esset inequale et civitati verecundum'. Florence had made the excuse that Giovanni degli Obizi had been granted citizenship of Pistoia when Lucca had requested his expulsion, and a clause in the comments on these proposals addressed to the Lucchese ambassadors in *Capitoli 32* shows that it was primarily the Florentines whom the Lucchese suspected of receiving and favouring her rebels; 'et primo quia comune Florentie vult posse retinere rebelles nostros ab superscripta causa quia sint cives vel municipes cum fideiussione tamen trium milium florenorum de non offendendo . . .' She rejected the idea of a guarantee of 3,000 florins on the grounds that it was not enough, considering how dangerous these rebels were, and that in any case Lucca would never be able to exact it.[16]

Lucca wished to retain as much fredom of action as possible in making terms with armed companies and others who might invade her territory. She was strongly against a proposal that a member of the league to whom another member had sent aid should not be allowed to make peace without that member's consent. She felt it would be enough if an ally was bound to include those who had aided her in any peace she made: 'et istam limitationem procuretis omnimodo quia necessaria est'. The reasons she gave for opposing the proposal illustrate her lack of trust in her neighbours and allies, and her fear that they might secretly be enemies; 'item quod si unus ex colligatis requisitus ut prestet gentem suam secundum formam lige, et quia forte gerit in animo odium occultum de gente sua servit fallaciter licet ex necessitate lige ut sine eo pax fieri non possit,

[15] *Capitoli*, 32, pp. 37–8.

[16] *Reg.*, no. 715, 29 Mar. 1379. *Capitoli*, 32, pp. 32, 40.

et paci rationabili talis iuvans consentire nolit, ut eius territorium destruatur, certe ex forma huius capituli omni carebit rimedio et pax haberi non poterit, quod est absurdum.'[17]

Lucca was finally able to enter the league on very favourable terms, gaining all the advantages of an alliance with her neighbours with the minimum of obligations and limitations on her freedom of action. Bernabò Visconti very quickly got to hear of the league and felt that his relations with Lucca were such that she owed him an explanation for entering a league without his knowledge. The Lucchese replied that it was true that they had entered a league with the other Tuscan communes, but that it was purely defensive and they had made no agreements detrimental to Bernabò's interests, ending 'nos enim illa que fecimus per tuitionem nostram speravimus vobis illa placere ad quem in omnibus nobis opportunum recurrimus tamquam devoti et filii zelatores et super hiis vestras favorabiles oblationes gratiose amplectimur toto corde tenentes indubie quod in nostris opportunitatibus nulli nisi Vestre Magnificentie recurremus'.[18]

This apparently satisfied him, for he troubled the Lucchese for no further explanations, and later in the year is found proposing a wider league against the companies, to include himself and his nephew, Giangaleazzo.[19] As the summer of 1380 had been much disturbed by threats and rumours of attacks by armed companies, this met with a favourable response.[20] But the Lucchese stressed their own comparative

[17] *Capitoli*, 32, p. 38. She also objected to a proposal that a two thirds majority should be sufficient to make decisions, insisting that they should be unanimous, 'quia quod omnes tangit debet ab omnibus approbari', *Capitoli*, 32, p. 22.

[18] *Anz. Temp. Lib.* 530, ff. 123v-124, 25 July 1380, *Reg.*, no. 770, in reply to a letter of Bernabò 20 July 1380. Lucchese letter printed in full in Landogna, 'La politica dei Visconti in Toscana', p. 105, and Doc. IX, pp. 123-4. Lucca also ordered certain officials to act with 'si facti et discreti modi, che lo loro signore messer Bernabò non abbia materia d'indignatione contro lo nostro comune', *Anz. Temp. Lib.* 530, f. 118v, 21 Feb. 1381, *Reg.*, nos. 760-1.

[19] The suggestion was first made 12 October, and again in more detail 8 Nov. 1380. G. Seregni, 'Un disegno federale di Bernabò Visconti 1380-1381', *Archivio Storico Lombardo*, Ser. iv, Vol. XXXVIII (1911), pp. 162-82. Letter of Bernabò 8 Nov. and Lucchese replies 17 Oct. and 19 Nov. 1380, Landogna, 'La Politica dei Visconti in Toscana', pp. 105-6 and Docs. X-XII, pp. 124-8. *Reg.*, no. 780, 17 Oct. 1380.

[20] *Reg.*, nos. 775, 781, 783-4, 791. *Rif.* 7, p. 340, 2 Oct., pp. 340-1, 17 Oct., p.

unimportance, 'nos sumus in Tuscia parvum signum, et oportet nos aliorum maiorum comunitatum colligatorum voluntatem sequi atque dispositionem'.[21] The Lucchese already enjoyed the protection of Bernabò Visconti and had not hesitated to appeal to him for aid, so presumably Lucca had less suspicion of him than did Florence and some of the other Tuscan cities, but as she herself recognized, and indeed stressed, she lacked the power to take the initiative, even if she had wished to do so and her part in the negotiations that followed was small. She deliberately tried to avoid playing an important part, not wishing to commit herself to views that might offend either Florence or Milan, should they fail to agree. When Florence discovered that Bernabò planned the league not only against the companies, but also against any foreign power that might attempt to disturb the peace of Italy, and that he wished the lord of Padua to be excluded, she consulted with her allies, asking Lucca to reply quickly, giving her opinion, 'quoniam . . . aliquid certum respondere non possumus nisi vestre fraternitatis intentione rescita'. But Lucca merely asked to be informed of the terms, and said that despite the importance of the matter she was content to trust in the Florentines, whom she regarded as fathers, and the other allies, whom she regarded as elder brothers, 'ad omnia que per vos et alios colligatos super dicta materia fuerint provisa contenti erimus in hiis que per ligam obligamur, in quibus parati sumus semper ad cuncta vestra et colligatorum servitia et honores'.[22] In fact, though negotiations continued

---

343, 28 Oct., p. 347, 9 Nov., p. 350, 14 Nov., p. 383, 31 Dec. 1380. In October Lucca had appealed to Bernabò for 200 lances to help her fight a company of Hungarians, *Reg.*, no. 2037, which should be dated 1380, not 1379. Bernabò had replied that 200 was not enough, 300 or 400 would be better. Seregni, 'Un disegno federale di Bernabò Visconti', p. 165, where dated 1380. Also *Reg.*, no. 791, Marchionne di Coppo Stefani, rubr. 880, Sercambi, I, pp. 219–20, who mentions only aid from Pisa, as Lucca feared the attack was instigated by Florence. G. Collino, 'la politica Florentino-Bolognese dall'avvento al principato del Conte di Virtù alle sue prime guerre di conquista', *Memorie della R. Accademia di Scienze, Lettere ed Arti di Torino*, 2, Vol. LIV, (1904), Doc. XV, 1 Dec. 1380. Seregni, 'Un disegno federale di Bernabò Visconti', p. 170.

[21] *Anz. Temp. Lib.* 530, f. 135, 19 Nov. 1380, *Reg.*, no. 790. Landogna, 'La Politica dei Visconti in Toscana', Doc. XII, p. 128.

[22] *Anz. Temp. Lib.* 530, f. 136v, 19 Jan. 1381, *Reg.* no. 805. Also nos. 788, 792–3, 795–6, 798, 802–3, 2067–8. Seregni, 'Un disegno federale di Bernabò Visconti', pp. 172–6. Landogna, 'La Politica dei Visconti in Toscana', Doc. XVII, pp. 132–3. Lucca

throughout 1381, no conclusion was reached.

The years 1381-4 were disturbed years for Lucca and the rest of Tuscany. She kept a close watch on the movements of armed companies and other events that might constitute a threat to her security,[23] but on several occasions she was obliged to make payments to save her territory from attack.[24] These dangers had repercussions on her relations with Florence, for Lucca suspected the Florentines of assisting her enemies. According to Sercambi the Lucchese suspected that Florence or some other power had incited a group of Lucchese *banniti* to raise Pallarosa in rebellion in 1383,[25] and Florence had certainly at one point backed the *condottieri* John Hawkwood and Richard Ramsey in claims they made against Lucca for settlement of debts owed to them by Alderigo degli Antelminelli, and though Lucca could in no way be held responsible, she was obliged to settle these claims, for 'hoc tempus ius sit in armis et opprimet leges timor'.[26] The

---

repeated her willingness to join the league in Jan. and Feb. 1381, *Reg.*, nos. 810, 817. She took the same line of willingness, as a minor power, to accept whatever the others should decide in negotiations with Florence about the possibility of admitting new members to the Tuscan league, *Reg.*, nos. 861, 871, 883, 886. She also suggested that she should act in concert with Pietro Gambacorta concerning the admission of d'Este and Malatesta, *Anz. Temp. Lib.* 530, f. 159, 20 Dec. 1381, *Reg.*, no. 883. Silva, *Governo*, p. 213.

[23] *Reg.*, nos. 840, 867-8, 879, 881, 884, 916, 920-1, 925. She kept Antonio of Pietrasanta as commissioner in Perugia, Nov. 1380, *Reg.*, nos. 2077-8, 2080, and Niccolò di messer Carlino in Florence, 6 Dec. 1381-10 Feb. 1382, nos. 999-1029. She sent aid to Perugia Oct. 1381, nos. 857-8, and to Florence, nos. 877, 914-16, 920-2, 926 and commission of ser Niccolò Dombellinghi, 16 Jan.-10 Feb. 1382, nos. 1038-48.

[24] Defence measures, *Reg.*, no. 882, *Rif.* 7, pp. 631-2, 3 Dec. 1381, *Rif.* 8, p. 155, 2 June 1382. The *contado* was 'sgomberato' in February and June 1382. Lucca had to pay 5,000 florins to one company, *Rif.* 8, pp. 111-13, 22 Apr. 1382, commission of Giovanni Sercambi, 7-15 Feb. 1382, *Reg.* nos. 1049-54 and Sercambi I, pp. 225-6. She granted Hawkwood Lucchese citizenship and a pension of 400 florins a year in order to preserve his friendship. He never took up the citizenship, but the pension was paid regularly in the following years, *Rif.* 8, pp. 54-5, 14 Feb. 1382, *Reg.*, nos. 1098, 1116-20, 1147, 1150-1, 1153, 1158. *Capitoli*, 32, p. 145 lists payments to him 1382-91. Lucca made gifts and loans to Lutz of Landau for the same purpose, *Rif.* 7, p. 347, 9 Nov. 1380, *Rif.* 8, p. 317, 13 Nov. 1382, *Min.* 3, 21 July 1381. Provision to Count Eberhard of Landau, *Capitoli*, 3, f. 31, 1,000 florins, 13 Sept. 1381.

[25] Sercambi I, pp. 234-6, where he dates it 1382. *Rif.* 8, p. 605, 9 Sept. 1383. Pallarosa was quickly recovered, apparently by 12 Sept. 1383, *Rif.* 8, p. 606, 10 Sept., p. 607, 12 Sept. 1383, but the rebellion might have been more serious for 1383 was a plague year and so many citizens had fled that Lucca was short of defenders.

[26] Florentine support for these claims, *Anz. Temp. Lib.* 530, ff. 157^{v} and 158, 22 Nov. 1381. These are *Reg.* nos. 874 and 875. Also no. 2079. *Rif.* 7, pp. 638-9, 7 Dec.

Lucchese had intercepted a letter to Ramsey from one of his captains, in which he said 'Fiorenze vedara elpasso a ongne vostro piacere e quello vifara bisongno, per chagione vorrebbeno volenthiere Lucca fosse disfatta. Questo ho daloro'.[27] There were other causes for tension between the two cities. Both had grievances about the reception of their rebels. Giovanni degli Obizi was not only still living in Florence as a Florentine citizen, but he had also been made Captain-General of the Florentine forces, and Lucca protested against this in vain.[28] Florence also complained that her rebels were taking refuge in Lucchese territory and using it as a base for attacks on Florence.[29] Lucca took steps to punish those guilty, but Florence renewed her demand for their complete expulsion 'multototiens et per oratores et per seriem literarum cum instantia'.[30] Lucca expelled some of these rebels, but firmly refused to drive out the rest, particularly those who had come to Lucca under the general immunities granted to workers in the *arte della lana*, the development of which the Lucchese government was trying to encourage.[31] Another cause for bad feeling was the existence of boundary disputes between communes in Lucchese territory and communes in Pistoiese territory. These disputes flared up into violence, and Lucca resented Florentine failure to give redress to her

---

1381 (discussion of a letter dated 18 Nov.). Lucca paid 7,300 florins to Hawkwood and 2,500 to Ramsey, who at one time claimed as much as 10,000, *Reg.*, no. 1183, 3 Jan. 1384. *Rif.* 9, p. 32, 7 Jan., p. 117, 3 June 1384, p. 321, 21 Mar. 1385. Lucca paid these sums to save her territory from attack when the company was planning to winter there. Her envoy wrote 'non si puo cavare loro del capo che Lucha non sia tutta piena doro e di drappi e non mi vale dire laimpotentia vostra'. *Anz. Temp. Lib.* 571, letter of 3 Jan. 1384. This is *Reg.*, no. 1188. Also nos. 1098, 1116–20, 1147, 1150–1, 1153, 1158, 1160–1, 1165, 2119–20, 1172–91.

[27] *Anz. Temp. Lib.* 439, the letter dated 6 Oct. 1383 was sent to Lucca 10 Oct. *Reg.*, nos. 1110, 1113.

[28] *Rif.* 9, p. 159, 12 Aug. 1384.

[29] *Reg.*, nos. 836, 17 July 1381; 875, 22 Nov. 1381.

[30] *Rif.* 7, pp. 614–15, 21 Nov. 1381. *Reg.*, nos. 1079, 9 May 1383; 1168, Dec. 1383. *Rif.* 8, pp. 672–3, 14 Dec. 1383. *Reg.* nos. 1202, Feb. 1384; 1204, 18 Mar. 1384.

[31] The Florentines claimed that these rebels were plotting against their state, and that Michele di Lando was planning to bring in foreign soldiers, *Reg.*, no. 1202. He had been made a Lucchese citizen 28 Mar. 1382, *Rif.* 8, p. 83 and was granted the right to carry arms, *Delib.* 133, f. 64^v, 2 Apr. 1382. Lucca complained that after she had driven out Florentines who had brought profit to her, they were allowed to stay in other places nearby, no less dangerous to the Florentines, *Reg.*, no. 1204. Also nos. 1079, 1168.

subjects and co-operate in reaching a speedy settlement. Peace was not finally made until 1386, and a local war raged along the border.[32]

But in the face of the more serious danger represented by the expeditions of Louis of Anjou in 1382 and the Sire de Coucy two years later Lucca consulted with her allies.[33] In fact the duke of Anjou took the route south via Bologna and the Romagna, and therefore did not involve the Tuscan communes in the embarrassments and difficulties they had at one time feared.[34] But the relief expedition under Coucy in 1384 did take the route through Tuscany. Florence warned Lucca of his arrival as early as 15 June 1384, before he actually entered Italy, and urged that preparations be made and the league strengthened in view of the danger to all Italy, 'et potissime civitatum qui libertate gaudentes cupiunt sub iustis legibus gubernari'.[35] Lucca sent observers to Lombardy to report on the plans of the Sire de Coucy, and especially on the all-important question of the route he would take on his way to Naples. The envoys reported the favour shown to Coucy by the Visconti, especially by Bernabò, and the 'pericolo che questa brigata non passi in Toscana in aiuto de'Senesi a petizione di Bernabo per la via di Pontremoli'. The news that he would travel south by way of Pontremoli, then through the territory of Lucca and Pisa, was confirmed at the beginning of

[32] *Reg.*, nos. 729, 742, 919, 927, 929-30, 950, 969-70, 974, 980, 982, 984-5, 1088, 1090-1, 1130, 1148, 1168, 1190-1, 1201, 1222, 1271, 1290, 1299, 1304, 1306, May 1379-July 1385. *Rif.* 8, pp. 247-8, 2 Sept., pp. 283-4, 6 Oct., pp. 286-7, 8 Oct., p. 330, 29 Nov., p. 358, 27 Dec. 1382, pp. 440-1, 5 Feb., pp. 564-6, 20 July 1383. *Rif.* 9, pp. 42-3, 10 Feb. 1384, pp. 365-6, 22 June 1385. *Rif.* 10, pp. 80-2, 28 June, p. 98, 22 Aug. 1386. *Min.* 3, 23 Sept., 11 Nov. 1382. *Delib.* 133, f. 75ᵛ, 20 May 1382. There were also boundary disputes between Lucca and Pisa that were sufficiently serious for Lucca to send mercenary soldiers to the border for defence, *Reg.*, nos. 979, 1070, 1072, Sept. 1382-Mar. 1383. *Rif.* 8, p. 475, 13 Mar. 1383, *Rif.* 9, pp. 121-2, 10 June 1384. There was also violence between Lucchese and Florentine subjects of Barga and Sommocolonia, *Rif.* 8, p. 260, 10 Sept., p. 330, 29 Nov. 1382.

[33] She expressed her willingness to do as the other cities did, and informed Charles of Durazzo that she was too weak to do anything on her own, *Reg.*, nos. 905-7, 932, 933, 943-50, 972. Similar evasive replies to Urban VI, who urged a crusade against Louis of Anjou, and the king of France and the dukes of Burgundy and Anjou, when they asked for aid, *Reg.*, nos. 909, 914, 944, 953.

[34] News of Anjou's expendition, *Rif.* 8, pp. 56-7, 19 Feb. 1382, *Reg.*, nos. 939, 948-9, Lucca kept an observer in Lombardy 29 June-22 July 1382, *Reg.*, nos. 1230-2, 1234-9, there wrongly dated 1384.

[35] *Rif.* 9, pp. 130-1, 18 June, p. 157, 10 Aug. 1384. *Reg.*, no. 1213, 18 June 1384.

August.[36] When he announced his intention of camping on Lucchese territory and staying there several days, she appointed a *balìa* to make terms with him, but although she granted him passage and supplies and a payment of 3,000 florins, her territory suffered severely.[37]

While Coucy was still in Tuscany negotiations began for the renewal of the league of Tuscan cities. Lucca took the opportunity of renewing her complaints against Florence about the reception of her rebels, but she did not allow this to prevent her from joining the renewed league, concluded 21 October 1384.[38] Once again she obtained favourable terms. She had to provide 25 lances, the same *taglia* as Città di Castello, and far less than Pisa with 120 lances and 150 crossbowmen of the Genoese riviera. She was explicitly exempted from any expenses beyond this *taglia*, and her forces were not obliged to fight outside the territory of the allies. The forces of the league were not to enter her territory except at her request, and she was again exempted from two clauses concerning the treatment of rebels. Some of these provisions gave great satisfaction in Lucca, for in the margin of the copy of the league in the Lucchese Archives there are a number of notes, such as 'nota utilem exceptionem pro comuni lucano' and 'nota pro comuni lucano bonam exceptionem'.[39] Lucca can be seen co-operating with her neighbours in a number of matters at this time. She joined with Florence, Pisa, and Perugia in sending ambassadors to Siena in an attempt to bring the warring factions there to peace.[40] She later interceded with Florence over the question of Lucignano at the request of Siena, and agreed to expel certain Sienese *banniti* from her territory and prevent it being used as a base for attacks on Siena, when the

[36] *Anz. Temp. Lib.* 571, commission of Niccolò di messer Carlino and others in Lombardy, 7 July–24 Aug. 1384. *Reg.*, nos. 1233 (which should be dated 1384), 1240–57. Also nos. 2121–3.

[37] *Rif.* 9, p. 164, 25 Aug., p. 179, 4 Sept., pp. 235–6, 30 Nov. 1384. Lucca was obliged to reduce the *estimo* of Massa, where he had camped because of the damage suffered, *Reg.*, no. 1221, 28 Aug. 1384. Defence measures during and after his passage, *Rif.* 9, p. 327, 27 Mar. 1385, *Reg.*, nos. 1258–70. *Rif.* 9, p. 191, 1 Oct. 1384.

[38] *Reg.*, no. 1220, 22 Aug. 1384.

[39] *Capitoli*, 25, pp. 261–91. The league included Florence, Perugia, Pisa, and Lucca with provision for Siena and Città di Castello to join.

[40] *Reg.*, no. 1228, Dec. 1384. *Cronaca Senese di Paolo di Tommaso Montauri*, R.I.S., n.s., Tom. XV, pt. vi, fasc. 8, pp. 705–6, 1–9 Jan. 1385.

Sienese, backed by Florence, asked for this.[41] At the same time as she joined the general league of Tuscan cities, Lucca also made a more restricted league with Pisa. Though a number of clauses dealt with relatively minor matters, such as the treatment of debtors who fled from one city to another, the league also provided for reciprocal aid and defence against attackers, and the two cities were to consult together regularly, and neither was to enter any other league without the other's knowledge.[42]

But if Lucca was on good terms with her immediate neighbours, her old close relations with Bernabò Visconti had weakened in the years 1382–5, and his place had to some extent been taken by his nephew, Giangaleazzo.[43] She still maintained friendly relations with him, asking his favour in a commercial matter, but when he wrote to the Lucchese of the plans of the duke of Anjou, they replied less warmly than they had to his letters in the past.[44] They were fully aware of the favour he had shown first to Anjou, and then to Coucy. They had kept a particularly close watch on Coucy's expedition, and their envoy reported 'questa inpresa si fa di consentimento e di volonta di messer Bernabo, e questo si vede di chiaro ed e dissposto a fare a quessto siri cio che vorra', and 'el siri e cosi venuto a possta di messer B[ernabò] come io sono alla vosstra'.[45]

Giangaleazzo had also shown friendship to Coucy, making preparations to receive him at Pavia, though he never in fact went there.[46] Giangaleazzo was able to win Lucchese friend-

[41] *Rif.* 9, p. 352, 18 May 1385, *Reg.*, no. 1304. *Rif.* 9, p. 359, 2 June 1385. *Min.* 3, 2 June 1385.

[42] *Rif.* 9, pp. 165–70, 26 Aug. 1384. *Reg.*, nos. 1218, 25 July; 1224, 28 Nov. 1384. The league was proclaimed 30 Nov. 1384.

[43] The Florentines too began to look to Giangaleazzo rather than to Bernabò in these years, Collino, 'La politica Florentino-Bolognese', pp. 121–2, 125–7, and docs. quoted there. Seregni, 'Un disegno federale di Bernabò Visconti', pp. 180–2, Landogna, 'La Politica dei Visconti in Toscana', pp. 115, 151–2.

[44] *Reg.*, no. 1166, Dec. 1383. *Anz. Temp. Lib.* 530, f. 178^{v}, 10 Aug. 1382, *Reg.*, no. 958.

[45] *Anz. Temp. Lib.* 571, *Reg.*, nos. 1056–8, 1233, 1242. He also reported that there was danger of Bernabò sending forces to intervene in Tuscan affairs, aiding the Sienese who were on bad terms with Florence at this time, *Reg.*, no. 1240.

[46] D. M. Bueno de Mesquita, *Giangaleazzo Visconti, Duke of Milan, 1351–1402* (Cambridge, 1941), p. 28. *Reg.*, nos. 1240, 1242, 2121–2.

ship by his intervention with Coucy to prevent them being attacked 'cum lucanos haberet in fratres et amicos precipuos et sibi ac suis reputet danna facta offerens pro conservatione status pacifici et libertatis lucane posse suum et vires'. This intervention, though ineffective, was much appreciated in Lucca, 'quod quidem si recta mentis acumine ponderetur servitium fuit numquam temporis vetustate delendum', and they made provision to retain his friendship. In January 1385 Giangaleazzo requested Lucchese aid when Coucy was returning to France through his lands, and the Lucchese were agreed that 'nullo modo videtur debere negari consensus multis causis et rationibus'.[47] The *Minute di Riformagioni*, which record the opinions of thirteen councillors, show that no one was against sending aid, opinions differing only on the best means of providing for the safety of the city during the absence of their forces. They agreed to send twenty-five lances, though these could so ill be spared that others would have to be hired to take their place in defending the city.[48] When a few months later after the fall of Bernabò, Giangaleazzo again requested aid 'propter novitates in partibus Lombardie occursas', Lucca again sent twenty-five lances 'considerata potentia et secundis successibus prefati domini et quod esse potest utilis lucano comuni si eius amicicia et benivolentia acquiratur'.[49]

Lucca was twice troubled by armed companies in 1385 and had to pay a total of 4,000 florins to buy them off,[50] so that she quickly joined the league against the companies concluded at Legnano 31 August 1385 between Giangaleazzo, Florence, and Bologna, which Lucca and Pisa were invited to join. The General Council voted in favour by 141 votes to six, though it involved a *taglia* of fifty lances, more than she had ever had

[47] *Rif.* 9, p. 180, 9 Sept. 1384, p. 281, 7 Jan. 1385. Bueno de Mesquita, *Giangaleazzo Visconti*, p. 29. Landogna, 'La politica dei Visconti in Toscana', p. 151.

[48] *Min.* 3, 7 Jan. 1385. They had sent only *balisterii* and 20 *pagis* of Lucchese *banniti* at a cost of 60 florins to Cortona at the request of Beatrice Castracani, when she appealed to them as particular friends and protectors, *Rif.* 9, p. 191, 1 Oct., pp. 213–14, 2 Nov. 1384.

[49] *Rif.* 9, p. 351, 18 May 1385.

[50] Company of Taddeo Pepoli and Boldrino da Panicale, *Min.* 3, 10 Apr. 1385, *Reg.*, nos. 1288–9. Company of Giovanni d'Azzo, called the Company of the Rose, *Min.* 3, 14 June 1385, *Reg.*, nos. 1292–5, 1297–8.

before.[51] Lucca also took part in the negotiations for the admission of Siena to the league of 21 October 1384, which were concluded 18 November 1385.[52] Lucca had to provide thirty lances, not twenty-five as in the league of 1384, and apparently lost some of the exemptions she had been granted, though she gained the right to make peace with any society which had been on her territory for ten days without being driven off the by forces of the league.

[51] *Rif.* 9, pp. 404–5, 15 Sept. 1385, ratified pp. 439–41, 26 Nov. 1385. *Reg.*, nos. 1308, 1219 (which should be dated 1385).

[52] *Capitoli*, 25, pp. 303–28, 18 Nov. 1385. It was not to prejudice the league of 31 Aug. 1385, nor the previous Tuscan league. *Rif.* 9, pp. 408–9, 6 Oct. 1385, ratification, pp. 446–7, 13 Dec. 1385.

9

1385–1392

In April 1386 Lucca received an embassy from the Pope which put her in some difficulties, for he wished to come to Lucca and make a brief stay there. Lucca had a lively sense of gratitude for the support of the Papacy since 1369, and Urban VI had only recently obliged her in the matter of the punishment of the Carmelites involved in the plot of messer Matteo Gigli.[1] Nevertheless, when the question was first raised many of her citizens were against granting the Pope's request, provided it could be done without forfeiting his support. Some wished to make excuses; others to receive him only on conditions.[2] The reason was not any opposition to the presence of the Pope himself, but fear of the men at arms and others whom he would necessarily bring with him, and the many strangers who would flock to Lucca from other states if the Pope were there. When the matter came up again in October it was finally agreed that the Pope should be received, but precautions were to be taken to avoid disturbances. No armed men were to enter Lucca or any other walled town. Extra guards were to be stationed in fortresses, the officer of the guard in Lucca was given emergency powers, and a special *balìa* was elected to ensure the safety of Lucca.[3] But once it had been decided that the Pope should be received, Lucca made whole-hearted preparations to do him honour.[4] He arrived just before Christmas 1386, and although in October he had only asked for passage and leave to spend one night in Lucca on his way to Modena, he in fact stayed in the city for nine months. When he came to leave in September 1387, the same kind of difficulties arose as had done on his arrival. He

[1] *Anz. Temp. Lib.* 530, f. 228^{v}, 8 Mar, 1385. *Reg.*, nos. 1277, 1285–6, 1309–10, 2126. *Rif.* 10, p. 50, 3 Mar. 1386.

[2] *Min.* 3 (not foliated), 3, 8, and 26 Apr. 1386.

[3] *Rif.* 10, pp. 127–8, 31 Oct., p. 143, 2 Dec. 1386. Also *Min.* 3 (not foliated) same dates.

[4] *Min.* 3, 9 Nov. 1386. Descriptions of the festivities in Sercambi I, pp. 252–8.

desired an armed escort to ensure his safety, but the Lucchese did not wish to permit men at arms to enter their territory. Efforts were made to induce the Pope to forgo the escort, and failing this a small number of men at arms were to be permitted to enter the Lucchese state at carefully chosen points, but on no account within the city itself.[5] Apart from the account of Sercambi there are no records of the way in which the Pope's presence affected the city. The Lucchese kept Florence informed of the Pope's intention of visiting Lucca,[6] but his presence in Tuscany was unwelcome to the Florentines, who may well have resented Lucca's willingness to receive him.[7]

There are certainly many other signs of suspicions between Lucca and Florence in the years 1385–8. In February 1385 a plot was discovered in Lucca. Messer Matteo Gigli, one of the leading citizens of Lucca, and certain others were in correspondence with messer Giovanni degli Obizi to procure his return to Lucca by force. One of the two Carmelites who acted as go-betweens was a Florentine and messer Giovanni himself claimed to have the power of Florence behind him.[8] Lucca professed not to believe this, but all her efforts in the preceding years had been insufficient to induce the Florentines to dismiss him.[9] When she sent to Florence to protest and demand redress, the Florentines sent apologies and excuses, but at least one Florentine councillor had pointed out that the Lucchese had received Florentine rebels, and in December Florence wrote begging for the release of the Florentine Carmelite.[10] There were other causes for irritation, though they were not in themselves very important. Florence

[5] *Rif.* 10, pp. 312–13, 24 Aug. 1387. *Min.* 3, 25 Aug. 1387. During the Pope's stay the debt of 50,000 florins was finally settled and Lucca freed from any further obligations, *Rif.* 10, pp. 312–13, 24 Aug. 1387, she apparently paid 4,835 florins that were still outstanding, p. 329, 13 Sept. 1387.

[6] A.S.F. *Cart. Sign. Miss.* 20, f. 117, 4 Dec., ff. 118v–119, 11 Dec., f. 120v, 14 Dec. 1386. Lucca asked for 20 lances from Florence and the Florentines agreed to send them, f. 119v, 12 Dec. 1386 and *Consulte*, 25, f. 150, 12 Dec. 1386.

[7] Sercambi I, p. 252. G. Collino, 'La guerra viscontea contro gli Scaligeri', *Archivio Storico Lombardo*, Vol. XXXIV (1907), pp. 111–12. A.S.F. *Consulte*, 25, ff. 155–157, 27 Dec. 1386, ff. 161–161v, 29 Jan. 1387 (Fl. style 1386), also ff. 165–166v, dated 7 Dec. 1386, but should probably be 7 Jan. 1387.

[8] *Sentenze e Bandi*, 70, ff. 35–6, Feb. 1385.

[9] She had tried again as recently as 19 Jan. 1385, *Reg.*, no. 1272.

[10] A.S.F. *Consulte*, 24 ff. 37–37v, 2 Mar. 1385, *Sign. Cart. Mis.* 20, f. 65v, 18 Dec.

supported the claims of an 'heir' under the will of the *condottiere*, Count Eberhard, against Lucca,[11] and she felt herself endangered, when Florence dismissed 500 lances which had been in her service.[12] In June Lucca asked to be assured of Florentine protection and that this should be made known to all.[13] Florence too felt she had cause for complaint. Lucca had pleaded the cause of Siena over Lucignano,[14] and in July she had to assure the Florentines that her negotiations with an armed company were not designed to direct the company against any neighbouring state.[15] In some respects the two cities acted as good neighbours and allies, as when Lucca asked Florence to intercede with John Beltoft and others who were demanding money,[16] and herself sent aid to Florence in October 1385.[17] In March 1387 Florence urged Lucca to send her orators to Bologna to confer on joint efforts to resist possible attacks from 3,000 lances, dismissed when peace was signed in Lombardy.[18] But in April 1387 the Florentines heard rumours that Lucca was leaning towards the Count of Virtù.[19] It was suggested in the Florentine council that their ambassadors should try to dissuade the Count of Virtù from undertaking the protection of the Lucchese, that the Florentines should write to Lucca saying they did not believe the rumours, at the same time giving Lucca assurances of friendship and protection by the allies, so that she would have

1385. When the plot was first discovered some Lucchese had been opposed to sending news of it to Florence as well as to Pisa, *Min.* 3, 18 Feb. 1385.

[11] *Rif.* 9, p. 328, 29 Mar. 1385.

[12] *Rif.* 9, p. 313, 1 Mar. 1385, *Min.* 3, 2 Mar. 1385.

[13] 'Humilmente pregate la loro signoria che si degnino la loro favore gratia et protectione a quelli loro figliuoli acostare per modo che ciascuno sia palese noi in la loro gratia esser lo quale favore et gratia avendo noi non si teme di cosa che potesse avenire', *Anz. Temp. Lib.* 530, ff. 232–232v, June 1385, no. 1290 in *Reg.*

[14] *Anz. Temp. Lib.* 530, ff. 236v–237v, July 1385, no. 1304 in *Reg.*

[15] *Reg.*, no. 1295, 7 July 1385.

[16] *Anz. Temp. Lib.* 571, *Ambascerie Carte Originali*, 17 Aug. 1385, no. 1219 in *Reg.* (where incorrectly dated 1384). Despite this Lucca had to settle Beltoft's claim *Rif.* 9, p. 395, 2 Sept. 1385.

[17] *Min.* 3, 1 Oct. 1385.

[18] A.S.F., *Sign. Cart. Miss.* 20, f. 123, 16 Mar. 1387.

[19] 'Et quod oratores ituri Papiam dicant Comiti qualiter dicitur quod Lucani volunt se sibi recommendare et quod hoc non creditur et removeritur ab intentione et hoc conferatur primo cum colligatis qui sunt hic', A.S.F. *Consulte*, 26, f. 28, 26 Apr. 1387. Collino, 'La guerra viscontea contro gli Scaligeri', p. 121, Landogna, 'La politica dei Visconti in Toscana', p. 156.

no need to turn to Milan.[20] But Lucca continued to regard the Florentines with distrust. The observers she kept in Siena during the summer and autumn of 1387 to report on the policy of the Florentines, especially towards Montepulciano, express suspicion of Florentine intentions not only towards Siena, but also towards Lucca herself. They reported 'qui e detto per certi che tornano da F[irenze], che apertamente parlano la prima cosa che faccino e anno sopra lo stomacho e defacti de Lucha. Dio tolgha loro la possa. Crediamo che sentiate cio, ma qui e divulgato il mal loro ragionamento e pensiero. Dio vi conservi in buono stato'.[21] The envoys warned the Lucchese government to keep a careful guard on their castles.[22]

Though Giangaleazzo was at this time expanding his possessions in Lombardy, the Lucchese do not seem to have sent any observers there, and there are virtually no references to Lombard affairs in Lucchese sources.[23] The Florentines sent an embassy to Pisa and Lucca after the fall of Padua, urging them to take precautions for the safeguard of their liberty, but not to fear, and assuring them of Florentine support.[24] But

[20] 'Et provideatur cum colligatis qui sunt hic quod Lucanis declarentur qualiter colligati intendunt ipsos habere pro fratribus ne devient propter metum ad aliud . . . cum consensu colligatorum per omnes colligatos assicurentur Lucani de statu suo, et per eos requirantur ad mittendum oratores Papiam sicut alii', A.S.F. *Consulte*, 26, ff. 28–9, 26 Apr. 1387.

[21] *Anz. Temp. Lib.* 571, letter of 5 July 1387, no. 1347 in *Reg.* Commission of Andrea da Volterra and Niccolò di messer Carlino in Siena, 22 June–30 Sept. 1387, *Reg.*, nos. 1341–54, 1358, 1364–70, 1411. Bueno de Mesquita, *Giangaleazzo Visconti*, pp. 90–2.

[22] *Reg.*, no. 1353, 6 Aug. 1387. This was in fact a time of crisis for the Lucchese contado; *banniti* were active there and it was necessary to make special provision against disorders, *Rif.* 10, pp. 281–4, 7 June 1387, p. 421, 4 Feb., pp. 546–7, 11 Sept. 1388, *Rif.* 11, pp. 111–12, 18 Aug. 1389. *Banniti* revealed a plot to betray the castle of Massa Lunense, *Reg.*, no. 2127, Feb. 1388. *Min.* 3, 26 Nov. 1387. Lucca had to buy off the company of Eberhard Suyler and Bertrand de la Salle, which was rumoured to be in Florentine pay. But this seems to have been untrue and Florence offered to make peace with them jointly, and included Lucca, Pisa, and Siena in the terms she made with the company April 1388, *Rif.* 10, p. 363, 23 Dec. 1387, A.S.F. *Cart. Sign. Miss.* 20, f. 165v, 20 Dec. 1387, *Dieci di Balìa: Miss. Legaz. Commis.* 1, f. 68, 2 Apr. 1388. News of other companies, *Reg.*, nos. 1374, 1377, 1379, 1381–2, 1387. Warning from Florence, *Dieci di Balìa: Miss. Legaz. Commis.* 1, f. 77, 21 Apr., f. 95, 24 May, f. 101, 5 June 1388.

[23] References to possible attacks by companies if peace or truce signed, *Rif.* 10, p. 485, 19 June, p. 581, 8 Dec. 1388 and to the Venetian occupation of Treviso, *Reg.*, no. 1384, 25 Dec. 1388.

[24] A.S.F. *Dieci di Balìa: Cart. Miss.* 1, f. 153, 27 Nov. 1388.

Lucca undoubtedly felt less alarm at Visconti gains than was felt in Florence. Verona and Padua were far distant and Lucca had no ambitions which Visconti expansion could threaten. If it occurred to her that sooner or later the ruler of Milan might attempt to take Lucca itself within the Visconti state, she must have reflected that the danger from Florence was nearer and more immediate, and that the good relations she enjoyed with Milan were a safeguard against any threats from her more powerful neighbour. So that when in May 1389 the Lucchese were invited by the Count of Virtù to enter the league which was being negotiated with Florence, Bologna, and other cities, they expressed themselves willing to do so.[25]

But if they had no hesitation about joining the league, they had some reservations about the terms to be made. They hoped in fact for the same kind of concessions and exemptions that they had been granted in previous leagues. They also wanted to avoid committing themselves until it seemed fairly certain that a league was going to be signed. Their ambassadors were instructed[26] to wait until the Count had reached agreement with the Florentines and Bolognese and then, but not before, to ask that certain concessions be made. These included exemption from the clause requiring the expulsion of rebels from other cities, and a provision that the forces of the league should not be permitted to enter her territory except at her express request, 'perche avemo provato che la gente che si manda in aiuto, ogni volta cia fatto piu damno che la gente inimica'. She also wished for a modification of the preliminary version of the league, which had been sent to her, and her ambassadors were instructed to speak to the Count in person about this, alone without his council. The chapter they objected to was one which provided that each of the allies should be recognized as owning by right the territory of which it was in fact in possession. Lucca did not feel she could consent to this because 'lo comune di Firenze tiene una grande e magiore parte del nostro contado', and

[25] Sindics were appointed for this 14 May 1389, *Rif.* 11, pp. 83–4. Florence had already informed her allies of the league that was under negotiation, A.S.F. *Dieci di Balìa: Cart. Miss.* 1, f. 181, 30 Mar., f. 191, 15 May 1389.

[26] Instructions to the ambassadors, *Anz. Temp. Lib.* 572, May 1389, no. 1397 in *Reg.*

suggested a modification in the wording of the clause which would save her rights to these lands. This is not the only indication that Lucca had not forgotten her claims to lands which were held by Florence, and that she was especially mindful of them at this time. She even seems to have had some hopes of recovering them, and was in negotiation with Giovanni d'Azzo, a *condottiere* and an enemy of Florence, to aid her in this should a favourable opportunity occur.[27]

The negotiations for the league were long drawn out largely owing to the Florentines' reluctance to accept the Count's terms. The Lucchese ambassadors knew that if the league were not concluded war would shortly follow, and felt that the Florentines were in the wrong, though they did not say so openly, in refusing terms which seemed fair and reasonable to the other envoys.[28] But despite her sympathy with Milan and her suspicion of Florence, it was soon clear that she was not prepared to side with Milan against Florence, let alone to fight the Florentines as an ally of Milan. The prospect of being urged to join a league which did not include Florence and Bologna, filled her with alarm. If such a league were proposed, the Lucchese ambassadors were first to consult with those of the other Tuscan cities in the hope that they would reject the proposal. But if the other cities accepted, the Lucchese were to speak privately with the Count to explain Lucca's position and induce him not to persist in the proposal. They were to urge that Lucca's membership of such a league would be of little advantage, for she was too small and weak even to control who should pass through her territory, so that she was not able even to grant passage to her allies and refuse it to her enemies. And if she joined such a league, it would enrage the Florentines, whose territory bordered on hers both in the Garfagnana and in the Valdinievole, so that she would be able to do Lucca irreparable damage long before the Count could send aid, however prompt and plentiful this was. The ambassadors were further to urge that the existing leagues, which still had some time to run, were adequate, and finally, as a last resort if the Count still insisted on a league without

[27] Letters of 5 and 6 Sept. 1389, *Anz. Temp. Lib.* 429, nos. 1423, 1424 in *Reg.*

[28] Letter of the Lucchese envoy, *Anz. Temp. Lib.* 429, 31 May 1389, no. 2133 in *Reg.*, and Silva, *Governo,* Doc. 20, pp. 325–6, where quoted in full.

Florence and Bologna, they were to say that they had not the authority to reply and must await new instructions from their government.[29]

The conference at Pavia broke down at the end of May, and although, owing to the efforts of Pietro Gambacorta, negotiations began again in July[30] and continued for much of the summer, no great optimism was felt about the outcome. Both sides were raising forces, and Lucca was making efforts to retain the goodwill of individual *condottieri* and maintained observers to report on military and political developments.[31] She watched events in Siena particularly closely, for Siena was threatened by an armed company part of which was in Florentine pay, and which was rumoured to be about to march on Pisa and Lucca. If that had been their intention, the leaders were dissuaded by the Florentines, who feared that such an attack would drive Pisa and Lucca into the arms of Milan.[32] The Lucchese continued to hope for the conclusion of the league, seeing the alternative as war between her two nearest and most powerful neighbours, in which she could hardly fail to find herself exposed to the attacks of mercenary soldiers, even if she suffered no more serious harm. But much as she desired the conclusion of the league, she was quite unable to influence events. The decision of peace or war lay in the hands of Florence and Milan, and Lucca could only hope that peace would be maintained, though she feared that the

[29] Giangaleazzo did propose such a league after the failure of the negotiations with Florence and Bologna, and although the Sienese and perhaps others were prepared to agree, the Lucchese were not, and their envoy, presumably after trying to dissuade the Count, referred the matter to Lucca as instructed, Bueno de Mesquita, *Giangaleazzo Visconti*, p. 104.

[30] Silva, *Governo*, pp. 248–51. The Lucchese sindic was appointed 19 June 1389, *Rif.* 11, pp. 90–2.

[31] *Reg.* nos. 1395, 1413. Commission of Niccolò di messer Carlino and Andrea da Volterra in Siena, 2 July–Oct. 1389, *Reg.*, nos. 1412–9, also nos. 1355–7, 1359, 1361–3, 1371. Commission of Niccolò Liena in Parma, 30 Aug.–6 Sept. 1389, *Reg.*, nos. 1420–4.

[32] *Anz. Temp. Lib.* 571, 16 Aug. 1389, no. 1355 in *Reg.* (where wrongly dated 1387). Silva, *Governo*, p. 253. In March the Lucchese ambassador in Siena, acting in concert with the Bolognese ambassador there, had tried to mediate between Florence and Siena, A.S.F. *Dieci di Balìa: Cart. Miss.* 1, f. 180, 19 Mar. 1389. The Florentines had thanked her, but their reply was discouraging. In March Lucca sent aid at the request of Siena, *Reg.*, nos. 1390–2, according to Minerbetti, p. 79, she sent 25 lances. lances.

spinning out of negotiations in Pisa while armies were being raised meant war.[33]

The league was concluded in Pisa 9 October 1389, but it brought only a few months of uneasy peace before war was declared in April 1390.[34] The day after the league with Milan was concluded another more limited league was signed by Florence, Bologna, Perugia, Pisa, Lucca, and Città di Castello.[35] Although it was declared to be without prejudice to the league of 9 October, it was inspired by Florentine distrust of Giangaleazzo. Nevertheless Lucca joined with her neighbours in this second league. But she remained neutral and took no part in the war. It would have been against the whole trend of her policy since 1369 to have done so. Lucca had reason to mistrust Florence and to see Milan as a useful counterbalance, but her mistrust of Florence was not strong enough to bring her out on the side of Milan. The reply she had instructed her ambassadors to make to the Count's proposal for a league without Florence and Bologna in 1389 probably expresses accurately enough her motives for keeping out the of Florentine-Milanese war.[36] When she was obliged to fight wars that directly concerned her, she quickly got into difficulties, as the period 1369–70 and 1397–1400 shows, and she felt no inclination to fight in a war that was not her direct con-

[33] *Reg.*, nos. 1416–17, 21 and 22 Sept. 1389.

[34] Lucchese sindics appointed 5 Oct. 1389, *Rif.* 11, pp. 136–7, ratified 13 Oct. 1389, *Rif.* 11, p. 140, and *Reg.*, no. 2138, 4 Jan. 1390. Copies of the league in *Capitoli*, 25, pp. 341–60 and *Protocolli* of ser Domenico Lupardi, *Archivio de'Notari* no. 282, ff. 2–12v. It was to last for three years and was directed against the companies. Lucca had a *taglia* of only 25 lances, but had to pay a share of the *condotta* of Hawkwood and Count Conrad. She paid about 1,035 florins for this, *Rif.*, 11, p. 142, 15 Oct. 1389. *Reg.*, nos. 1404–5, 6 and 8 Nov. 1389. Lucca watched events carefully, keeping observers in Pisa, Florence, Bologna and Modena in the early summer of 1390, *Reg.*, nos. 1433–9, 1451–66, 1467–86, 1487–93.

[35] League of 10 Oct. 1389 in *Capitoli*, 25, pp. 369–90. L. Osio, *Documenti Diplomatici Tratti dagli Archivi Milanesi*, Vol. I (Milan, 1864), no. cci, pp. 278–93. This league was to last for three years, and Lucca had the same *taglia* of 25 lances. She was also granted the same kind of concessions as she had had in previous leagues, express exemption from any expenses beyond the *taglia*, from clauses regarding the reception of *banniti* from other cities and a provision that the forces of the allies were only to enter her territory on her express request. These exemptions evidently gave satisfaction in Lucca, for they are marked 'nota pro comuni lucano', 'utili clausula' etc. in the margin of the text both in the copy in *Capitoli*, 25 and in another copy in *Protocolli* of ser Domenico Lupardi, *Archivio de'Notari*, no. 282, ff. 15–22v.

[36] *Anz. Temp. Lib.* 571, May 1389, no. 1397 in *Reg.*

cern and in which her interests were not directly involved. If she had taken one side such a small state would have suffered heavily at the hands of the other. In contrast to her attitude in the league against the Pope in 1375–6 Florence seems to have accepted Lucchese neutrality. Perhaps she felt that if she forced Lucca to choose one side or the other Lucca might choose Milan. She protested, however, at alleged breaches of Lucchese neutrality, when she heard that Milanese forces were cutting timber on Lucchese territory, or when an envoy visited Lucca asking for passage for Milanese forces.[37] Lucca's neutrality did not protect her from the passage of soldiers through her territory without her permission. The forces of both sides, but especially of Milan, passed through her lands, seizing supplies by force, and, though attempts at resistance were made, her territory suffered heavily, particularly the vicariates of Pietrasanta, Camaiore, and Massa Lunense.[38]

[37] *Reg.*, nos. 1457, 25 May; 1466, 20 June 1390. The Florentines wrote to Lucca protesting against favour they alleged had been shown to Milan, A.S.F. *Cart. Sign. Miss*. 22, f. 156, 26 Aug. 1391. Silva, *Governo*, pp. 272–3.

[38] Sercambi I, pp. 266–70. *Min.* 4 (not foliated), 21 and 22 Aug., 18 Nov. 1391. The forces of Florence and Milan camped on Lucchese territory for two and a half months, *Delib.* 133, f. 14, 19 Feb. 1392.

PART III

The Structure of Politics after 1369

10

THE GOVERNMENT 'A POPOLO'

In 1370, with the departure of Cardinal Guy of Boulogne, Lucca was once more free to rule herself as she wished. There can be no doubt of the delight of the Lucchese at the recovery of their freedom and independence after almost thirty years of Pisan rule. As in other Italian states of the period local patriotism and love of their city was strong among the Lucchese. It is a theme that runs through the public records as much as it does through Sercambi's chronicle. When the Gonfaloniere in 1397 spoke of Lucca as 'cara madre vostra e dolce' and said that Lucca 'nostra pietosa madre volendose a voi mantenere in sua liberta . . . ricorre a voi suoi cari e legittimi figluoli a voi si racomanda et voi con lagrime prega che non la lassiate perire che non li lassiate perdere lo nome de la sua liberta'[1] he was only giving particularly clear expression to a feeling that all shared.

As well as love for their city the Lucchese also had pride in her, and this implied the maintenance of certain standards in the conduct of public affairs. They felt that certain things were fitting in a free and independent city. They felt the need to excuse their somewhat inglorious foreign policy, their policy of 'flexibilitas et tractabilitas cum vicinis'.[2] They felt that it was just and honourable that pacts be observed,[3] that it was proper that Lucca should treat her creditors fairly 'sicuti decet in civitate libera' and that it was dishonourable that promises should be broken or debts remain long unpaid.[4] They were

[1] *Rif.* 13, p. 38, 18 June 1397.

[2] *Anz. Temp. Lib.* 530, f. 8, 24 May 1374, no. 460 in *Reg.* And above, Chapter 5 pp. 118–9.

[3] 'Et iustum sit et ad honorem comunis lucani pertineat pacta servari', *Rif.* 2, p. 134, 13 Nov. 1370.

[4] 'Conveniens sit quod per comune mutuantibus secundum id quod promittitur integre satisfiat nec contingat mutuantes ultra quam deceat suis pecuniis defraudari', *Rif.* 2, pp. 24–5, 6 Aug. 1370. 'Ser Marchese Gilii . . . consuluit quod sibi videtur pro honore et utilitate comunis lucani ut cuilibet sicuti decet in civitate libera suum ius et debitum tribuatur', *Rif.* 2, p. 30, 9 Aug. 1370.

quick to resent insults to the city, such as the building of the road at Stallatoio or the capture of Federigo Gonzaga on Lucchese territory.[5] Their pride in their city extended even to the smallest details, as when it was provided that Lucca should buy silver trumpets for use on ceremonial occasions when it was discovered that other cities had them, so that Lucca should not be in any way inferior to her neighbours.[6]

Love for their city and pride in her meant above all, a desire that she should be ruled in liberty. Much is heard of liberty in Lucchese records in the last thirty years of the fourteenth century, but as in other Tuscan communes the word is used in different senses to mean both independence from outside rule and a republican regime in internal government.[7] Liberty in the sense of freedom from outside rule was something particularly precious to the Lucchese, because for so much of the fourteenth century Lucca had been under the rule of a succession of outside powers culminating in that of her old rival and hated neighbour, Pisa. Over twenty-five years after Lucca had recovered her freedom, the Gonfaloniere expressed these feelings especially clearly in a speech designed to induce his fellow citizens to agree to financial sacrifices in order to defend Lucca against renewed Pisan attacks:

Manifesto e a ogni homo il quale ae dele cose vero cognoscimento et iudicio che de le piu care cose che dio ponesse al mondo fu liberta, la quale si conosce per lo suo contrario cioe per la servitu, la quale servitu quanto sia dura et aspra molti citadini viveno li quali per prova et experientia ne possono rendere et rendeno vera testimonanza. Certo veramente si tiene che ciascuno virtuoso citadino prima la morte volesse che ne le mani de crudeli et perfidi Pisani ne daltri ritornare. Et chi e che dubiti che chi governa Pisa non a mai adaltro inteso ne adaltro continuamente intende se non a pensare e tractare come possa la nostra cita occupare e a servitu riducere e socto li suoi calci mettere noi e la nostra liberta. La quale liberta tanti nostri honorevili citadini tanto tempo cercarono, tanto desiderarono et finalmente obtenneno con favore et gratia del cielo cioe di dio, e con favore e gratia di sancta chiesa, e del sacro imperio, et con gosto et pregio inextimabile de citadini.[8]

[5] See above, Chapter 6, pp. 137–8, Sercambi I, pp. 308–9. It is clear that he had no objection to the capture as such, only to the fact that it took place on Lucchese territory, for he asks why he could not have been captured somewhere else.

[6] *Rif.* 8, p. 87, 11 Apr. 1382.

[7] N. Rubinstein, 'Florence and the despots, some aspects of Florentine diplomacy in the fourteenth century', *Transactions of the Royal Historical Society*, 5th Ser. Vol. II (1952), pp. 29–31.

[8] *Rif.* 13, p. 38, 18 June 1397.

Liberty here is clearly used in the sense of independence from outside rule, but the Lucchese did not always distinguish so clearly between external and internal liberty. Like Florence and other Tuscan cities, they probably regarded the two as closely connected.[9] The Lucchese sometimes spoke of liberty in a way which suggests that they had primarily internal government in mind, using phrases like 'pro bono pacis et conservatione status atque libertatis Lucane civitatis' or 'pro bono felicis atque popularis status atque libertatis Lucane civitatis', which are common in Lucchese documents. But often internal and external liberty are linked, as when in 1390 the Gonfaloniere referring to the form of government spoke of how 'con li quali ordini et unita come voi chiaramente sapete dal principio de la nostra liberta fine a ogi siamo interamente conservati',[10] or in May 1392 the vice-Gonfaloniere, speaking of how peacefully Lucca had been ruled until mid-1390, said 'mirabantur cuncti qualiter tam parva civitas intra tot potentissimos populos et tam claras potentias posita in tanta libertate et tam tranquillo et pacifico statu se gubernaret et regeret'.[11]

The Lucchese were urged on these and other occasions to defend their liberty and their free and popular regime, which implies a claim that they enjoyed such a regime. From the time of the departure of Cardinal Guy of Boulogne in 1370 until the establishment of the *signorìa* of Paolo Guinigi in 1400 Lucca enjoyed liberty in the sense that she was ruled as a free republic with elected councils and Anziani, but in fact real control of the city soon fell into the hands of a bourgeois oligarchy. Changes took place in the first few years after 1370 which led to the exclusion of noble families at one end of the social scale and of the *popolo minuto* at the other, and left power in the hands of the wealthy merchant and business families, who shared it only with limited groups, like the judges and some of the notaries and a few lesser men.

There is evidence of friction in internal affairs very soon after Lucca had recovered her independence. There had already been complaints over alleged inequalities in the assess-

[9] Rubinstein, 'Florence and the despots', pp. 29–30.
[10] *Rif.* 11, p. 371, 16 Dec. 1390.
[11] *Rif.* 12, pp. 99–100, 15 May 1392.

ment of an *imposita*,[12] and one of the main reasons for rearranging the five *porte* of the city into three *terzieri* was to prevent friction, for the *porte* no longer reflected equal divisions 'ex quibus magna inest inequalitas in distribuendo honores munera et onera ob que rancores et errores non pauci in civitate sunt suborti'.[13]

But these were small irritations compared with the dispute that arose in the spring of 1370; for this was concerned with the form of government itself. The point at issue was whether the city should be ruled 'a popolo' or 'a comune'. It had since Lucca recovered her liberty been ruled 'a comune', which meant that nobles as well as *populares* took part in the government and held the highest offices,[14] but many were discontented with the existing state of affairs, complaining that a few citizens were trying to appropriate the direction of the city to themselves, allowing the rest to share the burdens, but not the honours or the power.[15] The dispute was serious. The *Riformagioni* make it clear that there was much discussion and that by early July feelings were running high, so it was essential to get the matter settled quickly. According to Sercambi the dispute had already lasted for several months, and both sides were ready for violence, which did in fact break out.[16] In a meeting of the General Council a *balìa* was authorized to settle the question in such a way that 'maiores, mediocres et minores pariter contentuntur'.[17]

[12] *Rif.* 1, p. 152, 13 Dec. 1369, 'grandis sit querela et murmur exortim propter inequalitatem observatam, ut asseritur, ab impositoribus'.

[13] *Rif.* 1, p. 214, 1 Feb., p. 220, 6 Feb. 1370. This was a long standing complaint. The Lucchese had petitioned Pisa in 1362 that the city might be redivided into *terzieri* because of the inequalities of the existing *porte*. The Pisans had agreed that the city should be redivided into new *porte*, but nothing further seems to have been done about this, *Anz. Av. Lib.* 42, p. 57, 21 Apr. 1362.

[14] The nobles appear in offices and on *balìe* with great frequency in the months before July 1370.

[15] In the General Council, *Rif.* 1, pp. 413-14, 4 July 1370.

[16] Sercambi, I, pp. 204-5. He dates it 1371.

[17] *Rif.* 1, pp. 413-17, 4 July 1370. As many as 46 *invitati* were present, and the *balìa* was voted by 203-25. Its thirty members included four nobles, ten or eleven artisans, a judge, two notaries, and a number of merchants. They were:

S. Paolino	*S. Salvatore*	*S. Martino*
d. Johannes de Opizis	d. Thomas de Opizis	Franciscus Guynisii
d. Ludovicus Mercati	Fridus Martini	Loysius Balbani
Conradus de Podio	mag. Federicus Trente	ser Tadeus Malpigli

A second meeting of the General Council was held 31 July 1370 with the unusually large number of fifty-three *invitati*, and it was there decided that Lucca should be ruled 'in libertà e a popolo'. This meant that members of noble families would in future be excluded from the college of Anziani and from the offices of *gonfaloniere* and *pennonieri*. Apart from that they would not be molested, and would be allowed to live peacefully in the city and to hold the office of vicar in the *contado* and any other offices from which they were not specifically excluded.[18] A number of nobles were present at this meeting of the General Council and messer Nino degli Obizi and Corrado di Poggio consented to this decree for themselves and their families and on behalf of the Salamoncelli and Quartigiani families and of messer Niccolò del Veglio and messer Niccolò Maulini.[19]

But this decision was not accepted equally peacefully by everyone. It led a number of citizens to plot to overthrow the regime. None of the plotters were nobles, and several of them were apparently artisans. Apart from Niccolò Lippi, Nuccino Sornachi, Stefano da Quarto, and Pieretto, *testore* named by Sercambi, a certain Bendinello Taddiccioni, maestro Lorenzo, a shoemaker, and Lotto Tardi, a weaver, were involved. Sercambi perhaps provides a clue to explain why artisans, some of them plainly humble men, should plot against the government in protest at the exclusion of nobles from power, when he describes Niccolò Lippi and Nuccino Sornachi as 'di parte guelfa amici' and asserts that Giovanni degli Obizi was behind the plot.[20] The Obizi were the ancient

---

Nicolaus de Versi	Loysius Buccelle	Dinus Vannis Malapresa
Franciscus Bussolini	Matheus Nuptini	Nicolaus cultrizarius
Orlandinus Volpelli	Nicolosus Bartholomei	Fastellus marescalcus
ser Marchese Gilii	Laurentius calzolar.	Lambertus Colucii faber
Franciscus Dini casaiolus	Johannes Puccini textor	Corsellinus Nuti battiloro
Pierus Baroncini calz.	Franciscus Vannini fillator	Landus Moriconis
Allexius pannarius	Pierus speciarius	(one name missing)

[18] Nobles did later hold offices like that of vicar, and the di Poggio family was able to play an important part in councils and *balìe*, even though excluded from the Anzianate.

[19] *Rif.* 1, pp. 454–8, 31 July 1370. Messer Niccolò Maulini and some others were affected because they were knights, not because they were of noble families.

[20] Sercambi I, pp. 204–6. Members of the Sornachi and Taddiccioni families were

champions and leaders of the Guelf party of Lucca and the plotters may well have been swayed by party feeling. Their aim, according to the sentences passed on them, was to turn out the Anziani and replace them by others, and to pillage and burn the houses of the Guinigi, Boccella, messer Simone da Barga, Orlandino Volpelli, and certain others, killing anyone who resisted.[21] These then were presumably the chief supporters of the regime 'a popolo' and the decree of 31 July 1370 should perhaps be seen as a victory for them and a defeat for the Obizi.[22]

Whatever the undercurrents of party feeling in this dispute, the fact remains that the nobles were for the future excluded from the highest offices in the state, though not from the vicariates, councils or *balìe*, and the Obizi, Quartigiani, Salamoncelli, di Poggio, and Antelminelli families were specifically named in the Statute of 1372 as ineligible for the Anzianate.[23] This exclusion was accepted peacefully by most of the nobles. Only Giovanni degli Obizi resisted, attempting to enter Lucca in arms.[24] He broke the confines that were then set for him and became the most dangerous of the rebels and

---

among the Guelfs who went into exile in 1314, returning and claiming their property only in 1331, *Curia de'Ribelli e de'Banditi 3*, ff. 70v-75, 83v-85, 101-2. The Sornachi, however, are listed by Civitali as among those favourable to Castruccio, *Historia della Città di Lucca dall'origine di essa città sino al 1572*, series *Biblioteca Manoscritti*, no. 38, f. 224. They were listed by the Pisans as rebels during the siege of 1341-2, but the Pisans apparently regarded as rebels all Lucchese except the few who had fled from Lucca to join their camp, *Curia de'Ribelli e de'Banditi*, 8, f. 2. Stefano da Quarto may have been a private enemy of the Guinigi, Sercambi I, p. 134. Decree against Lorenzo *calzolaio*, offering rewards for his death or capture, *Rif.* 2, p. 306, 11 June 1371. He had been one of the *balìa* of 4 July 1370.

[21] The attacks were planned for 25 July 1370, but were put off until 27 July. Some of the plotters went to the Guinigi houses to see what guard was kept there, but found they had got wind of the plot and were well prepared *Sentenze e Bandi*, 42 (undated) and 43, 28 July 1370. Pierotto di Giovanni *textor* came to council with a knife hidden under his cloak, but this was discovered and he fled, when there was a great 'rumor' and the cry of 'viva il popolo' was raised, *Sentenze e Bandi*, 43, 28 July 1370.

[22] It is doubtful whether it can also be regarded as a victory for the Ghibellines. Though all those named by the plotters had been active under Pisan rule and the Guinigi and Boccella were among those listed by Civitali as favourable to Castruccio, *Historia della Città di Lucca*, ff. 222v, 223v, the only one whose family can be definitely associated with either party is Orlandino Volpelli, and his family were Guelfs, who had left in 1314 and returned in 1331, *Curia de'Ribelli e de'Banditi*, 3, ff. 173–177v. For Ghibellinism after 1370 see below Chapter 11, pp. 229–35. Many aspects of this plot, however, remain obscure.

[23] *Statuto del Comune di Lucca* 1372, series *Statuti*, 6, Lib. I, viii.

[24] *Rif.* 2, pp. 127-8, 9 Nov. 1370.

exiles of Lucca, finding refuge in Florence and Pistòia, where he took military service and continually plotted to return to Lucca by force of arms.

The decision that Lucca should be ruled 'a popolo' did not mean that the regime was to be democratic, even by the standards of some other fourteenth-century Italian states. There were no laws to ensure that places in the college of Anziani or the councils should be shared in fixed proportions by the various classes or among the gilds, which played no part in political life.[25] The Anziani and councillors were chosen from the three *terzieri*, which were purely topographical divisions. There was no property qualification, and not even any regulation that citizens who owed money to the state or who had failed to pay an *imposita* should be ineligible. This might be thought to make it easier for artisans and other humble men to obtain a share in the government. Certainly there was no reason in theory why the humblest artisan should not hold office as Anziano, sit in the General Council and the Thirty-Six, and play an important part in the direction of affairs as a member of *balìe*. It was by no means unknown for a vintner or a weaver to become Anziano or sit in the Thirty-Six, and they sat in greater numbers in the General Council. But the real direction of affairs came to lie with the merchant and business classes. The government was controlled by the silk-merchants, cloth-dealers, goldsmiths, bankers, and others engaging in trade and industry as entrepreneurs, and some other groups, such as lawyers, notaries and doctors.

In the first years after 1369 there are occasional signs of some attempt to give the *popolo minuto* a share in the government. 'Minores' were sometimes included in *balìe*, as they had been in the *balìa* authorized to consider the form of government 4 July 1370. This was particularly the case where financial business was concerned. A certain 'Nicholaus coltricarius' was included in a *balìa* of nine to raise a loan of 10,000 florins in August 1370,[26] and it was provided that a third of those who were to make an *estimo* in October 1370 should be drawn from poorer citizens.[27] It was proposed in

[25] The only limitations were Lucchese citizenship, legitimate birth and a minimum age of 25, *Statuto* 1372, I, viii, xviii, xxii.

[26] *Rif.* 2, pp. 17-18, 4 Aug., p. 23, 6 Aug. 1370.

[27] It was to be done by five *gite* of three citizens per *terziere*, each consisting of 'unus

April 1371 that the adjustment of an *imposita*, which had aroused complaint, should be done by four citizens per *terziere* 'unus de maiori, unus de mediocri, unus de minori et alius de minima facultate', though the proposal was not passed.[28]

In these same years a number of artisans and others in humble occupations were elected members of the Thirty-Six or to important *balìe* or even became Anziani. One or two of them were Anziani frequently. Giovanni Puccini, a weaver, was Anziano thirteen times and a member of the Thirty-Six ten times between 1372 and his death in 1397. Lamberto Coluccini, a smith, was Anziano twelve times and Gonfaloniere once, and sat in the Thirty-Six twelve times.[29] Frediano Tempi, a vintner, Fastello Gaddi, *maliscalco*, and Giusto Lupucci, a tanner, also appear regularly as Anziani and in the Thirty-Six, and one or two others appear occasionally. These and other artisans also sat in the important *balìa* 'super regimine', elected to ensure the quiet of the city 31 July 1370 and renewed every three months in the next two years.[30] But these were not men in the humblest social position. They were substantial artisans with thirty or forty florins in the *Massa*, and employing a number of workmen in their trades.[31] Few even of these reached the highest offices, and even those who became Anziani rarely appear in

dives, alter de mediocri, alter de minori facultate', *Rif.* 2, pp. 102–3, 20 Oct. 1370. Another reference to things being done by a *balìa* 'de omni facultate', *Rif.* 2, p. 273, 28 Apr. 1371.

[28] *Min.* 2, ff. 13v–15, 27 Apr. 1371. It was also suggested that the *statutarii* be one judge, one notary, one doctor, three merchants and three *artifices*, but this was not passed, *Min.* 2, f. 20, 2–4 May 1371, similar provision *Min.* 2, f. 45v, 18 June 1371. Four ambassadors to Florence were to be one knight, one judge, one merchant and one *artifex*, *Min.* 2, f. 78, 16 July 1371.

[29] Lists of Anziani in *Regesto*, *Carteggio degli Anziani*, Vol. II, part ii, pp. xi–xxxv. Lists of councillors *Riformagioni*, *passim*.

[30] *Rif.* 2, p. 22, 5 Aug., pp. 98–9, 19 Oct. 1370, p. 220, 2 Mar., p. 223, 5 Mar., p. 316, 19 June 1371.

[31] The books of the Massa show that Giusto Lupucci had 109 florins, *Imprestiti* 10, f. 34v, Corsellino Nuti, goldsmith had 55, *Imprestiti*, 11, f. 41v, Lamberto Coluccini and his father 40, *Imprestiti*, 11, f. 64v, Giovanni Puccini and Frediano Tempi between 20 and 30, *Imprestiti*, 11, f. 248v. Fastello Gaddi had 12, which he had sold by 1373, *Imprestiti*, 11, f. 75v. Giusto Lupucci and his brother employed two workmen in 1372, *Corte de'Mercanti*, 83, f. 35v. Corsellino Nuti employed three in 1372 and five in 1371, *Corte de Mercanti*, 83, f. 18, 82, f. 19. He also attended meetings of the Court of Merchants and was one of the consuls in March and Apr. 1371, *Corte de'Mercanti*, 14, f. 4v.

the *balìe* which were elected so frequently and took so many of the most important decisions. In the first couple of years after 1369 obscurer men occasionally appear in *balìe*; Niccolò Cioli, a weaver, Bonuccio Lupori, called Megliorato, Giovanni Bruni, and Orsuccio Orsetti,[32] but such names disappear after 1372 or 1373.

Popolani minuti remained technically eligible for election to the college of Anziani and the Thirty-Six, but were simply not elected. Deliberate efforts were being made to keep the college of Anziani and certain other positions exclusive. As early as February 1370, when the city was to be redivided, it was agreed that twelve citizens 'de mellioribus' should do this.[33] The college of Anziani could be kept exclusive or widened by adjusting the duration of each *tasca*. As each citizen could be Anziano only once in each *tasca*, a larger number of citizens could be given the opportunity of holding the office by making the *tasca* for a longer period of time, or the college could be kept exclusive by making the *tasca* for a shorter period. The duration of each *tasca* came to be fixed at two years, but in the early years after 1369 this was more flexible, and there are clear indications that it was being manipulated in order to keep the college exclusive. In February 1371 it was agreed to make a *tasca* for eighteen months 'ad hoc ut hec dignitas pro contentatione populi ad plures debeat pervenire et ne si longius providere contingeret ad indignos se trasferat tante preheminentia dignitatis'.[34] Even with the *tasca* fixed at two years so that at least 120 persons could hold office, there was little chance of many *popolani minuti* being elected, for 120 places and more could easily be filled from the merchant and banking families and from judges, notaries, and a few other such groups. The members of the Thirty-Six were drawn from the same group that monopolized the Anzianate. The 'vacation' was only six months for ordinary councillors and a year for *gonfalonieri*, so that again there was little need to look outside the merchant and business class, and it was rare for artisans or obscurer citizens to be elected, especially after the first few years of independence.

[32] *Rif.* 2, pp. 217-19, 5 Mar., p. 320, 19 June 1371.
[33] *Rif.* 1, p. 214, 1 Feb. 1370.
[34] *Rif.* 2, pp. 201-2, 1 Feb. 1371.

The General Council was a slightly different matter. With 180 members and a year's 'vacation' there was a chance for at least 360 citizens to sit in the General Council, and thus take some part, however small, in the government. In fact both in the General Council and the Thirty-Six by no means all the members were re-elected at every possible opportunity, so that many more than the minimum possible number could sit in both councils. Nevertheless, surprisingly few lesser artisans and really obscure men sat in the General Council. Though some men in humble occupations, such as tailors, smiths, or barbers did sit in the General Council there were rarely more than about twenty of them, so that they were heavily outnumbered even there by members of the merchant and business class. Even those artisans who did occasionally sit in the General Council can have had little real say in the direction of affairs. They are never recorded as speaking in council, and a small group of obscure citizens of humble social position would hardly have been able to stand up against the representatives of the wealthiest and most powerful families in the city. Though they took some part in political life and were not totally excluded from a share in the government, that share must have been small.

One of the main reasons for the rare appearance of lesser artisans in the Thirty-Six and the General Council was the method of election. Both councils were elected by the Anziani and a *balìa* of four citizens per *terziere*, drawn from the retiring council of Thirty-Six. As very few artisans ever sat in the Thirty-Six, and in fact those chosen to elect the new councils and make the new *tasche* of Anziani usually belonged to the leading families of the city, there was little chance of humbler artisans being elected, unless for some reason it suited the merchant and business class to have them included. There was far less chance of *popolani minuti* being elected councillors than there had been under the method of election laid down in the Statute of 1308 after the popular victory. There the General Council numbered 550 with a year's 'vacation', so that at least 1,100 citizens could take part.[35] In addition ordinary citizens took part in the election of the

[35] *Statuto del Comune di Lucca,* 1308, in *Memorie e Documenti per Servire all' Istoria del Principato Lucchese*, Vol. III, part iii, Lib. I, xi.

councillors. Slips of paper were distributed to all the 'vicini' of each parish. Many of them were blanks, but each man who received a slip marked 'elector' nominated a councillor.[36] As the ordinary citizens themselves took part in the election there was far more chance of humbler men being elected than there was in the last thirty years of the fourteenth century, when only men who sat in the Thirty-Six took part in the elections and the councils were in a sense self-perpetuating. The same considerations apply to elections to the college of Anziani. Each of the Anziani, members of the Thirty-Six and the six *invitati* per *terziere* who made up the electoral council had the right to make nominations, and the same body then voted on each nominee. As the *invitati* were normally drawn from the same kind of business families that dominated the college of Anziani and Council of Thirty-Six there was little chance of artisans or *minuti* obtaining nomination.

With the nobility excluded from real power, and the *popolo minuto* and even quite prosperous artisans rarely sitting as councillors and even more rarely as Anziani, the control of affairs passed into the hands of the merchant and business families of the city, who shared power only with a few other, numerically small, groups, such as judges, doctors, and a small proportion of the many notaries. The judges, doctors, and notaries who played a part in affairs of state were often themselves members of the leading merchant and banking families. There are many citizens recorded in such sources as the books of the *Massa* who played no part whatever in public affairs. Excluding men who sat only in the General Council, or on just one or two occasions sat in the Thirty-Six, or held some minor post in the city, power was confined to members of about 170 or 180 families before 1392. Only members of these families ever held the office of Anziano, or even sat in the Thirty-Six more than once or twice, or ever appeared on any *balìa* of importance, except on perhaps one occasion. Even among these 170 or 180 families there were some whose members never rose beyond sitting in the Thirty-Six with some frequency, or occasional appearances on *balìe*. The number of families of real political importance was considerably smaller.

[36] *Statuto del Comune di Lucca*, 1308 Lib. I, xi. There was a year's vacation for electors also.

There was an inner oligarchy within this wider oligarchy. There were probably not more than fifty families that had several members holding the highest offices both regularly and frequently.

The vast majority of these were well-established in public affairs by 1369. Of the families active in political life in Lucca in the last thirty years of the fourteenth century many were among those named as 'potentes et casastici' in the Statute of 1308. These included the Anguilla, Bambacari, Beccuti, Boccansocchi, Bocci, Burlamacchi, Carincioni, del Caro, Cattani, Cenami, Dombellinghi, Faitinelli, Flammi, Forteguerra, Guidiccione, Guinigi, Malisardi, Malpigli, Martini, Mercati, Moccindente, Mordecastelli, Onesti, Panichi, Pinelli, di Poggio, Rapondi, Sartoy, Sbarra, Tadolini, and Testa. All these familes are represented among the Anziani before 1369, except the Bambacari, Bocci, Carincioni, Guidiccione, and Pinelli.[37] Many who were not named as 'potentes et casatici' in 1308 and who were therefore either *popolani* at that date or had risen to importance since took an active part in political life in the last thirty years of the fourteenth century. Of these the following had appeared among the Anziani in the period 1330–1369; Angiorelli, Antelmini, Arlotti, Arnolfi, Arnolfini, Balbani, Beraldi, Boccella, Buzolini, Busdraghi, Cagnuoli, Castiglione, Cimbardi, Cristiani, Dardagnini, Domaschi, Galganetti, Gentili, del Ghiotto, Gigli, Mattafelloni, Maulini, Mingogi, Moriconi, Perfettucci, Pettinati, dal Portico, Ronghi, Salamoni, Schiatta, Sembrini, Serpente, Spada, Spiafami, dello Strego, Tegrimi, Trenta, Volpelli da Volterra.[38]

The oligarchical tendency may have been accentuated by

[37] *Statuto del Comune di Lucca*, 1308, Lib. III, clxv, clxviii, clxix, clxx for the list of 'potentes et casastici' and the disabilities they suffered. C.p. F. P. Luiso, 'Mercatanti lucchesi dell'epoca di Dante, II, Gli antenati di Castruccio Castracani', *Bollettino Storico Lucchese*, Vol. X (1938), pp. 74-82, where it is argued that these were not very serious. The names of the Anziani do not survive complete for 1330-69, and the situation is complicated by political factors. Some families may have spent part of the period in exile, despite amnesties offered in 1331 and under the Pisans. A possible example of this is the Faitinelli, who went into exile as Guelfs in 1314, though some took advantage of the amnesty of 1331, *Curia de'Ribelli e de'Banditi*, 3, ff. 58v-59, 104. They continued to live mainly in Venice and the only member of the family recorded as Anziano before 1369 held office in February and March 1342, that is during the brief period of Florentine rule.

[38] Some other families are known, though not as Anziani, earlier, for example the

the period of Pisan rule. The Pisans can certainly be seen looking for men on whom they could rely. In 1353 they wrote to their chancellor in Lucca asking him to suggest men suitable to be Anziani there.[39] It would be in the interests of Pisa to seek an understanding with the more solid and stable elements in Lucca[40] and it is known from Sercambi that the Pisans had a number of strong supporters there, for example, Corrado di Chello di Poggio, Giovanni di messer Franceschino Onesti, Fredo Martini, Francesco Mordecastelli, and others, who took the side of the Pisans during the abortive rising against them in 1355, though this may have been due to Ghibelline party feeling.[41] Certainly many of the leading Lucchese families continued to hold office as Anziani under Pisan rule.

The same families continued to be prominent after 1369, and apart from the artisans already discussed, the only new families appearing in the years 1369–1390 are the Bandini, Bartolomei, Bernardi, Brilla, Borgognone, Campucci, Cionelli, Gregorii, Narducci, Parpaglione, Puccinelli, da Quarto, Saggina, Schiezza, Turinghelli, and Vannuccori[42] —none of them of the first importance. Though many of the families that held office both before and after 1369 were represented in the last thirty years of the century by men whose careers began about 1369[43] there was some continuity of personnel as well as of family; there are a number of men whose careers began in the 1350s or 1360s and continued into the 1370s and 1380s. In general, though a number of the families active in political life in the earlier fourteenth century had died out or abandoned the city, there were many others

---

Saggina and the da Quarto. See the interesting list of Lucchese merchants active in 1284 in T. Blomquist, 'Trade and commerce in thirteenth-century Lucca', Appendix I, pp. 150–8, which enables one to trace some of the leading families much farther back than it would be possible to do from purely political records.

[39] *Regesto*, *Carteggio degli Anziani*, Vol. II, part i, no. 607, 23 Nov. 1353.

[40] For this effect in other cities that had lost their independence, G. Chittolini, 'La crisi delle libertà comunali e le origini dello stato territoriale', *Rivista Storica Italiana*, Vol. LXXXII (1970), pp. 113–14.

[41] Sercambi I, pp. 108–9. Lucchese Ghibellines, as supporters of Pisa, were allowed to remain in Lucca when others had to leave, Sercambi I, p. 117.

[42] *Regesto*, *Carteggio degli Anziani*, Vol. II, part ii, pp. xi–xxxv.

[43] This impression is heightened by the lack of records of the names of Anziani and other officials after about 1362. Some of these men may have held office in the seven or eight years before 1369.

that were still in Lucca and still active in government. There were a few families whose political importance does not seem to go back much, if at all, beyond 1369, but the majority of the families that ruled the city in the last thirty years of the fourteenth century were among those who had ruled it in the previous thirty or forty years or even longer. Though some families may have concentrated on Lucchese politics with a new enthusiasm when the city regained its freedom, there was no break in the continuity of the ruling class in 1369.

This ruling oligarchy was primarily a mercantile and business class. An examination of the surviving records of the Court of Merchants shows that many of the most important political families were also the leading business families and that the men who were most active in communal politics were also those most active in the affairs of the Court of Merchants. The most important family politically, the Guinigi, had by far the largest company of silk-merchants and bankers, according to the declarations of companies of 1371, 1372, and 1381, and other leading families like the Balbani, Boccella, Buzolini, Cenami, Moriconi, and Onesti also had important companies.[44] Men like Luiso and Simone Boccella, Betto, Francesco, and Bartolomeo Buzolini, Niccolò Galganetti, Bartolomeo and Luiso Balbani, Turellino Bonucci, Lando Moriconi, Giuffredo Cenami, Forteguerra Forteguerra, Niccolò ser Pagani, and various members of the Guinigi family appear as regularly and frequently as consuls and councillors of the Court of Merchants as they do as Anziani and members of the communal councils. The names that appear most frequently and most predictably among the members of *balìe* appointed by the commune and are most regularly recorded as speakers in debates also played an equally prominent role in offices and among commissioners appointed by the Court of Merchants. These leading merchants with large companies were also, of course, among the wealthiest citizens, as evidenced by such sources as the books of the public debt.

So Lucca in the late fourteenth century was dominated by a

[44] Declarations of companies for 1371, 1372 and 1381, *Corte de'Mercanti*, 82–4, Deliberations of the Court of Merchants for 1370, 1380 and 1389, *Corte de'Mercanti*, 14–16.

bourgeois oligarchy of wealthy merchant families, long established in the political life of the city and accustomed to rule, dominating the Anzianate, the council of Thirty-Six and especially the informal *balìe* by which so much important business was conducted. It was to be among this inner oligarchy that divisions and rivalries grew up. Once parties had formed it became clear that the machinery of government that had enabled a social group to obtain a predominant position could also be manipulated in the interests of a faction.

11

THE FORMATION OF PARTIES 1369-1392

It was a commonplace of political speeches at this time that the strength of a city lay in the unity of its citizens and not in fortresses or soldiers. These sentiments were frequently expressed by the Lucchese, for they regarded their own disunity as one of the main causes of the period of foreign rule from 1329 to 1369.[1] But despite the fact that the Lucchese frequently found it necessary to remind their fellow citizens of the need for unity, it was claimed that Lucca had an exceptionally good record in this respect, and that her government from the recovery of liberty until about 1390 compared very favourably with that of other cities. It was claimed that Lucca had preserved her unity and liberty so successfully that her neighbours could scarcely believe it. Other much more powerful cities had been troubled by wars and famines, and forced to overtax their citizens and impose forced loans, while Lucca, on the other hand, had managed to save herself from the plots of her neighbours and the attacks of armed companies, and pay off her debts to the Papacy and other powers without recourse to forced loans. She had even managed to keep the price of corn lower than had any neighbouring city, and to save a little money for emergencies. And all this was due to the fact that her citizens had managed to live together in unity and concord under the Statutes.[2] This statement was made when serious internal disturbances had arisen. The period 1369 to 1390 was being viewed in retrospect, and past peace and unity contrasted with present troubles. The internal situation of the city had not been as idyllic as the speaker made out. But Lucca was one of the few republics that had no serious internal divisions in this period. There were factions and there were disputes, but they were not serious enough to

[1] For example *Rif.* 11, p. 371, 16 Dec. 1390, *Rif.* 12, p. 48, 20 Feb., pp. 98-9, 15 May 1392.

[2] *Rif.* 11, pp. 371-4, 16 Dec. 1390. Appendix Doc. V.

threaten the peace of the city. Lucca enjoyed about twenty years of comparative peace in internal affairs, and this was no small achievement in fourteenth-century Italy.

This period of comparative peace did not mean that there were no constitutional changes or that the relative position of the various groups within the city remained static. In fact the period 1369 to 1390 saw the Guinigi family quietly building up a party, and establishing itself in a powerful, perhaps dominating position within the framework of the existing constitution. Though harder to trace, the opposition, led by the Rapondi and Forteguerra families, was also building up a party. Serious faction disputes divided the city between 1390 and 1392 and the period 1369 to 1390 saw the formation of these two factions.

It is not easy to determine how soon after 1369 the two factions began to emerge. They were certainly in existence by 1390, and there are traces of them earlier. There is evidence in Sercambi that there were already two groups in the city in 1385. Francesco Guinigi, the head of the family, had died in June 1384, and this encouraged their opponents to form a movement 'per volere lo stato de'Guinigi mectere abasso'.[3] The terms Sercambi uses make it clear that the Guinigi had already acquired a position of influence within the city that set them apart from the other citizens, and that this was arousing opposition, so that when they were temporarily weakened by the death of Francesco they came in for much abuse, and it was even rumoured that their houses had been attacked and that they had been expelled from the city.[4] Sercambi speaks of the Guinigi and 'suoi'; they probably already had a recognizable group of supporters.

In fact the Guinigi can be found in a position of considerable power even before 1385. Their unpopularity in 1385 was due to the influence they had steadily been acquiring in the previous ten years. As early as 1376 their special position in Lucca was already apparent to neighbouring cities. When the Florentines were planning an embassy to Pisa and Lucca to dissuade them from receiving the Pope, it was advised that it

[3] Sercambi, I, p. 243.
[4] Sercambi, I, pp. 243–4.

should be 'amore domini Petri et Francisci de Guinigiis'.[5] They appear to have been conspicuous in the government of the city very shortly after Lucca was freed from Pisan rule. The anger of the plotters in the dispute about the form of government in July 1370 was directed against the Guinigi, along with the Boccella family, messer Simone da Barga, Orlandino Volpelli and others who were not named.[6] These were not necessarily Guinigi partisans later. Simone da Barga died in the plague of 1373, the Boccella did not apparently support either faction and Orlandino Volpelli was to be a leading member of the Forteguerra party. Nevertheless it does show that the Guinigi were among those prominent in 1370. This is confirmed in another condemnation in January 1371. When a dyer named Simone Vannis and certain others heard that Francesco Guinigi was to be made doge while holding the office of Gonfaloniere, they plotted to come to Lucca in the guise of an embassy from the Lucchese community in Venice to 'correre la città'. They were to kill Francesco Guinigi, messer Simone da Barga and others described as 'de regentibus', and then go to the palace of the Anziani, turn out the Anziani, 'et ipsius dominium pro ipsis et parte sua accipere et assumere'.[7]

Though others are named in these plots, it is clear that the Guinigi were already the most important family in the city by 1370. Sercambi supports this view when he describes how 'per lo senno di Francesco di Lazzari Guinigi padre del magnifico signor Paulo e per molti altri buoni & leali ciptadini, Lucha fu bene recta et governata dall'anno di MCCCLXX fine a l'anno di MCCLXXXIII, ripremiando i buoni et punendo quelli che male voleano vivere.'[8] The outstanding position of this family is one of the basic facts in the internal history of Lucca from 1369 to 1400. It is a little more difficult to speak of its position before 1369. It seems to have been an ancient family of feudal origin. It can be traced back to the tenth century in the

[5] A.S.F. *Consulte* 14, f. 101, 7 Nov. 1376. This probably dates from the establishment of the *conservatores*, *Rif.* 4, pp. 492–3, 4 Nov. 1374.

[6] *Sentenze e Bandi*, 42, 43, July 1370.

[7] *Sentenze e Bandi*, 44, 20 Jan. 1371. Francesco Guinigi was to be Gonfaloniere in Jan. and Feb. 1371. The plotters heard 'quod Franciscus Guinixii in isto suo regimine Vexilliferri iusticie debebat effici dux civitatis Luce'.

[8] Sercambi, III, p. 336. He had, of course, the benefit of hindsight.

contado and by the early twelfth century was of social and political importance in Lucca, where in 1308 the Guinigi were named among the 'potentes et casastici'. Until the thirteenth century they seem to have been mainly landed proprietors in both Pisan and Lucchese territory, but about this time they began to engage in trade.[9] There are records of the Guinigi as merchants from the mid-thirteenth century, and the fifteenth-century *Memorie* of Michele di Giovanni Guinigi record a large Guinigi company in 1294.[10] There are records of Guinigi abroad in the fourteenth century,[11] and by the last thirty years of the century the Guinigi company was the largest Lucchese trading company with between sixteen and twenty-two members, and branches in Bruges and London as well as in various Italian cities.[12] Evidence from such sources as forced loans suggests that the Guinigi were already the wealthiest family in the city before 1369. In an *imposita* of 1362 Francesco and Dino Guinigi were assessed at 343 florins, nearly twice as much as Jacomo and Guido Rapondi, who at 188 florins had the next largest assessment.[13] The Guinigi holding of 4,799 florins in the *Massa* in 1373 far exceeded that of any other family,[14] and Sercambi relates that Francesco Guinigi's wealth attracted the attention of Giovanni dell'Agnello, so that Francesco was obliged to flee to Genoa rather than make loans which he knew would never be repaid.[15]

The Guinigi were also of political importance before 1369. They are recorded as Anziani from 1331 onwards and served in councils and *balìe*. The political records for the period of

[9] For all this *Inventario del Archivio di Stato di Lucca*, Vol. VI, ed. D. Corsi (Lucca, 1964), Archivio Guinigi, introduction, pp. 357–60.

[10] *Inv.* VI, p. 359 and series *Archivo Guinigi*, 151, f. 60. Mirot, 'La colonie lucquoise', p. 52. Edler, *The Silk Trade of Lucca*, p. 95.

[11] *Inv.* VI, p. 359. Some took the oath of allegiance to John of Bohemia by proxy in 1331. List in F. Landogna, 'Giovanni di Boemia e Carlo IV di Lussemburgo Signori di Lucca', *Nuova Rivista Storica*, Vol. XII (1928) pp. 53–72. The originals are in series *Capitoli* 52.

[12] *Corte de'Mercanti*, 82, f. 11^{v}; 83, f. 7; 84, f. 11. *Libro della communità de'mercanti lucchesi in Bruges*, *passim*.

[13] Civitali, ff. 296^{v}–302. He lists 294 *poderie* and the total *imposita* was 5,146 florins. The lenders were probably selected without any very careful assessment of their capacity to pay, but the sums should give a rough indication of the relative resources of some of the wealthier families. Civitali interprets it in this way, f. 296^{v}.

[14] *Imprestiti*, 11, ff. 242^{v}–243.

[15] Sercambi, I, p. 134.

Pisan rule are less full than for the years after 1369, in particular there is very little for the last seven or eight years. Generalizations about the relative political importance of the various Lucchese families are therefore difficult. Nevertheless one gets the impression that, although the Guinigi were active in the political life of the city before 1369, they were only one of a number of important families and that they did not have the pre-eminent position they can be seen to enjoy almost immediately after 1369. Though they served on councils and *balìe* they were not so invariably included as they were after 1369, and when in 1355 the Emperor Charles IV asked that a number of leading Lucchese be sent to him for important negotiations, those elected did not include a member of the Guinigi family.[16] The Guinigi may have been gaining ground politically in the 1350s and 1360s—Francesco Guinigi was Anziano five times between 1352 and 1359—but the defectiveness of the records for the years after 1363 makes it impossible to state this with any certainty. The Guinigi may, therefore, have owed their political importance after 1369 to their contribution to the efforts to obtain the liberation of Lucca from Pisan rule. Francesco Guinigi was clearly active in this[17] and his prominent role in Lucchese politics after 1369 may reflect the leadership he gave at this important turning point in Lucchese history.

The wealth of the Guinigi family contributed greatly to their political importance in the last thirty years of the fourteenth century, and they can be seen carefully building up their fortune from both land and trade and banking after 1369. Land was acquired through marriages. Francesco Guinigi's eldest son, Lazzaro, acquired landed property with his first wife, Isabetta Rossiglione, who was the heiress of her father, Bindoccio, and her uncle, Pieretto, and died making Lazzaro her heir.[18] Francesco Guinigi married another of his

[16] Those elected in 1355 were Mingo Spada, Giovanni Onesti and Nuccio Boccansocchi, Civitali, f. 289^{v}.

[17] Sercambi, I, 176–82.

[18] *Protocolli* of ser Domenico Lupardi, *Archivio de'Notari*, 273 (not foliated), 26 Dec. 1379, *Archivio de'Notari*, 275, ff. 27–9, 29 Jan. 1382, referring to her will of 25 July 1380. She also left 600 florins to various charities. Her grandmother, Jacoba widow of Guidetto Rossiglione, also made Lazzaro her heir, *Archivio de'Notari*, 280, f. 60, 15 Mar. 1387.

sons, Roberto, to a wealthy heiress, Clara, daughter of Giovanni di Betto Anguilla, who had appointed him her guardian.[19] Roberto was no more than eleven years of age at the time of his marriage, and the property was therefore administered by Francesco and his son, Lazzaro.[20] Apart from land and houses acquired through marriages, there are other indications of attempts to build up Guinigi property in Lucca and the *contado*. Francesco Guinigi is found investing in land.[21] There is evidence in notarial records of purchases of land and houses in the city[22] and the *contado*,[23] and many references to leases, usually for rents in kind.[24] The Guinigi

[19] *Protocolli* of ser Filippo Lupardi, *Archivio de'Notari*, 160 (not foliated), 4 Mar. 1374.

[20] *Protocolli* of ser Simone Alberti, *Archivio de'Notari*, 248 (not foliated), 31 Jan. 1377. There are many references to their administration in the notarial records. They bought off possible claims against the inheritance by Clara's aunt, Gettina di Betto Anguilla, for 250 florins, *Protocolli* of ser Domenico Lupardi, *Archivio de'Notari*, 276, ff. 61v–63v, 25 Oct. 1383, and bought land and a house on Roberto's behalf from his uncle, Bonanno Serpente for 300 florins, *Archivio de'Notari*, 279, ff. 78–9, 7 Oct. 1386. There are many references to leases of land and houses in Lucca and the *contado* belonging to Roberto and Clara, *Protocolli* of ser Simone Alberti, *Archivio de'Notari*, 248, 31 Jan. 1377, 23 Feb. 1378, *Protocolli* of ser Domenico Lupardi, *Archivio de'Notari*, 278 (not foliated), 3 and 6 May 1385, *Archivio de'Notari*, 279, ff. 29v–30, 30 Jan. 1386. *Terrilogio di Paolo Guinigi*, series *Archivio Guinigi*, no. 130 bis, shows that much of the land held by Paolo had been acquired through Clara Anguilla. She died in 1383, *Archivio Guinigi*, 151, f. 5, and Roberto before 1394, *Archivio Guinigi*, 264, f. 280.

[21] *Inv.* VI, p. 360 and the contracts in the series *Archivio Guinigi* indicated there.

[22] *Protocolli* of ser Simone Alberti, *Archivio de'Notari*, 248, 31 Dec. 1378. *Protocolli* of ser Domenico Lupardi, *Archivio de'Notari*, 275, ff. 254v–255v, 14 Aug. 1382; 277, ff. 52v–54v, 1 Oct. 1384.

[23] *Protocolli* of ser Domenico Lupardi, *Archivio de'Notari*, 273, 14 Apr. 1379; 276, ff. 48v–49v, 24 Feb. 1383; 281, ff. 48v–49, 30 Apr. 1388; 283, ff. 93–4, 12 Mar. 1390, ff. 122v–123v, 7 May 1390; 284, ff. 69–70, 8 Oct. 1392. Also sales of land, *Archivio de'Notari*, 283, ff. 88v–89v, 8 Mar. 1390, ff. 158v–159, 15 Sept. 1390. There are also purchases of land and houses by Michele Guinigi, *Archivio Guinigi*, 151, f. 11v, 30 Apr. 1388, f. 16, 20 Nov. 1389, f. 17v, 30 Apr. 1390, ff. 20v, 23, 1388, f. 24v, 13 May 1393, and many leases recorded there.

[24] One improvement lease *Protocolli* of ser Simone Alberti, *Archivio de'Notari*, 248, 31 Dec. 1378. Other leases *Protocolli* of ser Domenico Lupardi, *Archivio de'Notari*, 273, 14 Jan., 2 Feb., 2 Sept. 1379, 30 Jan. 1380, 274, ff. 118v–119, 24 July 1381, 275, ff. 221v–222, 5 July 1382; 278, 16 May 1385; 280, ff. 65–65v, 28 Mar. 1387. *Protocolli* of ser Fedocco Scortica. *Archivio de'Notari*, 212, (not foliated), 16 and 18 Oct. 1381. Lease of a house in Lucca, *Protocolli* of ser Filippo Lupardi, *Archivio de'Notari*, 161 (not foliated), 8 Apr. 1376.

owned land in the Florentine *contado*[25] and that of Pisa,[26] as well as in the Lucchese state, and they also had money in the Pisan *Massa*.[27]

The Guinigi also continued to trade widely,[28] invest in other Lucchese trading companies and lend money to other Lucchese merchants, though this may have been partly with the aim of building up a party for themselves, rather than for purely commercial reasons.[29] One factor that must have contributed very greatly to the development of their wealth was their position as papal bankers. The Interdict against the Florentines during the War of the Eight Saints enabled the Guinigi to replace Florentine firms, and as early as 13 November 1376 they obtained a contract for the transfer of papal funds from England, Flanders, the Rhineland, Hungary, and Lombardy. On the outbreak of the Schism the Guinigi remained faithful to Urban VI and continued to act as papal bankers for almost fifteen years.[30] Their branches in Bruges and Venice acted as centres for the transfer of papal revenues to Rome, and the needs of papal business led to the development and expansion of the London branch.[31] Their activities as papal bankers involved far more than just the

[25] They sold a farm and other property in the commune of Sesto, in the Florentine contado, for 900 florins, *Protocolli* of ser Domenico Lupardi, *Archivio de'Notari*, 283, ff. 112–13, 23 Dec. 1389, 9 June 1390.

[26] *Protocolli* of ser Simone Alberti, *Archivio de'Notari*, 248, 15 Feb. 1377.

[27] *Protocolli* of ser Domenico Lupardi, *Archivio de'Notari*, 278, 20 Feb. 1385.

[28] There are many references in the notarial archives, e.g. *Protocolli* of ser Filippo Lupardi, *Archivio de'Notari*, 161, 20 Mar. 1376. *Protocolli* of ser Domenico Lupardi, *Archivio de'Notari*, 273, 28 Mar., 15 Oct. 1379; 278, ff. 22v–24, 30 Jan., ff. 26v–27v, 4 Feb. 1385; 284, f. 36v, 27 Sept. 1392. 23 July 1383 Giovanni Cagnuoli deposited 20,000 florins with Dino, Lazzaro and Jacobo Guinigi for a month 'pro ipsis convertendis in suis negotiationibus et mercantiis', *Archivio de'Notari*, 276, ff. 102v–103.

[29] *Protocolli* of ser Domenico Lupardi, *Archivio de'Notari*, 278, ff. 25–6, 30 Jan. 1385; 281, ff. 6v–7, 18 Jan. 1387; 280, f. 13v, 26 Jan., ff. 76–76v, 22 May, ff. 131v–132, 18 Sept. 1387; 282 (not foliated), 27 Aug. 1389.

[30] Y. Renouard, *Les Relations des papes d'Avignon et des compagnies commerciales et bancaires de 1316 à 1378* (Paris, 1941), p. 286. J. Favier, *Les Finances pontificales à l'époque du Grande Schisme d'Occident, 1378–1409* (Paris, 1966), p. 505. G. Holmes, 'How the Medici became the Pope's bankers', in N. Rubinstein (ed.) *Florentine Studies*, pp. 358–9. A. Esch, 'Bankiers der Kirche im Grossen Schisma', *Quellen und Forschungen aus Italianischen Archiven und Bibliotheken*, Band XLVI (1966), pp. 321–2. Also *Archivio Guinigi*, 1, *Contratti A*, f. 134. I would like to thank Dr. Holmes for drawing my attention to the importance to the Guinigi of their position as papal bankers and suggesting that it would repay further study.

[31] Esch, 'Bankiers der Kirche', pp. 321–3.

transfer of funds to Rome. They received papal revenues, and made payments directly on the Pope's behalf for forces in papal service, purchases of cloth, and other expenses, without the money ever passing through the hands of the papal treasurer. They advanced the Pope credit, paying items of expenditure in anticipation of revenues to be received. The sums that passed through their hands were considerable. They received 26,490 cameral florins between 7 February and 12 November 1377, and paid out 32,894 florins on behalf of the Papacy in the same period, so that they remained papal creditors for 6,404 florins.[32] They accounted for 110,743 cameral florins received and 110,662 expended in the period December 1380 to September 1384,[33] and 95,384 florins received and 97,154 paid out between 1 January and 23 November 1387.[34] Their activity at the Papal Curia declined after that, perhaps partly because of their preoccupation with Lucchese internal affairs, and by about 1392 they had been superseded first by other Lucchese, Lando Moriconi and Bartolomeo Turchi, and then by Florentine firms.[35]

[32] Holmes, 'How the Medici became the Pope's bankers', p. 359. Favier, *Les Finances pontificales*, pp. 506–8. Bini, *I Lucchesi a Venezia*, p. 132. Y. Renouard, 'Compagnies mercantiles lucquoises au service des papes d'Avignon', *Bollettino Storico Lucchese*, Vol. XI (1939), pp. 47–8. Original bull in series *Archivio Guinigi*, +5. Papal indebtedness to the Guinigi reached even higher figures later; 3 Jan. 1381 they were owed 13,891 florins, *Archivio Guinigi*, +22. See also Favier, *Les Finances pontificales*, pp. 507–8.

[33] Holmes, 'How the Medici became the Pope's bankers', p. 359, Favier, *Les Finances pontificales*, p. 508. *Archivio Guinigi*, +30.

[34] Holmes, 'How the Medici became the Pope's bankers', p. 359. They received 77,026 florins and paid out 75,411 between 1 Jan and 1 Oct. 1387, *Archivio Guinigi*, +32, and received 18,358 florins, counting the surplus of 1,514 florins from the previous account, and paid out 21,743 florins between 1 Oct. and 23 Nov. 1387, *Archivio Guinigi*, +33. There are many other original bulls in the series *Archivio Guinigi* relating to the transaction of papal business and many references in the notarial records e.g. *Protocolli* of ser Domenico Lupardi, *Archivio de'Notari*, 273, 8 Aug. 1379, 2 June 1380; 274, ff. 209–209v, 29 Jan, ff. 43–43v, 15 Mar., ff. 223v–224v, 4 July, ff. 156v–157v, 26 Sept. 1381; 284, ff. 47–47v, 12 Nov. 1392. *Protocolli* of ser Simone Alberti, *Archivio de'Notari*, 248, 19 June 1378.

[35] Holmes, 'How the Medici became the Pope's bankers', pp. 359–60, Esch, 'Bankiers der Kirche', pp. 323–6, Favier, *Les Finances pontificales*, pp. 508–20. The last account of Lazzaro di Francesco Guinigi with the Pope was dated 19 Mar. 1392. Lando Moriconi and Bartolomeo Turchi established themselves in papal finances in 1391–2, and like the Guinigi advanced credit as well as engaging in the simple transfer of papal revenues. Lando Moriconi was one of those excluded from the Anzianate and other offices in Lucca after the revolution of 12 May 1392, *Rif.* 12, pp. 121–2, 26 May 1392.

It is difficult in the absence of any account books or other business records of the Guinigi company, to speak with any precision of the contribution that their role as papal bankers made to the development of the Guinigi fortune. They must already have been wealthy and powerful bankers in 1376 or the Pope would not have had recourse to them. They were chosen because their network of branches in Italy and northern Europe and their wide trading contacts enabled them to ensure the safe and speedy transfer of papal revenues to Rome and because their financial strength made it possible for them to advance credit to the Papacy on a significant scale. Nevertheless, if their selection as papal bankers is evidence that the Guinigi were already important as international bankers, their role in papal finance must have brought a further development of their wealth. The profits that the Medici bank derived from papal finance in the fifteenth century are well known. The Rome branch of the Medici bank was the most lucrative of their various undertakings and came to require no capital of its own.[36] Though there is no evidence of the profits the Guinigi derived from papal banking, it seems not unreasonable to suppose that it brought them similar benefits. The only statement about the total wealth of the Guinigi is that of Bartolomeo Beverini, who wrote in the seventeenth century, but claimed to be basing his assertions on the public records, that Francesco and Dino Guinigi alone had a fortune of 200,000 florins. Though there is no way of checking this figure some accounts of Michele Guinigi give an indication of Guinigi wealth. His share of the profits of the Guinigi company for the two years ending 31 December 1384 was 3,066 florins. As he had a fifth share in the company total profits for this period were presumably 15,330 florins or 7,665 florins a year.[37] It has already been

[36] Holmes, 'How the Medici became the Pope's bankers', p. 379, Favier, *Les finances pontificales*, p. 523. Between 1397 and 1420 the Rome branch accounted for 52·1 per cent of the profits of the Medici bank, and had the highest yield in relation to capital invested, over 30 per cent. After 1426 the Rome branch required no capital of its own and was a source of capital to other branches. R. de Roover, *The Rise and Decline of the Medici Bank, 1397–1494* (Cambridge, Mass., 1963), pp.47–8, 205–10.

[37] B. Beverini, *Annali Lucchesi* (Lucca, 1830), Vol. III, p. 9. Michele Guinigi received only 1,569 florins 6*s*. *a oro* for the two years ending 31 Dec. 1386 (1387 Lucchese style, as the year began on 25 Dec.), *Archivio Guinigi*, 151, f. 2. There are

seen that the Guinigi had by far the largest holding in the *Massa* in 1373, and in the *Estimo* of 1397 various members of the Guinigi family had assessments that totalled 59,026 florins, again far more than those for any other family in Lucca.[38] The only other family for whom there is any indication of total fortune is the Rapondi family, who are said to have had 100,000 florins.[39] This is only half the figure Beverini gives for Francesco and Dino Guinigi alone, though the Rapondi were almost certainly the second wealthiest family of Lucca. The wealth of the Guinigi must have brought them great prestige and assisted them in building up a party of friends and supporters in the city.

Another extremely important factor in this was the personality and reputation of Francesco Guinigi himself. The weakening of the party on his death shows how greatly his personal prestige had contributed to it. He had been head of the family since the death of his uncle, Francesco di Bartolomeo in 1358.[40] By 1369 he had long political

no records of profits for earlier than 1384, so they cannot shed any light on the contribution to Guinigi wealth made by papal banking. They are also Michele Guinigi's personal accounts, not primarily concerned with the Guinigi company, and though there are some other figures for his receipts from the company it is not clear whether they represented his full share of the profits and what period of time they covered. But a statement dated 1384 gives some indication of the scale on which the Guinigi company operated 'Memoria come questo di primo gennaio 1384 fermo la nostra compagnia li ssuoi chonti e trovonsi tutte le male dette che avemo per tutto lmondo fiorini cinquantamilia secento settanta tre soldi sedici den. dieci cioe fior. 50673 s.16 d.10 a oro li quali sono lassati da parte nel quaderno de chonti a certe vii chel corpo della compagnia vecchia debia avere. E nelle faccia dalato sono per partita scritte tutte le dette delle quali quelle che piacesse a dio chessi rischotesseno si denno partire in questo modo cioe li due quinti a Dino e Lazari di Nicolao Guinigi uno quinto alli eredi di Nicolao di Lazari Guinigi uno quinto a Lazari di Francesco Guinigi e fratelli uno quinto a me Michele di Lazzari Guinigi, che dio per sua pieta le faccia buone', f. 2v. These figures may be compared with those for the Medici company later, which had profits totalling 151,820 florins 24*s* 4*d*. *a fiorino* for 1397–1420, about 6,600 a year, 186,382 florins 15*s*. 10*d*. *a fiorino* for 1420–1435, about 12,425 florins a year and 186,420 florins 22*s*. 3*d*. a *fiorino* for 1441–1451, about 18,642 florins a year, de Roover, *Medici Bank*, pp. 47–8, 55, 69.

[38] *Imprestiti*, 11, ff. 242v–243. Lucca, Biblioteca Governativa, MS. 925, ff. 256v–257.

[39] Mirot, 'La société des Raponde', pp. 300–2, 306. Jacobo di Giovanni Rapondi had 1,740 florins in the *Massa* in 1373 and 1,030 florins he had purchased from other creditors, *Imprestiti*, 14, f. 75v. His son, Giovanni, was assessed at 6,500 florins in the *Estimo* of 1397, Lucca, Biblioteca Governativa, MS. 925, f. 253v. Dino's will shows him to have been a wealthy man, Mirot, pp. 378–81. The Rapondi also had landed property in and around Lucca and abroad in France and Flanders.

[40] *Inv.* VI, p. 360.

experience. He had survived the period of Pisan rule, despite the difficulties this presented for a prominent and wealthy citizen, and had become the leading Lucchese adviser of Cardinal Guy of Boulogne, while he was imperial vicar in Lucca. He had played an important role in preserving Lucchese independence in the face of attempts of Bernabò Visconti to capture Lucca and of Alderigo Antelminelli to win the city for himself.[41] After the departure of the Cardinal he continued to be one of the leading citizens. He held office regularly as Anziano, Gonfaloniere, and councillor, and was frequently chosen for important embassies.[42] In addition he often spoke in council meetings and served on many important *balìe*. His exceptional qualities were recognized on his death. It was decreed that two of the Anziani should attend his funeral—an honour normally granted only to Anziani who died in office—as a tribute to his exceptional political wisdom and in recognition of his services to the city. He was described as 'non civitatis civis sed pater patrie, quam profunditate consilii non semel a servitute ac tyrannide liberavit, non solum presentibus periculis apponens remedium sed futura etiam mentis subtilitate previdens'.[43] Sercambi too pays tribute to his wisdom and foresight. He has nothing but admiration for him, and seldom mentions him without some word of praise, describing him, for example, as 'quello excellentissimo mercadante et famoso in virtù'.[44]

But although Francesco Guinigi was something of a hero to Sercambi and he could think of no better advice to Paolo Guinigi than to continue his father's policies,[45] he makes it clear that Francesco Guinigi was trying to build up a party for himself in Lucca. There can be no doubt that he was doing this deliberately. There is no question of him being simply a loyal citizen who accidentally acquired excessive influence in

[41] Sercambi, I, pp. 176–83.

[42] *Regesto*, pp. xi–xxxv for lists of Anziani, also *Riformagioni* passim.

[43] *Rif.* 9, p. 118, 5 June 1384. For the use of the term *pater patriae* and its significance at a slightly later date, W. L. Gundersheimer, *Ferrara, the style of a Renaissance despotism* (Princeton, 1973), p. 67 and A. M. Brown, 'Cosimo de'Medici, pater patriae', *Journal of the Warburg and Courtauld Institutes*, Vol. XXIV (1961), pp. 186–221.

[44] Sercambi, I, p. 236.

[45] Sercambi, III, p. 18.

the city because of his wealth and his personal reputation for patriotism and political wisdom.[46] Sercambi describes how Francesco Guinigi carefully built up and maintained a party both in the city and the *contado*. He names a number of Francesco's adherents in the *contado*, who were usually the Ghibelline party in each vicariate. According to Sercambi, Francesco Guinigi recognized that he had many enemies and that there were many within the city who wanted to see his power reduced. His answer to this was to make sure that he had a party of friends on whom he could rely, 'li quali sempre, a ugni hora che per lo dicto Francesco erano richiesti, comparivano alla salvessa di lui e del suo stato'.[47] This party of friends, both in the city and the *contado*, was the basis of Guinigi power.

There is a list of the Guinigi and Forteguerra parties about 1391, and a further list of citizens whom the Guinigi regarded as sufficiently reliable to be entrusted with arms after the revolution of May 1392. The first list is found in a manuscript in the Biblioteca Governativa in Lucca.[48] The heading states that it was drawn up by Dino Guinigi himself in 1391, and though it survives only in a copy made by the eighteenth-century antiquarian, Baroni, it is said to be taken 'dal 3° Quinterno delle memorie di famiglie fatte dal Civitali'. It has not been possible to trace the *Memorie di famiglie* of Civitali, but his manuscript history of Lucca, which is in the Archivio di Stato, is firmly based on contemporary documents and is one of the most reliable of the later histories of Lucca.[49] Though there is no contemporary evidence to connect the list with Dino Guinigi, it may well have been drawn up by him. It seems on the whole to be accurate in the men it names for each party. It lists 117 Guinigi supporters and forty-one for the Forteguerra party. The men it names as Forteguerra partisans were those 'che andorno di brigate a Palagio', that is those who took a really active part in the events of 1390 to 1392, so that it

[46] As appears to be suggested in C. Minutoli, 'I Guinigi ed i Forteguerra', in his *Frammenti di Storia Lucchese* (Lucca, 1878), pp. 17–18.

[47] Sercambi, III, p. 18.

[48] Lucca, Biblioteca Governativa, MS. 925, ff. 207v–208v. Appendix Docs. I and II.

[49] G. Civitali, *Historia della Città di Lucca dall'origine di essa città sino al 1572 (compilata l'anno 1572)*, series *Biblioteca Manoscritti*, no. 38.

almost certainly under-estimates the numbers of the Forteguerra party. Sercambi suggests[50] that the city was fairly evenly divided and that the Forteguerra party outnumbered that of the Guinigi at one point, so the number of Forteguerra sympathizers must have been larger than the number given as active supporters, though some might support them in particular matters, while remaining uncommitted to either party. The list of Guinigi supporters may well be more accurate and comprehensive. In many cases it finds confirmation in the list of citizens to whom arms were entrusted, though not all the fifty or so citizens it names appear in Dino Guinigi's list. Some citizens named in Dino Guinigi's list also appear as Guinigi partisans in Sercambi's chronicle, or there is evidence in the public records for the period before 1392 that they supported the Guinigi, or they can be shown to be men taking a full part in public affairs after the Guinigi victory in May 1392. The list in fact seems to be accurate.[51] It would not be possible to compile such a full list from other sources, and it and the list of citizens entrusted with arms after 12 May 1392 have been used as the criteria in judging who the supporters of each party were, occasionally supplemented by other names drawn from Sercambi or from the *Riformagioni*.

The chief disadvantage of the two lists is that one dates from 1391 and the other from 1392. Though they are probably reliable for the years 1390 to 1392, they are presumably less so the farther away from these dates one gets. This presents greater problems for the period 1370 to 1390 than it does for the years after 1392. An effort to determine the extent of Guinigi power at any point within this period by examining lists of office-holders, councillors, or members of *balìe* is rendered difficult by the fact that such lists contain the names

[50] Sercambi, I, pp. 261–2.

[51] One discrepancy is Turchio Balbani, whom Sercambi names as an enemy of the Guinigi in 1385 and 1400, Sercambi, III, pp. 9, 336–7. But as he appears regularly in office 1392–1400, Sercambi may have been mistaken. It is possible that he was one of those who turned against Paolo Guinigi in 1400 and that Sercambi was using hindsight in making him an enemy earlier; Sercambi himself mentions Turchio Balbani in office 1392–1400, I, p. 314, II, pp. 63, 349. Another discrepancy is that Galvano Trenta, listed as a Guinigi supporter, is named by Sercambi as an adherent of the Forteguerra, I, pp. 278–9. In this case Sercambi may have been right, as Galvano Trenta does not hold office after 1392. Sercambi also seems to imply that ser Simone Alberti may not have been a wholly reliable Guinigi partisan, I, 260.

of many citizens who died before 1391 and therefore do not appear on either list of Guinigi and Forteguerra partisans. In addition there is no means of knowing at what point before 1391 the citizens named in these lists became supporters of one party or the other. It would be dangerous to assume that a man named as a Guinigi supporter in 1391 was necessarily already a Guinigi supporter in, say, 1375, though occasionally membership of one group or the other can be traced back beyond 1391.[52] But despite these difficulties the two lists, and especially that of Dino Guinigi must be used as the basis for any discussion of the membership of the two factions.

The nucleus of the Guinigi party was, of course, the Guinigi family itself. The family was powerful because of its wealth, and it also had the advantage of being both numerous and united. The Guinigi seem, too, to have been in general men of ability, capable of taking a leading part both in commercial affairs and in politics. In Francesco Guinigi's generation the family consisted of himself, his two brothers, Niccolò, and Michele, and their three cousins, Dino, Lazzaro, and Jacobo. Niccolò died before 23 November 1381 and Jacobo seems to have taken little part in political life and to have died before 29 July 1383,[53] but Francesco could rely on the support of the others. The family seems to have been exceptionally close and united. The Guinigi company consisted of members of both branches of the family. Francesco's position as head of the family was never challenged, and there is no indication in his lifetime, or that of his son, Lazzaro, of any division of interest between the two branches of the family. Had the family not been so united it would have been much more difficult to pursue a policy of acquiring a powerful position in the city through a group of friends and supporters, holding offices and influencing councils without disturbing the forms of republican government.

In addition to Francesco Guinigi's two brothers and three cousins the family nucleus of the Guinigi party included their many sons. Of Francesco Guinigi's five sons, only the eldest,

[52] For example, Sercambi names certain Forteguerra partisans for the year 1385, III, pp. 336–7.

[53] *Protocolli* of ser Domenico Lupardi, *Archivio de'Notari*, 276, ff. 103–103v, 29 July 1383, *Rif.* 7, p. 618, 23 Nov. 1381.

Lazzaro, played an important part in political life before 1392, but Antonio, Bartolomeo, and Paolo all held office between 1392 and 1400, as did their cousin, Baldassare, son of Niccolò Guinigi, and the two sons of Michele and Lazzaro Guinigi, both called Giovanni.[54] Another of Lazzaro's sons, Niccolò, became bishop of Lucca in 1394. It was of great advantage that the Guinigi family should be numerous. A family that was numerous as well as wealthy commanded greater respect, and it would be possible too, to influence affairs by holding office frequently without arousing opposition by failure to observe the 'vacations', or weakening the family by neglecting its business interests in order to concentrate on politics.

The Guinigi were also able to build up their party by marriage alliances. There were even more daughters of the Guinigi family than there were sons, and a solid nucleus of the Guinigi party was bound to the family by marriage ties. Sometimes the Guinigi married outside the city. Francesco Guinigi's first wife had been a daughter of count Guglielmo de Mudigliano, and Dino Guinigi's first wife was a Malaspina.[55] Dea Malavolti, second wife of Michele Guinigi and Sozzina di Ruffi, the second of Lazzaro di Francesco Guinigi's three wives, were Sienese; Michele Guinigi's first wife had been Filippa, daughter of Rosso de'Buondelmonte and Lazzaro di Niccolò's son, Arrigo, married a daughter of Giovanni Cavalcanti of Florence.[56] But these marriages outside the city were comparatively rare.[57] The Guinigi generally married into

[54] *Archivio Guinigi*, 151, f. 5, family trees ff. 60v–61v. Niccolò Guinigi had had another son, Guaspare, but he died prematurely in 1389 when a large stone mortar, which a woman had left on her windowsill, fell on his head as he was passing down the Chiasso Barletti, *Archivio Guinigi*, f. 60v. The accident is described in detail in the petition of the 'lugubris et afflicte domine' responsible for it that her sentence be reduced. *Rif.* 11, pp. 230–1, 28 Jan. 1390. There was also a Niccolò di Francesco di Niccolò Guinigi, belonging to another branch of the family. Michele Guinigi sold him a house in Lucca for 50 florins, 15 July 1388 and he married the heiress of Giovanni Lazzari in May 1389, *Archivio Guinigi*, 151, f. 12. *Protocolli* of ser Domenico Lupardi, *Archivio de'Notari*, 282, ff. 29v–31v, 29 Apr., 5 May 1389. He held office regularly from 1390 onwards.

[55] *Archivio Guinigi*, 318, f. 5, *Archivio Guinigi*, 264, f. 330. *Archivio Guinigi*, 151, family trees, ff. 60v–61v.

[56] *Archivio Guinigi*, 151, f. 5, family trees, ff. 60v–61v.

[57] Several of them seem to have taken place before 1369. Francesco Guinigi's first wife died 29 Dec. 1358, *Archivio Guinigi*, 318, f. 5, *Archivio Guinigi*, 264, f. 330.

other Lucchese families, usually merchant families like their own. This assisted them in building up a party, though it would be an exaggeration to see all the marriage alliances made between 1370 and 1400 as having political aims. It was natural for the Guinigi to seek husbands for their daughters and wives for their sons from the other leading merchant families of the city. Nevertheless very many of those allied to the Guinigi in this way were to be Guinigi partisans. In some cases the marriages perhaps had political results even when they did not have political aims, though in others the Guinigi may have married into families that were already their partisans.

Francesco Guinigi's second wife had been Francesca, the daughter of the judge messer Giovanni Sbarra,[58] and his third Filippa, daughter of Albero Serpente. Her brother Bonanno was to be a member of the Guinigi party.[59] Of Francesco's own sons, only Roberto and Lazzaro were apparently married before 1392. Lazzaro's first wife was a Rossiglione,[60] and Roberto was married to Clara, the heiress of Giovanni di Betto Anguilla.[61] Francesco also had ten daughters. His daughter Filippa married Niccolò Pettinati, who died in 1369.[62] Beatrice married Giovanni Cagnuoli, who died in 1383, leaving two sons, Benedetto and Gherardo. Maddalena married Francesco Totti; Tommasina married Antonio Gigli; Agata married Stefano di Poggio; Petra married first Paolo Magghiari, who died about 1383, and second Giovanni di

---

Dino Guinigi's marriage also probably took place before 1369. Michele married his first wife 19 Oct. 1371 and his second 28 Oct. 1384, *Archivio Guinigi*, 151, f. 5.

[58] *Archivio Guinigi*, 318, f. 3v. The marriage may have been short lived. It cannot have taken place before 1359 and she made her will in 1360.

[59] Lucca, Biblioteca Governativa, MS. 925, f. 208. Will of Albero Serpente, Lucca, Archivio Notarile, series *Testamenti*, ser Fedocco Scortica, ff. 18–20, 8 Dec. 1371, codicil, ff. 20–20v, 9 Dec. 1375. Note in margin f. 18 that he died 13 Dec. 1375.

[60] *Protocolli* of ser Domenico Lupardi, *Archivio de'Notari*, 273, 26 Dec. 1379, *Archivio Guinigi*, 318, f. 3v. Mention of the betrothal 1365, f. 12v, and according to a loose folio dated 1363, when both were 'infante'.

[61] *Protocolli* of ser Simone Alberti, *Archivio de'Notari*, 248, 4 Feb. 1378. Chiara died in the plague of 1383, *Archivio Guinigi*, 151, f. 5. Bartolomeo di Francesco Guinigi married Maddalena, daughter of Luiso Tadolini, but this marriage took place after 1392. *Archivio Guinigi*, 312, f. 199, he acknowledged receipt of her dowry, 22 Jan. 1396.

[62] Niccolo Pettinati's will, *Protocolli* of ser Filippo Lupardi, *Archivio de'Notari*, 159 (not foliated), 12 July 1369.

Puccinello Galganetti; Margarita married Piero di Ciuchino Panichi, who went bankrupt and fled from Lucca in 1387.[63]

Francesco's son, Lazzaro, had many children. His son, Francesco, married Pia, daughter of Bonagiunta di Simo Schiezza, and another son Lorenzo, married Giovanna, daughter of Giuffredo Cenami.[64] Of his daughters, Isabetta married ser Niccolò, son of ser Pietro Manfredi of Camaiore,[65] Lagina married Bartolomeo Carincione, and Gettina married Nese, son of Giovanni Franchi.[66] Of the children of Francesco's brother Niccolò, who had married Jacoba, daughter of Matteo di Poggio, Baldassare married Caterina, daughter of Niccolò Onesti,[67] and Giovanna married Bartolomeo, son of Luiso Boccella.[68] Of the children of Francesco's other brother Michele, Antonia married Arrigo Arnolfini,[69] Ginevra married Antonio, son of Bonaccorso Bocci and Jacoba married Jacobo, son of Niccolò Ghiova;[70] Rabiluccia married first messer Guido Tegrimi and second Carlo Buzolini, while Gianella married Antonio, son of Quarto da Quarto.[71] Michele's son, Giovanni married

[63] Giovanni Cagnuoli's will, Lucca, Archivio Notarile, series *Testamenti*, ser Fedocco Scortica, ff. 97–99, 4 Aug. 1383. Paolo Magghiari's will, *Protocolli* of ser Domenico Lupardi, *Archivio de'Notari*, 273, 20 Sept. 1381. He went bankrupt in 1382, *Rif.* 8, pp. 84–5, 28 Mar., pp. 342–3, 16 Dec. 1382, p. 571, 28 July 1383. Marriage to Giovanni Galganetti, *Protocolli* of ser Domenico Lupardi, *Archivio de'Notari*, 277, ff. 24–24v, 26v–27, 29 Feb., 7 Mar. 1384. Marriage of Tommasina, *Archivio de'Notari*, 282, 3 Nov. 1389. For Piero di Ciuchino Panichi, *Archivio de'Notari*, 280, ff. 173v–174v, 19 Dec. 1387. See also family trees in *Archivio Guinigi*, 151, ff. 60v–61v.

[64] *Archivio Guinigi*, 151, family trees ff. 60v–61v. Lazzaro was the guardian of Pia and Margarita, the two daughters of Bongiunta Schiezza, and married both of them to Guinigi, *Archivio Guinigi*, 318, f. 18.

[65] *Protocolli* of ser Domenico Lupardi, *Archivio de'Notari*, 281 (not foliated), 4 July 1388. Ser Pietro Manfredi was one of ten men of Camaiore compelled to live in Lucca in 1375 after being involved in local disturbances, *Delib.* 132, ff. 131–132 and loose folio at the end, 26 Sept. 1375.

[66] Family trees, *Archivio Guinigi*, 151, ff. 60v–61v.

[67] *Protocolli* of ser Domenico Lupardi, *Archivio de'Notari*, 284, ff. 111–111v, 27 Sept. 1393.

[68] She was a widow by 1390, *Protocolli* of ser Domenico Lupardi, *Archivio de'Notari*, 283, ff. 278–278v, 28 Oct. 1390.

[69] *Archivio Guinigi*, 318, f. 6, f. 18, *Archivio Guinigi*, 151, f. 5, f. 33v, the marriage of Ginevra took place 14 Oct. 1397 and that of Antonia 7 Sept. 1399. Also *Archivio Guinigi*, 151, ff. 60v–61v, family trees.

[70] *Archivio Guinigi*, 318, f. 6, family trees *Archivio Guinigi*, 151, ff. 60v–61v.

[71] *Archivio Guinigi*, 318, f. 6, family trees *Archivio Guinigi*, 151, ff. 60v–61v.

Margarita, daughter of Bonagiunta Schiezza though this marriage did not take place before about 1399.[72] Francesco, Niccolò and Michele also had a sister, Chiara, who had married Bonifacio Boccansocchi.[73]

The other branch of the Guinigi family was connected with almost as many families. Dino Guinigi had by his third marriage to Jacoba Rossiglione a daughter, Taddea, who married first Francesco, son of Alderigo Antelminelli, and second Gherardo ser Bianconi.[74] Jacobo seems to have had only one child, Caterina, who married Betto Schiatta,[75] but the third brother, Lazzaro, who married Margarita dello Strego, had many children. Of these Giovanni married Clara, daughter of Giovanni Benettoni,[76] Beatrice married Ciuchino Avvocati,[77] and Isabetta married Michele, son of Bartolomeo Michelis.[78]

Many of those connected with the Guinigi by marriage appear in Dino Guinigi's list as Guinigi supporters. Bartolomeo Buzolini, Giovanni Galganetti, Antonio Gigli, Niccolò Onesti, Giovanni Benettoni, Ciuchino Avvocati, Gherardo ser Bianconi, Brunetto Pettinati, Quarto da Quarto, Bonanno Serpente, probably the Cagnuoli brothers, and members of the dello Strego, Boccansocchi, Anguilla, and di Poggio families, including Stefano di Poggio. The close connections by marriage between the Guinigi and di Poggio families is especially striking. The wife of Francesco's brother Niccolò was Jacoba, daughter of Matteo di Poggio, and Francesco's daughter, Agata, had married a di Poggio.[79] The mother of Dino, Lazzaro, and Jacobo Guinigi was a di Poggio, for their father, Niccolò, had married Caterina, a sister of

[72] *Archivio Guinigi,* 318, f. 18.

[73] *Archivio Guinigi,* 318, f. 4v. The marriage apparently took place in 1358.

[74] *Archivio Guinigi,* 151, ff. 60v–61v, family trees. Dino Guinigi had also been married to Chiara, daughter of Piero Rapondi, but she was dead by 1365, *Archivio Guinigi*, 318, f. 12v.

[75] *Protocolli* of ser Domenico Lupardi, *Archivio de'Notari*, 279, ff. 48v–49v, 17 Feb. 1386.

[76] *Archivio Guinigi*, 151, ff. 60v–61v, family trees.

[77] *Protocolli* of ser Domenico Lupardi, *Archivio de'Notari*, 278, ff. 26v–27v, 4 Feb. 1386.

[78] *Protocolli* of ser Domenico Lupardi, *Archivio de'Notari*, 280, ff. 88v–89, 8 June 1387. She died before 14 Jan. 1391.

[79] *Archivio Guinigi*, 151, ff. 60v–61v, family trees.

messer Dino di Poggio. In 1380 Jacobo, son of Chello di Lemmo di Poggio, married Ginevra, daughter of Francesco Dombellinghi, whose mother was a Guinigi.[80] With these close connections it is not surprising that the di Poggio family were among the Guinigi partisans.

But a connection with the Guinigi by marriage did not necessarily make a man a Guinigi partisan. Betto Schiatta was a leading opponent of the Guinigi despite his marriage to Caterina, daughter of Jacobo Guinigi, and the same applies to Michele, son of Bartolomeo Michelis, who had been married to a daughter of Lazzaro di Niccolò Guinigi, though she was dead by 1391.[81] The Dombellinghi family included Forteguerra supporters, despite the connection with the Guinigi family, and the Panichi, Rossiglione, and others who were related to the Guinigi by marriage were not apparently active supporters of either party. But the majority of those connected with the Guinigi family by marriage were Guinigi partisans and included some of their most active supporters.

Another probable source of recruits for the Guinigi party was the Guinigi company. A number of those named on Dino

[80] *Protocolli* of ser Domenico Lupardi, *Archivio de'Notari*, 273, 8 Mar. 1380. In the late fourteenth century the di Poggio were extremely numerous; they are distinguished from each other in documents by strings of patronymics. Although the kinship cannot have been very close in many cases, the di Poggio had a strong sense of identity and cohesion. When one of their number, Giovanni di Poggio, was fined for offences committed as vicar of Gallicano, seven of his *consortes* and others who were not named petitioned that he should be restored to office because of the 'verecundia' to the family, *Rif.* 7, pp. 247–8, 28 May 1381. The di Poggio were organized as a *consorteria* with an elected consul, assisted by two councillors. When the consul, Franceschino di Masino di Poggio died, ten of the family met in the church of S. Lorenzo di Poggio 'in qua dicti consortes soliti sunt congregari', to elect a successor, *Protocolli* of ser Domenico Lupardi, *Archivio de'Notari*, 278, 3 Apr. 1385. A meeting of the *consortes* was called later to arrange for the lease of some land within the city walls, which the family owned jointly. The family had a 'camerarius introytuum domus predicte de Podio', who was to receive the rent for this, *Protocolli* of ser Domenico Lupardi, *Archivio de'Notari*, 280, ff. 45–45^{v}, 12 Mar., 6 Aug. 1387, 23 Jan. 1390, 18 Apr. 1391, 24 Feb. 1396. The di Poggio were regarded as nobles in the fourteenth century and were one of the families excluded from the Anzianate in 1370, *Rif.* 1, pp. 454–8, 31 July 1370. They served extremely frequently on embassies, in councils and *balìe*, and as vicars and in other offices for which they were still eligible. Some concentrated on such administrative posts, but others were merchants. The di Poggio were among the leading Guinigi partisans, and alone of the families affected by the decree of 31 July 1370 were restored to full political rights after the Guinigi victory in 1392.

[81] *Protocolli* of ser Domenico Lupardi, *Archivio de'Notari*, 280, ff. 88^{v}–89, 14 Jan. 1391.

Guinigi's list as Guinigi supporters had been connected with the Guinigi company. Bartolomeo and Giovanni Bernardini had been in the Guinigi company in 1371, 1372, and 1381, and by 1381 Giovanni had risen to be a partner.[82] Giovanni del Ghiotto and Giovanni Boccansocchi had been members in 1381,[83] and Antonio da Volterra, who was one of the citizens entrusted with arms in 1392, had been a member of the Guinigi company in 1371 and 1372.[84] There are others who had been members of the company, who do not appear in either list of supporters, but who held office after 1392 and were probably Guinigi supporters. These include Bendinello Rossiglione, Giovanni Ganghi, and Francesco Vinciguerra. In oher cases relatives of members of the Guinigi company were supporters. Agostino Benettoni was employed in the Guinigi company, and his kinsman, Giovanni Benettoni, was a Guinigi partisan.[85] Kinsmen of other Guinigi employees, such as Dino Dardagnini, Folchino Tadolini, Lazzaro, Luiso, and Pagano dal Portico, and Niccolò di Pessino di Poggio were Guinigi supporters.[86]

There is no reason to believe that the Guinigi were deliberately trying to build up their power through their commercial company. But it is probable that a number of young men had got their first start in life in the Guinigi company. The Guinigi may have benefited from gratitude for this kind of patronage, and men who had begun in the Guinigi company, but later left it, may have kept in touch with their former patrons. Perhaps memories of earlier connections with the Guinigi company caused some men to look to Guinigi

[82] *Corte de'Mercanti*, 82, f. 11v, 83, f. 7; 84, f. 11.

[83] *Corte de'Mercanti*, 84, f. 11. Giovanni Boccansocchi was in London for the Guinigi 1377-8, *Libro della Communità dei mercanti lucchesi in Bruges*, p. 12.

[84] *Corte de'Mercanti*, 82, f. 11v, 83, f. 7.

[85] Agostino Benettoni was a member of the Guinigi company in 1371, *Corte de'Mercanti*, 82, f. 11v, and a factor in London in 1377, *Libro della communità*, p. 12.

[86] *Corte de'Mercanti*, 82, f. 11v; 83, f. 7; 84, f. 11. The Guinigi are also found investing sums with other merchants, some of whom were to be Guinigi supporters. This may have been partly a method of building up support, though also, of course, partly for commercial reasons. Examples of such investments, *Protocolli* of ser Domenico Lupardi, *Archivio de'Notari*, 278, ff. 25-26, 30 Jan. 1385 (Gherardo ser Bianconi), 280, ff. 76-76v, 22 May 1387 (Bartolomeo Balbani); 281, ff. 6v-7, 18 Jan. 1387 (Bartolomeo Vannuccori).

leadership and influenced them enough to make them Guinigi supporters in the crisis of 1390 to 1392. This cannot, of course, be proved, and connections with the Guinigi company were certainly not always enough in themselves to make men Guinigi supporters. There were at least two men who had been in the Guinigi company and who were leading supporters of the Forteguerra in 1390–2. These were Michele Michelis, who was in the Guinigi company in 1371 and 1372, and later connected with the Guinigi also by marriage, and Matteo Nutini, a member of the Guinigi company in 1381.[87]

There was another factor that might cause men to align themselves with the Guinigi party. The Guinigi had been to some extent in power in Lucca in the years before 1390, and especially between 1374 and 1385. Ambitious men might therefore hope for advancement by attaching themselves to the Guinigi. The chronicler, Giovanni Sercambi, was probably a man of this kind, though hope of advancement is not among the reasons he gives for supporting the Guinigi.[88] There was a group of notaries in the Guinigi party, who may have been hoping for advancement through Guinigi patronage. They included ser Domenico Lupardi, a notary frequently used by the Guinigi, and others, such as ser Gregorio Andreucci, ser Benedetto Bianchi, ser Fedocco Scortica, and perhaps ser Simone Alberti, who were poor men and who did not belong to families that were important politically. There were others, such as ser Niccolò dello Strego, ser Niccolò Turinghelli, ser Taddeo Malpigli, and ser Ubaldo Perfettucci, who were members of rather more important families,[89] but still not so important that they had no need of a patron, and these too were poor men. In addition to the notaries there were others who may have joined the Guinigi faction in the hope of gain or personal advancement, men like Pellegrino Lelli,[90] a tanner; Piero Manucci, tavern-keeper;

[87] *Corte de'Mercanti*, 84, f. 11.

[88] Sercambi, III, p. 337. In fact he specifically denies it.

[89] The Turinghelli and the Malpigli had been named as 'potentes et casastici' in 1308. Members of the Malpigli and Perfettucci had been Anziani before 1369, though only occasionally, but the Perfettucci had been prominent as *campsores* in the mid-thirteenth century, T. W. Blomquist, 'The Castracani family of thirteenth-century Lucca', *Speculum*, Vol. XLVI (1971), pp. 464–6, 470.

[90] Lucca, Biblioteca Governativa, MS. 925, f. 207v has 'Pellegrino Cielli coiarius', but this is almost certainly a misreading.

Piero Franceschi, *pannaio*; and Giovanni Talenti, a weaver. These and some of the notaries were outside the group of citizens who normally held political office. They probably could not hope to take part in political life, or even obtain non-political but profitable, offices without a patron, and were therefore perhaps attracted to the Guinigi party by the hope of personal advantage.

But the vast bulk of the Guinigi party, as listed by Dino Guinigi, was made up of members of political families. Some of these too may have supported the Guinigi in the hope of patronage. A number of Guinigi supporters, though of sufficient position to hold the office of Anziano, neither belonged to important families, nor were themselves wealthy men. Gherardo ser Bianconi, Giovanni del Ghiotto, Casino Vannis, Giovanni, and Bonifacio Cionelli or Prospero ser Conforti are examples of men of this type. Others, such as Bartolosso Angiorelli, Niccolò Pinelli, Quarto da Quarto, Niccolò Liena, the Avvocati, or Francesco Guinigi's brother-in-law, Bonanno Serpente belonged to more firmly established families but were not wealthy.[91]

The Guinigi also enjoyed the support of many who, though not in the very first rank of citizens for wealth, were men of substance, and often belonged to the leading families and appeared most frequently in offices, councils and *balìe*. Giovanni Mingogii, Franceschino and Bartolomeo Buzolini, Turellino Bonucci, Giovanni Boccansocchi, Dino Moriconi, and Niccolò ser Pagani are examples of men in this position.[92] There were others too who were among the very richest citizens

[91] Prospero ser Conforti was assessed at 4,166 florins in the *Estimo* of 1397, Biblioteca Governativa MS. 925, f. 255, but had no important family connections. He was called 'Prospero de Sorana, filius ser Conforti' (*Imprestiti*, 11, f. 331v) in 1373, so was perhaps a recent immigrant and therefore in need of a patron. The same perhaps applies to Bartolomeo Lottini; messer Matteo Lottini is described as 'de Camaiore', *Rif.* 10, p. 142, 18 Nov. 1386. The Avvocati were one of the most ancient families of Lucca, and they and the Pinelli and Liena were among those named as 'potentes et casastici' in 1308.

[92] The Boccansocchi had been named as 'potentes et casastici' in 1308. They and the Buzolini had been Anziani very frequently since 1330. Their assessments in the *Estimo* of 1397 were Giovanni Mingogi 1,900 florins, Biblioteca Governativa MS. 925 f.251v, Franceschino Buzolini, 2,466 florins, f. 249, Bartolomeo Buzolini, 1,600 florins, f. 249, Simone di Turellino Bonucci, 3,166 florins, f. 250v, Giovanni Boccansocchi 1,333 florins, f. 250v, Dino Moriconi 832 florins, f. 257, Niccolò di ser Pagani 2,000 florins, f. 255v.

in Lucca, as well as belonging to the leading families. Giovanni Benettoni, Niccolò Bocci, Pietro Gentile, Francesco di Giuntino Martini, and Giovanni Bernardi were among these.[93]

It is not easy to see why these men supported the Guinigi, especially if the party formed soon after 1369. Though there were external and economic difficulties, Lucca was internally at peace and there was no disorder or violence in the city that they might have looked to the Guinigi to cure. Men of their position can have had little to gain by supporting the Guinigi. Their own family and economic position would ensure them a regular and important position in public life. Indeed it might be thought that they had much to lose by the strengthening of Guinigi influence, especially if it led to a *signorìa*. They would be able to play a greater part in public affairs if the city remained a free republic, with control of the government in the hands of a bourgeois oligarchy, than if power in the city fell to one family. Indeed, if the choice genuinely lay between Guinigi power and a free republic, one might expect to find them among the most ardent opponents of the Guinigi. It would have been in their own interests, apart from the fact that the Lucchese, like the citizens of most Italian republics of this period, professed to prefer liberty and republican government to the rule of one man or family on ideological grounds.

But it seems probable that the choice did not lie between republican liberty on the one hand and Guinigi power on the other. There was as yet no question of a Guinigi *signorìa* and even after their victory in 1392 the Guinigi were careful to exercise their power with tact and restraint, and to maintain the outward forms of the old republican government. A passage in Sercambi's chronicle suggests that the alternative to Guinigi power was the power of some other family. He speaks of the motives of those who put themselves at the head of the opposition to the Guinigi, saying 'alcuni desideravano farsene

[93] The Martini, Onesti, Bocci and Benettoni had been named as 'potentes et casastici' in 1308 and had held the office of Anziano before 1369. In the *Estimo* of 1397 Giovanni Benettoni was assessed at 6,110 florins, f. 255v, Francesco di Giuntino Martini at 3,666 florins, f. 254v, Pietro Gentile at 11,666, f. 253v, Giovanni Bernardi at 11,333, f. 253v, and Bonaccorso Bocci at 16,666, f. 253, the richest citizen in Lucca, surpassing even any individual member of the Guinigi family.

signori, alchuni diventare ricchi per via di rubba & d'altri mali'. He asserts that he himself decided to become a Guinigi supporter because he thought 'lo regimento de'dicti Guinigi esser utile & buono & salvessa della ciptà di Luccha'.[94] Of course, Sercambi was one of the leading Guinigi partisans and might be expected to act as apologist for the Guinigi regime, so that unsupported statements of this kind cannot be taken at their face value. However, he is to some extent backed up by later writers, such as Dalli and Civitali, who see the internal troubles of Lucca in terms of two family groups, struggling for power and each trying to exclude the other.[95] They do not see the Rapondi-Forteguerra party as a group of right-minded citizens, attempting to defend the regular republican form of government against the irregular encroachments of the Guinigi. There are occasional incidents, too, which suggest that the Rapondi and Forteguerra were no less ambitious and self-interested than the Guinigi. Forteguerra Forteguerra was building himself an ostentatious house in Lucca,[96] and was capable of an act of arrogance and selfishness which Sercambi regarded as an insult to the city. He was Gonfaloniere in December 1386, when Urban VI visited Lucca, and as such he had been presented with a ceremonial cap embroidered with pearls and a sword with a scabbard and belt. He took them with him when his period of office ended, claiming that they were gifts to him personally, and not to the head of the Lucchese government.[97] This was just the kind of action that a patriotic Lucchese would regard as an insult to the city, and, if everyone felt as strongly about it as Sercambi apparently did, it may well have had some influence on the choice between the Forteguerra and Guinigi parties. It was certainly still remembered in 1392, for after the Guinigi victory action was taken to restore the cap and sword to the city.[98]

[94] Sercambi, III, p. 337.

[95] S. Dalli, *Cronica di Lucca dall'origine di essa città fino all'anno 1650* Tom. III series *Biblioteca de'Manoscritti*, no. 11, e.g. p. 347. Civitali, f. 360.

[96] *Rif.* 11, p. 31, 9 Feb. 1389. After his death it was sold to Bonaccorso Bocci for 4,000 florins, *Rif.* 12, pp. 476–83, 7 Aug. 1394.

[97] Sercambi, I, pp. 253–4.

[98] He was said to have 'ambitione ductus sibi temeraria presumptione ascripsit', *Rif.* 12, p. 190, 30 Aug. 1392. The cap and sword were in future to be assigned to each Gonfaloniere on taking office.

It is harder to speak of the Forteguerra-Rapondi party than that of the Guinigi. The only list of Forteguerra partisans is that drawn up by Dino Guinigi in 1391, and it contains only forty-one names. Sercambi names a few of the opponents of the Guinigi on the death of Francesco. They included messer Bartolomeo Forteguerra and his cousin, Forteguerra Forteguerra, Piero and Giovanni Rapondi, messer Giovanni Maulini, and Bartolomeo Michaelis, though Sercambi himself states that there were many others.[99] These were the leading opponents of the Guinigi in 1390–2, and this is the only real evidence for the existence of the party as early as 1384–5. But the Rapondi complained in 1371 that they had been heavily assessed in an *estimo*,[100] and in 1377 messer Bartolomeo Forteguerra refused the office of Anziano to which he had been elected.[101] This may mean that there was already tension between them and the Guinigi, though there is no sure indication of the membership or even the existence of a conscious opposition group before 1384. This makes it impossible to be sure whether the Guinigi and the Forteguerra-Rapondi parties developed in parallel, as rivals, or whether the Guinigi party grew up first, thus causing an opposition to develop in an attempt to check their undue influence. But it seems perhaps more likely that the two parties developed parallel.

The opposition centred round the Rapondi and Forteguerra families. They were both ancient families, well-established in Lucchese political life,[102] and the Rapondi, as the second

[99] Sercambi, III, pp. 336–7. He includes Turchio Balbani, who appears in Dino Guinigi's list as a Guinigi supporter. Sercambi also states that eight of the nine Anziani supported the Rapondi, though on the basis of Dino Guinigi's list four were Guinigi supporters, two Forteguerra supporters and three uncommitted. But the issue, the abolition of the *conservatores*, may well have attracted many supporters.

[100] *Rif.* 2, p. 323, 22 June 1371. They pointed out that messer Bartolomeo was a cleric and should not have been assessed at all. One Rapondi brother, Regolino was a captive in the hands of the English and others were in Northern Europe on business affairs. Other families with members abroad had not had them assessed.

[101] *Rif.* 6, p. 140, 2 Jan. 1377. There is no indication of his reason for doing this.

[102] Both were among those named as 'potentes et casastici' in 1308. The Rapondi can be traced back to the twelfth century and had claims to nobility. They had long engaged in trade, L. Mirot, 'La société des Raponde', p. 300. Members of the family regularly held office as Anziani before 1369 *Regesto*, Vol. II, part i, pp. xiii–xxix. The Forteguerra were another ancient family, apparently coming from the *contado*, where they held rights over the castle of Brancoli. They held office in Lucca as early as 1163

richest family of the city, were the natural rivals of the Guinigi. They were among the most active and influential merchants in France and Flanders, and had their centre in Paris and Bruges, rather than in Lucca itself.[103] After the outbreak of the Schism the Rapondi played an important part in the transfer of funds for the Avignonese popes. They had had no branch in Avignon in 1376, but they were able to fill the gap left in the financial administration of the Avignonese popes by the adherence of the Guinigi to Urban VI, and between 1381 and 1395 transferred at least 109,428 florins from Paris to Avignon on behalf of collectors within the Avignonese obedience.[104] The Rapondi were numerous;

---

and several of the family served as Anziani before 1369, L. Mirot, 'Forteguerra Forteguerra et sa succession', pp. 301–2.

[103] Mirot, 'La société des Raponde', pp. 324–76. The annual declarations of trading companies made to the Lucchese community in Bruges show that the Rapondi company numbered between five and eight persons, and that Jacobo, Dino, Giovanni, Andrea, Filippo, Piero, and Michele Rapondi were all members of it at one time or another, *Libro della communità, passim*. There were branches in Lucca, Venice and Avignon as well as Paris and Bruges, Mirot, 'La société des Raponde', pp. 311–13, 318, 324–5, 332, 385. Jacobo Rapondi and his son, Giovanni who belonged to another branch of the family, had a separate company, this time centred in Lucca, *Corte de'Mercanti*, 82, f. 8, 83, f. 2, 84, f. 10v.

[104] They established themselves in Avignonese finance about 1381, engaging mainly in the simple transfer of funds, rather than the more extensive banking and credit operations that the Guinigi carried out on behalf of Urban VI. The volume of business that the Rapondi transacted declined sharply after 1391, and ceased completely about 1395. At first sight the fact that the Guinigi were the leading bankers of the Roman popes and the Rapondi the leading bankers of the Avignonese line would seem to be a significant difference between them. But it is improbable that it had any political implications as far as Lucca was concerned. A state as small and politically insignificant as Lucca could hardly have taken an independent line on such a major European issue as the Schism. The notion of the Rapondi operating as a pro-Clementist group in Lucca is hardly conceivable. Lucca was and remained Urbanist. It is probable that Rapondi involvement in the finance of Clement VII was a matter of seizing an opportunity that offered commercial advantages, and that it sprang from their firmly established position in Paris, which was the main banking centre within the Avignonese obedience and the place from which Rapondi transfers to Avignon were effected. It was the local collectors who had the initiative in the choice of banker, and the Rapondi probably had the greatest resources and were able to offer the best service. In so far as their involvement in Avignonese papal finance had any political overtones it was the politics of France and Burgundy and not those of Lucca. It has been suggested that the decline of Rapondi activity in Avignonese finance was connected with the change of attitude to Clement VII on the part of the duke of Burgundy, to whom Dino Rapondi was heavily committed. It seems probable that the Guinigi role in the finance of the Roman papacy and the Rapondi role in that of the Avignonese popes was the natural result of the fact that the Guinigi company was centred in Lucca with branches in Bruges and London, while the Rapondi had their

Guido Rapondi had at least seven sons, including Dino, Piero and Bartolomeo,[105] and there were several other branches of the family. But many of the Rapondi spent long periods away from Lucca, and some of them must rarely, if ever, have set foot there. Because of their prolonged absences from the city few members of the family held office with any frequency. Dino and Giovanni held office occasionally, but only Jacobo di Giovanni and Piero di Guido Rapondi held office at all regularly.[106] The Forteguerra do not seem to have been very numerous, and only two members of the family took an active part in political life in the period 1369–92. Forteguerra Forteguerra was a wealthy merchant, much of whose business was conducted in Bruges, Paris, and London,[107] so that he was often absent from Lucca, and held office only intermittently

main centre in Paris, and that it had no real significance for Lucchese internal or external affairs. Though there is the possibility that commercial rivalry outside Lucca had an effect on the factions within the city, it is worth noting that neither party seems to have gained any commercial advantage as a result of the crisis of 1390–2, as both Guinigi involvement in Urbanist finance and Rapondi involvement in that of the Clementists declined after about 1391. For all this, Favier, *Les Finances pontificales*, pp. 483–501, 505.

[105] Mirot, 'La société des Raponde', p. 303. There was also a Regolino, son of Guido Rapondi, *Rif.* 2, p. 323, 22 June 1371. There were probably nine sons in all, as his property was divided into nine shares, Mirot, p. 380.

[106] Giovanni was Anziano in 1372 and Dino in 1388. Jacobo di Giovanni was Anziano nine times and Gonfaloniere once, and Piero di Guido was Anziano four times and Gonfaloniere once between 1369 and 1392. *Regesto*, Vol. II, part ii, pp. xi–xxxv. Both also sat regularly in councils and *balìe*. In 1383 the Lucchese tried unsuccessfully to secure the election of Bartolomeo di Guido Rapondi as bishop of Lucca, *Reg.*, nos. 1089, 1093, June and 21 Aug. 1383. He was later appointed Master of the Hospital of S. Jacopo of Altopascio, near Lucca, 23 Nov. 1387. He died in 1394, *Reg.*, nos. 1513–14.

[107] Apart from his own holdings of 214 florins in the *Massa* in 1373 he had purchased holdings of 725 florins as a speculation, *Imprestiti*, 14, f. 12^{v}. He had provided his daughters with the large dowry of 700 florins, which he raised to 950 florins with a further legacy of 3,500 florins to his only surviving daughter, Maddalena, in his will, *Rif.* 12, pp. 172–3, 16 Aug. 1392. Philip the Bold, duke of Burgundy had owed him 17,185 francs in 1370, Mirot, 'Forteguerra Forteguerra et sa succession', p. 303. After his death when his property was confiscated to the state, Lucca hoped to get 15,000 florins from it, as well as honouring legacies of over 12,000 florins. Apart from this he possessed houses and land, including the Forteguerra palace, which fetched 4,000 florins when sold, *Rif.* 12, pp. 172–3, 16 Aug. 1392, pp. 476–83, 7 Aug. 1394. As much of his business was conducted in Bruges, Paris, and London, it may be that he had further wealth, which escaped the Lucchese government. Mirot, 'Forteguerra Forteguerra et sa succession', pp. 303–20, and annual declarations of companies in Bruges, *Libro della communità, passim*. He also had a subsidiary company in Pisa, from which Lucca got 3,712 florins, *Protocolli* of

before 1386.[108] From 1386 onwards he appears regularly as Anziano and in councils and *balìe* until the crisis of May 1392, in which he was killed. His cousin,[109] messer Bartolomeo, was not a wealthy man,[110] but played, if anything, a more important part in political life. As a doctor of laws and a judge he frequently served in offices where legal knowledge was required and was often sent on embassies.[111] He had been one of the compilers of the new Statute of 1372, and was one of the original *conservatores.*[112] He sat regularly as Anziano, councillor, and on *balìe*[113] and by 1390 few citizens had had greater political experience.

A feature of the Forteguerra-Rapondi party was the number of judges who supported it. Almost all the Lucchese judges appear in Dino Guinigi's list as Forteguerra partisans, messer Ludovico Mercati, Guglielmo Flammi, Giovanni Maulini, Giovanni Cimacchi, and Giovanni Genovardi, as well as messer Bartolomeo himself. It is impossible to say whether they supported the Forteguerra-Rapondi party because, as judges, they were the natural defenders of the existing constitution against threats to it by the Guinigi, or out of solidarity with one of their number, messer Bartolomeo. But whatever their motives, the judges' support for the Forteguerra

ser Domenico Lupardi, *Archivio de'Notari*, 284, ff. 79v–80v, 4 Dec. 1394.

[108] He had held office in Lucca 1372–3, but was in Bruges 1376–7 and perhaps earlier, and again 1382–6, *Libro della communità*, pp. 9–12, 100–27.

[109] They were not, as Mirot stated, brothers. They were only distantly related, cousins, and not apparently first cousins. Patronymics show that Forteguerra was the son of Pagano and messer Bartolomeo son of Vanni or Giovanni, perhaps the same Giovanni who was active in Paris in the 1370s. Vanni's father was apparently called Jacobo, whereas Pagano's father was called Orlando, Mirot, 'Forteguerra Forteguerra et sa succession', pp. 302, 305–7.

[110] He owned houses and land in Lucca and a number of places in the *contado*, in the vicariates of Camaiore, Massa Lunense, Massa Pisana, Aquilea, Brancalo, Anchiano, Puticciano, Castagnore, and S. Colombano, *Rif.* 12, pp. 183–4, 30 Aug. 1392. He had only 35 florins in the Massa in 1373, *Imprestiti*, 14, f. 166v, and he had had a similarly modest assessment in the *imposita* of 1362, Civitali, f. 297. His widow was assessed at 516 florins in the *Estimo* of 1397, Lucca, Biblioteca Governativa, MS. 925, f. 254v.

[111] Ambassador to the Pope, Sept. 1370 and Sept. 1376; to Genoa, May 1372; to Pisa, Aug. 1384; to Florence, June 1385, Mar. 1388 and May 1389 and a number of other embassies.

[112] As *statutarius, Rif.* 2, p. 151, 23 Nov. 1370, *Min.* 2, f. 46v, 18 June 1371, *Rif.* 3, p. 154, 14 Dec. 1371. As *conservatore, Rif.* 4, p. 493, 4 Nov. 1374.

[113] He was Anziano six times and Gonfaloniere four times between 1369 and 1392, *Regesto*, Vol. II, part ii, pp. xi–xxxv.

was solid enough to attract acid comment from Sercambi,[114] and to cause the exclusion of all judges from the college of Anziani after May 1392.[115]

The rest of the Forteguerra party was made up of members of the same kind of merchant families who made up the bulk of the Guinigi party. In some cases they had trading or marriage connections with the Forteguerra or Rapondi families. Giuffredo Cenami, a wealthy merchant of an ancient Lucchese family, had married a Rapondi, and the connection with the Rapondi family was maintained.[116] Giovanni and Giacchetto Totti may have been influenced by Giovanni's marriage to Forteguerra Forteguerra's daughter.[117] The Maulini may also have been influenced by ties of kinship; Forteguerra's wife was probably a Maulini,[118] and Gherardino Maulini, as well as his brother messer Giovanni, a judge, was a Forteguerra partisan. The Sbarra family too were connected with the Forteguerra. Niccolò di Benedetto Sbarra was messer Bartolomeo's nephew, though the Guinigi regarded him as one of their party.[119] Forteguerra left a small legacy to a daughter of Bartolomeo Sbarra,[120] and Jacobo and Giovanni Sbarra were named by Dino Guinigi among the Forteguerra partisans. Another leading supporter was Bartolomeo di

[114] The Forteguerra also had the support of a number of notaries. For Sercambi's comments, Sercambi I, pp. 263-4, but he was prejudiced against judges and notaries, III, pp. 324-30. Judges could, of course, exercise an influence quite out of proportion to their numbers, L. Martines, *Lawyers and Statecraft in Renaissance Florence* (Princeton, 1968). Also J. K. Hyde, *Padua in the Age of Dante* (Manchester, 1966), esp. pp. 121-75.

[115] *Rif.* 12, pp. 121-2, 26 May 1392. Such an exclusion was not without parallel; judges, notaries and doctors were exluded from the *Nove* in Siena after 1287, W. M. Bowsky, 'The *Buon Governo* of Siena (1287-1355): a medieval Italian oligarchy', *Speculum*, Vol. XXXVII (1962), p. 370.

[116] L. Mirot, 'Études Lucquoises: Les Cename', *Bibliothèque de l'École des Chartes*, Vol. LXXXXI (1930), p. 103. Declarations of companies, *Libro della communità*, pp. 242, 249, 252, 1395-7.

[117] *Protocolli* of ser Niccolò Sartoy, *Archivio de'Notari*, 195, ff. 46-46^{v}, 10 July 1376.

[118] Forteguerra's daughter, Maddalena, named messer Niccolò Maulini, uncle of messer Giovanni and Gherardino, as her nearest kinsmen, *Protocolli* of ser Domenico Lupardi, *Archivio de'Notari*, 284, ff. 28-28^{v}, 27 Aug. 1392.

[119] In Dino Guinigi's list. The Guinigi were mistaken, for it was this Niccolò Sbarra who was one of the murderers of Lazzaro Guinigi in 1400. His marriage to one of Lazzaro Guinigi's sisters may have been before 1392, though Sercambi implies that it was later.

[120] *Rif.* 12, p. 173, 16 Aug. 1392.

Michele Moccindente, almost invariably referred to in Lucchese sources as Bartolomeo Michaelis. He seems to have been one of the richest Lucchese merchants with business interests in Venice, Genoa, Savoy, and Paris.[121] He and two of his sons, Giannino and Michele, were named as Forteguerra partisans in Dino Guinigi's list, and another of the Forteguerra party, Gherardo Burlamacchi, was married to his daughter.[122]

Apart from the preponderance of judges in the Forteguerra party, the composition of the two factions is markedly similar. This is underlined by the fact that in a number of cases different members of the same family took opposite sides, or men connected with the Guinigi family by marriage or business ties supported the Forteguerra. Matteo Nutini is an example of this. He was not a member of a particularly important family, nor outstandingly wealthy, but he was one of the citizens who had held office most frequently, and he had been connected with the Guinigi company.[123] Yet he was one of the leading supporters of the Forteguerra, while his brother, Jacobo, took the Guinigi side. Betto Schiatta,[124] despite his marriage to the daughter of Jacobo Guinigi, took the Forteguerra side, although his brother, Guaspare, was a Guinigi partisan. Giovanni Cattani supported the Forteguerra, although his brother, Matteo, sided with the Guinigi, and there were divisions in other families, too,

[121] *Protocolli* of ser Filippo Lupardi, *Archivio de'Notari*, 161 (not foliated), 5 Apr. 1376. *Protocolli* of ser Domenico Lupardi, *Archivio de'Notari*, 276, ff. 1–2, 31 Dec. 1382; 278, 22 Mar. 1385; 280, ff. 105^{v}–106^{v}, 8 July 1387. He was able to provide his daughters with the large dowry of 600 florins each, though there were several of them, as well as six sons. His will is in *Protocolli* of ser Jacobo Domaschi, *Archivio de'Notari*, 167, ff. 154–7, 23 Oct. 1378. He is found buying land in the Lucchese state on a large scale, *Protocolli* of ser Domenico Lupardi, *Archivio de'Notari*, 279, ff. 69–70^{v}, 7 Apr. 1386, and two of his sons had a joint assessment of 6,333 florins in the *Estimo* of 1397, Lucca, Biblioteca Governativa, MS. 925, f. 252^{v}, though much of his wealth must have been outside the city.

[122] Gherardo Burlamacchi had an assessment of 3,255 florins in the *Estimo* of 1397, Lucca, Biblioteca Governativa, MS. 925, f. 250^{v}. Marriage contract, *Protocolli* of ser Domenico Lupardi, *Archivio de'Notari*, 277, ff. 16–16^{v}, 11 Feb. 1384.

[123] He had 176 florins in the *Massa* in 1373, *Imprestiti*, 14, f. 72^{v}. He was in the Guinigi company 1381, *Corte de'Mercanti*, 84, f. 11.

[124] He had appeared regularly in the college of Anziani and councils, but less frequently in *balìe*. He had an assessment of 3,933 florins in the *Estimo* of 1397, Lucca, Biblioteca Governativa, MS. 925, f. 252^{v}. He had been a business associate of Guiffredo Cenami in Bruges 1377, 1380, 1382, 1384, 1386, *Libro della communità*, pp. 12, 64, 99, 122, 135.

though only between more distant relatives. Lando Moriconi was an especially fervent Forteguerra partisan and his cousin, Giovanni, took the same side, but Dino Moriconi, from a third branch of the family, supported the Guinigi. Castruccio Saggina supported the Forteguerra, although Alamanno, Lazzaro, and Piero, each of them from a different branch of the family, were all Guinigi adherents. To this extent there is truth in Sercambi's assertion that the events of 1390–2 divided brother against brother, father against son, partner against partner, neighbour against neighbour, and father-in-law against son-in-law.[125] The decision about which party to support may, therefore, have been made on principle in some cases, rather than resulting from family or business connections, though many supporters of the Guinigi party were probably attracted by the prospect of patronage and advancement.

Several of the leading members of the Forteguerra-Rapondi party seem to have spent quite long periods after 1369 outside the city and even had their centres in Bruges or Paris rather than Lucca itself. But this possible difference between the two parties should not be exaggerated. Members of the Guinigi party also spent some time outside the city, and residence abroad for long periods was normal for merchants and others whose business took them to France and Flanders or other parts of Italy. If the two parties differed in that the Forteguerra-Rapondi party had a rather larger element that had spent much time outside the city, the difference cannot have been very great. There was no social or economic cleavage between the two parties. The Guinigi, the Rapondi and the Forteguerra families were all old-established and wealthy. If the Forteguerra had the support of ancient families like the Mercati, the Moccindente, the Cenami and the Burlamacchi, who had been named as 'potentes et casastici' in 1308, the Guinigi had the support of the no less ancient Boccansocchi, Onesti, Martini, and di Poggio families. Both parties had the support of families which were not named as 'potentes et casastici' and were therefore either 'popolani' in 1308, or had risen to importance since then; the Maulini,

[125] Sercambi, I, p. 274.

Cimacchi, Genovardi, and Moriconi among the Forteguerra supporters, and the Mingogii, Galganetti, Mattafelloni, and dal Portico families among those of the Guinigi. If the Forteguerra had the support of very wealthy merchants like Bartolomeo Michelis or Gherardo Burlamacchi, the Guinigi had the support of others equally wealthy, such as Niccolò Bocci, Pietro Gentile, or Giovanni Bernardi. Both had the support also of men in a more modest position; Niccolò Bambacari, Giovanni Campucci, and Orlandino Volpelli and his sons in the Forteguerra party, and Giovanni Galganetti, Gherardo ser Bianconi, and Giovanni del Ghiotto in that of the Guinigi. It is true that the Guinigi party included more artisans and others in a comparatively humble social and economic position in Dino Guinigi's list. But this is very probably because the list of Guinigi supporters is much longer; the Forteguerra may well have had the support of men of similar position, who were not named in the much shorter list of their supporters because of their relative unimportance. If it was only the Guinigi who had the support of such men, it may have been because the Guinigi had greater power and could therefore offer greater advantages of patronage and advancement. But popular support does not seem to have been a feature of either party, and in any case the *popolo* does not seem to have played an important part in events. Both factions also had parties in the *contado*,[126] but neither probably had an advantage here, and in this respect too there seems to be no real difference between them.

If there was no real distinction between the Guinigi and Forteguerra parties as far as their social or economic composition is concerned, it remains to ask whether anything more than personal ambitions and rivalries can be discerned in the faction struggles of Lucca up to 1392. First of all one must ask whether the two factions took different lines on foreign policy, and whether either faction sought or enjoyed the support of any outside power. The factions were probably

[126] Sercambi, I, pp. 260–1, 265–6, 277–8, 280. Series *Sentenze e Bandi*, 82, ff. 45–8, 7 June 1392, where the Forteguerra party is said to have sought the support of 100 armed men from Barga, 200 from Coreglia and others from Licignane. They also approached three nobles (unnamed), one of whom promised 300 men and another 500.

fairly evenly balanced within the city in 1390, and it must have been tempting to look to outside powers to tip the scale. Lucca had, since the early 1370s, been playing Milan and Florence off against each other, and nothing would have been more natural than that one faction should have turned to Milan and the other to Florence. Milan and Florence too might have been expected to be quick to take advantage of such a situation, hoping by supporting one of the two factions to bring Lucca into a definite alliance to the exclusion of the rival city. But despite the fact that the crisis in Lucca was long drawn out, giving plenty of opportunity for outside intervention, there is no evidence of the intervention of outside powers to any significant extent. There is certainly no evidence that either party received forces from outside the Lucchese state. Both drew on support from the *contado*, but there is no mention in Sercambi or any other writer, nor in the sentences passed against the Forteguerra after their defeat, of either party receiving forces from Milan, Florence, or any other outside power.

But it does seem possible that there was some diplomatic intervention. Florence had provided on 26 April 1392 that an ambassador should be sent to Lucca to prevent any disturbances,[127] and on the 29th she provided 'quod mittantur oratores subite Lucam et sint confidentes et boni et non discedant donec dominus Nicholettus stet ibi'.[128] Florence clearly regarded the matter as urgent and important, and the mention of messer Nicholetto, probably Nicoletto Diversi, suggests that Giangaleazzo too was taking a hand in Lucchese affairs. It is tempting to assume that the presence of envoys from both Milan and Florence in Lucca at the end of April, only a fortnight before the final crisis, was connected with the internal factions, and this may well be so. But they may equally well have been there on some matter concerned with the negotiations for a new league and defence against the companies formed with the end of Florentine-Milanese war.[129] Even if their presence in Lucca was connected with the

[127] A.S.F. *Consulte*, 29, f. 69, 26 Apr. 1392, 'mittatur orator Lucam ita quod novitatibus obvietur'.

[128] A.S.F. *Consulte*, 29, f. 70^{v}, 29 Apr. 1392.

[129] See below, Chapter 14, p. 300.

internal factions, they were more likely to be there as observers to keep their own governments informed and make sure that the other side did not steal a march, than to influence events in Lucca. It may be doubted whether they could have influenced events in Lucca by diplomatic means alone in April 1392. By that time the crisis had been in existence for over eighteen months. The factions were deeply rooted, and it is unlikely that mere diplomatic intervention would have had any effect on either of the two parties.

It would be more probable that the Lucchese factions looked for and obtained outside support, if it could be shown that Lucca split on party lines in matters of foreign policy. But this again seems very doubtful. The Guinigi have sometimes been regarded as the Visconti party, opposed to Florence, and in favour of a Milanese alliance.[130] There is perhaps something in this for the period after 1392. Paolo Guinigi certainly had military aid from the Milanese forces in Pisa in his *coup* of October 1400, and Lazzaro Guinigi had visited Giangaleazzo in Pavia in May 1399, arousing the deepest suspicions in Florence. There are some indications of Lucchese hostility to Florence in the years after 1392, when the Guinigi were in control, and it is just possible that they connived at Jacopo d'Appiano's seizure of power in Pisa in October 1392.[131] But this is by no means certain, and they may well have been no more anti-Florentine than any other patriotic Lucchese. In any case it seems doubtful whether the Forteguerra can be regarded as the Florentine party; Piero Rapondi, messer Carlo Ronghi, Lando Moriconi, and other exiles of the Forteguerra party were prepared to turn to Milan and Pisa for support in 1395.[132]

In the exceptional circumstances of the hostility to Lucca of Jacopo d'Appiano, who was supported by Giangaleazzo, Lucca under the Guinigi made no bones about turning to Florence. Florentine documents make it clear that the Florentine alliance was the policy of the Guinigi. It might perhaps be argued that Lucca had little choice in the matter, and that even an anti-Florentine party would see the necessity of such

[130] For example D. Corsi, *Inv.* VI, p. 360.
[131] See below, Chapter 14, pp. 301–4.
[132] See below, Chapter 13, pp. 295–6.

an alliance in the circumstances of 1395. But there were undoubtedly elements in Lucca that did not think so. It is clear from Florentine sources that the Guinigi had by no means carried all their fellow citizens with them; Florentine envoys were frequently instructed to visit the Guinigi first and only reveal their embassy to the Anziani if the Guinigi thought it advisable. Sercambi confirms that there was a strong and vocal anti-Florentine party in Lucca,[133] and it was perhaps the existence of this and general disillusionment with the Florentine alliance that led to Lazzaro's visit to Pavia in 1399 and the *rapprochement* with Milan which by Lazzaro's death had perhaps gone no further than a restoration of the old friendly relations of the 1370s and 1380s. Even if the Guinigi did tend to be anti-Florentine, it was clearly not the mainspring of their policy; they were at any rate flexible enough to be prepared to enter into a close alliance with Florence in circumstances that did not seem to everyone in Lucca to warrant it.

In any case their policy in power was not necessarily the same as their policy before 1392. According to Sercambi, Francesco Guinigi always regarded the Florentines with suspicion and never consented to friendship with them.[134] The claim that he never consented to friendship with the Florentines is untrue; for it was he who advocated the renewal of friendship with Florence in 1374.[135] As for regarding the Florentines with suspicion, the same could probably be said of all Lucchese. Party lines on foreign policy before 1392 are not easy to distinguish. The internal situation is not clear enough for it to be possible to say that any course of action at a particular point is the policy of one party rather than the other. Full accounts of discussions of policy are rare in Lucchese documents, and by no means all those that do exist relate to foreign affairs. The few discussions of matters of foreign policy that do survive do not support a theory that the Lucchese factions took distinct lines on foreign affairs. They are in fact remarkable for the unanimity they show. When, in January 1385, Giangaleazzo asked for aid, Michele and Dino Guinigi, Niccolò ser Pagani, and Andrea dal Portico on the

[133] Sercambi, I, p. 316.
[134] Sercambi, III, p. 309.
[135] *Rif.* 4, pp. 476–7, 19 Oct., p. 492, 4 Nov. 1374.

Guinigi side, and messer Bartolomeo Forteguerra, Lando Moriconi, and Jacobo Rapondi on the other side were all equally in favour of sending it.[136] When in May of the same year he again asked for aid the Thirty-Six voted 39–0 that it should be sent.[137] When the rulers of Siena, backed up by the Florentine Priors, asked that Lucca should expel Sienese rebels from her territory, the Thirty-Six agreed to this 43–3, and messer Ludovico Mercati and Guglielmo Flammi are found seconding a speech made by Michele Guinigi.[138] Similarly in the matter of the Pope's visit to Lucca, though the discussion was rather more complicated, there was basic agreement between the two factions, and Matteo Nutini is found seconding speeches made by Michele Guinigi and Bartolomeo Michelis and Betto Schiatta agreeing with Giovanni Mingogii and Niccolò ser Pagani.[139] As late as 8 May 1392 the parties were agreed on the question of sending aid to Genoa. It was agreed 43–0, Piero Rapondi, messer Ludovico Mercati, Orlandino Volpelli, and messer Bartolomeo Forteguerra among the Forteguerra partisans and Niccolò ser Pagani, ser Domenico Lupardi, Pietro Gentile and Niccolò Onesti among those of the Guinigi all speaking in favour.[140]

In general there is nothing in the sources to support a view that the two factions took different lines on foreign policy. Perhaps the situation of Lucca in the late fourteenth century did not offer any real choice and the policy of playing one power off against another in the hope of emerging unscathed was the only one open to her.

Another possible distinction between the two parties remains to be discussed, and that is that they represented the old Guelf and Ghibelline factions. Such a discussion is made difficult by the fact that the use of the terms Guelf and Ghibelline had been prohibited in 1369.[141] They therefore never occur in Lucchese political records, and only very rarely in judicial records. The term Guelf is only used once with reference to Lucca in Florentine documents, and it is there not

[136] *Min.* 3, 8 Jan. 1385.
[137] *Rif.* 9, p. 351, 18 May 1385.
[138] *Rif.* 9, p. 359, 2 June 1385.
[139] *Min.* 3, 2 and 25 Apr., 30 Oct. 1386.
[140] *Rif.* 12, p. 95, *Min.* 4, 8 May 1392.
[141] *Rif.* 1, p. 86, 11 Sept. 1369. The use of the term 'ducalem' was also forbidden.

clear whether it refers to all the Lucchese or merely to a section of them.[142] Florentine chroniclers make no reference to the Lucchese as either Guelf or Ghibelline in this period. It is important to note, too, that no Lucchese writer, contemporary or otherwise, interprets the factions in terms of Guelf and Ghibelline. Sercambi's account of the faction disputes is mainly narrative, and comment is confined to attributing the disputes to pride, personal animosity and ambition, and to the machinations of the devil. The Lucchese writers Dalli and Civitali both interpret the Lucchese factions entirely in terms of the rivalries of the Guinigi and Rapondi families, and not in terms of Guelf and Ghibelline factions or of differences on foreign policy.[143] Neither was a contemporary, but both appear to be well-informed and might be expected to preserve a tradition that the two factions represented the old Guelfs and Ghibellines if this were so.

But despite this negative evidence the terms occur in Lucchese sources with sufficient frequency to make discussion of them worth while. Sercambi uses the world Guelf with reference to the Obizi party in the dispute between nobles and *popolani* in July 1370, and their defeat may possibly have been a victory for the Ghibelline party as well as the Guinigi family.[144] This view is supported by a statement in the condemnation of messer Matteo Gigli in January 1385. The death of Francesco Guinigi and the abolition of the twelve *conservatores libertatis*[145] encouraged him to attempt to procure the return of messer Giovanni degli Obizi by force with Florentine aid, 'et terra ista regatur ad partem guelfam'. Messer Matteo clearly felt that Lucca was ruled by a non-Guelf party, even if not by Ghibellines. It is to be noted, however, that the Obizi, the traditional leaders of the Lucchese Guelfs, are again involved, and this is underlined in the next words of the statement 'ita quod admodo dictus dominus Johannes cum suis consortibus non vagabundet'.[146] Though there is no clear

[142] A.S.F. *Consulte*, 10, f. 96v, 21 Apr. 1370, 'quod utile videtur sustinere guelfos lucanos donec illa civitas sit in quieto statu' may refer to the Guelf faction in Lucca rather than to the Lucchese in general, c.p. Silva, *Governo*, p. 48, but this is a rather strained interpretation.

[143] Dalli, III, pp. 324-5, 327-30, 333-6, 338-47, Civitali, f. 360.

[144] Sercambi, I, pp. 204-5. [145] Sercambi, I, pp. 243-4.

[146] *Sentenze e Bandi*, 70, ff. 35-7, Feb. 1385.

evidence that the Guinigi themselves were Ghibellines, there can be no doubt that they had some Ghibelline support. Sercambi, listing the supporters of Francesco Guinigi in the *contado*, makes it clear that they were in almost every case the Ghibelline party in that area.[147] Ghibelline feeling may have been more resistant in the *contado* than in the city itself, but it is clear that some of the most whole-hearted Guinigi supporters in May 1392, such as ser Giovanni da Castiglione and Andrea Stornelli, were Ghibellines. The attempt of Antonio Guinigi and Niccolò Sbarra to raise the cry of 'viva parte ghibellina' in February 1400 would seem to suggest that the Guinigi party was in some respects the Ghibelline party.[148]

This supposition would be strengthened if it could be shown that the Guinigi and a section of their party had been Ghibellines in the earlier fourteenth century. It is by no means easy to discover which families had been Guelf or Ghibelline before 1369, and most of the families which can be shown to have belonged to one or other faction were no longer resident in Lucca or active in political life by the last thirty years of the fourteenth century. But the evidence of party affiliations before 1369, slender though it is, clearly demonstrates that the Forteguerra and Guinigi parties cannot be identified with the earlier Guelf and Ghibelline factions and were not simply continuations of any pre-1369 groupings. Where it can be shown that some pre-1369 party or group contained members of families that later supported the Guinigi, this is always counterbalanced by the fact that it also included members of families that took the Forteguerra side. One of the few pieces of evidence for the membership of the Ghibelline party is a list

[147] Sercambi, III, p. 18. For the strength of Ghibellinism in the *contado*, Sercambi I, pp. 203–6. Factions in the *contado* continued to call themselves Guelf and Ghibelline throughout the sixteenth century, Berengo, *Nobili e mercanti*, pp. 343–4. I have not found any evidence connecting the Guinigi themselves with either the Guelf or the Ghibelline faction before 1369.

[148] Sercambi, II, pp. 408–9. Dalli's version makes this even clearer, adding that it was believed that the Florentines had killed Lazzaro and entered Lucca III, p. 475. A letter from the Genoese branch of the company of Francesco di Marco Datini of 25 Feb. 1400 relates that the murderers 'usciron di casa gridando: viva parte ghibelina e Guinigi; e davan boce uno de'Rapondi facea tratato per tor lor lo stato', quoted in R. Piattoli, 'Il problema portuale di Firenze dall'ultima lotta con Gian Galeazzo Visconti alle prime trattative per l'acquisto di Pisa (1402–1405)', *Rivista Storica degli Archivi Toscani*, Vol. II (1930), p. 157, note 1.

of Ghibelline councillors, probably belonging to 1330.[149] Most of those named were members of families no longer active in political life by the late fourteenth century, but the list includes messer Francheschino Onesti, messer Lancilotto Martini, messer Giovanni Sbarra, and Bonagiunta Dombellinghi. The Onesti and the Martini were Guinigi supporters in 1392, but the Dardagnini took the Forteguerra side, while the Sbarra were divided, members of the family appearing in both parties. There is a list of Lucchese citizens regarded as rebels by the Florentines during the brief period from November 1341 to June 1342, when they were in possession of Lucca.[150] These seem to have been Lucchese who were in the Pisan camp, and other really active partisans of Pisa, and were thus probably Ghibellines. Again the list includes a number of members of families which cannot be connected with either of the late fourteenth-century parties in Lucca, but it also names two members of families that later supported the Guinigi[151] and four members of the pro-Forteguerra Dombellinghi family.[152] Evidence of families that were Guelf in the early fourteenth century points the same way. Of the Guelf families that went into exile in 1314 the Brancaleoni, Cardellini, Morla and probably the Faitinelli later supported the Guinigi, while the Volpelli supported the Forteguerra. The Galganetti, who later supported the Guinigi, and the Moccindente, who later supported the Forteguerra, went into exile in 1329.[153]

Members of families that later supported both the Guinigi and the Forteguerra are found among the Lucchese who were active in political life under Ghibelline tyrant, Castruccio

[149] *Anz. Av. Lib.* 1, Aug. ? 1330 (badly damaged by damp).

[150] *Curia de'Ribelli e Banditi*, 7, ff. 7-51 and continues on unnumbered folios. The citizens whom Sercambi records supporting Pisa in the abortive rebellion of Lucca in 1355 were also perhaps Ghibellines. They included Corrado di Chello di Poggio, Nuccio Berlescia, Giovanni di messer Franceschino Onesti, Fredo Martini, Coluccino Peri, Puccino Mugia, and Francesco Mordecastelli, Sercambi, I, p. 108. Members of the di Poggio, Onesti, and Martini families were Guinigi partisans after 1369.

[151] Giuntino Dardagnini and Stregorino dello Strego, *Curia de'Ribelli e Banditi*, 7, ff. 10, 41^v.

[152] Bonagiunta and Bertuccio Dombellinghi and Pietro and Betto, sons of Francesco Dombellinghi, *Curia de'Ribelli e Banditi*, 7 (unnumbered folios).

[153] *Curia de'Ribelli e Banditi*, 3, ff. 13^v, 58^v, 104, 141^v, 173 (men leaving 1314), ff. 34, 87^v, (men leaving 1329). They were all among those taking advantage of an invitation to return to Lucca in 1331.

Castracani, and during the period of Pisan rule. Those who favoured the election of Castruccio as *signore* in 1320, or held office under him and were therefore presumably at any rate not hostile to him, included the Forteguerra and the Rapondi and the Dombellinghi, Genovardi, Moccindenti, and Mercati among their later supporters, and on the Guinigi side the Guinigi themselves and the Brancaleoni, Galganetti, del Gallo, da Ghivizzano, Gigli, Martini, Onesti, Orselli, di Poggio, dal Portico, Salamoni, dello Strego, Tegrimi, and Tadolini.[154] In view of what had already been said about the continuity of the leading families in political life before and after 1369 it is no surprise to find that members of many families that were later supporters of one or other of the factions in the late fourteenth century were active in Lucchese political life during the period of Pisan rule, and were among the Lucchese whom the Pisans regarded as particularly reliable. The Lucchese Anziani for April and May 1355, whom the Pisans considered sufficiently trustworthy to confirm in office for a further month after the rebellion in Lucca in May, included Guido Rapondi, as well as members of families that later supported the Guinigi, such as Francesco di Parente Onesti, Nuccino Boccanscochi, and Ciomeo Trenta. Their successors who were also presumably regarded by the Pisans as especially reliable, included Jacobo Rapondi and messer Guglielmo Mercati, of later Forteguerra families, as well as Filippo Gentile, Davino Buzolini, and Puccinello Galganetti of families that later supported the Guinigi.[155]

Clearly, then, the Guinigi and Forteguerra parties cannot

[154] Civitali, ff. 222^{v}, 223^{v}-224, where the same conclusion is drawn. They also included the Sbarra and Schiatta families, who had members of both the Guinigi and Forteguerra parties.

[155] *Regesto*, Vol. II, part i, nos. 684 (29 Mar. 1355), 692 (9 June 1355). A.S.P. *Comune A 60*, f. 17, 1 June 1355. Lists of Anziani *Regesto*, Vol. II, part i, pp. xiii–xxix show that those holding the office under Pisan rule included members of the Forteguerra, Rapondi, Burlamacchi, Dombellinghi, Maulini, Mercati, Moccindenti, Sartoy, and Volpelli families among those that later supported the Forteguerra and members of the Guinigi, Angiorelli, Arlotti, Arnolfini, Balbani, Benettoni, Boccansocchi, Buzolini, Dardagnini, Galganetti, Gentile, del Ghiotto, Gigli, Malisardi, Malpigli, Martini, Mattafelloni, Onesti, Perfettucci, di Poggio, dal Portico, Salamoni, Serpente, Tadolini, Tegrimi, and Trenta families among those that supported the Guinigi. Also the Cattani, Domaschi, Flammi, Moriconi, Sbarra and Schiatta families, which included supporters of both the late fourteenth-century factions.

be regarded simply as continuations of Guelf-Ghibelline or any other earlier groupings. There is evidence in Sercambi that earlier party distinctions had become less clear even before 1369. Although he sometimes refers to Lucchese Ghibellines during the period of Pisan rule as if they were a recognizable group, he himself states that it was by this time not always possible to prove who were Guelfs and who were Ghibellines.[156] The vicissitudes Lucca had undergone since the beginning of the fourteenth century might be expected to lead to the break-up of old factions and the blurring of old party distinctions, and there is evidence that this was happening. In 1355 Guelf and Ghibelline exiles of Lucca were able to reach an understanding among themselves and with the heirs of Castruccio Castracani for a joint attack on the city to free it from Pisan rule.[157] The recovery of Lucchese independence in 1369 might be expected to accentuate this weakening of old faction loyalties, and make many Lucchese ready to forget old rancours and make a new beginning. The government clearly felt in 1369 that the old party feelings had died down sufficiently to make it possible to forbid the use of the terms Guelf and Ghibelline, though, conversely, they presumably still had enough life in them to make the prohibition necessary.

Sercambi expressly states that the opposition to the Guinigi was drawn from diverse elements, 'tali guelfi, tali ghibellini, tali dugali, tali matraversi'.[158] The same was true of the Guinigi party, as we have seen. Nevertheless it did perhaps include a particularly strong Ghibelline element. There seems no reason to doubt Sercambi's statements that Guinigi support in the *contado* consisted largely of the Ghibelline party in each vicariate. Old Guelf-Ghibelline loyalties may have lingered longer in the *contado* than in the city, but as late as 1400 Antonio Guinigi and Niccolò Sbarra believed, though mistakenly, that 'viva parte ghibellina' would make an effective rallying cry in Lucca itself, which demonstrates both a belief that Ghibelline feeling still lingered there and its

[156] Sercambi, I, p. 117.

[157] M. Villani, Lib. V, caps. lxi, lxiv, lxix.

[158] Sercambi, III, p. 337. 'Dugali' were the supporters of the descendants of Castruccio Castracani.

association with the Guinigi. Sercambi records under 1409 a plot against Paolo Guinigi, which he claims was 'a stanza di parte guelfa e de Fiorentini'.[159] But if the Guinigi party included a Ghibelline element, even a strong Ghibelline element, it also drew its support from other earlier groupings, and association with Ghibelline elements seems to have had little or no implication for Guinigi policy. It is notable that the only occasion after 1369 on which Sercambi uses the term Ghibelline in an anti-Florentine sense was at a time when the Guinigi had led Lucca into a Florentine alliance.[160] The Ghibelline element in the Guinigi party might have made them a little more favourable to Milan, and perhaps to Jacopo d'Appiano, in ordinary circumstances, but in the last decade of the fourteenth century circumstances were not ordinary for Lucca. Guinigi foreign policy seems in general to have been opportunist, and they were certainly not deterred from an alliance with Florence, when necessity dictated it, by any ideological considerations. In terms of internal policy it is impossible to know how frequently the term Ghibelline was used after 1369, but if it was at all commonly applied to the Guinigi party in Lucca, it is unlikely that 'Ghibelline' in practice meant much more than 'Guinigi'.[161]

There seems to be no significant difference between the Guinigi party and their opponents in terms of social origin, position, occupation, or wealth, nor in terms of different lines on foreign policy or connections with the old Guelf and Ghibelline factions. The Lucchese faction disputes of the late fourteenth century seem to be purely about power with no issues of foreign or domestic policy dividing the two parties. They seem to be, as Dalli and Civitali saw them, purely rival factions, each trying to gain control of the government and exclude the other from power. They may have developed in

[159] Sercambi, III, p. 167.

[160] Sercambi, I, pp. 316, 407–8.

[161] Evidence in condemnations shows that opposition to the Guinigi after 1392 is simply in terms of resistance to them as the party in control with no use of the term Ghibelline, *Sentenze e Bandi,* 85, ff. 13–18v, 86, ff. 3–5, 12 Jan. 1394. There were occasional 'Guelf' plots, but they were not necessarily directed against the Guinigi. For a discussion of shifts in the meaning of Guelf and Ghibelline and the waning of their importance in Florence in this period, R. G. Witt, 'A note on Guelfism in late medieval Florence', *Nuova Rivista Storica,* Vol. LIII (1969), pp. 134–45.

parallel as rivals, but it is possible that the Guinigi party grew up first, gaining a degree of control over the government that caused the Forteguerra-Rapondi party to grow up in opposition to them. In that case the Forteguerra party might be regarded as representing a group of citizens banding together to protect republican government against the excessive influence of one family. The fact that it included most of the judges and doctors of laws may be thought to lend some colour to this view. In addition a number of the leading opponents of the Guinigi were merchants who spent much time outside the city, in some cases so much so that they may be said to have lived abroad rather than in Lucca. When these men returned, they may have seen the extent of Guinigi power which had been established during their absence more clearly than did the citizens who had been in Lucca all the time, and thus been led to oppose it. This might apply to Bartolomeo Michaelis, Giuffredo Cenami, Forteguerra Forteguerra, Orlandino Volpelli, the Totti, and most of the Rapondi.

But all this must be regarded as rather doubtful, and, although there is no real evidence of these men in opposition before 1385 at the earliest, they may well have been enemies and rivals of the Guinigi from the beginning. In any case, whether the Forteguerra-Rapondi party developed after 1370, parallel with the Guinigi party, or only later in opposition to an already established Guinigi party, the accounts of Sercambi, Dalli, and Civitali show them to have been no less ambitious and self-interested by 1390, when both parties were striving to gain control of the city and rule in their own interest to the exclusion of the other party.

12

THE STRUGGLE FOR POWER 1374-1392

ALTHOUGH the family was in an important position earlier, the turning point for the establishment of Guinigi influence in Lucca probably came in November 1374 with the setting up of the *conservatores libertatis*. On 4 November 1374 Francesco Guinigi recommended that three or four citizens from each *terziere* be elected with authority 'circa ea que sibi utilia et expedientia videbuntur ad conservandum libertatem civitatis lucane et pacificum et bonum statum ipsius'.[1] *Balìe* of this kind with general authority for the defence, peace, and well-being of the city were not new. A *balìa* referred to as the '18 super regimen comunis lucani' had been authorized 31 July 1370,[2] and regularly renewed with different members each time, 16 November 1370,[3] 5 March 1371,[4] and 19 June 1371.[5] Threats to Lucca by armed companies led to the election of similar *balìe* in 1373.[6] But the authority and especially the period of office of these *balìe* had always been strictly limited. Though it had been asserted in March 1371 'necesse sit et summe utile pro rebus et negociis arduis quotidie emergentibus ipsum officium semper esse',[7] the authority of any particular commission was limited to about three months, and there were occasionally other restrictions, such as that no member of the Thirty-Six could also be a member of a

[1] *Rif.* 4, pp. 492-3, 4 Nov. 1374. Also for keeping the friendship of the Florentines, which was the occasion of the discussion.

[2] *Rif.* 1, pp. 454-6, 31 July 1370. The members were elected 5 Aug. 1370, *Rif.* 2, p. 22.

[3] *Rif.* 2, pp. 98-9, 19 Oct. 1370, authorized to hold office for three months beginning 16 Nov. 1370.

[4] *Rif.* 2, p. 220, authorized 2 March 1371 for three months, elected p. 223, 5 Mar.,

[5] *Rif.* 2, p. 316, authorized 18 June 1371 (wrongly dated 28 June), to hold office until 1 Oct. 1371, elected p. 320, 19 June 1371.

[6] *Rif.* 4, pp. 242-3, 17 Oct. 1373, to hold office until 1 Jan., pp. 265-6, 4 Dec. 1373, p. 269, 6 Dec. 1371 it was decreed that twelve of a *balìa* totalling twenty-four were to reside in the Palace of the Anziani.

[7] *Rif.* 2, p. 217, 2 Mar. 1371.

particular commission.[8] These earlier commissioners had had wide powers, but these were mostly confined to the field of defence or internal security,[9] and the ordinary councils and other organs of government continued to function normally.

The *conservatores* differed from these earlier commissions in that there was no time limit to their period of office and the same twelve citizens continued to hold the office until 1381, and with another twenty-four citizens until 1385. In addition to the lack of any time limit for their period of office the terms of their authority were so vaguely worded that they were gradually able to bring more and more of the ordinary administration within their purview at the expense of the statutory councils, especially of the General Council, until with the Anziani they were virtually ruling the city. The omission of any time limit to their authority may well have been an oversight. Italian republics were usually extremely jealous of their republican institutions and it is very unlikely that the *conservatores* would have been authorized by the large majority of 146 to thirty-four, if the citizens had realized the use that would be made of them. But the election of the *conservatores* with wide powers and for an unlimited period of time may well have been a deliberate act of policy on the part of the Guinigi. The close connection between the *conservatores* and the establishment of Guinigi power is obvious both from the account of Sercambi and from a study of subsequent events. The *conservatores* had been proposed by Francesco Guinigi, and his death encouraged the opposition group to demand their abolition.[10] The *conservatores* were the main instrument that the Guinigi used to establish their power.

The *conservatores* began as an informal *balìa*, but they gradually acquired an apparatus of *invitati* and regulations about attendance that brought them into line with the General Council and the Thirty-Six. The *conservatores* soon ceased to be regarded as a *balìa* and thus temporary and informal, and came to be referred to as a council, 'consilium

[8] *Rif.* 2, p. 220, 2 Mar. 1371.

[9] They also had certain limited powers in matters of finance under authority from the General Council, *Rif.* 2, pp. 93–5, 6 Oct. 1370.

[10] Sercambi, I, pp. 243–4, III, pp. 336–7.

XII super baylia'.[11] There were *invitati* as early as December 1377, and occasionally in the next few years, and from 1381 onwards *invitati* appeared regularly at meetings of the *conservatores*.[12] In July 1379 the system of fines for failure to attend council meetings was extended to the *conservatores*.[13] This was only a temporary measure until January 1380, but in 1381 the *conservatores* were finally brought into line with the other councils when it was decreed that they too should be summoned by a bell, and that there should be the same payments for attendance and fines for non-attendance that there were for the other councils.[14]

But more important than these formal indications that the *conservatores* were now being regarded as a regular council was the gradual extension of their functions. One of their main concerns was defence, and they are found supervising the maintenance of fortresses,[15] making ordinances for the defence of the city,[16] intervening to keep order in the *contado*,[17] and even granting extraordinary powers to the captain of the guard and the Podestà in time of danger.[18] It was also the *conservatores* that carried out the reorganization of the *cerne* of the *contado*,[19] and authorized the hire of extra mercenaries, and mercenaries who were Lucchese *contadini*, something which could not be done without special dispensation.[20] They dealt also with finance and often made

[11] *Rif.* 6, p. 610, 11 July 1378 and frequently after that.

[12] *Rif.* 6, p. 415, 2 Dec. 1377, *Min.* 2, f. 201v, 19 July 1378, *Rif.* 7, p. 79, 28 Apr. 1379, pp. 340–1, 17 Oct., pp. 347–8, 9 Nov. 1380 and frequently after that.

[13] *Rif.* 7, p. 123, 29 July 1379.

[14] *Rif.* 7, p. 425, 4 Mar. 1381. The *conservatores*, of course, differed from the other councils in that the same twelve citizens held the office indefinitely until 1381, while the Thirty-Six was liable to renewal every six months and the General Council every year.

[15] *Rif.* 6, pp. 92–3, 18 Nov. 1376, p. 269, 8 June 1377, p. 543, 14 Apr., p. 610, 11 July, p. 621, 4 Aug. 1378. *Rif.* 7, pp. 304–5, 20 Aug., pp. 335–6, 9 Sept., pp. 337–8, 17 Sept. 1380.

[16] *Rif.* 7, p. 72, 21 Apr. 1379.

[17] *Rif.* 6, pp. 269–70, 8 June 1377, pp. 637–8, 24 Aug. 1378. *Rif.* 7, p. 59, 15 Mar. 1379.

[18] *Rif.* 7, p. 240, 12 Mar., pp. 340–1, 17 Oct. 1380.

[19] *Rif.* 7, p. 79, 28 Apr. 1379, p. 348, 10 Nov. 1380.

[20] *Rif.* 6, p. 429, 18 Dec. 1377, p. 610, 11 July, p. 621, 4 Aug., p. 712, 1 Dec. 1378. *Rif.* 7, p. 64, 2 Apr., p. 158, 30 Sept., p. 189, 25 Nov. 1379, p. 447, 24 Jan., p. 452, 4 Feb., p. 241, 12 Mar., p. 246, 20 Apr., p. 253, 26 Apr., p. 307, 20 Aug., p. 316, 29 Aug., p. 348, 10 Nov. 1380.

mandates for payments of Lucchese money.[21] Such an important decision as that authorizing the establishment of the *deposita* was taken by the *conservatores.* [22] They were concerned, too, with all kinds of administrative matters, such as agreeing to unions of communes in the *contado*,[23] considering the question of new coinage,[24] or extending the term for the payment of the salt gabelle.[25] They often issued whole strings of decrees on various administrative details on the same day.[26]

Often they were dealing with matters which were regarded as the special sphere of the General Council or the Thirty-Six. They dealt with petitions which would normally have been settled in the General Council or the Thirty-Six.[27] They are frequently found electing officials or authorizing their election. In many cases these were comparatively minor financial or law court officials,[28] though the election even of these minor officials belonged to the Thirty-Six. But the *conservatores* are also found electing more important officials, such as vicars,[29] and even the Podestà and major sindic.[30]

[21] *Rif.* 6, p. 559, 7 May, pp. 684-5, 10 Nov. 1378. *Rif.* 7, p. 60, 18 Mar., pp. 128-9, 8 Aug., p. 180, 17 Nov. 1379, p. 451, 4 Feb., p. 233, 5 Mar., p. 343, 28 Oct., pp. 347-8, 9 Nov., p. 365, 17 Dec. 1380.

[22] *Rif.* 7, p. 402, 8 Jan. 1381. This required a dispensation from the prohibition on discussing matters connected with the *Massa*.

[23] *Rif.* 7, pp. 315-16, 29 Aug. 1380.

[24] *Rif.* 5, pp. 35-6, 7 Mar. 1375.

[25] *Rif.* 7, p. 340, 17 Oct. 1380.

[26] *Rif.* 6, p. 610, 11 July, pp. 621-2, 4 Aug. 1378. *Rif.* 7, pp. 304-7, 20 Aug., p. 377, 28 Dec. 1380, pp. 401-2, 8 Jan. 1381.

[27] *Rif.* 6, pp. 668-71, 21 Oct. 1378. *Rif.* 7, p. 129, 9 Aug., p. 169, 6 Nov., pp. 171-2, 10 Nov., p. 181, 17 Nov. 1379, p. 246, 20 Apr., pp. 316-19, 29 Aug. 1380.

[28] *Rif.* 7, p. 207, 12 Dec. 1379, p. 436, 7 Jan., p. 263, 28 May, p. 272, 13 June, p. 296, 14 July, p. 305, 20 Aug., pp. 313-15, 28 Aug., p. 339, 28 Sept., pp. 348-9, 12 Nov., p. 364, 10 Dec., p. 377, 28 Dec. 1380.

[29] *Rif.* 6, p. 24, 29 July 1376, p. 404, 14 Nov., p. 411, 22 Nov. 1377 (these were replacements), p. 433, 27 Dec. 1377. *Rif.* 7, p. 189, 25 Nov. 1379, p. 277, 22 June, pp. 355-6, 23 Nov., p. 361, 6 Dec., p. 364, 13 Dec. 1380.

[30] They elected a vice-Podestà until the arrival of the new Podestà, *Delib.* 132, ff. 132-133, 27 Sept. 1375. They elected a vice-Podestà after Lucca had failed to find a suitable Podestà, *Rif.* 5, pp. 311-12, 28 Apr. 1376, and also authorized him to sindicate the retiring Podestà, p. 316, 30 Apr. Also *Rif.* 6, p. 102, 3 Dec. 1376. Also the chancellor of the commune, *Rif.* 6, p. 310, 27 July 1377, *Rif.* 7, p. 79, 28 Apr. 1379. *Major officialis fundaci, minor sindicus*, notary of the judge of appeal, *Rif.* 6, p. 610, 11 July 1378. Temporary sindic, *Rif.* 7, pp. 90-1, 13 May 1379. Exactor and captain of custody, *Rif.* 7, p. 253, 26 Apr. 1380. The advocate of the commune, *Rif.* 7, p. 271, 13 June 1380. The *conservatores* authorized the Anziani to grant the new Podestà an extension of the time limit for his arrival and to substitute the retiring Podestà until then, *Rif.* 7, p. 344, 28 Oct. 1380.

These were regarded as particularly important matters, which should be settled in the General Council or the Thirty-Six, and the *conservatores* were forbidden to interfere in the election of the Podestà and many other officials when they were re-established in 1392.[31] The *conservatores* also dealt with things that touched on foreign policy, chiefly gifts or loans to *condottieri*,[32] but also the repayment of debts contracted by Lucca in 1369,[33] or negotiations to secure the appointment of a particular man as bishop.[34] On at least one occasion they authorized an ambassador,[35] though the authorization of ambassadors belonged to the General Council.

They also issued decrees which altered or modified the statutes of the city, decrees concerning plots and treason,[36] minor changes in criminal procedure,[37] regulations for the office of the guard, the *abundantia* and various *proventus*.[38] Even though some of these matters were not in themselves of the highest importance, they were significant in that they modified the statutes of the commune, and they should properly have been decided in one of the statutory councils or by a *balìa* specially authorized to take such a decision. And in some cases the *conservatores* made decisions of much greater importance. They decreed that no cleric should hold office in the commune,[39] that no councillor should speak on anything not contained in the *proposita*,[40] and that no one elected to the college of Anziani could refuse if he was in the Lucchese city or state.[41]

The *conservatores* also did things which were specifically

[31] *Rif.* 12, p. 116, 26 May 1392.

[32] They granted citizenship to the *condottiere* John Thornbery, *Delib.* 132, ff. 107v–108, 8 Sept. 1375. *Rif.* 6, p. 621, 4 Aug. 1378. *Rif.* 7, p. 343, 28 Oct., pp. 347–8, 9 Nov. 1380.

[33] *Rif.* 6, p. 415, 2 Dec. 1377. *Min.* 2, ff. 192–3, 11 Aug. 1378. *Rif.* 7, p. 180, 17 Nov. 1379.

[34] *Rif.* 7, p. 337, 15 Sept. 1380.

[35] Messer Matteo Gigli to negotiate a treaty with Pisa regarding the treatment of *banniti*, *Rif.* 6, pp. 491–2, 27 Jan. 1378.

[36] *Rif.* 5, pp. 217–21, 15 Feb. 1376.

[37] *Rif.* 6, pp. 626–30, 13 Aug. 1378. *Rif.* 7, pp. 98–9, 25 May 1379.

[38] *Rif.* 6, p. 630, 13 Aug. 1378. *Rif.* 7, pp. 28–31, 16 Feb. 1379, pp. 327–8, 2 Sept. 1380.

[39] *Rif.* 7, pp. 98–9, 25 May 1379.

[40] *Rif.* 6, pp. 251–2, 14 May 1377.

[41] *Rif.* 6, p. 350, 25 Aug. 1377.

prohibited in the Statutes. Such things could be done if a dispensation from the particular prohibition were first granted, but this was regarded as a matter of great importance and was normally only done in the General Council. The *conservatores* twice granted a dispensation from the law forbidding the election of a man as Podestà, if he came from a city within sixty miles of Lucca or had recently held office in a city within 50 miles.[42] They authorized the new sindic to 'sindicate' the old one, despite statutory prohibition.[43] They interfered with one of the most important offices of the state, reducing the *conducterii* from six to three, and laying down new regulations for their election.[44] They even decreed the pardon of *banniti*,[45] and made grants of citizenship.[46] Though it cannot be said with certainty that they were exceeding their powers, which in any case were very vaguely defined, they were undoubtedly dealing with many things which properly belonged to the Thirty-Six or the General Council. It was probably felt at the time that they were overstepping the bounds of their authority, for in 1385 the office of commissioners of the palace, which took their place, was forbidden to readmit *banniti* or do other things that belonged to the councils, and in 1392, when the office was revived, further prohibitions were added, such as the granting of citizenship, interference with the main offices of state and making major decisions of foreign policy.[47]

The *conservatores* as a small group of citizens holding office for an indefinite period and encroaching on the power of the General Council and the Thirty-Six, were certainly unpopular by January 1385. They may already have been resented in 1380 or 1381; for in February 1381 the *conservatores* themselves decreed that their number should be increased from twelve to thirty-six, and a rota made out for these thirty-six to hold office twelve at a time.[48] Though the *conservatores*

[42] *Rif.* 6, pp. 623–4, 5 Aug. 1378. *Rif.* 7, p. 335, 9 Sept. 1380.

[43] *Rif.* 7, p. 436, 7 Jan. 1380.

[44] They were in future to be elected by the Anziani and three of the *conservatores*, *Rif.* 7, p. 365, 17 Dec. 1380.

[45] *Rif.* 5, p. 221, 15 Feb. 1376. *Rif.* 7, pp. 246–7, 20 Apr., p. 258, 7 May 1380, they reduced the fine for a homicide, p. 266, 1 June 1380, and for carrying arms, p. 273, 20 June 1380.

[46] *Delib.* 132, ff. 101^{v}–102, 29 Apr. 1378. *Rif.* 7, p. 338, 27 Sept. 1380.

[47] *Rif.* 9, p. 283, 10 Jan. 1385. *Rif.* 12, pp. 115–17, 26 May 1392.

claimed in the preamble to this decree that they were acting on their own iniative, they use phrases which suggest that there had been complaints at so much power being concentrated in the hands of the same few citizens, or at least that the *conservatores* were extending their number to forestall any such criticism. They speak of it being good 'honores dignitates et officia in plurimos saltem bene meritos propagare' 'ut res ipse publice bonorum consilio ceterorumque assensu semper in melius gubernetur et quisque sua gaudeat portione', and quote 'quod omnes tangit ab omnibus communiter approbetur' and speak of living 'in sancta . . . unitate . . . contentius et felicius'.

But if the *conservatores* thought it wise to disarm criticism by extending their number, they did not apparently think it necessary to use their authority with more discretion. For the next four years they continued to deal with very much the same kind of matters as before 5 February 1381. In fact they were encroaching even more seriously on the authority of the General Council and the Thirty-Six. The Thirty-Six and especially the General Council were meeting less frequently in the years 1380–4 than they had done previously. Ten or eleven meetings of the General Council are recorded each year from

[48] *Rif.* 7, pp. 417–18, 5 Feb. 1381. The *gite* were as follows:

Prima gita

* Bartholomeus Nuccii	* Matheus Captani	* Nicolaus ser Pagani
Andreas de Porticu	Jacobus Rapondi	* Lambertus Coluccini
Johannes Beraldi	Petrus Martini	Dinus Guinigi
Bartholomeus Busolini	Johannes Puccini textor	Bongagiunta Simi

Seconda gita

* Corradus de Podio	* ser Andreas Bellomi	* Loysius Balbani
* Puccinellus Galganetti	Simon Boccella	Nicolaus Pinelli
Johannes Mingogii	Juffredus Cenami	Guidus Arnolfi
Casinus Vannis	Opisus de Honestis	Quartus de Quarto

Tertia gita

* Franciscus Dati	* d. Bartholomeus Forteguerra	* Franciscus Guinigi
ser Nicolaus Mordecastelli	Janninus Arnolfini	mag. Johannes de Barga
Turellinus Bonuccii	Fredus Martini	Johannes Cagnuoli
Nicolaus Nardutii	Matheus Nutini	Landus Moriconis
(S. Paolino)	(S. Salvatore)	(S. Martino)

Those marked * had been the first twelve *conservatores*. Giannino Arnolfini was a replacement in the first twelve for Luiso Boccella, who had died.

1375 to 1379.[49] In 1380 this dropped to six, and in the next few years there were seven meetings in 1381, six in 1382, seven in 1383, and five in 1384. A similar pattern can be seen in the Thirty-Six. There had been between twenty-four and thirty-one meetings each year from 1375 to 1379.[50] In 1380 this dropped to thirteen and in the next few years there were fourteen meetings in 1381, nineteen in 1382, and thirteen in 1384.[51] It can hardly be a coincidence that in these years the number of meetings of the *conservatores* rose from fourteen or fifteen in the years 1377 and 1378[52] to twenty-seven in 1379, forty-seven in 1381, fifty-five in 1382, fifty-three in 1383,[53] and sixty in 1384. The number of meetings of the *conservatores* soared from twenty-seven in 1379 to forty-seven in 1380, just when those of the General Council dropped from eleven to six and those of the Thirty-Six from twenty-four to thirteen. It can hardly be a coincidence either that when in 1385 the *conservatores* were abolished the number of meetings of the General Council rose again to sixteen and those of the Thirty-Six to twenty-eight.[54]

An examination of the matters dealt with in the General Council and the Thirty-Six also shows the increasing encroachment of the *conservatores*. Before 1380, even though the *conservatores* had been dealing in many cases with matters of everyday administration or with important political or foreign policy decisions or the election of officials, this did not mean that the General Council and the Thirty-Six had entirely ceased to do so. They continued to exercise their normal

[49] Except for 1377 when there were only seven. There were 18 meetings in 1370, 19 in 1371 and 27 in 1373, but these were the early years of Lucchese independence, when her financial difficulties in particular caused frequent council meetings. There were 17 meetings in 1374, 10 in 1375 and 1376, 11 in 1378 and 1379.

[50] Again in the early crisis years the figures are higher, with 44 meetings in 1370, 52 in 1371, 33 in 1373, and 44 in 1372 and 1374.

[51] There are only eight recorded meetings in 1383, a plague year, when in addition to the *conservatores* there was a special *balìa* for the administration of the city.

[52] It is rather difficult to calculate the number earlier than 1377, as the *conservatores* were then a more informal *balìa* and, like the acts of the Anziani, many of their meetings may have gone unrecorded or the records not survived.

[53] As this was a plague year and many citizens were absent, the powers of the *conservatores* devolved on a smaller *balìa* of nine of them.

[54] These are the figures for 1385. Meetings of both councils were slightly less frequent later, ten to twelve for the General Council 1386-90, nineteen to twenty-seven for the Thirty-Six.

functions, dealing with many of the same kind of things as the *conservatores* were doing. But after 1380 the *conservatores* showed a strong tendency to replace the ordinary councils entirely, especially the General Council. Such few meetings of the General Council as there were dealt with such things as the amnesties for prisoners at Easter, S. Croce, and Christmas, formal grants of 'sindicatus' to ambassadors for leagues, the ratification of such leagues, the election of important officials, such as the Podestà and the granting of Lucchese citizenship. Though all these were matters which should be properly dealt with in the General Council and not elsewhere, many of them were formalities rather than decisions of real importance. Though meeting less frequently than it had previously done, and dealing with a smaller volume of business, the Thirty-Six continued for rather longer than the General Council to deal with the matters that were its usual concern. It is only after 1382 that it began to be confined to the formal drawing out of the names of the new college of Anziani, and trivialities, like the hiring of schoolmasters and surgeons and the authorization of small sums for public works. But even before 1382 the quantity of business it dealt with was much reduced, and the rest was being settled by the *conservatores*. It seems in fact that the *conservatores* were being used as Sercambi was later to advocate in his advice to the Guinigi 'acciò che quello che per consiglio generale vincere non si potesse, overo che a voi paresse non doversi a quel consiglio mettere, si possa per questo ottenere'.[55]

The *conservatores* had been proposed by Francesco Guinigi and were an instrument of Guinigi policy. The extent to which they were used before 1385, undermining the authority of the General Council and Thirty-Six, suggests that the Guinigi had already reached a position of great power in the city. This can to some extent be checked by an examination of the membership of the various councils and *balìe* of the period. However, as the only lists of Guinigi and Forteguerra supporters are that of Dino Guinigi and the list of citizens entrusted with arms in August 1392 and both date from after the faction disputes had broken out in 1390, this must be a rather hazardous business,

[55] Sercambi, III, p. 403. He calls them 'commissari', the name of the more limited *balìa* that succeeded the *conservatores* in January 1385.

and it would be unwise to place too great reliance on results obtained from it. Many citizens who had played a leading role in Lucchese affairs since 1369 were dead by 1390 and therefore do not appear in Dino Guinigi's list, so that there is no way of discovering to which party, if any, they belonged. Citizens named in the list as adherents of one party or the other in 1391/2 may not have supported any party in the 1370s or 1380s. In addition many of the citizens in Dino Guinigi's list were wealthy men and members of the leading families, so that they may well have held office earlier by virtue of their own position in the city, rather than as adherents of one party or the other. But bearing these difficulties in mind, an examination of the membership of the councils and *balìe* does suggest certain tentative conclusions.

The original twelve *conservatores* themselves included Francesco Guinigi and three citizens who were Guinigi supporters in 1391.[56] Four of the others died before 1391, but may have been Guinigi supporters as they belonged to families that sided with the Guinigi in 1391.[57] Of the remaining four, one, messer Bartolomeo Forteguerra, was certainly an opponent in 1390–2, and the other three do not seem to have supported either party.[58] Of the twenty-four added to the original twelve *conservatores* in February 1381, eleven were Guinigi supporters,[59] and four others possibly were.[60] Four were Forteguerra supporters in 1391,[61] and the remaining five probably supported neither party.[62] It seems probable that, although the opposition was not totally excluded, the Guinigi would always have a majority.

The same cannot be said of the college of Anziani, the

[56] They were Matteo Cattani, Niccolò ser Pagani, and Lamberto Coluccini.

[57] They were Puccinello Galganetti, Corrado di Poggio, Bartolomeo Nucci, and Luiso Balbani.

[58] They were Francesco Dati, Luiso Boccella, and ser Andrea Bellomi, who were dead by early 1384.

[59] Andrea dal Portico, Bartolomeo Buzolini, Giovanni Mingogi, Casino Vannis, Turellino Bonucci, Giovanni Puccini, Opizo Onesti, Dino Guinigi, Niccolò Pinelli, Quarto da Quarto, and Giovanni Cagnuoli,

[60] Fredo and Pietro Martini, Bonagiunta di Simo Schiezza and maestro Giovanni da Barga also Giannino Arnolfini.

[61] Jacobo Rapondi, Giuffredo Cenami, Matteo Nutini, and Lando Moriconi.

[62] Giovanni Beraldi, ser Niccolò Mordecastelli, Niccolò Narducci, Guido Arnolfi and Simone Borcella.

General Council or the Thirty-Six. The Guinigi themselves were well represented in the Anziani; a member of the family sat in three of the six colleges for eight of the seventeen years from 1369 to 1385, and in two of the colleges for each of the other years, and on eight occasions a Guinigi was Gonfaloniere. It seems that in general the Guinigi had the advantage in the college of Anziani. There are too few Anziani who can be attributed to one party or the other before the end of 1374,[63] even if the parties existed at that date, but in the period 1375–85 eighteen of the colleges did not include a member of the Forteguerra party.[64] The Guinigi seem to have had a simple majority in thirteen of the sixty-six colleges 1375–85,[65] and probably also in twelve others.[66] But seven votes were required to pass a measure in the college of Anziani,[67] and the Guinigi had this absolute majority in only four of the colleges for certain,[68] and perhaps also in seven others.[69] In no college did the Forteguerra have even a simple majority, but in five colleges for certain and perhaps also in two others they equalled or outnumbered the Guinigi.[70] On twelve occasions in this period a member of the Forteguerra-Rapondi party was Gonfaloniere,[71] and there were on a number of occasions as many as three Forteguerra partisans in the college, so that even if the Guinigi frequently had the advantage, they can rarely have been unopposed or certain of getting controversial measures passed.

Membership of the Thirty-Six shows a pattern in many ways

[63] The Guinigi perhaps had a majority in the colleges of Mar./Apr., July/Aug. 1372, and July/Aug. 1374.

[64] Four in 1375; two in 1376; three in 1377, 1378 and 1379; one in 1380; two in 1381; three in 1382; two in 1384; but none in 1383 and 1385.

[65] Two in 1375; one in 1376; two in 1378; two in 1382; four in 1384; and two in 1385.

[66] One in 1376; two in 1377; one in 1378; three in 1380; three in 1381; one in 1383; and one in 1384.

[67] *Statuto del Comune di Lucca*, 1372, Lib. I, xi.

[68] Mar./Apr. 1375; May/June 1376; July/Aug. 1382; Mar./Apr. 1384.

[69] July/Aug., Sept./Oct. 1378; Mar./Apr. 1380; Mar./Apr. 1381; May/June, July/Aug. 1384; Mar./Apr. 1385.

[70] July/Aug. 1375; May/June 1382; July/Aug., Sept./Oct., Nov./Dec. 1384; and perhaps May/June, Sept./Oct. 1381.

[71] Five of these occasions were in 1373 or earlier. The others were Nov./Dec. 1376; Jan./Feb., Nov./Dec. 1378; Nov./Dec. 1381; May/June 1382; May/June, July/Aug. 1383.

similar, except that there the Guinigi never had the two thirds necessary for a majority before the end of 1385. The Guinigi family itself was well represented; there was a Guinigi in each Thirty-Six except that elected in September 1385, and there were two members of the Guinigi family in the councils elected September 1384 and September 1385. There was always a strong group of Guinigi partisans, often numbering as many as eighteen to twenty with four or five others who were probably Guinigi supporters.[72] The number of Forteguerra-Rapondi adherents was always significantly fewer; it never rose above seven before 1385 and was frequently only two or three. But they often included judges, like messer Bartolomeo Forteguerra or messer Ludovico Mercati, or members of important merchant families, like Lando Moriconi, Giuffredo Cenami, Jacobo Rapondi, or Forteguerra Forteguerra; so that the opposition in the Thirty-Six probably carried a greater weight than its numbers would suggest.

In the General Council too, the number of Guinigi partisans greatly exceeded those of the Forteguerra, but they never came anywhere near the two-thirds majority of the 180 members required to pass a measure. The highest number the Guinigi reached before 1385 seems to be about fifty in that year. There were thirty-five Guinigi partisans in 1384 and forty-five in 1383; otherwise they never numbered more than about thirty.[73] The highest number the Forteguerra reached was fifteen in 1384, but eight to thirteen was more usual.[74] Nevertheless the Guinigi were so far from having a majority that they must have been even less sure of getting anything controversial through the General Council than through the Thirty-Six or the Anziani.

There was, however, the possibility of swaying the councils by having a large number of Guinigi partisans present as *invitati*. This was especially the case in the Thirty-Six, to which on occasion as many as twenty or more *invitati* were

[72] That is, members of families that supported the Guinigi later, but who themselves died before 1390. The councils of Mar. 1381, Sept. 1384 and Sept. 1385 had eighteen to twenty Guinigi partisans, and a number of other councils in the 1380s approached these figures.

[73] There are eight to ten others in each council who may have been Guinigi partisans because their relatives were later, but who died before 1390.

[74] In 1373 there were only six or seven.

added. More of these were Guinigi partisans than supporters of the Forteguerra, though Forteguerra supporters were by no means excluded. The Guinigi were perhaps making deliberate use of *invitati* in this way, for limitations were placed on the number of *invitati* who could be present in any one council in March 1385. Members of the Guinigi family, especially Francesco, or Niccolò ser Pagani, their ally, took a leading part in councils, and one of them is often the only recorded speaker on a particular measure in the *Riformagioni* accounts. The Guinigi would perhaps in many cases be able to influence councils where they did not have a majority, but they may frequently have found it useful to have the *conservatores*, whom they controlled much more closely, and who could pass things which the Guinigi preferred not to put to the ordinary councils.

One thing that may have helped the Guinigi is a measure of indifference to the conduct of public affairs on the part of many citizens. There are a number of complaints in the records that it was difficult to gather a quorum of councillors, so that it was often necessary to wait for one or two, or even that it was impossible to hold the council for lack of one or two. A system of small payments was ordered for those coming early and fines for those coming late or failing to come altogether,[75] but it was not really effective; in 1385 it was complained that the payments to those coming early were almost always made, but the fines were hardly ever exacted.[76] It was then decreed that the fines should be exacted within fifteen days, but this too seems to have been ineffective. There were further complaints of business being delayed because councillors failed to attend and further attempts to enforce attendance in 1390.[77] It is possible that if a number of citizens found it tiresome to attend council meetings they would be more willing to see much of the ordinary business of the councils pass into the hands of smaller bodies like the *con-*

[75] *Rif.* 7, p. 42, 23 Feb. 1379. There were similar complaints and a temporary system of fines earlier, *Delib.* 132, f. 121, 19 Sept. 1375, *Delib.* 133, f. 34v, 1 Dec. 1376, f. 42, 1 Jan. 1377. Lists of the names of councillors present at meetings often do show that few if any more than the bare minimum to make a quorum attended.

[76] *Rif.* 9, p. 296, 16 Feb. 1385.

[77] *Rif.* 11, p. 275, 20 May 1390.

servatores.[78] This indifference would also give an opening for a really determined body of citizens who did attend regularly to gain control of the affairs of the city.

But, however this may be, the Guinigi do seem to have acquired an undue influence by 1385. They and their supporters held office more frequently, not only in the college of Anziani and the councils and in the *conservatores*, but also in other offices such as the *secretarii*, the governors of the *dovana salis*, the *conducterii*, and the important *balie* which elected the new General Councils and Thirty-Six, and the special council of Thirty-Six with six *invitati* per *terziere* and nine sorters for the new *tasca* of Anziani. If they did not always have majorities in these offices, they always outnumbered the Forteguerra, though Forteguerra partisans were by no means excluded.[79] A comparison of the careers of individual Foretguerra and Guinigi partisans before 1385 shows the Guinigi supporters playing a fuller part in public affairs, holding office more frequently and sitting more regularly in councils and *balie*.

But opposition was growing. Though the city enjoyed comparative peace internally from 1370 to 1385, there are a number of indications that all was not entirely harmonious. There was the complaint of the Rapondi that they had been over-assessed in the *imposita*.[80] Lawsuits between the leading families sometimes threatened to disturb the peace of the city. In August 1371 the Thirty-Six was called upon to deal with such a dispute between Francesco Guinigi and his brothers on the one side and Jacobo and Bartolomeo Ronghi on the other, from which, it was said, 'dissentiones et odia provocentur propterque iam murmurationes insurrexerunt et possent de facili scandala exoriri que nedum partium ipsarum sed etiam civitatis de facili possent inquietare quietem'.[81] Shortly afterwards the *pacificatores* imposed a month's truce in a similar dispute between the Rapondi and the Panichi.[82] In

[78] There was, however, similar trouble in obtaining the attendance of the *conservatores*, *Rif.* 7, p. 123, 29 July 1379.

[79] It should be remembered that Dino Guinigi's list gives far more Guinigi than Forteguerra partisans.

[80] *Rif.* 2, p. 323, 22 June 1371.

[81] *Rif.* 3, pp. 25–6, 18 Aug. 1371.

[82] *Rif.* 3, p. 270, 14 Apr. 1372.

1375 the Guinigi were granted the right to carry arms despite the statutory prohibitions of this.[83] In 1376 it was decided to have chains put across the streets and squares of the city and close them at night 'ut tutius ab omni malignitate perversa civitas et libertas actentius conservetur',[84] though this was probably done more as a general precautionary measure than in any particular expectation of violence. In January 1377 messer Bartolomeo Forteguerra refused to accept the office of Anziano, to which he had been elected, and a special General Council was called just for this, which ordered that he must be compelled to accept.[85] Unfortunately his reasons for refusing the office are not recorded, but it may possibly be an indication of the strength of party feeling in the city, even at so early a date. At any rate the refusal was felt to be dangerous; 'multa varia et diversa scandala possent faciliter exoriri et rei publice lucane multa pericula generari.'[86]

It has already been suggested that there was probably discontent at the long continuance of the same twelve citizens in the powerful office of *conservatores*, and that the association of another twenty-four citizens in this office was intended to disarm criticism. There is evidence of similar discontent in the distribution of the office of vicar. It was petitioned that the vicars should be appointed by *terziere*, on the grounds that many citizens were discontented with things as they were and disputes arose each year when the elections were made.[87] The petitioners began by reminding their fellow citizens ominously that union and 'ben vivere' was the way to maintain the state and everyone should have a fair share of the honours as well as the burdens. But it is doubtful whether the dispute can be seen

[83] *Rif.* 5, pp. 121–2, 1 Nov. 1375. Such licences were fairly frequently granted.

[84] *Rif.* 6, p. 55, 29 Aug. 1376, p. 411, 21 Nov. 1377.

[85] *Rif.* 6, p. 140, 2 Jan. 1377. Later that year the *conservatores* decreed that no one who was in the city or state of Lucca when extracted as Anziano could refuse the office, *Rif.* 6, p. 350, 25 Aug. 1377. Messer Bartolomeo was one of those present at this meeting. The vote was 16–1.

[86] *Rif.* 6, p. 140, 2 Jan. 1377. But the tensions should not be exaggerated. Messer Bartolomeo Forteguerra was named along with Giovanni Bernardi as 'confidenti amici' 10 May 1384 in a division of jointly held property between Michele Guinigi, Lazzaro di Francesco Guinigi and Baldassare and Guaspare, heirs of Niccolò di Lazzaro Guinigi, *Archivio Guinigi*, 151, f. lv. In 1383 the Lucchese were attempting to obtain the appointment of messer Bartolomeo Rapondi as bishop of Lucca, *Rif.* 8, p. 587, 25 Aug. 1383, *Reg.*, nos. 1089, 1093.

[87] *Rif.* 8, pp. 516–17, 20 May, pp. 528–9, 1 June 1383.

as a party issue. If two of the petitioners, Giuffredo Cenami and Lando Moriconi, were Forteguerra supporters, two of the others, Andrea dal Portico and Dino Guinigi, and perhaps also the fifth, Fredo Martini, were of the Guinigi party, and both Francesco Guinigi and Jacobo Rapondi spoke in favour of the measure. If this was a blow struck at the Guinigi, they were quick to accept and associate themselves with the change.

But all these things are merely hints that there was already party feeling and tension in Lucca. The hostility of a group of citizens to the Guinigi became clear in January 1385, when the weakening of the party with the death of Francesco Guinigi the previous June encouraged them to demand the abolition of the *conservatores*. Sercambi names messer Bartolomeo and Forteguerra Forteguerra, Piero and Giovanni Rapondi, Turchio Balbani,[88] messer Giovanni Maulini, and Bartolomeo Michelis as the leaders of this movement, but asserts that 'grande quantità di ciptadini' favoured it.[89] Matteo Nutini, who was a Forteguerra supporter, at any rate in 1391, speaking as Gonfaloniere, said that many citizens had urged that for the sake of peace and unity the institution of the *conservatores* should be reconsidered, so that it came to include more citizens. Messer Bartolomeo Forteguerra then proposed that they should be abolished, and that to replace them four citizens per *terziere* should be elected with authority to provide for the defence of the city and state, and to take action against threatened attacks by any armed companies, spending money as necessary. They were to hold office for a year, after which they were to be ineligible for re-election for a further two years. They were to be called 'commissarii palatii super bono statu civitatis', and to prevent the kind of abuse that had grown up in the years 1375–85, they were specifically prohibited from pardoning *banniti*, authorizing other *balìe* or doing anything else that properly belonged to the General Council or the Thirty-Six.[90]

This was agreed in the General Council and the *Riformagioni* account records no other speakers. But the *Minute* records make it clear that it had already been

[88] Turchio Balbani appears as a Guinigi supporter in Dino Guinigi's list.
[89] Sercambi, III, pp. 336–7.
[90] *Rif.* 10, p. 283, 10 Jan. 1385. Appendix Doc. III.

discussed in a joint meeting of all three *gite* of *conservatores* along with a number of *invitati*. There is a brief list of these *invitati*, dated 9 January 1385, which shows that they included four Forteguerra partisans, messer Ludovico Mercati, Giovanni Campucci, Niccolò di ser Dino Lombardi and Gherardo Burlamacchi.[91] There are notes of a discussion in this meeting dated 10 January 1385, which show a surprising degree of unanimity among those present; messer Bartolomeo Forteguerra proposed that a General Council should be held with the three *gite* of *conservatores* as *invitati*, and almost everyone who spoke agreed to this. They included Dino Guinigi, Niccolò ser Pagani, Giovanni Mingogi, and Michele Guinigi on the Guinigi side, and Lando Moriconi, Bartolomeo Michelis, Turchio Balbani and messer Guglielmo Flammi on the Forteguerra side.[92] Jacobo Rapondi made the more moderate proposal that the *conservatores* be enlarged by the addition of a further forty citizens, and messer Ludovico Mercati the more extreme proposal that the Anziani, who were favourable to the Forteguerra, should elect whom they wished 'cum quibus habeant praticare et facere propositam'. But both these were Forteguerra partisans. The *Minute* also contain several pages of notes on the discussion in the General Council on 10 January. These show that citizens on both sides were in substantial agreement, except that Jacobo Rapondi was advocating that the *conservatores* should be increased to seventy-two. Such disagreement as there was turned on the question of whether the new officials were to hold office for a year or six months, and whether their term of office was to begin in January or March. But differences even on these comparatively unimportant matters did not follow party lines.[93] Michele Guinigi is found advocating that the *balìa* of *conservatores* 'sit sublata irrita et inanis'. Dino Guinigi and Niccolò ser Pagani can be found seconding recommendations

[91] *Min.* 3 (not foliated), 9 Jan. 1385. Also two Guinigi partisans, Giovanni Cardellini and ser Simone Alberti, and two others. But for ser Simone Alberti, Sercambi, I, p. 260.

[92] For Turchio Balbani see Chapter 11, p. 206, note 51. Niccolò Narducci, Francesco Dati and maestro Giovanni da Barga, who cannot be shown to have belonged to either party, also spoke, *Min.* 3, 10 Jan. 1385.

[93] Messer Tommaso da Ghivizzano said six months and Bartolomeo Michaelis 'sex mensibus vel uno anno arbitrio dominorum', as if it did not really matter.

made by Bartolomeo Forteguerra, and ser Niccolò Sartoy agreeing with Niccolò ser Pagani, and Andrea dal Portico with Lando Moriconi.[94] The abolition of the *conservatores* and the institution of the commissioners of the palace was eventually passed by 202–23, a surprisingly small percentage of votes against.[95]

But this show of unanimity resulted from the Guinigi making the best of a bad job. It cannot conceal the seriousness of their defeat. The names of the four per *terziere* would suggest this, even if there were no other evidence. Six of them, messer Ludovico Mercati, Bartolomeo Forteguerra, Giuffredo Cenami, Bartolomeo Michelis, Piero Rapondi, and Lando Moriconi, and according to Sercambi, also Turchio Balbani, were Forteguerra adherents. Only Michele Guinigi, Giovanni Mingogii, Turellino Bonucci, and perhaps Fasino Boccansocchi were Guinigi adherents.[96] Sercambi too makes it clear that the abolition of the *conservatores* was a serious defeat for the Guinigi. He associates the abolition with the desire of their enemies 'al tucto abassare lo stato della chasa de'Guinigi', and says that afterwards 'poco overo nulla i predicti Guinigi poteano in Lucha'.[97] According to him, it was rumoured outside Lucca that the houses of the Guinigi had been attacked and they themselves killed or driven out of the city.[98] There is no reason to doubt the assertion of Sercambi that the abolition of the *conservatores* encouraged the rebels and exiles of Lucca to hope for their return. It certainly seems to have been this that encouraged messer Matteo Gigli, one of the leading citizens of Lucca, a judge and a man frequently employed on embassies, to plot the return of messer Giovanni degli Obizi by force. The account of this plot contained in messer Matteo's condemnation says that he was approached by Luzo degli Obizi, Giovanni's kinsman and envoy, as soon as he heard of the abolition of the *conservatores*.[99]

94 *Min.* 3, 10 Jan. 1385.

95 There were 53 *invitati*, many of them Guinigi partisans.

96 *Rif.* 9, p. 283, 10 Jan. 1385. The twelfth was maestro Giovanni da Barga, who may have been a Guinigi supporter.

97 Sercambi, III, pp. 336–7.

98 Sercambi, I, pp. 243–4; III, p. 337.

99 'Cum fuit in dicta civitate remotio offitii baylie statim', *Sentenze e Bandi*, 70, f. 35, Feb. 1385.

It was probably partly as a result of this plot, as well as from a desire to consolidate the victory obtained with the abolition of the *conservatores* that in March 1385 a measure was passed to confirm the existing form of government and to prohibit any further changes. In the preamble it was stated that since the abolition of the *conservatores* certain Lucchese citizens had been plotting and threatening the liberty of the state, so that measures were necessary to prevent this 'cum omnis repens mutatio sit damnosa'. It was then agreed by 134–38 that the General Council and the Thirty-Six and the statutes on which they depended, and also the statutes concerning the *gonfalonieri* and *pennonieri*, the *dovana et massa salis*, and the *tasca* of Anziani should be confirmed. No changes could in future be made in them and very heavy penalties were laid down for anyone proposing such changes. In addition it was agreed that, in order that the votes of councillors should not be overwhelmed by crowds of *invitati*, a limit should be placed on the number of *invitati* who could be present at any one council. There were not to be more than six *invitati* per *terziere* at any meeting of the General Council or four per *terziere* at any meeting of the Thirty-Six. This decree may be seen as a reaction against the excessive use of *invitati* favourable to themselves by the Guinigi 1375–85, though as with the abolition of the *conservatores* they seem to have been quick to accept it.[100]

But if these measures greatly reduced Guinigi power, their effect does not seem to have lasted very long. The Guinigi quickly seem to have recovered their powerful position in the Lucchese state. The abolition of the *conservatores* must have been a serious blow, for the Guinigi had always had a majority among them and they had had very great power. Only the first set of commissioners of the palace had a Forteguerra majority; the Guinigi soon gained control, though the commissioners of the palace had much more restricted power than the old *conservatores*, and were nothing like so useful an instrument. But the Guinigi still had the advantage over the Forteguerra in the college of Anziani and the Thirty-Six. If there were only five colleges that contained no member of the Forteguerra

[100] *Rif.* 9, p. 324, and *Min.* 3, 23 Mar. 1385. Michele Guinigi, Niccolò ser Pagani, and Opizo Onesti were among those who spoke in favour. Appendix Doc. IV.

party in the period from January 1386 to May 1392,[101] and Forteguerra partisans were twelve times Gonfaloniere,[102] the Guinigi outnumbered the Forteguerra in all colleges except two.[103] There were five or more Guinigi partisans in thirty-five of the thirty-nine colleges, and they had the seven or more Anziani required for an absolute majority in at least ten of the colleges and perhaps also in six others.[104] The Guinigi family perhaps sat slightly less frequently than before 1385, but there were still members of the Guinigi family in two of the six colleges each year and three in 1390. In the Thirty-Six, too, they always exceeded the Forteguerra party, and in several councils came near to having the two-thirds necessary for a majority. Their number varied from sixteen to twenty-three, while the Forteguerra party numbered between six and twelve.[105] It seems that as far as the colleges of Anziani and the Thirty-Six were concerned the Guinigi were able to maintain their position.

The five years 1385–90 are almost bound to seem a mere interval between the anti-Guinigi movement that led to the abolition of the *conservatores* and the final crisis of 1390–2. There are a number of indications of tension and strife in the city. In December 1385 measures were taken to remove hatreds among the citizens. It was stated in council that rancour and enmity often arose among citizens from very small things, and a *balìa* of six per *terziere* was elected, to whom such disputes could be referred for arbitration and peace-making.[106] In 1387 there were disputes about appointments to offices made in the Thirty-Six. It was complained

[101] Mar./Apr., July/Aug. 1386; Sept./Oct. 1388; Mar./Apr., July/Aug. 1389.

[102] In two colleges in 1386; in four in 1387; one in 1389 and 1390; two in 1391; and two in the first six months of 1392.

[103] May/June 1386 equal numbers of Guinigi and Forteguerra supporters. Sept./Oct. 1389, four Forteguerra and three Guinigi partisans.

[104] One in 1386; three in 1388; two in 1389; two in 1390; two in 1391. The six where they possibly had a majority were one each in 1386, 1387, and 1388, two in 1390, and one in 1391.

[105] In September 1387 they numbered only three. Two of the highest figures, eleven in Mar. 1391 and twelve in Mar. 1392, were in councils elected during the crisis of 1390–2.

[106] *Rif.* 9, p. 448, 13 Dec. 1385. They were forbidden to intervene in civil cases or any other matter where intervention would be contrary to the statutes. The eighteen included five or six of the Forteguerra party and some independents, though over half were Guinigi supporters.

that many members of the Thirty-Six elected in September each year, and thus responsible for the annual election of officials in November and December, were greedy for offices for their own private profit and not for the general good. As a result there were many delays and disputes over the elections, and it was often difficult to get all the offices filled. It was therefore decreed that no member of the Thirty-Six elected in September could be appointed to any office that carried a salary.[107] There are also hints of disputes over the selection of ambassadors. In 1389 it was proposed that the regulations concerning ambassadors be reviewed 'ne multis exclusis prout hactenus factum est, pauci, seu honorabile id sit seu onerosum, semper mittantur'.[108] And despite the fact that their powers were much more restricted than those of the *conservatores*, the commissioners of the palace still seem to have been the subject of disputes. In December 1389 their period of office was reduced from a year to six months.[109] A year later it was further reduced to three months, and arrangements were made for the election of twelve citizens per *terziere* who had never held the office before, along with four more experienced citizens per *terziere*.[110]

The final crisis began with the making of the new *tasca* of Anziani in July 1390.[111] In this *tasca* messer Bartolomeo Forteguerra was named as *spiccinato*, that is one of the twenty-four citizens whose names were placed in a separate bag to be drawn out as replacements for any Anziano who was

[107] *Rif.* 10, p. 288, 12 June 1387. This applied only to offices filled by the Thirty-Six. It was proposed by Dino Guinigi and passed 37–3.

[108] *Rif.* 11, p. 131, 9 Sept. 1389.

[109] *Rif.* 11, pp. 186–7, 31 Dec. 1389 for 1390. The commissioners had also been discussed the previous day, *Min.* 4 (not foliated), 30 Dec. 1389. There were many speakers and differences of opinion, though these did not follow party lines.

[110] *Rif.* 11, pp. 366–7, 9 Dec. 1390 for 1391. Again the matter had been discussed the previous day. Some of the many speakers wished the commissioners to hold office for six months, but these included members of both parties, *Min.* 4, 8 and 9 Dec. 1390. The *gite* were to be arranged so that there would be one citizen per *terziere* who had held the office before and three who had not in every set of commissioners.

[111] Sercambi, I, p. 259 dates it Aug. 1390, but *Rif.* 11, p. 300 shows that the making of the new *tasca* for the period of two years from 1 Sept. 1390 was begun 6 July and completed by 8 July 1390. Sercambi shows his pro-Guinigi sympathies particularly clearly here, as he consistently describes the Forteguerra as troublemakers, when they had in fact reasonable cause for complaint, and it was the Guinigi who had begun the troubles by making messer Bartolomeo *spiccinato*.

dead or absent, when the time came for him to take office. The *spiccinati* were normally chosen from young men who were just beginning their careers, and had usually never held the office of Anziano before. In 1390 messer Bartolomeo Forteguerra was middle-aged. He had been Anziano for the first time as long ago as 1369, and had been Anziano five times and Gonfaloniere four times by 1390.[112] He was one of the college of judges and had very frequently sat in *balìe*; he had been one of the first *conservatores*, and had often served on embassies. It is not surprising, therefore, that he regarded his nomination as *spiccinato* as an insult, or that a large number of citizens shared his view.[113] He cannot have been elected as *spiccinato*. The election was done by the Thirty-Six and six *invitati* per *terziere*. These had included messer Bartolomeo himself, his cousin Forteguerra Forteguerra and a large number of Forteguerra supporters.[114] But the sorting was done by three of the Anziani and six of the Thirty-Six, and these were all Guinigi supporters.[115] It is clear from Sercambi that the insult to messer Bartolomeo Forteguerra was the work of the Guinigi party.[116] But it is difficult to see what they hoped to gain by it. There was bound to be trouble when he was

[112] Anziano, Sept./Oct. 1369, Jan./Feb. 1377, Sept./Oct. 1381, May/June 1386, Mar./Apr. 1388. Gonfaloniere, Nov./Dec. 1373, Nov./Dec. 1378, May/June 1383, Nov./Dec. 1389.

[113] Sercambi, I, pp. 259–60. All the citizens he names are listed as Forteguerra partisans by Dino Guinigi. *Spiccinati* were also selected from candidates who got enough votes to qualify for the Anzianate, but fewer than those who were put in the colleges in the first instance, *Rif.* 2, pp. 205–6, 3 Feb. 1371, also *Rif.* 11, p. 373, 16 Dec. 1390. There was therefore also the implication that messer Bartolomeo failed to get enough votes to be put into a college in the first instance.

[114] In the Thirty-Six, Niccolò di ser Dino Lombardi, Castruccio Saggina, Bartolomeo and Forteguerra Forteguerra, Piero Rapondi, Matteo Nutini, Betto Schiatta, and Giovanni Moriconi. Also three replacements on 5 July, Gherardo Burlamacchi, Giuffredo Cenami, and Lando Moriconi. Of the *invitati*, messer Ludovico Mercati, Giovanni Campucci, messer Guglielmo Flammi, and perhaps Michele Leonis.

[115] They were Nuccio di Giovanni, Opizo Onesti and Dino Moriconi as the three Anziani, Franceschino Buzolini, Giovanni Galganetti, Martino Arnolfini, Matteo Mattafelloni, Bonagiunta Schiezza, and Lazzaro di Francesco Guinigi of the Thirty-Six. The *sortitores* had considerable power, even when they did not abuse their position; they selected the Gonfalonieri from the candidates successful in the election for the Anzianate, they grouped the candidates into colleges, and they had some discretion in the selection of *spiccinati*, *Rif.* 2, pp. 205–6, 3 Feb. 1371, *Statuto del Comune di Lucca 1372*, Lib. I, vi.

[116] Sercambi, I, pp. 259–60.

drawn out as *spiccinato*, or when it was noticed that he had not appeared among the Anziani. It can only be regarded as a pointless insult, resulting from the bitterness of party feelings.

In fact the insult was soon revealed. Bonagiunta Schiezza, one of the sorters, told messer Bartolomeo some time before the first college of the new *tasca* took office in September 1390. Messer Bartolomeo then began to gather support in the city and the *contado* in order to destroy Guinigi power in Lucca, and by December 1390, according to Sercambi, who might be expected to underestimate rather than overestimate Forteguerra strength, well over half the city and *contado* of Lucca supported him.[117]

The college of Anziani for November and December 1390 was favourable to the Guinigi,[118] but in view of the large body of supporters messer Bartolomeo had won, they recognized the need for concessions. A meeting of the General Council was therefore called, and after a preamble recalling the past dangers of Lucca and the miseries of Pisan rule, and stressing the need for unity, the Gonfaloniere proposed that a further *tasca* of Anziani should be made for three years, not two, to begin when the two year *tasca* was finished, and that in future *tasche* should be for three years, not, as had become customary, two. He supported this change by the argument that it was not possible to include in a two year *tasca* all the citizens who deserved to be Anziani, and also that in the past many had been excluded because those who made the *tasche* had been influenced by 'parentado o amista o inganno di mente'.[119] He spoke of many new complaints about the *tasca* of Anziani that had arisen that year, and which had caused outside powers to believe that Lucca was seriously divided. Increasing the number of citizens who could be Anziani would, he hoped, bring peace and unity, and cause everyone to forget their differences and make any necessary sacrifices for the common good. The extension of numbers was also to be applied to the *invitati* to the Thirty-Six when the new *tasca*

[117] Sercambi, I, p. 261. Bonagiunta Schiezza died soon after; he was replaced in the Thirty-Six, *Rif.* 11, p. 329, 23 Oct. 1390.

[118] Michele Guinigi, Gerardino Benettoni, Simone Tegrimi and Giovanni Galganetti were all Guinigi supporters. Only Betto Schiatta and perhaps Galvano Trenta supported the Forteguerra.

[119] *Rif.* 11, pp. 371–4, 16 Dec. 1390. Appendix Doc. V.

was made there. There were to be twelve *invitati* per *terziere*, not six, in future, and there were to be three sorters per *terziere*, not two, though the number of Anziani acting as sorters remained at three. The sorters were to have a six-year 'vacation', which was an exceptionally long period, and in naming the *spiccinati* they were specifically instructed to choose those who 'siano di piu giovane eta et che non siano stati piu Antiani'. The names of the seventy citizens per *terziere* who were to be put into this first three year *tasca* of Anziani were then read out, which was not normally done, in order to remove suspicions.[120]

Both Forteguerra supporters, like messer Guglielmo Flammi, and Guinigi supporters, like Niccolò ser Pagani, messer Tommaso da Ghivizzano, Opizo Onesti, and Bartolomeo Buzolini, counselled that these changes be accepted.[121] The 'Ordines Super Tasca', as they were called, seem to be another example of the genius of the Guinigi for making a virtue of necessity. As in the case of the abolition of the *conservatores*, they were quick to associate themselves with a change that was unavoidable.[122] Their true attitude can be seen in May 1392, when they had the three year *tasca* repealed on the grounds that, though it had been made on the pretext of being for the public good, it was in fact the result of factions.[123] But in December 1390 the three year *tasca* probably served its purpose in quieting the more violent party feelings for some months.[124]

But Sercambi speaks of 'colloqui de 'ciptadini', which caused the Anziani to fear to summon the General Council shortly before Easter 1391 to discuss the amnesty for prisoners which was always granted at Easter, for fear that the councillors would insist on discussing other matters. The General

[120] Sercambi, I, pp. 261-2. *Rif.* 11, pp. 371-4, 16 Dec. 1390. Preference was to be given to the candidates who had obtained the most votes. The names include members of both the Guinigi and the Forteguerra parties and a number of citizens who had not been Anziani before.

[121] *Rif.* 11, pp. 371-5, *Min.* 4, 16 Dec. 1390. Passed by 145-41, and the preliminary dispensations by 168-21 and 171-18.

[122] It is possible that the *Ordines Super Tasca* aroused rather more controversy than appears from the account in the *Riformagioni* for 16 Dec. 1390. They may have been discussed in the General Council on consecutive days.

[123] *Rif.* 12, pp. 122-3, 26 May 1392. The three year *tasca* was certainly irregular.

[124] Sercambi, I, p. 262.

Council was finally summoned on the understanding that nothing except the amnesty would be discussed. But when the council did meet the Anziani were unable to make any proposal because they themselves were divided.[125] No *invitati* had been summoned to this meeting, but the Gonfaloniere, Gherardo Burlamacchi, and the preceptor of the Anziani, both of whom were Forteguerra partisans, claimed the right to summon any citizens they liked to the council. The rest of the Anziani failed to prevent this, and sixteen Forteguerra partisans entered the council.

One after another these citizens said that the *tasca* 'a beneplacito' had not been made with the consent of all the citizens, and that it should be abolished and a *balìa* elected to make all the necessary changes.[126] Since many of the council were of the other party, uproar resulted and the councillors almost came to blows. It was apparently while the council was sitting that some of the college of Anziani, who favoured the Guinigi party, without the knowledge of the rest of the Anziani, ordered the captain of the guard to arm as a precaution in case of violence.[127] In the council itself Dino Guinigi rose and pointed out that the council had been summoned only to discuss the matter of the prisoners and nothing else, but he was shouted down. This dangerous situation was resolved by a citizen, whom Sercambi does not name, who said that, while it was good to have heard what the sixteen Forteguerra partisans had to say, they were neither councillors nor *invitati*, and what they had said could not be put to the vote. If the council considered what they had said so urgent that it should be voted on, then an equal number of Guinigi partisans should be sent for. He himself did not consider it so urgent, and advised that the sixteen Forteguerra partisans should leave. The council should then consider the matter of the prisoners, and another council should be summoned with *invitati* to resolve the divisions and factions, and bring the citizens back to peace and unity. This advice was accepted and the council was able, after the Forteguerra partisans had with-

[125] Sercambi, I, p. 262.

[126] 'a rifermare ongni cosa che fusse da fare', Sercambi, I, p. 263.

[127] Sercambi, I, p. 264. The captain of the guard, ser Niccolò da Sanminiato, was shortly afterwards dismissed for this.

drawn, to settle the amnesty for the prisoners.[128] Nothing of this appears in the official records; Sercambi is the only authority for this council meeting. He does not date it very precisely, but it probably took place on 22 March, the date on which the *Riformagioni* records the amnesty to have been decided.[129]

The *Riformagioni* records a further meeting of the General Council a week later, of which there is no mention in Sercambi.[130] This is probably the council, which it had been agreed to call later; for it had eighteen *invitati* about half from each party,[131] and the subject of discussion was the three year *tasca*. It was first necessary to grant dispensation from the *Riformagione* of 23 March 1385, forbidding the proposal of any change in the government, and this was done.[132] The Gonfaloniere, Gherardo Burlamacchi, then said that there were great differences of opinion about the three year *tasca*, both about when it should be sorted, whether this should be done when the two year *tasca* was finished or before, and about whether, when it was sorted, it should be decided in advance which two months each college should hold office, as was apparently normally done, or whether they should be drawn out at random. He therefore proposed that the council should commit the decision on all these points to three citizens, Forteguerra Forteguerra, Matteo Nutini, and Pietro Gentili. This would seem to give a decided advantage to the Forteguerra party, as two of these three were Forteguerra adherents and only Pietro Gentili was a Guinigi supporter, but according to the Gonfaloniere, these three citizens had already been considering the different opinions in the city about the three year *tasca* and 'anno conducta la cosa con buon piacere di tutti a buona conclusione come da dicti citadini che unitamente a noi sono venuti avemo inteso sentito'. In any case

[128] Sercambi, I, pp. 264–5.

[129] *Rif.* 11, p. 447, 22 Mar. 1391. The only other business recorded for this council is the re-hiring of a *custos carcerum*, but the *Riformagioni* normally record only matters that were decided and decrees that were made, not discussions where no conclusion was reached.

[130] Sercambi, I, p. 265, the next entry concerns events in August 1391. *Rif.* 11, p. 449, 29 Mar. 1391.

[131] There were in fact eight of the Forteguerra, and nine, possibly ten, of the Guinigi party.

[132] *Rif.* 11, pp. 449–50, 29 Mar. 1391. The votes were 150–35 and 154–31.

the Guinigi appeared to be satisfied, as they made no difficulties about accepting these three citizens.[133]

The *Riformagioni* give the impression that everything went smoothly after this council meeting. The three citizens made a unanimous declaration about the *tasca* 20 June 1391. They divided it into two sections, one for the first eighteen months, and the other for the second, ensuring that the statutory 'vacations' were observed. The names of one Gonfaloniere and nine Anziani were to be written on separate pieces of paper and the papers sealed with wax of a different colour according to which *terziere* the Gonfaloniere represented. When the time came for a college to be drawn out, all those sealed with the appropriate colour of wax were to be taken out and one selected at random. The *spiccinati* were likewise to be divided into two sections and drawn out at random from the appropriate *terziere* as vacancies occurred.[134]

The sorting was duly done in December 1391.[135] There is no mention in the *Riformagioni* of any further disputes that year, and the records show that, to some extent at least, the ordinary business of government continued.[136] But Sercambi records serious disorders in the summer. According to him, both sides had bands of armed men, though they never actually came to blows with each other. Nevertheless the faction disputes that had broken out not only seriously hindered the business of government, but also imperilled the maintenance of law and order. Sercambi relates that castellans, soldiers, and officials were dismissed by one faction or the other. When ser Niccolò Dombellinghi was arrested by the Podestà, his friends in the Rapondi party had him released, and the Guinigi did the same when one of their men was arrested. Lucca remained in this state for several months. It was impossible to do justice, and on a number of occasions

[133] *Rif.* 11, pp. 450–1, and *Min.* 4, 29 Mar. 1391. Messer Bartolomeo Forteguerra proposed that these three citizens be accepted, provided that the actual sorting was done by the Anziani and three of the General Council per *terziere* in addition to these three citizens. Dino, Lazzaro and Michele Guinigi, Bartolomeo Buzolini and many others counselled that this be accepted and it was passed by the large majority of 155–31.

[134] *Rif.* 11, pp. 477–9, 20 June 1391.

[135] It was begun on 26 Dec. and finished by 29 Dec. 1391, *Rif.* 11, p. 558.

[136] Councils continued to meet, officials to be elected etc.

both in the city and the *contado* the two parties congregated their men with the intention of fighting it out. Sercambi claims 'era divenuta Luccha peggio ch'um bosco'.[137] Merchants and other citizens hid their goods for fear of robbery and work almost ceased both in the city and the *contado*.[138] There is no reference to disorders in the *Riformagioni* for 1391; it is hardly to be expected that there would be. But Sercambi's account is in part confirmed by reference to past disorders in February 1392, 'molte tracte et con armi et senza armi et per citadini et per altri sono state facte a casa di singulari persone et altro et simile molti ragionamenti et colloquii siano stati tenuti et avuti',[139] and in at least one case it proved impossible to find a vicar, as no suitable citizen would go because of the disorders.[140]

By the beginning of 1392 Lucca was thoroughly divided, even the women and children arguing about the rights and wrongs of each faction in the streets, according to Sercambi.[141] In these circumstances as soon as one issue was settled, another arose. In January 1392 messer Bartolomeo Forteguerra demanded three further changes in the government of the city. He demanded first that the last college of the *tasca* for two years made in July 1390 should not sit, but that instead the first college of the three year *tasca* should take office. If this proposal were not accepted, he suggested as an alternative that there should be ten other citizens, chosen by the Forteguerra faction, to act with this college of Anziani, living in the palace and with the same voting rights 'chome se fusseno xx antiani'.[142] His objection to the last college of the two-year *tasca* is understandable, as it included Lazzaro di Francesco Guinigi as Gonfaloniere and eight other Guinigi partisans. But it was felt to be important that the *tasca* of Anziani should not be tampered with, and the refusal to grant this demand would certainly be widely supported, except by ardent Forteguerra adherents.

[137] Sercambi, I, p. 274.

[138] Sercambi, I, pp. 265–6, 274–5.

[139] *Rif.* 12, p. 48, 20 Feb. 1392.

[140] *Rif.* 12, p. 50, 20 Feb. 1392, but it proved possible to send Giovanni Flammi as commissioner instead.

[141] Sercambi, I, p. 274.

[142] Sercambi, I, pp. 272–3.

The second demand concerned the *conducterii*, the Lucchese officials concerned with fortresses and especially the hiring and supervision of mercenary soldiers. The Forteguerra wanted the number of *conducterii* reduced from six to three. This is a little puzzling, because although there had earlier been six *conducterii*, their number had in 1380 been reduced to three,[143] and as late as 1386, and probably 1388, there had still been three, holding office for three months at a time.[144] The Forteguerra demand that they be reduced from six to three rests on the authority of Sercambi alone,[145] but it may well be that the number had been increased again to six some time before 1392. According to Sercambi, the demand that there should be three *conducterii* was refused on the grounds that one party or the other would always have a majority, but it was agreed that there should be four. Nothing of these disputes is recorded in the *Riformagioni*, but certain changes in the ordinances for the *conducterii* were made in January 1392, and there are references to 'grandi dubitationi sopra li ordini in ne quali lo dicto officio si fonda'. A *tasca* of twenty-four citizens was to be made each January, to hold office four at a time, beginning 1 February. They must therefore have held office for only two months each. There were also limitations on their powers, designed to prevent any *conducterii* making decisions that should be left to their successors; they were not to hire any castellan for more than six months, and castellans could not be re-hired more than two months before the end of their first term.[146] These changes were agreed by 136–15, and the first *tasca* which contained a number of Forteguerra partisans, was made almost at once.[147]

The third Forteguerra demand was that all captains in Lucchese service be dismissed, and new ones hired, presumably because the existing ones were thought to favour

[143] *Rif.* 7, p. 365, 17 Dec. 1380.

[144] *Min.* 3, 22 June 1388 names of the three *conducterii* for July, August and September. *Rif.* 10, p. 362, 11 Dec. 1387, p. 577, 27 Nov. 1388, the *tasche* of *conducterii* are said to have been made as usual for the coming year.

[145] Sercambi, I, p. 273. *Rif.* 12, pp. 43–4, 24 Jan. 1392 provides that there should be four *conducterii* in future, but does not say how many there were previously.

[146] *Rif.* 12, p. 44, 24 Jan. 1392.

[147] *Rif.* 12, p. 45, 26 Jan. 1392. They included eight Forteguerra supporters and thirteen or fourteen of the Guinigi party, but it is more likely that they were half and half.

the Guinigi. But this demand was refused on the grounds that it would be unjust to dismiss them for no reason, and that it would also be unwise, as it would make them enemies of the commune.[148]

An attempt was made in February 1392 to reconcile the two parties by Lando Moriconi, as Gonfaloniere, and his fellow Anziani. A sermon was preached by an Augustinian and all the members of the General Council swore on a crucifix to forgive any past injuries and not to support any factions in the future.[149] Sercambi dates this reconciliation before the three new demands made by messer Bartolomeo Forteguerra and his followers. But the changes in the office of *conducterii* appear in the *Riformagioni* under 24 January 1392, and there is no reason to doubt that an amnesty for past disputes and injuries and the re-establishment of 'buona concordia et unita per la gratia di dio con sanctissimo giuramento fermata', recorded in the *Riformagioni* under 20 February 1392, is the reconciliation described by Sercambi.[150]

There are no further references to the Lucchese factions in the *Riformagioni* until after 12 May 1392, so Sercambi is the only source for the events of the last weeks of the crisis. Forteguerra Forteguerra was Gonfaloniere in the college for May and June 1392, and Sercambi records that he summoned a 'colloquio' of citizens of both parties on 7 May 1392, in which he once again raised the question of reducing the *conducterii* to three and dismissing all the mercenaries in Lucchese service. Messer Bartolomeo Forteguerra made the interesting suggestion that instead of mercenaries Lucca should be guarded by her own citizens, organized under the traditional 'gonfaloni' and 'pennoni'. A number of the Forteguerra party agreed to this, and Lando Moriconi added that the mercenaries should be driven out of the city, and the money saved by employing citizens as guards should be used to lighten the gabelles.[151] It is not clear whether this represents a real difference of opinion on how Lucca should be guarded, or whether the Forteguerra party were simply improvising

[148] Sercambi, I, pp. 273–4.
[149] Sercambi, I, pp. 270–1.
[150] *Rif.* 12, pp. 48–9, 20 Feb. 1392.
[151] Sercambi, I, pp. 275–7.

methods of guarding the city, which would make possible the dismissal of mercenaries believed to support the Guinigi. Perhaps the latter is more likely, especially in view of the fact that there is no reference to the question before 1392. In any case Forteguerra views did not go unchallenged. A citizen, whom Sercambi does not name, was against appointing citizens as guards because it would encourage gambling and other vices, and advised that at least the present forces should not be dismissed until new ones had been hired in sufficient number to guard the city and fortresses. In fact no conclusion was reached, and the 'colloquio' broke up with some ill-feeling.[152]

A few days later the violence which had so long been threatening finally broke out. Both sides summoned large numbers of armed supporters from the *contado*, and fighting began on Sunday 12 May, before all the Guinigi supporters had arrived. A party of Guinigi supporters, after having been turned back by a hail of stones coming from the houses of the Moriconi, met a group of the other faction coming from the houses of the Rapondi. The Guinigi were victorious in a short sharp skirmish, in which ser Niccolò Dombellinghi was killed, several others wounded and the Rapondi put to flight. Meanwhile Lazzaro di Francesco Guinigi and some of his party had gone to the Palace of the Anziani. Finding it barred against them, they set fire to one of the doors and attacked the other with saws, but the doors were opened to them by some of the Anziani. Forteguerra Forteguerra tried to hide but was discovered. He was killed and his body thrown out of the window. According to Sercambi this was done by a 'forestiere', and was against the wishes of Lazzaro Guinigi and the citizens with him. Two other Forteguerra supporters among the Anziani, Galvano Trenta,[153] and Betto Schiatta, were able to escape, and the Guinigi saved the lives of other Forteguerra partisans, Piero and Giovanni Rapondi, Lando Moriconi, Giuffredo Cenami, Orlandino Volpelli, and his son, Duccio,

[152] Sercambi, I, p. 277.

[153] Galvano Trenta was in Dino Guinigi's list as a Guinigi supporter, but it seems more likely that he took the Forteguerra side. The records or the *Estimo* of 1397 show that he was still alive at that date, Lucca, Biblioteca Governativa, MS. 925, f. 254, but he did not hold any office in Lucca after May 1392.

by sheltering them in the house of Michele Guinigi.[154]

At this point having gained the victory, the Guinigi wished to put an end to violence and restore law and order. They had all the soldiers in Lucchese service confirmed for six months and summoned the leading citizens of Lucca to the palace to discuss what measures needed to be taken. When further reinforcements of Guinigi supporters arrived from the *contado*, it was resolved to admit only half of them, keeping the others outside in order to avoid violence and robbery.[155] But once violence had broken out the Guinigi found it difficult to restrain their followers. The council decreed on 13 May 1392[156] that messer Bartolomeo Forteguerra, as the cause of all the disputes, should be put to death. His hiding place was discovered, and he was arrested by the Podestà. But on the way to the palace they were intercepted by a band of men led by Andrea Stornelli, a Guinigi supporter who had already killed ser Conte Puccini and at least one other man on the previous day. Andrea had messer Bartolomeo summarily executed, and then removed ser Jacopo and Francesco di ser Angelo of Camaiore from the house of Giovanni Mingogii and beheaded them too, without the knowledge of the Anziani.[157] Three days later Andrea Stornelli and maestro Andrea of Florence 'cantatore'[158] caused further trouble. They started a riot in front of the Palace of the Anziani in support of a further extention of Guinigi power, demanding that the *tasca* of Anziani should be burned and Lazzaro Guinigi should have himself knighted. A number of citizens had to be sent out to quell the disorders, but Andrea Stornelli and Andrea of Florence were finally brought to recognize that they were at fault, whereupon they were pardoned. Order was restored by 16 May 1392.

The long period of rivalry and tension between the two parties, and the two years of crisis from 1390 to 1392, had ended at last in a clear victory for the Guinigi.

[154] Sercambi, I, pp. 277–9.

[155] Sercambi, I, pp. 279–80.

[156] Sercambi, I, p. 281. The *Riformagioni* contain no mention of council meetings on 12 or 13 May 1392.

[157] Sercambi, I, pp. 280–2.

[158] Andrea of Florence seems to have been a street-singer. For his career and that of Andrea Stornelli see S. Bongi's notes in Sercambi, I, pp. 452–5.

PART IV

The Consolidation of the Guinigi Regime

13

THE CONFIRMATION OF GUINIGI POWER

THE first few weeks after 12 May 1392 were occupied in measures necessary for the restoration of peace and order, rewarding those who had assisted the Guinigi and punishing their enemies and making certain changes in the form of government. In a meeting of the General Council 15 May a *balìa* of twenty-four citizens was authorized to hold office until 1 September with the fullest possible power. It could legislate, elect and remove officials, quash banns, impose any punishments or fines, authorize any expenditure, abolish gabelles and impose new ones, and even make peace or war. The eight citizens per *terziere* elected to this *balìa* were Bartolomeo Buzolini, Turellino Bonucci, Gherardo ser Bianconi, Andrea dal Portico, Giovanni di Poggio, Giovanni Galganetti, Giovanni Sercambi, and Giovanni Domaschi for S. Paolino, messer Tommaso da Ghivizzano, ser Domenico Lupardi, Niccolò Onesti, Giovanni Malisardi, Matteo Cattani, Matteo Mattafelloni, Francesco Orselli, and Niccolò Sbarra for S. Salvatore, and Dino and Lazzaro Guinigi, Niccolò ser Pagani, Pietro Ugolini, Ciuchino Avvocati, Giovanni Testa, Bartolomeo Balbani, and Giovanni Bernardini for S. Martino.[1] They were a fair selection of the leading families and the most experienced citizens, but they were also predominantly Guinigi supporters. As well as the two members of the Guinigi family and Niccolò ser Pagani, their close ally, Ciuchino Avvocati, messer Tommaso da Ghivizzano and Giovanni Sercambi were notable Guinigi supporters, and fifteen of the others had figured as Guinigi partisans on Dino Guinigi's list. These twenty four citizens virtually ruled the city for the next three months. The General Council met only three times and the Thirty-Six only five times in this period, and then rarely for matters of any importance.[2] All important decisions were taken by the *balìa*.

[1] *Rif.* 12, pp. 98–102, 15 May 1392.

[2] One of the meetings of the General Council was to authorize a sindic for the league

First of all they decided on rewards and punishments for the events of May 1392. In general the repression was not severe. Only messer Bartolomeo Forteguerra seems to have been sentenced to death. Six citizens had been sentenced to banishment 15 May 1392. Messer Giovanni Maulini had been confined to Rome, Niccolò Genovardi to Toulouse, Gherardo Burlamacchi to Venice, Giovanni Rapondi to Avignon, ser Antonio da Camaiore to Perugia, and Matteo Nutini to any place outside Tuscany that he chose to name. These six were among the leading opponents of the Guinigi and were sentenced in the General Council. Otherwise such decisions were left to the *balìa* of twenty-four. It was the *balìa* which decreed the exclusion of Orlandino Volpelli and his son, Piero Rapondi, Betto Schiatta, Jacopo Ronghi, and Lando Moriconi, from the Anzianate, councils and all other major offices, and decreed that no doctors or lawyers could in future be elected to the college of Anziani.[3] The *balìa* also decreed the removal of messer Carlo Ronghi from the office of vicar of Massa and messer Niccolò Maulini from that of vicar of Castiglione, as their loyalty was suspect.[4] In addition to these four or five *contadini* were banished, and two others deprived of Lucchese citizenship, and a number of officials were replaced,[5] but the number of those punished as a result of the events of May 1392 was not on the whole large, nor were the punishments very severe.

A number of citizens were rewarded. The most important of the decrees rewarding citizens was that which freed the di

---

of 1392, another to authorize *statutarii*. Two of the meetings of the Thirty-Six were for the drawing out of the names of the new Anziani. The others were for minor matters.

[3] *Rif.* 12, pp. 121-2, 26 May 1392. Banishments, *Rif.* 12, pp. 101-2, 15 May 1392. In addition Jacobo di Ciomeo Trenta was condemned for rebellion and Lorenzo di Simonello Sembrini banished by the Captain of the People. These condemnations are known only from petitions they presented later, so the date and cause of the sentences are obscure, *Rif.* 12, p. 278, 6 Mar. 1393. Jacobo Trenta was already an exile in Oct. 1392, see Chapter 14, p. 303, note 14.

[4] *Rif.* 12, p. 103, 16 May, p. 104, 19 May 1392. Messer Niccolò was, in fact, moved from Castiglione which controlled the whole of the Garfagnana to Massa. He cannot have been too seriously compromised in 1392 because he held the office of vicar regularly later.

[5] *Rif.* 12, pp. 140-1, 14 June, pp. 163-4, 11 July, p. 186, 30 Aug. 1392. *Sentenze e Bandi*, 82, ff. 95-6, ser Andrea ser Lemmi of Coreglia was ordered to Verona by the *balìa*, also Janetto Tracolini of Villa Basilica, ff. 96-97^{v}. They were condemned for failing to obey, 17 Oct. 1392.

Poggio family from the *Riformagione* of 31 July 1370, which had excluded them and other noble families from the college of Anziani and certain other offices.[6] Only the di Poggio family, who were notable Guinigi supporters, were restored to full political rights; the other noble families remained excluded. The Podestà, messer Giovanni de Palatio, was rewarded by having his period of office extended, and certain other offices and *proventus* were granted as rewards.[7] Niccolò and Agostino Avvocati, again notable Guinigi supporters, were pardoned a debt they owed to the commune,[8] and rewards were decreed for Andrea Stornelli of Lucca and maestro Andrea Gregori of Florence, because, it was said, they had done so much for the liberty of Lucca.[9] In addition the *secretarii* were entrusted with the sum of 500 florins, for which they were not required to render account, to reward secretly others who had worked for Lucchese liberty.[10]

Certain alterations in the constitution of Lucca were made as a result of the revolution of 12 May 1392. The chief of these was the re-establishment of the office of Captain of the People and that of the twelve *conservatores* or commissioners of the palace. The revival of the office of Captain of the People, a title which must have aroused memories of the popular government of the thirteenth and early fourteenth centuries, was probably intended as a propaganda move. But in fact the office bore little resemblance to the popular leader of the thirteenth century, and was nothing like so important. The old offices of major sindic, judge of appeals, and major official of the gabelle, which were customarily held by the same individual, were annexed to the office of Captain of the People, and it is difficult to resist the view that it was merely another name for the same offices, and a name which was

[6] *Rif.* 12, p. 122, 26 May 1392.

[7] *Rif.* 12, p. 127, 29 May , pp. 181–2, 29 Aug. 1392.

[8] *Rif.* 12, p. 134, 3 June, p. 182, 29 Aug. 1392. A *contadino*, Bonaturselli Juntini de Pariana, who had been killed in the fighting, was also freed from an obligation, p. 134, 3 June 1392.

[9] Andrea Stornelli was granted the *proventus baratterie* for three years at 800 florins a year, revoking a previous grant of it to Cecho Simonis of Pistoia at 1530 florins a year, *Rif.* 12, p. 134, 3 June 1392. Maestro Andrea was granted a pension of eight florins a month, *Rif.* 12, p. 134, 3 June 1392, raised to twelve florins, p. 181, 29 Aug. 1392. Also p. 104, 19 May 1392. For later rewards for Andrea Stornelli and maestro Andrea Gregori, see Bongi's notes in Sercambi, I, pp. 452–4.

designed to win popularity by arousing memories of a past popular regime. The Captain of the People was to be especially responsible for dealing with plotting, sedition, and attempts to collect troops or betray castles, but otherwise his functions were the same as those of the offices which had been annexed to his.[11] The office was closely connected with that of the commissioners of the palace; they elected him and his were the only sentences which they were authorized to quash.

The office of *conservatores libertatis*, which had been closely connected with the Guinigi family, was revived, though with the title of commissioners of the palace, which had been held by the officials who replaced the *conservatores* when they were abolished in 1385, and who had much more limited powers. The powers of the new commissioners were carefully defined. They were to be more extensive than those of the commissioners of 1385–92, but there were certain limitations upon them. They were not to make war or peace, enter into leagues or alienate Lucchese property, nor were they to interfere with the offices of the Anziani, *dovanieri*, *conducterii*, *gonfalonieri*, and *pennonieri* or Thirty-Six. They could not on their own authority free *banniti*, create Lucchese citizens, increase or reduce the gabelles, or impose new ones, interfere in legal cases between individuals, or elect the Podestà or other officials with the exception of the Captain of the People, and a few minor officials.[12] The things they could do were also laid down. They and the Anziani were to defend and maintain the state, making any necessary laws and ordinances for this. They were to make provision against wars and the danger of wars, and they could spend money as needed for the protection of Lucchese security.[13] These powers were later expanded a little; the commissioners could make ordinances concerning the government, administration, and defence of Lucca to preserve peace and order and the existing regime, hiring troops for this as necessary.[14] The commissioners were also to participate in the election of certain officials. They were to elect the Captain

[10] *Rif.* 12, p. 134, 3 June 1392.
[11] *Rif.* 12, pp. 113–15, 26 May 1392.
[12] *Rif.* 12, pp. 115–17, 26 May, pp. 179–80, 26 Aug. 1392.
[13] *Rif.* 12, p. 115, 26 May 1392.
[14] *Rif.* 12, pp. 179–80, 26 Aug. 1392.

of the People and had powers to review sentences imposed by him. With the Anziani and the *conducterii*, they were to elect the new *conducterii* who were not to hire more than a certain number of troops without their assent. They were also to join the Anziani in electing the four per *terziere* who acted as electors of the General Council and Thirty-Six. These twelve electors had previously been elected by the Anziani alone. The commissioners also had a share in the election of their own successors. A *tasca* of commissioners was to be made for two and a half years. Each group of commissioners was to hold office for six months, and when the *tasca* was finished, the Anziani and the last group of commissioners were to elect twelve from the previous *gite* to join with them in electing their successors, who were to be sorted by three Anziani and six of the commissioners.[15]

Certain important changes were made in the ordinances for the election of the Anziani. First of all the chapter of the Statute of 1372 concerning their election was revoked. The decree of 16 December 1390 was also revoked on the grounds that it had been made under pressure and not in the public interest. Instead a new *tasca* was to be made for two and a half years beginning 1 September 1392. After that the duration of each *tasca* was to be two years. The minimum age for Anziani was reduced from twenty-five to twenty-two, and the di Poggio were added to those eligible for election, but otherwise the regulations concerning eligibility and 'vacations' remained as before.[16] The rules governing the election and duties of some other offices were defined and clarified, but no other changes of importance were made. But more extensive changes were perhaps contemplated, for it was decreed on 13 July 1392 that a new statute of the commune should be compiled. Nine citizens were elected as *statutarii* for this on 30 August, and their task was to be completed by 1 November 1394. But although they several times issued decrees on important points, such as the number of citizens to sit in the General Council or the reduction of the 'vacation' between brother and brother or father and son in the college of Anziani from four

[15] *Rif.* 12, pp. 115–17, 26 May 1392.

[16] *Rif.* 12, pp. 121–6, 26 May 1392. Those declared bankrupt by the Court of Merchants were excluded along with the bastards, apostates, and those under 22.

months to two[17] the new statute was not finally completed until 12 February 1399. By that time it had been necessary to extend their authority on a number of occasions and to replace *statutarii* who died or became too ill to take part in the work of compilation.[18]

In the months immediately after the revolution of 12 May 1392 measures were taken to prevent plots and riots and to ensure the internal security of the new regime. A decree of the *conservatores* of 15 February 1376 against conspiracies and sedition was revived and penalties were laid down for these offences. The penalties were heavy, death and confiscation of property for sedition, plotting, collecting forces inside or outside the Lucchese state, or betraying castles, death for failure to reveal such plots, and fines for speaking against Lucchese liberty, the office of the Anziani, the statutes or councils, or saying anything to disturb the unity of the city.[19] Measures were also taken to ensure that a reliable body of armed men were always ready in case of emergency. A decree referred to as 'pro armando duecentos confidentes' provided that arms, including corselets and helmets, as well as lances and other weapons, should be kept in the houses of certain Lucchese citizens. The Guinigi themselves were to keep arms for fifty men and about fifty other Lucchese citizens were each to keep arms for three *contadini* who were to be assigned to them.[20] These fifty Lucchese citizens were, of course, men who had been prominent Guinigi partisans and others on whom the Guinigi felt they could rely. A year later ordinances were drawn up for the guard of the city in case of fire or other

[17] *Rif.* 13, p. 22, 10 Mar. 1397, p. 217, 8 Jan. 1399.

[18] New statute put into force, *Min.* 4, 12 Feb. 1399. A new statute was authorized, *Rif.* 12, pp. 165–6, 13 July 1392. Extensions of authority of the *statutarii*, *Rif.* 12, p. 473, 20 July, p. 485–8, 7 Aug. 1394, *Rif.* 13, p. 42, 20 June 1397, referring to earlier extensions of 16 Dec. 1395 and 15 Dec. 1396, p. 217, 8 Jan. 1399. Replacement of a *statutarius, Rif.* 13, p. 118, 22 Mar. 1398. The new statute was put into force by the *statutarii* themselves, not by a decree of any council, *Min.* 4, 12 Feb. 1399. But in June 1400 it was repealed on the advice of Lazzaro di Niccolò Guinigi on the grounds that it contained many things that were obscure, contradictory and ill-considered. The statute of 1372 was put into force again pending the compilation of a new one, *Rif.* 13, p. 337, 18 June 1400. Only fragments of the statute of 1399 survive, and there is not enough to explain why it was repealed after so short a time, *Statuti del Comune di Lucca 9*.

[19] *Rif.* 12, pp. 106–9, 26 May 1392.

[20] *Rif.* 12, p. 178, 26 Aug., p. 192, 31 Aug. 1392. Appendix, Doc. II.

disturbance. They were clearly more concerned with riots and revolutions than with fire. They included instructions for the soldiers of the guard to go to certain places in the city in times of disturbance, and also provided that some of the entrances into the main square should be closed to strengthen it and reduce danger.[21]

Some of these ordinances were designed to restore and maintain order, and were little more than police measures, such as any state might take to prevent disturbances. But in others the Guinigi family figures largely as more than just the most important of the leading families, and it seems opportune to ask at this point whether they had already reached a position of such power that they were the rulers of the city in all but name. Contemporaries had little doubt about this. The Florentine chronicler, ser Naddo da Montecatino, ends a brief account of the events of 12 May 1932 with the words 'e rimasero Signori i Guinigi'.[22] Minerbetti in a much longer account states that 'tutto il reggimento della terra di Lucca rimase nelle mani della setta de'Guinigi'.[23] There is an account of the death of Lazzaro Guinigi in the papers of Francesco di Marco Datini where it is said that Lazzaro 'si potea dire signore di quella tera'.[24] Sercambi too, who could not have been better placed to know about Lucchese and Guinigi affairs, makes it clear that they were the real rulers of the city between 1392 and 1400. His account of the revolution of May 1392 leaves the reader in no doubt that the Guinigi party emerged victorious and had great power in Lucca afterwards. He also specifically states that the Guinigi were making all the important decisions after 1392, when he says 'Et perchè sii certo, ongni volta che udirai dire che la diliberatione sia col comsiglio, intendi sempre con deliberatione della casa de'Guinigi, e con quelli che per li signori si eleggono'.[25] In 1394 on the death of the bishop of

[21] *Rif.* 12, pp. 314–16, 24 July 1393.

[22] *Chroniche Fiorentine di ser Naddo da Montecatino* in *Delizie degli Eruditi Toscani*, Vol. XVIII (Florence, 1784), p. 132.

[23] *Cronaca Volgare di Anonimo Fiorentino già attributo a Piero di Giovanni Minerbetti*, R.I.S., n.s. Vol. XXVII, part ii (Bologna, 1918), p. 159.

[24] Quoted in R. Piattoli, 'Il problema portuale di Firenze dall'ultima lotta con Gian Galeazzo Visconti alle prime trattative per l'acquisto di Pisa (1402–1405)', *Rivista Storica degli Archivi Toscani*, Vol. II (1930), p. 157, note 1.

[25] Sercambi, I, pp. 313–14.

Lucca, Giovanni, the Guinigi were able to secure their position still further by obtaining the election of Niccolò, son of Lazzaro di Niccolò Guinigi, as bishop.[26]

There are many indications of Guinigi power in Lucca between 1392 and 1400. The Florentine alliance of 1395 was their policy, and Lazzaro Guinigi openly played a leading part in affairs in the last years of the century, journeying to Florence in person in connection with the negotiations for peace with Pisa in 1398, and making his visit to Pavia in 1399.[27] There is evidence in official records as well as in chronicle accounts of this power. Florentine documents make it clear that the Florentines regarded the Guinigi, and especially Lazzaro di Francesco, as virtually rulers of Lucca, and as men with whom Florence could deal, relying on them to see that the other Lucchese followed their lead.[28] Lucchese judicial records show that certain plotters also regarded Lucca as being ruled by the Guinigi; there are a number of condemnations for conspiracies, whose aim is said to have been the overthrow of the Guinigi.[29]

The evidence of official records, contemporary writers and chroniclers and of events, in fact, all points to the same conclusion. The events of May 1392 established the Guinigi as virtual rulers of the city. Although they had no title or official recognition of their position, and although they left the republican constitution virtually unchanged, all real power and control of affairs was in their hands, and they were as much rulers of the city as if they had had the title of lord.

In practice they were careful to deal tactfully with the city, and to be content with the substance of power, even if this meant forgoing the shadow. Their rule was mild. The revolution of May 1392 had not been accompanied by much unnecessary bloodshed, although some accounts from outside Lucca give the impression that there were rather more deaths in and immediately after the fighting of 12 May than Sercambi records.[30] But the Guinigi family saved the lives of some of

[26] *Reg.*, no. 1509, 26 Jan. 1394. Sercambi, I, p. 302.

[27] See below, Chapter 14, pp. 316–7, 329–32. [28] See below, Chapter 14, pp. 310–2.

[29] This is made especially clear in an account of a plot involving Piero Rapondi, the aim of which was to find a 'modo di non esse piu sotoposto agli Guinigi', *Sentenze e Bandi*, 85, f. 13v.

[30] Ser Naddo da Montecatino, p. 132, Minerbetti, p. 159. For ser Francesco ser

their leading opponents by sheltering them in their own houses, and the number of banishments and sentences of exclusion from office after their victory was not large.[31] Some citizens who might well have been banished, such as Piero di Guido Rapondi, were merely excluded from office in 1392. A number of others who had been opponents of the Guinigi before 1392 were not punished at all, and there were a few, like Giuffredo Cenami or Castruccio Saggina, who continued to hold office, sitting in the councils and even the college of Anziani. This mildness must have done much to reconcile those who were committed to neither party and even some of the less whole-hearted supporters of the Rapondi and Forteguerra to Guinigi power.

Giovanni Sercambi, the chronicler, had proffered his advice to the Guinigi on how they should rule Lucca. The document is undated, but probably belongs to the period immediately after May 1392.[32] Sercambi's memorandum is a highly practical document. It contains no abstract political theories. Much of it is concerned with such things as the need to ensure adequate revenues and discussions of the number of soldiers required and where they might best be stationed in the city and the *contado*. But there are some sections concerning internal government, and these are of rather more immediate interest. Sercambi advised the Guinigi to ensure that they had control of certain offices; 'l'officio dell'ansianatico sempre a'vostri amici si dia, & così conductieri, gomfalonieri, vicario de Pietrasanta, Montecarlo, Camaiore, Castillioni, segretari, officio di balya overo comissari'. He advised that the council of commissioners with twelve or eighteen members should be revived with the same authority as the General Council, 'acciò

Angeli Bonaccorsi of Camaiore and his brother ser Jacopo decapitated during the disorders of May 1392, *Rif.* 13, p. 180, 20 Dec. 1398. *Cronaca Senese di Paolo di Tommaso Montauri*, R.I.S., n.s., Vol. XV, part vi, fasc. 8, p. 747, states that forty-five men were killed in May 1392.

[31] See above, Chapter , pp. . Sercambi, I, pp. 279–85.

[32] *Nota A Voi Guinigi*, addressed to Dino, Michele, Lazzaro, and Lazzaro di Francesco Guinigi, printed in Vol. III of *Le Chroniche di Giovanni Sercambi*, ed. S. Bongi, pp. 399–407. It probably belongs to the summer of 1392, for it advises measures which were in fact taken in August or earlier. Sercambi would scarcely advise the Guinigi to do things they had already done, and in certain details the *Nota* reads as if written shortly after their victory, e.g. p. 404, '& questo mi pare sia molto di necessità di farlo al presente prima che altro si facesse'.

che quello che per consiglio generale vincere non si potesse, overo che a voi paresse non doversi a quel consiglio mettere, si possa per questo ottenere'.[33] This would make it possible to fill the General Council from the citizens in general without any need to restrict membership to Guinigi adherents. This was obviously desirable 'acciò che non paia in tucto dalli honori di Lucca exclusi'.[34] To reduce suspicion and prevent complaints the general body of citizens, and not just Guinigi adherents, should be included in less important councils, such as the *abundantia* and *fundaco*, and be appointed to offices like that of treasurer, and called to councils as *invitati*, provided that the matters under discussion were not confidential.[35]

He several times stresses the importance of having and maintaining a body of friends 'intendendo vostri amici quelli che alla morte & alla vita colla voluntà vostra sono uniti'.[36] He sees this body of friends as large enough to monopolize the Anzianate, the offices of *conducterii*, *secretarii*, commissioners, *gonfalonieri*, and certain vicariates. In his view this body of friends was the basis of Guinigi power, and they should do everything possible to maintain them and ensure that their opponents should not entice any of them away 'conservandolo per quel modo che i buoni amici conservare si denno'.[37] It was, of course, the existence of this large body of reliable adherents, many of whom were among the leading citizens of Lucca, that enabled the Guinigi to control the city, while maintaining the outward forms of the old republican government, and to monopolize the most important offices without causing too much adverse comment.

The Guinigi can be seen adopting very much the policy advocated by Sercambi in the eight years before 1400, though whether as a result of his advice or not it is impossible to say. With regard to the college of Anziani, members of the Guinigi family themselves appeared very frequently, especially after 1394. There was a Guinigi in three of the six colleges of 1392 and 1394, though not in any of those of 1393. But after 1394 they appear even more frequently; there was a Guinigi in five

[33] *Nota*, pp. 401, 403. In fact they did not have the same authority as the General Council. See above pp. 274–5 and *Rif*. 12, pp. 115–17. 26 May, pp. 179–80, 26 Aug. 1392.

[34] *Nota*, p. 403. [35] *Nota*, p. 403. [36] *Nota*, p. 401. [37] *Nota*, p. 404.

of the six colleges in each year from 1395 to 1398 and in 1400, and in every single college in 1399. The frequent appearance of members of the Guinigi family was made easier by a decree of 8 January 1399, reducing the 'vacation' between brother and brother and father and son from four months to two. This was stated to be for the benefit of those belonging to large families, for by the four month 'vacation', 'multi in magna familia orti veniunt propter has vacationes ab huiusmodi officio excludendi'.[38] There can be little doubt which large family it was intended to benefit, and the purpose of 'vacations' of this kind was to prevent any one family gaining excessive influence. As well as sitting as simple Anziani, the Guinigi were also chosen as Gonfaloniere, the highest office in the state open to Lucchese citizens. Members of the Guinigi family were Gonfaloniere five times between May 1392 and December 1400. Lazzaro di Francesco Guinigi himself held the office twice, in July and August 1392 and January and February 1399. In July and August 1398 his younger brother, Bartolomeo, was chosen, when a vacancy occurred because of the absence of Giovanni Franchi.[39] The other two Guinigi to hold the office were Niccolò in January and February 1395 and Lazzaro in January and February 1397.[40]

But the Guinigi did not have to hold the office themselves to ensure favourable Anziani. When the names of the Anziani for the period 1392–1400 are examined, it is found that by far the greater number of them were Guinigi partisans.[41] The number of Guinigi partisans in any one college never seems to have dropped below five and was often much greater, sometimes eight or nine, or even all ten. The Gonfalonieri especially were almost always Guinigi supporters. Only Matteo Trenta, Gonfaloniere in May and June 1395 and May and June 1400,

[38] *Rif.* 13, p. 217, 8 Jan. 1399.

[39] *Rif.* 13, p. 131, 25 June 1398. He was elected 17–0 by the Anziani and commissioners. In this case Bartolomeo was chosen in preference to Dino Avvocati, a much more experienced citizen, who had held the office before.

[40] *Reg.*, pp. xi–xxxv.

[41] The criteria of Guinigi partisanship have been taken as either inclusion as supporters in Dino Guinigi's list, or having been allotted arms for the 200 *contadini* in the decree of 26 Aug. 1392. In a few cases such as ser Pietro Giuntori or Bonaccorso Bocci, men have been included who do not appear in either list, but who are known from later events to have been ardent Guinigi supporters.

and Giovanni Franchi, elected for July and August 1398, but absent, and actually holding the office in July and August 1399, are not known to have been Guinigi supporters, though neither of them appeared on Dino Guinigi's list as opponents. Giovanni Franchi perhaps was a Guinigi supporter, for his son, Nese, was married to one of Lazzaro di Francesco Guinigi's daughters.[42] Matteo Trenta, as a kinsman of Jacobo Trenta, who had been condemned for rebellion,[43] may perhaps have been regarded as less reliable from the Guinigi point of view; certainly in April 1400 he was replaced as Gonfaloniere by another citizen without any good reason being given.[44] Rather more independent citizens, who are not known to have belonged to either party before 1392, sat as ordinary Anziani between 1392 and 1400, and there was even one citizen, Castruccio Saggina, who had been a Forteguerra partisan. He had perhaps not compromised himself too seriously in 1392 and the Guinigi were inclined to be generous to their defeated opponents. At any rate he sat regularly as Anziano between 1392 and 1400,[45] and never gave any trouble after 1392. But in any case he is the only example of a Guinigi opponent holding the office of Anziano after 1392.

Packing the college of Anziani with leading citizens who are known to have been their supporters was not the only way of obtaining favourable colleges. The Guinigi also introduced many new men into the colleges, men who did not belong to important families, men whose ancestors had never held the office, and often men of a comparatively humble social position. At first sight it is surprising that the Guinigi, who had stood for a policy of confining the holding of the highest offices to a restricted group, and as late as 26 May 1392, had been accusing the Rapondi-Forteguerra party of trying to raise 'populares minutos infimos et ignobiles' to the government at the expense of the good, wealthy, and prudent citizens,[46] should themselves be introducing new men once they gained

[42] Family trees, *Archivio Guinigi*, 151, ff. 60v-61v.

[43] An exile by Oct. 1392, see above note 3. Matteo Trenta was apparently his nephew.

[44] *Rif.* 12, p. 323, 26 Apr. 1400.

[45] Nov./Dec. 1394, July/Aug. 1396, May/June 1398, May/June 1399. *Reg.*, pp. xi–xxxv.

[46] *Rif.* 12, p. 106, 26 May 1392.

control. Sercambi makes no mention of this, but the seventeenth-century chronicler, Dalli, perhaps preserves an earlier tradition when he says that the Guinigi had many new families put into the *tasca* of Anziani to the great wonder of other good citizens.[47]

The numbers of these new men are in fact most striking. Nearly eighty persons who had never held the office before were elected Anziani between 1392 and 1400. In some cases they were men who had long been abroad, like Francesco Vinciguerra,[48] or young members of families who had regularly held the office, and whose family and social position was such that they would naturally be elected Anziani early in their political careers.[49] But many of them were not. Over forty of them, and perhaps more, were men who could not normally have hoped to become Anziani and whose political careers belong entirely to the period after 1392, though few of them reached any great eminence or even held office very frequently. Many of them were probably not young men just beginning their political careers; Jacobo Comi, for example, had money in the Massa in 1373, but did not hold the office of Anziano until 1393;[50] Jacobo di ser Orso is mentioned as a *speziale* in 1371, but did not hold the office of Anziano until 1400.[51] They were often employed in humble occupations; Pellegrino Lelli[52] and Giunta Mattei[53] were tanners; Filippo Cecchi a *fornacerius*;[54] Donato Vannucci[55] and Luporino Puccini[56] were vintners. A number of others were in rather

[47] 'A disposizione de'Guinigi furono poste e intaschate molte famiglie nuove con grandissima ammirazione degli altri buon cittadini', Dalli, III, p. 347.

[48] He was in London and Bruges from 1377, *Libro della communità*, pp. 12, 41, 56, 64, 100, 139–40, 167, 170, 173, 184, 194, 197, 202, 212. He was still there as late as 1394, p. 226. He was Anziano for the first time in Mar. and Apr. 1397.

[49] For example Antonio Gigli Anziano for the first time Mar./Apr. 1393, Stefano Buzolini Anziano for the first time May/June 1394. Both were Anziani three times more before 1400. Gerardo Spada Anziano for the first time July/Aug. 1397, Guido Onesti Mar./Apr. 1397, Cristoforo Moriconi Mar./Apr. 1399 are further examples. They all appear in the Thirty-Six and other offices about the same time.

[50] *Imprestiti*, f. 59^{v}. Anziano Jan./Feb. 1393. *Reg.*, pp. xi–xxxv for him and other men to reach the Anzianate.

[51] *Corte de'Mercanti*, 82, f. 21^{v}. Anziano July/Aug. 1400.

[52] Anziano, Nov./Dec. 1392, Mar./Apr. 1397, Nov./Dec. 1400.

[53] Anziano, Nov./Dec. 1393.

[54] Anziano, July/Aug. 1393, July/Aug. 1400.

[55] Anziano, Sept./Oct. 1393.

[56] Anziano, Jan./Feb. 1394.

more dignified occupations, as *speziali* or notaries; Bartolomeo Giuntini[57] and Niccolò Bartolomei[58] were *speziali*; while ser Jacobo Vannini[59] and ser Antonio di ser Jacobo Nicolai[60] were notaries.

It is not difficult to see what the Guinigi hoped to gain by this policy. Only a handful of these new men had been Guinigi supporters before 1392, as Pietro Colucci, *speziale*,[61] ser Gregorio Andreucci,[62] or Pellegrino Lelli[63] were. But some of them became notable Guinigi supporters later. Jacobo Darii is an example of this. He was Anziano for the first time in 1394 and held the office twice later, and also held other offices, all after 1392. Although he was not one of the citizens deputed to keep arms for the *contadini*, nor in Dino Guinigi's list, he was one of the most devoted Guinigi supporters in 1400.[64] Another example is ser Pietro Giuntori. He was Anziano for the first time in 1393 and three times later, also sitting in the Thirty-Six and holding other offices, all after 1392. He too was a reliable Guinigi adherent by 1400, and was chosen to replace Matteo Trenta as Gonfaloniere in April 1400.[65] These two are almost certainly examples of men won over to support the Guinigi by the policy of raising new men to the college of Anziani and other offices, and there must have been many others. The Guinigi can be seen trying to win support by advancing men's careers in the *contado* too. It was decreed that notaries from the *contado* were to be treated as Lucchese citizens in appointments to offices in the *contado*, though not in their own vicariates.[66] This measure is specifically stated to be designed to cement the faithfulness of the most able and

[57] Anziano, Jan./Feb. 1396, July/Aug. 1397.

[58] Anziano, Jan./Feb. 1398.

[59] Anziano, Mar./Apr. 1396, July/Aug. 1398, July/Aug. 1400.

[60] Anziano, July/Aug. 1393.

[61] Anziano, Nov./Dec. 1399. Included in Dino Guinigi's list.

[62] Anziano, Jan./Feb. 1394 (as *spiccinato*), May/June 1395, Jan./Feb. 1398, May/June 1399. Included in Dino Guinigi's list.

[63] In Dino Guinigi's list, if Pellegrino Cielli is to be read as Pellegrino Lelli, see Chapter 11, p. 214 n. 90.

[64] Sercambi, III, p. 13.

[65] *Rif.* 13, p. 323, 26 Apr. 1400. Anziano Jan./Feb. 1393, Jan./Feb. 1397, May/June 1398, May/June 1400.

[66] 'Ad hoc ut hi de comitatu in quibus pollent scientia atque virtus multiplicatis beneficiis ad amorem et devotionem civitatis alliciantur', *Rif.* 12, p. 186, 30 Aug. 1392.

intelligent *contadini*. It must have been easy for the Guinigi to build up a party in the *contado* and the city once they were in power and controlled patronage. There must have been many ambitious men, especially perhaps notaries, who would support a government that advanced their careers. By appointing these to the college of Anziani the Guinigi would win their support. In appointing some of the obscurer and humbler men, they would at worst get Anziani who were unlikely to oppose them. It was not uncommon for a college of Anziani to consist of five or six known Guinigi supporters and three or four of these new men. Obscure figures like Gratiano Ciucchi or Micuccio Corsi would scarcely have been able to oppose a resolute group of Guinigi supporters, composed of members of the leading families of the city, even if they wished to do so. By raising these new men to the college of Anziani the Guinigi were able to broaden the basis of their support, killing two birds with one stone by obtaining both pliable Anziani and grateful supporters.

Sercambi had advised that certain other offices besides that of Anziano should always be given to friends of the Guinigi. Principal among these was the office of commissioner. Here too an examination of the names of those who held the office shows that they were predominantly Guinigi partisans. There was always at least one member of the Guinigi family among the commissioners, and often all twelve of them were known Guinigi supporters, though occasionally one or two citizens who are not known to have taken the Guinigi side before 1392, or who were even opponents of the Guinigi before 1392, appear among the commissioners. Castruccio Saggina held the office from September 1399 to March 1400, and Giuffredo Cenami, also named as a Forteguerra partisan in Dino Guinigi's list, held the office on 4 August 1400.[67] But the Guinigi party always had a majority, and it cannot be doubted that they controlled the office of commissioners by appointing their partisans.

This control of the commissioners was important because it was one of the most powerful instruments of government between 1392 and 1400. When the office was revived in 1392

[67] *Rif.* 13, p. 258, 23 Aug. 1399. Giuffredo Cenami sat as *subrogatus* for an absent commissioner for this one day only. *Rif.* 13, p. 349, 4 Aug. 1400.

certain limits were placed on the commissioners' authority, but they were granted very wide powers in defence, finance, and general administration, and without exceeding the limits of the authority granted to them they played a prominent role in the government of the city. They dealt with many and varied matters. They were particularly responsible for the internal and external safety of the city. They dealt with disturbances in the city and the *contado*,[68] they imposed and reduced sentences, granted safe-conducts, and quashed banns.[69] It was the commissioners who made the ordinances against fire and riots,[70] and who dealt with the plot of Niccolò di ser Dino Lombardi and Michele Leoni in January 1394.[71] They dealt too with the property of rebels, hearing and adjudicating claims upon them.[72] They could increase the forces in Lucchese service,[73] appoint additional guards for castles,[74] or appoint *podestà* for particular places in the *contado*.[75] They could authorize money for building work on fortresses,[76] and had in fact wide powers in finance generally. They are frequently found authorizing withdrawals from the *deposita*, and transferring money from the *dovana salis* or *abundantia* to the treasurer for immediate use.[77] They dealt too with very many minor administrative and judicial matters, which would earlier have been decided by the General Council or Thirty-Six.[78] They also dealt with matters that touched on foreign and domestic politics. They negotiated with armed companies, ratifying the agreements themselves.[79] They dealt

[68] *Rif.* 12, p. 289, 14 Apr. 1393, p. 407, 31 Jan. 1394. *Rif.* 13, p. 15, 26 Jan., pp. 50–2, 25 July 1397.

[69] *Rif.* 12, p. 278, 6 Mar. 1393. *Rif.* 13, p. 30, 14 Apr. 1397, p. 296, 5 Dec. 1399.

[70] See above, pp. 276–7, and *Rif.* 12. pp. 314–16, 24 July 1393.

[71] *Rif.* 12, p. 402, 9 Jan., p. 403, 11 Jan., p. 404, 13 and 15 Jan. 1393.

[72] *Rif.* 12, p. 204, 19 Sept. 1392, p. 408, 5 Feb., p. 433, 18 Mar., p. 474, 3 Aug., p. 491, 20 Aug. 1394.

[73] *Rif.* 13, p. 35, 4 May 1397, p. 323, 26 Apr., p. 340, 24 June 1400.

[74] *Min.* 4, 19 June 1397.

[75] *Rif.* 13, p. 15, 26 Jan. 1397.

[76] *Rif.* 12, p. 293, 5 May 1393.

[77] *Min.* 4, 21 Dec. 1392 and very many examples in the succeeding years. They could also reduce officials' salaries for the sake of economy, *Rif.* 12, p. 234, 27 Dec. 1392.

[78] For example confirming a union of communes in the *contado*, *Min.* 4, 8 Dec. 1392, *Rif.* 12, p. 232, 21 Dec. 1392, or deciding where appeal lay in a particular case, *Rif.* 13, pp. 327–8, 14 May 1400.

[79] *Rif.* 12, pp. 350–1, 16 Nov., pp. 351–2, 20 Nov. 1393. They also authorized

with the Marchese d'Este's request for aid against his rebellious subjects.[80] They replaced compilers of the new statute of Lucca who fell ill.[81] It was the commissioners who replaced an absent Gonfaloniere by another Anziano from the same *terziere* in 1398,[82] and in 1400 replaced a Gonfaloniere, not apparently absent, by another man, as 'eloquentiorem et aptiorem'.[83]

The commissioners, in fact, appear so frequently and deal with such varied matter after 1392 that there can be little doubt that the Guinigi were using them as Sercambi had advised—to supplement or replace the General Council and the Thirty-Six in the ordinary day to day business of government. Neither the General Council nor the Thirty-Six met frequently after 1392, and the business they dealt with was often trivial. The General Council, which from 1385 to 1390 had met nearly a dozen times a year, met only four or five times a year after 1392.[84] Similarly the Thirty-Six, which had met between twenty and thirty times a year between 1385 and 1390, met only between eight and twenty times a year after 1392.[85]

Certain things had been reserved to these councils and could not be done by any lesser authority, so that a certain number of council meetings each year were inevitable. But these were not always matters of great political importance. The General Council was often called to elect the Podestà, make grants of citizenship, or authorize the release of prisoners in the regular amnesties at Christmas, Easter, and S. Croce, which only it could do. It also is found granting formal authorizations to ambassadors,[86] or extending the time limit for the compilers of

---

certain other negotiations, *Rif.* 13, p. 103, 23 Jan. 1398, *Min.* 4, 26 Oct. 1398.

[80] *Rif.* 12, p. 318, 25 Aug. 1393.

[81] *Rif.* 13, p. 118, 22 Mar. 1398.

[82] *Rif.* 13, p. 131, 25 June 1398. They chose Bartolomeo Guinigi.

[83] *Rif.* 13, p. 323, 26 Apr. 1400.

[84] It met 16 times in 1385, 10 in 1386 and 1388, 11 in 1387 and 1390, and 12 in 1389. After 1392 it met five times in 1393, four times up to 23 Aug. 1394, after which there is a gap in the *Riformagioni*. It met six times in 1397, three in 1398, four in 1399, and five in 1400.

[85] It met 28 times in 1385, 24 in 1386, 26 in 1387, 23 in 1388, 19 in 1389, and 27 in 1390. After 1392 it met 13 times in 1393, 9 times up to 23 Aug. 1394, 19 times in 1397, 18 in 1398, 20 in 1399, and only 8 in 1400 (which was a plague year).

[86] *Rif.* 12, pp. 160–1, 6 July 1392, pp. 410–13, 17 Feb. 1394. *Min.* 4, 29 Mar. 1398.

the new statute.[87] These things required the authority of the General Council because of their importance from a legal point of view, but they had little political significance, and were in any case often merely the formal authorization of things which had already been decided elsewhere. Often, however, the council spent its time considering private petitions or other matters of little importance. Perhaps the only really important matters that the General Council dealt with, and which no other authority could have done, was the repeal of the new statute,[88] and the election during the plague of 1400 of the *balìa* of twelve citizens with the same authority as the council itself, which was the *balìa* that elected Paolo Guinigi captain of the city.[89]

The Thirty-Six, too, had to meet regularly as certain matters were reserved to it. It had to be called to make the new *tasche* of Anziani, and had to meet every two months for the extraction of the names of the new Anziani. Only the Thirty-Six could make the *tasca* of vicars, or replace vicars who were absent or who had refused the office. Though it still met with some frequency after 1392, most of the meetings were concerned with routine matters, such as the declaration of the names of the new Anziani or commissioners, the election of vicars and various minor officials, or the hiring of schoolmasters or doctors for the commune. It was rarely concerned with matters of finance or decisions about defence, fortresses, the authorization of expenditure or public building, or the many other administrative matters that had previously been its concern. Decisions about these matters were now being made elsewhere, either by the Anziani or commissioners, or in other more private meetings not recorded in the *Riformagioni* or other public records. In fact, even if there were no other evidence, the comparative scantiness of the records for the years between 1392 and 1400 would suggest that power had

[87] *Rif.* 12, pp. 485–8, 7 Aug. 1394, *Rif.* 13, p. 42, 20 June 1397.

[88] *Rif.* 13, p. 337, 18 June 1400.

[89] *Rif.* 13, pp. 345–6, 2 July 1400. The General Council also dealt with the sale of the Forteguerra palace and the claims of the duke of Burgundy against Piero Rapondi, whose goods had been confiscated by Lucca. This was because matters involving the alienation of Lucchese property and the rights of the city were therefore involved, rather than because of the importance of these matters, *Rif.* 12, pp. 476–83, 7 Aug. 1394.

passed away from the public councils. The volume of *Riformagioni* for September 1394 to December 1396 is missing, but fewer than 400 pages, 200 folios, are enough for the *Riformagioni* from May 1392 to August 1394, though there was much special business arising from the revolution of 12 May 1392. The last volume of *Riformagioni* before the gap of 1400–30 during the *signorìa* of Paolo Guinigi takes up well under 400 pages, by no means all of them written, for the four years from 1397 to 1400. This is only a half to a third of the volume of the records for earlier years.

Sercambi had advised the Guinigi to use the commissioners rather than the councils for important matters, so that the councils could then be chosen from among the citizens generally, which would prevent discontent among those excluded. This policy seems to have been followed. Both the Thirty-Six and the General Council contained a larger proportion of citizens who are not known to have supported either faction or who had supported the Forteguerra, than did the colleges of Anziani or the commissioners. Because of the gap in the *Riformagioni* from the end of August 1394 to January 1397 the names of the General Council for 1395 and 1396 are not known. But an examination of the lists for the other years shows that there was never a majority of known Guinigi supporters in the General Council, though there was always a solid group which included many leading citizens and which would probably be able to give a lead and influence the other councillors. This group did not increase sharply after 1392. There had been about fifty-five Guinigi supporters in the council of 180 members elected in March 1392, before the Guinigi victory of 12 May. In that elected in March 1393 there were sixty, but this had dropped to forty-nine in 1394. It varied from thirty-five to forty-five in the years from 1397 to 1400, but the council had by then reduced to 135 members. The proportion of Guinigi supporters may well be rather larger than appears from these figures, as only those included in Dino Guinigi's list or the list of those deputed to keep arms for the *contadini* in 1392 have been included. There were a number of sons or other close relatives of these men, who were probably also Guinigi supporters. In addition some of those who were Anziani for the first time after 1392 sat in the

General Council also, and they too may often have been Guinigi supporters. It is notable too that the General Council contained a larger number of obscure citizens in humble occupations after 1392 than it had done before, and these also may have supported the Guinigi. But even if the number of Guinigi supporters did not rise significantly, the number of their opponents fell sharply. There were seventeen Forteguerra partisans in the council elected in March 1392, and only two or three in the years that followed. This is only to be expected. Dino Guinigi had listed only forty-one Forteguerra supporters, compared with 117 for the Guinigi, and many of those forty-one were dead, in exile, or excluded from office after 1392. But nine or ten men who had supported the Forteguerra were elected to the General Council in the years from 1392 to 1400, though the colleges of electors were dominated by the Guinigi. There was never any sizeable group of known Guinigi opponents in the council, but there might be significant opposition to their proposals; forty votes were cast against a proposal by Niccolò ser Pagani to raise money to hire more forces,[90] for example, or twenty-nine against the proposal for an *Estimo*.[91]

A rather closer control was kept over the Thirty-Six. The number of certain Guinigi supporters never dropped below twenty, though for five of the twelve councils for which the names are known[92] it was below the two-thirds majority required to pass measures. But very few citizens who had been Forteguerra partisans sat in the Thirty-Six after 1392,[93] never more than one of them in any council, and it is probable the Guinigi could always be sure of a majority. They could probably always find the three or four votes needed from among the more independent citizens or among citizens who had become their supporters after 1392. New men were admitted to the Thirty-Six as well as to the college of Anziani. About thirty citizens who had not sat in the Thirty-Six before

[90] *Rif.* 12, p. 413, 17 Feb. 1394. 125 votes in favour.

[91] *Rif.* 13, pp. 38–40, 18 June 1397. 109 votes in favour. There were eight *invitati*, all Guinigi supporters.

[92] The names for the five councils from Sept. 1394 to Sept. 1396 are not known because of the gap in the *Riformagioni*.

[93] Giuffredo Cenami three times, Castruccio Saggina twice, and Michele Michaelis once.

or had relatives there sat after 1392, some of them also becoming Anziani.

The Guinigi had also been advised by Sercambi to keep control of certain other important offices, including the *secretarii*, *conducterii*, and vicariates of Camaiore, Pietrasanta, Montecarlo, and Castiglione. The names of the *secretarii* do not survive for the period after 1392, and those of the *conducterii* are recorded only for the years 1397, 1398 and 1399. These show that the majority of the *conducterii* were Guinigi supporters, but that a quarter or a third of them might be more independent citizens, and in 1398 Giuffredo Cenami, a former Forteguerra supporter, was elected.[94] The important vicariates were almost invariably given to Guinigi supporters, and the important *balìe* chosen to elect the General Council and the Thirty-Six and to make the new *tasche* of Anziani were also controlled by the Guinigi. An overwhelming majority of the citizens chosen for these were Guinigi partisans, but even here independent citizens were not entirely excluded and on two occasions Giuffredo Cenami was elected.[95] In the same way a majority of members of other important *balìe* were friends of the Guinigi, but independent citizens, and even men who had been opponents, were not totally excluded. Examples of this are the *balìa* of thirty citizens elected to raise money 17 February 1394, or the *balìa* of thirty for the *Estimo* 20 June 1397,[96] which included a handful of independent citizens and one or two men who had been Forteguerra partisans, such as messer Ludovico Mercati, Castruccio Saggina, or Giuffredo Cenami. Forteguerra partisans were not merely present in councils or *balìe*; they also spoke in debates, as messer Ludovico Mercati, for example, did in the discussion of a new statute in 1392.[97] Independent citizens were also represented on *balìe* for other less important matters, and are found holding financial or administrative offices. In fact Sercambi's claim that everyone held office

[94] *Rif.* 13, p. 104, 23 Jan. 1398.

[95] As elector of the General Council and Thirty-Six, *Rif.* 13, p. 110, 10 Mar. 1398, for the *tasca* of Anziani, *Rif.* 13, p. 216, 6 Jan. 1399.

[96] *Rif.* 12, p. 413, 17 Feb. 1394, names pp. 416–17. *Rif.* 13, p. 40, 20 June 1397.

[97] *Min.* 4, 13 July 1392.

equally is not without a certain justification.[98] Only in the *balìa* of twelve citizens to rule the city, elected on 2 July 1400, during the outbreak of plague were all the members Guinigi partisans, and that did not prevent them opposing Paolo Guinigi's desire for greater power. Bearing in mind the numbers of the Guinigi supporters, their personal distinction, and the fact that many of the Forteguerra party were dead, exiled, excluded from office in the city or had chosen to leave Lucca, the predominance of the Guinigi and their supporters in councils, offices, and *balìe* may not have appeared unreasonable. Many of those named as Guinigi partisans were members of the leading families, and were among the richest citizens and those who had held office most frequently before 1392. The frequent appointment of such men after 1392, as before, can have caused little comment; their personal qualities and position gave them a claim to a leading role in the city. The introduction of new men into the college of Anziani, councils, and other offices, probably caused more criticism, but none of them held office with any great frequency and none attained a position comparable with that of the leading members of the leading families who had held office regularly before 1392. Only two families reached this kind of position after 1392, probably as a result of their support for the Guinigi. Of these the Avvocati were among the most ancient Lucchese families.[99] The Bocci, though rarely appearing in office before 1392, must have been one of the richest families in the city; Bonaccorso Bocci was assessed at 16,666 florins in the *Estimo* of 1397—the only citizen with an assessment higher than that of Lazzaro di Francesco Guinigi.[100] So both these families had a claim to the highest office independent of their Guinigi partisanship.

[98] Sercambi, I, p. 318.

[99] N. Cianelli, 'De'Conti Rurali nello Stato Lucchese', Dissertazione XII, in *Memorie e Documenti per Servire all'Istoria del Principato Lucchese*, Vol. III, pp. 140-7.

[100] *Estimo* of 1397, Lucca Biblioteca Governativa, MS. 925, f. 253. His wealth could not compare with that of the Guinigi family as a whole, but according to the *Estimo* he was the richest individual in Lucca. It was he who in 1394 had bought the Forteguerra palace, *Rif.* 12, pp. 480-3, 7 Aug. 1394. Antonio, son of Bonaccorso Bocci, married Ginevra, daughter of Michele Guinigi, 14 Oct. 1397, *Archivio Guinigi*, 151, ff. 5v, 31.

It was possible for the Guinigi to control the city while maintaining the outward forms of republican government because they had the support of a strong and numerous group of the leading citizens. In many cases it can only be guessed what caused leading citizens, such as Turellino Bonucci, Opizo and Niccolò Onesti, Franceschino Buzolini, Matteo Cattani, or Dino Moriconi to support the Guinigi, but it is certain that without their support the Guinigi would either have been unable to establish and maintain their control, or would have been obliged to adopt measures that would have aroused hostility, taking over the government more directly, or making greater use of new men of humble origin, dependent upon themselves, whose elevation would have been resented. The support of a powerful and numerous body of leading citizens made it possible for the Guinigi to exercise a very real control without violating the traditional forms of government and without excluding those who had previously held high office and must have been regarded as the natural rulers of the city.

But despite this there seems to have been an atmosphere of tension in the city for much of the period from 1392 to 1400. Some of the measures taken after May 1392 show distrust and fear of disturbances, for example the decree to arm the 200 'confidentes' and the ordinances against fire and riots.[101] The slightest disturbance, springing perhaps from some private quarrel and not from a deliberate attempt to overthrow the government, could have serious consequences. A quarrel in which one man wounded another near the church of S. Cristoforo was taken very seriously because it might have caused a 'rumore'.[102] Giovanni Boccansocchi, who was a Guinigi supporter, was exiled to Pietrasanta for six months for causing a disturbance, though there was no question of suspecting him of disaffection or of any attempt against the government.[103]

[101] See above pp. 276–7 and *Rif.* 12, p. 178, 26 Aug., p. 192, 31 Aug. 1392, pp. 314–16, 24 July 1393.

[102] *Rif.* 12, p. 142, 18 June 1392.

[103] *Rif.* 12, p. 289, 14 Apr. 1393. The terms of the decree show the government's nervousness, 'periculosi sint motus et tumultuatio popularis, non enim facile regitur ensis in manibus furentium popularium'. Giovanni Boccansocchi had apparently gone through the streets armed, accompanied by a band of friends also armed, in pursuit of a private quarrel. He shortly petitioned and was allowed to return, *Rif.* 12, p. 295, 26 May, p. 304, 27 June 1393.

There were, however, plots by exiles and by malcontents within the city. The most serious of the plots in Lucca itself was that involving Piero Rapondi, Niccolò di ser Dino Lombardi, Michele Leoni and Niccolò Ronsini, discovered in January 1394. Piero Rapondi, though involved in the events of 1390–2, had merely been excluded from office, not banished. Niccolò di ser Dino Lombardi had been listed by Dino Guinigi as a Forteguerra partisan, but the other two had not previously appeared as opponents of the Guinigi. According to the sentences against them,[104] the plotters' aim was to procure the return of the Rapondi and other exiles by force and overthrow the Guinigi. The plot had begun in October 1392 when Piero Rapondi had revealed to Michele Leoni and Niccolò di ser Dino Lombardi his intention of going to Paris to confer with his brothers there and get their support. He hoped that Giovanni Rapondi, who had influence with certain captains, would join the plot and induce the captains to provide a force of a hundred lances. It was agreed that Piero should go to Paris and return within a year, and meanwhile Michele and Niccolò were to arrange to raise foot-soldiers in the *contado* and induce any other citizens likely to agree to join in the plot to raise further forces; 'e ben ci confidamo avere con noi de glialtri vestri amici che sonno male contenti de quessto stato come noi'.[105] But it was here that the conspirators came to grief; for one of the citizens they approached was Niccolò Ronsini, and although he at first agreed to join them, he later revealed the plot in return for promises of safety for himself.[106] Though the plot was unsuccessful it could have been very dangerous. In addition to the main plotters a number of others were involved,[107] and with a hundred lances from a mercenary captain, 300 foot-soldiers from the *contado*, and whatever forces and money Piero Rapondi could raise, the plot could have been a serious threat to the Guinigi position.

This was the most dangerous plot, but there were a number of others. In November and December 1393 a certain Stefano

[104] *Sentenze e Bandi*, 85, ff. 13–18^{v}; 86, ff. 3–5, 12 Jan. 1394.

[105] *Sentenze e Bandi*, 85, f. 13^{v}.

[106] *Rif.* 12, p. 403, 11 Jan. 1394. He was banished to Germany.

[107] *Sentenze e Bandi*, 85, ff. 14^{v}–18; 86, ff. 3–5. There were plans to seize various key points in the city.

Jacobi plotted with Niccolò Folchini of Lucca to admit men from the *contado* into the city, where they would seize the arms that were kept in Lucca and use them to start a revolution.[108] There were also attempts against places in the *contado*. In May 1394 three men of Pietrasanta, who were apparently Guelfs, plotted to raise Camaiore and Pietrasanta in rebellion, killing all the Ghibellines there 'et ipsa castra ad regimen et gubernationem partis Ghelfe reducere et domino alterius quam Lucani comunis subicere'. Their intention of seeking outside aid is interesting, but they do not seem to have leaned to any outside power in particular. They were apparently prepared to accept aid indiscriminately from any power willing to provide it. They planned to ask Florence for aid, as might be expected of plotters who were Guelfs, but they also sent a messenger to Giovanni Rapondi to say that if he could get enough men from either the Count of Virtù or Florence to besiege Lucca, they could undertake to put Pietrasanta and Camaiore in his hands. They also mentioned the possibility of having Castiglione 'et redurre tutta la Carfagnana a parte ghelfa'.[109] There was a further plot later in the year to raise Pietrasanta in rebellion by a combination of an attack by 400 lances under two captains hostile to Lucca and a rising of friends within the town. Half a dozen Lucchese were involved in this plot, which was hatched in Pescia, and they claimed to have 60,000 florins put at their disposal by enemies of Lucca.[110] These conspiracies were in time of peace. The situation deteriorated once Lucca became involved in an undeclared war with Pisa. Three Lucchese *banniti* of the vicariate of Camaiore raised Rocca a Pelago in rebellion and handed it over to Opizo da Montegarullo, an enemy of Lucca.[111] A number of Lucchese exiles, such as Piero

[108] *Sentenze e Bandi*, 86, ff. 21-3, Jan. 1394. Stefano was fined 60 florins and confined to Ancona for six months.

[109] *Sentenze e Bandi*, 86, ff. 71-4, 30 May 1394. Another plot had been discovered in Feb., ff. 22-4, 23 Feb. 1394.

[110] *Sentenze e Bandi*, 86, ff. 168-171, 19 Oct. 1394. *Capitano del Popolo*, 13 (not foliated), 2-19 Oct. 1394. The plotting took place in July and August 1394.

[111] *Sentenze e Bandi*, 89, ff. 15-15^v, 13 Apr. 1396, ff. 55-6 men of Soraggio, Silano, and Dallo were condemned for raising these places in rebellion in co-operation with Giovanni da Castiglione, 13 Oct. 1396. *Capitano del Popolo*, 15, ff. 66^v-67, the castellan of Dallo was condemned for betraying the castle to Giovanni da Castiglione for money, 18 Dec. 1398.

Rapondi, messer Carlo Ronghi and Lando Moriconi, returned to Tuscany and congregated in Pisa despite decrees prohibiting them to do so.[112] Their attempts against Lucca became merged in the greater issue of the war with Pisa, but they still found men in the Lucchese *contado* ready to co-operate with Lucca's enemies and admit them to Camaiore or other strongholds.[113]

The feeling of insecurity resulting from the frequent discovery of plots could not fail to have an effect on the internal government of the city. Already early in 1394 it had been decided that more forces must be raised and that all constables and hired soldiers should take an oath of loyalty to each college of Anziani, swearing to obey their orders implicitly and to do nothing without their instructions.[114] After 1395 Lucca had to face the hostility of Pisa, and the close alliance with Florence, which was the Guinigi answer to this, did not meet with the approval of all their fellow citizens. A speaker in the Florentine council said that Lucca had 'duas partes in se discordes, unam scilicet Guinigiorum amicam comunis aliam non.'[115] So the Guinigi had to reckon with a group within the city opposed to their foreign policy, as well as a full-scale war with Pisa and attempts by Lucchese exiles to return by force in co-operation with the Pisans and with the assistance of men in the Lucchese *contado* who sympathized with them.[116]

In the years 1397 to 1400 certain constitutional changes were made which increased Guinigi control over the govern-

[112] Sentences against messer Carlo and Jacopo Ronghi, Piero Rapondi, Pierino and Jacopo Michaelis, Giovanni di Niccolò Diversi, ser Giovanni da Castiglione, ser Antonio ser Tomasi da Camaiore, Giovanni de la Sala, Piero Francisci, Jacobo and Benedetto Campucci, Niccolò *presbiter*, Johannes called Grasso of S. Concordio a Moriano, ser Giovanni Acciai, ser Manne Junctaroni and Lotto Antonii of Camaiore, Giovanni Nerucci *faber*, and Domenico Bonucci, 4 Sept. 1396, *Sentenze e Bandi*, 89, ff. 41-2, *Capitano del Popolo*, 14 (not foliated). Messer Carlo and Jacobo Ronghi had already been declared rebels for failing to observe confines set for them, *Sentenze e Bandi*, 88, ff. 115-16, 11 Oct. 1395, similar sentence against Lando Moriconi, *Sentenze e Bandi*, 87, ff. 61-62^{v}, 31 Aug. 1395.

[113] *Capitano del Popolo*, 15, ff. 100-2, July and Aug. 1397, condemned Dec. 1397, ff. 103-6, Dec. 1397 another plot. *Sentenze e Bandi*, 92, ff. 105-7, details a plot to admit 300 *pedites* from Pisa into Camaiore by night, to be followed by 300 knights to ensure the exiles possession of the town, 19 Dec. 1397.

[114] *Rif.* 12, p. 413, 17 Feb., pp. 425-6, 10 Mar. 1394.

[115] A.S.F., *Consulte*, 31, f. 82^{v}, 18 June 1395.

[116] Sercambi, I, p. 321 *et seq*.

ment. In March 1397 the General Council was reduced from 180 to 135.[117] In June 1398 it was decreed that where the Gonfaloniere was unable to take office because of absence from the city or death another Anziano from the same *terziere* could be elected and the 'vacations' need not be observed, so that another member of the same family could be Gonfaloniere in the same *tasca*.[118] A third change came in January 1399 when the 'vacation' between brother and brother or father and son in the college of Anziani was reduced from four months to two.[119] These changes clearly benefited the Guinigi and facilitated their control. A smaller General Council would be easier to handle. The decree that 'vacations' need not be observed in replacing Gonfaloniere was immediately followed by the election of Bartolomeo di Francesco Guinigi, though his brother Lazzaro had been put in the same *tasca* as Gonfaloniere and held the office in January and February 1399. The reduction of the 'vacation' from four months to two was specifically stated to be for the benefit of members of large families, who found themselves excluded from such offices by the stricter four month 'vacation'. These changes cannot be called illegal or unconstitutional; they were made by the *statutarii*, the *balìa* which had been commissioned to undertake a complete revision of the Statute of 1372, making what changes they thought fit.[120] They undoubtedly had the power to make these changes. But the changes whittled away the safeguards that republics traditionally established against one family acquiring excessive power, and prepared the way for the establishment of a more openly Guinigi regime, in name as well as in fact.

If these changes were legal and constitutional, the same cannot be said of the replacement of Matteo Trenta as Gonfaloniere for May and June 1400 by ser Pietro Giuntori, a Guinigi supporter who probably owed his entry into the college of Anziani to the Guinigi.[121] Although the plague was

[117] *Rif.* 13, p. 22, 10 Mar. 1397.
[118] *Rif.* 13, p. 131, 25 June 1398.
[119] *Rif.* 13, p. 217, 8 Jan. 1399.
[120] *Rif.* 12, pp. 165-6, 13 July, p. 182, 30 Aug. 1392 and later renewals of their authority.
[121] See above, p. 284.

raging in Lucca in 1400, Matteo Trenta was not apparently absent, and the reason given for his replacement was that ser Pietro was 'eloquentiorem et aptiorem'.[122] It is very doubtful that the Anziani and commissioners, who made the decree, had the power to do this. In any case it was a flagrant violation of the statutory regulations governing the election of Anziani. Normally men elected to the college of Anziani were obliged to hold office, and could not be freed from the obligation or replaced except for reasons such as death, illness, or absence from the city. No one had ever been replaced because of his unsuitability, let alone because another man was more suitable. The college of Anziani and especially the Gonfaloniere was the most important office in the state, and the statutes governing the *tasca* were regarded as especially sacred and interference with them as an especially serious matter. The Guinigi had opposed interference with the *tasca* in 1390, when it suited them, but were now found tampering with it themselves. This particular act occurred at a time of crisis, when the Guinigi party was weakened by the death of Lazzaro di Francesco and when the city was endangered by the flight of many citizens to escape the plague. It may have been a panic measure, or at any rate an exceptional measure springing from particularly dangerous circumstances.

But the other changes certainly represent a departure from the old Guinigi policy of mild and constitutional rule, maintaining the outward forms of republican government intact. This greater stringency was probably due, at least in part, to changing circumstances. The Guinigi would naturally feel the need to tighten their control when faced with a full scale war outside the city and opposition to their policy within. But it may also be seen as part of a gradual movement by the Guinigi to increase their control and gather the reins of government more closely into their own hands. Their respect for the old forms of republican government may have been intended as no more than a temporary measure, and one may suspect that even without the crisis caused by the murder of Lazzaro Guinigi in February 1400 and the consequent need to take steps to prevent the complete collapse of Guinigi authority, the

[122] *Rif.* 13, p. 323, 26 Apr. 1400.

Guinigi would have gradually attempted to extinguish the old popular form of government altogether and eventually establish an open *signorìa*.

14

EXTERNAL PROBLEMS 1392-1400

THE events of 12 May 1392 in Lucca had no immediate effect on her foreign policy. The main concern in external affairs at this time was defence against the armed companies formed after the peace concluded in Genoa in January 1392 brought the war between Florence and Milan to an end.[1] These dangers led the Lucchese to join the league already concluded in Bologna on 11 April 1392 between Florence and her allies in the Romagna and Bologna, Padua and Ferrara.[2] But threats from the companies continued, and when Florence proposed a conference of the allies to discuss joint negotiations, Lucca availed herself of this offer and was included in the terms Florence made with Conrad Altimberg in August 1392.[3] She continued to co-operate with Florence and accept Florentine protection in negotiations with armed companies in the next few months.[4]

[1] The Tuscan cities had begun taking precautions against such attacks 15 Jan. 1392, A.S.F. *Consulte*, 29, f. 25^{v}. For these threats and negotiations with the companies *Consulte*, 29, ff. 54^{v}-55^{v}, 16 Mar., f. 57, 19 Mar., f. 57^{v}, 21 Mar. ff. 62^{v}-63^{v}, 4 Apr. 1392, *Cart. Sign. Miss.* 23, ff. 3^{v}-4, 5^{v}, 6-8^{v}. Despite efforts at resistance Lucca had to come to terms, paying 10,000 florins, *Rif.* 12, p. 162, 6 July, p. 164, 11 July 1392. The agreement is in *Capitoli*, 33, pp. 503-4, 3 July 1392, giving the payment as 9,000 florins and gifts of silks. Minerbetti p. 161 says 8,000 florins. Other Tuscan cities also had to pay, Silva, *Governo*, p. 277.

[2] Pisa and Lucca joined this league after some months of negotiations, Silva, *Governo*, p. 278. Copy of the league *Capitoli*, 25, pp. 397-414, 11 July 1392. A.S.F., *Consulte*, 29, ff. 65^{v}-66, 17 April, f. 67, 18 Apr., f. 69, 25 Apr., ff. 84-5, 10 June, ff. 86^{v}-87, 15 June 1392. Letters to Pisa and Lucca, *Cart. Sign. Miss.* 23, f. 14^{v}, 27 Apr., f. 17, 10 May 1392. Lucca granted authority to her sindic for this league, *Rif.* 12, pp. 160-1, 6 July 1392.

[3] Terms dated 29 Aug. 1392, *Capitoli*, 25, pp. 421-3, *Reg.*, no. 1500, 29 Aug. 1392. A.S.F. *Consulte*, 29, f. 118^{v}, 26 Aug. 1392, *Cart Sign. Miss.* 23, f. 33^{v}, 3 Aug., ff. 38-9, 17 Aug. 1392. Silva, *Governo*, p. 281.

[4] Florence made terms for Lucca as well as for herself with Biordo Michelotti May 1393, *Capitoli*, 26, pp. 3-6, 5 May 1393. A.S.F., *Consulte*, 30, ff. 20^{v}-21, 21 Apr., f. 21^{v}, 22 Apr., f. 23^{v}, 28 Apr., ff. 24-24^{v}, 2 May, ff. 25^{v}-27, 3 May 1393. There was also a joint renewal of the agreement with Conrad of Altimberg, Biordo Michelotti and others in November 1393, *Capitoli*, 33, p. 527, 15 Nov. 1393. Lucca appointed sindics for this *Rif.* 12, pp. 350-1, 16 Nov. 1393, ratified 20 Nov. 1393, pp. 351-2. Florence sent the terms for Lucchese approval *Reg.* no. 1505, 16 Nov. 1393. *Consulte*,

But if the change in government in Lucca had no real effect on Lucchese foreign policy an event occurred a few months later which was to have a very profound effect on her relations with her neighbours and completely change her whole external policy. This was the fall of Pietro Gambacorta and his replacement as ruler of Pisa by Jacopo d'Appiano in October 1392. Ser Jacopo d'Appiano was able to draw some of his support from Lucca and the Lucchese *contado* in his *coup d'état* against Pietro Gambacorta, and several chroniclers make the interesting suggestion that Lazzaro Guinigi himself connived at this.[5] There can be no doubt that forces for Jacopo d'Appiano's seizure of power were gathered on Lucchese territory, many of them Lucchese subjects,[6] and that some who had supported Lazzaro Guinigi against the Forteguerra faction in May 1392 were involved. Chief among them was Andrea Stornelli of Lucca and ser Giovanni Linelli of Castiglione. Andrea Stornelli had played a leading part in the fighting in May 1392, and was responsible for acts of violence, including the summary execution of messer Bartolomeo Forteguerra and the deaths of ser Jacobo and Francesco di ser Angelo of Camaiore, ser Conte Puccini and several others. He had been rewarded for his efforts by the Guinigi, but proved difficult to control and was still committing acts of violence several days after the Guinigi victory.[7] Ser Giovanni Linelli was listed by Sercambi as one of the leading members of the Ghibelline party in Castiglione and a firm Guinigi supporter.[8]

30, f. 81, 4 Nov. 1393, *Cart. Sign. Miss.* 23, ff. 156, 157v, 159, 162v, Pisa and Lucca were to pay Florence 160 and 80 florins a month respectively as their share of the cost of this agreement.

[5] Minerbetti, p. 164 'egli [ser Jacopo d'Appiano] fece una ragunata del contado di Lucca di ottocento fanti di consentimento di Lazero di Francesco Guinigi'. Similarly Soz. Pist. col. 1152. *Corpus Chronicorum Bononensium*, R.I.S., n.s. XVIII, pt. 1, Vol. 3, p. 439 does not specifically mention Lazzaro Guinigi, but refers to forces from Lucca. Also *Chroniche Fiorentine di ser Naddo da Montecatino, Delizie degli Eruditi Toscani*, Vol. XVIII, p. 113, Sardo, p. 253.

[6] 800 fanti according to Minerbetti, p. 164, Sardo, p. 253, has over 500. *Corpus Chron. Bonon.*, cit. p. 439, says over 1,000. O. Banti, 'Iacopo d'Appiano e le origini della sua signoria in Pisa', *Bollettino Storico Pisano*, Vols. XX–XXI (1951–2), pp. 29–34.

[7] Sercambi, I, pp. 278, 280, 282–4. Also pp. 453–4 for notes on his later career.

[8] Sercambi, III, p. 18. He was still employed by Lucca after the *coup d'état* against Pietro Gambacorta, e.g. as captain of the forces sent to aid the Marchese of Ferrara against rebels, Sercambi, I, p. 298, *Rif.* 12, p. 318, 25 Aug. 1393. See also Sercambi, I, p. 455, for notes on his later career.

He and Andrea Stornelli had already been involved in a plot against Pietro Gambacorta in June,[9] and in the successful *coup d'état* of 21 October they led men from the Garfagnana and Six Miles, 'e alcuni soldati di Luccha, senza saputa de'signori nè del consiglio'.[10] This force played a vital part in d'Appiano's seizure of power as Sercambi points out almost with pride, though he is at pains to assert that the Lucchese authorities had tried to turn them back.[11]

With forces from Lucca and leading supporters of the Guinigi involved it is not difficult to see how suspicions that the Guinigi had connived at Jacopo d'Appiano's seizure of power arose. But it is very doubtful that these suspicions were justified. The motive of ser Giovanni Linelli and Andrea Stornelli was presumably Ghibelline party feeling, which would cause them to assist ser Jacopo d'Appiano as a Ghibelline and a friend of Milan and enemy of Florence.[12] Ghibellinism and pro-Milanese feeling is the only possible motive for Lazzaro Guinigi to have connived at the fall of Pietro Gambacorta. But we have already seen that it is doubtful whether the Guinigi can be regarded as Ghibellines in any real sense, and even more doubtful whether they can be regarded as pro-Milanese and anti-Florentine. Even if they leaned slightly towards Milan it is unlikely that they would have been willing to take any risks in pursuit of a pro-Milanese policy. The Lucchese were always watchful and suspicious of their neighbours, especially the Pisans who were old enemies

[9] This involved bringing men into Lucchese territory from Florence and raising others in the vicariates of Pietrasanta and Castiglione. Sercambi, I, pp. 285–7, Minerbetti, p. 160. O. Banti, *Iacopo d'Appiano, Economia, Società e Politica del Comune di Pisa al suo Tramonto (1392–1399)* (Pisa, 1971), p. 13, Silva, *Governo*, p. 282.

[10] Sercambi, I, p. 288.

[11] Ibid., pp. 288–93 for Sercambi's account of the *coup* of Oct. 1392, pp. 293, 308–9 for assertions that Jacopo d'Appiano would never have achieved power in Pisa without Lucchese aid. He felt that Jacopo d'Appiano had cause to be grateful; in reproaching him for his later hostility he said 'u'è l'amicitia la quale avei col comune di Luccha', p. 308. On the importance of the role played by the forces from Lucca, Banti, *Iacopo d'Appiano*, p. 63.

[12] For the close relations of Stornelli and d'Appiano, Banti, *Iacopo d'Appiano*, p. 190, note 1. For the later careers of Stornelli and ser Giovanni Linelli as Ghibellines and friends of Pisa and Milan, see below, pp. 305, 313 and also Bongi's notes in Sercambi, I, pp. 453–5. On the Ghibelline element among d'Appiano's supporters in Pisa, Banti, *Iacopo d'Appiano*, pp. 72–5.

and rivals. Pietro Gambacorta had been a good neighbour and Lucca had only recently renewed her league with Pisa.[13] She would have been suspicious of any change of regime in a city as near as Pisa, especially when it replaced a tried friend by a comparatively unknown quantity. One vital question is whether or not Jacopo d'Appiano had as yet shown any signs of hostility towards Lucca. If he had not, it is just conceivable that the Guinigi might have connived at his seizure of power, believing him to be a friend of Lucca and the Guinigi family, only to get a very rude awakening later. But if the Florentines were to be believed, he showed hostility to Lucca very early. They wrote on 24 October 1392 warning Lucca that a Lucchese exile, Jacopo Trenta, had been detained in Pescia, carrying letters from ser Jacopo d'Appiano, and had confessed under torture that Vanni d'Appiano was plotting with certain Lucchese to put Lucca under Pisan rule with the support of the Count of Virtù.[14] A letter dated 1 March 1393 suggests that ser Jacopo d'Appiano was also trying to raise the fortress of Dallo in rebellion against Lucca.[15] No ruler of Lucca would have had cause to help such a man to achieve power.

Florence appears to have accepted Lucchese assurances about their attitude to Pisa. They may have had some

[13] A league 'ad sese invicem defendendum manutenendum et conservandum in eius statu et libertate pacificis in quibus ad presens sunt duraturam hinc ad quinquennium contra omnem et quamcumque personam intentem volentem seu intendentem facere vel attentare contra libertatem et statum liberalem utriusque comunis vel hostiliter invadentem molestantem turbantem occupantem vel inquietantem vel invadere molestare turbare occupare vel inquietare volentem per vim armorum sedictionis vel tractatus supradictas civitates vel aliquam earum vel earum [*sic*] vel alicuius earum territoria fortias et districtus. Et predicta intelligantur ad defensam vel offensam infra territoria predictorum comunium tantum dummodo gens armigera unius comunis non possit ingredi in territorium alterius sine dicti comunis in cuius territorio ingredi quereretur expressa licentia et consensu', *Delib.* 133, ff. 53–55^{v}, 28 Aug. 1392. The terms included the aid of fifty lances and 100 crossbowmen from Pisa to Lucca and half this from Lucca to Pisa, and clauses about the treatment of *banniti*, debtors etc. *Sindicatus* for the league, *Rif.* 12, p. 177, 26 Aug. 1392.

[14] Silva, *Governo*, p. 289 and letter in A.S.F., *Cart. Sign. Miss.* 23, f. 56^{v}, 24 Oct. 1392, quoted there Appendix Doc. 40. Also A.S.F., *Consulte*, 29, f. 143, 15 Nov. 1392. It was, of course, in Florentine interests to alarm the Lucchese and arouse their suspicions of Jacopo d'Appiano. The letters from d'Appiano were said to be unclear—'multum obscure et amphibologice loquebantur'—and the confession of Jacopo Trenta had been obtained under torture. The Florentines themselves expressed doubts about its reliability, but warned the Lucchese to be vigilant, Banti, *Iacopo d'Appiano*, pp. 15–16, 142.

[15] *Reg.*, no. 1502, 1 Mar. 1393.

suspicions. Speakers in the Florentine *pratiche* advised that 'unus orator mittatur Lucam qui hortetur eos ad conservationem domini Petri et quod gens de Lombardia non descendat', 'et mittatur unus orator Lucam qui sciat de intentione eorum et hortetur ipsos ad libertatem', 'et cum Lucanis et aliis procuretur quod ipsi sint nobiscum in pace'.[16] But if they did have doubts about the Lucchese attitude, it was apparently possible to allay them. They asked the Lucchese to send ambassadors to Pisa to help restore calm there, and thanked them cordially for having done so so promptly. In the same letter they said that although certain Lucchese had played a large part in the disturbances, 'quod certi sumus contra vestram voluntatem et beneplacitum processisse'.[17] They wrote accounts of the revolution in Pisa to a number of other states without mentioning that the Lucchese, much less Lazzaro Guinigi, were involved.[18]

The version of the events of October 1392 which the Florentines accepted and which is contained in Sercambi, in fact, seems the most likely; that is, that Jacopo d'Appiano did have assistance from the Lucchese *contado* and from Lucca itself, and that two prominent partisans of the Guinigi were among those chiefly involved, but that they acted without the approval of the Guinigi, who knew nothing of their intentions until it was too late.[19] There seems to be no very convincing reason why the Guinigi should have connived at the fall of Pietro Gambacorta and if Jacopo d'Appiano had already shown hostility towards Lucca, every reason why they should not. It is therefore probable that ser Giovanni Linelli and Andrea Stornelli were acting on their own initiative without the knowledge of the Guinigi.

Apart from the attempt to raise Dallo in rebellion Jacopo d'Appiano did not immediately show hostility serious enough to threaten Lucca's security or to lead to open war. But in

[16] A.S.F. *Consulte*, 29, ff. 138^{v}, 140, 140^{v}, 22 Oct. 1392.

[17] A.S.F. *Cart. Sign. Miss.* 23, ff. 56^{v}, 57, 24 Oct. 1392.

[18] Ibid., ff. 54^{v}-55 to Bologna, d'Este and other allies, 22 Oct. 1392, f. 55^{v}, to the Pope, 23 Oct. 1392.

[19] Sercambi, I, pp. 288-9. He also asserts that neither the Guinigi nor the vicar of Pietrasanta, Niccolò di Ceccorino di Poggio, nor anyone else in authority knew of the efforts to raise forces in Lucchese territory in June 1392, pp. 285-7.

September 1394 a force of mixed cavalry and infantry attacked Lucchese territory from Pisa, and this was sufficiently serious for the Lucchese to appeal to Bernardon de Serres, captain general of the Florentine forces, to send them aid quickly to enable them to defeat the Pisans.[20] In February 1395 Jacopo d'Appiano sent orders to Andrea Stornelli in Lucca to capture a certain Federigo Gonzaga. He was captured between Lucca and Pietrasanta, and taken first to Pisa, and according to Sercambi, was then sent bound and under guard to the lord of Milan.[21] This attack on a distinguished foreigner travelling through Lucchese territory was bitterly resented in Lucca. The government sent an embassy to Pisa to complain of the insult and hastened to punish those Lucchese who were involved. Andrea Stornelli confessed under torture and was executed. According to Sercambi the execution of Andrea Stornelli greatly angered d'Appiano and this was the origin of his hostility to Lucca, which was to result in open war in 1395–8.[22] When he heard of

[20] Letter of 24 Sept. 1394 *Anz. Temp. Lib.* 429, no. 1516 in *Reg.*

[21] Sercambi, I, p. 309. Tommasi, p. 278.

[22] Sercambi, I, pp. 310, 313. Banti, *Iacopo d'Appiano*, pp. 190–4 argues that Stornelli was probably innocent, and that the original reason for his arrest was the hope of exchanging him for the captured Gonzaga. His execution was not at first envisaged, otherwise Lucca would not have sent an ambassador to Pisa at the risk of his life. Banti suggests that Stornelli's execution was rendered necessary by his revelations under torture of plans for further internal revolutions in Lucca in support of 'quella delle due fazioni che era più favorevole al Visconti'. He suspects that certain of the Guinigi may have been implicated in this, and it was thus necessary to get rid of Stornelli quickly. The whole theory rests on the assumption that there were still two factions in Lucchese internal affairs, contending for power, and that one was pro-Florentine and the other pro-Milanese. This fails to take account of the completeness of the Guinigi victory. Though there were doubtless elements in Lucca that regarded the Guinigi and their policy with disfavour, the opposing faction had been crushed in May 1392 and could not provide effective opposition to Guinigi policy. In any case the two factions had not apparently taken different lines on foreign policy before 1392. Had the Guinigi wished to take a more openly pro-Milanese line in 1395 they could doubtless have done so without any need to engage in internal intrigues. As the Guinigi were in effective control in Lucca any plot to bring about a change in the government must have been directed against them. Andrea Stornelli had been an active Guinigi supporter in 1392, though his conduct after that may have been an embarrassment to them; apart from his involvement in the *coup* against Pietro Gambacorta he may have been one of those concerned in attacks on Florentine territory in November 1392 (see note 30). If he had to choose between his obligations to the Guinigi and those to d'Appiano, he would perhaps have chosen the latter, but he was probably still on good terms with the Guinigi in 1395; Civitali says that his execution took place 'nonostante che Nicolao Guinigi fosse gonfaloniere et amico dello

the execution he attempted to seize the Lucchese ambassador in Pisa, and finding he had already left, seized instead certain merchants and other Lucchese citizens who happened to be in Pisa. At the end of May 1395 Lucca was attacked by the company of Broglio and Brandolino at the instigation of Jacopo d'Appiano. They stayed on Lucchese territory for about ten days, robbing and burning and taking many prisoners before Lucca was able to collect some forces of her own and about 150 lances sent to her aid from Florence and 100 from Bologna and drive them off laden with booty towards Pisa.[23]

The Lucchese had also appealed to Giangaleazzo for aid, although they must have had doubts about his attitude. He had been involved in the capture of Federigo Gonzaga, who had been sent to Pavia, and he had interceded for the Lucchese condemned for this.[24] Broglio and Brandolino were in his service and he had sent them to the aid of Jacopo d'Appiano, his ally in Tuscany. He had instructed them not to attack the Lucchese and hastened to apologize for the damage they had done,[25] but he also attempted to excuse ser Jacopo,[26] and his response to the Lucchese request for aid was to offer fifty lances from the forces he had stationed in Pisa, which

---

Stornelli', f. 370. There is in fact no evidence that Stornelli was executed because of his connections with a conspiracy in Lucca. The evidence Banti quotes from the Florentine *Consulte* about divisions within Lucca on the question of foreign policy and the attempts of d'Appiano to overturn the Lucchese government belong to a period several months after the capture of Federigo Gonzaga and after the attack on Lucca by the company of Broglio and Brandolino had caused the Guinigi to move closer to Florence.

[23] Sercambi, I, pp. 311–12, Minerbetti, p. 197 says 100 and 60 lances. Minerbetti sees this attack as an attempt by d'Appiano against the regime in Lucca, 'Credesi che facesse per far rivolgere lo stato di Lucca'. Speakers in the Florentine *Consulte* also feared threats to the existing regime in Lucca, *Consulte*, 31, f. 83, 'quia senserat quod querebatur subvertere status Lucanorum per illos etiam de Carfagnana et dominum Jacobum de Appiano et quod illa civitas habet duas partes in se discordes, una scilicet Guinigiorum amicam comunis, alia non, et illi potentes sunt habeatur liga cum ipsi', 18 June 1395. Banti, *Iacopo d'Appiano*, p. 192, note 11.

[24] Sercambi, I, pp. 310–11. Lucca had agreed 'per meglio di comune' to quash the sentences against them on his request.

[25] *Reg.* nos. 1521–4, 1526–7, 2143–4, 2146. Full text of some of these letters in Landogna, 'La politica dei Visconti in Toscana', Docs. XXIII–XXVI. The originals are in *Anz. Temp. Lib.* 429.

[26] D'Appiano denied responsibility and Giangaleazzo supported him, Banti, *Iacopo d'Appiano*, p. 194, note 16. *Reg.*, nos. 1526–7.

would be sent on any request to d'Appiano.[27] He failed to realize that the Lucchese by now saw d'Appiano as an inveterate enemy, and would regard any Milanese troops coming from Pisa, where they were under d'Appiano's orders, as just as much their enemies as Broglio and Brandolino.[28]

The hostility of Jacopo d'Appiano was now Lucca's main preoccupation and the change of attitude in Pisa brought about a change in Lucchese foreign policy. While Pisa under Pietro Gambacorta had pursued a peaceful foreign policy, Lucca had been able to remain neutral and on friendly terms with all her neighbours. Her most immediate worry had been the excessive power and latent acquisitiveness of Florence. She had been able to balance this by remaining on cordial terms with the Visconti, so that she might if necessary rely on Milanese aid, should she find herself attacked from Florence. But this policy of balance was now no longer possible. The hostility of Jacopo d'Appiano changed and complicated Lucchese foreign policy. It was no longer a matter of finding a counterbalance to the power of Florence, and even if the Guinigi party would have preferred a pro-Milanese foreign policy, the first consideration now was to obtain adequate protection against hostile attacks from Pisa. D'Appiano, who threatened Lucca's security, had Giangaleazzo's complete confidence. He was supplied with Milanese forces, and Giangaleazzo had shown that he failed to realize the extent to which Lucca felt herself threatened. A ruler of Milan, who supported Lucca's most dangerous enemy and had complete confidence in him, could no longer be regarded as a reliable ally or used as a counterbalance to Florence. Lucca was in urgent need of protection against the ruler of Pisa and, as she could not find it in Milan , she turned to Florence.

Relations between Florence and Lucca had not been entirely cordial between 1392 and 1395. They had co-operated against the companies,[29] but each city had some cause for complaint against the other. There was hostility between

[27] *Reg.*, nos. 1522, 1527.

[28] Sercambi, I, pp. 312–13 records that the Lucchese felt that if they sent to Pisa for aid 'aremo i nimici dentro e fuori'.

[29] Above p. 300. Also A.S.F. *Cart. Sign. Miss.* 24, f. 12v, 31 Mar., f. 34v, 30 May 1394.

communes on the borders, and exiles of one city found refuge in the territory of the other, from where they plotted against their own city. In November 1392 Florence complained that attacks on her territory were being plotted from within the Lucchese state, and she claimed that those responsible were 'vestros illos amicos qui vobis insciis ad subvertendum statum civitatis Pisane pernitiosissime congregarunt', and demanded redress.[30] In 1393 Florence complained again about the plotting of Lucchese subjects against her, naming especially messer Giovanni Guarzoni of Pescia, a Florentine exile who was also a Lucchese citizen.[31] The causes for complaint were not all on the Florentine side. Lucca sent ambassadors to complain that Florentine subjects were involved in violence and wheel-breaking at Villa Basilica,[32] and Florence apologized for the damage done and assured the Lucchese that those guilty had been adequately punished.[33] In May 1394 Florence came under suspicion of plotting with Lucchese exiles to raise Pietrasanta in rebellion against Lucca. The Lucchese exiles involved in this do seem to have planned to seek foreign aid, though they seem to have been just as willing to seek it from Milan as from Florence.[34] But Florence vigorously protested their innocence, and claimed that the source of these rumours was Jacopo d'Appiano, who wished to make trouble and to sow discord between Florence and Lucca.[35]

These complaints concerned the activities of exiles and other private individuals. They were causes for irritation, but were not particularly serious. They did not involve the

[30] A.S.F. *Cart. Sign. Miss.* 23, ff. 61, 5 Nov., 61^{v}, 6 Nov. 1392. *Consulte*, 29, ff. 143, 5 Nov., 143^{v}, 6 Nov., 145^{v}, 11 Nov. 1392. The Lucchese must have given satisfaction because they were thanked, *Consulte*, 29, f. 150, 27 Nov. 1392.

[31] A.S.F., *Cart. Sign. Miss.* 23, ff. 83^{v}–84, 12 Feb. 1393 (Fl. style 1392), f. 87, 17 Feb. 1393 (Fl. style 1392). There were other similar complaints about Lucchese subjects later, *Cart. Sign. Miss.* 24, f. 94^{v}, 11 Dec. 1394.

[32] *Rif.* 12, p. 407, 31 Jan. 1394. A.S.F. *Cart. Sign. Miss.* 23, ff. 184–184^{v}, 10 Feb. 1394 (Fl. style 1393). Condemnations of eight Lucchese subjects to beheading for this, *Sentenze e Bandi*, 85, ff. 29^{v}–32, 23 Mar. 1394.

[33] A.S.F. *Cart. Sign. Miss.* 24, f. 12, 30 Mar. 1394. Other complaints about Florentine subjects later, ibid., f. 95^{v}, 17 Dec. 1394.

[34] See above p. 295.

[35] A.S.F. *Cart. Sign. Miss.* 24, f. 34^{v}, 30 May 1394. Protests of ser Jacopo, ibid., f. 35, 1 June, ff. 36^{v}–37, 6 June 1394.

Lucchese or Florentine states. More serious was the matter of Opizo da Montegarullo da Frignano, a neighbour of Lucca. Lucca had sent aid to Marchese d'Este on his reqest for the recovery of certain castles which Opizo da Montegarullo had raised in rebellion against him.[36] But Opizo was a Florentine protégé, and Florence was quick to protest at these attacks upon him, and attempted to mediate between Opizo, Ferrara, and Lucca.[37] She also protested at the support given by Lucca and Pisa to other nobles, Lancilotto and Guaspare da Montecuccolo, who were enemies of both Opizo and Florence.[38] Nevertheless she made efforts to minimize ill-feeling on account of these nobles. When early in 1396 Opizo seized the Lucchese fortress of Rocca a Pelago with the assistance of certain Florentine subjects, Florence hastened to assure Lucca that she had had nothing to do with this, and that every effort had been made to punish those responsible and to ensure that nothing similar could happen in the future.[39]

But these grievances and causes for complaint were quickly forgotten in view of the danger from Jacopo d'Appiano in 1395. The Florentines were very ready to send aid to Lucca. Many speakers in the Florentine *pratiche* urged that aid be sent to Lucca as quickly as possible, even suggesting withdrawing forces from elsewhere if need be.[40] They saw the hand of Giangaleazzo very clearly in the attacks on Lucca, and feared that he would seek to use Jacopo d'Appiano and disaffected elements in the Garfagnana to overthrow the regime in Lucca, taking advantage too of divisions within the city.[41] It was therefore urged that a league should be made with Lucca as quickly as possible. The Florentines were prepared to agree to keep forces in Lucca and to share the costs of fortifying the passes of the Lucchese state. There was a certain amount of

[36] Sercambi, I, pp. 295–304. *Rif.* 12, p. 318, 25 Aug. 1393.

[37] A.S.F. *Cart. Sign. Miss.* 23, f. 144, 3 Sept. 1393. *Consulte*, 30, f. 64^{v}, 4 Sept., f. 65^{v}, 5 Sept., f. 66^{v}, 9 Sept. 1394.

[38] *Consulte*, 30, f. 133, 19 June 1394. The Lucchese greatly resented Florentine attacks on them, Sercambi, II, pp. 35–6.

[39] A.S.F. *Cart. Sign. Miss.* 24, f. 183, 22 Feb. 1396 (Fl. style 1395). Sercambi, I, pp. 319–21.

[40] A.S.F. *Consulte*, 31, ff. 79–80^{v}, 29 and 30 May 1395.

[41] Ibid., f. 82^{v}, 18 June 1395.

haggling in the negotiations, the Lucchese wishing to ensure that they got the maximum amount of aid and financial assistance, and the Florentines wishing to limit their expenses and retain as much authority and initiative in the new league as possible, but agreement was in the interests of both cities and was quickly reached.[42] The league was concluded 19 July 1395, to last for five years. It was to be purely defensive, directed against the armed companies and other attackers. Lucca and Florence were the only members, though provision was made for the admission of Bologna, Perugia, and Siena, but not Pisa.[43]

The account of Sercambi shows that many Lucchese were reluctant to make a league with Florence and that it was only the extremely dangerous situation caused by the attacks from Pisa and fears for the future that caused her to do so.[44] This is confirmed by the report of a conversation the Lucchese envoys in Florence had with an imperial ambassador in 1397. The ambassador reproached the Lucchese for their alliance with the Florentines, who were the friends of France and the anti-Pope. The Lucchese envoys defended their city by recounting the attacks of ser Jacopo d'Appiano and the unsatisfactory replies of the Count of Virtù to their protests, 'le quali funno ultimamente che noi avessimo patientia, perchè era lo migliore remedio che potessemo avere'. Lucca had therefore been obliged to appeal to the Florentines for aid, and had had no choice but to agree when the Florentines proposed a league between the two cities, though it was Florence and not Lucca that had suggested this.[45]

These probably were the considerations that led the government of Lucca to accept the idea of a league with Florence, but Florentine sources make it very clear that the league was the policy of the Guinigi and their party, and that not all the

[42] Ibid., ff. 83, 84, 23 June, ff. 85v–86, 30 June 1395.

[43] Copy of the league of 19 July 1395 in *Capitoli*, 26, pp. 11–17. According to Sercambi one of the terms was that the Florentines were to keep 100 lances in Lucca, but there is no mention of this in the text, Sercambi, I, p. 316. Banti, *Iacopo d'Appiano*, pp. 195–6.

[44] Sercambi, I, p. 316. Landogna, 'La politica dei Visconti in Toscana', p. 184.

[45] *Reg.*, no. 1738, 19 May 1397. Letter of Niccolò di Ceccorino di Poggio and ser Guido da Pietrasanta, envoys in Florence. As they were excusing Lucca for having made the league they may well have exaggerated her unwillingness.

Lucchese supported it. There is perhaps a hint of this in Minerbetti, who says 'per questa cagione [i.e. the Pisan attacks] quelli che reggeano Lucca rimasono e furono poi molto amici de'Fiorentini, e lega e patti di concordie feciono insieme'.[46] The Florentines clearly regarded the Guinigi as men with whom they could negotiate. The Florentine ambassadors were to discuss with the Guinigi the amount the Lucchese were to pay for the joint forces.[47] They were to discuss with Lazzaro di Francesco the probable movements of the enemy.[48] They were to urge him to peace with Opizo da Montegarullo. They were to ask him to supply certain allies with victuals. They were to speak to him about capturing a certain Florentine rebel.[49] In one case the ambassadors were instructed to speak to the Guinigi, if they failed to get satisfaction from the Lucchese authorities, 'se i Lucchesi pur dinegassono la pace tra Opizo e loro, parlatene con Lazaro e con gli altri de Guinigi e con altri cittadini che vi paresse quanto fa per lo stato loro che pace sia . . . inducendogli a operare chella loro comunità sia contenta della detta pace'.[50] In other cases they were instructed to consult with Lazzaro and the other Guinigi first, and then discuss as much of their business with the Anziani of Lucca as the Guinigi thought fit, 'dicendo loro quello che parra a detti Guinigi che dobbiate dire delle dette cose e altro no'.[51] It is clear in fact that the alliance was the policy of the Guinigi. It is also clear that by no means all their fellow citizens were equally convinced of its necessity. The fact that the Florentine ambassadors did not feel free to discuss with the Anziani everything they discussed with the Guinigi would indicate this, even if there were not definite assertions in Sercambi that the alliance was unpopular in many quarters in Lucca and the *contado*. There can be no doubt that Lucchese opinion was divided about the league

[46] Minerbetti, p. 197.

[47] A.S.F. *Dieci di Balìa: Miss. Legaz. Commis.* 2, f. 30v, 3 July 1396. Instructions to Florentine ambassadors going to Lucca. Also ff. 34–34v, 16 July 1396. There is also one isolated letter from Florence to Lazzaro Guinigi earlier, A.S.F., *Cart. Sign. Miss.* 24, f. 22, 5 May 1394.

[48] A.S.F. *Dieci di Balìa: Miss. Legaz. Commis.* 2, f. 33, 14 July, f. 37, 18 July 1396.

[49] Ibid., ff. 29v–30, 3 July 1396.

[50] Ibid., ff. 28v–29, 23 June 1396.

[51] Ibid., ff. 31v–32, 11 July, f. 37, 18 July, f. 39, 22 July 1396.

from the very beginning. Indeed the Guinigi may have underestimated the opposition that an alliance with Florence would arouse. Sercambi relates that the Lucchese regretted the league almost as soon as it was concluded and would have liked to go back on it, but for the consideration of the promises she had made, the injuries she had received from Pisa and fears for the future.[52] Despite the unpopularity of the league in many quarters Lucca was to be a close ally of Florence for the next two or three years, looking to her for aid and protection.[53]

Lucca was soon to find herself in need of support, for in 1396 certain exiles tried to raise the *contado* in rebellion and procure their return to the city by force with the aid of Lucca's enemies. The attack was led by Count Giovanni da Barbiano, nominally in the service of the Lucchese exiles,[54] but Pisa provided money and forces despite an agreement signed in Florence in May 1396, which included an undertaking that the signatories would not attack each other and would resist armed companies.[55] Messer Carlo Ronghi and Lando Moriconi were in Pisa in the spring of 1396, and Opizo da Montegarullo, who in February captured the Lucchese castle of Rocca a Pelago, also found refuge there.[56] Lucchese *contadini* were involved and a certain Martino Guerra of Soraggio, who acted as a go-between, fell under suspicion, was

[52] Sercambi, I, p. 316, 'Della quale legha molto se ne mostrò il ducha di Milano mal contento, et tucti ghibellini di Luccha & del contado; intanto che, se con honesto modo se ne fusse potuto riuscire con honore et salvessa di comune, si sere'facto. Ma le'mpromesse facte, e anche le'ngurie ricevute da Pisa et etiando la paura dell'avenire, si mantenne quello che era fermato per lo dicto Nicolao come inbasciadore di Lucca & per Firenza'. A Milanese ambassador was in Lucca in Nov. 1395, urging the Lucchese to abandon the Florentine alliance, but he was dismissed by Lucca. A.S.F. *Dieci di Balìa: Relazioni di ambasciatori*, 1, f. 8, 23 Nov. 1395. Banti, *Iacopo d'Appiano*, pp. 196, 199-200.

[53] She was named as a Florentine adherent in the league with France of 29 Sept. 1396 and in other negotiations, *Reg.*, nos. 1538-9, 1738. Sercambi, I, pp. 354-5, Tommasi, p. 280.

[54] According to Minerbetti, p. 205, the company of Giovanni da Barbiano numbered 800 horsemen, Sardo, p. 270 says 1200. Also *Reg.*, nos. 1535-7. The duke of Milan was believed to be involved, nos. 1633, 1902.

[55] The signatories included Milan, Pisa, Siena, Lucca, and Florence, 16 May 1396. Minerbetti, p. 195. Copies of the agreement in A.S.S., *Capitoli*, 106 (not foliated), A.S.F., *Capitoli*, 50, ff. 165-70. Landogna, 'La politica dei Visconti in Toscana', p. 181, Banti, *Iacopo d'Appiano*, pp. 200-2.

[56] Sercambi, I, pp. 319-21.

interrogated, confessed, and was beheaded in May 1396.[57] There was fighting in Lucchese and Pisan territory in June and July with the Lucchese rebels aided by Giovanni da Barbiano and Pisa, and the Lucchese aided by the nominally independent company of Bartolomeo da Prato, which had Florentine backing,[58] and which was also supporting the Gambacorta and other Pisan exiles in their attempts to return to Pisa by force.[59] Lucca was by no means passive in the face of these attacks. She sent an army against Opizo da Montegarullo, which had some success,[60] and in a battle against Giovanni da Barbiano and the Lucchese exiles in July she captured many prisoners and horses and almost all the baggage including many banners, though part of this was later recaptured.[61] Inconclusive fighting continued into August, and Lucca suffered from the presence of both allied and enemy forces on her territory and had some difficulty in finding supplies for the Bolognese and Florentines.[62]

In August there was a further threat when ser Giovanni Linelli of Castiglione, Pierino, son of Bartolomeo Michaelis and other exiles with forces brought from Lombardy, according to Sercambi with the consent of the duke of Milan, attacked the Garfagnana and captured the fortress of Dallo. They were quickly driven off by a combined force of Lucchese and Florentines and Dallo recaptured, but a disturbing factor was that many Garfagnini had connived at the invasion, and it was considered necessary to sentence about thirty men of Lucca, Silano, Soraggio, and Dallo to exile and to ravage the area in reprisal in order to hold it more securely in future.[63] In

[57] Sercambi, I, p. 321. *Sentenze e Bandi*, 89, ff. 51–54^{v}, 20 May 1396.

[58] Florence could therefore deny responsibility, as she did to d'Appiano, A.S.F., *Dieci di Balìa: Miss. Legaz. Commis.* 2, f. 29^{v}, 30 June 1396. Also *Consulte*, 32, ff. 60^{v}–61^{v}, 30 July 1396. According to Minerbetti, p. 205, the Guinigi as rulers of Lucca hired the company of Bartolomeo, though the Florentines paid half the cost of this. Lucca was also aided by forces sent openly from Florence and Bologna, 400 lances according to Minerbetti, loc. cit. Sercambi, I, p. 323. Banti, *Iacopo d'Appiano*, pp. 204, 208.

[59] The duke of Milan sent aid to Pisa in the face of this attack, Minerbetti, p. 204, Sardo, pp. 263–6.

[60] Sercambi, I, pp. 328–32.

[61] Sercambi, I, pp. 332–5, 351–3, Minerbetti, p. 205; Sardo, pp. 271–3. Banti, *Iacopo d'Appiano*, pp. 203–4.

[62] *Delib.* 133, f. 92, 2 July, f. 97, 8 Nov. 1396. Sercambi, I, p. 335.

[63] Sercambi, I, pp. 349–51. C.p. Sardo, pp. 273–4.

August the Florentines as mediators were able to patch up a truce between Pisa and Lucca for six months,[64] but Pisan forces attacked Lucca again in January before the truce expired.[65] When Lucca sent an ambassador to protest to the Pisan government, an attempt was made to capture him on the way back, and he was injured in the scuffle.[66] Lucca hired forces to fight back,[67] and the war continued almost without intermission from February well into October with attacks almost daily at times. But it was almost entirely a matter of raids and counter-raids, capturing some castle, holding it for a while, and then abandoning it. Prisoners were taken and held to ransom, cattle were stolen and there was much burning and destruction, but neither side gained any permanent advantage.

The war of 1396–7 almost inevitably led to friction between Lucca and Florence. The Florentines had undertaken to protect Lucca from Pisan attacks; Lucca had made the league of 19 July 1395 for this purpose. She naturally looked to Florence for military aid when the Pisans began to raid her territory. Lucca kept one or more envoys in Florence for most of 1397, and their letters are full of reports of requests for aid.[68] The Florentines were fully aware of the need to defend

[64] Sercambi, I, pp. 352-3, Minerbetti, p. 205, Sardo, pp. 275-7. A.S.F. *Consulte*, 32, f. 56^{v}, 24 July, ff. 57-8, 28 July, ff. 59-60, 30 July, ff. 62^{v}-66, 3-5 Aug., ff. 69^{v}-70^{v}, 11 Sept., ff. 71-2, 25 Sept. 1396. *Dieci di Balìa: Miss. Legaz. Commis.* 2, ff. 31^{v}-32, 11 July, ff. 37-8, 20 July 1396. Earlier Florence had sought to involve Lucca more deeply in offensive action against Pisa, so that she would be more firmly committed to the Florentine alliance. Her change of heart was due at least partly to the desire to protect Florentine merchandise aboard a ship arrived in Porto Pisano, Banti, *Iacopo d'Appiano*, pp. 206110. Negotiations for a more lasting agreement in Sept.-Nov. came to nothing largely because Pisa and Florence could not agree on terms for Florence to use Porto Pisano, but there were difficulties to over Lucchese demands that Pisa should expel Lucchese exiles, especially Carlo Ronghi, Lando Moriconi, and Piero Rapondi. The Pisan government refused, on the grounds that they had been granted Pisan citizenship, but undertook to restrain them from attacks on Lucca, Banti, *Iacopo d'Appiano*, pp. 212-13.

[65] Sercambi, I, pp. 357-9. Banti, *Iacopo d'Appiano*, pp. 223-4. Lucca asked for aid in December 1396 because Pisa was collecting forces, A.S.F. *Consulte*, 32, ff. 81^{v}-84, 18 Dec. 1396. *Reg.*, nos. 1598-1625.

[66] Sercambi, I, p. 359. *Reg.*, no. 1542.

[67] *Reg.*, nos. 1703-6, 1709, 1713, 1715-16, 1718-21, 1723-4, 1726-8, 1731, 1740, 1744. Sercambi, I, pp. 403-4.

[68] Commissions of ser Guido da Pietrasanta and others in Florence 18 Jan. 1397-27 Jan. 1398, *Reg.*, nos. 1597-1637, 1673-1768, 1781-1898, 1946-62. Minerbetti, pp. 210-12, 221-2.

Lucca, and sent many assurances to the Lucchese and to the Guinigi that they would defend Lucchese liberty as if it were their own.[69] In some cases Florence did send aid in response to Lucchese requests, but more often she was obliged to refuse, make excuses, delay, or send far less than had been requested.[70] She was in financial difficulties and did not always have the forces available. Even when she had forces she did not always regard aid to Lucca as first priority. Most of the warfare between Pisa and Lucca was a matter of raids that were destructive and damaging, but not really dangerous. In 1397 Visconti forces were playing a larger part in the war and hostilities were directed more openly against Florence herself.[71] She therefore had to defend her own territory against attacks from Pisa, Siena, and elsewhere, and also to send reinforcements to Mantua. Lucchese ambassadors reported these difficulties, but Lucca became increasingly dissatisfied with Florence as the summer of 1397 wore on. The Lucchese envoy had written early in April that he was not listened to, and asked to be recalled.[72] Shortly afterwards he wrote in despair that, do what he might, he could not succeed in getting the Florentines to send reinforcements.[73] Sercambi's account is full of complaints of the failure of Florence to send adequate aid.[74] He complained that in November 1396 the Florentines had encouraged Lucca to oppose the passage of Paolo Savelli on his way to Pisa from Lombardy, but had failed to send adequate forces, so that the Lucchese were defeated.[75] Even when Florence did send forces they refused to counter-attack on Pisan territory and stayed only a short

[69] A.S.F. *Consulte*, 31, ff. 125v–126v, 26 Nov. 1395, *Consulte*, 32, f. 53v, 26 June, f. 55, 21 July, ff. 57–60, 28 and 30 July, ff. 62–6, 2–5 Aug. 1396. *Dieci di Balìa: Miss. Legaz. Commis.* 2, ff. 31v–32, 11 July, f. 39, 22 July 1396.

[70] For example Dec. 1396 or Jan. 1397 she sent 50 lances when Lucca had requested 150 lances and 50 *balestrieri*, A.S.F. *Dieci di Balìa: Miss. Legaz. Commis.* 2, ff. 68–9, 71.

[71] Visconti forces were massing in Pisa under Alberico da Barbiano for use against Florence, eventually numbering some 10,000 cavalry, Banti, *Iacopo d'Appiano*, pp. 124–6, 221–6.

[72] *Reg.*, no. 1699, 7, 8 Apr. 1397.

[73] *Reg.*, no. 1708, 19, 20 Apr. 1397. Also no. 1703, 13 Apr. 1397.

[74] Sercambi, I, pp. 361, 368, II, pp. 48–9, 52–4, 62–3.

[75] Sercambi, I, pp. 353–4, Sardo, p. 281. Banti, *Iacopo d'Appiano*, p. 213.

while.[76] Lucca even had to send aid to Florence when Sanminiato was threatened.[77] Sercambi believed that Florence was saving her own territory by allowing the war to be fought on that of Lucca, and, according to him, the failure of Florence to assist Lucca encouraged ser Jacopo d'Appiano to attack her 'vedendo che il comune di Fiorenza al bizongno è tardo a mandare genti a Luccha'.[78]

When peace negotiations began further disagreements arose. An attempt to bring about peace between Lucca and Pisa had already been made in June 1397 by Spinetta Malaspina, marchese di Villafranca, who was a friend and ally of Lucca and the father-in-law of Jacopo d'Appiano. At the end of October he made a further attempt, and was able to bring about an understanding that hostilities would cease for a few weeks so that the autumn sowing might take place, though this agreement was kept secret.[79] In January 1398 negotiations began again and at first there seemed good prospects of success. On 3 January 1398 the Milanese agents in Pisa, who included Piero Rapondi and Niccoletto Diversi of Lucca, had made a demand that Jacopo d'Appiano, who was old and ill and who had recently lost his warlike and resolute eldest son, Vanni, renounce his position in Pisa in favour of Giangaleazzo. D'Appiano and his son, Gherardo, resisted this demand in arms and the Visconti commissioners and their chief supporters in Pisa were arrested. Visconti forces were expelled from Pisa for a while and there were hopes in Lucca and Florence that d'Appiano would break off his alliance with Milan and be more ready to make peace.[80] Lazzaro Guinigi

[76] Sercambi, I, p. 364, end Feb. 1397. They refused to send forces to attack Pisa Sept. 1397, Sercambi, II, pp. 48–50, 52–4. Florentine sources show that they wished to avoid attacking Pisan territory if possible, at least in 1396, A.S.F. *Consulte*, 32, f. 55, 21 July, ff. 55v–56v, 24 July, ff. 59–60, 30 July 1396.

[77] Sercambi, I, pp. 364, 368–9. [78] Sercambi, II, pp. 52–4, 261.

[79] Sercambi, I, p. 405; II, p. 59. It became known to the Florentines causing them to fear the defection of Lucca. 18 Nov. 1397 the Lucchese envoy, Antonio da Cortona explained that it was untrue that peace had been made 'ma vedendo che mente se seminato et che Pisa a tanta brigata et voi non visete raconci fecesi pensiero che non era bene per uno prigione o due asini provocare il nimico anti starsi a buona guardia fine che le brigate fino rescripte et in punto et che si possa fare danno che vaglia qualche cosa al nimico facendo altramente poco senno serebbe', original letter in *Anz. Temp. Lib.* 572, no. 1877 in *Reg.* Also nos. 1878, 1881, 18–20 Nov. 1397.

[80] Sercambi, II, pp. 67–76, 78–9, 165–71. *Reg.*, nos. 1932, 1948–51, 1953, 1956. Banti, *Iacopo d'Appiano*, pp. 235–9, 243–5, 247. There are many references to the

journeyed to Florence in person to ask the Florentines to refrain from attacking Pisan territory for at least a month in the hope of coming to terms with Pisa. The Florentines were ready to agree to this, as they equally wished to bring the war to an end, but they insisted on taking part in the negotiations for fear that the Lucchese would make a separate peace.[81] This greatly reduced the chances of success, for ser Jacopo had already said that he did not wish the Florentines to take part.[82] Nevertheless the negotiations went ahead, at first with good hopes of success. The Lucchese ambassadors reported that the Pisans desired peace and that ser Jacopo would not wish to stand in the way of this.[83]

But disagreements soon arose between Pisa and Florence. Ser Jacopo complained that the Florentines had broken the peace and demanded securities, as he could no longer rely on Florentine promises. The Florentines also demanded securities before they could feel safe in returning to Pisa to trade.[84] But the negotiations were to turn on the question of Florentine trading privileges in Pisa. Florence insisted on the same concessions as she had enjoyed under Pietro Gambacorta; ser Jacopo d'Appiano flatly refused to consider this, though he was prepared to concede the Florentines the less extensive

---

peace negotiations in A.S.F. *Consulte*, 32, ff. 168v-178v, 8 Jan.-6 Feb. 1398, *Consulte*, 33, ff. 2-8v, 7-16 Feb. 1398. Also the account of the Florentine ambassadors, A.S.F. *Sign: Rapporti e Relaz. di Oratori*, 1, ff. 13-15v, Jan. and Feb. 1398, which is very similar to that of Sercambi.

[81] Sercambi, II, p. 76, Minerbetti, p. 226. *Reg.*, no. 1955. Mention of the arrival of Lazzaro and negotiations with him, A.S.F. *Sign. Legaz. Commis.* 1, ff. 172-172v, letter to the Florentine ambassador in Venice, 11 Jan. 1398. Also f. 173, ff. 104v-105, 10 Jan. 1398 (Fl. style 1397) the ambassadors to Pisa and Lucca were to thank the Lucchese for their efforts, but also to take precautions 'si per affectione di loro privato bene non si partissono in alcuno modo dal bene publico'. A.S.F. *Sign: Rapporti e Relaz. di Oratori*, 1, ff. 13-15v, Jan. and Feb. 1398, report of the negotiations. Reports that the Guinigi and the Lucchese had told Malaspina that they could do nothing without the Florentines with whom they were in league.

[82] Sercambi, II, pp. 76-7.

[83] *Reg.*, nos. 1899, 24 Jan., 1902, 26 Jan. 1398. Commission of Niccolò Onesti and ser Domenico Lupardi in Pisa, 24 Jan.-14 Feb. 1398, nos. 1899-1929. Also nos. 1927-8, 1960-2, 1965-8, 2151-2 (from Stefano di Poggio, not Stefano Forteguerra, as in *Reg.*) Minerbetti, p. 226. D'Appiano was probably also induced to agree to joint negotiations with Florence and Lucca because of the delicate state of his relations with Milan, following the attempt to subject Pisa to Giangaleazzo directly and his expulsion of Visconti forces and arrest of Visconti agents, Banti, *Iacopo d'Appiano*, pp. 243-4.

[84] *Reg.*, nos. 1902, 1906.

privileges they had enjoyed before 1369.[85] Lucca felt that the Florentines were being unreasonable; her ambassadors wrote 'li fiorentini fanno male a stare tanto duri in su le franchigie e dovrebbeno volere levare di Toscana tanto fuoco'.[86] The Lucchese were not prepared to support a war and pay taxes and forced loans to defend Florentine trading privileges, which they regarded as a side issue in any case.[87] Lucca sent envoys to Florence to urge her to come to terms, and finally Lazzaro Guinigi went himself to tell the Florentines bluntly, according to Sercambi, that they must be content to pay tolls as other merchants did, and that the negotiations could not be allowed to break down on this.[88] The Florentines agreed not to insist on the old trading privileges, but it was too late; ser Jacopo d'Appiano was no longer willing to make peace and the negotiations broke down.[89]

Lucca had been very anxious for peace. Her envoys even went so far as to make an agreement for the temporary cessation of hostilities without the knowledge of the Florentines, though the Lucchese Anziani reproved them for this. Lucca was already dissatisfied with Florence for failing to

[85] *Reg.*, nos. 1906, 1908. A.S.F. *Consulte*, 32, ff. 174v–175v, 30 Jan., f. 177, 6 Feb. 1398 (Fl. style 1397). Banti, *Iacopo d'Appiano*, pp. 242–3.

[86] *Anz. Temp. Lib.* 572, letter of 8 Feb. 1398, no. 1918 in *Reg.* Other complaints about the Florentine attitude, nos. 1908, 1911, 1913, 1915, 1917, 1920.

[87] *Reg.*, no. 1920, 9 Feb. 1398. Letter of 5 Feb. 1398 in *Anz. Temp. Lib.* 572, which is no. 1913 in *Reg.* refers to the *franchigie* 'le quali dalla pace e dalla guerra sono in tutto impertinenti'. The Lucchese were prepared to agree to a Pisan demand that they should close Motrone to the Florentines, Sercambi II, p. 76. Banti, *Iacopo d'Appiano*, pp. 240–1.

[88] 'E il dicto dì vennero novelle a Luccha chome l'acordio restava solo perche i Fiorentini voleano potere mectere et chavare di Pisa sensa gabella tucte mercantie, e i Pisani non voleano consentire. Per la qual cosa Lazzari di Francesco Guinigi cavalchò a Fiorenza con dire a'Fiorentini che piaccia loro stare contenti di pagare chome li altri merchadanti et che non voglino per questo che l'acordio rimagna', Sercambi, II, p. 77. *Reg.*, nos. 1911, 1913, 1938. Mention of a Lucchese envoy arriving in Florence, A.S.F. *Sign. Legaz. Commis.* 1, f. 175, 5 Feb. 1398, arrival of Lazzaro 8 Feb. Negotiations with him A.S.F. *Consulte*, 33, f.4, 8 Feb. 1398, when the Florentines agreed to commit the question of their trading privileges to him.

[89] Sercambi, II, pp. 77–8. *Reg.*, no. 1916. Also A.S.F. *Consulte*, 32 and 33, many references Jan. and Feb. 1398 (Fl. style 1397). In fact it is doubtful how seriously d'Appiano took the efforts to reach an agreement, and he was careful to ensure that the onus of the failure of the negotiations fell on the Florentines. He pointed out to the Sienese commissioner in Pisa that it would be clear that Florence was to blame for the failure and 'li Lucchesi aranno cagione di sdegno e levarsi da loro', quoted in Banti, *Iacopo d'Appiano*, pp. 245–6, note 62.

assist her adequately during the war; this dissatisfaction was increased when she saw the chances of peace ruined by Florentine selfishness and greed.[90]

In addition to these limited local negotiations for peace with Pisa, Lucca also took part as one of the members of the league of Bologna in the wider negotiations between the league and the duke of Milan. She kept Niccolò di Ceccorino di Poggio in Imola as her envoy from the beginning of June to the end of September 1397,[91] but the negotiations proved fruitless. Each side accused the other of starting the war and demanded the return of places captured and indemnity for damage suffered. The duke of Milan demanded that members of the league should not receive Pisan exiles, but refused to agree to a similar demand that Lucchese exiles should not be received.[92] There was little chance of agreement acceptable to the Lucchese being reached, for Pisa, with the support of Milan, made demands that could not have been conceded. Pisa and Milan demanded that the roads from Sarzana to Pisa be kept open, and especially that no obstacle be placed in the way at Motrone or Pietrasanta. This was of obvious importance for communications between Pisa and Milan, and might have been conceded; indeed Lucca and Florence denied that they had ever attempted to close the roads, and made counter-complaints of attacks on their merchants in Pisa territory.[93]

But Pisa also made territorial demands at the expense of Lucca. She laid claim to a number of Lucchese castles and to a large part of the Lucchese state, including the Garfagnana, Motrone, Viareggio, Pietrasanta, and Massa Lunense, and challenged the Lucchese right to navigate off Motrone and the strip of coastline that she controlled and to unload merchandise there.[94] Naturally Lucca could not consent to give up

[90] *Reg.*, nos. 1907, 1908. Florentine complaints of this nos. 1916, 1917. See also no. 1965 for Lucchese desire for peace. Spinetta Malaspina was able to make another secret agreement at the beginning of March that Lucca and Pisa would not attack each other except on three days notice, but this led to further Florentine complaints that Lucca was acting without her knowledge and had deserted her ally, Sercambi, II, pp. 155, 171.

[91] Commission of Niccolò di Ceccorino di Poggio 3 June–28 Sept. 1397, *Reg.*, nos. 1769–80. Sercambi, II, pp. 20–32.

[92] *Reg.*, no. 1771. Sercambi, II, pp. 22, 25, 27, 30.

[93] Sercambi, II, pp. 22, 25–6. *Reg.*, no. 1771.

[94] Sercambi, II, pp. 27, 29–30. *Reg.*, nos. 1771, 1775–6.

a large proportion of her territory. The right of sailing off the coast and unloading merchandise at Motrone was a particularly cherished privilege, and it had acquired greater importance for Lucca and for Florence since 1392. Florence could not use Porto Pisano while she was at war with Pisa, and the Sienese alternative of Talamone was also closed to her because of the hostility between Florence and Siena. She therefore turned to Motrone and had been using it during the war as a port of embarkation for ambassadors going to France and to Genoa, and also for shipping her goods abroad.[95] It was important to Lucca commercially; she received corn supplies via Motrone and she sent some of her goods from there, though she normally preferred to ship them from Genoa or to send them north by land. She also profited from tolls at Motrone and other points for goods passing through her territory. But her rights at Motrone were also a matter of civic pride, and the Lucchese replied indignantly that the Pisan demands were 'contra jus et antiquatem consuetudinem et in prejudicium juris publici'. The Pisans showed imperial privileges granting them rights over the Lucchese coast and the Garfagnana, and the Lucchese replied by showing their privileges and the declaration of their territory made by Charles IV in 1369.[96] The Lucchese ambassador reported with satisfaction that the Pisans were somewhat cast down at this, but he warned his government that they were seeking confirmation of their privileges from Wenceslas, king of the Romans, and with the support of the duke of Milan had good hopes of obtaining it, so that the Lucchese must take measures to ensure that it was not granted.[97]

Lucca countered Pisan territorial claims by making claims of her own. She demanded the restitution of villages and fortresses which had once belonged to the commune of Lucca

[95] e.g. *Reg.*, nos. 1626, 1691, 1808. Lucca getting grain through Motrone, no. 1717. Florentine ambassadors going to Genoa via Motrone A.S.F. *Sign. Legaz. Commis.* 1, f. 132, 10 Jan. 1399.

[96] *Reg.*, nos. 1771, 1775, also no. 1579, 18 Sept. 1397. Banti, *Iacopo d'Appiano*, pp. 230–1.

[97] *Reg.*, no. 1775, 12 Sept. 1397. 4 May a Lucchese envoy had spoken to Wenceslas' ambassador about having the privileges from Charles IV confirmed, but regarded it as a device to obtain money from Lucca rather than anything else. *Reg.*. no. 1738, 19 May 1397.

or to the bishopric, and had since been occupied by Pisa.[98] These were places that Lucca had not recovered in 1369, but they included claims to places lost in the wars of the early or mid-fourteenth century. Pisa was no more likely to concede these than Lucca was to give up a large part of her territory, and it is clear that neither side had any serious intention of making peace.

When the peace negotiations between Milan and the league began again in Venice in January 1398[99] these territorial claims and counter-claims were renewed. The Lucchese envoy had gone well armed with imperial privileges, and he and the merchants of the Lucchese community in Venice, who offered him every assistance, made a search for the privileges that had once been deposited there, though without success as the documents had long since been returned to Lucca.[100] In fact the negotiations for peace with Milan and her allies were soon transformed into negotiations for the renewal of the league, with Venice as one of the members.[101] Lucca's main concern in these negotiations was the familiar one of avoiding committing herself to any expenses from which she could get herself excused. Her envoy pleaded her poverty, expenses, and difficulties, but Mantua and Ferrara also wished to be spared any contribution and the other states demanded that everyone should pay their share. The Lucchese envoy advised his government to stay outside the league rather than commit itself to any expenses, but the Florentines supported the Lucchese in their claims to exemption, and it was finally agreed that Lucca should join the league as a Florentine adherent without any fixed obligations.[102] Sercambi criticized Lucca's entry into a league that was designed for war, but on

[98] A list of them *Reg.*, no. 1771, Sercambi, II, pp. 30–1.

[99] Commission of Niccolò di Poggio in Venice 16 Jan.–12 Apr. 1398, *Reg.*, nos. 1963–79.

[100] *Reg.*, nos. 1963–5. [101] *Reg.*, nos. 1968, 1970–5.

[102] *Reg.* nos. 1976–7. The league was concluded 21 Mar. Copy *Capitoli*, 18, ff. 150v–155v, Florence named Lucca as an adherent, ff. 155v–156. This was ratified by Lucca 27 Apr. 1398, ff. 156v–157v. Niccolò di Ceccorino di Poggio had a mandate to do so, dated 29 March, 'dummodo comune Lucanum non obligetur ad expensas guerre vel ad alia onera dicte lige nisi dumtaxat ad onera guerre et expensas guerre que principaliter fierat contra ipsam civitatem Lucanam vel eius territorium vel contra subditos dicte civitatis Lucane', *Min.* 4 (not foliated).

11 May 1398 a ten-year truce was concluded between Milan and the league and this was greeted with great joy in Lucca. It did indeed free her from some of her most serious preoccupations, and she took advantage of it to dismiss a part of the forces she had been maintaining for her defence.[103]

Lucca had in the years since 1395 taken a great interest in the internal affairs of Pisa. Any change in the government there, or even in the balance of parties within the city might affect Lucca very profoundly. Any rumours of changes were quickly reported to the Lucchese government.[104] The Lucchese had hoped that the efforts of Milanese agents to obtain the *signorìa* of Pisa for Giangaleazzo would cause Jacopo d'Appiano to desert the Milanese alliance and make him ready to make peace. But he chose to take the view that the attempt was an independent initiative on the part of Giangaleazzo's agents in Pisa in which the duke himself was not involved, and these hopes were disappointed.[105] Indeed in May 1398 d'Appiano made an agreement with Milan, whereby he and his heirs undertook not to make peace or war without the consent of Giangaleazzo for ten years in return for Visconti protection, and in August the company of Broglio and Brandolino, which had invaded Lucchese territory, was honourably received in Pisa, making it clear that despite the truce d'Appiano was by no means reconciled.[106] But in September 1398 he died and was succeeded by his weak son Gherardo. The insecurity of Gherardo's position made him even more dependent on Visconti support, and in February 1399 he sold Pisa to the duke of Milan.[107] The replacement of ser Jacopo d'Appiano by Giangaleazzo made a great difference to Lucchese foreign policy. She could now resume her old policy of remaining on good terms with Milan as a counterbalance to Florence, with whom her relations had become increasingly strained.[108]

[103] Sercambi, II, pp. 173, 190-5.

[104] e.g. *Reg.*, nos. 1542, 1887-8, 2157.

[105] Sercambi, II, pp. 67-75, 78-9, 165-71. *Reg.*, nos. 1932, 1948-51, 1953, 1956. Banti, *Iacopo d'Appiano*, pp. 235-9, 243-5, 247.

[106] Sercambi, II, pp. 224-6, Banti, *Iacopo d'Appiano*, pp. 239-40, 250-5, 261-2.

[107] Sercambi, II, pp. 244-55. Banti, *Iacopo d'Appiano*, pp. 262-4, 273-87.

[108] Landogna, 'La politica dei Visconti in Toscana', p. 185.

There had always been opposition in Lucca to the Florentine alliance of 1395. Sercambi records that it greatly displeased the duke of Milan 'et tucti ghibellini di Luccha & del contado', when it was made.[109] There were signs of hostility to it later in the *contado*. In February 1397 the Florentines heard reports that Lucchese subjects in the *contado* intended to treat forces coming from Florence to aid Lucca as enemies,[110] and Sercambi confirms that there was strong anti-Florentine feeling among the Lucchese *contadini*.[111] He also records an abortive rebellion in the Garfagnana in June 1397 in the middle of the most serious stage of the Pisan war by a large number of Garfagnani, many of them Ghibellines, 'con dire che non voleano esser in legha co'Fiorentini, et che certo di ciò erano molto mal contenti'. Sercambi represents this movement as the work of young hotheads, and records that other Ghibellines in the Garfagnana, older and firmly devoted to Lucchese interests, were able to reconcile them to the rulers of the city.[112] But there can be no doubt that the Florentine alliance was unpopular in many quarters. It involved a major departure from the policy Lucca had pursued earlier of avoiding committing herself to any one of her neighbours, and put her in something approaching a client relation to Florence. Sercambi was quick to deny that it made Lucca any less independent or her own mistress, when he heard that Antonio degli Ubaldini, an enemy of Florence captured while fighting for the Pisans, feared to be taken to Lucca because of the authority he believed the Florentines to enjoy there, but he himself claimed that Lucca's obligations to her Florentine ally were such as to prevent her making an independent peace.[113]

If there was objection to the Florentine alliance in principle in many quarters, a few years experience served only to strengthen it. The Lucchese had not had the assistance they

[109] Sercambi, I, p. 316.

[110] *Reg.*, no. 1623, 19 Feb. 1397.

[111] Sercambi, II, p. 262, 'l'animo de'tuoi contadini è si contrario a quello di Firenza'.

[112] Sercambi, I, pp. 407–8.

[113] Sercambi, I, pp. 405, 410–11, II, 77. The league provided that neither Florence nor Lucca could make peace without the consent of the other unless the other party were included, *Capitoli*, 26, f. 13.

felt was due in the war against Pisa, and their *contado* had suffered heavily. They believed that, if their alliance with Florence had not prevented them making a separate peace, they could have come to terms with Pisa, and they attributed the failure of the joint peace negotiations to Florence's selfish insistence on the same commercial privileges as she had enjoyed under Pietro Gambacorta.[114] Florence's search for a port was to cause further trouble with Lucca. In June 1398 after the failure of the peace negotiations with Pisa she had begun to negotiate with Lucca for a formal agreement for the use of Motrone. Lucca wished the terms of the agreement to include an undertaking by Florence that she would not later make an agreement with another city and transfer her trade elsewhere. The Florentines refused to accept this kind of limitation on their freedom of action, though they assured the Lucchese that they had no intention of abandoning Motrone lightly if an agreement was concluded.[115] But no agreement was reached in the summer of 1398, and it is clear from the discussions in the Florentine councils that most Florentines would have preferred either Porto Pisano or Talamone to Motrone as a port.[116]

After the death of Jacopo d'Appiano Florence resumed negotiations for the use of Porto Pisano without consulting Lucca.[117] The Lucchese resented the fact that they had not

[114] It is by no means certain that Jacopo d'Appiano ever intended the negotiations seriously, but he encouraged Lucca to believe that she could have obtained a separate peace and fostered the idea that the joint negotiations had failed over the question of Florentine commercial privileges, in order to lay the blame for the failure on Florence and thus sow dissension between Florence and Lucca, Banti, *Iacopo d'Appiano*, pp. 234-5, 240-1, Sercambi, II, pp. 77-8.

[115] A.S.F. *Sign. Legaz. Commis.* 1, f. 182, 5 July 1398, letter to the Florentine ambassador in Lucca. Also f. 114, 27 June 1398. *Sign: Rapporti e Relaz. di Oratori*, 1, f. 20^{v}, 28 June-17 July 1398. *Consulte*, 33, f. 45^{v}, 29 May 1398. There were also negotiations with Siena for the use of Talamone and with Pisa, Banti, *Iacopo d'Appiano*, pp. 260-1.

[116] *Consulte,* 33, ff. 83^{v}-86, 10 and 11 Oct., ff. 87^{v}-88^{v}, 18 Oct., ff. 93^{v}-95^{v}, 21-3 Oct., ff. 96-96^{v}, 29 Oct., ff. 100-1, 14 Nov., ff. 106-107^{v}, 16-19 Dec. 1398. For the whole question of Florence's problems in finding an outlet for her trade in this period, R. Piattoli, 'Il problema portuale di Firenze dall'ultima lotta con Gian Galeazzo Visconti alle prime trattative per l'acquisto di Pisa (1402-1405)', *Rivista Storica degli Archivi Toscani*, Vol. II (1930), pp. 157-90.

[117] Ambassadors to Pisa for the use of Porto Pisano, A.S.F., *Sign. Legaz. Commis.* 1, f. 124, 7 Oct. 1398-8 Jan. 1399. Florence was still negotiating with Siena, as much playing the governments of Pisa and Siena off against each other and trying to

been consulted or included in the negotiations and felt that Florence was abandoning them despite the sacrifices Lucca had made to enable the Florentines to use Motrone.[118] Lucca's attitude to the question of Florentine use of Motrone was not always consistent. On the one hand she valued the profits and revenues that Florentine trade brought, and therefore did not wish Florence to come to terms with Pisa;[119] on the other hand she felt that the presence of Florentine merchants in Lucchese territory might give the Florentines an excuse for intervention that could threaten Lucchese security. The Florentines might bring forces into Lucchese territory on the pretext of protecting their merchants using Motrone 'per la qual cosa ti potre' intervenire che le dicte genti a pititione di Firenza ti potrenno prendere o veramente disfare il tuo contado'.[120] Nevertheless negotiations for the use of Motrone were resumed in April 1399. On this occasion the trouble seems to have been that Florence demanded more than she was prepared to concede. She desired to have the same commercial privileges in Lucca as she had had in Pisa, granting the Lucchese the same privileges in Florence as the Pisans had had. Lucca would not hear of this, and was prepared to grant only more limited privileges to the Florentines, demanding identical privileges for her merchants in Florence.[121] Again no agreement was reached, but by April and May 1399 the general political situation was in any case unfavourable to a commercial agreement between Lucca and Florence.

Sercambi's account of these last years of the fourteenth century is full of hostility to Florence. As he is virtually the only authority for Lucchese history and the Lucchese attitude to her neighbours in this period it is difficult to be sure whether his attitude was typical of that of his fellow citizens or whether his views were coloured by party feeling. He was one

---

encourage pro-Florentine parties within these cities and wean them from alliance with Milan as trying to reach an agreement, Banti, *Iacopo d'Appiano*, pp. 266–72.

[118] Sercambi, II, pp. 242–4. He spoke of the 'sconcio e spesa à ricevuto et riceve Luccha per potere fare che le tuoi mercantie et victuagle sposassero in nel porto nostro di Motrone, et per tucto il terreno di Luccha secure a Firenza le potessi conducere'.

[119] e.g. *Reg.*, no. 1903, 27 Jan. 1398.

[120] Sercambi, II, pp. 262–3.

[121] A.S.F. *Sign: Rapporti e Relaz. di Oratori*, 1, f. 29, report of Giovanni Biliotti, ambassador to Lucca, 27 Apr.–18 May 1399. *Consulte*, 33, ff. 150v–152, 11 Apr. f. 157v, 9 May 1399.

of the leading adherents of the ruling Guinigi party in Lucca. The Guinigi had made the league of 1395, and had therefore presumably accepted the necessity of an alliance with Florence then. Sercambi gives no indication that he had disagreed with Guinigi policy in this, or that he was exceptionally anti-Florentine. But some of his complaints are echoed in such sources as the reports of Lucchese envoys and it seems likely that his views would be shared by many Lucchese, and that there would be others who were even more resolutely anti-Florentine than he was. His views are therefore worth discussing.

Sercambi had a long memory and recalled old scores from wars in the earlier fourteenth century. He felt that when Florence had assisted Lucca and lent her money in 1369 this had not been from altruistic motives but 'a intentione che Luccha si governasse socto il governo di Fiorenza'. When the Florentines saw that Lucca was not prepared to be a client state, they made many attempts to subjugate her, according to Sercambi. He lists the Lucchese villages and castles held by Florence, and points out that despite the league of 1395, Florence had shown no signs of returning them, so that she clearly intended to keep them permanently. He complained that 'quelli che compuosero Firenza, per la sua grandessa, vuole il suo e l'altrui possedere'.[122] His chief complaint against Florence as an ally was her selfishness. He felt that this was particularly clear in the way that Florence had allowed Lucca to bear the brunt of the war of 1397, and in her attitude in the peace negotiations in January and February 1398, but he saw it in other things too. When Florence requested that Lucca join with her in protesting at Giangaleazzo's acquisition of Pisa, he felt that Florence was doing this in her own interests, not those of Lucca. He pointed out that if the war should begin again it could only do harm to Lucca. She had nothing to gain. She would be attacked as she had been in the war of 1396–8, and scarcely dare call on Florentine forces to guard the city and fortresses for fear of being enslaved. Even if the war were successful, Lucca would gain nothing. She would not even recover what she had lost, for Florence would keep for

[122] Sercambi, II, pp. 122–5, 127, 171.

herself anything that she or her allies conquered. He therefore concluded 'che meglio è per te, Luccha, a vivere im pace con ongni persona che prendere guerra a pititione e a stanza de'Fiorentini'.[123]

In 1399, after the Milanese acquisition of Pisa, Lucca was able to resume the old policy of neutrality and peace with all her neighbours. This meant above all a resumption of her old friendly relations with Milan. There are many expressions of anti-Milanese feeling in Lucchese documents of 1396 and 1397, when Giangaleazzo was supporting Jacopo d'Appiano, but Sercambi was probably again fairly typical of the Lucchese attitude when he stated that despite the fact that in the war with Pisa Lucca had been 'lo dicto dugha alquanto incontra', she should remember that she had received far more benefits than harm from the Visconti. 'E però, quanto a te serà possibile, col dicto dugha manterai buono amore'. Lucchese policy should be to maintain her independence honourably with regard to all her neighbours, not subjecting herself to Giangaleazzo or to anyone else, but living at peace with everyone. It might have been expected that Lucca would have become more suspicious of the duke's intentions after his support of Jacopo d'Appiano and his acquisition of Pisa. He might then have lost some of his attraction as a counter-balance to Florence, and when he began to acquire possession of cities in Tuscany so near to Lucca, she might have come to feel, like Florence, that her independence was threatened. But, if Sercambi is typical of the Lucchese attitude, this does not seem to have happened. He advised that Lucca should keep certain fortresses well guarded in case Giangaleazzo or his successors should wish for 'magior dominio' over Lucca, but he apparently regarded this as a very remote possibility, saying that 'si de'stimare che il prefato dugha vorrà con buono animo techo stare, non stringendoti a quello che fusse tuo danno nè vergogna'.[124] In fact if the Milanese acquisition of Pisa aroused Lucchese suspicions of anyone it was of Florence, for Florence, seeing herself surrounded by the lands of the duke of Milan, might try to cut his communications by capturing Lucca.[125]

[123] Sercambi, II, pp. 259–63. Other complaints of Florentine selfishness II, p. 265.

[124] Sercambi, II, pp. 138–40.

[125] Sercambi, II, p. 262, 'così come Firenza si vede esser intorniata da tucte parti del

The Florentines had long feared that Lucca might desert the alliance and be reconciled with Milan. They had shown nervousness on this score during the peace negotiations with Pisa.[126] They listened anxiously to news from Lucca, and in January 1399 sent the Lucchese news of a plot there, offering Florentine assistance.[127] Florentine fears of a Lucchese defection increased when news arrived first that Gherardo d'Appiano had made himself lord of Pisa, and then that he had sold the city to the duke of Milan. Speakers in the Florentine council urged that an embassy should be sent to Lucca, and that orators acceptable to the Lucchese should remain there continuously to exhort them to remain faithful to the Florentine alliance. The Lucchese should be assured of Florentine support, and forces sent to aid them, 'Lucani hortentur et maxime familia de Guinigiis', 'conservetur Lucana civitas sicut status proprius', 'conserventur Lucani sicut oculus capitis nostri'.[128] But the Florentines soon had to recognize that Lucca was wavering. By the end of March they feared that she had already reached an agreement with Milan. It was advised in the Florentine council 'octo provideant scire an Lucani fecerint cum tiranno concordiam', 'sciantur de factis Lucanis an sint vera que dicta sunt honesto modo', 'de Lucanis valde dubitant et ideo habeatur diligentia ut sciatur de factis eorum ita quod reparetur si fieri potest'.[129]

Florentine suspicions were well-founded. The Guinigi party in Lucca had accepted the necessity of an alliance with Florence in 1395, and probably made it willingly enough. But when Pisa passed into the hands of the duke of Milan the *raison d'être* of the alliance was gone. In view of the anti-Florentine feeling of a section, perhaps an important section,

---

dominio del duga di Milano che i Fiorentini desidererebero prendere te, Luccha, acciò che mediante te fusse risegata la via al predicto duga'. While there is no evidence in Florentine documents that they had hostile intentions towards Lucca at this time, there are references to Florentine attempts to induce the Lucchese to 'serrare la via da Pisa et per terra et ancho per mare'. Letters from Florence to Giovanni Biliotti in Lucca, A.S.F. *Sign. Legaz. Commis*, 1, f. 169v, 2 May 1399, also 4 May and an undated letter slightly later.

[126] A.S.F. *Sign. Legaz. Commis.* 1, ff. 104v-105, 10 Jan. 1398 (Fl. style 1397).

[127] *Consulte*, 33, f. 100v, 14 Nov. 1398, f. 120, 20 Jan. 1399 (Fl. style 1398). There is no other record of a plot in January 1399.

[128] *Consulte*, 33, ff. 121-137v, 22 Jan.-17 Feb. 1399 (Fl. style 1398).

[129] *Consulte*, 33, ff. 144v-152, 24 Mar.-11 Apr. 1399.

in Lucca and the *contado*, the Guinigi were probably glad of the opportunity for reconciliation with Milan. When Gherardo d'Appiano had made himself lord of Pisa, many in Lucca hoped that he had done so with the intention of handing the city over to the duke of Milan.[130] Lucca sent an embassy to Milan at the end of March 1399 to congratulate Giangaleazzo on his acquisition of Pisa, which, she hoped, would bring peace to the whole of Tuscany, and also to recommend the city of Lucca to him. The duke received the embassy graciously, offering to do all that he could for the benefit of Lucca. He also made a request that Lazzaro Guinigi should visit him in person 'per buona chagione'.[131] This reply was felt in Lucca to be most encouraging. Lazzaro discussed the proposal that he should visit Pavia with other members of the Guinigi family, and it was decided that he should go. Efforts were made to keep the visit secret, but despite this it soon became known.

When the Florentines heard of Lazzaro's proposed visit to Pavia, they did everything that they could to dissuade him. One of the Florentine councillors said 'quod profectio Lazari de Guinigiis ad comitem est nimium suspiciosa'. News of the visit combined with the latest proposals from Lucca concerning the use of Motrone convinced the Florentines 'quod non sit mens eorum recta ad factum', and they resolved to seek an outlet to the sea either in the Sienese state or anywhere else. Meanwhile an embassy was to be sent to Lucca 'et quod dehortentur cum omnibus rationibus quas scribere scient hoc iter et scribant Johanni quod ex eorum parte faciat quicquid potest non vadat.'[132] There is no indication in Florentine documents of the arguments their ambassadors used, but according to Sercambi they warned that once the duke had Lazzaro in his power he would ask something unacceptable, and put Lazzaro to death if he refused. They urged that Lazzaro's mission could not be so important that no one else could be sent, and that it would ruin the peace negotiations in Venice. Florence claimed that her motive was consideration for Lucca and for Lazzaro Guinigi and the rest of his family, but it was

[130] Sercambi, II, p. 247.
[131] Sercambi, II, p. 264.
[132] *Consulte*, 33, ff. 157v–158, 9 May 1399. Other speakers agreed.

perfectly plain to the Lucchese authorities that 'la paura di Firenza era che l'andata del dicto Lazzari non fusse per riconciliarsi col prefato dugha di Milano'. Despite Florentine representations it was decided that Lazzaro should go to Pavia. The Lucchese gave out that his mission was connected with the recovery of Guinigi property in Pisa, confiscated under Jacopo d'Appiano, but the Florentine ambassador departed unconvinced.[133]

Nothing is known of the precise nature of Lazzaro's conversations with the duke of Milan. According to Sercambi, Lazzaro achieved his intention and arranged matters to the benefit and satisfaction of Lucca, his family, and his party.[134] The expressions of Sercambi are vague, but it is unlikely that Florentine fears that Lucca had come to an understanding with Giangaleazzo were without foundation. Sercambi protests indignantly at the calumnies put about by Florence, but there is no doubt that she had grounds for suspicion. Lazzaro's visit to Pavia was in itself provocative. It must have been well-known in Lucca that Florence would regard the visit of her near neighbour and ally to her greatest enemy with suspicion, and fear that Lucca was going the same way as Pisa.[135] It is hardly surprising if, as Sercambi says, everyone in Florence believed that Lazzaro had made an agreement with Milan to the detriment of Florence.[136] Rumours that Lazzaro had dismissed the Anziani and made himself lord of Lucca were false, and it is unlikely that he had given Lucca to the duke. But it is very probable that he had received assurances of Milanese support and in some way commended the city to Giangaleazzo. Perhaps he had been offered Milanese aid if he wished to turn his unofficial, but very real, authority in Lucca

[133] Sercambi, II, pp. 267–8. The Florentines were also urging the Lucchese at this time to send their envoy to Venice for the negotiations for peace with Milan. The Lucchese were reluctant, delaying as long as they could before sending an envoy on 24 June 1399. Sercambi, II, pp. 258–9, 265–6.

[134] 'avendo avuto dal duga di Milano sua intentione di quello perchè v'era andato . . . Dalla qual tornata il comune e li amici del dicto Lazzari funno molto contenti, sperando che avesse ordinato in tal maniera, che Luccha e loro casa e li amici si potrenno assai contentare e con salvessa mantenersi'. Sercambi II, pp. 278–9.

[135] A.S.F. *Sign. Legaz. Commis.* 3, ff. 3v–4v, 24 July 1399 in a letter to their envoy in Venice the Florentines wrote of Lazzaro's visit to Pavia 'a paura si parla variamente e chi ne stima una cosa e chi un altra'.

[136] Sercambi, II, p. 270.

into an open *signorìa*. The Visconti commissioners in Pisa stated that they had orders 'che a tucti i bizongni della casa de'Guinigii fussero presti'. According to Sercambi, they offered 200 or 300 lances as a guard for Lazzaro's return, and this was accepted by Michele, Dino, and Lazzaro di Niccolò Guinigi, should the need arise.[137] Milanese diplomacy seems to have been active in Lucca in the early months of 1400. On 2 January 1400 the duke of Milan wrote to Lazzaro di Francesco, Lazzaro di Niccolò, Dino, and Michele Guinigi that he was sending Zanardo Lanzavecchi as his ambassador.[138] Two months later, after the death of Lazzaro di Francesco, he sent another embassy to Dino, Lazzaro, Michele, Bartolomeo and Paolo Guinigi.[139] The nature of these embassies is not known, but they may perhaps be taken as an indication of some kind of understanding between Giangaleazzo and the Guinigi in the early months of 1400. The theory that Lucca and the Guinigi had some kind of understanding with the duke of Milan by the summer of 1399 would explain the lack of alarm in Sercambi at the advances of the duke in Tuscany and Umbria, and even satisfaction at the plight of Florence. Alarm as Giangaleazzo gradually added Siena and Perugia to Pisa would have been natural enough, and Lucca might well have begun to feel that Florence had been right all along about the danger of Milanese expansion. It is difficult to explain the lack of alarm and apprehension in Lucca at Milanese advances except on the theory that Lucca had had some kind of assurances from the duke.

Relations with Florence were seriously strained with Florence showing her distrust by fortifying her castles on the Lucchese border.[140] She promised satisfaction for an attack on a Lucchese village by men from Pescia, but Lucca had little faith in her promises 'posto che poca speranza fusse data che i Fiorentini debbiano volere ben vicinare'.[141] Sercambi reports a

[137] Sercambi, II, pp. 271–2, 279.

[138] *Regesto del R. Archivio di Stato in Lucca*, Vol. III, *Carteggio di Paolo Guinigi*, ed. L. Fumi and E. Lazzareschi. Appendice alla Parte Seconda, p. 474, no. 12, 2 Jan. 1400.

[139] Ibid. no. 13, 5 Mar. 1400. The ambassador was Bongaiunta da Fondo.

[140] Sercambi, II, pp. 270, 286–7.

[141] Sercambi, II, pp. 269–70. The Florentines certainly seem to have been rather lukewarm in their efforts to satisfy Lucchese complaints. In the *consulta* some advised

story that certain Florentines, in collusion with Lucchese exiles, planned to ambush Lazzaro Guinigi on his way back from Pavia, but he was warned by Milanese officials in Pisa when a letter was intercepted, and was able to take precautions.[142] The Lucchese believed that a company, which in July 1399 attacked Siena and threatened Lucca and Pisa, was in Florentine service, and sent ambassadors to protest about this, only to be met by Florentine denials. When the Milanese officials in Pisa asked for the aid of 200 Lucchese foot-soldiers to help resist the company, Lucca sent them, partly to keep the company from attacking her own territory.[143] Despite Florentine attempts to remedy the situation,[144] there are many expressions of anti-Florentine feeling in Sercambi's chronicle, and he reports that the Florentines were everywhere spreading slanders about Lazzaro Guinigi's visit to Pavia, adding with satisfaction 'più tosto tu, Firenza, diverrai serva che Luccha'.[145]

This was the way things stood, with Lucca on good terms with Milan, and relations with Florence very strained, when in February 1400 the murder of Lazzaro Guinigi, combined with threats of attack by Lucchese exiles, and a further outbreak of plague, plunged Lucca into a serious crisis.

---

further inquiry and punishment of those guilty, but others felt that enough had been done. In any case Florence was more concerned to protest her innocence in the matter. *Consulte*, 33, ff. 165^v–166^v, 9 June 1399.

[142] Sercambi, II, pp. 270–2. The Florentines had certainly informed their envoys in Rome of the situation in Lucca, sending copies of letters from their envoys in Lucca. A.S.F. *Sign. Legaz. Commis.* 1, f. 169, 1 May, f. 169^v, 4 May 1399.

[143] Sercambi, II, pp. 279–83.

[144] A.S.F. *Consulte*, 34, f. 7, 1 Aug. 1399 'et mittantur oratores Lucam qui sint confidentes et accepti Lucanis'. Ibid. f. 67, 24 Jan. 1400, ff. 77–9, 11 Feb. 1400 (Fl. style 1399) ambassadors to be sent to Lucca to exhort them to preserve their liberty. The Florentines had tried to get the league of Bologna to give the Lucchese assurances of protection, 'non ci parrebbe fusse altro che grande bene e utile confortarli a perseveranza e dare buona speranza di loro favore siche voglino conservare in liberta e in fratellanza chon la lega'. The Florentine ambassador in Venice was to speak to the doge about this. A.S.F. *Sign. Legaz. Commis.* 3, ff. 3^v–4^v, 24 July 1399.

[145] Sercambi, II, pp. 283–5.

15

THE ESTABLISHMENT OF THE SIGNORIA OF PAOLO GUINIGI

LAZZARO was murdered by his younger brother, Antonio, and his brother-in-law, Niccolò di Benedetto Sbarra on 15 February 1400. They called at his house in the evening, asking to speak to him. Having no reason for suspicion, Lazzaro let them in, whereupon they drew their swords and killed him. Niccolò Sbarra belonged to a family that had supported the Forteguerra before 1392, and was a nephew of messer Bartolomeo Forteguerra on his mother's side. Yet he had been listed by Dino Guinigi as a Guinigi partisan, and according to Sercambi Lazzaro had saved his life in the disorders of May 1392, and later enriched him and married one of his sisters to him.[1] But Sercambi relates that he still remained a secret enemy despite the many favours he had received, and that it was he who took the lead in the plot, inciting Antonio Guinigi to murder his brother. Antonio's motive is more difficult to determine. Sercambi relates that he had taken offence for no reason, but Minerbetti asserts that he was incited to murder his brother and make himself *signore* of Lucca by Giangaleazzo's vicar in Pisa.[2] According to Minerbetti the duke of Milan wished to be rid of Lazzaro Guinigi because he was too friendly to the Florentines. He makes no mention of Lazzaro's visit to Pavia the previous summer, and his account contains a number of inaccuracies. He makes no mention of the part played by Niccolò Sbarra. Michele Guinigi was not, as he asserts, Gonfaloniere; he was not even an Anziano, and he

[1] Sercambi, I, p. 281; II, p. 406. The precise date of the marriage and the identity of the sister are not recorded.

[2] Minerbetti, p. 246, Soz. Pist. col. 1169. Antonio had, as Minerbetti states, served as a *condottiere*, Sercambi, I, p. 412, *Reg.*, nos. 1782, 1856. When serving under Paolo Savelli he had taken part in attacks on Florentine territory to the great indignation of the Florentines, *Reg.*, no. 1673, 14 Mar. 1397. He may also have been in financial difficulties; in 1398 he was taken to court for a debt by Tegrimo Fulcieri and his holdings of 212 florins 2*s.* 2*d.* and 966 florins 12*s.* 1*d.* *a oro* in the *Massa* were adjudged to his creditor, *Imprestiti*, 18, ff. 140^{v}, 265^{v}, 306^{v}, 8 Aug. 1398.

did not, according to Sercambi's account, play a leading role in the capture of Antonio and Niccolò. It is unlikely that Giangaleazzo was implicated in the murder. There is no hint of this in Sercambi, and far from being too friendly to Florence, Lucca and the Guinigi party had been moving steadily away from Florence and closer to Milan, a development culminating in Lazzaro's visit to Giangaleazzo in Pavia in May and June 1399. The account of the plot in the sentences against Antonio and Niccolò says nothing of any outside power being involved; it agrees with the version of Sercambi, except that it makes Antonio and not Niccolò the instigator.[3] Two of the later chroniclers of Lucca attribute a different motive to Antonio. They assert that his grievance was that Lazzaro had given the heiress, Caterina Castracani degli Antelminelli, whose guardian he was, to his brother, Paolo, and not to Antonio, who felt that as the elder of the two he had the better claim.[4] It seems likely, in fact, that Niccolò's part in the murder was a long-meditated act of revenge, and that Antonio's sprang from this, or some other, private grievance.

After they had murdered Lazzaro, Antonio and Niccolò tried to rouse the city, not to overthrow the Guinigi party, but to defend it, raising the cry of 'viva parte ghibellina', and shouting that their enemies had entered the city to overthrow the regime.[5] But it was not long before the truth became

[3] According to his condemnation Antonio said to Niccolò 'Nicolae vis esse una mecum ad interficiendum Lazzarum Francisci de Guinigiis meum fratrem carnalem quia ego intendo omnino ipsum interficere considerato quod idem Lazzarus michi intulit quamplures varias et diversas iniurias insupportabiles et alia innumerabilia oppropria et dedecora. Et me ut vides non . . . [lacuna where outside top edge of page torn] . . . sed cotidie ut inimicum. Et tu Nicolae bene debes huic assentire ex eo . . . ipse Lazzarus fuit causa mortis tui avunculi et hoc facto nos elevabimus . . . civitatem et de facili presentem liberum et pacificum statum dicte civitatis subvertemus . . . Lazzarus non avera questa torta cosi in pacie come sicrede. Cui Nicolaus . . . dixit ego sum contentus hoc facere et venire una tecum ad interficiendum . . . zarum et vindicare me de morte dicti mei avunculi quam semper in animo gexi . . . ad esse omnibus que dicis'. *Sentenze e Bandi*, 97, loose folio torn where the number should be, before f. 29, dated 16 Feb. 1400.

[4] Civitali, ff. 378–378v, Dalli, III, pp. 473–4. No contemporary source refers to this motive, but serious internal disturbances arose in Pistoia in 1401 over just such a dispute over the marriage of an heiress, Herlihy, *Medieval and Renaissance Pistoia*, pp. 206–7.

[5] Dalli, III, p. 475, asserts that when Antonio and Niccolò raised the cry of 'viva parte ghibellina' the captain believed the Florentines had killed Lazzaro and entered the city. As Niccolò joined with Antonio in trying to rally the city to the defence of the Guinigi after the murder his rancour was perhaps directed against Lazzaro personally.

known to other members of the Guinigi family, and the forces of the city, led by Bartolomeo and Paolo Guinigi, captured Antonio and Niccolò and handed them over to the Podestà. They confessed and were executed the next day.[6]

The Florentines hastened to send an embassy to Lucca to offer their condolences and to urge the Lucchese to take action for the conservation of their liberty and the existing regime and the Guinigi family, offering them the full support of Florence in this. The embassy was well received, and the ambassador reported to his government later that the Lucchese and the Guinigi had said that they knew they could not preserve their liberty without Florentine assistance, and called the Florentines their fathers and benefactors.[7] In part this was ordinary diplomatic courtesy, but the Lucchese must have been anxious not to offend the Florentines in the changed situation, and in May 1400, even when refusing to renew the league with Florence, they did so with many expressions of goodwill.[8]

In fact, though Minerbetti records that quiet was restored in Lucca and that the Guinigi remained in power,[9] their position was greatly weakened. Their power had no institutional basis; the outward forms of the old republican government had been maintained and the authority of the Guinigi rested entirely on intangible personal factors. The death of Lazzaro was a serious blow. He had inherited something of his father's prestige, and was himself a man of ability. In 1400 he was a little over fifty years of age,[10] and had behind him many years of experience as a man of affairs and as a statesman, and had been virtual ruler of the city since 1392. The blow to the Guinigi party was made more serious by the death in 1400 of a number of other leading members of the family, some of whom perhaps stayed in the city at the risk of their lives during

[6] Sercambi, II, pp. 408–10. *Sentenze e Bandi*, 97, cit.

[7] A.S.F. *Consulte*, 34, ff. 82–82ᵛ, 18 Feb. 1400. *Dieci di Balìa: Relaz. di Ambasciadori*, 1, ff. 61–61ᵛ, 19–23 Feb. 1400 (Fl. style 1399).

[8] A.S.F. *Consulte*, 34, ff. 102–4, 20 May 1400. *Dieci di Balia: Relaz. di Ambasciadori*, 1, f. 62, 14–22 May 1400. The Lucchese refused the alliance, 'ma che sempre vogliono essere figliuoli di questo comune'.

[9] Minerbetti, p. 246, Soz. Pist. col. 1169.

[10] He gave his age as over thirty in 1378, *Protocolli* of ser Simone Alberti, *Archivio de'Notari*, no. 248 (not foliated), 23 Feb. 1378.

the plague in order to ensure Guinigi authority.[11] Bartolomeo, one of the two remaining sons of Francesco Guinigi, died in May 1400. Lazzaro di Niccolò died of plague at the end of June, and his son, Giovanni, followed him early in July. This left few active and experienced members of the family. Michele Guinigi, Francesco's brother, and a man who carried great weight in the city, was suffering from an incurable disease and died in October 1400. Dino Guinigi, their cousin, was too old to take a really active part in public affairs, though he lived until 1411, and Paolo, Francesco's only surviving son, commanded nothing like the same respect and was in any case seriously ill in the summer of 1400. Niccolò ser Pagani, another experienced citizen, who had played a large part in public affairs and been an important Guinigi supporter, died in the summer of 1400.[12]

The position was made more serious by an exceptionally severe visitation of the plague which had begun in September 1399[13] and raged throughout the summer of 1400, only beginning to die down in September and October. A visitation of the plague always meant problems for the government. Citizens fled to escape it, causing difficulties in obtaining sufficient Anziani, councillors and officials and perhaps in defending the city. The situation was particularly serious in 1400. The plague seems to have been worse than in some previous attacks. There are long lists of citizens who were absent and had to be replaced in the councils; sixty-five of the 135 members of the General Council had to be replaced on 2 July 1400,[14] and according to Sercambi 150 citizens a day were dying at the height of the plague.[15] Private houses and even villas and castles were said to be standing empty and more citizens fled daily.[16] Emergency measures had to be taken. Extra forces were hired,[17] and in June 100 foot-soldiers were summoned from the *contado* to guard Lucca.[18] It was decreed

[11] Sercambi, III, p. 4.
[12] Sercambi, III, pp. 4–8, 11.
[13] Sercambi, II, pp. 396–7.
[14] *Rif.* 13, pp. 343–4, 2 July 1400. Officials fleeing from the plague, *Rif.* 13, p. 347, 5 July 1400.
[15] Sercambi, III, pp. 4–5. Also Minerbetti, p. 251.
[16] *Rif.* 13, p. 333, 9 June 1400.
[17] *Rif.* 13, p. 323, 26 Apr. 1400.
[18] *Rif.* 13. p. 340, 24 June 1400.

that the names of the new Anziani should be published early, so that they could be forced to return to Lucca. But despite the heavy fines laid down for those who failed to do so, it was still necessary to appoint replacements for Anziani who had ignored the summons.[19] In order that Lucca should not be completely deserted, and in order to forestall any attacks from outside, many *banniti* were readmitted. All those condemned to fines and also some who were guilty of more serious offences were offered pardon.[20]

But the danger that the city would be left totally deserted and undefended, and the difficulty of maintaining the ordinary government during the plague were not the only problems. The city was threatened from outside and the position the Guinigi family had built up over the last decades trembled in the balance and seemed in danger of collapse. The deaths of the most senior and most respected members of the family and the lack of any adequate candidate to take their place encouraged their enemies within the city and Lucchese in exile outside to make an effort to overthrow them. Lucchese exiles had taken refuge in Bologna, Florence and Pisa, and there was much talk there of the decline of the Guinigi party. A letter written to Giovanni Testa, the Gonfaloniere of Lucca for July and August, shows how uncertain the position was. The writer reported rumours of the death of Dino Guinigi and wrote

> perche ame pare che tu si remaso governadore di Lucca, pregote che la sapi bene governare, perche tu non sai di chi fidarte che tale fue amicho di Lazari che non sere forse, tuo. Ogi e maiore pericolo di Lucca che mai fosse che voi non vegnate soto altrui.[21]

The plots and threats of attack from exiles outside the city would have been less serious had there not also been much talk and sympathy for them from certain quarters within the city. But according to Sercambi, though the Guinigi party was fully aware of this, with the clemency which had always marked their rule and which was to be continued by Paolo Guinigi

[19] *Rif.* 13, p. 333, 9 June, p. 339, 22 June, Turchio Balbani, the Gonfaloniere, had fled to Bologna and did not want to return to hold the office, p. 341, 29 June 1400.

[20] Sercambi, III, p. 9

[21] Letter of 5 July 1400, *Anz. Temp. Lib.* 439, no. 1984 in *Reg.* The writer was Giovanni de Sala, a Lucchese exile, who desired to return. He was one of those involved in the attacks on the Garfagnana in 1396, *Sentenze e Bandi*, 89, ff. 41–2, 4 Sept. 1396. Zerbi, *I Visconti di Milano e la Signoria di Lucca*, p. 57.

after 1400, they did not molest known adherents or relatives of the exiles, who wished to stay in Lucca.[22]

They did, however, take action to safeguard the city and the position they had acquired within it. According to Sercambi the extra forces hired and the men brought from the *contado* were Guinigi supporters.[23] Provision was made that the college of Anziani along with such councillors as were present could fill any positions that fell vacant through death, illness or absence, except in the General Council or the Thirty-Six, without the need to observe vacations, and if there were no councillors remaining or present the Anziani could make the substitutions on their own.[24]

In July the Guinigi went a step further. Messer Tommaso da Ghivizzano, one of the firmest adherents of the Guinigi party,[25] proposed the setting up of a *balìa* of twelve citizens to whom the entire administration of the city should be entrusted for a year. They were to have full power and jurisdiction 'prout habet totus populus et comune Lucanum et cives ipsius civitatis Lucane ac consilium generale ipsius comunis'. This seems to have been intended as more than just a temporary emergency measure. The preamble to the discussion speaks of providing for the future as well as the present, 'non enim minora pericula finita peste imminere videntur si recte consideratur et cernitur'. The decree itself gave the *balìa* power to replace any of their number who should die, fall ill or be absent, and they were also empowered to elect others with the same authority as themselves 'pro eo tempore de quo eis videbitur et placebit'.[26] The *Riformagioni* account of this provided that the *balìa* was to act in concert with the Anziani, but Sercambi relates that it could act alone without the need to

[22] Sercambi, III, pp. 5–6.

[23] Sercambi, III, p. 6. The chapter in which he records the provision of extra defenders is headed 'Come a Luccha vennero alla guardia molti amici della casa de'Guinigi'.

[24] 'Et si nulli de consiliariis superessent aut presentes non forent possint illud idem domini per se facere', *Rif.* 13, p. 330, 25 May 1400. This is not entirely clear, but presumably means that the Anziani could elect replacements on their own, rather than that they could perform the functions of these councillors themselves. This was proposed by Lazzaro di Niccolò Guinigi.

[25] Sercambi, III, p. 7.

[26] This was cancelled in the text, but not replaced by any clause laying down a time limit, *Rif.* 13, pp. 345–6, 2 July 1400. Passed by 101–30.

consult the Anziani, and that, further, it could 'rimuovere l'officio dello antianatico, e cassare officiali et soldati, et di nuovo elegere; e tucto poteano fare e a ugni ora sensa contasto'.[27] It seems doubtful, however, whether his account is wholly reliable. He claims to have addressed the council himself, but the *Riformagioni* show that the proposal was made by messer Tommaso da Ghivizzano, and that Sercambi was not even present,[28] though he may have played a leading part in some preparatory discussion or unofficial meeting that has not been recorded. He does not give the date, except to say that it took place in July or August, while Giovanni Testa was Gonfaloniere. It is therefore just possible that his account refers to some later modifications of the decree of 2 July, not recorded in the *Riformagioni*. But this is unlikely, and Sercambi's own account of later events shows that the Anziani retained their importance and that the *balìa* did not live permanently in the room he says was prepared for them in the Palace of the Anziani.[29] The Thirty-Six continued to meet,[30] as did the twelve commissioners. In fact only two of the twelve commissioners who took office 1 March 1400 remained; the rest were dead, or had fled to escape the plague. Absent ones were relaced mainly by members of the *balìa* of 2 July 1400.[31] But the new commissioners took office normally on 1 September 1400, and the commissioners still did things, such as electing the Captain of the People and a captain of the *contado*, which could easily have been done by the new *balìa* under the authority granted to it 2 July 1400.

Nevertheless even if the old organs of government continued to function and the *balìa* of 2 July 1400 acted with the Anziani and not alone, the authority granted to it was very great, and it prepared the way for the total extinguishing of the

[27] Sercambi, III, p. 8.

[28] *Rif.* 13, p. 346, 2 July 1400. S. Bongi, *Chroniche Lucchesi di Giovanni Sercambi, Prefazione I*, p. xxiv, note 1, Tommasi, p. 287.

[29] They had to be fetched 14 October, Sercambi, III, p. 15.

[30] *Rif.* 13, p. 347, 5 July, pp. 252-3, 23 Aug., p. 362, 23 Oct. 1400. The last two meetings were for the extraction of the names of the Anziani, however.

[31] Five of the six replacements 4 Aug. 1400 and nine of the ten replacements 18 Aug. were from the members of the *balìa* of 2 July 1400. Also four of five replacements 6 Sept. 1400 for members of the new group of commissioners whose office began 1 Sept. 1400. Three of these new commissioners were also members of the *balìa* of 2 July 1400.

republican form of government. Two of the members of the *balìa* were drawn from the Guinigi family, and the others were all regarded as firm adherents of the Guinigi party.[32]

In September and October 1400 the Guinigi obtained an exceptionally favourable college of Anziani. Several of those drawn as Anziani were dead or absent, so that it was possible to substitute Giovanni Sercambi as Gonfaloniere and Paolo Guinigi and Andrea Orsucci as Anziani.[33] Of the others Ciuchino Avvocati and Jacobo Darii were notable Guinigi supporters. But the death of Michele Guinigi 11 October 1400 struck a further blow at Guinigi authority.[34] There had, according to Sercambi, already been much plotting and talk among Lucchese absent from Lucca during the plague. Lucchese in Rome, Genoa, Bologna, and above all Florence, were discussing means of putting an end to Guinigi power. Sercambi asserts that the commune of Florence itself was involved in these plots.[35] Among the Lucchese he names it is not surprising to find men like Lando Moriconi, who had long been enemies of the Guinigi regime, but some of the others, such as ser Domenico Lùpardi or Turchio Balbani had earlier been Guinigi supporters. These were apparently not the only defections; according to Sercambi, one of the leading members of the di Poggio family, who had been among the most whole-hearted supporters of the Guinigi earlier, had now gone over to the opposition.[36] There may be a number of explanations for these changes of view. It is possible that they had only supported Guinigi rule when the alternative was the rule of the Forteguerra and Rapondi, and that they now saw in the weakening of the Guinigi party an opportunity to free the city from the control of any one family. But it seems probable that, at least in part, the reason for their change of attitude

[32] They were Giovanni Sercambi, Nuccio Giovanni, Francesco Berindelli, Franceschino Buzolini, messer Tommaso da Ghivizzano, Antonio da Volterra, Paolo Guinigi, Bonaccorso Bocci, Dino Guinigi, Giovanni Bernardini, Giovanni Testa, and Niccolò di Filippo da Signa, *calzolaio*, *Rif.* 13, p. 346, 2 July 1400, Sercambi, III, p. 8.

[33] This was done by a *balìa* authorized for the purpose 9 June, *Rif.* 13, pp. 333–4, 9 June, p. 354, 23 Aug. 1400, not by the *balìa* of 2 July, as Sercambi states, III, p. 9.

[34] Sercambi, III, p. 11.

[35] 'Il comune di Firenza, con alquanti usciti di Luccha et etiando con alquanti asentati, preseno pensiero e molti ragionamenti del modo di mandare per terra la dicta case de'Guinigi e loro amici', Sercambi III, p. 10.

[36] Sercambi, III, pp. 10–12.

was objection to Paolo Guinigi personally. The unnamed member of the di Poggio family is said to have declared 'che non si sosterrà che Paulo Guinigi maestri, e prima che consentisse . . . voremmo prima morire'.[37] Paolo Guinigi was not yet thirty years of age in 1400,[38] and as a comparatively young man did not carry the same weight as his brother Lazzaro, or Michele or Lazzaro di Niccolò had done. He was relatively inexperienced, and was perhaps regarded as unfit to rule. Sercambi himself, one of his chief supporters in 1400, later criticized him for weakness of character and excessive and ill-judged clemency, and he certainly showed himself timid and irresolute in the crisis of 1429.

But he acted resolutely enough in 1400. When the death of Michele Guinigi led some Lucchese both inside and outside the city to look for the fall of the Guinigi, Paolo resolved to forestall any attempts against his position by having himself elected Captain and Defender of the city. He had the support of Giovanni Sercambi, the Gonfaloniere, and Jacopo Darii, who like Paolo himself was an Anziano, and messer Tommaso da Ghivizzano, Agostino Avvocati, and the chancellors ser Guido da Pietrasanta and ser Marco Martini. They summoned the supporters of the Guinigi party from the *contado*, who seem to have been the Ghibelline faction in each vicariate.[39] They also requested forty or fifty lances from Giangaleazzo's captain in Pisa. According to Sercambi, the Guinigi party believed Florence to be behind the efforts of Lucchese exiles to bring about their downfall, and he asserts that the Florentines had stationed forces in the Valdinievole and Valdarno, ready to march against Lucca when called upon.[40] If this was true, or if Paolo Guinigi and his supporters believed it to be true, his request for aid from Milan is understandable, particularly if there had been some kind of agreement between the duke and

[37] Sercambi, III, p. 12.

[38] Series *Archivio Guinigi*, no. 312, f. 155 records the date of his birth as 1372. This is probably correct, as he was Anziano for the first time Mar./Apr. 1395, and the minimum age for this was 22. He sat in the Thirty-Six elected September 1393. The minimum age for this was 25, *Statuto* 1372, I, xviii, but the reduction of the minimum age for Anziani from 25 to 22 after May 1392 probably applied to the Thirty-Six as well, *Rif.* 12, p. 121, 26 May 1392.

[39] Sercambi, III, p. 13. See also III, p. 18 for Sercambi's list of Francesco Guinigi's Ghibelline supporters in the *contado*.

[40] Sercambi, III, p. 12.

the Guinigi during Lazzaro's visit to Pavia in May 1399. But whatever his immediate motives for making the request, the fact remains that Paolo Guinigi obtained the captaincy of Lucca with the aid of Visconti forces, for Giangaleazzo's captain agreed not merely to send aid, but to come to Lucca himself.[41]

The *coup* was planned for 14 October 1400. Paolo summoned his friends and supporters to Lucca and during the night managed to win over the constables of the hired forces in Lucchese service to his side, Paolo remained armed in the piazza, while members of the *balìa* of 2 July were summoned to the palace early in the morning. There Sercambi as Gonfaloniere explained to them that the plots of exiles and outside powers against the city of Lucca and the Guinigi made it necessary for Paolo to take arms for the safety of the city and the existing regime. There was much grumbling from the *balìa*, especially from Giovanni Testa and Antonio da Volterra, who objected to Paolo's taking arms. Even when the *balìa* was informed of the forces summoned from the *contado* and from Pisa, and requested to elect Paolo Captain and Defender of the city, there was still resistance. But one of the *balìa* was messer Tommaso da Ghivizzano, and he urged the others to agree. Paolo also had the support of the Podestà and the Captain of the People. Finally the *balìa* of 2 July and the Anziani agreed to elect Paolo Captain and Defender of the People, as he had desired, and he then rode through the city with the banner of the people carried before him.

It is interesting to see the strength of the opposition to Paolo's desire to be made Captain and Defender of the city, even from the *balìa* of 2 July, composed largely of men the Guinigi had regarded as their supporters. They too may have hoped for an end to Guinigi rule in the city with the death of the strongest and most influential members of the family. But it may have been that while they had been willing enough to accept Guinigi power when it was indirect and not accompanied by any official title, they were unwilling that it should be openly acknowledged. They too may have regarded Paolo

[41] Sercambi, III, p. 14. Communications between the Guinigi and Milan had been maintained. *Regesto*, III, *Carteggio di Paolo Guinigi, Appendice alla Parte Seconda*, p. 474, nos. 12-14, Jan.-Mar. 1400.

as unfit to hold even the unofficial position that his father and brother had had.

Even after Paolo had achieved the position of Captain and Defender of the People there was still opposition. In November 1400 a plot was discovered, in which Paolo's cousin, Niccolò Guinigi, bishop of Lucca, Bartolomeo di Duccio da Aramo, and certain canons of Lucca cathedral were involved. One of the great sources of strength of the Guinigi family had been their unity. The several branches of the family had been able to co-operate and no quarrels or rivalries, which would have greatly weakened the family, had hitherto broken out. Sercambi attributes bishop Niccolò's participation in this plot to jealousy of Paolo's title of Captain.[42] As an ecclesiastic and a member of the Guinigi family he was pardoned, and in fact continued to live in Lucca, as bishop, on good terms with Paolo after 1400, giving no further trouble. The other chief plotter, Bartolomeo da Aramo was executed. He too had previously been a Guinigi supporter; Sercambi names his father as among Francesco Guinigi's reliable friends in the *contado*, and a member of the Ghibelline party of Valdriana.[43]

According to Sercambi, it was this plot which caused Paolo Guinigi to wish for a further change in his position. He had been content since 14 October to rule with the Anziani and councils.[44] But in November he had himself elected *signore* by the *balìa* of twelve and the Anziani. Sercambi describes his position as 'signore a bachetta' with 'mero e misto inperio di potere tucto fare'.[45] He allowed the college of Anziani then in office to finish their term, but after that no new colleges took office. There were no Anziani, General Councils, or Councils of Thirty-Six between 1400 and 1430. Paolo Guinigi ruled the city alone.

[42] Sercambi, III, p. 21.
[43] Sercambi, III, p. 18.
[44] The Thirty-Six met once, *Rif.* 13, p. 362, 23 Oct. 1400.
[45] Sercambi, III, p. 22.

CONCLUSION

It is illustrative of the difficulties of republican government in late fourteenth-century Italy that the 'liberty' and republican regime restored with such high hopes in 1369 proved so short-lived. Liberty in the sense of freedom from outside rule was to prove remarkably resilient; Lucca never again fell to one of her neighbours and was to retain her independence until 1799. But liberty in the sense of a republican form of government proved more fragile; it lasted formally for little over thirty years and effectively for an even shorter period.

For much of the last three decades of the fourteenth century Lucca seems to have enjoyed relative peace and order internally. There is little sign of class struggle, social unrest, or an unruly magnate element. Judicial records certainly show, as in Florence and other cities, the existence of an underworld of criminal elements and a tendency to easy recourse to violence in minor quarrels, but cases involving important citizens are not unduly frequent and there is no sign of social unrest among the lower classes.[1] The *popolo minuto* does not seem to have played any significant role in political life; there are few mentions of it in such sources as chronicles or the council records, and there are certainly no records of the kind of industrial unrest that has been illustrated for Florence.[2] This was perhaps because the silk industry, Lucca's main industrial activity, did not involve the large class of wage-earning artisans in a weak economic position that the Florentine wool

[1] For violence in other cities in this period L. Martines (ed.), *Violence and Civil Disorder in Italian Cities 1200–1500* (Berkeley and Los Angeles, 1972), especially the articles by Chojnacki and Brucker.

[2] Brucker, *Florentine politics and society*, pp. 54–6, 107–11, 197–8, 367–8, 378–86. M. B. Becker, 'Some aspects of oligarchical, dictatorial and popular *signorie* in Florence, 1282–1382', *Comparative Studies in Society and History*, Vol. II (1959–60), p. 424. N. Rodolico, *La democrazia fiorentina nel suo tramonto (1378–82)* (Bologna, 1905), pp. 101–12. For Siena, D. L. Hicks, 'Sienese society in the Renaissance', *Comparative Studies in Society and History*, Vol. II (1959–60), pp. 113–14. V. Rutenberg, 'La vie et la lutte des Ciompi de Sienne', *Annales* Vol. XX (1965), pp. 101–9, and more generally *Popolo e movimenti popolari nell'Italia del '300 e '400*, tr. G. Borghini, Bologna, 1971.

industry produced. Nor does the decline of the Lucchese silk industry seem to have brought with it the unemployment and economic distress that a similar decline produced in late fifteenth- and early sixteenth-century Genoa.[3] One of the main causes for the decline of the Lucchese industry seems to have been emigration and this probably meant that it involved little unemployment. Petitions suggest that the problem was reduced production rather than difficulty in selling products. There was, therefore, no tradition of social and industrial unrest in Lucca and no memory of an uprising like that of the Ciompi to dominate the thinking of the upper classes, as it has been argued was the case in Florence.[4] If Lucca had any memory of the recent past to dominate her thinking, it must have been the memory of Pisan rule, and the determination not to allow the city to fall again under foreign domination perhaps did something to bind her governing classes together, especially in the first years after 1369.

But delight at once more enjoying independence and determination never again to fall under outside rule did not mean that there were no disagreements about the way Lucca should be ruled. It has already been seen that little more than a year after the Emperor had freed her from Pisan rule and within a few months of the departure of Cardinal Guy of Boulogne Lucca was seriously divided. The government 'a comune' that came to an end in July 1370 lasted too short a period for it to be possible to discuss its precise character and to understand why it aroused such opposition. The role of Guelf party feeling and the influence of particular families like the Obizi or the Guinigi is also unclear.

One can speak with more confidence of the regime that emerged from these disputes. It is clear that, though government 'a popolo' involved the exclusion of certain noble families, it did not mean a broadly based popular regime. Lucca is yet another example of the tendency for government to fall into the hands of an oligarchy, whatever the nominal

[3] P. Coles, 'The crisis of Renaissance society, Genoa 1488–1507', *Past and Present*, no. 11 (1957), pp. 27–8.

[4] A. Molho, 'Politics and the ruling class in early Renaissance Florence', *Nuova Rivista Storica*, Vol. LII (1968), pp. 416–17 and 'The Florentine oligarchy and the *balìe* of the late Trecento', *Speculum*, Vol. XLIII (1968), pp. 26, 28.

character of the regime.[5] In Lucca as in other cities 'popolo' meant not the whole people, but only the richest and most influential section of it, the merchants, bankers, and entrepreneurs. Oligarchy, it has been said, was everywhere the predominant form of government. In republics there was always a tendency for power to concentrate in the hands of a limited group, and it was rare for it to be shared more widely. Even the popular victory of 1343 in Florence did not establish a regime dominated by artisans and shopkeepers or give more than a very small proportion of the population a share in the government.[6] Certainly in Lucca after 1370 government 'a popolo' meant a government dominated by an oligarchy of wealthy merchants, bankers, and entrepreneurs, usually belonging to old-established families.[7] Though it was by no means unknown for a weaver or a tanner or a smith to sit as a member of the college of Anziani or Council of Thirty-Six, and there was a handful who held such positions regularly, they were usually substantial men with thirty or forty florins in the *Massa* and employers of workmen in their trades. Even they were not very numerous, and there were many men recorded in such sources as the books of the *Massa* who played

[5] W. L. Gundersheimer, *Ferrara, the Style of a Renaissance Despotism* (Princeton, 1973), p. 8.

[6] P. J. Jones, 'Communes and despots: the city state in late-medieval Italy', *Transactions of the Royal Historical Society* ser. v, Vol. XV (1965), pp. 74-5. D. M. Bueno de Mesquita, 'The place of despotism in Italian politics' in J. L. Highfield, B. Smalley, and J. R. Hale (eds.), *Europe in the Late Middle Ages* (London, 1965), p. 310. L. Martines, 'Political conflict in the Italian city-states', *Government and Opposition*, Vol. 3 (1968), pp. 77-80. B. Pullan, *A History of Early Renaissance Italy* (London, 1973), pp. 118-22. G. Chittolini, 'La crisi delle libertà comunali e le origini dello stato territoriale', *Rivista Storica Italiana* Vol. LXXXII (1970), pp. 102-3. Molho, 'Politics and the ruling class', pp. 404-5, 408-11, 417, 'The Florentine oligarchy', p. 28. M. B. Becker and G. A. Brucker, 'The *Arti Minori* in Florentine politics 1342-1378', *Medieval Studies*, Vol. XVIII (1956), pp. 96-7, 101-4.

[7] For 'popolo' in a similar sense, Martines, 'Political conflict', pp. 79-80, Jones, 'Communes and despots', p. 76. For the cry 'viva il popolo' in movements involving wealthy middle class elements and even magnates, W. M. Bowsky, 'The anatomy of rebellion in fourteenth-century Siena: from Commune to Signory ?', in Martines (ed.), *Violence and Civil Disorder*, pp. 247-63 and Brucker, *Florentine Politics and Society*, p. 113. The government of Lucca in the late fourteenth century may be compared with that of the Nine in Siena 1287-1355, when certain noble *casati* and also judges, doctors, and notaries were ineligible, and artisans and men in other humble occupations were occasionally included, but the government was dominated by men who also dominated the consulate of the Guild Merchant. The chief difference was perhaps the role played in Siena by the lesser nobility, Bowsky, *'Buon Governo'*, pp. 373-8.

no part at all in political life. Surprisingly few men in humble occupations ever managed to enter even the General Council, and those that did were heavily outnumbered by members of the merchant and business class and can have had little influence on affairs. They are virtually never recorded as speaking in council, and even if they did their views would not count for much against those of wealthy citizens whose businesses took them abroad and gave them outside contacts and an experience of foreign affairs that no shoemaker or vintner who rarely left the city would be able to rival.

Power then was in the hands of a relatively small group of leading mercantile and banking families. There were perhaps 170 or 180 families that had members holding the office of Anziano, sitting in the Council of Thirty-Six and elected to *balìe* with any frequency. But as in other Italian republics there was an inner oligarchy within this wider oligarchy.[8] There were something like fifty families that had several members holding the highest offices regularly and frequently. Most of these were already well-established by 1369. Many of them are recorded as holding the office of Anziano between 1330 and 1369 or had been among those named as 'potentes et casastici' in 1308. The records of the Court of Merchants show that this oligarchy was primarily a mercantile and business class. The men who played the leading part in communal politics were equally active in directing business affairs; they controlled the most powerful companies, held office as consuls and councillors, and spoke most frequently in the deliberations of the Court, as they did in those of the Commune.

It is important to note that though the ruling class was an oligarchy of wealthy and usually old-established families, it was not a closed aristocracy. There were none of the 'serrate' described by Ventura for the Venetian terrafirma with council seats held for life and treated as a piece of private property.[9] There were no parties on an organized basis or lists of office holders, only the descendants of whom could hope to gain

[8] Martines, 'Political conflict', p. 81, Jones, 'Communes and despots', p. 78. For the role of the inner oligarchy in Medici Florence, N. Rubinstein, *The Government of Florence under the Medici 1434 to 1494* (Oxford, 1966), esp. pp. 131–5.

[9] A. Ventura, *Nobiltà e popolo nella società veneta del '400 e '500* (Bari, 1964), pp. 11–29.

entry to the highest posts, such as were being compiled in Siena in the late fifteenth century.[10] The oligarchy that dominated Lucchese affairs was still loose and informal, not hereditary and exclusive. It was still possible for new men, even those in a less solid economic position or less dignified occupations, to gain entry. There was no theoretical or legal exclusiveness; it was simply that in practice the government of the city was dominated by members of a relatively small number of usually long-established families, with the resources, experience, contacts, and prestige that must have seemed in the 'deferential society' of the times to have given them a claim to power.[11]

It was from within this oligarchy that the Guinigi *signorìa* arose and it is to this oligarchy one must look for its origins. No other group was of any real importance. It was within the ranks of the oligarchy that the rivalries and divisions grew up, which eventually led to the domination of the city by a single family, and finally to the emergence of a single man as *signore*. One of the great weaknesses of Italian republics was their tendency to factionalism. Even where a relatively homogeneous group had established itself as a ruling class, it was rare for it to remain united. There was a tendency to split into two parties, each headed by a great family, and there were struggles between rival families, groups, and factions with no political, economic, or class content. From these struggles a *signorìa* frequently emerged, either by the direct victory of one faction over the other or because the city, exhausted by the struggles, gave itself to a *signore* in the hopes that he would bring peace and order.[12] The Guinigi, like

[10] Hicks, 'Sienese society', pp. 415-16. For the crystallization of aristocratic society at tyrant courts and in republics in the Renaissance, Chittolini, 'La crisi delle libertà comunali', pp. 115-16.

[11] Martines, 'Political conflict', pp. 77-9.

[12] A. Anzilotti, 'Per la storia delle signorie e del diritto pubblico italiano del Rinascimento', *Studi Storici*, Vol. XII (1914), p. 86. G. B. Picotti, 'Qualche osservazione sui caratteri delle signorie italiane', *Rivista Storica Italiana* Vol. XLIII (1926), pp. 14-15. F. Cognasso, 'Le origini della signoria lombarda', *Archivio Storico Lombardo*, ser. viii, Vol. VI (1956), pp. 8-9. F. Chabod, 'Di alcuni studi recenti sull'età comunale e signorile nell'Italia settentrionale', *Rivista Storica Italiana*, Vol. XLII (1925), pp. 39-41.D. Waley, *The Italian City Republics* (London, 1969), pp. 230-2. J. Larner, *The Lords of the Romagna* (London, 1965), p. 57. G. Masi, 'Verso gli albori del principato in Italia', *Rivista di Storia del Diritto Italiano*, Vol. IX (1936),

many Italian *signori* came to power as the head of a faction, and it was within the ruling oligarchy that these factions first formed.

It has already been seen that the composition of the two factions was markedly similar. There was no social or economic cleavage between them. Certainly neither can be seen as representing popular as opposed to oligarchical forces. Both were led by wealthy old-established families engaged in industry as entrepreneurs and in international trade and banking. It is significant of the extent to which power followed wealth that one faction was headed by the richest family in Lucca and the other apparently by the second richest. The parties were bound together by a network of interests, and wealth must have been an important factor in building these up. The nucleus of each party was a family grouping, with its own kinsmen and connections by marriage and business associates. There are examples of men connected with one group by marriage ties or past business contacts taking the other side, and there were cases of kinsmen taking opposite sides, but these are not very common and serve only to emphasize the social similarity of the two factions. The Forteguerra-Rapondi party certainly had the support of the vast majority of Lucchese judges, perhaps out of solidarity with messer Bartolomeo Forteguerra. The Guinigi party included a number of notaries and other men in a less solid social and economic position, who may be seen as clients motivated by ambition and interest in choosing which party to support, but it is probable that the Forteguerra-Rapondi party would be seen to have included similar men, had fuller lists of their adherents survived. If this was a feature of the Guinigi faction alone, it can probably be explained by the fact that they were to some extent in power in the 1380s and therefore attracted men who were looking for a patron.[13]

---

pp. 68–70, 76. Jones, 'Communes and despots', pp. 77–9, 83–6, Chittolini, 'La crisi delle libertà comunali', pp. 102–3. J. Heers, 'Partis politiques et clans familiaux dans l'Italie de la Renaissance', *Revue de la Méditerranée*, Vol. XX (1960), pp. 261–5. Molho, 'Politics and the ruling class', pp. 406–12, 417. E. Sestan, 'Le origini delle signorie cittadine: un problema storico esaurito?', *Bullettino dell'Instituto Storico Italiano per il Medio Evo e Archivio Muratoriano*, Vol. LXXI (1962), pp. 47–9, 54–6. Also L. Simeoni, *Le signorie*, 2 vols., Milan, 1950.

[13] For the building up of parties by favours and ties of interest in other cities,

The factions were purely internal groupings, concerned with establishing themselves in a position to dominate their city. There is no evidence that either had the support of any outside power, nor do there seem to have been divisions along party lines on foreign policy questions. Also, although the Guinigi seem to have had the support of the Ghibelline factions in the various vicariates of the *contado*, it is difficult to connect the two factions with any earlier party grouping in the city. There is reason to believe, as one might expect, that the vicissitudes Lucca had undergone in the earlier fourteenth century had caused the break-up of old factions and the blurring of old party distinctions. Both parties drew their support from families connected with a number of previous groupings, and although the term Ghibelline does seem to have been used in connection with the Guinigi, it is unlikely that it had more than local meaning. The Guinigi party seems to have had no *raison d'être* beyond support of the Guinigi and their ambitions.

The Lucchese factions were city-based. It is true that their influence was by no means confined to the city. Both parties had supporters in the *contado*, and when it came to an open struggle drew or hoped to draw forces from there. The leading members of the two parties held land in the *contado*. Their families were probably of *contado* origin, perhaps even feudal origin, and they may have kept up their connections with the particular part of the *contado* from which they had come, though the Guinigi at least had groups of supporters all over the *contado*. But whatever the antecedents of the leading families, they had their roots in the city by the late fourteenth century. They were merchants, bankers, manufacturers, lawyers, and their sources of strength were in the city. They were city factions, whose activities and influence stretched into the *contado*, not noble and feudal families deriving their strength from the number of armed followers they could raise from their lands and jurisdictions, who were intervening in the city, like the great families of the Romagna or even the rival

Anzilotti, 'Per la storia delle signorie', pp. 81–2, Masi, 'Verso gli albori del principato', pp. 150–1, Sestan, 'Le origini delle signorie', pp. 47–9. For patronage as a source of strength to a ruler in a rather different situation, I. Robertson, 'The *signorìa* of Girolamo Riario in Imola', *Historical Studies*, Vol. XV (1971), pp. 98–104, 115.

factions in early fourteenth century Padua.[14] Many northern Italian *signori* had feudal backgrounds and the establishment of the *signorìa* has been seen as the victory of landed power.[15] This applies primarily to an earlier period, but the importance, even the increasing importance, of signorial or 'feudal' elements in city factions and the need to look beyond the city to include the *contado*, when considering the rise of *signori* in the fourteenth and fifteenth centuries in certain areas has been stressed by Chittolini. But this is less important in cities that were commercial and manufacturing centres than in primarily agricultural areas.[16] It certainly seems to have had little application to Lucca. She had few feudal families of any real importance within her territory by the late fourteenth century, and noble families with their base in the *contado* play little part in Lucchese internal affairs. The di Poggio seem to have some of the characteristics of such families, but their leading members included men active in trade and industry, and they are in practice indistinguishable from other leading Lucchese families. Also they were not, of course, at the head of either faction.

The essence of the Guinigi faction was a group of predominantly wealthy and old-established merchant and business families, headed by the richest family in the city, who with supporters including clients attracted by the prospect of patronage were trying to dominate their city by the manipulation of the republican forms of government. The Forteguerra-Rapondi party may have developed parallel or grown up slightly later in reaction to the progress the Guinigi had made. But whichever was the case they cannot be seen as

[14] Larner, *Lords of the Romagna*, pp. 18-77. J. K. Hyde, *Padua in the Age of Dante* (Manchester, 1966), pp. 262-82.

[15] Waley, *The Italian City Republics*, pp. 221-32, Bueno de Mesquita, 'The place of despotism in Italian politics', pp. 314-15, Cognasso, 'Le origini della signoria lombarda', p. 10, Pullan, *A History of Early Renaissance Italy*, pp. 143-5. Also E. Salzer, *Uber die Anfänge der Signorie in Oberitalien*, Berlin, 1900. For the d'Este, Gundersheimer, *Ferrara*, pp. 18-24.

[16] Chittolini, 'La crisi delle libertà comunali', pp. 105-6, 111-13, 119. For the need to distinguish between different places and different societies, Masi, 'Verso gli albori del principato', pp. 141-4, 154-6, Sestan, 'Le origini delle signorie', pp. 56-7. For the role of feudatories in Florence, M. B. Becker, 'The republican city state in Florence: an inquiry into its origins and survival (1280-1434)', *Speculum*, Vol. XXXV (1960), pp. 39-41.

right-minded citizens, striving to defend the republican constitution against the manipulations and encroachments of the Guinigi. They were clearly no less ambitious and self-interested. The choice for Lucca, as for so many Italian cities of the period, was between two factions, not between a regular republican government and domination by a faction. The nature of the choice would go some way towards explaining why it was that so many leading citizens, whose wealth and social position would seem to ensure them a leading place in any republican regime, and who would seem to have much to lose if a faction succeeded in gaining control of the government, are nevertheless found among the active supporters of one party or the other. Also many citizens may have been prepared to tolerate or even support factions that were manipulating the government while maintaining outward republican forms, when they would not have been prepared to support an effort to establish an open *signorìa*.

The most obvious and direct parallel to these efforts by Lucchese factions to dominate the city by manipulating republican institutions is in Florence. In late fourteenth- and early fifteenth-century Florence groups that differed little from each other in social and economic composition and outlook struggled for power and influence,[17] and after 1434 the Medici were able to establish a greater degree of control by similar methods. The Medici are, of course, the classic example of a concealed *signorìa* by men who were in theory no more than ordinary citizens. The Lucchese factions pursued a similar policy of trying to establish and strengthen their position by the manipulation of councils and offices, but with the difference that they had a far better chance of exercising a really close control, because the form of government made such manipulation relatively easy. The Lucchese constitution was much less complex than that of Florence, and selection by lot played a very minor role. The Thirty-Six was elected by the Anziani and six per *terziere* of the retiring Thirty-Six, and in September they also elected the General Council. Many other

[17] Molho, 'Politics and the ruling class', p. 417, Masi, 'Verso gli albori del principato', pp. 150–6, Sestan, 'Le origini delle signorie', pp. 47–9, L. F. Marks, 'Fourteenth-century democracy in Florence', *Past and Present*, no. 25 (1963), p. 77. I regret that I was not able to consult G. Brucker, *The Civic World of Early Renaissance Florence* (Princeton, 1977) and F. W. Kent, *Household and Lineage in Renaissance Florence* (Princeton, 1977) until this book was in proof.

offices, such as vicar and *conducterii* were also subject to direct election, not sortition; even when there was a 'tasca' for these offices it was made by the direct election in advance of the number of citizens necessary to fill the office for the stated period, though the particular term for which they served and in the case of vicars the vicariate may have been decided by lot. But the limited role of sortition was most significant in the case of the Anziani. They were elected normally for two years at a time by the current Anziani and Thirty-Six reinforced by six *invitati* per *terziere*. Each of the electors had the right to make a certain number of nominations, and the nominees were then voted on one by one. Though there were elaborate arrangements to ensure secrecy during voting, the names of the successful candidates were to be declared, and the grouping into colleges was done at the same time by an Anziano and two of the electoral council per *terziere*. Not only did they select the Gonfalonieri and decide which of the successful candidates were to hold office in the same college, something of great importance in neutralizing suspect or unreliable citizens, they may even have decided the order in which the colleges were to hold office. The ordinary method of election in Lucca thus made control relatively easy. The use of direct election instead of sortition on the basis of lists of men declared eligible in a scrutiny meant that there was not the same danger of potential enemies holding office because their names had been left in the bags.[18] Nor was there any need for the kind of laborious efforts the Medici had to make to obtain the authorization and renewal of elections *a mano* to the Signoria. This was unpopular and met with setbacks, and it gave a far more limited degree of control of the personnel selected to the highest office than the ordinary republican constitution provided for any group seeking to control political offices in Lucca.[19]

[18] It has indeed been argued that the failure to consolidate the regime in Florence after 1382 was the direct result of reliance on appointment to offices by lot, and that Cosimo de'Medici imposed electoral controls because he learnt from these mistakes, Molho, 'Politics and the ruling class', pp. 412–13, Rubinstein, *Government of Florence under the Medici*, pp. 7–8. For the complexities of the Florentine electoral system, also Brucker, *Florentine politics and society*, pp. 66–71. Lottery did not, however, prevent the repeated appearance of the same men among the Nine in Siena, Bowsky, *'Buon Governo'*, pp. 370–1.

[19] Rubinstein, *Government of Florence under the Medici*, esp. pp. 10–49.

Once a majority had been obtained in the college of Anziani and the Thirty-Six its maintenance was a relatively simple matter, as between them they controlled the elections of succeeding Anziani and the General Council and Thirty-Six. There were, of course, vacations, but these presented no real problem as the ruling oligarchy was large enough to provide men to fill all important offices without the need to arouse criticism by failure to observe vacations. As the principle of vacations and the rotation of offices in Italian city-states was designed to prevent excessive power falling into the hands of any one family or group, one can only observe that this proved remarkably ineffective in the case of Lucca, though it must be doubted whether any constitutional arrangements could have been proof against a really determined effort to evade them. A further loophole was provided by the practice of adding *invitati* to councils and the use of *balìe* for much important business. Those who were ineligible for membership of a council because of a vacation might nevertheless be present at a particular session as *invitati*, and the numbers of *invitati* at times rose to a point where it was complained that they might swamp the ordinary members. *Invitati* were selected by the Anziani, and this might be a further instrument in the hands of a ruling group. So might the use of *balìe*. Many individual matters discussed at the General Council or Thirty-Six were not decided outright, but were committed to a *balìa* to be elected by the Anziani. The council usually decided its numbers and its duration, and might restrict its freedom of action even on the very limited business committed to it. Nevertheless the frequency with which *balìe* were used and the range of business committed to them could mean some erosion of the powers of the ordinary councils. *Balìe* must have given some continuity to the government and done something to ensure that business was in the hands of capable and experienced citizens, but they must also have contributed to the passing of control into the hands of a limited group of men. The same predictable names occur among the membership of *balìe* with great regularity, and even if the motive in their appointment was executive efficiency, it involved in practice the passing of much power into the hands of the same limited group.

The *conservatores* were in a rather different category. Here it was not a question of manipulating traditional republican institutions, but of establishing a completely new office. In fact it developed gradually. It is difficult to believe that it would have been authorized, and by the large majority of 146–34, had it been realized that the same twelve citizens would hold the office indefinitely, and gradually extend their sphere of action, encroaching on the powers of the General Council and Thirty-Six until there were few even of the most important matters of state that they did not deal with and until they came near to ousting the ordinary councils from most of the real decisions, relegating them to dealing with formalities or trivia. It is in connection with the *conservatores* that it becomes possible to distinguish the establishment of the influence of the Guinigi party from that of the oligarchy generally. It has been observed that it is not always easy to draw a firm line between a republic under a tight oligarchy and a *signorìa* of the concealed type; the commune and the *signorìa* shade into each other.[20] This is so in the case of Lucca. It is difficult to distinguish the establishment of the influence of the Guinigi party, consisting of wealthy members of the leading families, from the merchant and business oligarchy generally. The republican institutions could be manipulated by an oligarchy just as easily as by a faction. But the Guinigi party does begin to emerge more clearly in connection with the office of *conservatores*. It is clear from the account in Sercambi's chronicle, and especially from his Nota ai Guinigi, and from the history of the office itself, that it was an instrument of the Guinigi party. The enormous importance that the *conservatores* attained, and the position the Guinigi faction reached in other offices and councils is therefore evidence that the party already had great power in the city between 1380 and 1385, and perhaps earlier. The extraordinary honours paid to Francesco Guinigi on his death provides a further indication of the special position of the Guinigi within Lucca, something which seems also to have been apparent to outsiders. Indeed many of the developments

[20] Waley, *The Italian City Republics*, p. 239. For the similarities of oligarchy and tyranny, Sestan, 'Le origini delle signorie', p. 44 and W. L. Gundersheimer, 'Toward a re-interpretation of the Renaissance in Ferrara', *Bibliothèque d'Humanisme et de la Renaissance*, Vol. XXX (1968), p. 280.

associated with a *signorìa*—the concentration of power in the hands of fewer citizens, the use of extraordinary *balìe*, the declining frequency and importance of the meetings of the ordinary councils—can already be seen in Lucca in the 1380s.[21]

This did not go unchallenged and there was a struggle for power in the later 1380s and especially 1390–2. One feature of this was its non-violent character before 1392. It was a struggle for influence in councils and offices and for the limitation of the functions of offices like the commissioners of the palace, the successors of the *conservatores*, which were still associated with the Guinigi. Undoubtedly one of the main reasons that this power struggle took a peaceful form, and did not involve an open confrontation or resort to violence before 1390, was the attitude of the Guinigi themselves. They were always a group of peaceable merchants and businessmen with no unruly feudal or magnate element, and they were also very sensitive to the general feeling in the city. They were quick to accept measures like the abolition of the *conservatores* and associate themselves with the change. They were not prepared to stand out against a demand that had wide support, even if it meant the temporary loss of something that contributed to their power. They accepted the setback and set about quietly rebuilding their position.

It was, however, an event that represents a departure from this policy that precipitated the crisis of 1390–2. The naming of messer Bartolomeo Forteguerra as *spiccinato* was the kind of pointless insult that sprang from factiousness and party feeling. It could bring no possible benefit to the Guinigi; on the contrary it was bound to lead to open conflict in conditions unfavourable to them, for it would bring many uncommitted citizens out on the Forteguerra side. It seems to have been a temporary aberration, though it is worth noting that Lazzaro di Francesco Guinigi was one of the *sortitores*, so that it cannot be argued that it was the work of a few over-enthusiastic Guinigi supporters. By December 1390 the Guinigi had returned to their old policy and were ready to compromise and associate themselves with the Ordines Super Tasca, but by that

[21] Martines, 'Political conflict', p. 85.

time it was too late. The factiousness that was latent in so many Italian republics had come into the open. Once a confrontation between the two factions had begun a new cause for dispute arose as soon as an old one was apparently settled. This could only have one outcome, the victory of one party or the other in a violent conflict. This was some time in coming. The crisis was long drawn out, lasting some eighteen months, disrupting the ordinary business of government, and threatening the maintenance of law and order, if Sercambi is to be believed. The issue was finally settled, as so many Italian cities settled their internal faction disputes, by the victory of one party in streetfighting.

Between 1392 and 1400 the trends in Lucchese internal affairs that can already be distinguished in the 1380s become more clearly apparent. The events of May 1392 established the Guinigi as virtual rulers of the city. Contemporaries had no doubts about this. Sercambi makes it clear, and several non-Lucchese chroniclers speak of the Guinigi as effective rulers of the city. The Florentines saw the Guinigi as men with whom they could deal, relying on them to carry their fellow citizens with them. It is clear that they controlled the foreign policy of the city to the extent of making and maintaining an alliance with Florence in 1395, despite strong feeling against it in certain quarters. In the last years of the century Lazzaro Guinigi openly played a leading role in foreign affairs, making important visits to Florence in 1398 and Pavia in 1399. Their opponents too had no doubts that the Guinigi were the effective rulers of Lucca, and the aim of some plots was to bring them down.

As the events of 1392 clearly established the Guinigi as effective rulers of Lucca it is instructive to see how they used their power. It was their policy to control the city indirectly, without seeking any title or open recognition of their rule. They left the republican constitution virtually unchanged, at any rate to begin with, but were able to manipulate it so that all real power was in their hands. As they can be seen more clearly pursuing the policy that had been foreshadowed before 1392, their rule of Lucca from 1392–1400 suggests interesting reflections for the earlier period also. Sercambi's Nota ai Guinigi is extremely valuable here, as it demonstrates that the policy the Guinigi can be seen pursuing was a conscious and deliberate one. He advised them to control the government by ensuring the election of reliable adherents to the most important posts, using the office of commissioners of the palace as a means of getting measures passed which it was thought that the statutory councils might reject, or which it was felt better not to put to them. Discontent could then be prevented by filling the less important offices and councils from the citizens generally, so that they would not feel totally excluded. It is instructive to examine the internal government of the city from 1392 to 1400 with Sercambi's counsels in mind, for whether as a consequence of his advice or independently, the Guinigi can be seen pursuing a policy very like the one he advocated. They did indeed control the Anzianate, members of the Guinigi family themselves holding the office more frequently than before 1392. Guinigi adherents appeared in large numbers, almost all the Gonfalonieri being of their party, and many new men, often relatively obscure men, were introduced into the college, perhaps in an attempt to broaden the basis of their support. The commissioners too were predominantly Guinigi partisans and played an extremely important role between 1392 and 1400. They were being used to supplement and replace the ordinary councils, which met far less frequently than before 1392, and the business conducted there was often of a formal nature or concerned only with trivial matters. A less close control was kept over these councils, and although the Guinigi party was strongly represented in the Thirty-Six, more independent men were not excluded and even men who had been listed as Forteguerra supporters before 1392 appeared occasionally. With control of the Anzianate and the important office of commissioners of the palace, and with a large body of adherents, including members of some of the leading families, strongly represented in the other offices and councils, the Guinigi were easily able to control the city while maintaining republican institutions and including some citizens who did not belong to their party.

Sercambi stresses the importance to the Guinigi of having a body of friends on whom they could rely. He saw this as the basis of their power. Though he describes it as those who 'alla morte & alla vita colla voluntà vostra sono uniti', which might be thought to imply a restricted group, he clearly envisages it as sufficiently numerous to monopolize the Anzianate, commissioners, *conducterii*, *secretarii*, *gonfalonieri*, and certain vicariates. It must, therefore, have numbered scores if not hundreds of citizens. This body of friends, the Guinigi party, was indeed the foundation of their power. Without such a body of supporters it would have been impossible to control the city while maintaining the outward forms of republican government. It was also vital that they should include a strong element drawn from the leading families of the city. Though the Guinigi did introduce a number of newcomers into the highest offices, this seems to have attracted adverse comment, and they would probably have aroused serious opposition had they been obliged to rely more heavily on such men. But as their party included members of some of the wealthiest and most firmly established families, whose personal position would have given them a claim to power, they were able to manipulate the government by ensuring the appointment of their adherents without any obvious breach with past republican government. The motives of such men in supporting the Guinigi are less easy to discern, but it was by no means uncommon for the establishment of a *signorìa* to have the support of an oligarchy, and the oligarchs did not usually lose by it, as they became the leading men at the court of the *signore*, and their social and political position could thereby be confirmed and strengthened.[22]

In fact this system of indirect rule through the control of offices and councils by means of a party of reliable adherents was to be relatively short-lived. Only eight years after their victory of May 1392 the Guinigi had converted their position into an open *signorìa*. There were special factors at work in 1400, the murder of Lazzaro Guinigi, the character of Paolo and the weakness of his position, the crisis caused by the

[22] For the willingness of men, including members of old oligarchies, to serve *signori*, Chabod, 'Di alcuni studi recenti', p. 47, Chittolini, 'La crisi delle libertà comunali', pp. 111-16, Jones, 'Communes and despots', pp. 79, 93, Ventura, *Nobiltà e popolo*, pp. 19, 39-51. For the Medici party as the basis of their strength, N. Rubinstein, 'Politics and constitution in Florence at the end of the fifteenth century', in E. F. Jacob (ed.), *Italian Renaissance Studies* (London, 1960), pp. 149-51 and *Government of Florence under the Medici,* pp. 108-9, 131-5, 174-80, 191-2, 229-35. I regret that I have not seen D. Kent, *The Rise of the Medici Faction in Florence, 1426-34*.

plague and the threats from exiles, but one may doubt whether these were decisive. It would be difficult to argue that the Guinigi wished to maintain the previous position and were only reluctantly pushed into claiming greater and more overt power by the crisis situation of 1400, for there are clear signs in the previous three or four years that they were gathering the reins of power more firmly into their own hands. The reduction of the numbers in the General Council from 180 to 135, the decree permitting absent Gonfalonieri to be replaced without the need to observe vacations, and the reduction of the vacation between brother and brother and father and son, all point to the concentration of power in the hands of a narrower group. The replacement of a Gonfaloniere, who was not apparently absent, by another as 'eloquentiorem et aptiorem' indicates a departure from the scrupulous observance of even the outward forms of republican government.

The final establishment of a Guinigi *signorìa* in 1400 suggests a number of interesting reflections. It took place, as did the establishment of so many *signorìe*, in an atmosphere of crisis. But it was a time of crisis for the Guinigi rather than for Lucca. There is no question of the Lucchese turning to a *signorìa* to save them from internal disorders or external threats. Though there had been occasional conspiracies Lucca had been relatively peaceful internally since 1392. The external threats from exiles, made more serious in 1400 by the absence of many citizens because of the plague, were directed against the Guinigi. It was rumoured that their power was on the verge of collapse since the death of Lazzaro and exiles hoped to procure their return. But Lucca itself, as opposed to the Guinigi position there, was not seriously threatened. Had Lucca turned to a single man for her salvation at a time of external threats, it would have been in 1396 or 1397 at the height of the war. By 1400 this danger had passed. Though Lucca was on bad terms with Florence with Lazzaro's visit to Pavia, this was because of Florentine suspicions of Lucchese intentions. Florence was in no position to threaten Lucca in 1400, and it would have been easy enough to have improved relations had the Lucchese really wished to do so.

It was, then, the Guinigi position that was in danger and was felt to need shoring up by obtaining a more open recognition of their power. The ambitions of Paolo himself also need to be taken into consideration here, for it is doubtful if it was a wise move from the Guinigi point of view and really did serve to strengthen their position. One of the most striking things about Paolo Guinigi's bid for the title of Captain, which was a preliminary to that of *signore*, was the strength of the opposition shown, even by some of those who had been the closest adherents of the Guinigi. Even the *balìa* of 2 July 1400, who had been Guinigi supporters and were presumably considered their most devoted and trustworthy adherents, resisted Paolo's demands, and not even the presence of large numbers of armed men, some of them from the Visconti forces in Pisa, prevented them from voicing their opposition. Unfortunately it is not clear whether their reluctance sprang from residual feeling for republican institutions or from hostility to Paolo personally. Personal factors, a reluctance to accept the leadership of a relatively young and inexperienced member of the Guinigi family, possibly combined with doubts about his character and ability, do seem to have played a part, but republican sentiment was important too. Attachment to republican institutions was strong, and despite the fact that they had for many years been being eroded by manipulation in the interests of a faction, many of the leading citizens were reluctant to see them extinguished completely, even though they themselves might hope to find a place at the court of the new *signore*. The strength of this resistance should not, however, be exaggerated. The rule of Paolo Guinigi lasted thirty years and survived crises such as that following the death of Giangaleazzo Visconti in 1402. He certainly did not rule by force nor rely on the support of an outside power, and must have been able to count on a measure of assent in Lucca. But the fact that there should have been this resistance to the Guinigi as late as October 1400 is of great interest.

There was a cleaner break between oligarchical rule and that of a *signore* in the case of Lucca than there was in many other cities, for Paolo Guinigi at once dispensed with the Anziani and the old communal councils; there was no 'diarchy' to give some continuation, however formalistic and empty of real meaning, to communal institutions.[23] But the

[23] For the thesis of F. Ercole on the 'diarchy' of communal and signorial

signorìa in Lucca was the culmination of a long and continuous line of development. It had arisen from a number of factors, the tendency for power to concentrate in the hands of an oligarchy, the factiousness inseparable from Italian republics, but perhaps above all the will and ambitions of the Guinigi themselves. They had come first to dominate their city and become *de facto* rulers, and then to obtain an open *signorìa*, not because of some inherent weakness in republican government or some inevitable tendency towards one-man rule, but because of an act of will on their part. They had gradually and deliberately built up a group of supporters, connected by ties of kinship and a web of interests and clientage, and established a tighter and tighter grip on the city, successfully beating off challenges from a rival group. Their rule can be seen becoming more and more open, and they were gathering the reins of power more closely into their own hands before the crisis of 1400.[24] Their position was already sufficiently entrenched and the trend towards Guinigi rule sufficiently well-established to carry even the not particularly well-qualified Paolo to power in 1400, despite the doubts of some of the Guinigi party. The final establishment of an open Guinigi *signorìa* did no more than set the seal on a continuous line of development going back more than twenty years.

---

government, 'Comuni e signori nel veneto', *Nuovo Archivio Veneto*, Vol. XIX (1910), reprinted in *Dal comune al principato* (Florence, 1929), pp. 103-18, but see also Picotti, 'Qualche osservazione sui caratteri delle signorie italiane', pp. 22-3. Waley, *The Italian City Republics*, p. 237, describes the commune's role in the signorial period as posthumous.

[24] For *signorìe* resulting from the efforts and ambitions of a man or party, Waley, *The Italian City Republics*, pp. 234-5, Picotti, 'Qualche osservazione sui caratteri delle signorie italiane', pp. 14-15, Masi, 'Verso gli albori del principato', pp. 76, 150-6, Sestan, 'Le origini delle signorie', pp. 47-9.

TABLE I

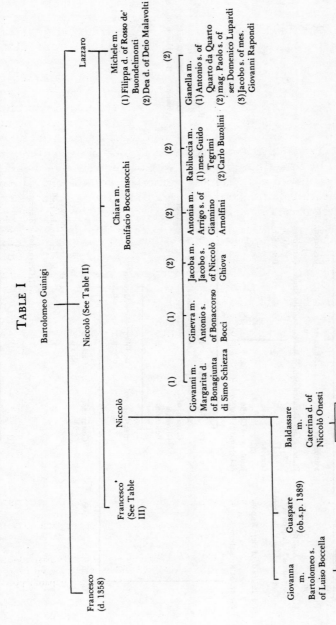

- Bartolomeo Guinigi
  - Francesco (d. 1358)
  - Niccolò (See Table II)
  - Lazzaro
    - Francesco (See Table III)
    - Niccolò
      - (1) Giovanni m. Margarita d. of Bonagiunta di Simo Schiezza
      - (1) Ginevra m. Antonio s. of Bonaccorso Bocci
      - (2) Jacoba m. Jacobo s. of Niccolò Ghiova
      - (2) Antonia m. Arrigo s. of Giannino Arnolfini
      - (2) Rabiluccia m. (1) mes. Guido Tegrimi (2) Carlo Buzolini
      - (2) Gianella m. (1) Antonio s. of Quarto da Quarto (2) mag. Paolo s. of ser Domenico Lupardi (3) Jacobo s. of mes. Giovanni Rapondi
      - Giovanna m. Bartolomeo s. of Luiso Boccella
        - Niccolò
        - Caterina
      - Guaspare (ob.s.p. 1389)
      - Baldassare m. Caterina d. of Niccolò Onesti
        - Niccolò ob.s.p.
        - Michele ob.s.p.
    - Chiara m. Bonifacio Boccansocchi
    - Michele m. (1) Filippa d. of Rosso de' Buondelmonti (2) Dea d. of Deio Malavolti

TABLE II

Niccolò di Bartolomeo Guinigi
m.
Caterina sister of mes. Dino di Poggio

- Dino
  m.
  (1) d. of mes. Azzo de mes. Corradino Malaspina of Cadrebaschi di Valle Trebbia
  (2) Chiara d. of Piero Rapondi
  (3) Jacoba Rossiglione
  - Niccolò ob.s.p.
  - Asso ob.s.p.
  - Costanza ob.s.p.
  - Caterina ob.s.p.
  - Taddea
    m.
    (1) Francesco s. of mes. Alderigo Antelminelli
    (2) Gherardo ser Bianconi
    - (1) Jacoba m. Filippo Rapondi
    - (1) Ysabetta m. Jacobo Mugni
    - (1) Filippa m. Federigo Salesi
    - (2) Margarita
- a daughter
  m.
  Franceschino Dombellinghi
  - Ginevra
    m.
    Jacobo s. of Chello di Lemmo di Poggio
- Lazzaro
  m.
  Margarita dello Strego
  - Giovanni
    m.
    Clara d. of Giovanni Benettoni
    - mes. Lazzaro
    - ser Filippo ob.s.p.
    - Antonio ob.s.p.
  - Gherardo ob.s.p.
  - Niccolò bishop of Lucca (1394–1435)
  - Dino ob.s.p.
  - Arrigo m. a d. of Giovanni Cavalcanti
  - Jacobo ob.s.p.
  - Beatrice
    m.
    Ciuchino Avvocati
  - Isabetta
    m.
    Michele s. of Bartolomeo Michaelis
- Jacobo (d. 1383)
  - Caterina
    m.
    Betto Schiatta

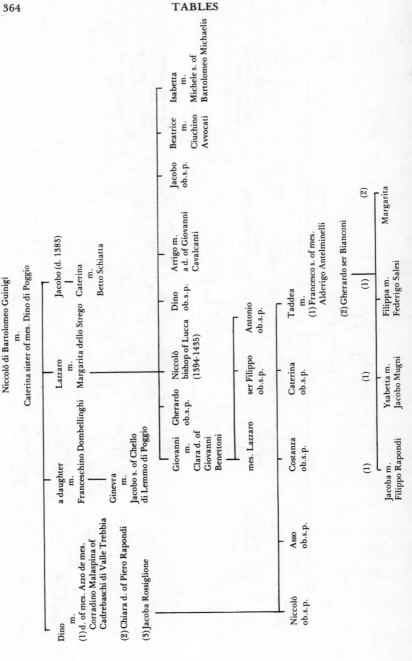

Table III

Francesco di Lazzaro Guinigi
m.
(1) d. of count Guglielmo de Mudigliano
(2) Francesca d. of mes. Giovanni Sbarra
(3) Filippa d. of Alberto Serpente

Children:

- **Lazzaro** m. (1) Isabetta d. of Bindoccio Rossiglione; (2) Sozzina d. of Ruffo di mes. Naldino of Siena; (3) Caterina d. of Bartolomeo Buzolini
- **Bartolomeo** ob.s.p. m. Maddalena d. of Luiso Tadolini
- **Roberto** m. Clara d. of Giovanni di Betto Anguilla
- **Antonio** ob.s.p.
- **Paolo** lord of Lucca (1400–30)
- **Filippa** m. Niccolò Pettinati
- **Margarita** m. Piero s. of Ciuchino Panichi
- **Petra** m. (1) Paolo Magghiari; (2) Giovanni s. of Puccinello Galganetti
- **Beatrice** m. Giovanni s. of Tommasino Cagnuoli
  - Benedetto
  - Gherardo
  - Jacobo
  - Caterina
- **Maddalena** m. Francesco Totti
- **Tommasina** m. (1) Antonio Gigli; (2) Vincente Spada
- **Agata** m. Stefano di Poggio

Children of Lazzaro:

- (1?) **Isabetta** m. ser Niccolò s. of ser Pietro ser Manfredi of Camaiore
- (2) **Francesco** m. Pia d. of Bonagiunta di Simo Schiezza
- (2) **Niccolò** ob.s.p.
- (2) **mes. Lorenzo** m. Giovanna d. of Giuffredo Cenami
- (2) **Lagina** m. Bartolomeo Carincione
- (2) **Gettina** m. Nese s. of Giovani Franchi
- (2) **Giovanna**
- (3) **Selvaggia**
- **Luciano** (dashed line)

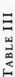

APPENDIX OF DOCUMENTS

DOC. I.

List of Guinigi and Forteguerra Partisans

(Lucca, Biblioteca Governativa MS. 925, ff. 207^v–208^v)

Nota fatta da Dino Guinigi di suo [*sic*] mano scrive gli uomini confidenti et amici di casa Guinigi per ordine di terzieri il 1391 in circa —

S. Paolino

Giovanni Mingogi
Bartolomeo e Franceschino Buxolini
Turellino Bonucci
ser Simone Alberti
Nuccio Giovanni pannaio
Jacopo di Bartolomeo Nucci
Giovanni Sercambi
Andrea dal Portico
Giovanni Parducci
Michele Brancaleoni
Gherardo Serbianconi
Agostino Puccinelli
Lessio Giovanni
Giovanni Geraldi[1]
Giovanni del Ghiotto
Giovanni Galganetti
Giovanni Gigli pannaio
Francesco Berindelli
Bianco Delli
Casino Vanni
Nicolao Neri pannaio
Filippo Fornacieri
Pietro Colucci speziale
Giovanni Boccansocchi
Nicolao Liena
Bartolomeo Lottini
Ruberto dal Portico
Alamanno Saggina
Michele ser Federighi
Nicolao Ceccorini e Stefano di Poggio
ser Grigorio Andreucci
Giovanni Lupicini
Simone Simoni
Pellegrino Cielli cuoiaro[2]
Giovanni Guidelli cuoiaro
Piero Manucci tavernaro
Pietro Saggina
Giovanni Domaschi
Stefano Buxolini

sono numero 41

S. Salvatore

Giovanni Puccini textore
ser Nicolao dello Strego
ser Nicolao Turinghelli
Meo Buongiovanni
Piero Franceschi pannaio
Prospero Serconforti
Bartolomeo Serjacobi
Matteo Cattani
Matteo Mattafelloni
Guaspari Stiatta
Giovanni Perfettucci filatore
Giovanni e Bonifazio Cionelli
Jacopo . . . [sic]
Gherardo Anguilla
Nicolao Onesti
Galvano Trenta
Giovanni Bernardi
Bartolosso Angiorelli
Simo Tegrimi
Bartolomeo Vannuccori
Martino Arnolfini
Pietro Gentili

[1] Giovanni Geraldi is otherwise unknown, and this is perhaps a misreading for Giovanni Beraldi.

[2] This is probably a misreading for Pellegrino Lelli.

Giovanni Malizardi
Luiso Tadolini
Francesco Orselli
Jacopo Nutini
Nicolao Sbarra
Michele Gregori
Francesco Giuntini Martini
Francesco di Sandoro Lapi
Giovanni Sernicolai
Nicolao Bocci
M° Jacopo fizico
Lotto Martini merciaro
ser Domenico Lupardi
il figlio di Bartolomeo di fr. Vanni

sono 38[1]

S. Martino

Nicolao Provenzali
Giovanni Frammi
ser Ubaldo Perfettucci
Jacopo Galganetti
Nicolao Pinelli
Gherardo Salesi
Giovanni Benrettani
Nicolao Morla
Bernabò Arlotti
Paulino Salamoni
Ciuchino e Dino Avogadri
Turchio Balbani
ser Piero Sercioni
Orso di Giovanni Serorsi
Pietro, Giovanni e Bartolomeo Bernardini
ser Taddeo Malpigli
ser Fedocco Scortica
Nicolao di Puccinello Bandini
Piero Ugolini
Giovanni Benettoni
Giovanni Cardellini
Nicolao Dardagnini
Brunetto Pettinati
Nicolao di Gallo
ser Benedetto Bianchi
Bonanno Serpenti
Nicolao Filippi da Signa
Quarto da Quarto
Francesco di Tomuccio tintoresso
Dino Moriconi
Giovanni textore
Tegrimo Fulcieri
Tomazo Ricciardi
Ugo Borgognoni
Giovanni Talenti textore

sono in tutto 38

In tutto con gli addietro sono 117 persone tutte confidenti e fautori de Guinigi.

Ora si noteranno i contrari a casa Guinigi quali loro chiamavano delle *Setta* che andorno di brigate a Palagio.

messer Lodovico Mercati
messer Bartolomeo Forteguerra
messer Guglielmo Frammi
messer Giovanni Maulini
messer Giovanni Cinacchi
messer Giovanni Genovardi
messer Michele da Coreglia
Giusfredi Cenami
ser Nicolao Sartori
Forteguerra Forteguerra
Matteo Nutini
Betto Stiatta
Giovanni Cattani
Bartolomeo, Giannino e Michele Micheli
Piero e Giovanni Rapondi
Gherardino Maulini
Castruccio Saggina
ser Jacopo Domaschi
Jacopo Volpelli
ser Nicolao Dombellinghi
ser Antonio da Camaiore
Gherardo Burlamacchi
Nicolao Sardini
Lando e Giovanni Moriconi

[1] They are in fact 37.

ser Jacopo Turchi
ser Piero da S. Gennaro
Jacopo e Giovanni Sbarra
Lorenzo Seralinni [sic]
Nicolao Bambacari
Giacchetto Totti
ser Jacopo di ser Angelo
Giovanni Campucci
ser Jacopo Turchi[1]
Michele Trentacoste
Nicolao Genovardi
Giovanni Totti

In tutto sono 41

DOC. II

Names of the citizens entrusted with arms for the 200 contadini
(*Rif.* 12, p. 192, 31 Aug. 1392)

Bartolomeo Buzolini
Lazzaro Saggina
Andrea del Portico
Gerardo ser Bianconis
Giovanni Galganetti
Nuccio Johnannis
Stefano di Poggio
Giovanni di Poggio
Nicolao ser Pagani
Turellino Bonucci
Nicolao Simoni
Giovanni ser Cambi
Giovanni Gigli pann.
Antonio Gigli
Giovanni Boccansocchi
Francesco Berindelli
Nicolao Liena
Nicolao Sbarra
ser Domenico Lupardi
d. Thomas da Ghivizzano
ser Andrea da Ghivizzano
Nicolao Honesti
Giovanni Malisardi
Matteo Mattafellonis
Matteo Cattani
Jacobo Faytinelli
Tomas Ricciardi
Luyso Tadolini
Opizo Honesti
Nicolao Arnolfini
ser Antonio di ser Jacobo Nicolai
Bartolomeo Loctini
Nicolao Gelli
Brunetto Pettinati
Michael Bocci
Nicolao Puccinelli Bandini
Petro Ugolini
Giovanni Texta
Ciuchino Advocati
Giovanni Berettani
Giovanni Cardellini
Giovanni Bernardini
Bartolomeo Balbani
Paolino Salamonis
Nicolao Philippi calz.
Bernardo Arlotti
Prosper ser Conforti
Lamberto Coluccini
Giovanni Benettonis
Nicolao Dardagnini
Petro Gentilis
Antonio de Vulterris
Turco Balbani

DOC. III.

Abolition of the Conservatores

(*Rif.* 9, p.283, 10 Jan. 1385)

Matheus Nutini vice-Vexillifer Justitie proposuit . . . cum hoc sit pro bono pacis et conservatione status atque libertatis lucane civitatis et ad pacem et concordiam omnium bonorum civium lucane civitatis multi lucani cives venerint et exposuerint collegio dominorum fore bonum utile et necessarium

[1] This name occurs twice.

providere ordinare atque disponere super consilio trium gitarum balie lucane civitatis quod illud in maiori numero civium augeatur et dilatetur et per modum ordinem atque tempus sicut crediderint convenire pro bono pacis et concordie omnium civium lucane civitatis et tollenda scandala que absint. Et quod unicuique consiliario presentis consilii liceat impune consulere et arengare super dicta materia addere et minuere prout sibi placuerit pro bono pacis et conservatione libertatis lucane civitatis ita quod auctore deo libertas lucane civitatis in omnibus et per omnia conservetur. In dei nomine quid videtur consiliariis dicti consilii feliciter consulatur.

Famosus et egregius legum doctor dominus Bartholomeus Forteguerra unus ex consiliariis dicti consilii surgens in dicto consilio ad arengheriam publicam et concionantibus deputatam dixit atque polito affamine consuluit pro bono pacis et concordie atque unitate et pacifico statu civitatis lucane quem deus sua ineffabili misericordia augeat et conservet quod autoritate presentis consilii intelligatur et sit sublata annullata irrita et inanis omnis balia consilii XII super balia et cuiuslibet gite illius et qualibet alia balia et autoritas dependens ab ea salvo quod in negotiis et casibus terminatis nec illa vel illo deinceps uti possit quomodolibet seu frui, sed in presenti consilio eligantur et electi esse intelligantur quatuor lucani cives per terzerium boni sapientes et experti de quibus infra fit mentio cum quibus vel maiori parte quorum domini Antiani possint providere circa adventum sotialium et hostilium gentium circa guerram tam que moveretur quam que moveri sperararetur contra civitatem lucanam et circa custodiam civitatis et castrorum lucani comunis cum auctoritate expendendi propterea dumtaxat de pecunia lucani comunis prout expediens fuerit. Quorum balia duret a die electionis facte usque ad Kalendas Januarii proxime secuturas. Et quilibet qui electus fuerit vacet a dicto officio duobus annis a die depositionis officii. Et finito anno predicto de mense Novembris et Decembris proximis eligantur alii XII cives in generali consilio cum auctoritate et balia providendi circa predicta. Et vocentur commissarii palatii super bono statu civitatis. Et in omnibus per eos agendis debeat obtineri victoria per tres ex quatuor. Declarantes etiam quod aliqua ex occasionibus superscriptis non possint ribannire bannitos vel reducere in civitatem ribelles vel estitos vel aliud actum facere qui spectet ad aliquod consilium generale vel XXXVI lucane civitatis salvis commissis. Et cum hoc quod virtute dicte balie non possit creari in lucana civitate aliquis officialis cum balia.

This was agreed 202–23, and the following twelve citizens were elected:

S. Paolino
mes. Ludovico Mercati
Giovanni Mingogi
Turellino Bonucci
Fasino Boccansocchi

S. Salvatore
mes. Bartolomeo Forteguerra
Bartolomeo Michaelis
Giuffredo Cenami
Piero Rapondi

S. Martino
mes. Giovanni de Barga
Michele Guinigi
Lando Moriconi
Turchio Balbani

DOC. IV.

Confirmation of the Existing Form of Government

(*Rif.* 9, pp.324–5, 23 Mar. 1385)

Proposuit dominus Vexillifer . . . cum lucana res publica retroactis temporibus sub statutis et ordinamentis nunc vigentibus ut res ipsa demonstrat fuerit in optimo atque tranquillo statu feliciter gubernata adeo ut vera pax et unio semper crescens inter lucanos cives per dies magis atque magis sumpserit incrementum fueritque pro maiori civium unitate atque firmiori auree libertatis quiete pridie in maiori et generale consilio lucani comunis balia consilii XII super conservatione libertatis civitatis lucane consensu omnium cum tranquillitate sublata. Ex cuius sublatione nonnulli lucane civitatis optimo statui invidentes aliter quam res se habuerit existimantes elatis animis multa in libertatis preiudicium sunt moliti ex quibus lucanis civibus periculum atque iactura maxima redundabat cum omnis repens mutatio sit damnosa. Eriganturque continuo in miserande sinu Italie sotiales et effere gentes armorum quorum viribus plerumque pessimi exaltantur sceleraque diu mente concepta atque optata geruntur. Que omnia si recto mentis cernuntur acumine quilibet nisi prorsus desipiat potest verisimiliter dubitare et vigilanti atque insomni lumine promptus stare circa conservationem libertatis atque pacifici status civitatis lucane. Quid ergo ne futuris temporibus lucana et quieta res publica concuti possit videtur in dei nomine salubriter super predictis omnibus et eorum connexis et dependentibus consulatur.

Jacobus Rapondi unus ex consiliariis dicti consilii surgens in dicto consilio ad arengheriam superdictam in ipso consilio dixit et consuluit quod auctoritate presentis consilii ut lucana res publica gubernetur felicius et salubrius sub ordinatis statutis et ordinamentis lucani comunis prout hactenus usque in hodiernam diem feliciter factum est et ne a pacis invidis et bonorum emulis ipsa res publica quod benignus deus avertat quomodolibet possit impelli. Maius et generale consilium lucani comunis et populi consilium trigintasex prudentium virorum civitatis lucane et statuta et ordinamenta unde dicta consilia processerunt et statuta de confaloneriis et pennoneriis et ordinamenta dovane et masse salis lucani comunis nec non Tasca Antianorum lucani comunis et ordinamenta et statuta unde dicta tasca procedit et que de ipsa seu circa ipsam tascam et eius reformationem disponunt stent et illibata serventur deinceps prout et sicut in statutis et ordinamentis lucani comunis latius et diffusius continetur. Et ne deinceps voluntas consiliariorum alicuius consilii possit ab invitatorum multitudine superari prout aliquando forsitan factum est, quandocumque futuris temporibus celebrabitur maius et generale consilium lucani comunis non possint esse in illo vel fieri nisi usque in sex lucani cives invitati per terzerium. In consilio autem trigintasex quando contingerit in futurum teneri non possint in illo esse vel fieri nisi usque in quatuor lucani cives invitati similiter per terzerium. Et hoc quod dictum est de invitatis non referatur ad reformationem tasche dominorum in qua servetur statutum lucani comunis . . .

These proposals were passed 134–38.

DOC. V.

Ordines super Tasca

(*Rif.* 11, pp.371–4, 16 Dec. 1390)

Come voi carissimi et honorevili consiglieri vi potete racordare o la magior parte di voi Idio o per li nostri peccati o per quelli de nostri antichi et loro divisione sottopuose per lunghi tempi questo comune a diverse et extranee signorie da quali come i citadini di Luca furono tractati chil provo lo sa bene et puone rendere vero testimonio. Et ancora li altri se ne denno potere ricordare per che non pure la nostra natione et vicini dintorno sentio liurli de nostri doloro ma li Franceschi Inghilesi et Fiaminghi e quasi ogni cristiana regione da cui ne nostri bisogni fummo ricevuti per pieta sentinno pena de nostri tormenti. Et desi certissimo tenere che le voci de nostri dolori passarono a dio la cui pieta diede opera da non potere extimare humana ma divina a la liberta nostra e cosi e da credere che li fu di piacere mettere ne cuori de citadini unione e concordia e tale ordine prendere ne loro regimento che seguisseno la conservatione tale quale egli avea donato liberta.

Con li quali ordini et unita come voi chiaramente sapete dal principio de la nostra liberta fine a ogi siamo interamente conservati advegna che neuno nostro vicino lo credesse perche non pure a citadini di Luca e stata gloriosa utilita ilben vivere ma etiando et da lungi et da presso di meglio vivere che alcuna altra cita di questo paese a preso fama et non senza cagione per che dove laltre terre con viva ragione via piu di noi potenti non senza graveze a molestie di compagne non senza graveze dimposte e dismesurate carestie e mortali guerre sono state dove idio a noi a conceduto gratia diripararsi da le insidii de vicini da le graveze de le compagne senza cavare di borsa sforsatamente denaio a persona. Etiando de le carestie preservati in forma che sempre a meno valuto qui lo biado che in terra vicina quantunque di sua natura sia via piu di noi abondevile oltra la satisfatione de debiti che avavamo con sancta chiesa e con altri come sapete. Et ancora mediante la gratia di dio qualche cosetta e avanzato in comune. Et questo si de et potete credere dovere esser advenuto perche li ordini et li ordinati concordevilmente sono stati conformi a dio onde glia acresciuti et multiplicati et cosi essendo per lavenire e da sperare bene et meglio.

In tra quali ordini come voi honorevili consiglieri sapete fu lordine de la tasca de li antiani la quale come per li statuti si vede servato e difarsi per due anni. Et avegna chel tempo di due anni sia grande pur non a potuto ne puote includere tutto lo numero di citadini che meritevilmente potrebeno esser stati da quali patientamente e stato comportato. Et anco signori advegna che non si debia non e pero che ne consigli quando la tasca se facta non abia di quelli che amano piu uno che uno altro o per parentado o amista o ignanno di mente il perche puote esser advenuto la exclusione di molti di cui e stato et e da increscere sempre.

Et noi che hora siamo a questo officio avendone sentito questo anno nuovi et varii lamenti di che si crede fuor di qui noi esser in gran divisione e veduto quanto e ben vivere li citadini uniti et pacifici si considerati li tempi pistilentiali si etiando affannati di gravi carestie et di pessime conditioni di mestieri come ancora vedere li danni pericoli et subiectione in che gia per la divitione incorremmo a cio che li comuni honori piu comunamente et in magior numero ampliati siano cagione a ciascuno citadino le comune fatiche piu concordevilmente sopportare et accio che con chiaro animo et senza alcuno sospecto la citadinanza salarghi di benevolentia procuri a bisogni et beni del suo comune et accio che per lessere honorati mettano loro ingegni a virtuosamente vivere. A noi parre in quanto a voi paresse che ben fusse a provedere in questa materia in forma che fusse ragionevile contentamento a ciaschuno siche ogni scandalo e diferentia che fusse intra citadini silevi et pognasi in buona et tranquilla pace.

Or noi come vavemo dicto avendone sentito alcuni lamenti et vedendo li bisogni e lutilita grande avemo posto pensieri ne rimedii e ne modi e piaceci dirveli cio che dove vipiacciano vi possiate dare executione.

Noi vedemo che nel tempo de la tasca de due anni secondo li ordini a lofficio del antianato non si po includere tutta la meritevile citadinanza a quello officio. E per tanto a noi parre che dove li statuti dispognano che la tasca de li antiani si faccia per due anni per li tempi avenire sia per tre anni. Et avemo noi veduto che commodamente et di buoni citadini la tasca per tre anni sadempiera come ancora a voi sevi piacera li potrete udire nominare. Et accio che si faccia per levar via ogni sospecto et ogni incredulita di non far lo bene come si dice, et etiando per ralegrare et confortare lo cuore de citadini vegendo loro esser saliti ad honore vegendo la unita et benivolentia di tutto il consiglio et possino prendere conforto de loro buono regimento presente et che de venire et levisi via ogni rancura possa ciascuno andare e stare securamente dove meglio creda fare et viva certo del suo buono stato et de la sua cita. A noi parre che nel presente consiglio tutti li dicti citadini meritevili a quello officio per tre anni cominciando quando sera finita la presente tasca cioe septanta per tersieri fussero qui nominati et anno partito vinti accio chel consiglio nabia lonore etiando perche quelli che non viseranno vegiano la citadinanza disposta altra volta a metterli pero che per piu di tre anni non sivede abilmente poter farla.

Et accio che sempre sia materia di dovere includere tutti buoni citadini a lofficio delantianato ci parre che fusse per li tempi avenire perpetualmente a fare la tasca per tre anni. E da questa volta in la sempre per lultimo collegio de la tasca si debia fare insieme col consiglio di trentasei et dodici buoni invitati per terzieri li quali solamente in quel consiglio a quello acto si possano fare non potendo esser tra li antiani di quello collegio consiglieri et invitati piu che due dalcuno casato o consortato in tale acto. Et intendasi la victoria de nominati esser avendo la magior parte de le pallocte la quale sia una piu che la meta preferendo sempre che ara piu pallocte.

Et dove erano due citadini per terzieri a sortire insieme con uno Antiano per terziere perche la tasca come vedete si crescie siano insieme con li dicti tre Antiani del dicto numero de consiglio o invitati tre citadini per terzieri. Et ciascuno de dicti primi sortitori e li altri che seranno vachi dal dicto officio per tempo di sei anni. E li dicti sortitori del dicto numero cosi obtenuto et vinto come dicto e ne possano et debiano trahere dieci per terzieri per questa prima volta tanto li quali siano Antiani succedenti a quelli che per legitime cagioni ne collegi de la tasca mancasseno li quali siano di piu giovana eta et che non siano stati piu Antiani avendo in cio quella discretione che si richiede preferendo da poi ne laltre tasche sempre quelli che aranno le piu pallocte con questa dichiaratione che quelli che al fine de la tasca non fusseno stati tracti succedano et siano Antiani ne le tasca seguente senza fare altro scrutinio.

Et perche poche cose piu pericolose potrenno per comune advenire che rompere o attentare di rompere li ordini de la tasca de lantianato perche si po dire essere il fondamento di tutto lo governo di Luca onde la fermeza di quelli si po dire esser fermeza del buono stato de la cita. E veduto etiando che la legie et comune utilita siano tenuti li antiani ne lentrata de loro officio giurare di mantenere e far mantenere li dicti ordini e la executione de dicti ordini sotto pena di spergiuro oltra quelle che li ordini del comune impognano.

Nomina autem dictorum septuaginta civium per terzerium de quibus supra fit mentio sunt hec viz.
primo pro terzerio Sancti Paulini:

d. Lud. Mercati
mag. Michele da Coreglia
Andreas de Porticu
Francesco ser Angeli
Giovanni Domaschi
Nuccio Johannis
Andreas Dati
Bartolomeo Buzolini
Alamanno Saggina
Giovanni Mingogii
Gerardo Burlamacchi
Gerardo ser Bianconis
Giov. Gigli di S. Giusto
Agostino Puccinelli
Castruccio Saggina
Bianco Delli
Giovanni Beraldi
Giov. Gigli (pann.)
Simon Rodolfini
Franceschino Buzolini
Francesco Berindelli
Fanuccio Franceschi
Bartolomeo ser Justi
Giovanni ser Cambi
Nic. ser Giov. Folchini
Bindo Galganetti
Giovanni Campucci
Amerigo Paganelli
Bartolomeo Finati
Giovanni Boccansocchi
Giov. Luporini Vite
ser Jacobo Domaschi
Giovanni del Ghiotto
Giovanni Ganghi
Masseo Aitanti
Orlandino Volpelli
Jacobo Bianchi
Francesco Dombellinghi
Paolo ser Nicolosi
Natus Vannucci (vint.)
Nicolao ser Dini
Nicolao Bambacari
Nicolao Liena
Nicolao Diodati
Piero Saggina
Nicoloso Nieri
Roberto de Porticu
Nicolao ser Jacobi Turettini
Simon Simonis
Jac. Francesci Martini
Turellino Bonucci
Giovanni Parducci (biad.)
ser Nicolao Dombellinghi
Manfredo Cagnuoli
Michele ser Frederici
Giovanni Giudelli (coiar.)
Lessio Johannis
Michele Brancaleone
Piero Trenta
Nicolao Simonis
Giovanni Perotti
Cristoforo de'Chiatri
Giovanni Sbarra
Francesco Johannis Panici

Pardino Palmieri
Jacobo Nucci
ser Simon Alberti
Agostino Gianelli
Casino Vannis
Giovanni Galganetti

San Salvatore:

d. Bartolomeo Forteguerra
d. Tommaso da Ghivizzano
d. Giovanni Maurini
Bartolomeo Michelis
Betto Schiatta
Piero Rapondi
Andrea Domaschi
Gerardo Anguilla
Gerardo Martini
Giovanni di Landuccio Bernardi
d. Giovanni Cinachi
d. Giovanni Genovardi
Giovanni Dati
ser Andrea da Ghivizzano
Forteguerra Forteguerra
Francesco Juntini Martini
ser Domenico Lupardi
Francesco Orselli
Nicolao Ronsini
Domenico Cosciorini
Giovanni Petri (spet.)
Jacobo Ronghi
Jacobo Nutini
Paolo Gucci
Bartolomeo Scortica
Jacobo Sbarra
Luyso Tadolini
mag. Jacobo Coluccini
Michele Lomori
Bartolomeo ser Jacobi
Matteo Cattani
Martino Arnolfini
Piero Francisci (pann.)
Matteo Santucci Martini
Simetto Tegrimi
Bartolomeo Vannuccori
Matteo Mattafellonis
Michele Gregorii
Meo Bongiovanni
Francesco Sandori Lapi
Francesco Mattafellonis
Giovanni Cionelli
Giovanni Malisardi
Agostino de'Chiatri
Bartolomeo Sbarra
Guaspar Schiatta
Giovanni Cattani
Filippo Fecis
Giovanni Puccini textor
Labruccio Cerlotti
Matteo Trenta
Nicolao Guidiccione
Giuffredo Cenami
Jacobo Antelmini
Matteo Nutini
Petro Corsi
Opizo Honesti
Petro Gentilis
Nicolao Genovardi
Nello Faytinelli
ser Nicolao dello Strego
Nicolao Sbarra
ser Nicolao Sartoy
ser Nicolao Turinghelli
Michele Leonis
Nicolao Honesti
Galvano Trenta
Francesco Guidiccione
Simon Tegrimi
Lando Sartoy

S. Martino:

d. Guglielmo Flammi
Dino Guinigi
Lando Moriconi
Bartolomeo Balbani
Giovanni Bernardini
Arrighino Arrighi
Quarto da Quarto
Savino Bartolomei
ser Taddeo Malpigli
Giachetto Totti
Ciuchino Advocati
ser Fedocco Scortica
Giovanni Moriconi
Jacobo mag. Johannis
Lazzaro di Nicolao Guinigi
Nicolao ser Pagani
Nicolao Morla
ser Ubaldo Perfectucci

Tomas Ricciardi
Dino Moriconis
Gerardino Benettoni
Giovanni Franchi
Pinello Astolfi
Nicolao Guinigi
Nicolao Puccinello Bandini
Nicolao Provenzalis
Rafael Tegrimi
ser Benedetto Bianchi
Tegrimo Fulcieri
Francesco Ronghi
Petro Ugolini
Bartolomeo Bernardini
Paolo Tangrandi
Taddeo Busdraghi
Turco Balbani
Dino Advocati
Fastello Gaddi
Camporo Parpaglione
Bonanno Serpentis
Giovanni Testa
Lazzaro di Francesco Guinigi
Giovanni Flammi
Giovanni Berettani
Brunetto Pettinati
Nicolao Dardagnini
Berto da Quarto
Giovanni Francesci Perfectucci
Gerardo Salesis
Giovanni Cardellini
Giovanni mag. Gerardi
Nicolao Pinelli
Uberto ser Pagani
Pietro Bernardini
Piero Tegrimi
Belometto Pinelli
Simon Mansi
Giovanni Turchi
Urso Johannis ser Ursi
Giovanni Benettoni
Jacobo Gratta
Jacobo Moriconi
Bernabò Arlotti
Frediano Tempi
Nicolao Ghiova
Nicolao Filippi de Signa
Francesco Tomucci
Jacobo Galganetti
Nicolao Lighi
Paolino Salamonis
Michele Guinigi

The Ordines Super Tasca were accepted by 145–41, and the citizens named above were accepted by 145–43.

BIBLIOGRAPHY

ARCHIVE AND OTHER UNPRINTED SOURCES

Comune di Lucca, Archivio di Stato

Series *Statuti del Comune di Lucca*, no. 6, Statute of the Commune, 1372; no. 9, Statute of the Commune, 1399 (Fragments).

Series *Capitoli*, nos. 3, 4, 17, 18, 24–6, 31–4, Leagues and agreements with outside powers; no. 52, Oath to John of Bohemia 1331–1333; no. 19, Agreements with Pisa 1342–1362.

Series *Consiglio Generale*, nos. 1–13, *Riformagioni Pubbliche*, 1369–1400.

Series *Anziani al Tempo della Libertà*, nos. 2–4, *Minute di Riformagioni*, 1371–1400 (some lacune).

Series *Anziani al Tempo della Libertà*, nos. 131–3, *Deliberazioni*, 1370–97 (some lacune).

Series *Anziani al Tempo della Libertà*, no. 439, *Lettere originali*, 1369–1400.

Series *Anziani al Tempo della Libertà*, nos. 529–30, Copies of outgoing letters 1369–85.

Series *Anziani al Tempo della Libertà*, nos. 571–2, *Ambascerie, Carte Originali* 1379–1400.

Series *Anziani Avanti la Libertà*, nos. 1–46, Decrees of councils, proclamations, etc. 1330–69.

Series *Camarlingo Generale*, nos. 7 and 8, *Introito-esito*, 1334; nos. 79–83, *Introito-esito*, 1369–81, and fragments for later.

Series *Camarlingo Generale*, nos. 103, 110, *Mandatorie*, 1377, 1397.

Series *Ragionieri della Camera e del Comune*, nos. 3–14, accounts of the official auditors, 1341–81.

Series *Gabella Maggiore*, no. 1, *Statuto della Gabella Maggiore 1372*, with additions 1372–1443.

Series *Gabella Maggiore*, nos. 10–50, Accounts of the payment of customs duties at the *gabella maggiore* for the years 1329–1433, with many lacune.

Series *Offizio Sopra il Sale*, no. 1, Decrees relating to the salt tax and the public debt.

Series *Imprestiti*, nos. 9–20, Books of the public debt, 1369–1411.

Series *Corte de' Mercanti*, nos. 14–16, Acts of the Court of Merchants for the years 1370, 1380, and 1389.

Series *Corte de' Mercanti*, nos. 82–6, Declarations of companies etc. for the years 1371, 1372, 1381, 1407, and 1488.

Series *Sentenze e Bandi*, 538. List of immigrants for the *Arte della Lana*, 1382–1417.

Series *Sentenze e Bandi*, nos. 42–4, 70, 82, 85–9, 92, 97, Sentences of the Court of the Podestà and others, 1370–1400.

Series *Capitano del Popolo*, nos. 13–15, Sentences of the Captain of the People, 1394–7.

Series *Curia de'Ribelli e de'Banditi*, nos. 3 (1331); 7 (1341–2); 8 (1342).

Series *Milizie della Campagna*, no. 1, *Cerna del Contado*, 1376.
Series *Estimo*, nos. 39 (1368); 69 (1374); 75 (1394–5); 76 (1347–8); 83 (1346); 135 (1410), Valuations of property in the *contado* for the *estimo*.
Series *Archivio de'Notari*, no. 123, *Protocolli* of ser Bartolomeo Buonmese, 1376.
Series *Archivio de'Notari*, nos. 159–61, *Protocolli* of ser Filippo Lupardi, 1369–76.
Series *Archivio de'Notari*, nos. 167–8, *Protocolli* of ser Jacobo Domaschi, 1378–83.
Series *Archivio de'Notari*, no. 195, *Protocolli* of ser Niccolò Sartoy, 1369–83.
Series *Archivio de'Notari*, no. 212, *Protocolli* of ser Fedocco Scortica, 1380–1.
Series *Archivio de'Notari*, no. 242, *Protocolli* of ser Niccolò Turinghelli, 1376.
Series *Archivio de'Notari*, nos. 247–8, *Protocolli* of ser Simone di ser Jacobo Alberti, 1370–8.
Series *Archivio de'Notari* no. 262, *Protocolli* of ser Orso Barsellotti, 1373.
Series *Archivio de'Notari*, nos. 273–84, *Protocolli* of ser Domenico Lupardi, 1379–92.
Series *Archivio de'Notari*, no. 295, *Protocolli* of ser Pietro di Vanello Saraceni, ser Niccolò Dombellinghi and ser Niccolò Pantassa, 1380–9.
Series *Archivio Guinigi*, no. 1, *Contratti A* (916–1452).
Series *Archivio Guinigi*, no. 131 bis, *Terrilogio di Paolo Guinigi*.
Series *Archivio Guinigi*, no. 151, *Memorie di Michele Guinigi*, 1384–1460.
Series *Archivio Guinigi*, no. 264, *Notizie di Lucca B+* (1190–18th century).
Series *Archivio Guinigi*, no. 312, *Notulario di contratti* (900–1399).
Series *Archivio Guinigi*, no. 318, *Guinigi: Notizie*, (9th–18th centuries).
Series *Archivio Guinigi*, +5, +22, +30, +32, +33, original bulls.
Series *Biblioteca Manoscritti*, nos. 9–14, Salvatore Dalli, *Cronica di Lucca (dall' origine di essa città fino all'anno 1650)*, 6 vols.
Series *Biblioteca Manoscritti*, no. 38, Giuseppe Civitali, *Historia della Città di Lucca (dal'origine di essa città sino al 1572)*.

Comune di Lucca, Archivio Notarile.

Testamenti, ser Fedocco Scortica, ser Bartolomeo Buonmese, 1338–91

Comune di Lucca, Biblioteca Governativa

MS. 925. Dino Guinigi's list of Guinigi and Forteguerra supporters, 1391 (ff. 207v–208v), Names of *estimati* and their assessments for *Estimo* of 1397 (ff. 249–58).

Comune di Firenze, Archivio di Stato

Series *Capitoli*, no. 50, League of 16 May 1396.
Series *Consulte e Pratiche*, nos. 10–34, 1370–1400.
Series *Signori Carteggi: Missive 1 Cancelleria*, nos. 15–25.
Series *Signori Carteggi: Missive Legazioni e Commissioni, Elezione e Instruzioni a Oratori*, nos. 1–3.

Series *Signori Carteggi: Rapporti e Relazioni di Oratori*, no. 1.
Series *Dieci di Balìa: Carteggi: Missive Legazioni e Commissioni*, nos. 1-2.
Series *Dieci di Balìa: Relazioni di Ambasciadori*, no. 1.

Comune di Pisa, Archivio di Stato

Series *Comune A*, nos. 56, 60, 79.
Series *Diplomi Roncioni*.

Comune di Siena, Archivio di Stato

Series *Capitoli* no. 106, League of 16 May 1396.

PRINTED STATUTES AND COLLECTIONS OF DOCUMENTS

L'Arte della Seta in Firenze, anonymous treatise of the late fourteenth or early fifteenth century, ed. G. Gargiolli, Florence, 1868.

Inventario del R. Archivio di Stato in Lucca, ed. S. Bongi, E. Lazzareschi, and D. Corsi. 6 vols., Lucca, 1872-1964.

E. Lazzareschi, 'Gli Statuti dei Lucchesi a Bruges e ad Anversa', in *Miscellanea di Studi Storici ad Alessandro Luzio*, 2 vols., Florence, 1933.

E. Lazzareschi and L. Mirot, 'Lettere di Mercanti Lucchesi da Bruges e da Parigi, 1407-1421', *Bollettino Storico Lucchese*, Vol. 1 (1929), pp. 165-99.

Libro della Communità dei Mercanti Lucchesi in Bruges, ed. E. Lazzareschi, Milan, 1947.

J. C. Lünig, *Codex Italiae Diplomaticus*, 4 vols., Frankfurt and Leipzig, 1725-35.

Memorie e Documenti per Servire all'Istoria del Principato Lucchese, 11 vols., Lucca, 1813-60.

E. Molinier, 'Inventaire du Trésor du Saint-Siège sous Boniface VIII, 1295', *Bibliothèque de le'École des Chartes*, Vol. XLVII (1886), pp. 646-67.

L. Osio, *Documenti Diplomatici Tratti dagli Archivi Milanesi*, 3 vols., Milan, 1864-72.

La Pratica della Mercatura di Francesco Balducci Pegolotti, ed. Allan Evans, Cambridge, Mass., 1936.

Regesti del R. Archivio di Stato di Lucca: Vol. II, pt. i, *Carteggio degli Anziani 1322-1369*; Vol. II, pt. ii, *Carteggio degli Anziani 1369-1400*, ed. L. Fumi, Lucca, 1903; Vol. III, *Carteggio di Paolo Guinigi*, ed. L. Fumi and E. Lazzareschi, Lucca, 1925-33.

A. Segre, 'Dispacci di Cristoforo di Piacenza, procuratore mantovano alla corte ponteficia', *Archivio Storico Italiano*, Ser. v, Vols. XLIII-XLIV (1909).

G. Sercambi, 'Nota ai Guinigi', in *Le Chroniche Lucchesi*, Vol. III, pp. 399-407.

Statuto del Comune di Lucca 1308, in *Memorie e Documenti per Servire all'Istoria del Principato Lucchese*, Vol. III, part iii.

Lo Statuto della Corte dei Mercanti in Lucca del MCCCLXXVI, ed. A. Mancini, U. Dorini, and E. Lazzareschi, Florence, 1927.

A. Theiner, *Codex Diplomaticus Dominii Temporalis Sancti Sedis*, 3 vols., Rome, 1861-2.

PRINTED CHRONICLES AND HISTORIES

B. Beverini, *Annali Lucchesi*, Lucca, 1830.

Corpus Chronicorum Bononensium, 3 vols., R.I.S., N.S., Vol. XVIII, Città di Castello, 1909–22.

Cronica di Pisa 1089–1389, R.I.S., Vol. XV, Milan, 1729.

Cronaca Senese di Donato di Neri., R.I.S., N.S., Vol. XV, part vi, Bologna, 1936–44

Cronaca Senese di Paolo di Tommaso Montauri, R.I.S., N.S., Vol. XV, part vi, Bologna, 1923–46.

G. Dati, *Istoria di Firenze dal 1380 al 1405*, ed. L. Pratesi, Norcia, 1904.

Diario d'Anonimo Fiorentino dall'anno 1358 al 1389, ed. A. Gherardi, in *Documenti di Storia Italiana*, Vol. VI (Chronache dei Secoli XIII e XIV), Florence, 1876.

Cronaca Volgare di Anonimo Fiorentino già attributo a Piero di Giovanni Minerbetti, R.I.S., N.S., Vol. XXVII, part ii, Bologna, 1918.

Cronaca Fiorentina di ser Naddo da Montecatino, Delizie degli Eruditi Toscani, Vol. XVIII, Florence, 1784.

Cronaca di Pisa di Ranieri Sardo, ed. O. Banti, *Fonti per la Storia d'Italia*, Rome, 1963.

G. Sercambi, *Le Chroniche Lucchesi*, ed. S. Bongi, 3 vols., *Fonti per la Storia d'Italia*, Rome, 1892.

Sozomeno Pistoriensis, Specimen Historiae, R.I.S., Vol. XVI, Milan, 1730.

Marchionne di Coppo Stefani, *Cronaca Fiorentina*, R.I.S., N.S., Vol. XXX, Città di Castello, 1903.

N. Tegrimi, *Vita Castruccii Antelminelli, Lucensis Duci, 1301–1328*, R.I.S., Vol. XI, Milan, 1727.

Donato Velluti, *La Cronica Domestica*, ed. I. del Lungo and G. Volpi, Florence, 1914.

G. Villani, *Cronica*, ed. F. Dragomanni, Florence, 1844–5.

M. Villani, *Cronica*, ed. F. Dragomanni, Florence, 1846.

SECONDARY WORKS

A. Anzilotti, 'Per la storia delle signorie e del diritto pubblico italiano del Rinascimento', *Studi Storici*, Vol. XXII (1914), pp. 77–106.

O. Banti, *Iacopo d'Appiano, economia società e politica del comune di Pisa al suo tramonto (1392–1399)*, Pisa, 1971.

——'Iacopo d'Appiano e le origini della sua signoria in Pisa', *Bollettino Storico Pisano*, Vols. XX–XXI (1951–2), pp. 3–42.

——'Un anno di storia lucchese (1369–70): dalla dominazione pisana alla restaurazione della libertà', in *La "libertas lucensis" del 1369, Carlo IV e la fine della dominazione pisana*, Accademia Lucchese di Scienze, Lettere e Arti, Studi e Testi IV (Lucca, 1970), pp. 33–53.

B. Barbadoro, *Le finanze della repubblica fiorentina*, Florence, 1929.

H. Baron, 'The social background of political liberty in the early Italian Renaissance', *Comparative Studies in Society and History*, Vol. II (1959–60), pp. 440–51.

C. C. Bayley, *War and Society in Renaissance Florence, the de Militia of*

Leonardo Bruni. Toronto, 1961.

M. B. Becker, 'An essay on the "Novi Cives" and Florentine politics, 1343–1382', *Medieval Studies*, Vol. XXIV (1962), pp. 35–82.

——'Economic change and the emerging Florentine territorial state', *Studies in the Renaissance*, Vol. XIII (1966), pp. 7–39.

——*Florence in Transition*, Vol. I, *The Decline of the Commune*, Baltimore, 1967.

——*Florence in Transition*, Vol. II, *Studies in the Rise of the Territorial State*, Baltimore, 1968.

——'Florentine *libertas*: political independents and *novi cives* 1372–8', *Traditio*, Vol. XVIII (1962), pp. 393–407.

——'Problemi della finanza pubblica fiorentina della seconda metà del Trecento e dei primi del Quattrocento', *Archivio Storico Italiano*, Vol. CXXXIII (1965), pp. 433–66.

——'Some aspects of oligarchical, dictatorial and popular *signorie* in Florence 1282–1382', *Comparative Studies in Society and History*, Vol. II (1959–60), pp. 421–39.

M. B. Becker and G. A. Brucker, 'The *Arti Minori* in Florentine politics, 1342–1378', *Medieval Studies*, Vol. XVIII (1956), pp. 93–104.

K. J. Beloch, *Bevölkerungsgeschichte Italiens*, 3 vols., Berlin, 1939–61.

M. Berengo, *Nobili e mercanti nella Lucca del Cinquecento*, Turin, 1965.

T. Bini, *I lucchesi a Venezia*, 2 vols., Lucca, 1853.

T. W. Blomquist, 'The Castracani family of thirteenth-century Lucca', *Speculum*, Vol. XLVI (1971), pp. 459–76.

——'The drapers of Lucca and the marketing of cloth in the mid-thirteenth century' in D. Herlihy, R. S. Lopez and V. Slessarev (eds.) *Economy, Society and Government in Medieval Italy*, Essays in memory of Robert L. Reynolds (Kent, Ohio, 1969), pp. 65–73.

——'Trade and commerce in thirteenth-century Lucca', Unpublished doctoral dissertation, Department of History, University of Minnesota (Minneapolis, 1966).

G. Bolognini, 'Le relazioni tra la Reppublica di Firenze e la Repubblica di Venezia nell'ultimo ventennio del secolo XIV', *Nuovo Archivio Veneto*, Vol. IX (1895), pp. 5–109.

S. Bongi, *Bandi lucchesi del secolo decimoquarto*, Bologna, 1863.

——'Della mercatura lucchese nei secoli XIII e XIV', *Atti della R. Accademia Lucchese*, Vol. XXIII (1884), pp. 443–521. Reprinted with additions, Lucca, 1884.

——*Di Paolo Guinigi e le sue ricchezze*, Lucca, 1871.

W. M. Bowsky, 'City and contado: military relationships and communal bonds in fourteenth-century Siena', in A. Molho and J. A. Tedeschi (eds.) *Renaissance Studies in Honor of Hans Baron*, (Dekalb, Ill., 1971), pp. 75–98.

——'The anatomy of rebellion in fourteenth-century Siena; from Commune to signory?', in L. Martines (ed.) *Violence and Civil Disorder in Italian Cities, 1200–1500* (Berkeley and Los Angeles, Cal., 1972), pp. 229–72.

——'The *Buon Governo* of Siena (1287–1355): a medieval Italian oligarchy', *Speculum*, Vol. XXXVII (1962), pp. 368–81.

——*The Finance of the Commune of Siena 1287-1355*, Oxford, 1970.

——'The impact of the Black Death upon Sienese government and society', *Speculum*, Vol. XXXIX (1964), pp. 1-34.

——'The medieval commune and internal violence: police power and public safety in Siena, 1287-1355', *American Historical Review*, Vol. LXXIII (1967), pp. 1-17.

L. BRENNI, *La tessitura serica attraverso i secoli*, Como, 1925.

A. M. BROWN, 'Cosimo de'Medici, pater patriae', *Journal of the Warburg and Courtauld Institutes*, Vol. XXIV (1961), pp. 186-221.

G. A. BRUCKER, *Florentine Politics and Society 1343-1378*, Princeton, 1962.

R. CAGGESE, *Classi e comuni rurali nel medioevo italiano*, 2 vols., Florence, 1907-9.

——'La Repubblica di Siena e il suo contado nel secolo decimoterzo', *Bullettino Senese di Storia Patria*, Vol. XIII (1906), pp. 3-120.

E. CARPENTIER, *Une Ville devant la peste, Orvieto e la Peste Noire de 1348*, Paris, 1962.

E. CARUS-WILSON, 'The woollen industry', in *Cambridge Economic History*, Vol. II (Cambridge, 1951), pp. 355-428.

B. CASINI, *Aspetti della vita economica e sociale di Pisa dal catasto del 1428-9*, Pisa, 1965.

F. CHABOD, 'Di alcuni studi recenti sull'età comunale e signorile nell'Italia settentrionale', *Rivista Storica Italiana*, Vol. XLII (1925), pp. 19-47.

G. CHERUBINI, 'Qualche considerazione sulle campagne dell'Italia centro-settentrionale', *Rivista Storica Italiana*, Vol. LXXIX (1967), pp. 111-57.

G. CHITTOLINI, 'La crisi delle libertà comunali e le origini dello stato territoriale', *Rivista Storica Italiana*, Vol. LXXXII (1970), pp. 99-120.

L. CIUCCI, *L'arte della seta in Lucca*, Como, 1930.

F. COGNASSO, 'Le origini della signoria lombarda', *Archivio Storico Lombardo*, Ser. viii, Vol. VI (1956), pp. 5-19.

P. COLES, 'The crisis of Renaissance society, Genoa 1488-1507', *Past and Present*, no. 11 (1957), pp. 17-47.

G. COLLINO, 'La guerra veneto-viscontea contro i Carraresi nelle relazioni di Firenze e di Bologna col Conte di Virtù', *Archivio Storico Lombardo*, Ser. iv, Vol. XXXVI (1909), pp. 5-58, 315-86.

——'La guerra viscontea contro gli Scaligeri nelle relazioni diplomatiche fiorentino-bolognesi col Conte di Virtù (1386-7)', *Archivio Storico Lombardo*, Ser. iv, Vol. XXXIV (1907), pp. 105-59.

——'La politica fiorentino-bolognese dall'avvento al principato del Conte di Virtù alle sue prime guerre di conquista', *Memorie della R. Accademia di Scienze, Lettere ed Arti di Torino*, 2, Vol. LIV (1904).

——'La preparazione della guerra veneto-viscontea contro i Carraresi nelle relazioni diplomatiche fiorentino-bolognesi col Conte di Virtù (1388)', *Archivio Storico Lombardo*, Ser. iv, Vol. XXXIV (1907), pp. 209-89.

E. CRISTIANI, 'Città e campagna nell'età comunale in alcune pubblicazioni dell'ultimo decennio', *Rivista Storica Italiana*, Vol. LXXV (1963), pp. 829-45.

——*Nobilità e popolo nel comune di Pisa*, Naples, 1962.

C. M. de la RONCIÈRE, 'Indirect taxes or "gabelles" at Florence in the fourteenth century', in N. Rubinstein (ed.), *Florentine Studies* (London, 1968), pp. 140–92.

R. de Roover, 'The organisation of trade', in *Cambridge Economic History*, Vol. III (Cambridge, 1963), pp. 42–118.

——*The Rise and Decline of the Medici Bank, 1397–1494*, Cambridge, Mass., 1963.

F. Edler, 'The silk trade of Lucca during the thirteenth and fourteenth centuries', Unpublished doctoral dissertation, Department of History, University of Chicago (Chicago, 1930).

F. Ercole, 'Comuni e signori nel veneto (Scaligeri, Caminesi, Carraresi)', *Nuovo Archivio Veneto*, Vol. XIX (1910), reprinted in *Dal Comune al Principato* (Florence, 1929), pp. 53–118.

A. Esch, 'Bankiers der Kirche im Grossen Schisma', *Quellen und Forschungen aus Italienischen Archiven und Bibliotheken*, Band XLVI (1966), pp. 277–398.

J. Favier, *Les Finances pontificales à l'époque du Grande Schisme de l'Occident, 1378–1409*, Paris, 1966.

E. Fiumi, *Demografia, movimento urbanistico e classi sociali in Prato dall'età comunale ai tempi moderni*, Florence, 1968.

——'Fioritura e decadenza dell'economia fiorentina I', *Archivio Storico Italiano*, Vol. CXV (1957), pp. 385–439.

——'Fioritura e decadenza dell'economia fiorentina II', *Archivio Storico Italiano*, Vol. CXVI (1958), pp. 443–510.

——'Fioritura e decadenza dell'economia fiorentina III', *Archivio Storico Italiano*, Vol. CXVII (1959), pp. 427–506.

——'L'imposta diretta nei comuni medioevali della Toscana', in *Studi in onore di Armando Sapori*, Vol. I (Milan, 1957), pp. 327–53.

——*Storia economica e sociale di San Gimignano*, Florence, 1961.

——'Sui rapporti economici tra città e contado nell'età comunale', *Archivio Storico Italiano*, Vol. CXIV (1956), pp. 18–68.

Fondazione Treccani degli Alfieri, *Storia di Milano*, Vol. V, Milan, 1955.

V. Gay, *Glossaire archéologique du Moyen-Age et de la Renaissance*, 2 vols., Paris, 1887–1928.

A. Gherardi, 'La guerra degli Otto Santi', *Archivio Storico Italiano*, Ser. iii, Vols. V–VIII (1867–8).

W. L. Gundersheimer, *Ferrara, the Style of a Renaissance despotism*, Princeton, 1973.

——'Toward a reinterpretation of the Renaissance in Ferrara', *Bibliothèque d'Humanisme et de la Renaissance*, Vol. XXX (1968), pp. 267–81.

J. Heers, 'Partis politiques et clans familiaux dans l'Italie de la Renaissance', *Revue de la Méditerannée*, Vol. XX (1960), pp. 259–79.

D. Herlihy, 'Direct and indirect taxation in Tuscan urban finance, ca. 1200–1400', in *Finances et comptabilité urbaines du XIIIe au XVIe siècles*, Colloque internationale-Blackenberge, 6–9 Sept. 62, Actes (Brussels, 1964), pp. 385–405.

——*Medieval and Renaissance Pistoia, the Social History of an Italian Town, 1200–1430*, New Haven, Conn., and London, 1967.

——*Pisa in the Early Renaissance, a Study of Urban Growth*, New Haven, Conn., 1958.

W. Heyd, *Histoire du commerce du Levant au moyen-age*, tr. Furcy Raynaud, 2 vols., Leipzig, 1923.

D. L. Hicks, 'Sienese society in the Renaissance', *Comparative Studies in Society and History*, Vol. II (1959–60), pp. 412–20.

G. Holmes, 'How the Medici became the Pope's bankers', in N. Rubinstein (ed.), *Florentine Studies* (London, 1968), pp. 357–80.

J. K. Hyde, *Padua in the Age of Dante, a Social History of an Italian City-State*, Manchester, 1966.

P. J. Jones, 'Communes and despots: the city-state in late medieval Italy', *Transactions of the Royal Historical Society*, Ser. v, Vol. XV (1965), pp. 71–96.

——'Medieval agrarian society in its prime: Italy', in *Cambridge Economic History*, Vol. I (2nd edn., Cambridge, 1966), pp. 340–431.

F. Landogna, 'Giovanni di Boemia e Carlo IV di Lussemburgo, signori di Lucca', *Nuova Rivista Storica*, Vol. XII (1928), pp. 53–72.

——'La politica dei Visconti in Toscana', *Bollettino della Società Pavese di Storia Patria*, Vol. XXVIII (1928), pp. 65–133, 149–236.

——'Le relazioni tra Bernabò Visconti e Pisa nella seconda metà del secolo XIV', *Archivio Storico Lombardo*, Vol. L (1923), p. 136–43.

F. C. Lane, 'The funded debt of the Venetian republic, 1262–1482', in *Venice and History* (Baltimore, 1966), pp. 87–98.

J. Larner, *The Lords of the Romagna: Romagnol Society and the Origins of the Signorie*, London, 1965.

E. Lazzareschi, 'Angelo Puccinelli e gli altri pittori lucchesi del Trecento', *Bollettino Storico Lucchese*, Vol. X (1938), pp. 137–64.

——*L'Arte della Seta in Lucca*, Seconda Settimana Lucchese, May 1930.

G. Livi, 'I mercanti di seta lucchesi in Bologna nei secoli XIII e XIV', *Archivio Storico Italiano*, Ser. iv, Vol. VII (1881), pp. 29–55.

F. P. Luiso, 'Mercatanti lucchesi dell'epoca di Dante, II, gli antenati di Castruccio Castracani', *Bollettino Storico Lucchese*, Vol. X (1938), pp. 69–94.

G. Luzzatto, *Il debito pubblico della repubblica di Venezia dagli ultimi decenni del XII secolo alla fine del XV*, Milan, 1963.

——'Il debito pubblico nel sistema finanziario veneziano dei secoli XIII–XIV', in *Studi di Storia Economica Veneziana* (Padua, 1954), pp. 211–24.

M. E. Mallett, *Mercenaries and their Masters, Warfare in Renaissance Italy*, London, 1974.

A. Mancini, 'Emigrati italiani del Trecento', *Annali della R. Scuola Normale Superiore di Pisa*, Ser. ii, Vol. I (1932), pp. 335–46.

——*Storia di Lucca*, Florence, 1950.

G. Marcotti and G. Temple-Leader, *Giovanni Acuto, storia di un condottiere*, Florence, 1889.

L. F. Marks, 'Fourteenth-century democracy in Florence', *Past and Present*, no. 25 (1963), pp. 77–85.

——'The financial oligarchy in Florence under Lorenzo', in E. F. Jacob

(ed.), *Italian Renaissance Studies* (London, 1960), pp. 123–47.
L. MARTINES, *Lawyers and Statecraft in Renaissance Florence*, Princeton, 1968.
——'Political conflict in the Italian city-states', *Government and Opposition*, Vol. 3 (1968), pp. 69–81.
——(ed.), *Violence and Civil Disorder in Italian Cities 1200–1500*, Berkeley and Los Angeles, Cal., 1972.
G. MASI, 'Verso gli albori del principato in Italia', *Rivista di Storia del Diritto Italiano*, Vol. IX (1936), pp. 65–180.
C. MASSEI, *Dell'Arte della Seta in Lucca*, Lucca, 1843.
A. MAZZAROSA, *Storia di Lucca dalle origini al MDCCXIV*, 2 vols., Lucca, 1833.
C. E. MEEK, 'The trade and industry of Lucca in the fourteenth century', in T. W. Moody (ed.), *Historical Studies VI* (London, 1968), pp. 39–58.
——'Il debito pubblico nella storia finanziaria di Lucca nel secolo XIV°', *Actum Luce*, Vol. III (1974) pp. 7–46.
D. M. BUENO DE MESQUITA, *Giangaleazzo Visconti, Duke of Milan, 1351–1402*, Cambridge, 1941.
——'The place of despotism in Italian politics', in J. L. Highfield, B. Smalley, and J. R. Hale (eds.), *Europe in the Late Middle Ages* (London, 1965), pp. 301–31.
F. MICHEL, *Recherches sur le commerce, la fabrication et l'usage des étoffes de soie, d'or et d'argent et autres tissus precieux en occident, principalement en France, pendant le moyen-age*, 2 vols., Paris, 1852–4.
C. MINUTOLI, 'I Guinigi ed i Forteguerra', in his *Frammenti di Storia Lucchese* (Lucca, 1878), pp. 15–25.
L. MIROT, 'Études lucquoises: la colonie lucquoise à Paris XIII–XV', *Bibliothèque de l'École des Chartes*, Vol. LXXXVIII (1927), pp. 50–86.
——'Études lucquoises: les Isbarre monnayeurs royaux, Augustin Isbarre', *Bibliothèque de l'École des Chartes*, Vol. LXXXIX (1928), pp. 299–389.
——'Études lucquoises: Forteguerra Forteguerra et sa succession', *Bibliothèque de l'École des Chartes*, Vol. XCVI (1935), pp. 301–37.
——'Études lucquoises: les Cename', *Bibliothèque de l'École des Chartes*, Vol. XCI (1930), pp. 100–68.
——'Études lucquoises: les Isbarre monnayeurs royaux, Ausustin Isbarre', *Bibliothèque de l'École des Chartes*, Vol. LXXXVIII (1928), pp. 275–314.
——*La Politique française en Italie de 1380 à 1422*, Paris, 1934.
——*La Politique pontificale et le retour du Saint-Siège a Rome en 1376*, Paris, 1899.
A. MOLHO, *Florentine Public Finances in the Early Renaissance, 1400–1433*, Cambridge, Mass., 1971.
——'The Florentine oligarchy and the *balìe* of the late Trecento', *Speculum*, Vol. XLIII (1968), pp. 23–51.
——'Politics and the ruling class in early Renaissance Florence', *Nuova Rivista Storica*, Vol. LII (1968), pp. 401–20.
R. PIATTOLI, 'Il problema portuale di Firenze dall'ultima lotta con Gian Galeazzo Visconti alle prime trattative per l'acquisto di Pisa (1402–1405)',

Rivista Storica degli Archivi Toscani, Vol. II (1930), pp. 157-90.

G. Picotti, 'Qualche osservazione sui caratteri delle signorie italiane', *Rivista Storica Italiana*, Vol. XLIII (1926), pp. 7-30.

G. Pirchan, *Italien und Kaiser Karl IV*, 2 vols., Prague, 1930.

F. Podreider, *Storia dei tessuti d'arte in Italia*, Bergamo, 1928.

B. Pullan, *A History of Early Renaissance Italy*, London, 1973.

Y. Renouard, 'Compagnies mercantiles lucquoises au service des papes d'Avignon', *Bollettino Storico Lucchese*, Vol. IX (1939), pp. 42-50.

——, *Les Relations des papes d'Avignon et des compagnies commerciales et bancaires de 1316 à 1378*, Paris, 1941.

I. Robertson, 'The *signoria* of Girolamo Riario in Imola', *Historical Studies*, Vol. XV (1971), pp. 88-117.

N. Rodolico, *I Ciompi, una pagina di storia del proletariato operaio*, Florence, 1945.

——*La democrazia fiorentina nel suo tramonto (1378-1382)*, Bologna, 1905.

N. Rubinstein, 'Florence and the despots, some aspects of Florentine diplomacy in the fourteenth century', *Transactions of the Royal Historical Society*, Ser. v, Vol. II (1952), pp. 21-45.

——'Politcs and constitution in Florence at the end of the fifteenth century', in E. F. Jacob (ed.), *Italian Renaissance Studies* (London, 1960), pp. 148-83.

——*The Government of Florence under the Medici 1434 to 1494*, Oxford, 1966.

J. C. Russell, *Medieval Regions and their Cities*, Newton Abbot, 1973.

V. Rutenberg, 'La vie at la lutte des Ciompi de Sienne', *Annales: Economies, Sociétés, Civilisations*, Vol. XX (1965), pp. 95-109.

——*Popolo e movimenti popolari nell'Italia del '300 e '400*, tr. G. Borghini, Bologna, 1971.

E. Salzer, *Uber die Anfänge der Signorie in Oberitalien*, Berlin, 1900.

C. Sardi, *Le contrattazioni agrarie del medio evo studiate nei documenti lucchesi*, Lucca, 1914.

G. Seregni, 'Un disegno federale di Bernabò Visconti 1380-1381', *Archivio Storico Lombardo*, Ser. iv, Vol. XXXVIII (1911-12), pp. 162-82.

E. Sestan, 'Le origini delle signorie cittadine: un problema storico esaurito?', *Bullettino dell'Istituto Storico Italiano per il Medio Evo e Archivio Muratoriano*, Vol. LXXI (1962), pp. 41-69.

H. Sieveking, 'Studio sulle finanze genovesi nel medioevo', tr. O. Soardi, *Atti della Società Ligure di Storia Patria*, Vol. XXXV (1905), pp. 3-261.

P. Silva, 'Il governo di Pietro Gambacorta in Pisa e le sue relazioni col resto della Toscana e coi Visconti', *Annali della R. Scuola Normale Superiore di Pisa*, Vol. XXIII (1912), pp. 1-352.

L. Simeoni, *Le signorie*, 2 vols., Milan, 1950.

G. Temple-Leader and G. Marcotti, *Giovanni Acuto, storia di un condottiere*, Florence, 1889.

G. Tommasi, 'Sommario della storia di Lucca dal MIV al MDCC', *Archivio Storico Italiano*, Ser. i, Vol. X (1847).

R. Vaughan, *Philip the Bold*, London, 1962.

A. Ventura, *Nobiltà e popolo nella società veneta del '400 e '500*, Bari, 1964.

C. Violante, 'Imposte dirette e debito pubblico a Pisa nel medioevo', in *L'Impôt dans le cadre de la ville e de l'état*, Colloque internationale—Spa 6 Sept. 64 (Brussels, 1966), pp. 45–95.

D. P. Waley, 'The army of the Florentine republic from the twelfth to the fourteenth century', in N. Rubinstein (ed.), *Florentine Studies* (London, 1968), pp. 70–108.

——*The Italian City-Republics*, London, 1969.

R. G. Witt, 'A note on Guelfism in late medieval Florence', *Nuova Rivista Storica*, Vol. LIII (1969), pp. 134–45.

L. Zerbi, *I Visconti di Milano e la signoria di Lucca*, Como, 1894.

INDEX

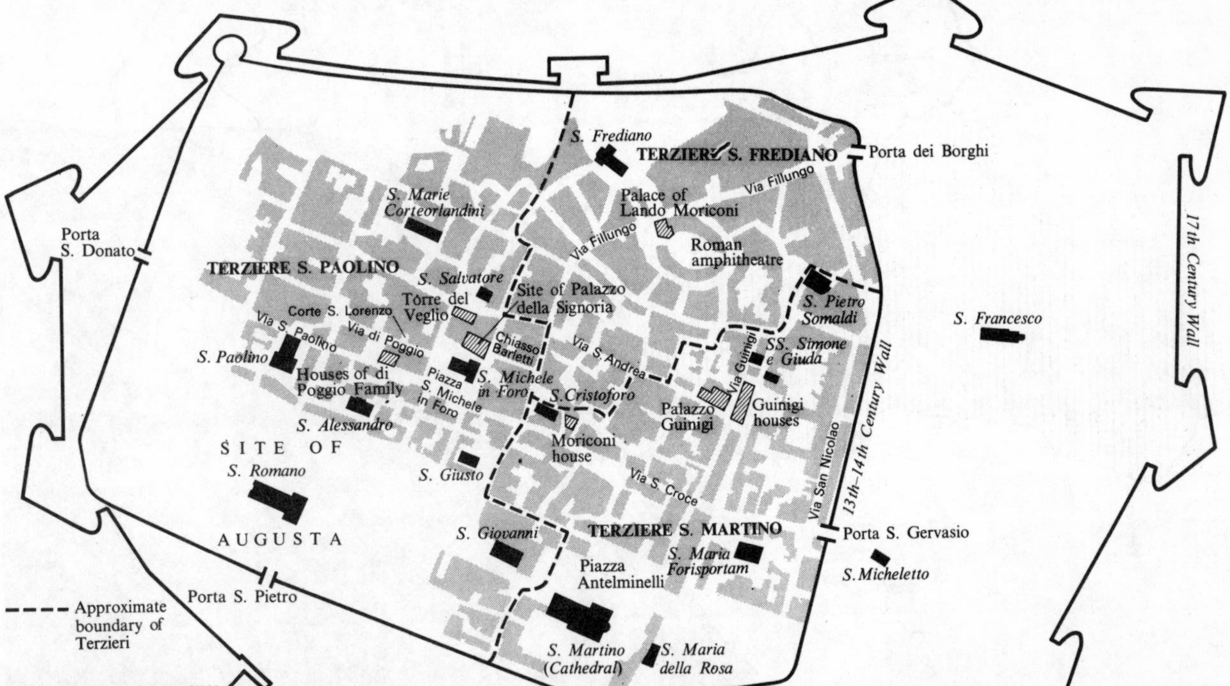

Based on G. Matraia, *Lucca nel'200* (Lucca, 1843), P. Pierotti, *Lucca, edilizia urbanistica medioevale* (Milan, 1965) and I. Belli Barsali, *Guida di Lucca*, 2nd edn. (Lucca, 1970).

Lucca in the Fourteenth Century

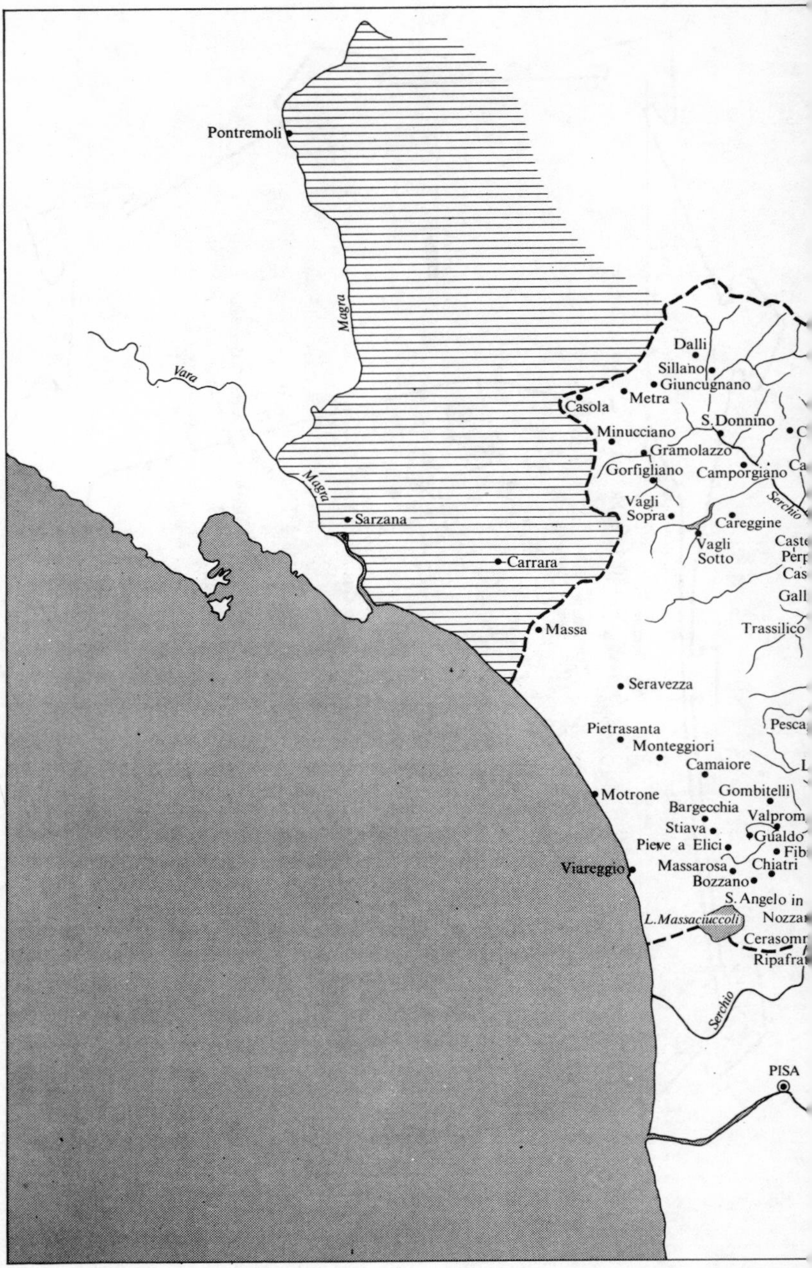

The Lucchese State

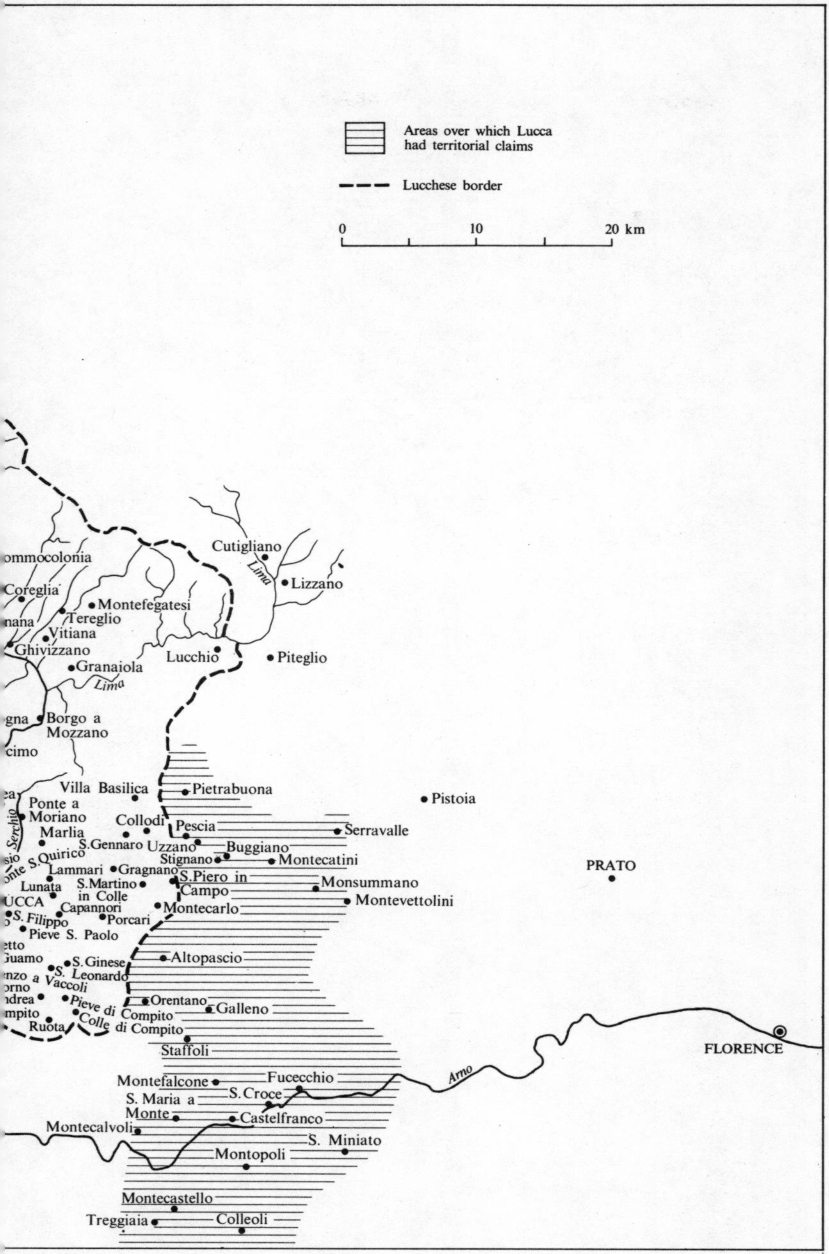

ourteenth Century